Penguin Handbooks
Baby and Child

Penelope Leach was educated at Cambridge University, where she read History, and the London School of Economics, where she obtained a Ph.D. in Social Psychology. She has researched into juvenile crime for the Home Office and into the development and upbringing of children for the Medical Research Council. As Jane Adrian, she contributed regularly to *The Times* and to the *Sunday Times*, and she writes under her own name for *Mother and Baby*, *Mother*, *Family Circle* and other magazines. She has broadcast frequently, including series for 'Woman's Hour' and for BBC further education, as well as on many phone-in programmes. She is a vice-president of the Pre-School Playgroups Association and the Health Visitors' Association, has served on the committee of the Developmental section of the British Psychological Society and is a sponsor of the Society of Teachers opposed to Corporal Punishment. Her first book, *Babyhood*, was published by Penguin in 1974 and a revised and expanded edition appeared early in 1983. In 1979 her appeal for a better deal for parents and young children appeared as a Penguin Special called *Who Cares?*. Her latest book, *The Parents' A–Z: A Guide to Children's Health, Growth and Happiness*, was published by Allen Lane in 1983 and will be published by Penguin in 1984.

Penelope Leach is married to an energy specialist and they have two children, a girl and a boy.

Baby and Child

Penelope Leach

Photography by Camilla Jessel

Penguin Books

BABY AND CHILD was edited and designed by Dorling Kindersley Limited,
9 Henrietta Street, London WC2E 8PS.

Penguin Books Ltd, Harmondsworth, Middlesex, England
Penguin Books, 40 West 23rd Street, New York, New York 10010, U.S.A.
Penguin Books Australia Ltd, Ringwood, Victoria, Australia
Penguin Books Canada Ltd, 2801 John Street, Markham, Ontario, Canada L3R 1B4
Penguin Books (N.Z.) Ltd, 182–190 Wairau Road, Auckland 10, New Zealand

First published in Great Britain by Michael Joseph Limited 1977
Published in Penguin Books 1979
Reprinted 1981 (twice), 1982, 1983 (twice)

Photographer Camilla Jessel wishes to thank all those who allowed
their children to be photographed and also the Save The Children Fund
for permission to reprint the photographs on pp. 277, 428, 446 and 447.
Photographs on pp. 19, 205, 359, 360, 425, 445 and 448 reproduced
by kind permission of Penelope Leach.

Printed in England by Pindar Print Limited, Scarborough, North Yorkshire
Set in 'Monophoto' Apollo by Filmtype Services Limited, Scarborough

To all the children of the Maze.
Past, present and future.

A book of this kind relies on knowledge from so many sources that to thank each individual is impossible. I gratefully acknowledge my debt both to the research workers and to the parents and children whose work I have been privileged to share over the years.

Because I have the good fortune to be part of a close extended family, my own education in parenthood began with my own mother and sisters. In part it is this knowledge, taken in while I was too young to be conscious of learning, which I am trying to share.

The learning went on through the births of our own children and is still going on now as they grow up. All three generations, especially my husband, Gerald Leach, my mother, Elisabeth Ayrton, and my sister, Prue Hopkins have helped in the preparation of this manuscript.

I owe a particular debt of thanks to Camilla Jessel for her brilliant photographs and to Bridget Morley for her sensitive designs. Together these brought the book alive. Also to the many people at Dorling Kindersley who have worked to put it together.

Finally, I should like to thank Christopher Davis whose patient editing has made it all just possible.

PENELOPE LEACH

Contents

Introduction

"Baby and Child" is written from your baby or child's point of view because, however fashion in child-rearing may shift and alter, that viewpoint is both the most important and the most neglected.

This book looks at what is happening within your child — let's say a boy — from the moment of birth until the time when you launch him into the wider world of school. It looks at the tasks of development with which he is involved, the kinds of thought of which he is capable and the extremes of emotion which carry him along. Babies and children live minute by minute, hour by hour and day by day and it is those small units of time which will concern you most in your twenty-four-hour caring. But everything he does during those detailed days reflects what he is, what he has been and what he will become. The more you can understand him and recognize his present position on the developmental map that directs him towards being a person, the more interesting you will find him. The more interesting he is to you the more attention he will get from you and the more attention he gets the more he will give you back.

So taking the baby's point of view does not mean neglecting yours, the parents', viewpoint. Your interests and his are identical. You are all on the same side; the side that wants to be happy, to have fun. If you make happiness for him he will make happiness for you. If he is unhappy, you will find yourselves unhappy as well, however much you want or intend to keep your feelings separate from his. I am on the same side, too. So although this is a book and one that I hope you will find useful, it will not suggest that you do things "by the book" but rather that you do them, always, "by the baby".

Rearing a child "by the book" — by any set of rules or pre-determined ideas — can work well if the rules you choose to follow happen to fit the baby you have. But even a minor misfit between the two can cause misery. You can see it in something as simple and taken-for-granted as the "proper" way to keep a newborn clean. Bathed each day according to the rules, some babies will enjoy themselves, adding pleasure for themselves and a glow of accomplishment for you to the desired state of cleanliness. But some will loudly proclaim their intense fear of the whole business of nakedness and water. However "correctly" you bathe such a baby, the panic-stricken yells will make your hands tremble and your stomach churn. You are doing what the book says but not what your baby needs. If you listen to your baby, the central figure in what you are trying to do, you will abandon the bath and use a washcloth. Then both of you can stay happy.

Through your love,
the newborn,
wrapped in mystery,
unfolds . . .

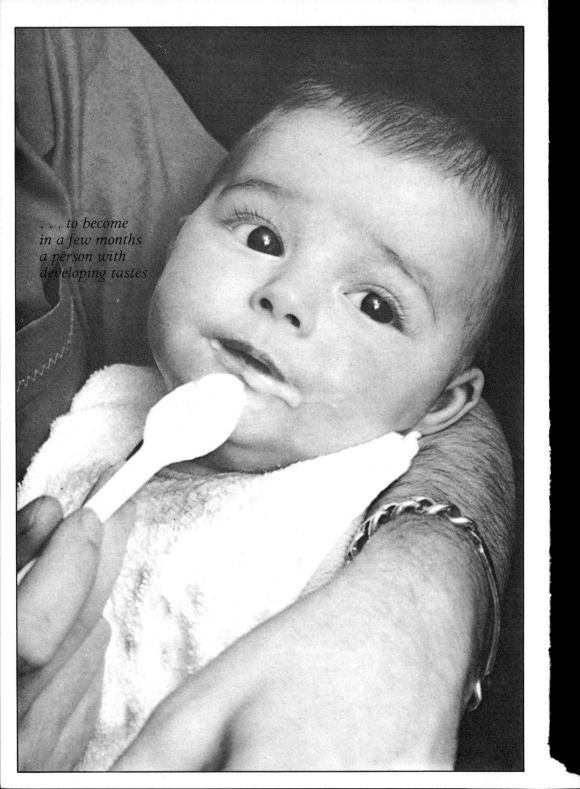

*. . . to become
in a few months
a person with
developing tastes*

. . . and then a toddler,
venturing out from beneath
your sheltering wing

. . . and eventually a child who, secure in your love, can discover the pleasures of other children.

This kind of sensitively concentrated attention to your own real-life child who is a person-in-the-making, is the essence of love. Loving a baby in this way is the best investment that there is. It pays dividends from the very beginning and it goes on paying them for all the years that there are. He is, after all, a brand new human being. You are, after all, his makers and his founders. As you watch and listen to him, think about and adjust yourselves to him, you are laying the foundations of a new member of your own race and of a friendship that can last forever. You are going to know this person better than you will ever know anybody else. Nobody else in the world including your partner, however devoted, is ever going to love you as much as he will in these first years if you will let him. You are into a relationship which is unique and which can be uniquely rewarding.

Loving a baby or child is a circular business, a kind of feedback loop. The more you give the more you get and the more you get the more you feel like giving. . . . It starts in the very first weeks. You chat to your baby as you handle him and one day you notice that he is listening. Because you can see him listening you talk to him more. Because you talk more he listens more and cries less. One magical day he connects the sound he has been hearing with your face and, magically, he smiles at you. Less crying and more smiling from him means that you feel like giving him even more of the talk that so charmingly pleases him. You have created between you a beneficial circle, each giving pleasure to the other.

It goes on like that too. A crawling baby tries to follow you every time you leave the room. If his determination to come too makes you increasingly determined to leave him behind, each trivial journey to the front door or the washing line will end in miserable tears from him and claustrophobic irritation for you. But if you will accept his feelings and willingly wait for him and help him stay with you, he will pay you back in contented charm and turn the chore you had to do into a game you both enjoy. Later still your pre-school child will chatter endlessly to you. If you half-listen and half-reply the whole conversation will seem, and become, tediously meaningless for both of you. But if you *really* listen and *really* answer, he will talk more and what he says will make more sense. Because he talks and says more, you will feel increasingly inclined to listen and to answer. Communication will flourish between you. So this whole book is orientated towards you and your child as a unit of mutual pleasure giving. Fun for him is fun for you. Fun for you creates more for him and the more fun you all have the fewer will be your problems.

I have written the book in this way because experience with my own children and the children of the many families who let me share their relationships with each other as part of my research has convinced me that the whole baby-business is in danger of becoming unnecessarily grim and forbidding. All through time people have loved and enjoyed their offspring. They must have done so or our ancestors would all have been exposed at birth by people who did not share our respect for life. Yet now we assume that every permanent couple will want to have children and at the same time we refuse to take the business of loving those children, of minding about them, seriously. We are in danger of taking away the joy, leaving only guilt and hard work in its place. I have worked with women who felt guilty because they were enjoying life at home with a two-year-old person who was learning life. They felt that they ought to do, or at least ought to *want* to do, something "more fulfilling" . . . . I have worked with women who felt guilty because they were not enjoying life at home with a two year old. They felt that they ought not to enjoy their outside jobs because their children needed them. There have been men who felt guilty too—guilty because they put their careers before their families or their families before their careers; spent too much time at work making money to spend on the children, or too much time at home with the children not making enough money to spend on them. It sometimes seems to me that we have edged parents into a no-win situation, into an emotional trap.

This book is meant both to help you find the courage to guard yourself against unnecessary guilt and to find positive courses of action which will actually benefit your child where your self-reproach will not. Guilt is the most destructive of all emotions. It mourns what has been while playing no part in what may be, now or in the future. Whatever you are doing, however you are coping, if you listen to your child and to your own feelings, there will be something you can actually *do* to make things right. If your new one cries and cries whenever he is put in his cot, guilty soul-searching about your "mishandling" will get none of you anywhere. Stop. Listen to him. Consider the state that his crying has got you into. There is no joy here. Where is he happy? On your back? Then put him there. Carrying him may not suit you very well right this minute but it will suit you far better than that incessant hurting noise. Only when peace is restored to you all will you have the chance calmly to consider more permanent solutions. If your three year old panics when you put out her bedroom light, stop. Listen to her; listen to your own feelings. There is no luxurious rest for her nor well-earned adult peace for you. Put the light on again and let both of you be content. It does not matter whether she "ought" to be scared of the dark; it only matters, to everyone present, that she *is*.

Bringing up a child in this flexible thoughtful way takes

birth canal facing towards your backbone. So his final position in readiness for birth will be head down and back to front.

As the time for birth approaches and his position is settled, baby and womb drop down together in your abdomen so that his head is engaged in the basin-shaped bones of your pelvis, through the still closed cervix. Now he is held still and quiet. His movements will no longer kick the bar of soap off your belly in the bath. You can breathe more easily too, with a little more room between the top of your loaded womb and your diaphragm.

When labour begins even the best prepared parents tend to be taken by surprise. It is not that the beginning of the process is difficult to recognize; it is that even the most careful words cannot describe the overwhelmingly physical nature of the birth process nor prepare you for the extraordinary feeling of having your body taken over by forces which are outside your conscious control. We are brought up to control and manage our bodies' functions, holding back coughs and yawns, fending off sleep in public. . . . But childbirth cannot be controlled in this sense. Once labour begins, your baby is going to get himself born with or without your conscious cooperation. The con-tractions will go on at their appointed rate and strength until the birth canal is fully open. The muscles of your uterus will push the baby down that canal and go on pushing until he emerges. You cannot call a rest-pause, decide to make a telephone call or wait for the doctor, change your mind about having the baby at all. . . . There is no way out of the experience except through it, because it is not really your experience at all but the baby's. Your body is his instrument of birth.

You cannot see your baby turned, forced and moulded by the muscular contractions which you feel as labour pains. You cannot watch his slow progress down the birth canal, forced by your body's convulsive and irresistible pushing. You cannot know whether he feels pain and fear. But that baby is the point of the whole labour process. It is his safe arrival with which your body is concerned. He, not you, is the star of the show. It may help you if you can think of him while your body strives to produce him. It will certainly help him if you can consider his likely feelings, at least from the moment that he emerges.

Giving birth is an experience which often threatens to be over-whelming. Your body has a demanding job to do and it will do it, but your mind and your emotions can protest violently at being taken over. If they do, you will tense up to each contraction instead of softening to it; you will fight your body's control instead of going along with it. Ante-natal training helps enormously by taking the mystery out of labour and teaching you how to help it along rather than hampering it. But an involved partner, who has trained with you and will see you right through the birth, makes all the difference. Although he is totally involved emotionally, he is unaffected physically. With him to watch over you, abandoning your normal self to the birth process feels safer. He has the same knowledge that you have been given so, if the physical sensations should threaten to overwhelm you, he can remind you to do as you have been taught. If accumulated minor discomforts, like backache and a dry mouth, should bother you, he has the time to offer the backrub or the wet sponge that will relieve them. As labour progresses, drawing you deeper and deeper into the vortex of birth, he may become the most important person in the room to you. Nurses and doctors come and go doing whatever is physically necessary, but he is there for you to hold on to emotionally. When the world becomes a blur of strange effort, his is the face you can still see clearly; his words are the ones you can still understand. By the time the baby emerges, even the most reluctantly participant father will be sure of his vital role in the whole affair. Yours will be a truly mutual baby from the start.

Although more and more fathers are nerving themselves to total involvement and being welcomed by an increasing number of hospitals, there will always be some couples who do not want it that way. A father who cannot face witnessing the birth can ensure that his partner feels adequately supported if he can only bring himself to talk about it.

You, the new mother, have been through a tremendous experience; a major physical and emotional crisis. You will almost certainly find that you need to re-live it; to talk about it detail by detail, work it out, understand it, think about your feelings. There may be practical details which confuse you and which need sorting through before you can stop thinking about them: How did it manage to get dark without you noticing? How long was it between your going into the delivery room and the baby's arrival? Emotional details may feel important too: Did the nurses think you had done well? Did they understand why you were upset about this, that or the other? Is everyone proud of you and can you feel proud of yourself? Until the birth experience has been talked through, it will not slip comfortably away to the back of your mind, leaving you free to give yourself wholeheartedly to mothering the baby you have produced. It is the women who can find no one to talk to or who are too shaken by the birth experience to make themselves talk, who tend to find themselves brooding over it. The birth becomes something they do not want to think about but cannot clear from their thoughts. Clearing your mind for mothering is vital because your baby needs you. His experience has been far more shattering than yours. Because we cannot know exactly what he feels during birth we tend to behave as if he felt nothing. We concentrate on his safety, leaving consideration of his comfort or happiness for later. But with highly developed birth technologies, there is no reason why a baby should not be safe *and* comfortable. We must learn to look at his birth with his likely feelings in mind.

Brutally forced through a tight passage from a soft, quiet, warm, dark haven into a world of light and noise and texture, every bit of the baby's nervous system reacts with shock. But his struggles are not over. The placenta which fed his circulation oxygen from your bloodstream, has finished its work. He must breathe. His lungs have never expanded before. The effort of that first breath must be fearful. But if he can make it alone, we need not add the pain of a slapped bottom. We are so used to slapping newborns and hearing their first cry that we have almost forgotten that there can be breath without crying.

If he is to breathe easily, his nose and mouth must be clear of amniotic fluid and mucus. But if he can clear them himself, we need not torment him with tubes. We are so used to routine suction for new babies that we have forgotten how those tubes must feel to him.

Safely breathing, the baby needs time to rest and to discover that even though the womb has ejected him, there is still comfort in his world. Your belly, soft and slack now, forms an ideal cradle. On it, he can be almost as comfortable as he was in it. There he can rest.

But he cannot rest unless his surroundings are toned down. The midwives needed those glaring lights for a safe delivery, but he is safely delivered now. Turn them down. They hurt the baby's eyes. He has never seen light before.

The midwives needed to talk and to move around during the delivery. But there is nothing now that cannot wait. Be quiet. Your noises frighten him. All sounds have been muffled for him until now.

If all is dim and quiet, warm and peaceful, the baby will relax after his traumatic journey. His breathing will steady. His crumpled face will smooth itself out and his eyes will open. His head will lift a little and his limbs will move against your skin. Put very gently to your bare breast, he may suck, discover a new form of human contact and feel a little less separated. These are his first contacts with his new world: let him make them without distress. These are his first moments of life; let him have them in peace.

The baby must be weighed. But why must he be weighed now? His weight will not change in half an hour. He must be washed. But why now? The vernix that has protected his skin for months is not harming it just because he has been born. He must be dressed. But why now? Your warmth, a soft wrapping and the heat of the delivery room are all he needs. He must have drops in his eyes, a dressing on the cord stump, a physical examination, a cot to lie in. You must be washed and changed, moved to a bed, given a drink, settled to sleep. All these things must indeed be done, but why must they be done right now? The baby is born. He is living independently. The time for high-powered technology and efficient nursing is over. The time for warm and peaceful intimacy among the three of you has come.

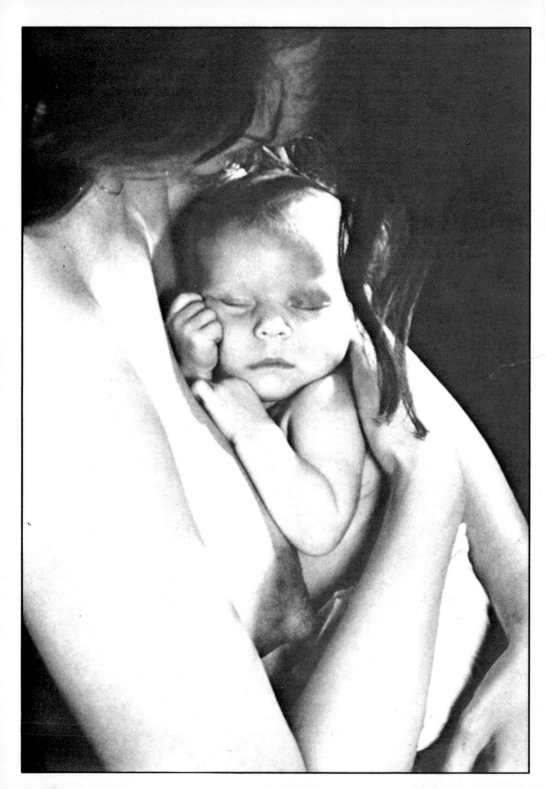

CHAPTER TWO

THE NEWBORN

The first days of life

Birth feels like the climax to long months of waiting but it is not really a climax at all. You were not waiting to give birth, you were waiting to have a baby. Your labour has produced that baby and there is no rest-pause between the amazing business of becoming parents and the job of being them. Don't expect too much of yourselves during these first, peculiar days. All three of you have a tremendous amount of adapting to do. The feelings and behaviour of today have very little to do with next month because by then all three of you will have changed. Your baby will have settled into life outside the womb and you will both have settled into parenthood.

Most couples remember this as an intensely emotional and confusing time. Everything is felt too much: stitches and pleasure, responsibility and pride, selfishness and selflessness. You are still desperately tired. Your hormone balance is disturbed, your milk neither fully in nor finally suppressed, your body striving for equilibrium. Your partner has no direct physical effects but he has an emotional tightrope to walk. He has to concede to you the prime role as the one who laboured yet he has to make you feel that this is the child of you both, that he too is deeply involved. If he pays too much attention to the baby, he risks making you feel that you are no longer his central person. If he concentrates on you he risks the charge that he does not care for his newborn. Many men remark wryly that during these first days after birth there is no way that they can get it right.

As for the baby: what he has to cope with is without parallel in human experience. While he was inside you your body took care of his. It provided his food and his oxygen, took away his waste products, kept him warmly cushioned and protected, held the world at bay. Now that he is separated from you his body must take care of itself. He must suck and swallow food and water, digest it and excrete its wastes. He must use energy from that food to keep his body functions running, to keep himself warm and to go on growing. He must breathe to get oxygen and keep his air passages clear with coughs and sneezes. While accepting all these new duties he must also cope with a positive bombardment of stimuli as the world rushes in on him. Suddenly there is air on his skin, there is warmth and coolness, there are textures, movements and restrictions. There is light and darkness and there are things to see, coming into focus and blurring out again. There is hunger and emptiness, sucking, fullness and burping. There are sounds and smells and tastes. Everything is new. Everything is different. All is bewilderment.

Your newborn baby's behaviour is a series of reactions to what he perceives as random stimuli. He has instincts and reflexes and working senses but he has no knowledge and no experience. He does not know that he is himself, that the object he sees moving in front of his face is his own hand or that it remains part of him when it has vanished to lie beside him on the blanket. He does not know that you are people either. He is programmed to pay attention to you, to look at your faces and listen to your voices. He is programmed to suck when you offer him a nipple. He is programmed for survival but he knows nothing.

While he remains a newborn, rather than a baby who has settled into life outside the womb, his behaviour will be random and unpredictable. He may cry for food every half hour for six hours and then sleep without any for another six hours. This morning's "hunger" does not predict this afternoon's because his hunger has no pattern or shape as yet. His digestion has not settled; hunger signals have not taken on a clear and recognizable form for him. He simply reacts to momentary feelings. His sleep is similarly formless; ten minute snatches through the night and a five hour stretch in the day tell you nothing about how he will sleep tomorrow. He may cry, too, for no reason that you can discover and stop as suddenly and inexplicably as he began. His crying has no definite pattern of cause and effect because he has not yet discovered how to differentiate between pleasure and displeasure.

When you start looking after this small, new human being, you lack that first essential for watchful care: baselines. The baby is brand new. However much you know about babies in general, neither you nor anyone else knows anything about this one in particular. You do not know how he looks and behaves when he is well and happy so it is difficult for you to know when he is ill or miserable. You do not know how much he "usually" cries because he has not been around for long enough for anything to be usual. So there is no easy way of knowing whether this crying suggests that anything is amiss. You do not know how much he usually eats or sleeps so you cannot judge whether today's feeding or sleeping is adequate or excessive. Yet his wellbeing is in your hands. Even without baselines of usual behaviour against which to judge, you have to make continual assessments and

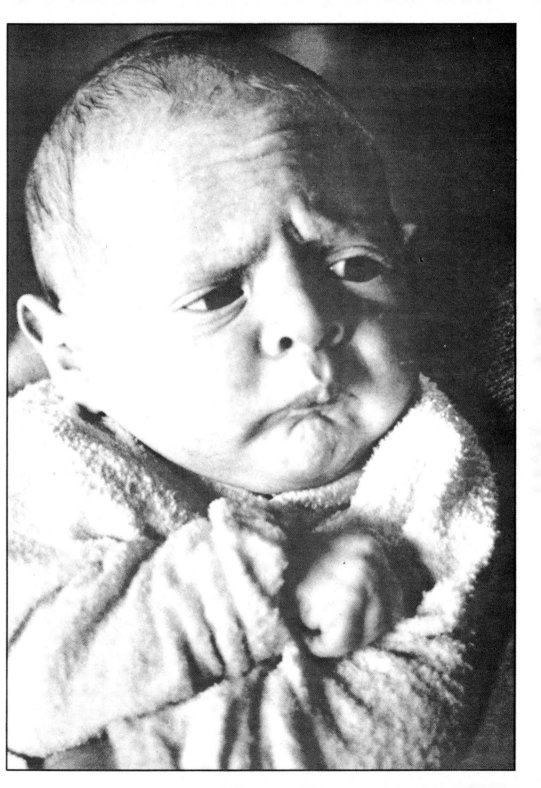

adjustments while you learn your baby and he learns life. There is a lot of learning for all of you. It may take only a week after his birth for you to feel secure in your care and for him to feel secure in his world. But it may take a month. It has taken some eighty pages of this book to lay down the basic essentials and they are the most down-to-earth and the hardest working pages the book contains. Once you and he have learned them, established your baselines, got to know each other, everything will suddenly seem much easier and smoother for all of you. You will be dealing with a baby person rather than a newborn. The next chapter and all the chapters after that are incomparably easier.

During this settling period don't torment yourselves by expecting love. Love will come but it will take time. However you define the word it must have something to do with interaction between people who know each other, who like what they know and want to know more. If there is love, there must be a sharing, a giving and taking of affection and support. A brand new baby is neither lovable nor loving. He is not truly lovable because he has not yet got himself into predictable, knowable shape nor had time to produce the characteristics which will make it clear for evermore that he is a unique person. You may love him because he is your baby; the fulfilment, perhaps, of a plan or a dream; but you cannot love him as one person loves another. He is not fully a person until he is settled. He is not loving because he does not yet know of his own existence, let alone yours. He will learn to love you with a determined and unshakeable passion unequalled in human relationships. But it will take time.

You cannot turn on your love for the baby at the flick of a switch or the cutting of the umbilical cord. The mixed feelings you have towards him now are neither a guide nor a warning for the future. The overwhelming tenderness that sweeps over you as you cradle his heavy, downy head can give way in a moment to furious irritation at his crying. Your pride in being a parent can turn suddenly to over-whelming claustrophobia as you realize that you are committed to him for ever and will never again be free to be an entirely separate individual person.

If you can let it, your body will start loving the baby for you even before he is properly a person. Whatever your mind and the deeply entrenched habits of your previous life may be telling you, your body is ready and waiting for him. Your skin thrills to his. His small frame fits perfectly against your belly, breast and shoulder. That hard, hot head is there for your cheek to rub and your thumb moulds itself to the startling grip of those small, bony fingers.

If you can revel in the baby physically, you will speed up the time when he can join in this essential business of loving. Given the chance, he will not lie passively, leaving it to you to make all the advances. If you will have him close, he will make advances to you,

too. He has a built-in interest in you because your loving care is essential to his survival. He will see to it that love comes.

If you can let your body's commands and your baby's physical reactions govern your behaviour during these very first days, you will handle him as he needs handling. Child-rearing plans and policies are no use to you yet. Plans and policies can only be judged by the consistent responses they evoke and nothing you can work out will get consistency from an unsettled newborn.

The baby needs to be handled so that his new and independent life seems as little different as possible from the old dependent life in your womb. His needs are simple and repetitive. They need to be met simply and immediately. He needs food and water in the combined form of milk; he needs warmth and comfort from cuddling arms and soft wrappings in a small, safe bed; he needs just enough cleanliness to keep his skin from getting sore and he needs protection. That is all he needs. The gadgets and gimmicks, the baths and changing mats, powders and lotions, brushes and bootees that tempt you in every baby shop will be fun for you to buy and nice for him later. But for now he is a bundle and he should be a bundle. Wrap him warmly, hold him closely, handle him slowly, feed him when he is hungry, talk to him when he looks at you, wash him when he is actually dirty and leave him peacefully alone to come to terms with life. Unless he is actually ill and under medical care, there is absolutely nothing which it is your duty to do to him if it makes him jump or cry. Peaceful contentment means that you have got it right. Distress means that you have got it wrong. Let his reactions guide you.

If you can manage this, tired and overwrought though you are, the baby will gradually come to realize what he needs and to realize that he gets what he needs when he needs it. By the time he is a settled, knowable, lovable small person who has been outside your body for ten or fifteen or twenty days, he will know the world to be a good place to be alive in. And that, after all, is the best start you can possibly give him.

Birthweight

After the sex, your baby's weight is usually the first thing you are told about him or her. Babies come in a large variety of shapes and sizes, so why does it matter to everybody exactly what this one weighs? Because the birthweight, whatever it may be, is your baby's own personal starting point for growth.

Average babies The average birthweight for babies is just over 7lbs (3.2kg). But that average conceals many variations. Boys are usually a few ounces heavier than girls; first babies are usually rather lighter than their younger brothers and sisters, while on the whole large parents have large babies and small parents have smaller ones. So your baby can be the right size for him without being that average 7lbs (3.2kg). All three of the babies below were perfectly normal and healthy. The difference in their size is obvious.

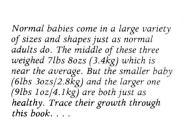

Normal babies come in a large variety of sizes and shapes just as normal adults do. The middle of these three weighed 7lbs 8ozs (3.4kg) which is near the average. But the smaller baby (6lbs 3ozs/2.8kg) and the larger one (9lbs 1oz/4.1kg) are both just as healthy. Trace their growth through this book. . . .

Heavy babies   If you give birth to a 10lb (4.5kg) baby you will be rightly proud of yourself for having delivered him. And he will probably look more beautiful than most of the other newborn babies in the ward as he will be well covered with fat. But for a day or two the hospital staff may keep a special eye on him. This is because a very few exceptionally heavy babies are the result of the mother having diabetes or pre-diabetes. It is important to be sure that this particular one is just a well-grown baby whom nature meant to be large, rather than a baby whose metabolism has been disturbed in the womb and whose exceptional weight comes from water which has been retained in his body.

Light babies   If your baby is below average birthweight but weighs more than 5½lbs (2.5kg) he will be treated like an average birthweight baby except that he will probably be fed more often. The chances are that you are smaller than average too and that this is a healthy baby who is meant to be small.

   If the baby weighs 5–5½lbs (2.3–2.5kg) he will probably be put in an incubator, however healthy and lively he seems to be. This is because babies who are born weighing less than 5½lbs (2.5kg) are liable to have trouble with breathing, with keeping warm and with sucking. So to play safe, *all* babies who are under this weight are started off with special care. Look upon it as a precaution only. Don't jump to the conclusion that there is something wrong with him. If there are no problems he will probably be out of the incubator and in a cot by your bed within a couple of days.

   You may have one minor problem to face, though. However well he does, the light baby will not be allowed to go home until he has stopped losing weight after birth (see p. 50) and regained his birthweight plus enough on top of that to bring him over that 5½lbs (2.5kg) mark. If you were planning to stay in hospital for a week or ten days, he may be ready to leave with you. But if you had intended to go home after 48 hours or so, you will either have to change your plans or go home a few days ahead of him.

   If your baby is born weighing less than 5lbs (2.3kg) then he probably is lighter than nature meant him to be. The lighter he is the more special the care he will need. The particular kind of care will depend partly on whether he is premature or small-for-dates.

Premature babies   Most very small babies are small for the simple reason that they have been born prematurely – before the completion of the usual 40 weeks in the womb. Missing time in the womb means that the baby has missed out on some growing time. It also means that he has missed out on some getting-ready-for-independent-life time. The more weeks inside the womb he has missed, the more difficulties he is likely to face. A baby born after 36–38 weeks gestation will probably only need to have things made very easy for him, by being kept in an incubator with extra warmth, extra oxygen and tiny feeds of a very easily digested mixture at frequent intervals. A "younger" baby may need more help than that. He may need to have some of the responsibilities of independent life taken right off him for a while, being fed, for example, by a tube passed down his nose into his stomach so that he does not have to suck or swallow.

Hair

Any amount of hair on the head, from almost none to a luxuriant growth, is normal. Babies born late, after extra time in the womb, may have a great deal of rather coarse hair. Whatever it is like at birth, most of the newborn hair will fall out and be replaced. The colour of the new hair may be quite different.

Body hair. In the womb babies are covered with a fine fuzz of hair. Some, especially premature babies, still have some, usually across the shoulder blades and down the spine. It will rub off in the first week or two.

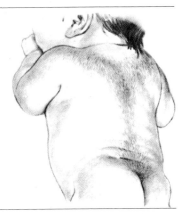

Head

Oddities of shape. These are almost always due to pressure during birth and will right themselves over a few months. The head may become slightly flattened if the baby is always put to sleep on one particular side. It is worth making sure that new babies are put on alternate sides, at least until they learn to roll themselves over.

Fontanelles. These are the soft areas where the bones of the skull have not yet fused together. The most noticeable lies towards the back of the top of the baby's head. It is covered by an extremely tough membrane and there is no danger whatsoever of damaging it with normal handling.

In a baby without much hair, a pulse may be seen beating under the fontanelle. This is perfectly normal. If the fontanelle ever appears sunken, so that there is a visible "dip" in the baby's head, it is a sign of dehydration (usually due to very hot weather or a fever). The baby should be offered diluted fruit juice, or water.

If the fontanelle should ever appear to be tight and tense and to bulge outwards, the baby should see a doctor immediately as it could be a sign of illness.

Eyes

Swollen, puffy or red-streaked eyes. These are often noticed soon after birth and result from pressure during it. Swelling and inflammation resolve over a few days. Any recurrence of trouble with the eyes, once newborn problems have resolved, should be promptly reported to the doctor.

Yellowish discharge and/or crusting on lids and lashes. This is the result of a very common mild infection known as "sticky eye". It is not serious but the baby should be seen by the doctor who will recommend drops or a solution for bathing the eyes.

Squinting. Many babies whose eyes are perfectly normal have a squinting appearance in the early days of life.

If you look at your baby closely you will probably find that it is the marked folds of skin at the inner corners of the eyes which make you think they are squinting. These folds of skin are perfectly normal and become less and less noticeable during the baby's first few weeks.

Until the baby has strengthened and

learned to control the muscles around the eyes, it is quite usual for there to be difficulty in holding both eyes in line with each other so that they can both focus steadily on the same object. As your baby looks at your face, you may suddenly notice that one eye has "wandered" out of focus. A "wandering eye" almost always rights itself by the time the baby is six months old. But point it out to the doctor at your next visit so that a check can be made on its progress. A true squint means that the baby's eyes never both focus together on the same object. Rather than moving together and then one wandering off, the eyes are permanently out of alignment with each other. If you are the first to notice that your baby has a "fixed squint" you should report it at once to the doctor. Early treatment is both essential and highly successful (see Enc/Eyes – vision disorders).

Ears

Discharge. While it is normal for a baby's ears to produce wax, it is never normal for them to produce any other kind of discharge. If you are not sure that the substance you see coming from the ear is wax, consult your doctor. If it is wax, he will only be pleased to reassure you. If by any chance it is pus, treatment is urgent.

Sticking out. It used to be common for new babies to have their protruding ears strapped flat to their heads with adhesive tape. A few authorities still believe that this treatment can persuade the ears to flatten themselves. However most would agree that such treatment would be impracticable. The tape would need to be used continuously for months and would undoubtedly make the skin sore. It would also be ineffective, because the set of the ears is not malleable to such measures.

If you think that your baby's ears are obtrusive, it is worth making sure that you smooth back the one your baby is just going to lie on . A good long nap each day with the ear bent forward under the head will not improve matters. Otherwise you can only wait and see whether the ears become less noticeable as your baby's head assumes a more mature shape and as more hair grows.

Mouth

"Tongue Tie". The tongue of a new baby is anchored along a much greater proportion of its length than is the tongue of an older person. In some babies the anchoring fold of skin is so long that the baby has almost no tongue which is free and mobile.
In the past such babies were thought to be "tongue tied". It was believed that unless the anchoring skin was cut so that the tongue was free, the baby would not be able to suck properly or to learn to talk. Now we know that a true "tongue tie" – one which will not right itself with normal growth – is exceedingly rare. Most of the growth of a baby's tongue during the first year of life is in the tip so that by the first birthday the tongue is fully mobile. In the meantime its close anchorage has no effect on sucking, eating or speech.

White tongue. While they are being fed only on milk, babies often have tongues which are white all over. This is absolutely normal. Infection or illness does not produce all-over whiteness but patches of white on an otherwise pink tongue.

Blisters on the upper lip. These are called "sucking blisters" and are due simply to the baby's sucking. They can occur at any time while the baby is purely milk-fed. They may vanish between feeds. They are unimportant.

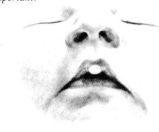

Breasts

Swollen breasts are perfectly normal for babies of both sexes in the first three to five days after birth. They are caused by hormones flooding through the mother just before the birth. The hormones are intended for her but they sometimes get to the baby, too. The swollen breasts may even have a tiny quantity of milk in them. They should be left strictly alone as any attempt to squeeze milk out might introduce infection. The swelling will die down in a few days as the baby's body rids itself of the hormones.

In these first days
wrap her warmly,
hold her closely,
handle her slowly . . .

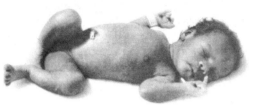

. . . your newborn is still unused to being free of your womb and out in the bewildering world.

Abdomen

Umbilical hernia. *A small swelling close to the navel, which sticks out more when the baby cries, cannot actually be called "normal", but is very usual indeed. It is caused by a slight weakness of the muscles in the wall of the abdomen, which allows the contents to bulge forward. Most such hernias right themselves completely by one year and most doctors believe that they heal more quickly if they are not strapped up. Very few ever require operation.*

Sex organs

The genitals of both boys and girls are larger, in proportion to the rest of their bodies, at birth than at any other time before puberty. During the first few days after birth they may look even larger than normal because hormones from the mother have crossed the placenta, entered the baby's bloodstream and caused temporary extra swelling. The scrotum or the vulva may also look red and inflamed. All in all the baby's sexual parts may look conspicuous and peculiar. But don't worry. The doctor or midwife who delivered the baby will have checked that all is normal. The inflammation and swelling will rapidly subside during the baby's settling period and he or she will rapidly "grow into" those apparently over-large organs.

Tight foreskin (Phimosis). *The penis and the foreskin develop from a single bud in the foetus. They are still fused at birth and they only gradually become separate during the first few years of the boy's life. A tight foreskin is therefore a problem which a new baby cannot have. You cannot retract his foreskin because it is not made to retract at this age. You cannot wash underneath it because it is not meant to be cleaned from outside in babyhood. Circumcision (surgical removal of the foreskin) is medically advisable in only a minute proportion of babies. When it is necessary it has usually become so because attempts have been made to retract the foreskin forcibly before it was ready to retract of its own accord (see Enc/Circumcision).*

Elimination and secretions

Meconium. *This is a greenish black sticky substance which fills babies' intestines in the womb and has to be evacuated before ordinary digestion can take place. Almost all babies pass meconium in the first 24 hours. If a baby is born at home, the midwife or nurse must be told if none is passed by the second day. Failure to pass meconium might mean an obstruction in the bowel.*

Blood in stools. *Very occasionally blood is noticed in the stools in the first day or two. It is usually blood from the mother, swallowed during the delivery. Keep the nappy to show to the midwife or nurse.*

Reddish urine. *Very early urine often contains a substance called "urates" which looks red on the nappy. As it looks like blood you may prefer to keep the nappy to show the midwife or nurse.*

Frequent urine. *Once the urine flow is established the baby may pass water as often as 30 times in the 24 hours. This is entirely normal. On the other hand a baby who stays dry for 4–6 hours at this stage should be seen by the nurse or a doctor. It is just possible that there is some obstruction to the flow of urine.*

Vaginal bleeding. *A small amount of vaginal bleeding is common in girls at any time in the first week of life. It is due to maternal oestrogens passing into the baby just before birth.*

Vaginal discharge. *A clear or whitish discharge from the vagina is also quite normal. It will stop in a very few days.*

Nasal discharge. *Many babies accumulate enough mucus in the nose to cause snuffles or some visible "runniness". This does not mean that the baby has a cold or other infection.*

Tears. *Most babies cry without tears until they are 4–6 weeks old. A few shed tears from the beginning. It does not matter either way.*

Sweating. *Most babies sweat a great deal around the head and neck. This has no importance unless the baby shows other signs of being feverish or unwell. It is a good reason, though, for rinsing the head and hair frequently as the sweat may irritate the skin in the folds of the neck.*

Vomiting. *Posseting of a little milk after feeds is normal. (For a full discussion see p. 75).*

Feeding

Only you can decide whether to breast or bottle-feed. It is your body and your baby. Nobody has the right to pressure you either way or to condemn you whatever you decide. Breast milk is *physically* better for babies because it is the milk that nature intended for them rather than milk which nature meant for calves. But modern baby formulae can be very nearly as good, and may even be better for the baby emotionally if using a bottle makes you happier. Of course breast-feeding gives you both close, warm, physical contact, but you can make that contact by using a bottle, too. So don't listen to partisan arguments. Instead, think about yourself, the baby and your whole family unit:

What kind of person are you? If you welcome physical contacts and are looking forward to the physical relationship your baby will want to have with you, then you will probably enjoy breast-feeding. There is an obvious, natural connection between the baby's hungry, seeking mouth and your full breasts. It feels very right and very pleasurable too.

But if you find the whole idea embarrassing, you may not enjoy it. If you don't enjoy it, then it will not work very smoothly. Both you and the baby may be happier using a bottle.

What kind of life do you want to lead? If you mean to stay at home and devote the next few months mainly to nursery routines, either method will suit you.

If you mean to go back to full-time work within a few weeks of the birth, then obviously you will have to use a bottle. But you might still want to breast-feed while you can.

If you mean to look after the baby yourself but want to preserve as much freedom to go out and about, visiting and travelling, as you can, then breast-feeding will be much easier for you. Holidays, camping, boating, hiking are all simpler with a breast-fed baby. They need real organization with one who is bottle-fed.

Are you uncertain which you want to do? If you want to keep your options open while you make up your mind, then you will have to start off with breast-feeding. You can always switch your baby from breast to bottle but you cannot easily change from bottle to breast – without the stimulation of regular sucking, your breasts will not have milk available.

If you do decide to give breast-feeding a try, you will be giving your baby an excellent start even if you switch over to a bottle quite quickly. But although even a few days at the breast will be better than nothing they will not really tell you whether you are a person who enjoys breast-feeding or not. As we shall see, most mothers have to ride over a variety of minor problems and discomforts before breast-feeding becomes something they can take for granted. Only after two or three weeks will you be able to see how easy it is.

If you have not made up your mind whether to breast or bottle-feed, a look at some of the pros and cons of each method may help you to decide.

Some pros and cons of breast and bottle-feeding	Breast-feeding	Bottle-feeding
	Before the real milk comes in, the breasts produce "colostrum". This gives the baby water, protein, sugar, the necessary minerals and many important antibodies. Even a few days of breast-feeding will give your newborn a head start.	*There is no artificial equivalent to "colostrum".*
	Breast milk is the easiest to digest. Babies who are breast-fed even for a few weeks are less prone to digestive upsets.	*Although most babies thrive on bottle-feeding, a few find a full-strength formula difficult to digest at first.*
	Breast milk is suitable for all babies. It cannot be too rich, too watery or in any way "wrong" for your baby.	*You may need a period of trial-and-error before the best milk for your baby is found.*
	Breast milk never needs any preparation. It is ready packed in its own sterile container at the right temperature. And it is with you and ready wherever you go.	*Bottle-feeds have to be made up, sterilized, stored safely, carried with you when you go out. You will probably warm them, too, although babies only object to icy milk.*
	Travelling is easy; you need not give a thought to the baby's food.	*You need a lot of equipment even if you only go out for the day.*
	Night feeds are easy.	*Night feeds mean a trip to the refrigerator to get the bottle, and boiling water to warm it in.*
	Babies are unlikely to get gastro-enteritis or any other form of stomach upset while they are fed on breast milk alone. They will also have some protection against other illnesses.	*Gastro-enteritis or stomach upsets need not occur. But making sure that they don't means being very careful, always, about sterilizing bottles, teats, mixing jugs, etc. (see p. 65).*
	The baby will not get too fat. A plump breast-fed baby is meant to be plump. You cannot overfeed your baby on breast milk alone.	*Bottle-fed babies need not get too fat. But they will if you put too much milk powder or extra sugar or cereals in their feeds (see p. 66).*
	The baby's food needs will be met first out of whatever you eat. So breast-feeding mothers usually get their figures back quickly.	*Getting thin again is more difficult if your baby is not helping by taking some of those calories.*
	You cannot tell how much milk the baby has had. The supply varies according to the baby's demand. It is sucking which stimulates your breasts to make more milk; on a rigid schedule you may not make enough.	*You can see exactly how much milk the baby has taken, and the amount offered is up to you.*
	Fatigue, worry, illness, menstruation can all temporarily lessen the milk supply. Many drugs can pass into the milk and dose the baby, too, so check with the doctor about taking medicine or alcohol.	*The baby's feeding is physically separate from your well-being.*
	Although your baby's milk is free, it is manufactured from what you eat. It is essential that you have enough protein, vitamins and fluid.	*Babymilks have to be bought, but the baby's feeding is independent of your eating habits.*
	You cannot delegate feedings, at least until the supply is well-established.	*Other people can stand in for you at feeding times.*
	Feeding means baring the breasts. Some mothers will feel a need for privacy and may dislike feeding the baby in public.	*The baby can be fed anywhere, without embarrassment.*

First feeds

Newborn babies don't need much food in the first three or four days of life. Breast-fed babies get colostrum, which is mostly water with protein, sugar, and a lot of valuable antibodies in it. Bottle-fed babies are offered milk, but the water part of that milk is what they need most. They probably will not take much, anyway. As we shall see, feeding is something babies have to learn.

Because they take little food, babies usually lose weight for four or five days before they start to gain. It is quite usual to lose half a pound (225g) over days and then gain it back over the next five. A baby's weight at ten days is therefore expected to be roughly the same as it was at birth.

When a newborn baby is thirsty or hungry he feels uncomfortable so he cries. But at this early stage he does not cry *to be fed*. He does not know that his discomfort comes from hunger; or that sucking will bring him food; or that food will make him feel better. He has to learn the sucking = food = comfort sequence by experience.

Some babies are so ready to suck that this vital learning takes place quickly and easily. They may have been practising sucking their fingers in the womb (we know that some babies do) and once they are born they suck anything that comes their way. Of course, when such a baby is offered the breast or a bottle he sucks that too. Sucking gives him milk. Milk makes him feel good. The feeding lesson is learned.

Other babies are not at all like this. They cry piteously with hunger-pain but when their mothers try to put a nipple or teat in their mouths they yell around it. Even a taste of colostrum or milk does not stop the crying. The connection between that taste and comfort has not been made yet. With a baby like this early attempts at feeding can be a struggle.

However, whether yours is a "sucky baby" or not, you can be quite sure that he has been born with a set of sucking reflexes. If instead of trying to force your nipple or a teat into his yelling mouth you use these reflexes, he will suck. Once he has sucked a few times and discovered the food-comfort, all will be well.

Evoking the sucking reflex

A baby who is hungry turns his head *towards* a gentle touch or stroke on the cheek. So if you are holding him in the crook of your left arm, ready to feed him from your left breast or from a bottle held in your right hand, stroke his right cheek and he will turn his head in towards you.

As he turns his head his lips will purse. Both these manoeuvres are reactions to your touch on his cheek, but once he has made them he is ready for a further cue: the touch of nipple, finger or anything suckable on his pursed lips. As soon as he feels it he will latch on and begin to suck. It sounds very simple and it is. But it is easy to give contradictory cues, by touching *both* cheeks, for example; to give them in the wrong order, by touching his lips first; or to spoil the timing, by not being ready with a nipple for that pursed mouth. Above all, it is easy to be too active. You cannot force him to suck. Give him the cues and trust him.

If a baby's sucking reflexes are respected and used in his very first feeding experiences he will quickly learn the lesson sucking — milk — comfort. But it helps him to learn and it helps him to get enthusiastic about the whole feeding business if the feeds are kept as comfortable and as peaceful as you can possibly manage. It is not always easy to arrange life for your baby exactly as you would like it, especially if you are in a busy hospital, but these are some of the things you should try to avoid:

Don't try to feed a baby who is really upset and screaming. He will not suck well. He is overwhelmed by his feelings. He cannot respond to your invitations to suck himself better. In a hospital this can be a problem. The staff may want your breast-fed baby to wait for his feed because they want you to get a reasonable amount of rest—especially at night. The bottle-fed babies on the ward may be fed on a schedule, with nurses making up all their feeds at certain hours. If you are breast-feeding make it clear to the night staff that you do want to be woken up whenever your baby is hungry. If you are bottle-feeding insist on an extra bottle if he seems really hungry at the "wrong" times. If, despite all your efforts, he has been kept waiting and is upset, then he needs comforting by close wrapping, rocking or walking before you attempt to persuade him to suck.

Don't let noise and movement distract your baby from sucking. If you are at home, try feeding him quite alone at least for a few days. If you are in hospital, bend down over him so that your face is directly above his. If you can get him to focus on you, other things will be less distracting. Wherever you are, keep up a gentle stream of talk. Your voice will block out the other sounds.

Don't try to force a sleepy baby to stay awake. In the very first days many babies are too sleepy to suck for long. It does not matter if he goes to sleep after a few sucks. He will wake again when he needs a few more (see p. 72). But it *does* matter if he is bounced and jolted and has his feet flicked in misguided attempts to wake him up enough to take the "proper" amount. Feeding should be gentle bliss.

You want the baby to discover that sucking brings milk and that milk feels good, so it is important that the sucking should be properly rewarded. In breast-feeding a somewhat pendulous breast (especially one that is not yet full of milk but only has some colostrum in it) can block the baby's nose when he tries to suck so that instead of reward he gets a panic because he cannot breathe. The answer is to use the fingers of your free hand to depress the breast a little just above the areola so that his nose is kept clear (see p. 61).

In bottle-feeding the baby may be offered a teat with too small a hole. Instead of an easy reward for his sucking he has to work for every sip and in these early days he may easily give up. If you up-end the bottle, milk should drip out of the teat at a rate of several drops per *second*. If it is slower than that, ask for a larger holed teat if you are in hospital, or enlarge the hole with a red-hot needle if you are at home.

Breast-feeding

Getting started with breast-feeding is not always easy. Just as many babies need to be tactfully shown how to use their sucking reflexes, so many breasts have to be gradually persuaded into easy performance of the function for which they are designed. Many first-time mothers find the first few days worrying, strange and uncomfortable; as a result some abandon the attempt to breast-feed within a week of the birth. Don't give up at least until you have given yourself a chance to experience the glorious time ahead when these early problems are over and the milk is there, like magic, whenever the baby wants it. Because they know, from experience, that this happy state is coming, second-time mothers who have breast-fed before hardly ever let early difficulties put them off. They know that once the milk supply is fully established, breast-feeding will be worthwhile.

If you have small breasts, don't let glimpses of more lavishly endowed women, feeding their babies in the hospital, make you feel inadequate. The size of your breasts has no relevance to their ability to produce an abundant supply of milk, Milk is produced in deeply buried glands, not in the surrounding fatty tissue.

Don't be surprised or disheartened if the whole feeding business is a struggle as long as you remain in hospital. A busy ward is not the best place to combine learning yourself with teaching your baby. The availability of expert help seems comforting but may not be of very much practical use. Helping someone persuade a new baby on to the breast is rather like helping her tie a necktie. You can do it yourself or let her do it; two of you together make a muddle. You will probably work things out better when you and the baby can be alone together in your home surroundings, with everything under your own control and the privacy you need to experiment without feeling a fool.

It will probably be three to five days after the birth before your milk comes in. In the meantime don't make the mistake of thinking that your colostrum is milk which is "watery" and "no good", and that your baby would be better off with a nice creamy-looking formula. Colostrum is meant to be watery because water is what your baby needs most. It is irreplaceably good.

Your baby should be put to the breast regularly during these first days, both to get that vital colostrum and to practise sucking while your breasts are still soft. Without practice in the whole business of sucking, the newborn will find your larger, harder, milk-filled breasts more difficult to cope with.

When the milk does come in there are various minor, short-lived but uncomfortable problems which may arise:

Engorgement   After the birth, tremendous hormonal activity in your body instigates milk production. Often the milk "comes in" overnight so that your breasts suddenly become large and tightly swollen both with milk and an increased supply of blood. Sometimes the chemical messages the breasts receive are over-emphatic. The breasts become rigidly hard, hot and painful with even the areolae around the nipples distended. If this happens, then your breasts are engorged.

Breasts in this state are always uncomfortable and may be extremely painful. Fortunately the hormonal imbalance will settle down within a day or two. Your breasts will never again be so large, tight or uncomfortable, even when you are producing three times as much milk for a larger and hungrier baby.

The cure for engorgement is to get rid of some of the excess milk. You will not be able to do this at once by suckling the baby because he will not be able to get hold of the swollen areola. You must first soften the breasts a little, by bathing them repeatedly with hot water, and then express some milk by the method described on page 63.

If your baby does not take enough milk at intervals frequent enough to keep you comfortable, you will get some relief from very cold washcloths or wrapped ice-cubes laid on the breasts. A simple pain-reliever will help, too.

Sore nipples If your baby sucks enthusiastically, the unaccustomed use may make your nipples sore. Massage and cold-water bathing during late pregnancy should have toughened them a little, but now you must limit the baby's sucking time to about two minutes each side, increasing by only a minute each day, until they are used to their new job.

Keeping the nipples dry between feeds, and being careful not to pull the sucking baby off them forcibly will help too (see p. 62).

Cracked nipples If a sudden, thin, sharp pain darts through your nipple as the baby latches on, continuing with the sucking, there may be a tiny crack in it. A cracked nipple must be rested and reported to your doctor who will probably give you some cream to put on it to aid healing and prevent infection. Healing will only take a day or two, but during this time the baby must be fed only from the other breast. You can gently express the milk from the affected side (see p. 63).

Hard, sore lumps in the breast Very occasionally one of the tiny tubes which carries the milk from glands to nipple gets blocked. Milk gathers above the blockage and cannot escape. You will be able to feel a small, hard, painful lump.

Bathe the breast repeatedly with hot water and massage it gently, then feed the baby. If the lumpiness and pain subside, you have helped the milk duct to clear itself. If they do not, see your doctor the same day. The lump could be due to an abscess forming rather than to a simple blockage.

Breast abscesses These are usually the result of infection getting into the breast through an untreated crack in the nipple. One area of the breast will be hard, red and painfully throbbing. You may have some fever and feel unwell. It is important to see your doctor on that same day although you can safely continue to feed the baby from the affected breast while you wait.

If a breast abscess is treated in the early stages (usually with antibiotics), you will be able to go on feeding the baby normally throughout the treatment period and you need have little pain. If the abscess is neglected you may have to confine the baby to the other breast for many days and it may be memorably painful.

Your baby is helped to get the milk from your breasts by the draught or "let down" reflex. Sucking, hunger cries, or the baby's mere presence when your breasts are full, causes the release into your blood of "Oxytocin". This hormone makes the muscle fibres around your milk glands contract, forcing their milk down into the milk ducts. "Oxytocin" also makes the muscles of your womb contract and some women feel the contractions as mild colicky pains. They stop being noticeable after two or three days.

Sometimes the draught reflex makes the second breast leak milk while the baby sucks from the first, or it makes both breasts leak when they are overfull or when the sight or sound of any young baby reminds your body of your own. Some suggestions for dealing with this are on p. 62.

Supply and demand

How much milk have you got? How often should the baby have it? In breast-feeding these two questions go together because your breasts will make as much milk as your baby sucks from you. The more he takes the more you will make. The more often he takes it the quicker you will make more. This is why a mother can make exactly the right amount of milk for a 6lb (2.7kg) baby *or* exactly the right amount of milk for twins who weigh 13lbs (5.9kg) between them. This is why she can make enough for the baby in his second week of life and just the right amount in his twenty-second week. . . .

Breast-feeding is a natural supply and demand system. It therefore depends on the baby being allowed to behave naturally. The system often fails if he is kept to an unnaturally rigid schedule. The natural system works like this:

The breasts make milk and the baby drinks it. The breasts are left empty, so they at once start to make more milk. If the baby had enough at that first feed, he will be satisfied for some time – probably around three hours – so the breasts will only make about that same amount of milk again. But if he did not get quite enough at that first feeding, he will be hungry quite soon. He will want to suck again. If he is allowed to, he will empty the breasts yet again and they will be stimulated to make more milk.

The more often he empties the breasts, the more milk they will make. Eventually, perhaps after a day, perhaps after a week, the breasts will be making so much milk that the baby will stop being hungry so often. He will only empty the breasts every three or four hours, so they will slow their production down to that level.

Let the baby suck as often as he or she is hungry, however often that may be. For a few days he may want to be put to the breast as often as 10 or even 12 times in the 24 hours. As long as your nipples do not get sore or cracked (see pp. 53 and 62) and as long as you can use these almost non-stop feedings as periods of physical rest for yourself, it does not matter how often you suckle him.

Make sure the baby has emptied both breasts at every feed so that they receive maximum stimulation. If, due to the variable demands of these unsettled early days, he sometimes leaves some milk, express it by hand (see method, p. 63).

Believe that babies who suck when they want to, will get what they need. But if you find yourself worrying continually

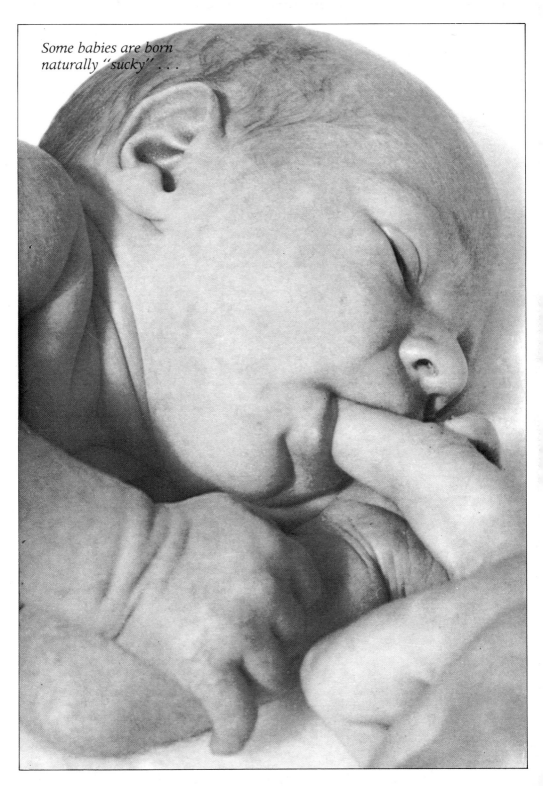

Some babies are born
naturally "sucky" . . .

*. . . others need to be helped. The baby
has reflexes which tell him what to do
if you give him the cues . . .*

*. . . a gentle touch on his cheek from breast
or finger, and he will turn in towards you*

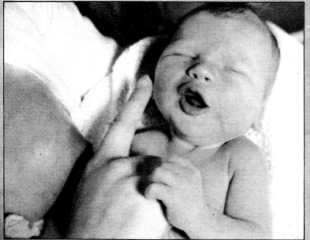

*. . . mouth open, lips pursed,
the right moment is now*

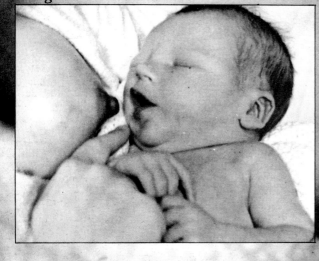

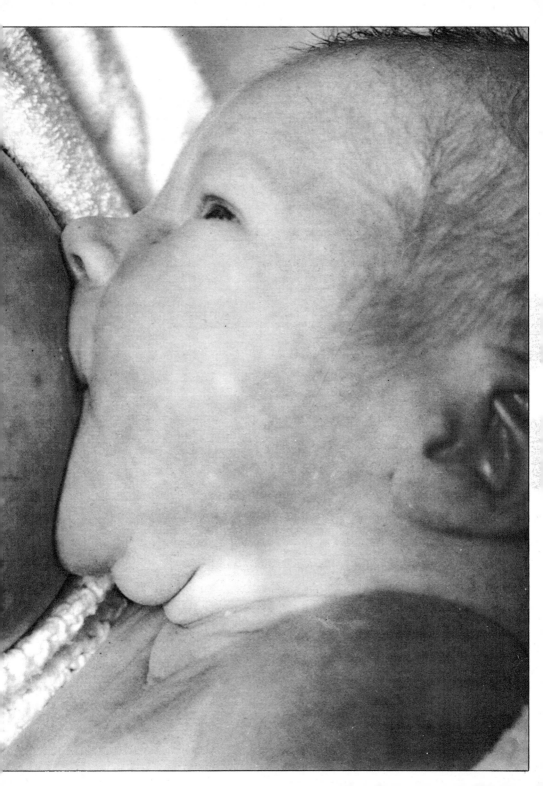

. . . sucking gives him milk
. . . milk makes him feel good . . .
the feeding lesson is learned.

because you cannot see how much milk he is taking, consider test weighing him to set your mind at rest (see below).

Don't try to make your baby wait for feeds. This will prevent him from giving your breast that vital message "I need more, make it", so it will ensure that he goes on being hungry, restless and unable to wait for a reasonable interval between feeds.

Don't offer a bottle instead of the breast, even if he sucked so recently that you are sure there cannot yet be any more milk for him. There will always be a little, and preventing him from taking it will make your breasts fill up more slowly.

Don't offer a bottle as well as the breast because his demands are so frequent that you feel he must have more at each meal. This will conceal the extent of his hunger from your breasts so that their supply cannot increase to match it.

Expressing At the beginning, the baby's demands may be very variable, because he is not very settled yet nor very efficient at sucking. It is worth expressing any milk that he leaves, so that your breasts make plenty for the next feed when he may be hungrier.

Don't try to express until no milk comes out. As you drain the breast, it makes more milk, so you will never completely empty it. Stop when the milk stops squirting and only appears in drops (see method p. 63).

Test weighing Some mothers find it difficult to stay calm about their baby's feeding when they have no idea how much milk he is getting. The correct advice is "leave it to the baby; he will take what he needs if you just feed him whenever he wants". But if you are worried, you may find it hard to follow this advice. In fact worry over whether the baby is getting enough is one of the most common reasons for mothers changing to bottle-feeding: it is a relief to be able to *see* 3 or 4ozs (85 or 115ml) vanishing into the baby.

If you and your baby are both enjoying breast-feeding, *don't give up*. You can set your mind at rest by borrowing or hiring a set of babyscales. Your local clinic may lend you a set, or a chemist will tell you the firms that hire them out.

To find out how much milk your baby is getting in 24 hours: weigh him, in his clothes, just before you feed him. Write down the weight. Then feed him, without altering his clothes. Anything he puts in his nappy must stay there. Weigh him again.

The difference between the second and the first weights is the quantity of milk the baby took at that feed. Do the same for the other feeds in the 24 hours and you know what he has had altogether. But don't weigh him just for one feed. That will not tell you anything. It may be an extra big feed or an extra small one. Only the total feeds for a whole day and night will assure you that he is getting enough.

Of course it is a pity if you get so anxious about the whole feeding business that you feel you have to keep on weighing the baby. Your real assurance that he is adequately fed is his contentment, his energy and his weight gain. But if an occasional test weighing day can keep you calm and stop you feeling that you must add in bottles or cereals, it is worthwhile.

Starting breast-feeding

You and your baby will soon take breast-feeding pleasurably for granted, but while you are getting used to it, mutual comfort is important. Clothes that open down the front, for example, make it easier to bare your breasts than "fishing" down the neck of a sweater; they give the baby a good sucking position, too. A controlled milk flow, a comfortable chair, plenty of time and all the privacy you personally want will all help you both to enjoy yourselves.

Feeding position

Cradle the baby in the crook of your arm so that her well-supported head is above the level of her stomach. If you hold her flat, the air she takes with the milk will not be able to rise to the top of her stomach for easy burping. Leave her outside hand free – she will soon enjoy stroking the breast as part of active feeding rather than passively being fed. Don't hold her head forcibly against you. She must be able to turn away for a rest.

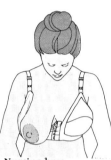

Nursing bras

These open in front and have a separate flap for each breast, which means that you can release one breast at a time. Wearing a nursing bra also helps to reduce milk leakage.

Comfort during feeds

It is important that you are comfortable during feeds and able to relax completely. The ideal nursing chair is low enough for you to sit with your feet flat on the floor, upright enough to support your back all the way up, and armless so that you do not bump the baby's head. If you feed lying down, use plenty of pillows to support your full weight. Don't try to lean on your elbow – it will ache.

Avoiding backache

Pillows support your arm and the weight of the baby on it . . . or pillows support the baby so that your arm takes no weight.

You will get backache if you try to put your baby's mouth to your nipple by leaning over to her or by lifting her up to you.

So, sit forward with a pillow supporting your back and cross your legs so that your raised knee brings the baby within reach.

Alternatively, sit back so that the chair supports you all the way up your spine. Put a pillow on your lap and lie the baby on that.

Putting the baby to the breast

The whole technique of breast-feeding will soon become obvious to you because it is based on making the baby comfortable and you will be able to see when she is not! After a few days she will need little encouragement or stimulation of her sucking reflexes because she will have learned the sucking = food = pleasure sequence by experience. But starting off right is important, and it remains important to avoid making her feel smothered, choked or forced.

Helping her to suck

If your baby takes only your nipple into her mouth she will get no milk. Her suction and the compression of her lips will actually close the openings. Her attempts are very likely to make your nipples sore.

Milk will flow out of the openings in your nipple when she uses her jaws to press rhythmically around the base of the areola, while simultaneously exerting suction. Help her to take the nipple and the areola right into her mouth. When she is sucking, her lips should be sealed around the meeting edge of the areola and the skin of your breast.

Sucking reflexes
1 *When you are ready to give the breast, prepare the baby to take it by gently stroking the cheek nearest to you.*

2 She will respond by turning inwards towards the breast. After a few days the touch of your bare breast against her cheek will be enough to evoke this response.

3 As she turns inwards, her lips will purse. If the nipple touches them now . . .

4 . . . she will take it and settle to nursing.

Giving her breathing space

Your baby has to breathe through her nose while she is sucking. A feeling of smothering will panic her and might even put her off breast-feeding, so make sure your breast does not obstruct her nostrils. You can do this by depressing the breast gently just above the areola. This will give her a "breathing hole".

Reducing the flow

Sometimes the "let down" reflex works too well for a new baby. As soon as she starts to suck, milk pours out, making her gulp and choke. You can slow up the flow by putting your middle and forefinger on either side of the areola, just above the baby's lips, and pressing gently upwards. Remove them when her sucking rhythm steadies.

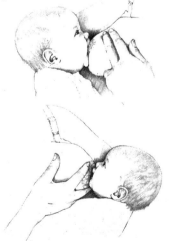

Breast care

Don't let your baby suck for long at each breast until your nipples have become hardened. Two minutes on each side, increasing by about one minute per day is enough. If you have no problems she can suck as long as she likes by her third week. Start each feed at the breast she ended up with last time. Each breast will then get the stimulation of her hungriest sucking at alternate feeds.

Don't try to remove the baby from your breast by pulling against her suction. She exerts a tremendous pull and it will hurt your nipple. Wait, if you can, until she stops for a rest. If not, break the suction by slipping your forefinger down between the areola and her lips.

"Which breast first at this feed?"

The baby is having the left breast first this time, but will you remember which to offer first at the next feed?

If you are liable to forget, use a code: tuck a tissue into your bra on the side she sucked first.

Next time start her on the breast with no tissue. Easy to remember as the other will leak into its tissue.

Looking after your nipples

Nipples vary in their sensitivity. You may find that to avoid soreness, you have to look after yours throughout the breast-feeding period; but if you take trouble during the early weeks, they may toughen up sufficiently to look after themselves thereafter. Preventing your nipples getting sore is rather like preventing your baby getting nappy rash. Like her bottom, your nipples are exposed to continual friction, which can make them dry and flaky, and to continual damp, which can make them soggy. The combination of damp and friction can make for chapping. Some suggestions for avoiding these discomforts are shown below.

Dry both nipples carefully after feeds. Leave them exposed to the air for a while whenever you can.

Keep leaking nipples dry with squares of one-way nappy. Avoid waterproofed pads which exclude air.

Wash carefully to remove milk traces at least twice each day. Use plain water without soap.

Plain lanolin cream rubbed in twice daily will help replace the natural oils and keep the nipples supple.

Expressing

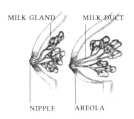

MILK GLAND MILK DUCT

NIPPLE AREOLA

Milk is produced by glands distributed through the breast tissue. It gathers in minute sacs (the alveoli) and travels down milk ducts which widen into ampullae, placed inside the areola. There the milk stays until the sucking baby presses the areola between her gums to squirt it from the ampullae through the openings in the nipple. At the same time her suction draws further milk down the ducts and calls the draught reflex into play.

When you want to express – to get milk out without the baby's help –

you have to replace her stimulation by using gentle massage to start the milk moving down the ducts and pressure on the areola to move it from the ampullae through the nipple. If you are ridding yourself of unwanted milk or ensuring emptied breasts, express into the washbasin or wherever you please. But if the baby is to drink the milk, use a sterile jug and refrigerate it. Don't go òn trying to express until the breast is empty. That time is never. Stop when the milk comes in drops instead of jets.

How to express

1 *Support the breast in one palm and use the other to stroke repeatedly downwards as far as the areola. Work evenly all round the breast.*

2 *Now support the breast in your right palm. Place your thumb about halfway up the breast . . .*

3 *. . . and run it firmly down.*

4 *As your thumb reaches the edge of the areola, press in and up and milk will squirt from the untouched nipple.*

Where to squeeze

Don't squeeze the nipple; you will close the ducts. Squeeze the edge of the areola up and in. You will know you are right if your action makes the whole nipple stand out.

Expressing from overfull breasts

The breast in front is full, ready for sucking; the one behind is overfull; the baby cannot grasp the engorged areola so she cannot suck.

Breasts which become overfull usually leak out the milk they cannot hold. Sometimes they become engorged with blood so that the swelling of the breast actually prevents milk escaping. Engorged· breasts are painful. The normal massage technique of expression is impossible. So, bathe the breasts in water as hot as they can comfortably bear. Soaking in the bath is the easiest way, otherwise keep applying washcloths. The breasts may spontaneously leak milk after a few minutes. If not, apply alternate gentle pressure with your fingers above the areola and more wash-cloths until milk comes.

Bottle-feeding

We have no real alternative to the breast-fed baby's colostrum, so while the bottle-fed baby may start life with one or two drinks of sugared water, formula will be offered by the second day. This is much sooner than a breast-fed baby would find milk, so your baby may take very little. The water content is needed much more than the food content, so don't worry.

If your baby does take all the milk offered, weight gain may start from birth instead of after a few days weight loss. Although early weight loss often worries parents, don't be too enthusiastic about every ounce your bottle-fed baby gains; babies can get too fat.

Choosing a formula Cow's milk is ideal for calves but it is not the natural food for babies. It contains too little sugar and the wrong kind of fat. Its protein makes indigestibly solid curds in the baby's stomach and it contains more minerals – especially sodium – than human milk. Adapting it to make it more like breast milk is a complicated procedure, so ignore all forms of ordinary cow's milk and stick to a special babymilk.

The best babymilks are those which have been most extensively modified. They are often described as "humanized" and while this does not mean that they are exactly like breast milk, it does mean that they have been made as similar as possible. Complex processing makes these the most expensive milks, but they will suit your baby whether he has a resilient or a sensitive digestive system and they will help him to grow sturdy and firm rather than become fat and flabby.

The least satisfactory babymilks are simply dried cow's milk with added iron and vitamins. They are the cheapest but they cannot be recommended. Even if your baby digested them easily he would be receiving too much sodium. This would place a strain on his kidneys and might actually be dangerous if he was already unwell and/or feverish.

Between these extremes of safety and price there are many formulae available and your baby will probably thrive on any of them. Study the labels of several brands carefully so that you know exactly what you are feeding to him:

Does your formula need added sugar? Most have the right amount incorporated but a few leave you to add it yourself. A complete formula is easier to use; the fewer items you have to measure out, the less likely you are to get the exact mixture wrong when you are in a hurry or half asleep.

Are iron and all necessary vitamins included? They almost certainly will be but it is important to check. Consult your doctor if you are unsure on this point.

How easily can it be mixed? Many powdered formulae can simply be shaken up with the correct amount of cooled boiled water. Some need to be stirred in to the water while a few go lumpy if they are not made into a paste first.

Some formulae are sold as a liquid concentrate rather like ordinary evaporated milk. Although the tins are heavy to carry home and need refrigerating once opened, these are very simple to measure and mix.

If you really want to save yourself trouble and do not mind what you spend on your baby's milk, you can buy feeds which are ready-mixed and sealed into pre-sterilized disposable bottles.

Preparing bottle-feeds You cannot safely take a happy-go-lucky approach to preparing bottles, especially while your baby is very young. Hygiene is important if he is to stay well, and correct preparation of the formula is important to proper nourishment.

Hygiene There are bacteria everywhere. We all carry germs on our hands and our clothes. We breathe them, eat them and excrete them. Most of them are harmless. Very few types will make us ill unless we take in such a large number all at one time that our bodies' defences are overwhelmed.

A new baby, especially one who is not breast-fed, has few defences against common germs. It takes time for him to build up immunity to them. In an ordinarily clean home, he will cope with the germs that he sucks off his hands or breathes in the living room. But when he is feeding it is different. Milk, especially milk which is around room temperature, is an ideal *breeding ground* for germs. So while he might pick up a few off his own fingers and deal with them perfectly well, he will pick up an enormous, and possibly overwhelming number from a bottle which has been left standing around in a warm room. Gastro-enteritis is still one of the most common reasons for young babies being admitted to hospital. To keep the baby's milk as free from bacteria as possible:

Wash your hands before handling the milk, especially after using the lavatory or handling pets or their food.

Use a sterile babymilk and keep the packet closed or the tin closely covered and refrigerated once it has been opened.

Sterilize everything you use in measuring, mixing or storing the made-up milk. That means measuring spoons, mixing jugs and the water in the feed itself.

Sterilize bottle, teats and teat covers. Provided that you put a sterile teat cover over the sterilized teat on your ready-filled bottle, that teat will still be sterile and safe when you take the cover off to feed the baby.

Bacteria which escape your precautions (by landing on the sterile teat as you put it on the bottle, for example) cannot multiply dangerously while the milk is boiling hot nor while it is icy cold. It is the in-between temperatures that help them to flourish. To minimize the chances of bacteria breeding:

Cool the made-up milk quickly, preferably by putting it in the refrigerator while it is still hot.

Keep it cold until the baby wants it. Don't put a bottle to warm in advance of him waking up, nor keep it warm for him if he drops off to sleep for more than a few minutes in mid-feed. *Never* put warm milk in a vacuum flask or electric bottle warmer.

Throw away any milk the baby leaves. Don't try to save that half bottle for next time and don't pour the remains back into your jug of sterilized formula in the refrigerator.

Making up the formula

When you combine milk powder or liquid concentrate with boiled water, you are constructing food and most of your baby's drink. If you do it in exactly the proportions the manufacturer suggests in the mixing instructions, you will end up with a feed that is as close to the composition of breast milk as it is possible to get with that particular formula. The baby will get the right amount of nourishment and the right amount of water.

Research workers have found that a great many bottles are not made up accurately. It is largely this inaccuracy which makes bottle-feeding unsatisfactory for many babies. *Follow the manufacturer's instructions exactly.* Making a bottle is not like preparing instant coffee. You cannot make it better by putting in just a little extra powder, or more thirst quenching by adding extra water. If you add too much powder, the milk will be too strong. The baby will get too much protein, too much fat, too many minerals, and not enough water. He will get fat because you are giving him too many calories, and thirsty because you are giving him too much salt. Because he is thirsty, he will cry, and because he cries you will give him another bottle. If that bottle is too strong, too, he will be even more thirsty. So it will go on. The result is a baby who cries a lot, does not seem terribly well or happy, puts on a lot of weight, and seems to need a lot of feeding.

Don't be afraid to offer extra, plain, boiled water, but don't add anything extra to the formula. If the milk needs sugar, the instructions will tell you to add it. If they don't say so, don't add it.

Never guess at quantities. Measure milk powder accurately by filling the scoop provided and slicing off the surplus at scoop level with a knife. Wiping the surplus off on the edge of the tin or smoothing it off with a spoon will not be accurate; you will almost certainly end up with a somewhat packed and heaped scoop. Shaking off the surplus may leave you with either too much or too little powder.

Measure liquid concentrate accurately by pouring it either directly into the bottle or into a marked-off measuring jug and then holding it up to your eye level to read off the marked ounces. If you check the level with your eye above it, you will think there is less milk than there really is.

Measure the water accurately by boiling it (to sterilize it) *first*, and pouring it into your bottle or measuring jug when it has cooled. If you measure the water first and then boil it, some will be lost in evaporation.

Measure any needed sugar accurately by using a 5ml pharmacist's or measuring spoon heaped and levelled as for milk powder scoops. If you use any teaspoon which comes to hand it may hold more or less than that standard amount.

Once you have made the correct mixture – assembled the milk according to the manufacturer's formula – the baby can have as much or as little as he wants. You don't need to carry your scientific accuracy in *making the milk* on into *feeding it*!

The way your baby behaves will affect your handling, teaching you to be more gentle . . .

*. . . your handling will affect
the way she behaves,
teaching her to be more relaxed.*

Starting bottle-feeding

Your baby's bottles, teats and the equipment used to prepare the milk need scrupulous attention to prevent a build-up of bacteria. The amount of equipment you buy depends on which type of formula you use and on how you organize your sterilizing. The number of bottles and accessories suggested below are for maximum convenience.

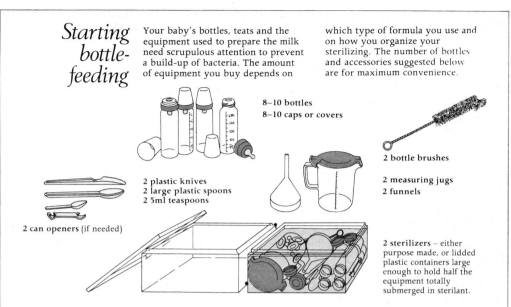

8–10 bottles
8–10 caps or covers

2 bottle brushes

2 plastic knives
2 large plastic spoons
2 5ml teaspoons

2 measuring jugs
2 funnels

2 can openers (if needed)

2 sterilizers – either purpose made, or lidded plastic containers large enough to hold half the equipment totally submerged in sterilant.

Easy sterilizing

You can sterilize feeding equipment by boiling it for 20 minutes, but chemical sterilants make the job easier. Mixed according to the instructions they can take up to 2 hours to make clean equipment sterile. Everything must be totally submerged – a bottle that floats will not be sterilized.

Equipment can be kept in the sterilant for twenty-four hours but then it must be renewed. If you have enough bottles and other equipment you can divide it between two sterilizers. This keeps sterilizing down to a twice-daily chore, and means that you always have enough bottles ready for use.

In the morning . . .

Wash all bottles, jugs etc. used during the night. Use hot water, detergent and a bottle brush.

Turn teats inside out. Rub with salt if slimy. Rinse salt off very thoroughly.

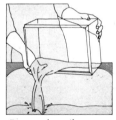

Empty stale sterilant from sterilizer and replace with a fresh mixture.

Carefully submerge all the clean bottles, teats etc. so that everything is below sterilant level.

Add any dummies, plastic rattles, teething rings etc. Everything will be sterile by evening.

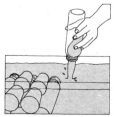

In the evening, once the sterilizing period is over, take bottles out as you need them. Drain but do not rinse.

After the feed, rinse bottle and teat and leave by the sink ready for the morning wash-up session.

In the evening . . .
Sterilize the bottles you will use during the next day in exactly the same way; they will have all night to become safe.
In the morning, take them out as you need them; after use, drain, rinse and leave them by the sink for the evening wash-up session.

Preparing bottle-feeds

Formulae must be made up accurately if the bottle is to contain the right number of calories. Use only the scoop provided for milk powder and level off with a knife to avoid overfull measures. If sugar is required, use a 5ml measuring spoon and level that off too. Sterilize water by boiling *before* measuring as some will evaporate. If you want to make up feeds for 24 hours, you can store them in a sterile jug in the refrigerator, but you will only have enough sterile bottles for 12 hours.

Making up powdered formulae

Boil water and let it cool to hand-heat. Wash your hands.

Take measuring jug, mixing spoon and knife from sterilizer. Drain.

Pour water into jug. Check correct quantity by holding at eye level.

Add required number of scoops of milk powder, levelling each with knife.

If your formula requires it, add carefully measured sugar.

Stir the mixture thoroughly with the sterile spoon.

Either *cover jug and refrigerate* or take bottles from sterilizer and drain.

Fill the bottles from the jug, putting more in each than the baby will drink.

Screw the teats upside down on the bottles. Cover with their sterile caps.

Put in refrigerator.

If you have no refrigerator . . .

Each feed must be made as needed; it is not safe to leave prepared feeds standing at room temperature. Choose a powdered formula that will mix when shaken in the bottle. Put warm boiled water in bottle; check quantity at eye level. Add correct number of carefully levelled scoops of powder. Screw on teat and teat cover. Shake well.

Making up a liquid formula

Wash top of can. Sterilize by pouring boiling water over it. Punch two holes with sterilized opener.

Pour correct amount into individual bottles or into jug. Check quantity by holding at eye level.

Add water, checking quantity as you do so.

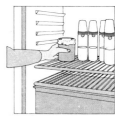

Cap bottles or cover jug. Refrigerate. Remaining concentrate must also be covered and refrigerated.

Giving the bottle

Being physically close to you during feeds is just as important to the bottle-fed baby as to the breast-fed one. Always give her the bottle while she is cradled in your arms: resist any temptation to prop it for her so that she can feed herself.

Choose a chair that supports your back while your feet are flat on the floor. Have a table nearby to hold the bottle in its warming jug. Support the baby's head well above the level of her stomach, and support your cradling arm too or it will ache.

Testing temperature and flow

Cold milk is not harmful but the baby will prefer it warm. Stand it in a jug of hot water for a few minutes. Then uncap the bottle; put the teat upright and test the milk's temperature on the inside of your wrist. It should feel just warm. Milk should come out at several drops per second. Enlarge a too-small hole with a red-hot needle.

Tilting the bottle

Make sure the baby gets the bulbous tip of the teat well back in her mouth. Always keep the teat full of milk.

Sucking reflexes
1 Make sure that you are settled and ready before you alert the baby to the bottle.

2 Using one finger of the hand that is holding the bottle, gently stroke the cheek nearest to you.

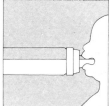

This bottle is being held too flat, the teat is only half full of milk and the baby will suck in air with her feed.

As the baby sucks, she removes both milk and the air from the unfilled space in the bottle. If no air can get back in, a vacuum will form. The teat will go flat and the baby will not be able to get any more milk. To prevent or cure this, pull gently against her suction so that the vacuum is momentarily released and you see air bubbling back in. Hold the bottle firmly all the time so that the baby

3 She will turn her head towards your touch, pursing her mouth as she does so.

4 At the touch of the teat on her pursed lips she will take it deeply into her mouth and settle to sucking.

can pull against it with her suction. If you hold it too loosely, her efforts will move the bottle around instead of pulling milk out.

Carrying bottles with you

Never carry warm formula. It is a dangerously ideal breeding ground for bacteria. Carry the baby's milk icy cold from the refrigerator. Keep it that way by putting the sterile sealed bottles in an insulated picnic box (safe for up to 8 hours) or by burying them in ice cubes in a plastic bag (safe for around 4 hours). Warm the bottles as you need them by standing them in hot water from a thermos flask. Wide-necked flasks will take a bottle

direct; narrow-necked ones mean carrying a jug as well. If you are going to need more bottles than you can safely keep cold, measure milk powder (*not* liquid) into empty sterile bottles and seal. Mix with boiled water from a thermos flask as you need each one. Always carry at least one more feed than you think you will need during the trip. This will help in case of breakdowns or delays.

Supply and demand for the bottle-fed baby

How much and how often should bottle-fed babies be fed? They do best if they are treated exactly as if they were breast-fed. Milk should be offered whenever the baby seems to be hungry and the feeding should only be stopped when eager sucking ceases. If you stick to these principles in the very early weeks, you will never have to face problems over whether or not to feed "on schedule" because a schedule will gradually evolve out of the baby's digestive pattern.

A new baby is used to having his food needs continually replenished by transfusion feeding in the womb. Now they must be met by digestion of food from a stomach that starts full and gradually empties. While he gets used to this change he may demand food at irregular and frequent intervals. If he cries only an hour after drinking 3ozs (85ml) of formula, you may ask yourself whether he can possibly be hungry again already. The answer is that although his stomach cannot yet be empty, he feels a need to have his food topped up.

If you offer him a bottle whenever he seems hungry, he will only take the amount he needs. If he drinks it all, you can assume he needed it. If he takes a little, the comfort of sucking and of your care will make him feel better. If he drinks none, what have you lost? One bottle of formula.

If you meet these irregular demands willingly, they will stop by themselves in a few weeks. It takes around three to four hours for the baby to digest a full feed. True hunger signals are tied in to the near-completion of the digestive process. Once his digestion is working more maturely and he has got used to this new kind of hunger, he will neither feel nor express distress until he *has* digested the last meal so his demands will fall into the same pattern as a conventional schedule.

Exactly the same process of maturing and settling into a feeding pattern will take place if you keep your baby to a strict four hourly schedule from the beginning. Offered feeds only at 6am, 10am, 2pm, 6pm and 10pm, he will eventually expect food at these natural intervals. The difference is that these early weeks will be miserable for you all. The baby will wake and cry. If you do not feed him because it "isn't time" you will try every other method of comforting him, which will be hard work. Because what he really wants is food, and because he will get hungrier and hungrier while you are working away at other methods of comfort, nothing you do will really soothe him. By the end of the session you will be feeling that unhappy mixture of guilt and anger and helpless despair. To crown it all, when the clock does at last say the "right time" and you give him a feed, he will probably not suck well or take enough milk to keep him happy until the next scheduled meal. All that crying will have tired him and filled his stomach with air. He will probably fall into exhausted sleep after an ounce or two and wake up again an hour later to repeat the whole performance.

So don't fall into the trap of thinking that if you feed your baby whenever he seems hungry he will get into the habit of demanding food frequently. He does not wake from habit, he wakes from hunger. When he is mature enough not to be hungry so often he will not wake up and cry.

Patterns of feeding, sleeping and crying

This unique record is taken from the notes kept by the mother of a little boy who was bottle-fed "on demand". Whenever he cried he was offered milk. If he accepted it, a "feed" was recorded. The time it took includes sociable time he spent awake. If he would not accept the offered milk, every other possible method of comfort was offered. His recorded crying periods are not therefore solid crying but times when he would have cried if left alone.

No schedule was imposed on the baby. Yet even these three separate days, taken from his first, second and fourth weeks, clearly show the development of a pattern. Where Day 5 is every parent's nightmare – a day without pattern and almost without rest – by Day 10 the number of feeds is dropping, the periods of distress are shorter and the baby is just beginning to do most of his sleeping by night.

By Day 28 the baby has settled down. He has adopted for himself a pattern which is almost identical to the conventional schedule of feeds at 6 am, 10 am, 2 pm, 6 pm and 10 pm. He has dropped that horrible 2 am feed and usually accepts a feed when he wakes and is then contented.

Day 5
He awakens after periods of sleep which vary from one hour (11 pm–midnight) to four hours (6–10 am). When he wakes he does not always want to eat (4 am). When he has eaten it does not always make him content (11 am). He spends more of the night than of the day awake, and more of his waking time in the miseries than in contentment and feeding added together.

Day 10
Day 10 already shows some patterning. Despite a bad patch between 5 am and 8 am, he has slept for five hours of night-time. He seldom cries when he does not want food and usually settles happily after feeding.

Day 28
Day 28 is a totally different picture. He is hungry roughly every four hours. He sleeps from 11 pm to 5 am. There are only six episodes of crying and five feeds. Each feed readies him for contented sleep except for brief fussing at 3 pm. He sleeps, feeds and socializes for longer periods because, being settled now, he spends far less time crying.

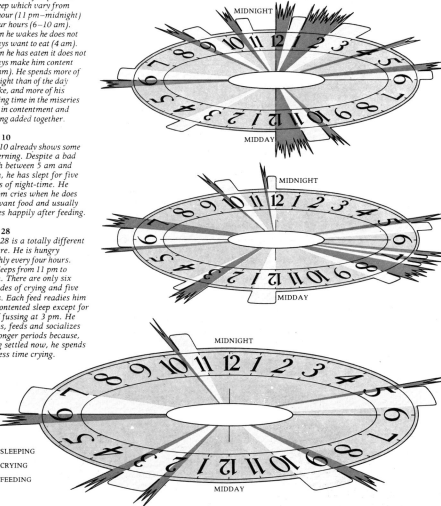

SLEEPING
CRYING
FEEDING

Burping or bringing up wind

Whether feeds are from breast or bottle your baby will suck and swallow air along with the milk. If you feed with the baby in a fairly upright position, the heavier milk will find its way to the bottom of the stomach and the lighter air will gather at the top. When the stomach is uncomfortably distended with milk and air the baby will burp some of the air out and relieve the pressure.

Burping midway through feeds

Some babies swallow so much air that their stomachs get uncomfortably distended before they have had enough milk. They need a half-time burp to make room for the rest of the feed. A breast-fed baby who needs to burp will probably do so when she is shifted across from the first breast to the second. A bottle-fed baby will stop sucking. If you hold him upright for a moment, he will burp and then return to his feed.

Many babies do not need to burp until they have finished feeding. There is no need to remove the teat from the mouth of a baby who is sucking happily, just in case he has too much air in his stomach. If he is still sucking, he is not uncomfortably full and should be left to suck in peace.

Burping after feeds

All your baby needs is the opportunity. Hold him upright against your shoulder; rub his back or pat it gently, and see what happens. If he has not burped after three minutes, he does not need to.

Don't feel that you must not put him in his cot until he has burped. He may not have taken in much air this time. If he needs to burp later, he will do so, with or without your help.

Don't use the sitting up position if you are trying to get your baby to burp. While he is sitting forward with his chin supported in your hand, his stomach is folded so that it is difficult for the air to rise above the milk level and escape. Don't try to force air out of him; force will certainly bring milk with it.

If your baby is one of the few who really seems uncomfortable until he has burped, but is slow to do so, he may manage better if you put him to sleep lying on his stomach. In this position he can burp when he needs to, and if he brings any milk up with the air (see below), there is no risk of him choking on it.

Burping

Burping is an overrated problem. Your baby will get air in her stomach. Milk, which is heavier than air, will fall below it if you hold her upright, so she will usually burp the air out. But if she does not, don't waste time thumping her. Her stomach may not be uncomfortably distended this time; she may burp later in her cot; either way it does not matter.

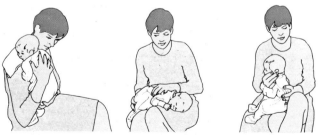

The best burping position: the baby is stretched out straight and upright. Rubbing or patting her back may help.

A burp in this position will almost certainly bring milk with it as air cannot rise above the milk level.

In this position the baby's stomach is folded, making it difficult for air to rise above the milk level and escape.

Bringing up milk   Almost all babies sometimes bring up some milk along with the air. Usually the quantity is very small. It may look a lot because it is mixed with saliva and spread all over your shoulder! If you are worried, spill $\frac{1}{4}$oz on purpose to give you a standard of comparison. If it really *is* a lot, there are several possible reasons for it:

The baby may have sucked more than he could comfortably hold. He is sensibly bringing back the overflow.

You may have fed him in too flat a position, preventing the air from rising above the milk. Try holding him more upright.

You may have bounced him about, mixing the air with the milk, or banged him on the back before the air had reached the top of the stomach. Handle him gently immediately after feeds.

You may have delayed his feed while he cried, or you may have made him cry in mid-feed by trying to make him burp when he wanted to suck. The crying will have put a lot of extra air into his stomach, followed by the rest of his milk.

You may not have tilted the bottle sufficiently to ensure that the entrance to the teat was always covered with milk. The baby will have had sucks of pure air between sucks of milk and it will all be mixed up together in his stomach.

The hole in the teat may have been too small so that the baby had to suck very hard and swallowed air with each mouthful of milk. Check that when you hold the bottle upside down, milk drips out at several drops per second. (Don't check with water; this is thinner and comes out faster than milk.)

Vomiting   If a baby brings up milk some time after feeding, it will be curdled because digestive juices will already have been working on it. If an hour or more passed since the feeding, it may smell nasty. The baby may only have had some air trapped inside the stomach which has now come up bringing the partly digested milk with it, or there may be a digestive disturbance or the beginning of an illness. If the baby seems unwell and especially if there is any fever or any sign of diarrhoea, consult your doctor or clinic. If the baby seems perfectly well let hunger guide feeds as usual and just keep an eye open for any symptoms.

Projectile vomiting   This is quite different either from hiccuping milk up with some air or from ordinary vomiting. The baby spurts milk out towards the end of a feed with such force that it may hit the floor or a wall as much as three or four feet away.

A baby who does this regularly probably has a condition called "pyloric stenosis". This is a fault in the muscles of the stomach outlet. It is much more usual in boys than in girls and is easily and permanently corrected by a small operation.

If you think that your baby's vomiting is projectile, tell your doctor immediately. The urgency is not because pyloric stenosis is dangerous in itself but because this particular kind of vomiting does take a large proportion of the feed away from the baby who will not thrive until it is prevented. Your doctor will probably arrange for your health visitor to watch one of the baby's feeds and report on the vomiting. If pyloric stenosis is diagnosed, medicine may be prescribed which will improve the condition while your baby waits for the operation.

Food and growth

New babies need as much breast milk or properly made formula as they willingly drink; the offer of some cooled boiled water a couple of times each day and, if they are bottle-fed, a measured dose of a vitamin C enriched fruit syrup. They do not need anything else until they are at *least* three months old (see p. 137).

Once the birthweight has been regained at around ten days old (see p. 50) the baby will gain weight at around 1oz (28g) per day. Of course there will be day-to-day variations, but he will average 6–8ozs (170–225g) each week.

Many parents find it difficult to leave it entirely to the baby to decide how much milk to take. They feel a great need to know exactly what he "ought" to have so that they can be sure he is having enough. But feeding a baby is not an exact science because babies vary just as much as older people in their food needs. A baby with a slow, efficient metabolism will have plenty of energy and grow well on fewer calories than a baby who burns his food up faster and less completely.

Most adults are bad at adjusting their food intake to suit their individual metabolisms. Our eating is mixed up with habit, social customs and pure greed. But a small baby's adjustment is almost always perfect, at least until we confuse it for him by introducing solid foods. Whatever quantities your baby takes, you can be quite sure that they are right for him provided he is offered as much as he wants whenever he wants it; he is contented most of the time and becoming more contented as he gets older and more settled; he is active whenever he is awake and becoming more so with age and he gains weight steadily at around that expected 6–8ozs (170–225g) each week.

Most babies will take something like 3ozs (85ml) of breast milk or made-up formula for each pound of their bodyweight in an average 24 hour period. A 7lb (3.2kg) baby is therefore likely to drink about 21ozs (595ml) and a 9lb (4.1kg) baby about 27ozs (765ml). But there are very few circumstances in which you should allow that information to affect your feeding. If the baby is breast-fed, you will not know how many ounces he takes unless you have such cause for worry that you test weigh him (see p. 59). If he is bottle-fed, you will know what he takes at each feed, but you should neither encourage him to take the "proper" amount nor refuse to give him more because he has had his "ration".

Expected weight gain

If you find yourself worrying about your baby's weight gain or you want a scientific way of supporting your own observations of his or her abundant good health, you need to understand the importance of the rate of weight gain we expect and therefore of your baby's *expected* or *ideal* weight.

Your baby's birthweight is his personal starting point for growth. Whatever that birthweight was, he will grow roughly the same amount and at approximately the same rate as all other babies. His overall growth follows a pre-set trajectory rather like a rocket which, once launched, follows a pre-determined pattern. You fuel his growth with proper food and adequate care and as long as you do so the upward growth curve will be steady. If illness, starvation, serious neglect or emotional disturbance should lead his weight gain to dip downwards off that expected curve, he will need an extra boost of food-energy to put him back on course. If over-concentrated bottles or concealed cereals should lead his weight gain to peak upwards off his personal curve, he will need it reduced to its proper composition so that he can get back on course.

So a baby needs to be fed, always, according to his expected weight. If he has gained much less than average, feeding him as if he had gained normally will give him the chance to gain fast for a while. If he has gained very fast, feeding him as if he had not will give him the chance to slow his rate of gain for a while. Of course if he is being fed on demand, with neither restriction nor forcing, he will see to this for himself. But if his food is limited by a scanty breast milk supply or strict scheduling, or if it is pushed on him by an over-strong formula or too-early solids, he may not be able to make the adjustment for himself. Assuming that the weight the scales tell you that he *is* equals the weight he is *meant to be* could lead you into a vicious circle of mis-feeding. Let's look at how this might happen in practice.

Imagine that your baby was born weighing 7lbs (3.2kg) but was ill after birth, lost more weight than average and now, in his third week, weighs just over 6lbs (2.7kg). You will undoubtedly have been worrying about him and you may have had trouble establishing breast-feeding, so you test weigh him (see p. 59) and discover that he has taken 18ozs (510ml) of milk in the 24 hours. If you accepted that 6lbs (2.7kg) actual weight as being normal for him, you would assume that he was getting enough. But you would be wrong. His *expected* weight is not 6lbs (2.7kg) but 8lbs (3.6kg). So 18ozs (510ml) of milk is not enough for him. He needs to have around 24ozs (680ml) available if he wants it.

Calculating your baby's expected weight	Calculation	Example baby's expected weight	
	Start with the birthweight	*Birthweight*	*7lbs*
	Subtract 1oz per day for days 1–5	*Weight at 5 days*	*6lbs 11ozs*
	Add 1oz per day for days 6–10	*Weight at 10 days*	*7lbs*
	Add 1oz per day or 6–8ozs per week from 10 days to 3 months		
		Weight at 30 days	*8lbs 4ozs*
		Weight at 2 months	*10lbs 2ozs*
		Weight at 3 months	*12lbs*

Height or length matter too Weight gain is not the only way to assess a baby's growth. Children are not meant to get fatter and fatter but bigger overall. Getting taller (or longer) matters too. Your baby's length will change much more slowly than the weight and it is far more difficult to measure accurately, but whatever the length at birth, approximately $\frac{3}{4}$ inch (1.9cm) will be gained each month or just over 2 inches (5cm) in three months.

Just as there is an expected *weight* for a baby of any age, related to birthweight, so there is an expected *length* at any age, related to birth-length. A complete record of your baby's growth means charting both measurements. You will find that if all is going well, they rise in a consistent relationship to each other.

Having said all this, babies do not continue to grow at the same rate as each other forever. We interfere with the regularity of growth by overfeeding or underfeeding, or introducing solid foods early or late. Life interferes too, making one child subject to many infections and another resistant to them. Eventually the child's own hormones interfere: the pre-puberty growth spurt takes place at different times and rates in different people. But for most babies the pattern shown on the chart on page 506 will be the norm for at least the first year and often for the first three years.

The most common exceptions are premature babies (see p. 38). They may be very slow to get started with feeding and therefore with growing. They may do no more than hold their low position, relative to average babies, for a long time.

Small-for-dates babies (see p. 39) may make startling growth during their early weeks, especially if they were partly starved in the womb. With excellent care such babies may change position from the very bottom of the lowest section of the chart to somewhere near the top of that "small baby section".

Babies who are ill immediately after birth or in their first weeks may fail to start gaining weight or may actually lose some. Again excellent care may lead to a spurt of "catch up growth" so that the baby's personal growth curve shifts upwards and then settles down on the new, higher trajectory.

Babies who are bottle-fed from birth with wrongly mixed formula may lose no weight in the first days. They may even gain very fast from the beginning. An even greater rise in such a baby's weight curve may be seen if solid foods are added early to the full quota of over-concentrated milk. It is in a case like this that the importance of recording length as well as weight becomes clear: a baby who is gaining weight faster than nature intended will not gain length to match it. The disparity is your cue that your child is getting obese rather than simply growing large.

"Average"
is easier

Society is geared to average babies. If your baby was not of average birthweight you need to be aware of it and allow for the difference. Baby clothes which are sized by age may mislead you. A stretch suit for "birth to three months" means 7–12lbs (3.2–5.5kg) and length to match. It will not last your ten pounder for long. Over-the-counter medicines may advise dosage by age rather than weight and that can be extremely misleading. A small baby needs less of any medicine than a larger one.

Above all, don't be taken in by the various "sayings" about weight gain which you may hear quoted as gospel truth. This one, for example: "A baby should double his birthweight by six months and treble it by a year". Well, should yours? If you look at the chart on p. 506 you will see that the average birthweight baby in the middle will indeed double his birthweight in six months and treble it in a year, but the small baby at the bottom will almost double his in *three* months and treble it in six. If he gained "by the saying", he would be half starved. As for the big baby at the top, while his birthweight will double by six months it will be nowhere near trebled by a year. If he gained "by the saying", he would be grossly fat.

Normal patterns of growth

The expected pattern of growth for each of the babies pictured on p. 37 is charted here. The small baby at the bottom, the average baby in the middle and the large baby at the top are all expected to grow the same amount and at the same rate. So the "growth curve" made by joining up successive weekly or monthly measurements is the same shape for each of them. You can see that babies are expected to lose weight in the first five days and regain it by ten days. You can see too that the curve of a baby who was gaining exceptionally slowly would drop below the average curve for his or her birthweight while the curve for a baby who was getting fat rather than big overall would rise above it without the length curve rising fast enough to keep in the usual relationship to it.

You can keep a permanent record of your own baby's growth on the chart provided for you on p. 506. It will help you to spot obesity; assess setbacks and give your doctor useful information. Above all it will be a fascinating record to look back on, especially if you have another child, unwise though it is to compare them!

To find the expected weight/height of any baby, find the birthweight/length on the left margin; now follow that growth curve with your finger until it crosses the vertical line corresponding to the age in weeks along the bottom. Now go horizontally back to the weight/height scale and read off. Go to p. 126 to see if these three grew as they were expected to.

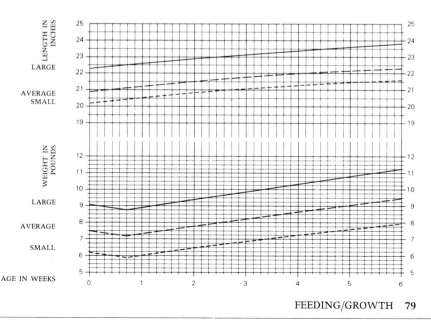

Keeping your baby warm

Warmth is important to new babies. If their environment is kept very warm, they do not have to use any energy in warming themselves and they also tend to be relaxed and contented. If their environment gets cool, they have to use energy on heat-production instead of using it for the activities of living and growing. They tend to be fretful and restless too. If they are allowed to get cold, there is a possibility of dangerous chilling (see below).

Ideal warmth

All human beings make heat for their bodies in the same way. When we need more warmth, our metabolic rate goes up, with a faster heart beat and quicker breathing. We use up some of our food-calories to release energy in the form of heat. This process of heat-production is efficient in a baby from the moment of birth, but unlike older people the new baby cannot *conserve* the heat that he makes. Instead of getting warm and staying warm, he loses heat as fast as he makes it. He has to go on and on using energy to make warmth until extra heat provided from outside relieves him of the necessity.

Experiments have shown that a *naked* baby does not stop using energy to make warmth until the temperature immediately around his body reaches about 85°F (29°C). While this is too hot for an ordinary family room, it is a reasonable temperature to aim at in a room where you bath a brand new baby. The rest of the time you can ensure that the air around his body stays at this ideal temperature simply by dressing him. Three light layers of clothing (such as a vest and nappy, a stretch suit and a shawl) will keep the air inside the bundle warm enough with room temperatures around 68°F (20°C).

Cooler temperatures

A baby's ability to conserve his own warmth improves with age and weight. His ability to spare some energy for heat-production improves too. A baby who was premature and now weighs only around 6lbs (2.7kg) should definitely be kept indoors at a steady temperature and should only be undressed in really warm places. On the other hand, a three month old baby weighing around 12lbs (5.5kg) will have begun to be able to conserve warmth and can well afford to use some energy on keeping himself warm for at least some of the time.

Between those extremes, commonsense precautions will keep your baby warm enough to be both safe and contented. Exposure to very cool temperatures should be kept brief. A short trip in his pram with the air temperature in the '50s will not hurt him. The insulation of his wrappings will conserve his warmth for some of the time, and making his own heat for the rest of it will not drain him of energy. A whole morning in the pram in the garden is a different matter. Why should he be forced to work at keeping warm for so long when he could get just as much fresh air beside an open window?

Don't let him cool right off while he is deeply asleep. As long as he is awake or merely dozing, his heat-producing mechanism will "switch on" as soon as it is needed and prevent him from getting chilled. But if his sleep is so deep that the cold does not disturb him, the mechanism will not come into play and he could go straight from sleep into a chilled state (see below). If your house cools off markedly during the night, you must make sure that his room is separately heated at least for a few weeks.

Signs of chilling A baby who is managing to keep himself warm but would be happier if outside conditions relieved him of the task will be restless. His breathing will be faster than usual and he may cry. While his hands and feet may feel cool, his chest and stomach, under his clothes, will still feel normally warm. As soon as you take him to a warmer place (especially out of a cool breeze), he will become calmer and more relaxed.

A baby who is losing the battle to stay warm and is in danger of becoming chilled, behaves quite differently. He is very quiet and still. He will not cry until he is beginning to get warm and can therefore spare the energy which crying takes. His hands and feet will feel cold and even the skin of his chest under his clothes will feel cool to your hand. Do not simply add more wrappings. He is already cold and is showing you that he cannot make more heat for himself at the moment. Extra wrappings will insulate the coldness in. He needs to get warmer first – perhaps by being taken into a warm room and given a warm feed or by being cuddled under a wrap or blanket. After that, extra wrappings will insulate in the warmth that he needs.

If such a baby were given no help in getting warm or was left asleep with his heat-producing mechanism not working, he could slip into the next stage of chilling which is called the "neo-natal cold syndrome". This is very rare but it is dangerous. Vital bodily functions run so slowly that the baby is lethargic, floppy, difficult to wake up and unable to suck. His hands and feet look swollen and bright pink. His skin is very cold to touch. A baby in this condition needs urgent medical attention as he will have to be re-warmed slowly and with great care.

High temperatures High air temperatures seldom bother babies. Yours may be at his brightest when you are wilting because it is 90° in the shade. Keep clothes as few and as light as possible; it is sweat evaporating off his skin which keeps him comfortable. Banish plastic pants. They will keep his bottom so warm and wet that steam may rise when you remove them, and under these circumstances nappy rash is very likely. If the baby should become irritable because he is too hot, consider his skin. If he is damp with sweat, fanning him will assist evaporation and cooling. If his skin is dry, sponge him with warm water to provide more moisture to evaporate. Sponging and then fanning will cool the hottest baby.

Direct heat Direct heat is a different matter. Until the friction of clothes and exposure to air, wind and sun have toughened it, the baby's skin is very fragile. Guard it not only from obvious hazards like sunburn and hot water bottles, but from unexpected ones too. Don't put him down on a rug close to the fire or leave him close to light bulbs or radiators.

Everyday care

Handling your baby

New babies have an instinctive fear of being dropped which shows whenever their heavy heads are allowed to flop or their uncontrolled limbs dangle in space. They can neither support their own heads nor control their own muscles and they are only relaxed and happy when someone does it for them. In a cot or pram the mattress provides support; in someone's arms the adult body supports the baby's, but being picked up or put down introduces a potentially alarming moment when one kind of support is removed before the other is established.

The answer is to give new babies a moment with *both* kinds of support before either is removed. If you are picking your baby up, arrange your hands and arms under and around him or her while the mattress is still supporting the weight. Don't even begin to lift until the baby has felt the new security your hands are providing. When you put the baby

down, reverse the process: keep your supporting hands in place as you put him or her down so that the baby has time to register the security of the mattress before you remove them.

Arranging your hands and arms takes practice before it becomes an unthinking skill. But you will not go far wrong if you think of new babies as badly wrapped parcels. If you pick them up around the middle, both ends will flop. If you concentrate on supporting their heads, their legs will dangle. You have to gather them together so that you can move them in a compact bundle. Above all, do make sure that your baby is aware of what you are going to do before you do it, that you move slowly and that you keep to a minimum the distances through empty space which he or she must travel. If, for example, you are picking your baby up from a carry cot on the floor, kneel down to take the baby into your arms. Don't stand up until he or she is nestled against you.

Picking up and putting down

Give the baby a few moments supported by your hands *and* the mattress before you take one of them away. Never pick her up without alerting her to your presence by talking to her and touching her. Would you like to be swooped into the air by an invisible giant?

Put your left hand under her neck and your right hand under her bottom. Spread the fingers to support her head and thighs.

Lean down so that your left wrist and forearm follow her spine right down to her waist level.

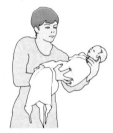
Lift slowly. Your arms support her in the same position as the mattress.

Your arms are in the right position to put her to your shoulder without any more jouncing around.

You can even free your right hand by shifting your left elbow around to brace her against you.

To put her down, lower her slowly until her head and back are on your left hand and arm on the mattress.

Lower her bottom and when it too is supported, gently slide your hands from beneath her.

Dressing and undressing

Dressing and undressing upsets many babies. They fear the feeling of air on bare skin and dislike being pulled around. So keep nakedness to a minimum and try to pull the clothes rather than the limbs. At the beginning you will probably feel that you do not have enough hands to support that wobbly neck *and* hold the whole baby steady *and* pull the clothes on or off.

Use a firm surface, such as a bed or changing table, and lie the baby on that while you deal with the bottom half. This is much easier than doing it on your lap because it keeps the baby properly supported and both your hands free.

It is the top half that causes problems, and here the type of clothes you use will help or hinder you (see below). Take the baby on your lap and cross your knees so that the upper one supports the lower back. That leaves a hand for the head and another for clothes.

Undressing

Settle him on a shawl on your lap with your legs crossed, your left arm around him, and his head against your bosom.

Lift the top garment to shoulder level, concertina each sleeve with your left hand and lift it off his arm with your right.

Now shift your left arm so that the wrist supports his neck and he sits with his head just clear of your bosom.

Stretch the neck of the garment wide open, using your right hand and the thumb of your left.

Lift it cleanly over his head without scraping his nose or ears or jerking his head back.

Wrap him immediately in the shawl he is sitting on and cuddle him against you.

Clothing

Try to buy clothes that will be easy for both of you. If everything the baby wears fastens down the front, for example, you will not have to turn him or her over to do up the back.

If all long sleeves are raglan type, you will be able to use your hand to guide the baby's through, instead of trying to push that soft little fist through a tight sleeve by itself.

If none of the clothes have ribbons or strings to tie, you will not find them in a knot just when you are in a hurry, and you will not find them chewed or wrapped around the baby's neck either.

If most of the clothes are made of stretch materials, the whole business will be far easier.

Dressing

Settle him as for undressing. Use your right hand and the thumb of your left to stretch neck of garment.

Pop it over his head, keeping it open so that it goes on without scraping his nose or ears.

To pull on each sleeve, first put your left hand up the sleeve in reverse and grasp his hand.

Then, with your right hand, pull the sleeve over his arm rather than his arm through the sleeve.

Cleanliness

Babies do not need to be kept nearly as clean as most of us keep them. It is adults who like them to smell of baby powder. The chief purpose in washing a new baby is to remove from the skin anything which might irritate and make it sore. The skin would take care of itself if it did not get drenched with urine, smeared with faeces, splashed with sticky milk and lightly speckled with dust.

Most mothers will be taught, by hospital staff or visiting midwives, to bath their new babies every day. If you want to carry on with this, a reasonably easy method is given on p. 152. But if, like many mothers, you find that the bath is something that neither you nor the baby can enjoy just yet, you don't have to do it. You can make your baby perfectly clean by "topping and tailing", and what is more you can do it without frightening him or her or putting yourself through the horrors of trying to hold a slippery screaming mite safely in a bath full of water. . . .

The topping and tailing method of washing a new baby concentrates on cleaning thoroughly the bits that really need it: the eyes, nose and ears, the face, hands and bottom. It keeps undressing (and therefore re-dressing) to a nappy-changing minimum and it can all be done without picking the baby up.

Notice that the method does not include any interference with any *inside* part of the body. It does not include poking bits of cotton wool up the nose, cleaning out the ears with "Q-Tips", or pulling back the foreskin of a little boy. All of a baby's orifices are lined with mucous membranes which are designed to bring out any dirt. The slight flow of mucus from the nose will carry dirt out with it; wax will work its way out of the ears and within reach of your cotton wool in its own good time; tears bathe the eyes continually and far more efficiently than you can. So concentrate on wiping away what appears on the outside. Don't go hunting up the nostrils or into the ears with twists of cotton wool; if you do, you may actually push back the dirt. It is a good principle never to interfere with any part of a baby's body which is not visible from the outside.

Always use warm boiled water and a separate swab for each eye and wipe from the inner to the outer corners. This will avoid the risk of spreading any minor infection from one eye to the other.

Topping and tailing

Put the baby on a towel on a bed or changing table. Gather together a bowl of warm *boiled* water – this is for his eyes – another of ordinary warm water, cotton wool balls, washcloths, a soft towel, clean nappies and any cream, powder etc.

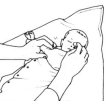

Wipe each eye with a separate cotton ball dampened in boiled water. Wipe always from inner corner outwards.

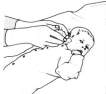

With another cotton ball, wipe around ears and neck to get rid of dried sweat which might cause soreness.

Use a further cotton ball to clean around his mouth and chin creases to remove dried milk and dribble.

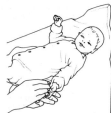

Use a clean washcloth dampened in warm water to wipe his hands, checking for any sharp fingernails (see p. 151).

Now take off his nappy. If he is merely wet, wipe him with a damp washcloth.

If he is soiled, get the worst off with the nappy, then use soap on one washcloth and rinse it off carefully with another.

Dry every skinfold, not forgetting the crease between his buttocks; apply cream if you like, powder if you must!

Nappies

Your basic choice is between washable nappies and disposables. There are many types of each but whatever type you select, the washable ones will all have to be washed, sterilized (see p. 87) and dried, while the disposables will all have to be bought, carried and disposed of.

If your washing and drying facilities are good, washable nappies may be the right choice for everyday use. Even though you will need artificial heat to dry them during most of the year, they will work out cheaper and are probably more comfortable for the baby. If washing and drying space are a problem, disposables are the answer, although using plastic pants all the time could make your baby's bottom sore, and disposing of disposables is a frequent cause of blocked drains!

Many mothers find that a compromise works best. You could use washable nappies at night, for maximum comfort and absorption, keeping disposables for use in the daytime when the baby can be frequently changed. The advantages and disadvantages of some of the most widely available types of nappy are listed below:

Gauze squares
These are ideal for very new babies because they are very soft and un-bulky. The baby will soon need more absorbency, but the squares remain useful for protecting the cot sheet from dribble etc.

Terry squares
The basic washable nappy. It is quick drying when hung out un-folded, but very absorbent when folded to several thicknesses. You can fold it so that you get most thickness where there is most wetness – at the front for boys, at the back for girls.

Shaped terry
These are made of several thicknesses of a softer and finer terry towelling. They need no folding and look neater than squares, but they are more expensive and they take a long time to dry.

Disposables
These are absorbent pads, either plastic-backed or for use in special plastic holders. Search for a type which does not crumble when wet (messy and liable to make the baby's skin sore) and which is highly absorbent. Few brands will be adequate when used singly on a baby who sleeps through the night.

One-way nappies
These are for use with, rather than instead of, ordinary washable or disposable nappies. They are small oblongs of a special material which lets urine through one way but not back the other. Placed against the baby's skin, a one-way nappy ensures a comparatively dry bottom even when the nappy outside it is soaked. They are a real aid to comfort and to nappy rash prevention; they dry so quickly that eight will probably be enough. They are well worth using even if you are determined to avoid all other nappy washing by using only disposables.

Nappy liners
These are squares of disposable material designed to be placed inside washable nappies to catch the worst of the baby's bowel movements. Unfortunately a liner is only effective if you put it next to the baby's skin and if you do that, you cannot use a one-way nappy properly. Unless you find your baby's bowel movements revolting (and at least while he or she is milk-fed, you probably will not) a one-way nappy seems better.

Plastic pants
A necessity with most disposables, they are a voluntary extra if you use washable nappies. Some babies can wear them night and day without ill-effects, others get soggy, red, sore bottoms after a few hours. Only experimentation will tell you how your baby reacts. Remember that the more efficiently a particular type keeps bedding dry the more efficiently it will keep the baby's bottom wet. A good compromise may be a comparatively *inefficient* type of plastic protection which keeps most of the moisture off the bedding, but still allows some air circulation and evaporation. The type which is like a pre-shaped plastic sheet, put on like a nappy and tied at the hips, is probably best.

Changing nappies

A changing mat or table is easier than your lap: you have both hands free. Keep cotton wool, nappies etc. beside it. In a big house a second "changing place" downstairs will save effort. Washable nappies must only be fastened with special guarded safety pins. Keep your own hand between the pin and her skin.

You need not wash a wet baby at each nappy change. Twice a day is enough. If the baby is soiled, use the front part of the nappy to remove the worst, lifting the bottom by holding both ankles in one hand with a finger between the ankle bones to stop them grinding together. Clean off the last traces with cotton wool and baby oil unless it is a regular topping and tailing time.

Experiment with various ways of folding washable nappies until you find the one that is easiest for you and most effective on your baby. Different ways of folding suit different sizes and sexes.

Triangle method (for larger babies, especially boys).

Spread the nappy diagonally on the mat.

Fold down the top half to make a double-thickness triangle.

Lie the baby on it with the triangle base at waist level, the point between his legs.

Bring the point up between his legs.

Hold the point with your left hand while you fold one side over to meet it.

Tuck the end neatly under itself and hold all four layers with your right hand.

Now use your left hand to bring the other side over to the centre.

Hold with your left hand, fingers protecting his tummy, while you pin all layers at the centre.

Kite-shaped method (for all sizes and both sexes).

Spread the nappy diagonally. Fold down the top corner, then the two lower sides.

Now fold the bottom corner up. Experiment to find the right length to fit your baby.

Lie the baby with the base of the larger triangle at waist level, the smaller between her legs.

Bring between-legs portion up, then bring each side up in turn and pin on each hip.

Rectangle method (for small babies, both sexes).

Fold the nappy in half so that you have a double-thickness oblong.

Fold top third down for a girl, or bottom third up for a boy.

Lie baby with top edge at waist level. A girl needs extra padding at the back.

Bring between-legs portion up, fold sides to meet it and pin on each hip.

Nappy sterilizing

If keeping the baby's body clean is less important than many people think, keeping clothes and equipment clean is vital. That soft skin will get sore if traces of ammonia from urine or of detergent from the washing machine are left in nappies which have not been properly washed and rinsed. Soiled nappies which have not been sterilized can lead to infected nappy rash with actual sores all over the bottom.

Sterilizing nappies, like sterilizing feeding equipment, used to be a chore which took up an enormous amount of time. Nowadays there are chemical sterilants for nappies as well as feeding equipment which make the job easy and quick.

So, buy a product sold as a nappy sterilant. Change the solution daily as the chemicals lose their effectiveness after about 24 hours. Remember that the chemicals can only do a complete job on nappies that are totally submerged in the sterilant solution and that they take time to work. Most manufacturers' instructions will recommend that nappies stay submerged in the solution for at least six hours.

In the early days when you may be tired and flurried and every detail of babycare is new, it can help to have a planned routine for this boring but necessary chore. Here is one suggestion:

Nappy routine Buy two large plastic buckets with lids. Make sure that you can tell them apart, by having two different colours or putting a blob of paint on one. Fill them with fresh nappy sterilizing solution each morning. Drop wet nappies into one and soiled nappies (with the worst of the solid matter scraped off into the lavatory) into the other, right through the day.

During the night put any nappies you remove into a plastic bag. If you put them into your sterilizers they would not have enough time in the solution. They must wait for the morning's new mix.

In the morning, put all the nappies from the "wet only" bucket straight for rinsing. They do not need any detergent but they must be rinsed thoroughly in your washing machine or in the bath.

Put all the nappies from the "soiled" bucket into your washing machine, set to its "hot" programme, or into a bath full of hot water and detergent. Rinse them thoroughly.

Refill your now empty buckets with fresh sterilizing solution and drop in the nappies from your plastic bag.

In this way you can be sure that all your nappies have an adequate number of hours in the sterilant and that you never have to wash nappies that, once sterilized, only need rinsing.

If nappies cannot be tumble-dried, hang them outside if you can. Drying them on radiators or hot pipes will make them very stiff. If this happens, a "fabric softener" in the rinsing water will help, but, contrary to some manufacturers' instructions, the softener must be rinsed out of the nappies because it can cause irritation to the baby's skin.

Remember that nappy sterilants are poisonous. Rinse your hands before handling baby or bottles. They also contain bleach. Don't put a coloured garment in with the nappies, even if it is soiled. Boil it, or use a biological detergent.

Excreting

"Changing" stools

Once the baby's bowel is cleared of meconium (see p. 47) and milk feeding, whether from the breast or from a bottle, has begun, "changing" stools will be passed. As the name suggests, their rather peculiar character is due to the changeover from transfusion feeding in the womb to ordinary digestion.

Changing stools are usually greeny-brown, semi-fluid and frequent. But sometimes they are bright green, full of curds and mucus and violently expelled. If they look like this, don't automatically assume that the baby has violent diarrhoea. Peculiar looking stools are a feature of these early days.

If the stools really worry you, take the baby to the doctor, with one of the soiled nappies in a sealed plastic bag, so that he can check that there is no infective diarrhoea (gastro-enteritis). If the baby is being breast-fed, gastro-enteritis is extremely unlikely. If feeding is by bottle, it is a possibility, but it is still a remote one if the baby seems contented and sucks well.

It may be three weeks or even more before your baby settles to passing normal or "settled" stools.

"Settled" stools

As long as your baby is having only breast milk and extra water, his stools will be an orangey-yellow colour with a consistency like mustard and a mild sour-milk smell.

He may have so many motions each day that you never change a nappy that is not soiled as well as wet. On the other hand, he may have only one motion every three, four or even five days. Both extremes and everything in between them are absolutely normal. And it is normal for him to swing from one to the other.

A breast-fed baby cannot be constipated – however seldom his motions appear, they will be normally soft and easy to pass. He cannot have diarrhoea without seeming ill. So as long as he seems well in other ways, don't worry about his stools.

Bottle-fed babies have stools which are more solid and formed than those of the breast-fed baby. They are a pale brown colour and smell more like ordinary stools. They are usually less frequent.

A breast-fed baby's food is always perfect for him. A bottle-fed baby's food may not be. If the formula is not right, then you may get your first clue from your baby's stools.

Constipation

If a bottle-fed baby goes for a day or two without passing a stool and then passes a hard one which causes obvious discomfort, he is constipated. Lack of fluid is a common cause; offer extra drinks of water. If the stools remain hard, the remedy is to adjust the amount of sugar he has. Sugar loosens the stools by fermenting in the intestine and hurrying the passage of waste.

If the formula the baby is having always has sugar added to it, then a very little extra (say half a teaspoon) can be added for a few days. If the formula is already complete, it should not be altered without consulting the doctor. In that case a little sweetened diluted fruit juice as a mid-morning or mid-afternoon drink will serve the same purpose.

Diarrhoea   If a bottle-fed baby suddenly starts to have diarrhoea he should see the doctor in case he has got gastro-enteritis. If he is vomiting as well, goes off feeds and/or seems feverish or ill, then the appointment should be made as an emergency. Gastro-enteritis can be extremely dangerous to babies, especially to very young ones. The immediate danger is loss of fluid from the body due to the diarrhoea and exacerbated by any vomiting. The baby should have as much cooled boiled water as he will drink.

But most loose stools will be found to be due to diet not to infection. Too much sugar can cause diarrhoea, just as extra sugar corrects constipation. Are you adding extra to the bottles when the formula does not require it? Or giving the baby lots of fruit juice? Or giving him drinks of sugar water?

Too much fat can also cause loose stools. If fat is the cause, the stools will smell very nasty. Once again, take baby and nappy to the doctor. If he feels that the fat in the milk is not agreeing with the baby, he may recommend that you change to a half strength milk for a while. If so, the baby will probably need rather frequent feeding. Half strength milk means many fewer calories, so he will be hungry. Don't switch formulas before you consult your doctor.

Colour changes   Even before you introduce any solid foods, some "extras" can cause quite alarming colour changes in the stools. That half strength milk, for example, will make a far darker stool than the full strength. Rosehip syrup will turn the stools reddish or purple, while if the doctor has prescribed iron for the baby, the stools may be blackish.

Urine   It does not matter if the baby wets himself very often; it may matter if he wets himself infrequently.

A new baby who is dry after a couple of hours needs watching. His body may be using up more fluid than usual because he is starting a fever. Or he may need more than usual because it is a hot day or because he is wearing a very warm shawl. Give him plenty of extra drinks of water or juice, and see if he is still dry after another two hours. If he is (and he almost certainly will not be), ring your doctor. He just might have an obstruction.

Too little fluid, especially when the weather is hot or when he has fever, can make the urine extra strong and concentrated. If it is really strong, it may stain the nappy yellow and redden the baby's skin. Once again, he needs more to drink.

If the urine goes on being very strong, even though the baby is drinking plenty, and especially if it begins to have a nasty fishy smell, then you should take him to the doctor. It is possible he has a urinary infection.

Of course if you think there is blood in your baby's urine, you will make an immediate appointment with the doctor. But pause to think for a moment. If your baby is a girl and the redness you can see is blood at all, it may be coming from the vagina rather than from the bladder. Vaginal bleeding is quite normal during the first few days of life (see p. 47), and on a wet nappy can easily look as if it is part of the urine. Equally, the redness on the nappy may not be blood at all if, for example, it follows the baby's first drink of diluted blackcurrant juice.

Sleeping

New babies sleep exactly the amount that their personal physiology tells them to sleep. There is nothing that you can do to make your baby sleep more than this amount and nothing that the baby can do to sleep less. Unless he is ill, in pain, or extremely uncomfortable he will do his sleeping wherever he finds himself and under almost any circumstances. So your power over his actual hours of sleep is very limited. By making him comfortable you can ensure that he sleeps as much as he wants to, but you cannot put him to sleep. On the other hand if you are somewhere where you cannot make him very comfortable–in a bus, for example–you need not worry about him being kept awake. If he stays awake, it is because he does not need to sleep.

Separating sleep from wakefulness

At the very beginning of life the baby often drifts so gradually from being awake to being asleep that it is difficult to tell which state he is in at any given moment. He may start a feed wide awake and ravenous; suck himself into a blissful trance so that only his occasional bursts of sucking tell you that he is still at least a little awake; and then drift into sleep so deep that nothing you do can wake him.

This kind of drifting does not matter at all from his point of view. He is simply doing what he needs to do when he needs to do it. But from your point of view it is a good idea to help him gradually to make a more complete difference between being awake and being asleep. It will be much easier for you to organize your life later on if you know that the baby is either awake (and therefore bound to need some attention and company), or asleep (and therefore unlikely to need anything at all for a while). Babies who do learn early to be either fully awake or fully asleep are likely to be the ones who sleep for reasonably long periods at night, too.

So, rather than letting him drift and doze on somebody's lap, it is a good idea to start from the very beginning to "put him to bed" when he needs to sleep and to "get him up" when he is awake. If he is always put into his pram or cot when he is really sleepy, he will soon come to associate those places with being asleep. If he is always taken into whatever company is available when he is awake, he will make that association too.

Disturbances to sleep

A sleeping baby need not mean a hushed household. Ordinary sounds and activities will not disturb him at this early age. But if everybody creeps about and talks in whispers while he is asleep, there may come a time when he cannot sleep unless they do. It is therefore important to let him sleep through whatever sound level is normal for your household so that he does not come to expect a quietness that will make all your lives a misery.

At this stage he will be disturbed most often by internal stimuli. Hunger will disturb him; being cold may disturb him if he is not in a very deep sleep; pain will wake him and so may passing a bowel movement or burping. Sometimes the jerks and twitches of his body as it relaxes towards deep sleep will disturb him too.

A newborn baby will sleep whenever he needs to and wherever he finds himself . . .

Of course, outside stimuli can disturb the baby, but when they do it will usually be because they change very suddenly. He will drop off to sleep quite happily with the television set on, but he may wake when it is switched off and the room becomes quiet. A toddler playing around the room will not keep him awake but one who suddenly comes in may wake him.

Helping your baby sleep more at night than by day

Although human beings are mainly diurnal creatures, sleeping by night and active by day, babies do not seem to have a clear and inbuilt mechanism instructing them accordingly. They start off sleeping and waking randomly through the 24 hours. It takes time and sensible handling to persuade them to do most of their sleeping at night and most of their being awake in the daytime. The majority learn to adopt this pattern fairly rapidly, if not as rapidly as their exhausted parents would choose!

You can speed up the process by making a clear difference between going to bed for the night and ordinary daytime naps, from the beginning. "Topping and tailing" him and changing him into nightclothes can be part of this. Giving the suppertime feed in his room can be part of it too. Above all, put him down to sleep in the cot and the room that he is going to use all night, rather than putting him in his pram somewhere else in the house as you might during the day.

Take extra trouble to make the baby comfortable. If you are merely putting him to bed for a daytime nap, it may not matter very much to you if a burp wakes him a little while later. When it is night, try to ensure that he has finished with burping and that nothing that you can foresee is going to disturb him.

Wrap the baby up securely (see p. 98). In the daytime it does not matter if his own movements bring him fully awake as soon as his sleep lightens. At night you want him so securely wrapped that he will not wake even during the normal periods of light sleep which intersperse heavy slumber.

Darken the room sufficiently to make it seem different from daytime, and to ensure that when he opens his eyes (as all babies do from time to time during the night) his attention is not caught by anything brightly lit or clearly visible. But leave a dim (15 watt) light on so that you can attend to him during the night without switching on more lights.

Make sure the room is warm and that it stays warm. Getting chilly will wake him if it happens while he is in light sleep, and can be risky if it happens while he is in deep sleep (see p. 81).

Keep night feeds as sleepy and as brief as possible. The baby is bound to wake up because he cannot yet get through the night without food and drink, but the less completely he awakens, the better. Make sure, before you leave him, that everything you will need during the night is gathered together. You don't want to have to carry him around while you search for a dry nappy.

When he cries, go to him immediately so that he has no time to get into a wakeful misery. Don't play and talk while you feed him; concentrate on soothing cuddles instead. Daytime feeds are social playtimes but night feeds are for sustenance only.

Places to sleep

New babies can sleep almost anywhere provided they are comfortably wrapped up. A well-padded cardboard box or drawer (taken out of its chest!) would do instead of the usual crib, carry cot or pram. Although your baby will need a drop-side cot later, don't use one now. The slatted sides are draughty and it is difficult to make such a small person feel cosy in such a large space.

Most first beds are portable; a bed on wheels means that you can move the baby still asleep. The solid sides of carry cots keep draughts off but their plastic linings can feel cold and clammy to the touch. If the cot tipped so that the baby's face became wedged against them, they might even obstruct breathing. A cotton lining, put in with snap fastenings so that it can be removed for washing, is therefore practical as well as pretty. A water- and wind-proof hood and apron is useful when you carry the baby outside – even from house to car. Warmth beneath the baby is important. The bed needs a thick mattress and it should fit well (not more than 1in. space all round) so that your baby's face cannot get wedged between mattress and cot-side.

Remove protective plastic *bags* from mattresses – they can be dangerous. Plastic tight-covering is safe: it could not lift and stick to the face.

Making up your baby's bed

Use a thick plastic sheet – quilted is safest and most comfortable. Cover with flannelette undersheet. Elasticized corners will keep both smooth.

Cellular blankets combine lightness and warmth. Put them under the mattress; fold sides over baby and tuck in. He or she is secure and draught-proof.

Your new baby does not need a pillow. It is better for her to lie flat, and although she would almost certainly turn her head if her face got covered, it is foolish to take even the smallest risk.
Lie her, wrapped in her shawl on the bottom sheet. If you put her on her side alternate which she lies on so that her still-soft skull does not flatten. Smooth her ear back beneath her head. Many babies are more comfortable on their stomachs. Don't put her to

lie on her back, she cannot deal easily with burped-up milk in this position. Cover securely, using several light layers for warmth rather than one weighty quilt.

By day . . .

It is good for the baby to be in the midst of family life. You can have her bed in the kitchen, living room or wherever you please. But make sure she is in easy earshot of any rooms you are likely to be in. Watch out for toddlers and for pets. A toddler is unlikely to attack the baby directly, however jealous he is feeling, but many a brick gets thrown towards the pram by-accident-on-purpose.

Dogs who have been in the family longer than the baby can be unexpectedly and even dangerously jealous. Don't leave baby and dog alone together unless the baby is completely out of reach. Cats like nothing better than to sleep in a cot with a baby for a hot water bottle. Apart from hygiene, a cat on her face could smother her. A cat-net is therefore a wise precaution. It will fend off those bricks and discourage the dog as well as keeping the cat in its place. A cat-net is a "must" in most back gardens.

Fresh air
It is good for your baby to spend time in the open air and later on she will enjoy the different sights, sounds and feelings. But don't make a fetish of it in these first weeks. She can get plenty of fresh air near a window opened at the top. This will let stale warm air

out so that cool fresh air is drawn in.
If it is foggy, especially if your area is subject to "smog", the less "fresh" air she gets, the better. Foggy air is dirty air; smog is filthy. Keep her indoors with the windows closed. When you do put her in the garden, remember that wind will chill her much more than cold still air. Put the pram hood up and turn its back to the breeze. Use the storm apron to wind-proof her blankets. Direct sunlight on her face will bother her and could burn. In winter, put the

pram hood up and work out where the sun will come from at the end of her sleep as well as now. In summer, the hood will trap hot, stale air. Use a pram canopy, lined with a non-dazzling colour, unless you have a friendly tree.

At night . . .
She must be close enough to wake you as soon as she cries, but ideally she should not be in your room after the first days (see p. 94). If you have no separate room for her, consider carrying her into the living room when you go to bed. If her sleeping room is too far away for you to be sure of hearing her, invest in a "cry-call" or "baby alarm". You will probably find this battery-operated microphone/speaker system useful for years as you can take it with you to strange houses, hotels, even when you go camping.

Helping yourselves to sleep longer at night

Being a parent means broken nights. If you are very lucky you may only have to live with them for a few weeks. Most will have to survive for months and some for longer still. So it is worth organizing things so that your night duties are as easy as possible, and using self-discipline to ensure that you actually *sleep* whenever the baby will permit.

Wake the baby for a late-night feed at your bedtime. If you wait for him to wake, you will be losing sleeping time. It will not hurt him to be fed before he knows he is hungry.

Think of your own small-hours comfort. If you are bottle-feeding, leaving the bottle ready in the refrigerator and a vacuum flask ready-filled with hot water to warm it will cut down your work. If a hot drink helps you get back to sleep, leave that ready in a vacuum flask, too. If cold feet keep you awake after feeds, you could think about an electric blanket. . . .

Feed the baby as soon as crying begins. If you "leave him to cry" he may indeed cry himself back to sleep, if he was not very hungry. But he will keep you awake while he is crying and then wake again, *extremely* hungry, just as you have got back to sleep yourself. If you "make him wait a bit" he will keep you awake with his crying and when you finally feed him he may be too tired and upset to take a full feed. He will wake you again sooner than he might have done if you had fed him promptly. If you "give him sugar water" the sucking and thirst-quenching may put him back to sleep. But once again the peace will not last; his stomach will soon remind him that you fooled him.

Discipline yourself to sleep the moment the baby is settled. It is easy to lie awake wondering if he is going to need another burp or another ounce. If he does need you, he will soon let you know. If he does not, waiting for him to cry will lose you yet another piece of sleeping time.

Move the baby out of your room as soon as possible. His small snufflings and movements at your bedside may disturb you more than you realize. If they mean that you peep into the cot every half hour you may actually disturb him. Of course you *must* be sure that you will hear even the smallest cry, but you will get far more rest if you cannot hear anything quieter and less urgent than that.

Decide whether one or both parents are going to cope. Although the very early night feeds seem part of the excitement of having a baby and you may both want to be involved, there is a long stint of too little sleep ahead of you. There is not really much point in both of you waking for every feed unless doing it together makes it all much quicker. Breast-feeding mothers usually decide that a snack and a chat is not enough compensation for having a husband who is exhausted too. Most of them prefer to manage alone and perhaps get paid back with afternoon naps at the weekends. Bottle-feeding parents sometimes work out a sharing system, with one parent doing one night and the other the next. But for many couples even that does not really work because the mother finds that she wakes up anyway. If she cannot get back to sleep until she knows the baby is settled again, she might as well give the feed herself.

Crying and comforting

Parents often wish that their babies never cried at all. But crying is the only reliable way in which very young babies can signal to the adults who take care of them. It is their way of communicating and they have different kinds of cry for communicating different information (see p. 156). Babies cry when they need something and it is because you know that yours will do so that you can assume, under all normal circumstances, that a baby who is not crying needs nothing. It would take really serious illness, severe chilling, or smothering, to make a baby suffer in silence.

Babies never cry for nothing. The statement that they cry "to exercise their lungs" is nonsense. Their lungs get all the exercise they need in breathing. A baby cries for a reason; he needs something. If you can find out what it is that he needs, and provide it, the crying will stop. Usually the need is simple. Hunger. Feed him and he stops crying. But sometimes the baby cannot be satisfied so easily. The parents offer everything they can think of but the crying goes on and on.

A baby who cries and cannot be comforted is extremely difficult to cope with calmly. The sound churns his parents up emotionally. He seems to reject all their efforts to help him. They feel useless, frustrated and, eventually, angry. If the crying and the ineffectual attempts to comfort go on for long, it begins to seem to the parents that the baby *will not* stop crying. They lose sight of the fact that he *cannot* stop until he has been understood. The parents get more and more tense. Because they are tense they handle the crying baby less calmly and he therefore cries more. Some bouts of crying which have no other obvious cause may even be set off by some tension or unhappiness in the parents which the baby senses through their handling, their facial expressions or their voices.

The causes and the "cures" for crying which are outlined here are designed to answer those frantic questions which come into the mind of almost every parent at some time: "What is the *matter* with him?"; "What can I *do*?" Somewhere in the list there is something that will comfort (or at least explain) your baby.

Causes and cures of crying

Hunger Hunger is the most common cause of crying in a young baby and the easiest to deal with. Research studies have shown that if the baby is hungry, only milk will stop the crying. The baby may suck sweetened water, fruit juice or a dummy, but he will start to cry again after a few seconds. His need can only be met by food going into his stomach. Just sucking, or even sucking combined with a pleasant taste, will have no effect.

Pain Pain certainly causes crying from the first minutes of life, but it is often difficult to be sure whether a crying baby is distressed by pain or by something else. For example, he may stop crying when he is picked up, and immediately pass wind from one end or the other. Can we assume that the wind was causing pain? It may have been giving him "bellyache"; it may have been making his stomach feel uncomfortably distended or it may have had nothing to do with the crying, being passed merely by chance when he was picked up (see p. 74).

Certain kinds of pain cause a very clear reaction: the baby will probably cry heartbreakingly if his bottle or his bath is even a few degrees too warm. He will not appreciate being pricked with a safety pin either. But minor knocks and bangs may pass unnoticed in these early weeks, especially if it is the baby's hands or feet which are affected. The myelin sheathing of some nerves is not completed for months after birth, so the baby is less sensitive to some kinds of pain than is an older child.

Over-stimulation, shock and fear

Too much of any kind of stimulation will cause crying. Loud sudden noises, unexpectedly bright lights, sharp or bitter tastes, cold hands, hot face flannels, too much laughter, tickling, bouncing or hugging can all overcome the new baby.

Sudden happenings, particularly if they involve a sense of being about to fall or be dropped, tend to cause shock and real fear. As well as crying the baby may tremble and pale.

If there is a minor accident, such as a bang on the head while being carried through a doorway, the baby's crying is as likely to be due to the shock of the bang as to actual pain.

Mistiming

The amount of any kind of stimulation which is "too much" depends on the baby's mood and state. What he enjoys when he is awake, content and well-fed may make him cry when he is sleepy, irritable or hungry. For example, physical games which he enjoys when he is feeling sociable will reduce him to despair if they are used to "cheer him along" when he is not. Tired, sad babies need cuddles, not play. Hungry ones need food.

Mistiming feeds will obviously cause crying from hunger, but mistiming the rate at which the baby gets the milk can cause trouble too. If you offer food too slowly – by having the hole in the teat too small or by taking him off the breast or bottle to burp – the distress of his hunger breaks through the relief of feeding, so that the baby who was crying because he was hungry stays hungry because he is crying too much to suck.

Bathing or changing a baby who is very hungry will cause crying, both because it delays the arrival of food and because being handled when he needs a feed tends to irritate him. He should not be bathed immediately after a feed as a great deal of jouncing around is likely to make him bring up milk, so choose a wakeful period for baths, or wake him to be bathed before he has woken himself from hunger. Nappy changing after feeds does not matter if it is gently done. But if the baby is one who needs to burp at half-time, or drops off to sleep and needs waking up, you can change him in mid-feed.

Getting from a sleepy state to sound slumber is often difficult for small babies. Try not to make it more difficult by changing his surroundings when he is just getting drowsy. If you must push him to the shops in his pram, start the expedition before he begins to drop off so that he can go to sleep to smooth motion, or wait until he is sound asleep and then start.

Being undressed   Many parents assume that it is their own clumsiness and in-experience which make babies cry when their clothes are taken off. Although skill certainly helps by making the process as quick and smooth as possible, many babies cry literally for the loss of their clothes. What often happens is that the baby gets increasingly tense as his outer garments are removed and finally howls when the garment next to his skin–vest or undershirt–is taken off. This reaction has nothing to do with being cold: it can happen however high the temperature of the room or the undressing hands. The baby misses the contact between the fabric and his bare skin. He does not like the feeling of his skin exposed to the air.

He will stop crying as soon as he is dressed again. But he can usually be kept completely calm while he is naked if a piece of textured material (a towel, a nappy or a shawl) is laid across his chest and stomach.

Cold   As we have seen (see p. 81), feeling chilly will cause crying if the baby is awake or almost awake at the time. Much of the crying that goes on when babies are first put to sleep outside in their prams is due to feeling cold. It is not a dangerous kind of cold–the crying reaction will keep the baby making heat for himself–but he does not like it. The crying will stop as soon as he is brought into a warm room.

Jerks and twitches   Most new babies jerk and twitch when they are in that drowsy state of near-sleep. A few are startled awake over and over again by their own movements. They cry, drowse, jerk and cry again, unable to get themselves past the twitchy state and into deep sleep.

Efficient wrapping up or swaddling (see p. 98) will always deal with this kind of crying.

Lack of physical contact   Babies who cry until they are picked up, stay cheerful while they are being held and then cry again when they are put down, are usually crying because they are uncomfortable without physical contact. This kind of crying for lack of "contact comfort" is often misunderstood. Parents are told that the baby is crying "because he wants you to pick him up". The implication is that he is making an unreasonable demand on you and that if you "give in" you will start "bad habits". In fact, the reverse is true. The baby is not making unreasonable demands, you are. He is not crying to make you pick him up but because you put him down in the first place and deprived him of contact comfort. It is natural and instinctive for a small baby to be most easily content when he is being held by somebody. In many parts of the world (and not only in "primitive" societies either) babies are held and carried almost all the time. Grandmothers and older sisters take turns when mothers must be free, but most chores are carried out with the baby carried on the mother's back.

Picking the baby up and cuddling him will almost always stop the crying. If it does not, then holding him against your shoulder, so that his stomach and chest are pressed against your breast, will. If whimpers still break through the contact comfort, walk with the baby in this position; the rocking movement will soothe him and peace will descend.

You probably cannot hold and walk your baby for hours on end even if there are two of you to take turns. But you can deal with most of your baby's need for contact comfort by wrapping him up in such a way that the wrapping shawl gives him the same feeling of warmth and security that he gets when he is held closely in your arms against your body.

Wrapping your baby up is rather like old-fashioned swaddling except that it is not intended to "keep his back straight" or any nonsense of that kind. It is intended simply to give him tactile comfort, by surrounding him with a warm, soft, gentle holding layer of material which prevents his own little jerky movements from disturbing him.

Efficient wrapping is magically soothing to most babies. Wrapping which is too loose may have the opposite effect. Your aim is to encase the baby completely so that his limbs are gently held in their preferred position and so that, when he moves, he moves as one complete bundle rather than feeling himself moving within the shawl. If you use the method outlined here, you need not worry about getting the wrapping too tight. It is held in position only by the baby's own weight, and this is not enough to hold it

Wrapping up

Wrapping your baby up is the most effective of all ways of giving overall physical contact with a warm, soft surface. Once wrapped the baby will also stay warmer than with ordinary covering. Stray draughts will not easily penetrate the parcel. Although wrapping is most often used to promote sleep, it will also help your baby to feel securely held when being carried around.

Lie the baby on a soft, light shawl or cellular blanket.

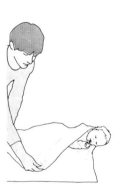
Take one side up, level with the back of the head.

Bring it down diagonally over the shoulder; elbow held, hand free. Tuck the end under the baby's knees.

Take the other side up with as much tension as you can without shifting the baby.

Fold this side straight down.

Lift the baby a little to secure the end beneath the body.

The result: a secure bundle; warm, relaxed, ready for sleep.

tighter than is comfortable. The ideal wrapping material is light and slightly stretchy so that it moulds itself a little to the baby and "gives" with him. A shawl or small cellular blanket will do in winter. In hot weather a flannelette cot sheet will be comfortably warm to feel without being too hot to wear. In extremely hot weather a baby who enjoys the comfort of being wrapped but is too hot will be happy if a soft gauze material is used.

The baby's natural position is with his arms bent at the elbow and his legs flexed. Wrap him like this, making no attempt to straighten him out before you start. Above all, leave his hands where he can suck them if he wants and is able to do so.

Babies vary widely in the length of time they continue relaxing best when wrapped up. Let your baby be the judge: when he wants to rid himself of the wrappings he will begin to kick and struggle to get them undone.

You can also keep crying for contact comfort to a minimum by making sure that all the surfaces the baby lies on are warm and soft. Plastic laminates and sheets may make life easier for you but they are horrible for him. So cover all plastic mattresses, mats, etc with a textured fabric such as terry-towelling. Even a nappy spread under him will make a difference.

If all else fails . . . If you have looked for all these causes and tried all these "cures" and your baby still cries, inexplicably, maddeningly, there are a few other techniques you can try:

Rhythm A baby who cannot relax can be helped to do so by a variety of constant rhythmical stimuli. These seem to work by blocking out whatever internal or external discomforts were bothering him. You apply a soothing blanket of overall stimulation which wipes everything else out for the baby. It will not work if there is a simple cause for the crying which you have failed to discover. Hunger, for example, will break through everything. But it will work if the trouble is some kind of general and diffuse irritability or a tenseness which is preventing a tired baby relaxing into sleep.

Rhythmical sounds. You can buy a recording of a mother's heartbeat, as heard by a baby in the womb. It is very effective.

Soft rhythmical music on the radio or stereo works almost as well but make sure that it does not stop before the baby is properly asleep. If it does, the change in stimulation will wake him.

The burring sound of a fan heater works excellently. So does the sound of a car engine. Most babies sleep peacefully in cars while they are running but tend to wake again the moment the engine is switched off, so a desperate drive round the block in the small hours may not really solve your crying problem!

Rhythmical movements. Rocking a baby is universally effective in stopping crying and inducing sleep. Parents who find that it does not work are almost certainly rocking too slowly. Research has shown that the effective rate is at least 60 rocks per minute through a travel of about three inches. Such a rate is difficult to achieve by hand, even if you have a rocking cradle. It is probably easier to walk with the baby. Time yourself and you will find that a walk round the room rocks him at just about this rate. It seems likely that the soothing effect of this rate of rocking comes directly from his experiences in the womb, when you walked about with him inside you.

You can provide this kind of rocking and lots of contact comfort while leaving yourself free to get on with at least a few other things, if you carry the baby on your back. There are a variety of commercial carriers available, but for soothing crying babies a simple sling made out of a small cot sheet is probably best. A stiff canvas carrier puts a barrier between his body and yours. A sling holds him warmly against you.

Sucking Sucking will not stop a hungry baby crying unless it brings him food, but it will almost always soothe a baby who is not hungry.

Dummies. There are pros and cons to the use of dummies (see p. 157). Reasonably contented babies can manage perfectly well without them and it is better that they should do so. But babies who are often miserable and difficult to comfort in any other way can be kept much more contented if they are allowed to use them. The furious howling mouth latches on to the dummy and all that energy goes into sucking instead of crying. Gradually the rhythm of the sucking becomes gentler. Eventually the baby goes to sleep. Even while he sleeps, having the dummy in his mouth protects him against a fresh bout of crying: whenever something begins to disturb him, he starts to suck again instead of waking.

If you decide that your baby does need a dummy, do guard against the habit of popping it into his mouth whenever he cries without first trying to find out what he needs, and provide it. His dummy should be a last resort, used only when you have tried everything else.

Thumbs and fingers. Some babies find and suck these before they are born and use them efficiently for comfort sucking from the first day of life. Others cannot find their own hands without help until they are several weeks old (see p. 165). If a lot of crying that is difficult to "cure" is worrying you and you do not like the idea of a dummy, you might compromise by helping the baby's hand to his mouth to see whether he can quiet himself by sucking it.

Extra warmth As we have seen (see p. 81), wakeful babies tend to be fretful if they are having to make warmth for themselves, and they tend to flourish when temperatures around them are high. If your baby is crying and you cannot discover any reason for it and therefore cannot persuade him to stop, you can use *extra* warmth to calm him down and help him to relax. Although the warmth will not cure whatever discomfort is making him cry, he will react to the discomfort less if you can get the temperature of the room up to around 75°F (24°C) and keep it there until the episode is over.

A baby who is often miserable and difficult to comfort will give you and himself more peace if you keep him extra warm right through the newborn period. Wrap him carefully when you carry him. Don't put him outside in his pram on chilly days or take him for trips in a cold car until he has grown up a bit. Keep his own room and any other rooms he regularly uses as near 75°F (24°C) as you can manage.

Colic

Apart from serious illness or acute pain, colic is the one cause for long-continued crying which will not respond to any of the above methods of comfort. People often talk of babies being "colicky" when they only mean that they seem miserable and behave as if their stomachs troubled them. True colic is much more specific than this—and much rarer too, fortunately.

True colic is often called "three months colic" but the name is not an appropriate one as a baby who is going to have it almost always starts in the first three weeks after birth and finishes by three months old. The alternative term "evening colic" describes the syndrome better as the trouble occurs exclusively during a particular period of the early evening.

The typical behaviour pattern of "evening colic" often builds up slowly over a couple of weeks. But it is easy to put your baby's restless distress in the evenings down to colic when in fact it is due to some other cause. It may be just because the baby is still unsettled, it may be because your breast milk supplies are low in the evening. The chart below may help you to discover whether your baby really has "evening colic" or not.

Does your baby have "evening colic"?	A baby may have "evening colic" if:	A baby does not have "evening colic" if:
	She cannot settle down after her late afternoon or early evening feed. She either screams as soon as she has finished feeding, or goes to sleep but wakes screaming within the hour. *Her crying at this time is quite different from any other time of day. She appears frantic and beside herself.* *She draws her knees up to her stomach and seems to have acute tummyache.*	*He cannot settle down after his late afternoon or early evening feeding, but cries at this time in exactly the same way that he cries at other times of day. Not colic. Just part of his unsettled newborn behaviour.*
	Everything seems to help a little for a few minutes, but nothing stops the crying completely or for long. For example, she stops crying when she is picked up but starts again as she is cuddled. She belches and quiets but screams again. She sucks furiously for a few moments, then drops the teat or nipple to cry some more. Wrapping her tightly soothes her for a few minutes, then suddenly it maddens her. Lying her on her tummy across your knee relaxes her for a few minutes but then she struggles and screams.	*He cries in the evening—perhaps more than at other times of day—but takes a feed and then settles. Not colic, just hunger. Perhaps extra hunger due to reduced evening breast milk supplies (see p. 127).* *He cries in the evening, burps and then settles down. Not colic, just wind.*
	The most acute "attacks" are spasmodic. In between them the baby is shaky and sobbing. *The whole episode may last up to three hours.*	*He cries in the evening, stops when picked up, stays happy while held but cries again when put down. Not colic, just a need for contact comfort and company.*
	The same pattern repeats itself every evening until it stops altogether as suddenly as it began.	*He cries a great deal in the evening on some days but not on others. Not colic, if not a regular pattern.*

If, after going through the chart, you do think that your baby may be suffering from colic, take him or her to the doctor. But don't expect too much from the interview. Nobody understands colic very well—not even pediatricians. It is not an illness; there is no easy way to diagnose or cure it. The point of seeing your doctor is only that by discussing the baby's behaviour with you he will be able to help you decide whether this is a baby who really has colic or not. If together you decide that the answer is "no", he will help you to look for other explanations for the behaviour that worries you. If the answer is "yes", he will give you authoritative reassurance as to the baby's general health and the fact that, although he or she appears to spend two or three hours each evening in intermittent agony, colic does no permanent harm.

Living with colic There is very little you can do for a baby suffering from colic. Your helplessness, together with the fact that the dreadful bouts of screaming occur at the time of day when you are most tired and in need of peaceful time together, makes colic one of the most difficult things for new parents to cope with.

Try to accept the fact that the cause is unknown. If you continually search for a cause, you will only confuse every other aspect of your babycare by changing feeds, feeding techniques and routines, all to no avail. Colic has been variously put down to overfeeding, underfeeding, too rich, strong or weak feeds, milk which was too hot or too cold, milk which flowed too fast or too slowly, allergies, hernias, appendicitis, gall bladder trouble, wind and nervous exhaustion in the mother! All these contradictory explanations share one decisive fallacy: if any one of them was the cause of colic, why should the trouble occur after one and only one feed in the 24 hours? However you feed your baby, you do not do it in a particular way at 6pm. If the baby had a physical problem, it would not reveal itself only at this time of day. If maternal fatigue was a cause, rather than a result, of colic, the trouble would not occur when father took a turn with the bottle....

So instead of worrying about *why*, worrying in case you are doing something wrong, worrying in case the baby is ill, try for a mood of constructive resignation. You are faced with a bad few weeks. Although you cannot cure the baby's attacks you cannot leave him to suffer them alone, either. He will need all your time and attention while they last, so concentrate on organizing life so as to free yourself to cope with the least possible stress.

If you are desperate, ask your doctor about a medicine called *Dicyclomine hydrochloride* which reduces the mobility and muscular spasms of the colon. Some doctors believe (and the behaviour of some babies supports them) that this drug, given half an hour before the feed which precedes colic, can solve the whole problem. If your doctor does not consider it worth trying, or if it does not work for your baby, don't dose the baby with anything else. Concentrate on trying to stay sane, supporting each other and believing that there is nothing the matter with your child. He is physically perfect. It is just that he is still very immature and his nervous system and his digestion are showing their immaturity in this particularly stressful way. However awful the "evening colic" may be, it will not last for more than eight weeks.

Adjusting to your baby's behaviour

Some babies are much more difficult to look after happily than others. You cannot choose your baby's temperament any more than you could have chosen his or her sex. You may have the "kind" of baby you find easy to understand, sympathize with and handle, or a "kind" of baby who needs handling that does not come at all naturally to you.

All healthy newborn babies have many characteristics and behaviours in common. But each one of them is also a unique individual who has already had a unique set of experiences in the womb, during birth and immediately after it. All these things play a part in how the new baby settles in to life; how he or she reacts to you and to the world. You also are unique individuals with years of complex experiences behind you. All this will play a part in what you expect your baby to be like; in how you react to him or her.

If your expectations match the reality of your baby and the ways of handling that come "naturally" to you happen to suit that baby the interaction between you will be comparatively smooth and easy from the beginning. But if these things do not match, you and the baby will have to do much more adjusting to each other. Suppose, for example, that this is your second baby and that your first was a child who was basically calm and placid and thrived on lots of stimulation and rough and tumble play. You will probably start off by handling the new baby as you handled the first; if his reactions are similar all will be well. But if he happens to be a particularly sensitive and jumpy baby, who is terrified by anything fiercer than a gentle cuddle, your interaction will not be easy at all. Both of you will have to learn. His behaviour will affect your handling, teaching you to be more gentle; your handling will affect his behaviour, teaching him to be more relaxed.

At this very early age you have to try to combine handling your baby in ways which suit him *now* with allowing for the fact that some of his most extreme behaviours may be reactions to prenatal and birth experiences and may therefore change radically when he has settled down. You have to accept him for what he is today but leave it open to him to be something quite different next month or next year. A mother whose natural behaviour is outgoing and energetic but whose baby is jumpy may make tremendous efforts to adjust her handling to suit her son. Having done so, she may get so used to thinking of the baby as "nervy" or "highly strung" that she goes on treating him extra carefully long after the baby has grown out of his newborn jumpiness and become ready for more robust handling. If the mother's mind is closed to the possibility of her baby changing, she may quite forget to offer him noisy toys and rough and tumble play at six months and she may try too hard to protect him from bumps and falls when he learns to walk at around a year. The little boy may have to fight for his independence during the toddler stage.

So whatever your baby is like now, handle him in the ways which seem to keep him happy and calm. But while you react sensitively to his present needs, try not to label him. You will affect him and he will affect you; what kind of person will eventually come out of the interaction between you, nobody can know. That is part of the excitement of rearing a new human being.

Miserable babies Just as there are adults who always look on the black side of everything, so there are babies who are inclined to the miseries. Babies who are miserable are usually those who take a long time to settle happily into patterns of being soundly and comfortably asleep, awake and ravenous, full, awake and happy and then asleep again. They behave as if little bits of all those states stayed jumbled up together, keeping their behaviour unpredictable and preventing them from settling down to enjoy life.

Typical behaviour: The baby is tired and fretful but he cannot relax enough to go to sleep. He whimpers and dozes his way through the afternoon and then he is irritably hungry but not joyful about sucking. He is probably slow and difficult to feed. When the feeding is over he is awake but not very sociable. He soon gets tired of being held; does not seem to take much notice of being talked to but is not pleased to be returned to his cot. He probably wakes often in the night.

A baby like this may gain weight more slowly than most and be slow to start smiling or playing with his hands (see p. 165). Often he even looks unhappy. He is the opposite of all those "bonny babies" in the babyfood advertisements.

Living with it: A baby you cannot make happy is very depressing. Like the baby who cries without apparent reason (see p. 95) he will tend to make you feel inadequate as a parent. If his miseries go on for very long you will probably feel put-upon too. You will be lavishing love and care on a baby who seems to give nothing in return. While these feelings about a miserable baby are very natural it is important to try to keep them at bay. Don't let yourself feel that his unhappiness is a criticism of you. It is life outside the womb that your baby does not like very much, not you. You must stay on his side or you will not be able to offer the warm, gentle, patient attention which will, eventually, help him to feel happier. Work to get him to look at you, listen to you, smile at you. If you can only get him to the stage where he responds, the worst of his miseries will be over.

As well as loving the baby whether you get any response or not, try all the suggestions for crying babies on pp 95–100 and the following:

Keep the baby indoors in a very warm room and see if that makes him more relaxed. If it does, you could keep him in for a month – he can get plenty of fresh air with a window opened at the top.

See that the baby gets plenty of milk, as much as he will willingly take whenever he seems to want it.

See if the baby sleeps more easily when carefully wrapped (see p. 98). There is no harm in wrapping him for every sleep-time until he starts to kick the wrappings off.

See if the baby is happier with a great deal of contact comfort. If he likes being carried around, make a sling so that you can carry him on your back most of the time he is awake for a few weeks.

Don't introduce new aspects of life until he seems much happier with what he is already experiencing. Don't, for example, try a new baby hammock or a first car ride or even a first drink of fruit juice until he has stopped being so miserable.

Jumpy babies All newborns are startled by loud noises, turn away from bright lights and throw up their arms and cry if they feel they are going to be dropped. Jumpy babies take this kind of behaviour to extremes. They may startle and cry, tremble and pale at quite low grade stimuli. They seem to be frightened of almost everything, and perhaps they are. Perhaps it is life outside the safe, warm, dark haven of the womb which frightens them.

Typical behaviour: The baby overreacts to every kind of stimulation, whether it comes from inside him or from outside. Hunger takes him rapidly into a frenzy of desperate crying. His own jerks and twitches stop him relaxing into sleep. Picking him up makes him tense; putting him down makes him jump. Any change in his surroundings, however slight it may be, alerts and may alarm him. With this kind of baby even a telephone ringing in the next room may be enough to make him jump.

Living with it: The baby is not going to learn not to be frightened by being frightened. His nervous system is not going to become better able to accept minor shocks by being shocked. He is going to become calmer only by a combination of maturing and being handled so gently that he finds less and less in his daily life to upset him.

Caring for a jumpy baby can be a real challenge. If you see it as such, it can even be enjoyable. You set yourself to get through each day, or each bit of a day, without ever doing anything or letting anything happen which startles the baby or makes him cry. Your aim is to keep the stimulation which the baby receives below his tolerance level while he matures enough to be able to accept more stimulation happily.

Never hurry when you are handling the baby. When you pick him up, for example, he needs due warning so that his muscles can adjust to the change of position. When you carry him he needs you to move slowly and smoothly, supporting his head so that it does not wobble and never letting him feel insecurely held.

Keep handling to a minimum. For example, a jumpy baby will certainly hate being bathed and should be simply "topped and tailed" until he is calmer. He will probably hate bumpy pram rides and wide open spaces too. Let him move only from cot or pram to lap and back again for a few weeks.

Cut down on physical stimulation by careful wrapping. Changes of position and being moved from one place to another will be far less worrying for him if he is properly wrapped up (see p. 98). The wrappings will provide a protective cocoon between him and the outside world.

Make sure that everyone who handles the baby is quiet and gentle. You want him to discover that the world and the people in it are safe. A jolly uncle with good intentions and a loud laugh can frighten a jumpy baby in a way that makes him want to retreat even more from his new world. Protect him; he has plenty of time for learning to make social contacts.

Sleepy babies

Babies who seem to have an almost unlimited capacity for sleep probably feel just as unready for life outside the womb as do miserable or jumpy babies. But they react to it quite differently: instead of protesting or recoiling they avoid life by staying asleep.

Typical behaviour: The baby is "no trouble". He makes almost no demands and probably has to be woken up for most of his feeds. It is often difficult to persuade him to stay awake for long enough to suck very much at a time and once he has sucked himself back to sleep he may be unwakeable. He does not seem to care very much about his surroundings. He seldom cries for long but he seldom seems particularly happy either. He is playing a sleepy, neutral game.

Living with it: Although the baby's lack of responsiveness may disappoint you, this is a comparatively easy "type" of baby to cope with. While he is so sleepy, you can be regaining your strength and collecting your wits in readiness for the active motherhood which will come when the baby matures a little.

Make sure that the baby wakes up enough to eat. Occasionally an exceptionally sleepy baby who is being fed on demand fails to gain as much weight as he should because he does not demand as much food as his body needs. If you have to wake him for feeds, then of course there is no harm in waking him to suit your convenience, but make sure that you do so at least every four hours. Add in a couple of extra feeds if his sleepiness means that he only sucks for five minutes at a time.

The baby may be perfectly willing to sleep through a twelve hour night from the beginning. Don't let him. That is too many hours without water, quite apart from the food itself. Wake him at your bedtime and bless the fact that he probably will not wake you in the small hours!

Don't take the baby's sleepy isolation for granted. In other words, don't let his willingness to be shut away in his cot for hours lead you to *expect* him to behave like that. Give him lots of opportunities for sociable cuddles and talk. Try to get him interested in looking at things and being talked to. If he is fast asleep on your lap after two minutes, it is fair enough to put him back to bed, but try again to play with him at the next feed. You want him to realize, gradually, that being awake is fun.

Wakeful babies

Babies vary in the amount of sleep they need, right from the beginning of their lives. Most babies will sleep for something like 16 hours in the 24 to start with. Very sleepy ones may sleep for 22 hours in every 24. A really wakeful baby may never sleep for more than 12 hours and may seldom do that sleeping in stretches of more than two hours at a time.

Typical behaviour: The baby is not especially miserable or especially jumpy. There is nothing "keeping him awake", he just does not sleep for the number of hours we expect of very small babies. He will take a feed and drop off to sleep immediately. But an hour or two later he is awake again, not because he is ready for more food but just because he has stopped being asleep. Because he spends so much time awake he will probably show more interest in the things around him at an earlier age than most babies. His development in every area may be rapid because he is spending so much more time looking, listening and learning.

Living with it: This is not the kind of baby you can care for in short concentrated bursts of time and then forget about in between. He makes himself felt almost all day and often for a good deal of the night, too. How you react to him will probably depend at least partly on how much else you have to do. A very jealous toddler, for example, will suffer much more from a very wakeful baby than from one who naps in a corner for much of the toddler's day. The main trouble with a wakeful baby is that he is spending a lot of hours awake at an age when it is difficult to find entertainment for him. He cannot handle toys yet; he is not ready for physical play nor even for being propped up. Start by reminding yourself that he would sleep if he needed to; try to accept his wakefulness, and don't feel that he "ought" to be asleep. If you try to make him behave as other babies do, you will waste a lot of time tucking him away for naps he does not want, and you will make him miserable too because he will be bored and lonely.

Find different ways of keeping the baby company. Perhaps his pram could come into the kitchen? If so, you can park it close beside you and get into the habit of stopping for quick chats as you move around. If he has a carry cot that lifts off its stand, he could lie in that beside you while you are reading or watching television.

Find easy ways of carrying your baby. Although you obviously cannot carry him around all the time, being carried is perfect entertainment for a wakeful newborn. A sling inside the house might let you do simple housework with the baby on your back. A canvas carrier (see p. 159) will let you take him into shops instead of leaving him to be bored in his pram outside. (Don't use a cot-sheet sling outdoors with a new baby; it is not warm enough.)

Arrange different places where the baby can lie on the floor. A spare pram mattress that you can carry from room to room is useful. He will get less bored if he has lots of changes of scene.

Give the baby interesting things to look at. This will help him entertain himself. Hang things from the pram hood or above the cot, and change them often so that he always has something new to look at. Make or buy a mobile or two, so that he can watch something that moves. (For further suggestions, see p. 178.)

Be prepared to treat your baby like a somewhat older one. He will be packing a lot of learning into all those hours awake, so you need to keep an eye on his development and be sure that you offer new kinds of entertainment as soon as he shows that he is ready for them. The next chapter (see pp. 156–195) should help.

Using his or her body

There is much to learn about looking after very new babies and because they have not yet settled down, caring for them is a very demanding job. It is easy to get so involved in daily care that you find yourself treating your child like a very precious kind of object rather than a developing person; a new human being.

But your baby is human and your baby is developing – every moment of every day. Don't let night feeds and wet nappies take up so much of your attention that you miss the fascinating changes that are taking place; the signs of your baby beginning to grow up.

Postures and head control

Newborns are very scrunched-up looking creatures. Whatever position you put your baby in he will curl himself inwards with his body taking up its position in relation to his head. This is because at this stage of life his head is so large and heavy in relation to the rest of him that it acts as an anchor and a pivot.

Until the rest of him grows a little so that his head becomes relatively lighter, and until he can get some control over the muscles of his neck, the baby's voluntary movements will be restricted. At the beginning he can lift that head a little and he will always turn it to avoid smothering, but movements of his limbs are restricted by his curled position while the fact that his head is always turned to one side prevents him from seeing things which are directly above him.

A baby's muscle control starts from the top and moves gradually downwards (see p. 160). When you hold him against your shoulder in the first hours after birth, he rests his head against you. If you do not support his neck for him, that head will simply flop. Within a week he can force those neck muscles to lift the head away for a second or two. A few days later he practises head control so continually that when you hold him it feels as if he were deliberately bumping his head against you: effort-flop-effort-flop, again and again. By three to four weeks he can balance his head for several seconds provided you keep absolutely still. He still needs your supporting hand when ever you carry him and especially when you lift or put him down.

Reflex physical activities

During the first week of life, this baby, whose muscles are still so incompetent even in balancing his head, exhibits some remarkably mature-looking behaviours which sometimes fool parents into believing that they have produced an infant who will crawl or even walk at a few weeks of age! But these are not voluntary or controlled movements. They are simply reflexes which will die out over a few days and then be re-learned months later at the appropriate stage of development.

False crawling

If you put him on his stomach, the baby's naturally curled-up position leads him to flex legs and arms so that he looks as if he were about to crawl off. He may even "scrabble" so that he wrinkles his cot sheet. The position will be unlearned when the baby becomes able to uncurl himself and lie flat (see p. 161).

The newborn's natural position is curled inwards. But for the first few days she sometimes varies it with strangely grown up postures. They are not what they seem. They are passing reflexes

. . . placed on her tummy she looks as if she is about to crawl

. . . startled, jerked or too roughly handled, she throws out her arms and legs, instinctively clutching for support

. . . without your support in the first weeks she cannot even manage to hold up her large and heavy head

. . . her hand will react to anything that touches her palm by gripping

*. . . in the first hours
this reflex hand grip
is powerful enough to
support the baby's weight . . .
but the strength will go
from it overnight*

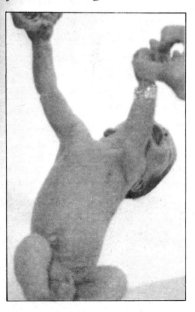

. . . the soles of his feet react to a firm surface, with deliberate "steps". But, like the other reflexes, this vanishes in a few days. It will be almost a year before he can really walk.

False walking If you hold the baby upright with his feet just touching a firm surface, he will take quite deliberate "steps", placing one foot after another while you support his weight. Once again he will unlearn this. By the time he is a week old he will simply sag if you hold him upright.

False clinging In the first days of life a baby's hand grip is incredibly strong. In theory, you could hang him up by his hands and he would cling on tightly enough not to fall. But don't try it. The ability passes between one day and the next. You might choose the next for your experiment!

But although the baby's extraordinary strength of grip passes off, some degree of reflex hand grip remains. If you put your finger or a rattle into his closed fist, his hand will grip itself around it. When you try to remove it, his fist will close even more tightly in a reflex attempt to hang on. This reaction to the feel of a grippable object in his palm will remain through all the weeks that must pass before the baby is ready to learn to take hold of objects on purpose. So hanging on with his hands is not something which, like crawling or walking, he has to unlearn and then learn all over again. In this instance the reflex action eventually gives way to deliberate action.

The reflex response which leads a baby to hang on to whatever he finds in his hands may be left over from pre-history when our ape-like ancestors' children kept themselves safe by clinging to their mothers. Today's human babies cannot cling on to an adult with their hands, arms and legs, as baby monkeys cling to their mother's belly fur. Yet they seem to want to. They are happiest and most relaxed when they are carried in a face-to-face position, legs straddling your belly, arms around your neck. When they are not being carried, being closely wrapped up, or even having a piece of warm textured material laid across their chests and stomachs as if they were pressed against a warm mother, calms and pleases them.

A reminder to be careful . . . If your baby, who would like to cling to you, feels that he is about to be dropped, he produces a violent and obviously distressed reflex which is called the "Moro response". If you jerk him while you are holding his hands, you will see his arms snatch up at yours and his legs curve convulsively upwards as if seeking a body around which to clasp themselves. If you put him down carelessly, so that your hands start to release him before he feels the firm security of the mattress, he will throw out both his arms and legs and then flex them violently; his head will jerk back because the reflex movements have upset his head control; he will probably cry out in fear.

Like other reflexes, the Moro response has lost its direct usefulness to the baby because, unlike his furry ancestors, he does not have the muscle power to save himself from a fall by holding on. But the response is still a useful one. Every time your baby reacts in this violently startled way you will know that you have handled him too roughly, too unexpectedly or without taking enough care to support his heavy head. Moro responses are a hint to parents to take more care.

Using his or her senses

Each of your baby's five senses is in working order from the moment of birth. A baby does not have to learn to see, to hear, to sense touch through the skin, or even to smell or taste. The equipment for all these activities is in-built. What is lacking is experience: knowledge of what things look or sound like; how different things feel or smell or taste. All five senses are bombarded with stimuli as soon as the baby comes out of the womb. Learning through the senses goes on from that moment.

Finding out exactly *what* a new baby senses is exceedingly difficult because he cannot tell us what he is feeling. Research workers have to find ways of measuring the baby's responses without his direct cooperation. Often we cannot say more than that babies respond with pleasure to certain kinds of sensory stimulation and with distress to others. The sense of touch is an instance in point. We know that babies react with calm pleasure to warm, soft, firm pressure, especially up the front surface of their bodies. We know that they react by gripping to the feel of an object in their fists; we know that they react with sucking reflexes to a stroking touch on the cheek. But we do not know exactly what they feel nor what difference they sense when their skins are tickled with a feather or stroked with sandpaper.

Smelling and tasting

We assume that newborn babies have a sense of smell because we know they have a sense of taste and the two are intimately linked. But experiments in smell-differentiation would be impossible. Offered bad eggs and daffodils, babies can neither tell nor show you whether they can distinguish between them nor which they "prefer". They have to go on breathing even if each breath brings a noxious odour. They are not yet able to hold their breath on purpose.

Taste is easier to test. Bitter, acid or sour tastes make the baby screw up his face, turn his head away and/or cry. He can also differentiate accurately between plain, slightly sweetened and very sweet water. We know this because while he will suck a bottle containing any one of these, he will suck longer and harder as the sweetness increases. No wonder it is so difficult to control the sugar-intake of older children!

Hearing and making sounds

Your baby's only deliberate sounds during these early days are crying. It may seem to you that all the crying sounds the same, but in fact there is a repertory of different cries which represent different states of feeling. Whether or not you feel you can recognize, by ear, the difference between one kind of cry and another, you will almost certainly find yourself reacting differently to each. When the types of cry are analyzed by sound spectrograph you can actually see the differences between them, differences of tone, of duration and of rhythm (see p. 156).

A baby's pain cry has a particular intensity and rhythm. Instinct will tell you to take the stairs three at a time. You will find that you are thinking of nothing but getting to the baby—fast.

A hunger cry is quite different. It has particular patterns of sound and pause which are the same for all babies but quite different from any of your baby's other cries. If you are breast-feeding, that particular cry may start the "let down" reflex so that your milk starts to flow even as you get up to go to the baby. If you are bottle-feeding, the cry probably directs you to the kitchen to start warming the bottle. In this case, however, although you will have no doubt at all that the baby needs you, you will not have the sense of urgency that comes with the pain cry.

Fear sounds different again. The fear cry is a sound of pure desolation and is highly infectious. By the time you reach your baby your own pulse will be racing and adrenalin will be flooding through your body, readying it to fight any danger to protect him.

By the time he is around four weeks old your baby will begin to make other sounds besides crying. He will make small gurgly googly noises when he is relaxed after a feed and little tense whimpery sounds when he is building up towards hunger cries. He is moving towards the next stage in communication – cooing.

Listening

Babies can hear from the moment of birth and may be able to sense sound vibrations while they are still in the womb. Certainly they react with soothed pleasure after birth to recordings of heartbeat sounds, which they have lived with before it.

Loud, sudden sounds will make your baby jump. The sharper the sound the more extreme will be his reaction. Thunder rolling round the house will not bother him nearly as much as a plate smashing on a hard floor. Just as clearly as he dislikes these sounds, the baby enjoys (or at least is soothed and relaxed by) repetitive rhythmical sounds. He will enjoy music, but he will enjoy the rhythmical pounding of a drum or the steady whirr of your vacuum cleaner just as much – as far as we can tell.

But while the baby clearly *hears* all these sounds, the ones to which he *listens*, with obvious concentration, are the sounds of people talking. He has a built-in interest in voices and in voice-like sounds. Because they come from the caretakers without whom he cannot survive, he is programmed to pay attention to them.

Unless you are on the look-out for it, you may not notice how much your baby enjoys your voice during these first weeks. At this stage his looking and listening systems are still separate. He listens without looking for the source of the sound he hears, so he often listens to your voice without looking at you. But if you watch him carefully, you will see his reactions to your loving prattle. If he is crying, he will often stop as you approach the cot, talking. He does not need to see you or to feel your touch first. If he is lying still when you begin to speak to him, he will start to move excitedly. If he is kicking, he will stop and freeze to attention, concentrating on your voice.

It will be a long time before the baby can understand your words but from the first days of his life he will react to the tones he hears in your voice. When you talk softly and caressingly he reacts with pleasure, but if you speak sharply to an older child while handling the baby, he will probably cry, while if something should make you cry out in fear while you are holding him, he will be instantly panic-stricken.

Looking   Babies can see, clearly and with discrimination, from the moment of birth. If your baby seems to spend a lot of waking time gazing blankly into space or looking towards a brightly lit window or blowing curtain, this is not because babies are incapable of seeing anything more detailed, but because you do not put anything else within visual range. New babies' focusing range is very short.

A new baby's eyes work rather like an old-fashioned fixed-focus camera with the focal length set at 8–10 inches (20–25 cm). At that precise distance he can see clearly but objects which are further away are blurred. If he lies in his cot with nothing within his focal distance to look at, he will look across the room at whatever he can perceive through the distance-blur. Brightness and movement (as every short-sighted person knows) are the two things that will be visible to him.

If, armed with this information, you deliberately put things close enough to your baby's eyes for him to see them clearly, he will "choose" to pay attention to much more subtle stimuli than brightness or movement. You can test his "choices" for yourself by holding pairs of objects where he can look at them. He will look at a simple circular red rattle if there is nothing else close enough for him to see, but if you add a sheet of paper with a complicated black and white pattern on it he will turn his attention to that instead. He will look at a simple cube but add a more complex shape such as a tea strainer and he will look at that. He is programmed to give his attention to complex patterns and shapes because he must learn a complex visual world.

His fixed-focal distance is not a matter of random chance. On the contrary, it is exactly the distance which separates his face from yours when you hold and talk to him or when you are breast-feeding. Just as voices are the most important things for him to listen to, so faces are the most important things for him to look at and he is innately programmed to study them intently whenever he can. It may even be that the blurring out of more distant objects is developmentally useful to him as it helps him to concentrate on those vital faces undistracted by other things.

New babies do not know that people are people so your baby cannot know, when he studies your face, that what he is looking at is *you*. He simply gives his full visual attention to any face or to anything he sees which is face-like. His criteria of "face-like" have been studied in detail. If an object or a picture has a hair-line, eyes, a mouth and a chin-line, the baby will react to it as a face. If you watch his eyes carefully you will see that he starts at the top, scans that hairline, moves his gaze slowly downwards to the chin-line and then returns it to the eyes. Once he is looking the stimulus in the eye, he will go on gazing for much longer than he will look at anything else.

While it is interesting to try out this reaction by showing your baby a simple sketch of a face, or a balloon with a face drawn on it, looking at real faces is much more valuable to him. When he has learned faces you will get your reward for patiently giving him yours to study. One day soon that intent scanning will end as usual at your eyes but it will culminate in his first true social gesture to the outside world which you represent. It will end with his first smile.

Your face is the most interesting thing in your baby's early world . . .

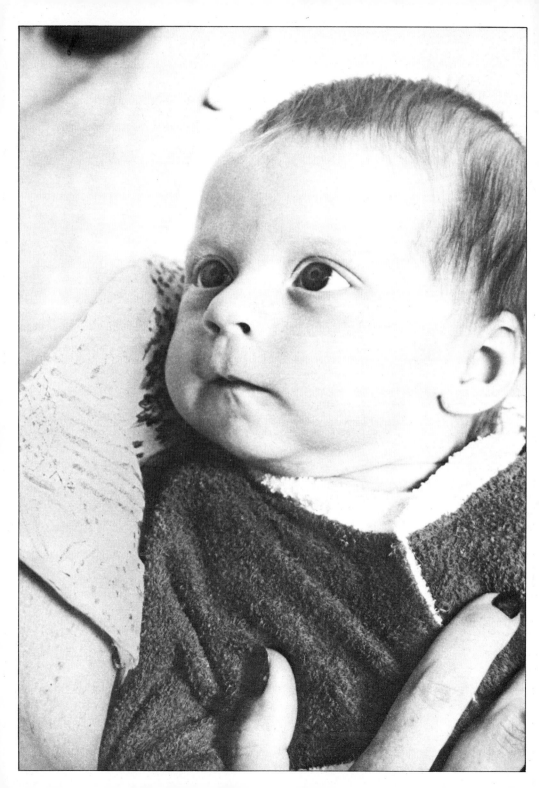

CHAPTER THREE

THE SETTLED BABY

The first six months

One day you will find that you have stopped regarding your baby as a totally unpredictable and therefore rather alarming novelty, and have begun instead to think of him as a person with tastes, preferences and characteristics of his own. When that happens you will know that he has moved on from being a "newborn" and has got himself settled into life. Nobody can date that moment except you. An easy birth, close satisfactory contact immediately after it, and a good fit between his needs and your expectations, will all tend to bring it forward. Post-natal depression, feeding difficulties, or a baby who needs handling in a way that does not come naturally to you, will all tend to keep it back. But whether he is settled at two weeks or at two months, that moment will come.

A settled baby is a manageable proposition. He may be a little devil, but he is a little devil you know. You can tell how he likes to be handled even if it is not the way you would choose to handle him. You know what to expect from him even if it is the worst. You know what frightens him even if it is almost everything. Above all, you can tell when he is happy, however seldom it may be, and when he is miserable, even if that is almost always. So once your baby is settled you know what you are up against. Instead of trying to survive from hour to hour, get through another day, avoid thinking about another week, you can begin to work and plan for reasonable compromises between his needs and those of everyone else.

The baby will make it clear that his prime need is for people, in the shape of you, his constant caretakers. Your love for him may still be problematic, but the dawn of his attachment to you is a matter of sheer necessity. If he is to survive, he has to attach himself to you and ensure that you take care of him. As these first few weeks pass, his interest in people becomes increasingly obvious. Your face fascinates him. Every time it comes within his short focusing range he studies it intently from hairline to mouth, finishing by gazing into your eyes. He listens intently to your voice, kicking a little when he hears it, or freezing into immobility as he tries to locate its source. Soon he will turn his eyes and his head to see who is talking. If you pick him up, he stops crying. If you will cuddle and walk him, he is content. Whatever else he likes or needs, he clearly likes and needs you. You can begin to have some confidence in yourselves as the parents of this new human being.

But in case these settled responses to your devoted care are not enough to keep you caring, the baby has a trump card still to play. Somewhere between four and eight weeks he is going to smile at you. One day, when he is studying your face in his intent and serious way, he scans down to your mouth and back to your eyes as usual. But as he gazes, his face slowly begins to flower into the small miracle of a wide toothless grin that totally transforms it. For most parents that's it. He is the most beautiful baby in the world even if his head *is* still crooked, and the most lovable baby in the world however often he wakes in the night. Few adults can resist a baby's new smiling. Even the most reluctantly dutiful visitors have been known to sneak back to the cotside to try for one more smile, all for themselves. . . .

When the baby smiles it looks like love, but he cannot truly love you yet because he does not know one person from another. His early smiles are an insurance policy against neglect and for pleasant social attention. The more he smiles and gurgles and waves his fists at people, the more they will smile and talk to him. The more attention people pay him, the more he will respond. He will tie them ever closer with his throat-catching grins and his heart-rendingly quivery lower lip. His responses create a self-sustaining circle, his smiles leading to your smiles and yours to more from him.

There is no harm in your assuming that these enchanting early smiles are meant for you personally. They soon will be. It is through pleasant social interaction with adults, who find him rewarding and therefore pay him attention, that the baby moves on from being interested in people in general to being able to recognize and attach himself to particular ones. By the time he is around three months old it will be clear that he knows you. He will not smile at you and whimper at strangers. He still smiles at everyone. But he saves his best signs of favour, the smiliest smiles, for you. He becomes both increasingly sociable and increasingly fussy about whom he will socialize with. He is ready to form a passionate and exclusive emotional tie with somebody and you are elected.

Under what we think of as "normal family circumstances" most babies select their mothers for this first love. But it is not the blood-tie which gives you the privilege. It is a privilege and it has to be earned. You earn it not by just *being his mother* but by *mothering him*. Mothering, in this sense, does not just mean taking physical care of him. The love he is forming is not cupboard-love, based on the pleasures of feeding.

One day, when he is studying your face,
his face will slowly begin to flower . . .

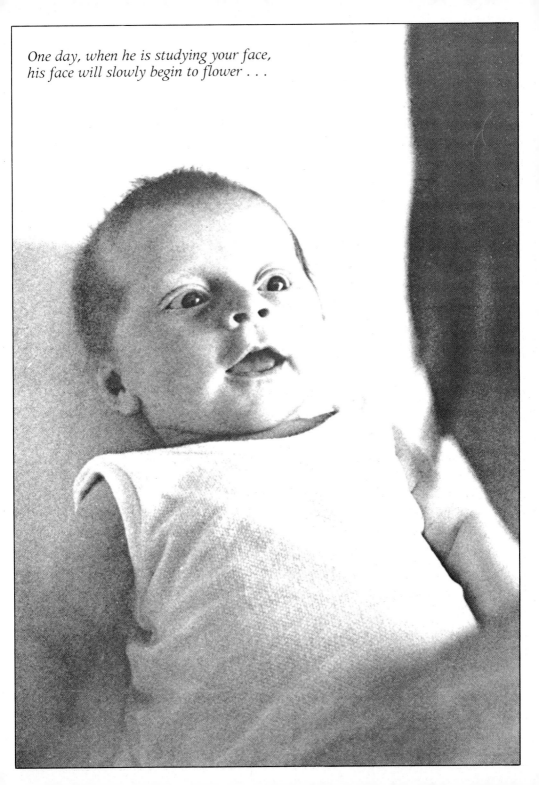

He will fall for the person who mothers him emotionally, talking to him, cuddling him, smiling and playing. If you had to share his total care with someone else and you handed over all the physical tasks, using your limited time for loving, you would keep your prime role in his life. But if you used your time for his physical needs and left the other person to be his companion, it would be the companionable adult to whom he attached himself. He needs some one person who always comes when he needs help or company, who notices when he smiles and smiles back, who hears when he "talks", listens and replies. Somebody who plays with him and shows him things, brings little bits of the world for him to see. These are the things which really matter to three month babies. These are the things which make for love.

Every baby needs at least one special person to attach himself to. It is through this first love relationship that he will learn about people and about the world. It is through it that he will experience emotions and learn to cope with them. And it is through this baby-love that he will become capable of more grown-up kinds of love; capable, one far-distant day, of giving to his own children the same kind of devotion he asks for himself now. Babies who never have a special person, receiving adequate physical care but little emotional response, or being looked after by a succession of caretakers, often do not develop as fast or as far as their innate drive and their potential for personality allow. But provided he does have his special person, your baby can use any number of other people too. His capacity for love is not rationed any more than yours is. The reverse is true. The more he is allowed to attach himself to you, the more he will be able to respond affection-ately to others. Love creates love.

Few fathers are in a position to receive their baby's first attachment because mundane matters like jobs prevent them from being that ever-present, always-responsive person. But a father who can accept, support and encourage the unique relationship between his partner and his child will find that there is one waiting for him too. It comes a little later and it is built on the first, but it is just as vital to the child.

At four or five months, the very fact that the father cannot be the person who is always there and continually involved in the baby's routine care, makes him especially valuable. When he does come home, or stays home because it is a weekend, his face, his talk and his play strike the baby as fresh and interesting. Because he has not spent the day trying to fit a sufficiency of chores and sanity-preserving adult activities around the baby's needs, he may actually be able to offer more of the social contact the baby craves. As the baby grows up a little and becomes able to remember and anticipate pleasures, a father can concentrate on building his own, peculiarly fatherly, relationship with his child. Instead of competing with the mother for her special mother-relationship, he can create his own and may find himself with a prime place in his baby's affections.

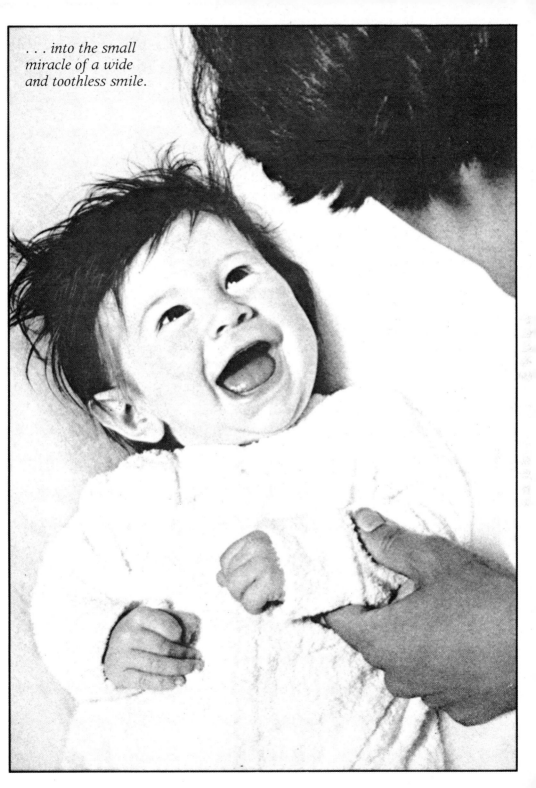

. . . into the small miracle of a wide and toothless smile.

Many women passionately enjoy this stage of motherhood. The baby flatters you with his special attentions, making you feel special, beloved, irreplaceable. He needs you for everything. He must have adequate physical care but he must have emotional and intellectual care too: play, toys, help and opportunity to practise each tiny new ability. Whatever the baby becomes able to do, he needs and will want to do it; it is up to you to make it possible for him. Yet, with all this needing, his hour-by-hour care is comparatively easy. He is no longer irrational and incomprehensible as he was when he was newborn, yet he is not awake most of the day and into everything as he will be once he can crawl in the second half of the year. You still get daytime periods of peace and privacy and you can still put the baby on the floor and know that he will be safely where you put him when you next glance around.

But some women hate it. Instead of taking pleasure in being so much enjoyed and needed, they feel shut in and consumed by the baby's dependence. They yearn for at least a little time when the baby needs nothing practical and nothing emotional either. The continual effort of identifying with his feelings, noticing his needs and padding his journey through the passing days makes them feel drained. Feeding a hungry baby or cleaning a dirty one seems easy compared with coping with his loneliness or boredom.

Giving yourself the high importance-rating you truly deserve is both the prevention and the cure. All the vital developments of these months are waiting inside your baby. He has a built-in drive to practise every aspect of being human, from making sounds, using his hands or rolling over, to eating real food or roaring with laughter. But each aspect is also in your hands. You can help him develop and learn or you can hinder him by holding yourself aloof. You can keep him happy and busy and learning fast or you can keep him discontented, bored and not learning as fast as he could.

If you do help him, you and the whole family will gain because the baby will be cheerful and easy and a pleasure to have around – most of the time. If you refuse to help him, trying to ration your attention, everyone will suffer and you will suffer most of all. The baby will be difficult, fretful and no pleasure to anyone. You will be unhappy because, however much you may resent the fact, your pleasure and his are tied together. If you please him, his happiness will please you and make it easier for you to go on. If you leave him miserable, his misery will depress you and make it more difficult. You may resent his crying; resent the fact that he needs you – again. But ignoring the crying not only condemns him to cry, it also condemns you to listen to his crying. So when you try to meet his needs, tune in to him, treat him as he asks to be treated; you do not only do it for him, you do it for yourselves, too. Like it or not, you are a family now. You sink or swim together.

Feeding and growing

By the time your baby is around two weeks old, he or she will be settled into feeding either at the breast or from a bottle. Those first confusing days, when neither of you knew quite what you were doing, are over.

The baby wants to eat. He wants you to feed him because he cannot feed himself. You want to feed him because you know that he must eat if he is to grow and be healthy. So you and your baby are both on the same side. To worry or to fight over feeding is a waste of both your energies and a waste of fun for you both.

The fun part is important. If you watch the baby at the beginning of a feed you can see that he is hungry and that the feeling of the milk going down inside him is lessening the hunger pain. You can see that he is enjoying being held and cuddled while he sucks. And you can see that the actual sucking is important to him too. After three or four gulping minutes he settles into a perfect rhythm; a burst of sucks and then a breath and a rest and another burst of sucking. Soon an expression of blissful satisfaction spreads across his face. The rhythm slows a little; the rest pauses get longer, the bursts of sucking shorter. Now he is drunk with milk and pleasure; almost asleep. Just giving the odd suck now and again to remind himself that the milk is still there for him.

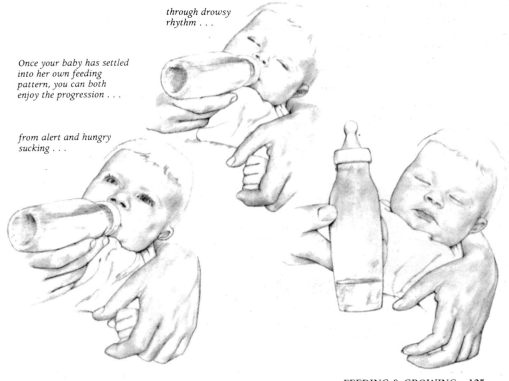

through drowsy rhythm . . .

Once your baby has settled into her own feeding pattern, you can both enjoy the progression . . .

from alert and hungry sucking . . .

It all sounds easy. And for some parents with some babies it is easy. But for others it is not. The baby may go on with the unsettled and unsettling behaviour which is typical of the newborn period for longer than you expect. This is especially likely if he was a premature baby or if he had any particular difficulties immediately after birth. He may produce some new and puzzling behaviour over feeding, or you may be so anxious to do right by him that you cannot believe it is meant to be as easy and straightforward as it seems.

If your baby is reasonably contented most of the time, is gaining weight steadily and is getting increasingly active when he is awake, you can be sure that there is nothing the matter with his feeding from *his* point of view.

If he does not seem to be thriving in this easy, cheerful way, you will, of course, consult your health visitor or your doctor. But consider first the possibility that he is not getting enough to eat at the times when he is hungry.

Growth As we have seen (see p. 76), babies gain something like 1 oz (28 g) each day from the time they are ten days old until they are around three months. But after the first quarter year, the rate of growth slows down a little. In the second three months your baby will gain around 5–6ozs (140–170g) each week, and around $2\frac{1}{2}$ inches (6cm) overall. As we stressed before, *regularity* of gain is more important than amount. A baby whose weight gain, week by week, has been neatly following the shape of the curves on the average growth chart (see p. 506) but who suddenly slows right down so that the curve flattens off, may be being underfed. However, if the baby has always gained more slowly than average, so that the curve has always been flatter than average, you may just have a baby who is meant to gain rather slowly.

These are the heights and weights during the first six months of the three babies introduced on p. 37. All three grow at the same rate although their different starting points make their actual measurements different. Growth slows a little in the second three months, giving a curve, from successive measuring points, which is typical for all babies. A flatter curve or sudden dip might be a clue to underfeeding.

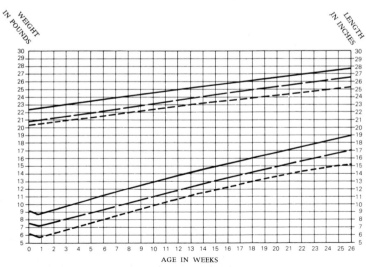

HEIGHT

LONG

AVERAGE

SHORT

WEIGHT

HEAVY

AVERAGE

LIGHT

Breast-feeding

Underfeeding Underfeeding in a breast-fed baby can creep up on you very gradually in a way which is unfairly difficult to spot. What often happens is this: having got breast-feeding started, your milk supply is plentiful during the first two or three weeks while you are getting plenty of rest and not (we hope) worrying too much about the rest of your household. The baby settles down to some kind of feeding pattern and you rightly assume that demand and supply are dovetailing nicely.

But eventually you have to step back into running your household again. Many mothers embark on a spurt of activity instead of getting back into the rhythm gradually. Whether it happens when the baby is two weeks old or four weeks old, suddenly taking up all your old activities *plus* caring for the new baby is bound to make you very tired.

Getting tired and harassed tends to reduce the milk supply. And meanwhile the baby is growing. He needs more milk this week than he did last, so if your fatigue means that there is less available, he is bound to be hungry.

This kind of situation is not easy to spot. The baby's behaviour may not tell you very much because discontent and crying, a tendency to wake only two hours after his last feed and a demand for two feeds in every night, are not *new* behaviours. They seem like his unsettled behaviour in the newborn period, so you may not realize that he would be settling by now if he were not hungry. The behaviour of your own breasts may also mislead you. You probably wake each morning with more milk than you know what to do with and in urgent need of a clean nightdress! So how can your baby be short of milk?

The answer is that your supply is copious when you have been resting, but gets less and less adequate as your busy day wears on. If you think carefully back over the past few days you will probably recognize a pattern of your baby being content for reasonable periods between each feed you give him – from, say, 4am to 4pm – but getting less and less contented from 4pm until you have had your first good sleep of the night. In busy households your milk will often be at its lowest for the baby's 6pm feed because it follows that chaotic couple of hours during which older children need picking up from school, the house needs tidying and supper must be cooked.

What to do depends on how much you want to go on breast-feeding. If you do want to, then the baby has to be given the chance to make more milk for himself, just as he did at the very beginning when you were getting breast-feeding going (see p. 54). The milk is stimulated by his sucking. The more often he sucks, the more milk you will make. When his frequent sucking has built up the supply until it meets his needs, he will suck less often. It is a beautifully simple system and it really does work. But remember that it will take at least two weeks to make a real difference to the baby. He will need the first week to stimulate you to make the extra milk he needs. It is only in the second week that you can expect to get a nice surprise from the scales and to find yourself caring for a calmer and more contented baby.

Keeping up the milk supply

Once you have got your milk supply up to the level where it meets your baby's needs, you will want to make sure that it remains ample. As well as offering him the breast whenever he seems to be hungry, a few other things will help you both:

More rest for you, especially towards the end of the day. This is important. Discipline yourself to rest for a while each afternoon, however difficult it may be to make arrangements for older children or to resist the waiting chores.

Expressing any milk left over from feeds early in the day when you have got plenty. The baby probably cannot drink all that is available to him then, but if you empty the breasts for him they will produce more at the next feed.

Taking the time and trouble to drink when you are thirsty. The baby will be taking more than a pint of fluid from you. While it will not help your milk supply to flood yourself with fluid, it does help to make sure that you really drink what you need. That means noticing when you feel thirsty and doing something about it. If you do not have time to make yourself a cup of tea or coffee, at least take a drink of water.

Taking the time and trouble to eat properly. As long as your diet is adequate the quality of your milk will be fine. Your body meets your baby's needs first, now, just as it did while you were pregnant. But if that diet is only *just* adequate, the fact that the baby's milk is using up a lot of calories, protein and vitamins may leave you short. And that will mean that you are more liable to feel tired and droopy; you will be less able to cope with the demands being made on you.

Some things will not help . . .

Worrying. We do not entirely understand the mechanisms by which worry and anxiety affect some physical functions such as breast-feeding, but there is no doubt that they do. Many mothers see this most clearly if they try to feed the baby in circumstances which are too public for them to feel relaxed: the breast is full, the baby sucks, but the mother's tension prevents the "let down" reflex which, under normally relaxed circumstances, lets the milk flow in response to the stimulation of the sucking. As farmers say when dealing with a nervy cow, "you have to gentle her or she won't let it down". You have to try and "gentle" yourself, relax, go easy on yourself.

Trying to keep the baby to a schedule, even if it is one which he seemed to have settled on for himself a week or so ago. Your breasts must have the stimulation of extra sucking if you want them to produce extra milk.

Giving the baby a bottle-feed as well. If you give him a bottle he will be less hungry; he will not therefore instruct your breasts to make the full amount of milk he needs. The time for complementary bottles is after you have decided that you cannot or do not want to bother to produce more milk.

Leaving a baby-sitter to give occasional feeds by bottle. Breasts which are left full of milk for several hours receive the signal "you have made more than is needed; make less". Once your supply is consistently adequate you will be able to use a bottle occasionally, but while you are trying to increase your supply it is better to take the baby with you when you go out.

Patent medicines which claim to increase breast milk. Like "tonics" and medicines which claim to increase your sexual vigour, most of these are merely multivitamins and magic. They probably will not do you any harm but unless your diet is very deficient in vitamins they will not do you any good either.

Birth control pills. It is known that these decrease the milk supply. Discuss an alternative method of contraception with your doctor or Family Planning clinic. If the "pill" is the contraceptive you prefer, you will certainly be able to start it again when your baby is four to five months old. If you have breast-fed successfully for that length of time, the whole supply-demand situation will be perfectly adjusted and will override the slight lessening caused by the "pill". Furthermore you will have started your baby on some extra foods by that time so that he will no longer be dependent on you for every single calorie.

If things don't improve . . .
Two weeks of trying to increase your breast milk and your baby's contentment will usually put matters right. But not always. If there is no improvement, you need to assess the situation. Just how short of milk is he? If you are keen to go on breast-feeding and therefore do not mind how much trouble you take, the best way to find out is given in the Newborn chapter: calculate the baby's "expected" weight (see p. 77), calculate his probable needs (see p. 76), test weigh him for a complete 24 hour period (see p. 59), and compare the amount of milk the test weighing shows he has taken with the amount he is likely to need.

If you find that there is very little difference between what he probably needs and what he has had, it is unlikely that you need consider giving him any food other than breast milk. Unless your doctor is worried about him, you can safely go on dealing with his discontent and your breast milk supplies by letting him suck as often as he likes. If you repeat the test weighing after a further two weeks, you will almost certainly find that he is getting plenty.

If you find that there is a considerable difference, you will have to give him complementary bottle feeds (see below) while you go on trying to increase your breast milk supplies. You should be guided on this by your doctor, but you can usually assume that extra food will be needed if the baby is only getting three quarters, or less, of his calculated needs. This would mean, for example, that a baby whose expected weight was 9lbs (4.1kg) and whose calculated needs were therefore 27ozs (765ml) per 24 hours was shown by test weighing to be getting only 20–21ozs (570–595ml).

Of course all this is quite a lot of trouble for you. There is an easier method of discovering how much extra milk your baby needs, but it makes it more likely that he will end up bottle-fed:

Complementary bottles
Choose and prepare a bottle formula as for a bottle-fed baby (see p. 64). Feed the baby from the breast as usual, but at the end of each feed, when he has taken all he can from both breasts, offer him a bottle of the prepared formula. The amount of formula he

drinks will be roughly the amount he still needs after taking all your breast milk. It may be nothing at some feeds, several ounces at others.

If he is only willing to drink formula after certain feeds of the day (it will probably be the late afternoon and evening ones when your milk supply is at its lowest), you need only offer bottles at those feeds.

This method sounds simpler than the first one – for one thing it involves no arithmetic! – but it has some snags and is not advisable for mothers who would be sad to abandon breast-feeding:

Disadvantages of complementary bottles

It may be several days before the baby will accept the bottle. Babies who have settled to breast-feeding do not usually take easily to a teat. If yours refuses to drink any formula at all, you may not be sure whether he is refusing it because he is already getting enough from the breast or because he dislikes the new method. The only way to be sure is to persist in offering the formula for at least five days. If he is hungry, the baby will have given in and accepted it within that time. If he has not accepted it, he is probably not hungry.

Complementary bottles tend to reduce breast milk. Once the baby accepts the bottle and takes all the extra he needs from it, he will be hungry less often than before. Your breasts will receive less stimulation because he will suck less often, so it will be difficult for you to maintain, far less increase, your supply.

Complementary bottles tend to reduce your motivation to breast-feed. Even if your baby is only taking a few ounces per day from a bottle, you still have the trouble of sterilizing feeding equipment and preparing formula. You may soon feel that you are getting the worst of both worlds and might as well let breast-feeding tail off.

Complementary bottles tend to reduce the baby's motivation to breast-feed. Once he has learned that milk comes out of bottles as well as breasts, the baby is likely to get "lazy" about breast-feeding – especially about bothering with that last half ounce which takes considerable sucking effort. As soon as the breast milk stops flowing freely he looks around for the bottle.

In theory you can breast-feed and give complementary bottles as necessary right through to weaning time. Some mothers actually do this. They are usually the ones who very much enjoy breast-feeding and are therefore prepared to take double trouble in order to go on. However, most mothers find that starting on complementary bottles means a gradual end to breast-feeding and a switch to full bottle-feeding.

Overfeeding

You cannot overfeed a breast-fed baby unless you give something else as well as milk.

A hungry baby who has a mother with a copious milk supply and is not a very active type may get fatter than the baby next door who is also breast-fed. But he will not get too fat unless you start adding solid foods before he needs them, or giving him too many syrupy drinks (see p. 133).

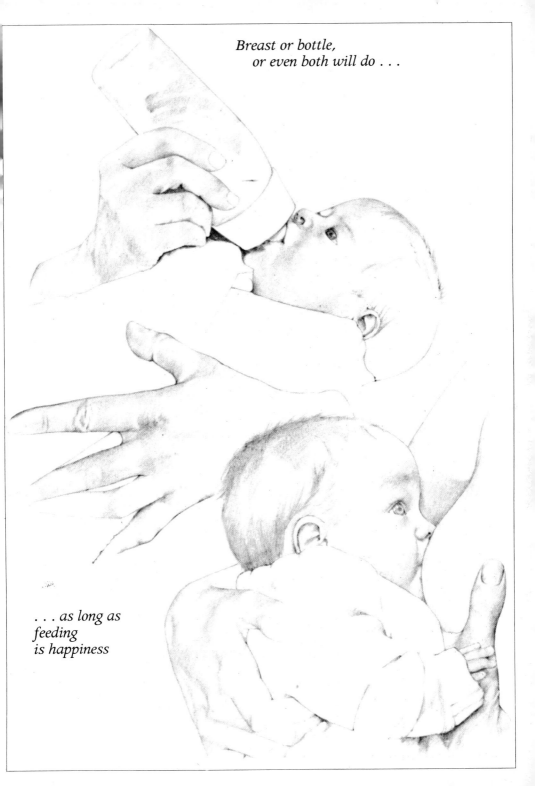

Breast or bottle,
or even both will do . . .

. . . as long as
feeding
is happiness

Bottle-feeding

Underfeeding is rare in bottle-fed babies but it can happen. A baby who cries a great deal, seems generally discontented with life and is gaining weight slowly, is probably not getting enough to eat. Check the following points:

You may be working out your baby's needs too rigidly. Although it is true that his body will require about 3ozs (85ml) of formula for each pound of his "expected" weight (see p. 76) this does not mean that you should prepare exactly that number of ounces, divide it equally between the number of bottles he takes, and then wait for him to drain each one.

If you do this you are not allowing for the fact that, like anyone else, he will be hungrier at some times than at others. Suppose that his "requirement" is 30ozs (850ml) of milk per day and you divide this into five bottles of 6ozs (170ml) each. If he drains the first two, leaves 2ozs (57ml) in each of the next two and then drains the fifth, he will have had 4ozs (115ml) less than he is likely to need during the 24 hours. Regularly emptied bottles are a reproach, not a cause for congratulation. If the bottle is emptied, how can you be sure that the baby would not have liked another ounce or two?

Use your calculations of his requirements as a rough guide only. Put at least 2ozs (57ml) more than you think he will drink into each bottle. Only in this way can you be sure of giving him the chance to drink all he wants and to compensate for a small breakfast by having a huge lunch.

You may be scheduling feeds too strictly. The baby's digestion will take around four hours to deal with a full feed, so most of the time he will not demand food much more often than this. But his appetite will vary; he will not always take a full feed. If you do not allow him to make up for a small breakfast by having a mid-morning snack, but make him wait until the next "proper" mealtime, he may not then be able to hold enough extra milk to make up. Suppose that he only drinks 3ozs (85ml) of milk at breakfast time instead of the usual 6ozs (170ml). A couple of hours later he will be hungry. If you make him wait until lunch time he will not be able to drink the usual 6ozs (170ml) *plus* the 3ozs (85ml) he missed earlier. His stomach simply will not hold 9ozs (255ml) of milk. Repeated day after day this kind of situation can lead to a great deal of fretfulness as well as to low weight gain.

You may be using a teat with too small a hole. A baby who is really hungry will work hard and patiently to get milk however slowly it flows. But once he has had 2 or 3ozs (57–85ml) the acute hunger pains stop. Then the effort becomes too much; the feeding is taking a long time; the baby gives up and goes to sleep.

He will wake again in a couple of hours and demand more food, but if the same thing happens repeatedly you may find that you have a baby who demands frequent feeds, never takes much at any of them, never stays contented for very long and does not gain much weight.

So make sure that the milk drips rapidly out of the teat when you turn it upside down. The baby should be able to get at least half the feed during the first five minutes of sucking.

You may be dealing with an exceptionally sleepy baby (see p. 106). This will right itself in a few weeks as he grows up enough to be more alert. In the meantime watch the clock, wake him for feeds at reasonable intervals and use the things that will interest him most – your face and voice – to keep him awake while he sucks. If he drops off despite your efforts, don't try to pour milk into his sleeping mouth; you cannot force him to feed. He will not starve if you feed him little and often while you wait for him to grow up a bit.

Overfeeding Many bottle-fed babies gain rapidly from birth and are fat by the time they are six weeks old. The risk of obesity is one of the reasons for preferring breast to bottle-feeding.

Unfortunately it is not a risk that many people take seriously because a fat baby looks cuddly and sweet. But it is not good for him to be fat now and there is evidence to suggest that if you let him get fat during the early months he will be more liable to obesity later in life. A fat child may be laughed at; a fat teenager may suffer agonies of self-consciousness, while a fat adult is extra liable to many illnesses and may go through misery trying to keep his weight down. So don't let yourself envy the parents of roly-poly babies: you want fitness not fatness.

Bottle-fed babies do not get too fat from being allowed to drink as much properly-made formula as they want, whenever they want it. They get fat either because the formula is not made up accurately or because they are given extra foods as well. Remember that unless your doctor specifically recommends it (which he might if your baby is exceptionally large) he should not have "solids" until he is at *least* three months old (see p. 137). Remember, too, that when he does have solids they should never be concealed in his bottle, but should be given separately, from a spoon, so that he can take all his milk, if he wants it, without having a lot of extra hidden calories forced down.

Make those bottles up accurately. Extra milk concentrate means a bottle containing the usual number of ounces but more than the usual number of calories.

Remember that formulae which are not "low sodium" may cause thirst. A drink of water will break the vicious circle of formula-thirst-crying-more formula-more thirst-more crying.

Remember that vitamin C fruit syrups contain a lot of sugar. Your baby must have at least the correct dosage of vitamin C each day, but the syrups should be well-diluted and should not be used casually instead of water. Teaspoon for teaspoon they are almost as fattening as pure granulated sugar.

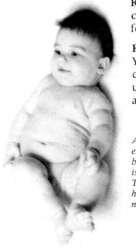

Although this roly-poly baby is enchanting, it is not good for him to be so fat. While steady weight gain is important, fat does not mean fit. The fatter he gets the less exercise he will take, and treble chins will not be charming when he is older.

*Fretting for food
when weight gain
is normal*

Although there are many reasons for fretfulness which have nothing to do with food, the way a baby is fed can cause discontent even if the weight gain is normal.

This fully-fed baby may be hungry. That sounds like a contradiction but it is not. His normal weight gain shows that his body is receiving enough food for its needs every 24 hours. But that does not mean that there cannot be many times during any 24 hour period when he feels hungry enough to be miserable. Think of a child at boarding school. He is fed a carefully planned diet which keeps him growing at an appropriate rate. Yet he complains that he is always starving. Why? Because that careful diet is doled out to him at pre-determined times and in pre-set quantities; he is fed according to his overall *needs* but not according to his immediate *appetite*. If you jettison all your ideas about "proper" feeding times and feed the baby when he is hungry, he will probably drink exactly the same number of ounces as before and gain the same number too. But he may do it with half the number of crying jags.

This fully-fed baby may be thirsty. If the baby is allowed to feed whenever he is hungry, is gaining weight normally, but still seems very fretful, it may be his water intake that needs adjusting. Milk is food and drink in one. There is no way a baby who is thirsty but not hungry can get the water without the food. Breast-fed babies are better off in this respect because, as we have seen, breast milk contains less sodium than most formulae and sodium can be thirst-making. But even breast-fed babies often need extra water in hot weather or when they are feverish.

Any baby who cries for the breast or a bottle, sucks eagerly for a few seconds and then stops and cries again should be offered a couple of ounces of water which has been boiled and cooled.

Apart from this, babies should be offered the chance of at least two extra drinks of boiled water every day. One can be plain water, the other can have his vitamin C syrup added. There is no harm in offering water much more often than this. If he is not thirsty, he will not drink it.

Night feeding

Most babies will go on needing six feeds in the 24 hours until they are at least six weeks old. Many will need five feeds until they are somewhere around four months. As long as your baby has six feeds, you are bound to have to wake up once during your normal sleeping hours, but if you are clever you need seldom wake twice. Once the baby is content with only five feeds a day you should be able to get a solid stretch of six or seven hours sleep almost every night.

Being woken, night after night, is a tremendous strain; more of a strain than doctors or nurses, friends or relations often realize. It is not the hours of sleep lost which make you so tired. Most of those can probably be made up by going to bed earlier or having an afternoon nap at a weekend. The exhaustion comes from the continual disturbance of your sleep *patterns*. Being woken, even for a few minutes, twice or three times every night for weeks on end can make you feel like sleepwalkers.

Juggling feeding times so that you get more sleep

Maximum rest for you as well as contentment for the baby depend on your managing to take a flexible approach to his night-time hunger. Keeping him waiting for feeds or trying to enforce a schedule will doom you to unnecessary weeks of broken nights

The secret of juggling night feeds to suit you all is to stop yourself thinking in disciplinary terms. Don't let yourself believe that doing without a sixth feed is "good" of the baby; virtue does not come into it. Nor should you feel that feeding him before he is ravenous, or giving him a few extra sucks by way of a snack, is "spoiling". It is simply good sense.

If you can genuinely accept this, you will realize that you can always anticipate and prevent a demand for food which is going to come up at a totally uncivilized hour. You do it by waking the baby up and feeding him instead of waiting for him to wake you. Why fall exhausted into bed at midnight, knowing that the baby will want food at around 2am *and* around 6am, when you can wake him just before you go to sleep and thus ensure that he will only disturb you at around 4am?

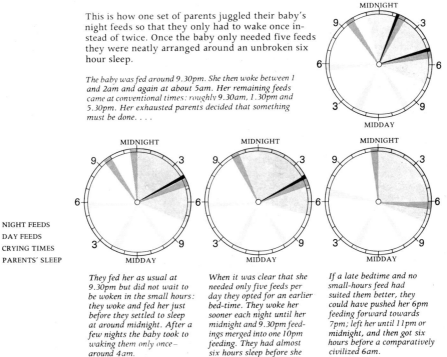

This is how one set of parents juggled their baby's night feeds so that they only had to wake once instead of twice. Once the baby only needed five feeds they were neatly arranged around an unbroken six hour sleep.

The baby was fed around 9.30pm. She then woke between 1 and 2am and again at about 5am. Her remaining feeds came at conventional times: roughly 9.30am, 1.30pm and 5.30pm. Her exhausted parents decided that something must be done. . . .

■ NIGHT FEEDS
□ DAY FEEDS
■ CRYING TIMES
□ PARENTS' SLEEP

They fed her as usual at 9.30pm but did not wait to be woken in the small hours: they woke and fed her just before they settled to sleep at around midnight. After a few nights the baby took to waking them only once – around 4am.

When it was clear that she needed only five feeds per day they opted for an earlier bed-time. They woke her sooner each night until her midnight and 9.30pm feedings merged into one 10pm feeding. They had almost six hours sleep before she woke around 4am.

If a late bedtime and no small-hours feed had suited them better, they could have pushed her 6pm feeding forward towards 7pm; left her until 11pm or midnight, and then got six hours before a comparatively civilized 6am.

Going through the night without being fed

Not all babies willingly abandon their sixth feed at six weeks or cooperate in having their fifth feed "juggled" for their parents' convenience by three or four months. If yours is one of the babies who seems to need more feeds by night than by day and who is still waking you twice every night when he "ought" not to be waking you at all, you may well find that your patience and good sense are being eroded by sheer exhaustion. Try to hang on to them. Your baby wakes (usually) because he is hungry. Because he is hungry he cries. A feed will stop him crying immediately but nothing else will stop him for any useful length of time. So don't feel under any moral pressure to resist feeding him. Don't decide that fobbing him off for half an hour with a drink of sweetened water means that you have won a disciplinary battle. Your baby will sleep through the night when he is ready to do so. In the meantime any method of *forcing* him to go without a feed will only make him unhappy and lose you even more sleep.

Leaving the baby to cry is a common but nonsensical prescription. If he is not hungry, then some other need is being communicated and he should have immediate attention. If he is hungry, food is the right, quick and easy answer.

The longer you leave a hungry baby to cry the more hungry and tired he will get. When you finally give in, the tiredness may mean that he takes only a small feed before sleep overcomes him; he will wake again all the sooner.

If you refuse to give in and you leave the baby to scream for an hour or more, he may go back to sleep because he is exhausted. But you will still have gained nothing. Half an hour's nap will revive him and his now ferocious hunger. You will have been kept awake through the first crying bout and now you are awake again. . . .

These miserable fights are totally useless. You cannot teach your baby not to wake up in the night. He cannot wake himself up on purpose any more than you can so he cannot "learn" to stay asleep on purpose either.

Giving drinks that are not food may put your baby back to sleep for a few minutes if he was only a little bit hungry. But the sweetened water or juice and the sucking only give him a few calories, a temporary feeling of fullness and a warm cuddle. It will not take him more than half an hour to discover that his tummy is still empty; he will wake you again just as you have sunk back into heavy sleep.

If your baby wakes, crying, so soon after a feed that you cannot believe he is ready for more milk, by all means offer a drink of water. He may simply be thirsty. Under all other circumstances it will be just as quick and infinitely more effective to give him what he is actually asking for: food.

Giving an extra-large feed in the evening will not help unless you were actually underfeeding him before (see p. 132).

Babyfood manufacturers sometimes try to cash in on parents' need for more sleep with advertising copy which says "for a peaceful night for your baby *and* you, give . . . ." But a baby's appetite and digestion do not work like an engine; you cannot make him go for longer without a refill by forcing in extra fuel. If he is already taking a full feed in the evening, it will consist of as much as he wants and, by definition, he will not want any more. If you force extra calories into him, by putting cereals into his bottle, for example, he will still digest it at the normal rate. The extra will affect his figure but it will not affect his sleep.

Mixed feeding

Breast milk or formula is a complete food and drink except that breast-fed babies may need a little extra iron by the time they are four months old. In theory your child could go on living on milk alone forever but in practice a milk-only diet would not work out very well.

Although the foodstuffs in milk are complete they are very diluted: milk contains far more water than anything else. As the baby gets heavier he needs more calories so he drinks more milk. Eventually he reaches a point where he is drinking all the milk that his stomach can hold at every feed, yet four or five 7 or 8oz (200–225ml) stomachfuls per day do not give him quite as many calories as his body requires. Since he literally cannot hold any more milk on each occasion, the only way he could get more food would be to feed more frequently. If you had nothing but milk available for him, you would find that he began to demand back the night feeds he had just abandoned and to demand the bottle or breast at more and more frequent intervals through the day. Fortunately you do have something else available: solid foods which are far more concentrated sources of calories than milk. Tiny quantities of a solid food give the baby the extra calories he is beginning to need without stretching his milk-distended tummy much further.

There are social reasons too for offering your baby solid foods. You are trying to bring up a human being and human beings eat "real" food. He needs to get used to a wide variety of tastes and textures; he needs to learn that good food can come from a plate as well as a breast or bottle. Until he has learned these things he cannot join you, happily, at your family meal-table.

Once a baby is ready for solid foods, do give them all from a spoon rather than adding any to his bottle. Feeding your baby a bottle which has a spoonful of cereal mixed into it is forced feeding – it means that he cannot get his accustomed quantity of milk (and that means water, too) without getting the added cereal as well. It deprives him of any chance of saying "no" to the cereal without saying "no" to the milk as well.

When to start   While there are no hard and fast rules that apply to all babies, no baby should start solid foods before he is three months old without special medical reasons. After this age, your baby's weight, hunger and feeding pattern will cue you when to start.

Your aim should be to spot the time when he is coming near to the limits of milk-only feeding so that you introduce him to the brand new experience of minute tastes of solid foods before he really needs their food value. If he is over three months and bottle-fed, you can estimate this time quite accurately enough if you consider the baby's milk consumption, the number of feeds he is having and his weight.

Milk consumption. If your baby is taking 7ozs (200ml) at most feeds, you can assume that he or she is near the limits imposed by the capacity of the stomach. To get more food there would have to be more meals rather than larger ones.

Number of feeds. If 7ozs (200ml) is all he can take at a meal, then 7 times the number of feeds he has each day will tell you how many ounces of milk he could take. If he has five feeds, then he could drink as much as 35oz (995ml). If he only has four feeds, then he will not manage much more than 28ozs (795ml).

Weight. Your baby's daily needs are likely to be around 3ozs (85ml) of milk for every pound that he weighs (see p. 76). So consider whether the maximum number of ounces he could take in his chosen number of feeds adds up to somewhere near this figure. For example, a 10lb (4.5g) baby is likely to need 30ozs (850ml) of milk per day. Five feeds (maximum 35ozs; 995ml) is probably still plenty, but four feeds (maximum 28ozs; 795ml) would be barely enough.

If the baby is breast-fed, so that you do not know exactly how much he drinks, you can use his weight combined with his demands for food to tell you when to introduce solids. If he weighs as much as 12lbs (5.5kg), he cannot be getting enough for his needs in less than five feeds each day. A baby's refusal to lengthen the interval between feeds and/or a sudden demand for an extra, sixth, feed, will tell you that he needs something more than milk.

An average birthweight baby who has gained weight at the normal rate, will probably reach 12lbs (5.5kg) when he is around three months old. Since this is also about the age when he will be ready to go for longer intervals between feeds, cutting out the fifth in the day, this may be a sensible time to start solids. A very large baby may reach 12lbs (5.5kg), and therefore his stomach's limits on five feeds per day, much earlier than this. Consult your doctor about whether milk on demand is still enough. A very small baby will not reach 12lbs (5.5kg) until he is much older, but he should start tastes of solid foods by his fifth month anyway. If you leave the new experience until he is much older than this, he may find the new tastes and feeding methods hard to accept.

First solid foods are extras
These early tastes of solid foods are intended more for education than for nutrition. You start offering them while your baby is still getting enough from his milk alone, to cover the possibility of his needing a tiny bit extra and to get him used to them before they are essential to him. They are extra to the diet he is already on and they are not meant to change it or to replace any part of it. The beginning of mixed feeding is not the beginning of weaning.

Keep the quantity of solids down and the quantity of milk up. Don't let advertising by babyfood manufacturers convince you that your baby should match increasing quantities of solid foods to decreasing quantities of milk. Instead, feed very small quantities of solid foods and the usual amount of milk, increasing the solids only if the baby wants more as well as the milk.

Never force solid foods on the baby. Offer tastes and let him decide whether he wants them or not.

Offer a wide variety of flavours. Find out, by experiment, what the baby likes and what he does not. Even at this early stage he will have definite preferences which you should respect.

What solid foods should the baby have? Most of the baby's diet will consist of milk for weeks yet. Even when he does begin to reduce his milk intake because he positively wants more solid foods, the milk that he goes on drinking will provide almost all the protein, minerals and vitamins he needs. His first solid foods are needed only for their calories—their fuel—and there are calories in every kind of food. So it does not matter which particular foods you choose to give him, provided that they are of a semi-liquid texture, that the baby likes the taste and that the food does not give him indigestion. He will get no more benefit from an expensive "high protein" cereal than from an ordinary one. He does not need the extra protein in the expensive one, only the calories which are in both.

Cereals Cereals are the traditional first solid foods. They are marketed specially prepared for babies and they only need mixing with formula for a bottle-fed baby or with boiled cow's milk or expressed breast milk for a breast-fed one.

Cereals have the advantage of being rich in iron which is important to breast-fed babies. They also have a bland milky taste which is sufficiently like the baby's accustomed food to make them acceptable. On the other hand most babies refuse cereals unless they are sweetened, and once you add sugar, even a tiny portion of cereal will add a lot of calories to the day's diet. So keep quantities very small indeed. A single teaspoon of the dry cereal mixed with three teaspoons of milk and a quarter teaspoon of sugar will be plenty.

Strained fruits Many babies prefer strained fruits to cereals. While the taste of fruit is more surprising to him than the taste of cereal it is also more interesting and pleasurable. If being given fruit makes him enthusiastic about these early lessons in eating, give it to him. The more he enjoys solid foods now, the more easily he will accept them later on when they become important in his diet.

Once your baby happily accepts one or two solid foods it is good for him to be offered a wide variety. You can buy special babyfoods for him or put tiny portions of your own cooking through a liquidizer or food-mouli (see p. 145). If you want him to like your cooking, make sure he has some home-cooked foods from the beginning. If he gets very used to the bland sameness of commercially-prepared babyfoods, he may later reject the stronger and more definite tastes of your foods. Fresh stewed apple, for example, is nothing like "apple dessert".

Home-prepared foods Since you do not have to worry, at this early stage, about feeding your baby a "balanced diet" of solid foods, you can simply put a tiny portion of any bland food which you have available through a food-mouli. A teaspoon of mashed potato mixed to a semi-fluid texture with milk or gravy would be excellent. So would carrots or other bland vegetables similarly treated. Any fruit except strawberries (which occasionally cause an allergic reaction), or very pippy ones like raspberries, will be good for him if they are stewed and pureed. They can be made less strong tasting by being mixed with milk or custard.

Commercially-prepared foods

Cans and jars are an extravagant way to feed a baby at this early stage. He will only need one or two teaspoons of food at a time, yet the cans hold three tablespoons. You cannot use the remainder up over several meals because the foods will not stay fresh and safe for more than 24 hours after opening, even in a refrigerator, and you do not want to offer the same food three times running.

Dehydrated foods can be used as gradually as you like. Buy several different kinds, both sweet and savoury, so that your baby can explore variety. You can also ring the changes by occasionally mixing the food with stock or water instead of milk.

Feeding your baby's first solids

There is no hurry; go slowly. Learning to eat solid foods is a big task for your baby. Up to now he has connected being hungry with sucking for milk. Now he has to learn that hunger can be satisfied by foods other than milk and that these foods can be taken in ways other than sucking. To begin with he will not understand what you are trying to do when you put a spoon to his mouth. He will not know that what you are offering is something that will quell his hunger so he will have no reason to cooperate. If he is hungry, he will want his bottle or the breast. If you upset or frustrate him, by trying to force food into his mouth when he is rejecting it, you may put him off the whole business.

Timing the meal. Don't offer solid foods before milk at meals for which your baby is always frantic. The early morning feed, for example, is not usually a good one to begin with. He is barely awake but he is ravenous. Let him suck in peace.

Don't try to give spoon foods to your baby when he is desperate to suck. If you do, he will yell with hunger and frustration around every spoonful. On the other hand don't wait to offer them until he is full of milk. He will be too sleepy and lethargic to bother. A sandwich system can often work best: a few minutes sucking to allay the worst of his hunger and assure him that the breast or bottle is still safely there for him; then the offer of some solid food; and then as much more milk as he wants.

Feeding the meal. Taking food without sucking is very difficult for babies until they get the hang of it. If you put the food on his tongue, he does not know how to get it far enough back in his mouth to swallow. It will simply dribble out again. If you dump it at the back of his mouth, he may gag and will probably then reject spoonfeeding, sometimes for weeks. The technique that usually works best is to use a tiny spoon—an old-fashioned salt or mustard spoon is ideal—and to hold it just between the baby's lips so that he can suck the contents off. If he sucks at it, he will get some of it far enough back in his mouth to swallow. If he likes the taste, he may become positively enthusiastic.

Knowing when to stop. If you use this method of spoonfeeding, he will be able to "tell" you when he does not want any more: he will turn his head away from the spoon or close his lips instead of sucking. But if you put food right into his mouth, you will not be able to tell when he has finished. Dribbling the food out, gagging, crying may all be signals to stop, but they may also be the result of bad feeding technique or a baby who is not very good at eating yet.

Spoonfeeding

Your baby has no reason to suppose she is going to enjoy her first solid foods. You have to help her. She has to discover that the tastes are pleasant and she has to learn to get the food far enough back in her mouth for swallowing. Only after that will she discover that the food copes with hunger!

Don't force her. Let her suck the food off for herself; stop the meal if the taste makes her cry, or when her closed lips say "enough".

Hold a tiny spoon to the baby's lips and let her suck off the contents. She will get enough to taste. If she likes it she will go on. . . .

If you put too much food on the spoon and put it too far back in the baby's mouth, you are forcing her to swallow; she may gag and she has no chance to "say" whether she likes it.

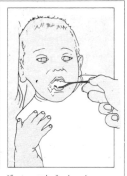

If you put the food on the front of the baby's tongue, it will simply dribble out again. She cannot get it far enough back to taste or swallow. You will both be frustrated.

Digesting early solids

Most babies can digest a wide range of foods easily. Conventions about "suitable" foods have little factual basis. For example, a British mother might not give her baby avocado pear because in Britain it is a luxury food. Yet in California or Israel avocado pears are commonplace and often fed to babies.

It is important not to add salt to the baby's food because extra salt puts a strain on young kidneys. It is sensible to avoid spices and exotic seasonings as these may burn the baby's mouth or even inflame his stomach, and it is essential to avoid coffee, tea and alcohol which are all drugs. Otherwise, he can try any food which the rest of the family usually eats. But try it out *slowly*. Introduce any food which is new to him on its own and as a single teaspoonful the first couple of times. If it should disagree with him you will then know exactly which food to avoid for a few weeks.

Remember that he cannot chew yet. If you feed him lumps he will have to swallow them as lumps. He will not like doing so and he may choke. So sieve, mouli or liquidize his early meals. Remember too that liquidizing does not get rid of pips or tough skins. His digestion will not deal well with these things at first, so sieve foods which contain them.

Too much sugar or too much fat can upset the baby's digestion. Remember that he has been accustomed to that perfectly balanced milk diet and he will need time to adjust to a sudden excess of sugar in a chocolate pudding, or a sudden raising of his fat intake because you have put butter with his vegetables.

Allergies

If yours is a family which suffers from allergic disorders like asthma or hay fever, consult with your doctor before you start mixed feeding. If the baby has already shown signs of being prone to allergy—if he has eczema, for example—he may advise you not even to try possible culprits like egg-white or strawberries at this early stage. Otherwise don't worry. An allergic reaction to a tiny quantity of food is unlikely to be violent. Just withold that food until he is older.

*Juggling feeding
times once
your baby is
having solids*

An average baby will be ready to abandon the fifth feed by about four months old. By this time feeds will include some solid foods as well as milk so the four feeds will really consist of three meals each day with a fourth bottle or breast-feed. The baby will need these four feeds every day until at least six months old, so it is worth taking the trouble to make sure that you arrange them in a convenient way. The "meals" will probably be at whatever breakfast, lunch and supper times are normal for your family. But you have plenty of flexibility about that fourth milk feed. The baby cannot go from a 6pm supper to an 8am breakfast without feeding, but that stretch of time can be broken either by a late night bottle or by an early morning one, whichever you prefer. If your household wakes early and you like to go early to bed, you will probably prefer it to be an early morning feed. If you like to sleep in but always go to bed late anyway, a late evening bottle or breast-feed may suit you better.

Three common feeding patterns for this age group, each suiting a differently organized household, are given below:

Feeding pattern	Comments
Early waking baby in early rising household. *The baby has a bottle between 5am and 6am and then sleeps again. The morning rush is over when the baby next needs attention: breakfast at 9–10am. She has lunch rather late, between 1.30 and 2pm and, with the help of a drink of juice, lasts until supper which is served with the rest of the family at around 7pm.*	*The whole pattern is dependent on the baby having that early morning feed. If she begins to sleep later in the mornings, she must either be woken for it or have her feeding pattern altered, as below.*
Later waking baby in family that stays up late. *The baby wakes and has breakfast with the rest of the family at around 8am. He has lunch at about 12.30pm and then an early supper served specially – at about 5pm. He wakes or is woken for a milk feed at the parents' bedtime.*	*This pattern gives the father more opportunity to be with the baby as he will see him at breakfast and at his late night feed. It gives the mother more peace in the evening as the baby can be put to bed before the adult evening meal, but it also gives her more of a rush in the morning if she has to cope with the baby's breakfast at the same time as everyone else's.* *The pattern is dependent on that late night bottle. If he is allowed to sleep through without it, the baby will not last until breakfast time.*
The middle road. *The baby wakes at around 7am. She is happy to accept breakfast at once, in which case her lunch and tea will come early and she will have a late-evening milk feed.* *But she is equally happy to be given milk alone when she wakes and then to have a late breakfast, lunch and supper.*	*This pattern need not be fixed one way or the other. You can probably keep it flexible from day to day as long as you are willing to give the baby something extra to keep her going. She might need an instantly available snack while she waits for breakfast on "early" days, and something between lunch and supper on "late" days.*

Turning first solids into meals

By around five months babies who have enjoyed their first tastes of solid foods will have learned that food from a spoon can satisfy hunger. Although sucking milk will go on being vitally important for many months, they will have learned to look forward to solids as well. Such babies are ready to begin, very gradually, to eat more spoon and finger foods and to rely less on the breast or bottle.

The "sandwich" system makes it easy to recognize this stage. You prepare the baby's solid food and then settle down to feed him from the breast or bottle. Recognizing his dish, he will begin to hurry that first sucking in order to get to the dish sooner. If he likes what is in it, he may eat it all and then want only a token amount of milk to finish up with.

Once he begins to behave like this you can offer rather more solid food (perhaps three teaspoons instead of one) and be prepared to abandon the "sandwich" system when he shows, by gesture, that he wants to start a meal with his solids or that, having sucked and then eaten, he does not want any more milk. He is *beginning* to wean himself by very gradually shifting his allegiance from milk to "real" food. But he is doing it because he wants to, not because anything is being forced on him. It is important to let him set the pace. There may be days or even weeks when he reverts to wanting only milk and there may be certain feeds in each day when he continues to need two sucking sessions. If you let him lead, you can be sure that he will take the milk/food combination that he wants and that what he takes will also be what he needs.

Eventually he will probably arrive at a pattern. First thing in the morning he will almost certainly need to suck before he can eat. If this first meal is his fourth milk-only feed, being given now rather than in the late evening, he will obviously have only milk. But if the meal is breakfast, let him suck as much as he wants and then have his solid food afterwards.

At lunch-time he will probably be eager for his solids and he may be generally less interested in sucking at this time of day. Offer him the breast or bottle after his meal, but once he shows you he is uninterested, offer a drink from a cup instead.

At suppertime he may need a suck first, to calm him down after his bath and playtime. Then he will be ready to eat his solid food before having a long peaceful suck (perhaps in his own room) to ready him for bed.

If he still has a milk feed to come in the late evening, this will obviously be a time just for simple, sleepy sucking.

During this in-between stage your baby is learning to manage with fewer but larger meals than he has been accustomed to. He will learn fast and happily if you keep the whole business of eating pleasurable for him. Often he will need a snack to keep him going. Instead of an extra milk feed he will enjoy something hard and edible to hold and chew. The more practice he gets in managing finger-foods the sooner he will get some actual nutrition as well as enjoyment out of them. He will want to play with his solid foods, too, and the more you encourage him to dabble with his fingers and mess with a spoon the sooner he will learn to feed himself. All in all, happy meals at this age mean lots of mess, so it is a good idea to get organized and equipped for it.

Starting solid foods

As soon as your baby begins to take a real interest in solid foods and to cut down on sucking, it is time to get organized so that meals are quick and easy for you and comfortable for the baby. This is no longer a tiny baby to be held on your lap to suck a tiny portion of puree off a spoon. This is a person who is going to eat with gusto. Your baby still needs to be held and closely cuddled while sucking, but the rest of the time a chair will be more comfortable and will leave you freer to help the baby and get things you have forgotten! There is going to be a fantastic mess too, so instead of trying to prevent it, organize things so it does not bother you.

There is a lot of baby-feeding equipment on the market, but here are some types to guide you. Choose carefully – this equipment is going to be around for more than a year.

High chair
If you buy its own stand. this seat turns into a stable, easy-clean high chair which supports the baby comfortably. You can still detach the chair to use on picnics. Keep a harness permanently clipped to it and spread newspaper underneath at mealtimes. A plastic sheet looks more elegant but needs washing instead of just throwing away. You are now all set for maximum fun and minimum mess. . . .

Bibs
The ideal bib. Its stiff plastic cannot smother. It has no strings to tangle. and spills are caught in the pocket, not in the lap.

Terrycloth or fabric bibs look pretty but need constant laundering.

Thin plastic bibs are best avoided – the strings tangle and the baby might smother.

Chairs and tables
The more traditional high chairs are not as stable nor as easy to keep clean as the newer models. They may seem longer-lasting because they can collapse into a low-chair/table for later. But a separate little table and chair are much easier for a toddler to use.

Dishes
In this dish you can serve two things separately, while the warm water compartment keeps food warm. It has a suction cup on the bottom so the baby cannot turn it over. Ordinary plastic dishes will do, of course, but they are all too good as hats. . . .

Cups
A teacher-beaker is easy to hold, easy to drink from, and will not spill. The worst it can do is drip. . . .

This mug makes it easy for the baby to get the angle right, but it is weighted and heavy to handle.

A mug without a lid? Then it must be for pouring. . . .

Helping your baby to eat

Try to think of yourself as helping the baby to eat rather than feeding her. Once she sits up to meals she will certainly want to join in with her hands as well as her mouth. Let her dabble and smear, dip her fingers in the dish and suck them and try to find out what a spoon is for. It is messy but it is vitally important. The more she feels that what she eats is under her own control rather than simply being ladled into her, the more she will enjoy the whole eating-game. The more she enjoys it now, the less trouble you are likely to have later with fads and food refusal. Lots of practice now will mean that she can feed herself completely independently at an early age, too.

So try not to boss her. Skin washes, her bib protects clothes, and paper protects the floor; let her dig in and enjoy herself.

Don't discourage any method of getting food from plate to mouth. Enthusiasm is what matters.

Let her have her own spoon; only by playing with it can she learn to use it.

When she knows what it is for but cannot get a load to her mouth, fill yours and swap it for her empty one.

Finger-foods

Foods that are meant for fingers are good for morale; they make eating easy and fun. Hard foods are good for the baby's jaws, too, while a finger-snack can bridge the gap until the next proper meal is ready.

 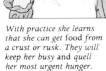 

Begin with a raw carrot, an apple slice or a cooked smooth chop-bone: just like a toy, but nicer-tasting than plastic.

With practice she learns that she can get food from a crust or rusk. They will keep her busy and quell her most urgent hunger.

Later she will feed herself with cut up finger-foods: much nicer than spoonfuls of lumpy food. Pat her on the back if she chokes.

Preparing food

At this age all but finger-foods will have to be smoothly pureed. Most babies prefer the texture of heavy cream; a stiffer, mashed-potato texture tends to make them gag. Try to avoid anything which may disgust your baby. A piece of gristle can upset eating for weeks.

Some foods simply need reducing to semi-liquid texture. You can use a liquidizer and adjust the final puree with extra stock, milk or water. Pippy, stringy or very rough-textured foods, like raspberries, cabbage or minced meat, need sieving too. A "mouli" will both liquidize and sieve.

Plates, dishes and spoons do not need sterilizing but should be drip-dried (if not machine-washed). Drying-up cloths are bacteria-traps. Teacher-beakers can trap drops of milk in the spout; wash them carefully and sterilize at least once a day.

Don't open canned foods with the opener you use for cat food! And scald the top of the can with boiling water first. Don't prepare foods with unwashed hands or on a surface you have used for raw meat. Cover cooked food and cool it quickly. If you must serve leftovers, reheat them to full boiling point so that the food is re-sterilized.

Sleeping

While newborn babies often drift randomly in and out of sleep, sometimes spending long periods suspended between the two states, settled babies are much more definite about the difference between the two. Once asleep you can be fairly sure that they will not wake up again for a while; once awake you can be equally certain that they will not go to sleep again until they have been fed. At three or four weeks of age sleeping and feeding still go hand in hand. Left to follow their own inclinations babies wake up because they are hungry and go to sleep because they are full. Their waking time is therefore concentrated around feeds – the physical care given before them and the affectionate attention given after them.

Wakeful periods By around six weeks, the relationship between feeding and sleeping begins to slacken a little. The baby will still be inclined to go to sleep when he is fully fed, but he will not always sleep until he is ravenously hungry again. He may begin to wake up, sometimes, just because he has had enough sleep for the moment.

Most babies adopt one particular time of day for being wakeful. A common one is the second part of the afternoon. The baby sleeps after breakfast through most of the morning. He has his lunchtime feed and sleeps again, but this time he does not sleep right through until hunger wakens him. He naps for a couple of hours and then wakes anyway. Many mothers encourage this pattern because it is a convenient time to pay social attention to the baby. He could have his daily drink of fruit juice when he wakes up, and then a pram ride to the shops or a period of free kicking on the floor with no nappies and plenty of your attention. An hour or two of this and the baby will be very ready for his bath and the next feed. The physical exercise and the play will have tired him. He will probably sleep well until his late evening feed.

Of course some babies adopt a different and less convenient time of day for being awake. If your baby tends to nap for only an hour or so after breakfast and then stays awake all morning and sleeps all afternoon you can probably alter the pattern by juggling the feeding times. An extra "snack" feed when he wakes in the middle of the morning may well put him back to sleep again. If you then let him sleep on until a late lunch time, he will, over a few days, shift towards being awake in the afternoon.

By the time the baby reaches three to four months he is likely to have two or even three wakeful periods in the day. As before, a good feed makes him inclined to sleep, but as he gets older his naps get progressively shorter.

Sleeping difficulties In this age-group any difficulties are yours, not the baby's. He will sleep as much as he needs to sleep; he is still not capable of keeping himself awake and he is no more capable than you are of waking himself up on purpose. You need never add worry about whether he can be getting enough sleep to worry about the fact that you certainly are not!

*Leave his daytime sleeping to him,
his naps will get shorter as he gets older*

At night If your baby does not sleep soundly for reasonable periods at night, it is worth checking back to page 92. He may not yet have made a complete difference between night behaviour and day behaviour and you may need to help him become a diurnal creature.

Check for sources of outside disturbance too. If he still shares your bedroom, your own sounds and movements may be stimulating him to full wakefulness whenever his sleep lightens. And frequent peeps into the cot may be making matters worse. Energetic kicking which dislodges wrappings and covers may mean that he gets cold and uncomfortable. A baby bag, shaped like a dressing gown with the bottom closed, will help him to feel both safe and warm. If you start using one now, you may save yourself serious problems later on when he gets to the climbing out of bed stage (see p. 303).

A lot of evening wakefulness can be the result of colic (see p. 101) which has got him accustomed to spending those particular hours awake. If he did have colic but it is now over, get him up when he wakes, give him a good cuddle and then put him down again. With no pain to keep him awake he will soon drop off. If the evening fretting has nothing to do with colic and the baby is fully breast-fed, check that your milk supply is adequate for his early suppertime feed. He might just need a snack.

Remember that as he gets older he needs to spend more and more time awake. If he sleeps practically all day, he is bound to choose the evening or night for wakefulness. You may need to juggle his pattern.

Waking at an ungodly hour of the morning usually simply means that the baby has had enough sleep, even if you haven't. While he has five feeds per day his early morning feed will probably buy you another couple of hours peace. Once he is down to four feeds per day you will have to choose between peaceful baby-free evenings or a later start to your morning. You will not be able to have both (see p. 142).

By day In the very early weeks you may well find it almost impossible to relax or get on with anything other than babycare while your baby is awake. Only when he goes to sleep can the rest of life start up again. If he does not go to sleep, or if he keeps waking up, you will probably feel that you have accomplished nothing all day. While this kind of feeling is very natural while you are coping with a new and unsettled baby, it is important to get yourself over it as quickly as you can. It is only for a very few weeks that being asleep remains the baby's usual state, with being awake as the exception. He is a human being and very soon being awake will be his usual daytime state with sleep—in the form of separate naps—the exception. You have to teach yourself to accept and enjoy the baby as a wakeful member of the family. Once you can get over the phase of saving everything you need to do until he is next asleep, you will find that there are ways of doing almost everything you have to do while keeping him pleasant company. Once you have accepted that he is a person, to whom you can chat while peeling potatoes, babycare and the rest of your life will join up. You will find that you have learned to do two (or three or four) things at once while enjoying all of them..

Excreting

New babies' digestions gradually settle down with the rest of them. Once this has happened you will be able to recognize the type and frequency of stool which is normal for your baby. A baby who is fed only on breast milk is most unlikely to suffer any digestive disturbance, to get diarrhoea or to become constipated. Don't be concerned if there are sometimes several stools per day and then there are days without one. Frequency does not matter either way. Even four days without a stool does not mean constipation if the final product is soft and easily-passed.

Cow's milk leaves a baby with more waste to dispose of, so bottle-fed babies will produce larger, firmer stools and will usually pass them 1–4 times per day. As we have seen (see p. 89), gastro-enteritis is a real and serious possibility in a bottle-fed baby, so a *sudden* attack of diarrhoea, with unusually frequent and watery stools, means a same-day trip to see the doctor. Take one of the soiled nappies with you. If the baby also seems ill, with fever and/ or vomiting, get to a doctor quickly.

Stools that loosen gradually over several days are more likely to be due to diet than infection. Take a baby who seems off-colour to the doctor, otherwise consider sugar intake. Perhaps you have been putting extra sugar in bottles or giving extra fruit juice or sweetened water to drink. If you give nothing but accurately-made formula and plain boiled water for a few days, the stools will probably return to normal. You can then re-introduce the correct dose of vitamin C syrup.

Bottle-fed babies can suffer from constipation. If a baby's body requires extra water (due to hot weather, or fever, for example), it will extract every possible drop from the food waste and the stool will be dry, hard and difficult to pass. Plenty of extra drinks of plain water will help, but if uncomfortably hard stools continue, try giving the baby diluted fruit juice once or twice a day.

When you start mixed feeding

Whether your baby is breast or bottle-fed, the stools will change when you introduce solid foods. Colour changes or particles of undigested food simply mean that the baby's digestion is not yet breaking down the new substances completely. If you go on with tiny quantities it will soon adapt. A stool which contains obvious mucus as well as undigested food means either that the baby cannot yet digest that particular food, or that it was given in a form which contained too much roughage. Withhold that food for two or three weeks and then re-introduce it in an even smaller quantity and more finely sieved.

Regular motions

Filling the stomach sets off a reflex which shifts waste down the intestine into the rectum. Once your baby feeds regularly regular movements may be passed during or immediately after feeds. Don't be tempted to try and "catch" these in a pot. The few soiled nappies you might avoid could not possibly be worth the discomfort to your baby or your inevitable irritation when you "miss" (see pp. 225 and 305).

Careful handling will give him confidence . . .

Confidence will help him to enjoy being handled.

Everyday care

Handling your baby

Tiny babies feel insecure and frightened when they are unbundled. That is why changing their clothes and bathing them and generally mucking them about needs to be kept to a hygienic minimum. But gradually, as babies get confidence in their own bodies, all that changes. You can see the change in what they do when you are not handling them. At the beginning your baby chose to lie all scrunched up as if still in your womb. And the baby liked to be closely wrapped with the whole skin surface in contact with something warm and soft. During the second and third months the baby straightens out. Arms and legs move. Wrappings are fought off. Now the baby is ready to enjoy physical freedom, and to enjoy being handled and bathed.

Cleanliness

"Topping and tailing" is still the easy way to keep your baby clean enough for comfort between baths. But physical activity is increasing now; don't use a table, put the mat on a low bed or the floor.

Your baby handles many objects and sucks her hands, so wash them twice a day by rubbing between your soapy ones. The baby will like the feeling but will not like soap in either eyes or mouth. . . .

Short fingernails are hygienic and will stop gouging of the face during hand play. Use tiny, blunt-ended scissors or try peeling the soft surplus nail off with your teeth. Your sensitive mouth will feel every wriggle; you will not hurt the baby.

Sticky milk or spilled solids left on the face will make it sore. Wash with plain water or use baby lotion or oil if the skin is dry or chapped. Your baby's head needs wiping over to

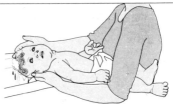

get rid of city dust or dried sweat. If it is matted with food, shampoo the hair, with non-sting shampoo. Hold the baby along your arm and damp hair with a washcloth. Lather once, then rinse with a washcloth repeatedly dipped in clear water.

The baby's bottom needs careful washing as traces of urine and faeces will make the skin sore. But the genitals need no special attention in either sex. Don't try to pull back a boy's foreskin or wash between a girl's labia. Hidden parts look after themselves, better than we can.

Nappy rash

Nappy rash can mean anything from slight redness and heat to severe inflammation with sores or pustules. One can lead to the other. Skin gets chapped by friction and damp or irritated by traces of detergent left in nappies. Acid urine stings and makes it worse. Bacteria from stools or unsterilized nappies then infect the sore skin.

To prevent it: take care in sterilizing and rinsing nappies; and keep the baby's bottom as dry as possible with frequent changing, discretion in the use of plastic pants and as much time as possible with no nappy on at all. If her bottom tends to get sore, wash urine off whenever you change her, and coat it with a silicone-based barrier cream, or with castor oil ointment.

If nappy rash does develop, consult your doctor if there are actual sores or yellow spots. Otherwise keep her lying *on* rather than *in* a nappy for as much of the day as you can. Banish plastic pants. Change her the moment she is wet or soiled and clean her with oil or vaseline rather than water and soap. Don't use protective creams until the rash is better as these keep air off the skin. Be patient: the baby is bound to be irritable – her bottom is sore.

Bathing

If your baby has uncurled his body and begun to kick, he is probably ready to enjoy being bathed. Instead of lying tensely in the water, on the edge of panicked crying, he feels the water floating his body and it makes him feel light and free and powerful. Because the water supports some of his weight, he can do his best and hardest kicking with its help. You will need a waterproof apron!

Although you can manage without one, a baby bath–on its own stand or put on a firm table or bed–makes bathing much easier. A small portable bath means that you can choose both a warm room and a height that doesn't give you backache. If you have no small bath, a fixed basin or sink will do but watch out for fixed taps. It is easy to bang the baby on them or scald him with a drip from the hot one.

By around three months, a bath may be one of your baby's favourite games. If so, do allow plenty of time and let him revel. Bathing before his evening feed is often better than in the morning. A long glorious splash leaves him beautifully exercised and relaxed, ready for supper and bed.

Collect everything you need. Undress the baby on a towel on your lap. If he is soiled, get the worst off with the nappy, then wrap him in the towel while you test the water. 85–90 F (29–32 C), or warm to your elbow, is right.

Rinse his hair and wash his face while he lies on your lap still snugly wrapped. . . .

Unwrap and hold him with the fingers and wrist of the left hand supporting his head, the right hand supporting his bottom and thighs.

Lower him into the water and hold him while he gets used to it. When he has relaxed you can withdraw your right hand.

With his head supported on your left wrist and your fingers grasping his left upper arm, your right hand is free to wash and play.

To lift him out, keep the same grip with your left hand and put your right under his bottom, grasping his left thigh. He's slippery.

Wrap him in the towel, pulling it up around his head. Pat him dry, and check that his creases are dry before you re-dress him.

Going in the big bath

Somewhere between three and six months babies and their thrashing limbs will get too big for any form of small bath and you will have to transfer to the adult one. Be tactful about it. Your baby may find the vast expanse of water and the towering walls frightening at first. If the baby does seem worried, try putting the usual small bath inside the big but empty one for a few days so that the baby can get used to the look of it.

Holding your baby securely is more of a problem at floor level. Don't try to bend down to it; kneel on the floor with everything you need beside you. A rubber mat or old bath towel in the bottom of the bath will stop the baby slipping away from you and make him feel more secure too. Keep the water shallow. If it is deep he will float and if it is more than 4–5 inches (10–13 cm) deep it will cover his face if he should slip from your grasp. Be sure that the hot tap is properly turned off before you put him in.

Remember that the bath is wide. Unless you grasp the baby's shoulder with your fingers as well as supporting the head on your wrist, he could roll over and get his face in the water.

Doubtful babies

If your baby is doubtful about bathing – not really afraid but not quite happy either – there are a number of things you can do which will probably help him or her to relax and enjoy it. If you have taken trouble over all the following points and the baby still seems unhappy, you should treat him or her as a frightened baby (see below).

Do	Don't
Get the room really warm so that she does not get tense and shivery as you undress her. A temperature as high as 75°F (24°C) is ideal if you can manage it.	*Bath her in a room which is actually cool. If the temperature must be below 65°F (18°C), abandon the bath for today.*
Make the water pleasantly warm to your wrist or elbow (don't test it with your hand which is probably accustomed to really hot washing up water). Run the cold water in first and then warm it from the hot tap.	*Use water that feels cooler than your wrist or elbow – it will feel chilly to her skin – or risk putting her into water which is too hot – it will give her a shock.*
Put her in the water as soon as you have undressed her. Soap her by using your free hand, wearing a soap mitt if you find this helpful.	*Soap her on your lap first and only put her in the water to rinse. She will feel uncomfortably chilly and sticky while being soaped and worryingly slippery while being lifted into the water.*
Let her splash herself – and you.	*Splash her.*
Avoid getting soap in her eyes. If you do, lick it out.	*Try to get soap out of her eyes by splashing water in them.*
Give firm support with your hand to her neck and the back of her head, as shown opposite.	*Hold her under her shoulder blades. She will feel as if her head might go back and under the water.*
Make sure that you lift her straight out of the water and into a really large, soft, warm towel. Pat her dry through it and give her time to adapt to being out of the water before you open the wrapping towel to check that her skin folds are dry.	*Let her feel cold even for a second while you reach for a towel or try to wrap her in one that is damp or too small. Rub her dry, or leave her naked while you dry her skin folds.*

Frightened babies

Some babies take a long time to learn that a bath can be fun. Babies who still dislike being undressed and put to kick on a big surface probably will not enjoy being bathed either. Stick to topping and tailing them while they grow up a bit.

Even a baby who enjoys free kicking may dislike being bathed. No baby will get over a fear by being frightened. Don't bath a frightened baby. Don't even sit beside the bath to wash him or her. Wrap a big towel on a bed or changing mat and wash the baby bit by bit instead. This gets the baby just as clean and accustomed to feeling wet all over.

If you resist the temptation to try a bath for at least a month, even the most frightened baby will have

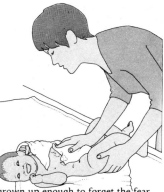

grown up enough to forget the fear. Then, with infinite care and tact, you can try again. You may well find that you now have a water baby.

Teething

The fact that a baby is in the process of cutting a tooth is too often used to explain fretful or irritable behaviour or even illness. A baby who cries a lot and is difficult to keep cheerful is very hard to bear, as we have seen. But don't fall into the trap of automatically assuming that troubled behaviour is caused by teething. A physical cause for crying may make it easier for you to stay patient and loving with the baby, but at this age putting it down to teething is neither accurate nor safe.

Teething seldom causes trouble in babies under five months. Since the first tooth will not be cut until five to six months it is absurd to assume that irritability in a three month old baby is due to that future event.

When a tooth is nearly due it is still most unlikely to cause anything more notable than a slightly inflamed gum, a bit of dribbling and a lot of chewing. The first teeth are cut very easily. It is the first molars, cut at around a year, which can cause real pain.

Believing that your baby's behaviour is due to teething may lead you to neglect real illness. A few babies each year reach hospital in a bad state because parents assumed that signs which were really symptoms of illness were only due to teething and therefore did not call their doctor in time.

Teething cannot cause fever, diarrhoea, vomiting, loss of appetite, convulsions or "fits". So if your baby seems ill, consult your doctor irrespective of the state of his or her coming teeth. If the baby seems well, wipe the dribble off his or her chin so that the continual wetness does not make it sore. Give hard rusks or teething rings if he or she seems to want to bite a lot. Be sympathetic if the baby is *occasionally* fretful when he or she bites too hard on the inflamed gum. Otherwise ignore the whole matter.

Babies cut their teeth in a particular order and roughly at certain ages. But there is a wide variation in those average ages. A baby who cuts teeth earlier than average is not brighter or more forward than the baby who cuts them later. The actual age at which they appear has no importance – except that once your baby has a tooth you will never again see that particular toothless grin!

Teeth and chewing
First teeth are not chewing teeth, they are biting-off teeth. A baby cuts the front teeth first, and does not chew with those any more than an adult does.

Babies start chewing with their gums and perfect it long before they acquire teeth at the back of the mouth to help them. So don't assume that a baby with one solitary front tooth cannot chew. He or she can and must.

Babies start teaching themselves to chew as soon as they can get their hands and the toys that they hold into their mouths (see p. 166). It is important that they should be given *foods* to chew soon after this, and certainly before six months.

Babies who are fed entirely on semi-liquid foods until they have some chewing teeth at around a year often refuse to chew food at all. They have got so used to slops that really solid food revolts them and makes them gag. If your baby is given hard foods to mouth at the four to five month stage when objects are being explored by mouthing, he or she will take much more easily to family meals later on. Chewing hard foods is good for the baby's developing jaw, too. It makes it less likely that orthodontic treatment (braces and so forth) will be needed later on. Feeding themselves, with their own hands, long before they can feed themselves with a spoon, also gives babies a good start towards feeling enthusiastic and independent about eating.

So as soon as toys go in your baby's mouth, he or she should be given hard foods to put in too. Peeled pieces of apple are good; so are hard crusts or rusks, raw scrubbed carrots and even cooked, smooth chop-bones.

But your baby should never have any of these things when lying down – he or she might choke or might poke an eye with the carrot or the bone. Once babies cut a tooth or two you need to be extra watchful even when they have these foods while sitting in their chairs. New teeth are sharp. Your baby might grate a tiny piece off that apple and choke on it. If you are there, a quick pat between the shoulder blades will help him or her cough it out of the windpipe.

Teeth and weaning

Your baby's first tooth will be visible as a small, pale bump under the gum for days before it emerges. When its point breaks through, it will be sharp. You may be tempted to regard it as a signal to speed up weaning. But there is no need to worry about the possibility of the baby biting your nipple. This first tooth, and the second one which will follow it two or three weeks later, is a bottom tooth. The baby has no matching top tooth against which to pincer anything. It will be months yet before he or she can bite you.

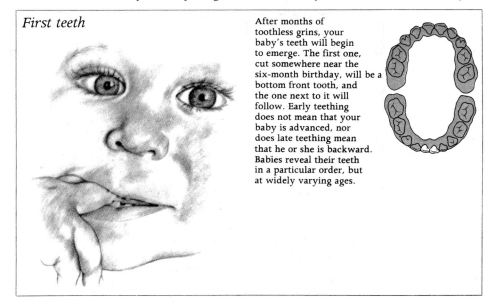

First teeth

After months of toothless grins, your baby's teeth will begin to emerge. The first one, cut somewhere near the six-month birthday, will be a bottom front tooth, and the one next to it will follow. Early teething does not mean that your baby is advanced, nor does late teething mean that he or she is backward. Babies reveal their teeth in a particular order, but at widely varying ages.

Crying and comforting

Some babies cry more than others. Even once they are "settled" there are babies who seem more inclined to the miseries, more jumpy or just generally less contented than other babies.

But there are changes during the second and third months which make even "difficult" babies easier to live with and love. Your baby may still *begin* to cry many times every day, but will no longer go on and on despite all your efforts at comfort. You will be able to stop the crying now. Pick the baby up and talk and the crying will stop. If there is real distress – pain, for example, or acute hunger – the crying may start again. But usually a baby of this age will stay calm just as long as you will go on cuddling.

So instead of those dreadful times in the newborn period when you felt like the most useless parents in the world, you will now know that you are magic. Maybe you wish the baby did not need your magic quite so often, but at least it is better to feel useful! The crying becomes more meaningful, too. The baby still uses that basic hunger cry. He still lets out that pain cry which makes your heart thud. But he adds a "grumbly" cry, a sort of whimpery, fretful, almost whiny sound. And he uses that one first on most occasions. He is not saying "disaster!" or "I'm starving!": just "I don't seem to be quite happy just now". Soon afterwards he adds an "anger" cry, quite unlike any of the others. It is an indignant roar: "Come back!" it seems to say, or "I want it!" or "Don't!"

. Maybe you could not describe all these different cries in words. But you will know them apart when you hear them. When he starts to grumble, you know that he is *getting* hungry or *getting* bored. You know it is time to do something for him and it is easier to think what to do because you are not overwhelmed by the urgency of a full-throated roar.

So at least you can begin to understand his crying better, and you can always stop it, at least for the moment. But what can you do to make him happier, make him *start* crying less often?

Typical cries

The baby's repertoire of cries grows. Presented visually from a sound spectrograph you can see the differences in volume, pitch and rhythm in three typical ones. More important, you will soon be able to distinguish the cries when you hear them and know what it is he or she needs.

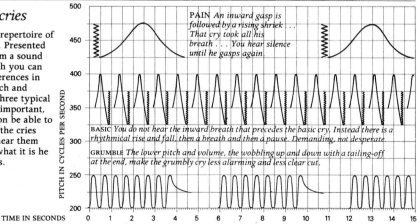

PAIN *An inward gasp is followed by a rising shriek . . . That cry took all his breath . . . You hear silence until he gasps again*

BASIC *You do not hear the inward breath that precedes the basic cry. Instead there is a rhythmical rise and fall, then a breath and then a pause. Demanding, not desperate.*

GRUMBLE *The lower pitch and volume, the wobbling up and down with a tailing-off at the end, make the grumbly cry less alarming and less clear cut.*

PITCH IN CYCLES PER SECOND

TIME IN SECONDS

500 450 400 350 300 250 200

0 1 2 3 4 5 6 7 8 9 10 11 12 13 14 15

Causes and cures of crying

All the causes and cures of crying that were suggested for the Newborn baby (see p. 95) may still apply to this older one. But there are some new aspects to consider now, too.

Sucky babies   Some babies are better soothed by sucking than by anything else. Your baby may already have learned to suck fist or fingers. If not, you can help.

Make quite sure you don't wrap the baby with arms and hands trapped. Try helping the fist to the mouth a few times, and see if the baby would like to suck it. If the comfort of sucking is needed it is much better if it is under the baby's own control. It is much more hygienic for a baby to suck his or her own hands than anything else, too.

Dummies   If your baby cannot or will not suck his fingers, you could give a dummy. It is rare for books to suggest dummies, but there is no doubt that they can make a miraculous difference to a few miserable or jumpy babies. Let us look at some pros and cons:

Advantages	Disadvantages
If the baby takes to it, the dummy will soothe him to sleep, or soothe him after a fright.	*Once he is used to it he may not be able to do without it. He may want it through babyhood. Can you stand the look of it?*
If he sleeps with a dummy in his mouth, disturbances will make him start sucking again (thus soothing himself) rather than waking him right up.	*If the dummy falls out of his mouth in the night, he may wake and cry for it.*
A dummy will probably mean that he will not take to sucking his thumb.	*If he often has a dummy in his mouth, it will prevent him from putting toys etc. in his mouth, which he needs to do in order to explore them properly (see p. 167).*
	Unless you are very fussy about sterilizing them, dummies are unhygienic.
	Unless you are very careful, you will find yourself shoving the dummy in his mouth every time he is unhappy, instead of trying to find out what is the matter.

On balance it is probably better to try and do without a dummy altogether, but if your baby is *really* miserable, you could try giving one for a few months, at bedtime only. Peaceful evenings and nights may raise the morale of the whole family. If the baby is a happier person by around six months, you could try taking it away altogether before the baby is old enough to remember it or miss it for long. It is at the crawling and toddling stages that dummies seem most unaesthetic, unhygienic and limiting to a child's explorations.

Whatever you decide about dummies, *don't* compromise with a "dinky feeder" filled with sweet drinks. These are the shortest road to rotted first teeth; there is also a risk of your baby sucking and choking while asleep. If you want to give your baby a drink, give it in a bottle on your lap.

Wakeful babies who are bored

A lot of your baby's crying may be due to your expecting him to sleep more often and for longer periods than he needs. He may be a baby who needs much less sleep than average – remember that some three and four month old babies never sleep for more than 12 hours in the 24. Or you may not yet be able to get on with life when he is around, so that you keep trying to tuck him away.

If he is a very active baby (and many wakeful ones are), the physical restrictions of wrappings and covers will frustrate him. When he must be alone in his cot or pram, try leaving him free to kick. If the weather is cold, a baby bag will keep him warm without restricting him too much.

Even with freedom to move around, he will get very bored if he spends a lot of time alone but awake. Interesting things to look at, swipe at and eventually touch will do a great deal to keep him happy (see pp. 178–179). If he has always slept on his stomach, try putting him on his back with his pram under a tree or near your dancing washing or with lots of interesting objects hung close over his cot.

Even interesting objects are no replacement for people. If your baby spends a lot of time awake but alone, he is probably crying because he is lonely. After all a baby who is *asleep* in the garden does not know that he is alone; a baby who is awake is alone and conscious of it. If you take him into the family circle whenever he is awake, the excess crying may stop overnight. You are fascinating to your baby and so is everything that you do. Now that he is old enough to be propped up it is easy to arrange for him to be part of whatever you are doing.

He can be propped in his pram with a cushion under the mattress and the pram parked close to you. He can sit in his infant seat on the draining board or the dining table or wherever you are working. No matter how tedious the chores you are doing, they will not bore him. You may be fed up with peeling potatoes but he has never met a potato before; introduce him.

When he is tired of being propped, a rug on the floor is an ideal playground unless your home is full of dogs and toddlers. He will not watch television but he will be happy to watch you doing so. But perhaps the best of all solutions for wakeful babies is a baby bouncer. A canvas seat harness attached by elastic cords to a door frame or ceiling hook gives him a perfect all round view of the world and, at the touch of his toes on the floor, a delightful freedom to dance and twirl and jump. . . . Baby bouncers make miserable babies happier and happy ones happier still. As soon as your baby can hold his head and upper back straight he is ready to learn his world from this entrancing new angle.

When your baby is awake . . .

she wants to be with you . . .

there are several ways in
which she can be safely part
of what you are doing . . .

Using his or her body

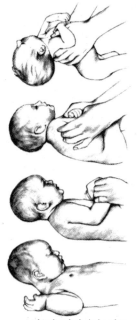

At birth a baby's head is simply too heavy, but by 6 weeks he can hold it for a second while by 3 months he brings it with him if you pull him up. By 6 months he is trying to get up by himself. . . .

As we have seen (p. 108), babies are born with very little control over their limbs or their bodies and with their postures dominated by their over-heavy heads. Muscle control starts from the top; babies learn to support their heads on those wobbly neck muscles. It moves downwards in an orderly and unvarying sequence. By the middle of the first year the baby can hold the back muscles steady enough to sit up. By the end of the year he or she is fighting for control of the leg muscles so as to stand upright.

All babies follow the same pattern of physical development but each one goes down that path at his or her own particular rate. Like runners they set off together and follow the same track, but some spurt along one stretch and stand still at another, while others jog steadily all the way. So perfectly normal babies may be weeks ahead of, or behind, equally normal babies of the same age, yet they will all be learning their new physical skills in the same order. A baby may learn to sit alone early or late. But yours will certainly learn to sit before standing.

Because the rate at which a child moves on from one accomplishment to the next is so variable, children continually shift their positions relative to each other. For example, your niece may learn to sit alone weeks earlier than your daughter, but having got herself to sitting position she may not go on to crawl for a couple of months. Meanwhile your daughter "catches up" by learning to sit and then, instead of pausing, goes straight on to crawl within a week of first sitting.

So while milestones like learning to roll over, sit up, crawl, stand and walk are quite a useful guide to *what* you can expect your child to do next, they are not at all a useful guide to *when* the next development will take place. If milestones are used to compare different children, they can make mothers feel competitive and can lead to quite unwarranted jealousy and heartbreak. Your baby is not better or worse than your neighbour's child because he learns to manage something sooner or later than he. Your baby is an individual person taking his or her own time along the developmental track. Comparing this person with anyone else is as foolish as comparing an apple with an orange. *Your baby is unique.*

Head control

By six weeks most babies will have got their necks sufficiently under control to be able to balance their heads upright as long as whoever is holding them keeps still.

If you walk around carrying the baby, or bend down while you are holding him, his head will still flop. He still needs your hand at the back of his neck as he is lifted and put down, or whenever you tip him even a little off centre.

Over the next six weeks or so those neck muscles get firmer and his control moves gradually down to include his shoulders. He is growing and putting on weight, too, so his head is getting lighter in relation to the rest of him. By the time he is three months old his control of his head will be complete. Your supporting hand will be needed only when you pick him up or move him unexpectedly.

Postures As the baby's head control improves, so all his postures—the physical positions that he adopts spontaneously—change too. He gradually uncurls from that newborn position (see p. 108). He learns to lie flat on his back with the back of his head on the mattress and both arms and legs free. On his stomach he learns to stretch his legs out from underneath him, and to turn his head to either side instead of keeping it always turned in one preferred direction. Held at your shoulder he keeps himself upright instead of curling himself in to rest his head in the hollow of your neck. If you pull him gently to sitting position by his hands, he learns to bring his head with him instead of letting it drop backwards or resting his chin on his chest.

These small and gradual physical developments are vitally important. The baby's postures and muscle control affect both the things he can do himself and the use he can make of the world around him. Curled in foetal position, his head always turned to one side, he could see nothing above his cot. Now, when he lies flat he has a clear view above him and one that he can enlarge by turning his head. Now he can enjoy toys, mobiles and faces hung there for his delight. Now, too, his limbs are freed. He will begin to discover the joys of physical activity.

Uncurled and kicking, the three month baby discovers the joys of vigorous play.

Kicking Most babies will have "uncurled" by the time they are three months old. Once your baby has reached this stage, he will begin to look as if he is happy in his body, and having fun learning to use it.

Now, if he is awake he is moving. As he lies on his back, he kicks, moving one leg after another in a smooth bicycling action, quite different from the jerky little movements he made earlier. His arms wave too. We shall see later that his hands, moving in and out of view, become his most important "toys" (see p. 165).

As he lies on his stomach, he practises a new kind of head control. He bobs his head up off the mattress, rather as he bobbed it off your shoulder a few weeks earlier. Soon he learns to hold this head up position for a few seconds. Once he can do that, he learns to take some weight on his forearms too, so that not only his head but also his shoulders come clear off the mattress.

Once he can lift his head off the mattress it will not be long before he discovers how to get his shoulders off too by taking his weight on his forearms.

Rolling Even at nine or ten weeks, babies are so physically active that if you put them down to sleep on their sides, they will roll themselves on to the broader base of their backs. There is no point in putting your baby on the side once this has begun. The days when the baby's sleeping position was entirely up to you are over.

By three months the baby will have learned a much more difficult trick – and one which leads to many a bump on the head. He has learned to roll from his back on to his side. That changing table which seemed so safe and convenient may become a danger between one nappy change and the next.

Think what a lot of entertainment and independence these tiny physical developments give the baby. He can exercise himself; watch his feet and his hands; roll enough to shift position and change his view of the room; lift his head so that he can see something different.

But think, too, how little it takes to spoil all this for him. Restrictive clothes or blankets will stop him kicking; a crumpled sheet will stop him rolling; a bare white wall will take away his pleasure in being able to look around. If he is to get the most out of his own development, he needs your help.

The beginnings of learning to sit up Once your baby can hold his head steady as you carry him gently around, and hold it clear of the mattress when he lies on his tummy, his muscle control will move downwards to his upper back. If you pull him gently to sitting position, he will not curl right over so that his head almost touches the floor, as he did earlier; he will hold up his head and shoulders, so that only the middle of his back and his hips are still saggy.

Between three and four months, being pulled to sitting may become one of your baby's favourite games: you only have to take his hands for him to try and pull *himself* up, using your hands as handles. Even without adult hands he will try to sit up by this stage. Lying on his back, resting after an energetic kicking bout, he will lift his head clear of the floor. A month later he can

At 3 months he can manage his head and shoulders; it is his back that is still saggy. It will be a few more weeks before the sag is confined to hip level.

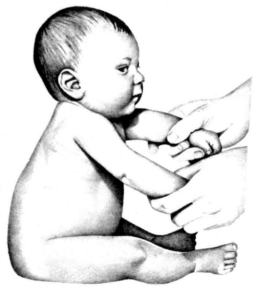

Propping

Propping is good for babies. It brings them into the family circle and gives them a view of everything that is going on. There is no truth in the old myth that being propped up can strain your baby's back. But if she is to be comfortable, she needs to be propped carefully, with a firm straight slope from her bottom to her head.

Upholstered furniture is not the best place for propping. The baby's bottom has slipped, her back is bent and her head pushed forward.

A pillow under the baby is also inadequate, but put under the mattress it makes just the right slope for comfort and a good view.

Best of all, an adaptable chair like this will keep her comfortably propped anywhere.

lift both his head and his shoulders and may get an amazing glimpse of his own feet as he does so!

All this means that the baby now needs to spend at least some of his waking time propped up. Propping him up brings him into the family; he can see what is going on; people catch his eye as they pass, pause for a smile and a chat; propping him makes him more of a person and less of a "thing".

But it needs care. Propped in the corner of a sofa or armchair, he gradually slips down, his back bends more and more and his head is pushed forward. He cannot wriggle back to get comfortable again, either. He can be made comfortable in his pram, if pillows are put *under* the mattress so that he leans against a firm smooth slope. But much the best solution is a baby chair which can be adjusted from a nearly reclining position to a nearly upright one. A chair like this lets the baby tell you how upright he is ready to sit. If you strap him into the chair set at around its halfway mark when he is about two months old, he will relax comfortably in it. After a few days or weeks you will see him craning his head and shoulders forward from the backrest as he tries to sit more upright. If you then notch the chair up one more hole, the process will be repeated. The chair is light, portable and stable enough to be put on tables, draining boards or anywhere that allows the baby to be close to you and watch what you are doing. It is ideal for early mixed feeds too. Of course, as the baby gets heavier and has the chair in increasingly upright positions, the combination makes it less stable, so that it is only safe on the floor, but if you then buy its own stand and tray, you can turn it into a high chair and use it right through toddlerhood (see p. 144).

By 5–6 months, his muscle control will have moved downwards again. Now his back will be under control although his hips still sag. When you pull him to sitting he may provide all the muscle power himself, only needing your hands for balance. When you prop him he may only need support at the bottom of his spine, sitting in his pram, for example, with a pillow wedged under his bottom. By six months, you may be able to sit him on the floor and take your hands away for a second. There will only be the problem of balance left for him to solve before he sits alone.

The beginnings of learning to crawl

Once babies have learned to hold their heads up and take their weight on their forearms as they lie on their tummies, it does not take them long to learn to pull their legs up under them and get their bottoms in the air. By four or five months, many babies have learned that they can get more purchase on the mattress or floor if they pull their legs right up and push with their feet rather than their knees. At about the same time they may learn to lift their shoulders by pushing up with their hands rather than their elbows. Now the baby has both ends organized for crawling but still cannot put the two together so as to get on to both hands and knees simultaneously.

Often babies try so hard to put these two positions together that they look as if they are see-sawing: head-down-bottom-up and then bottom-down-head-up. A real crawl, moving along deliberately with his tummy right off the floor, is very unusual before six months. But a see-sawing baby often covers quite a lot of ground; enough ground to go off the edge of the bed or over the top of that flight of stairs. . . . Your baby is not fully mobile yet, but it is nevertheless high time for commonsense safety precautions (see Enc/Safety).

Some babies cut out these preliminaries to crawling because they dislike being put to lie on their tummies at all. They are usually babies who are especially interested in looking at things and in interacting with people. They object to having their view of the world restricted, so they fight to roll over on to their backs again, and may even succeed before they are six months old.

A baby who reacts like this will stop objecting to lying on his tummy as soon as he can get there of his own free will by rolling over from his back. He will probably manage this soon after he has perfected rolling in the other direction. There is no reason to suppose that his refusal to practise crawling preliminaries will make him late in successful crawling. He will probably just leave *trying* to crawl later than most babies but manage to perfect the process and get moving rather faster.

The beginnings of learning to stand

Standing is a later accomplishment than sitting or crawling. Muscle control moves downwards. Babies cannot control their legs until they have acquired control over their backs and hips.

But practice starts early. Held in "standing" position on your lap, your three month baby sags pathetically; but he soon begins to take a tiny proportion of his own weight by pushing down with his toes while he practises straightening his knees. By four to five months the knee-straightening has become rhythmical so that it feels as if he were "jumping". Once he reaches this stage he will probably refuse to *sit* on your lap at all: he will turn himself inwards, fasten his fists in your clothes and fight to get himself upright. Standing gives him warm contact with your body, a chance to gaze into your face and a delightful view of the world over your shoulder, that moves as he "jumps".

By the time he is six months old you may have decided that he is a gymnast in the making who is convinced that you are a trampoline. . . .

Bottom down, head up and head down, bottom up: the see-sawing baby will soon put the two positions together.

Seeing and understanding

As we have seen (see p. 116), newborn babies have a built-in interest in looking at faces and at complicated shapes and patterns. Babies are born interested in people because people must care for them. They are born interested in complicated-looking objects because they must learn to manage a complex world.

During these months your baby will begin to understand things he or she sees. The baby learns to know one thing from another and *do something* about each, adding action to looking.

Finding you

In his first days your baby will study any face or any object or picture with the hairline-eyes-mouth pattern which makes it seem like a face. But he quickly learns to distinguish real faces from phoney ones. When his smiling starts, at around six weeks, he smiles at you, your neighbour or a face-sketch. But by eight weeks, you or your neighbour will get faster, wider smiles.

By three months the baby not only knows real faces from fake ones, he also begins to know one face from another – especially the familiar from the strange. He still smiles and "talks" to that smiling, talking neighbour but he smiles more readily at you.

By four months he knows you and he infinitely prefers you. He is not alarmed by strangers – that stage comes later – but he is restrained with them whereas he is free, confident and joyous with you. Before he reaches six months, the signs of his emotional attachment to you as individual people are flatteringly clear. On your lap he behaves as if your body belonged to him; he explores your face, sucks your nose, puts his fingers in your mouth. . . . Handed to the stranger he is polite but decorous. When you hold out your arms to take him back, he comes to you with grins and crows of delight. He has understood that those people he keeps on seeing are his special people. He forces you to accept the role by singling you out for charming attention.

Finding his or her hands

It takes a baby longer to find his hands than to find you. Your face is deliberately put within his focal range many times each day, but his hands are usually out of sight and out of mind until he himself can do something that leads to their discovery.

As long as they are continually fisted, the baby is not ready for his hands. Only when they are open during most of his waking time is he ready to have things put in them; to start finding them.

A six week old baby finds his hands by touch. He grasps one with the other; pulls them; opens and shuts the fingers. But even at eight weeks, when those hands are open, he behaves as if he does not know that they are a part of him. He uses one hand to play with the other as if it were an object. He does not bring his hands up to look at them. If, at eight weeks or so, a rattle is put into the baby's hand, he will grasp it and finger it just as he does his own "other" hand. But because he can now use his arms freely, as he lies flat on his back, he is likely to make that rattle sound. When it sounds, he follows the noise with his eyes and sees, for the first time, his own hands and the rattle in them.

For the next two or three weeks, toys that are easy to grasp and make some sound when they are waved around are of real importance. They direct the baby's eyes and attention to what his hands are doing. They help him to establish the relationship between himself and his hands; the relationship between what those hands do (wave around) and what happens (the noise).

By ten to twelve weeks the baby does not need the sound any more, though he may still enjoy it. He has truly found his hands by now, by eye as well as by touch. He knows where they are and plays with them constantly, watching them all the time. He lies for minutes on end, bringing his hands together; spreading them apart so that they go out of sight; bringing them back again; pulling the fingers. . . he is as concentrated as a five year old watching television.

Once the baby's hands are under this much control, at around three months, he will explore them with his mouth as well as his eyes and the other hand. One finger goes into his mouth; it is taken out again; inspected, put back in the mouth with a thumb for company, looked at again and so on.

Now that his hands go in and out of his mouth, so will everything else. His mouth has become part of his exploring equipment. He will not fully understand an object unless he *does* put it in his mouth. If you are worried about hygiene, you must find the

Hands are the three month old baby's very best toys. They come and go, they move, they feel nice, taste nice and are always available. This is the most vital stage in learning the fine manual skills which make a human baby so different from any other creature. . . .

baby toys which are suitable for sucking as well as for holding and looking at. Trying to stop him putting things in his mouth is wasted effort and wrong too. It is better to spend the time and energy on washing his toys from time to time.

Because the baby's mouth is part of his exploring equipment, it is obviously a pity if it is continually occupied by a dummy. Very sad and fretful babies, who really need their dummies almost all the time, probably are not ready for much play with their hands yet. But most babies can now have their comfort-sucking saved for bedtime so that their mouths as well as their hands can take part in playtime.

Guiding his or her hands

As we have seen, babies start out by using their hands and their eyes separately. They finger a toy without looking at it and they look at a toy without touching it. As long as looking and touching stay separated, the baby is passive: only looking; unable to do anything about what is seen. To become an active participant in life, the baby has to put these two things together and learn to reach out and touch and take the things that he or she sees.

Getting hold of things is a very complicated business. You have to see something, want it, estimate how far away it is, and then use complicated movements of the arm to get your hand to it. Even then you have to make fine adjustments of that hand in order to get hold of the object. Learning to do this is called learning "hand-eye coordination" – learning to put what the hands do together with what the eyes see. The development of hand-eye coordination in the first half of this vital year is as important as the development of crawling and walking is in the second half. What is more, this coordination of hand and eye remains important right through life. The child who is good with a ball is one whose hand-eye coordination is well developed. The competent driver will be well coordinated too.

Helping your baby to coordinate hands and eyes

You cannot *teach* a baby to coordinate hands and eyes: babies cannot start learning until they have grown up enough to be ready. As soon as they are ready, they will start learning.

But once the learning does start, you can help it along. Research has shown that babies brought up in old-fashioned residential nurseries, with few toys, not much adult attention and hours and hours spent in their cots with nothing to do, are very slow in learning to reach out and grab things. The minute those babies are given attention and interesting things to look at and to handle, their hand-eye coordination develops much faster. So obviously it is important for parents to make sure that their babies *do* have this kind of stimulation.

Even babies reared by the most conscientious parents sometimes get less help with this kind of "play" than they could use. It is not that the parents do not *want* to give the baby everything he can use, it is because the stages of development of hand-eye coordination are not very obvious. If you do not know what stage your baby has reached, you cannot tell what he will enjoy using. So let us look at the order in which babies do learn these skills, the ages when most of them manage each stage, and the particular things that parents can do to help the whole process along.

Using hand and eye together

0–8 *weeks* The baby's curled up position and "nearsightedness" mean that he does not see much except when he is picked up or something is deliberately shown to him at about 8 inches (20cm) from his nose. If this is done, he will focus his eyes on the object and indicate his interest in it with his body. If he was lying still, he will start to wriggle; if he was kicking, he will "freeze to attention". If the toy is moved slowly, still within his limited focus range, he will follow it with his eyes. If it is moved too fast or taken too far away for him to see it clearly, he will lose interest at once. The minute he loses sight of the toy he has forgotten that it ever existed.

What you can do to help. Until the baby opens his hands (at about 8 weeks) and begins to play with them, he does not actually *need* toys to play with. But practice in focusing his eyes on things is good for him. Remember that his best focusing distance is 8–10 inches (20–25cm), and that your faces are the most interesting objects in the world to him.

2–2½ *months* The baby is beginning to uncurl his body, to open his fists and to watch his own hands when they happen to come into view. He is still very short-sighted, but he is much quicker to focus his eyes on things that are shown to him. He is better at following a moving object with his eyes, and will probably turn his head, too, to keep it in view.

What you can do to help. Those open hands are asking to have things put in them. Toys (such as many kinds of rattle) which make a sound as they are moved are very useful. The sound will attract the baby's attention to what his hands are doing, and will speed up the moment when he makes that vital connection between what his eyes see and what his hands do.

2½–3 *months* Most babies now watch their hands while they play with them. The baby who does this is connecting seeing with doing. If you watch carefully, you will soon see that when you show him an object he does not only look at it and try to keep it within view, he also tries to do something about it. Usually what he does is to take a vague swipe at the object with whichever hand is nearest to it. He may also look from his hand to the object and back again.

What you can do to help. The baby needs practice in controlling his hands and in estimating, by eye, the distance between them and the object he wants. He also needs as much experience as possible of his own power and control over objects. He needs games which give him the message "I see that, I do this, and something happens". Things to swipe at are superb toys at this stage. A woolly ball can be hung from a string above his cot, so that the ball is about 10 inches (25cm) above his face. He will hit at it and sometimes his hand will connect so that it swings. The same kind of thing hung from a twig when his pram is outside will keep him even happier. His successful swipes will make the twigs move as well as the ball. A light rattle, hung up in the same way, makes a change – the baby will discover that his swiping makes noise as well as movement.

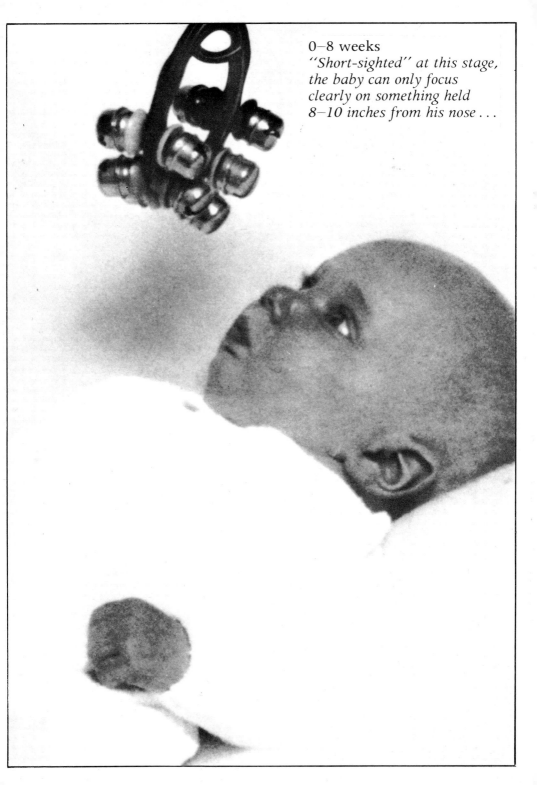

0–8 weeks
*"Short-sighted" at this stage,
the baby can only focus
clearly on something held
8–10 inches from his nose ...*

2–2½ months
*Although still "short-sighted", the baby is now quicker
to focus and can follow a moving object with his eyes . . .*

. . . he follows it from side to side

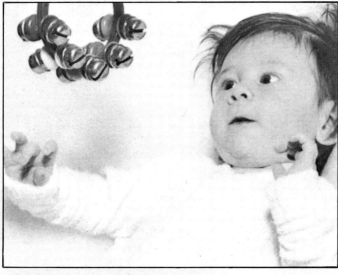

. . . and up and down too

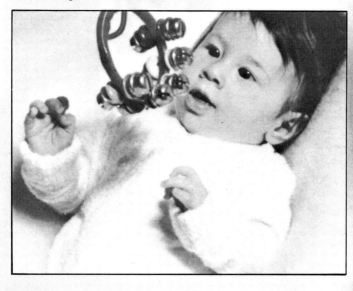

. . . the sound a rattle makes when put into his hands will help him to connect what his eyes are seeing with what his hands are doing.

2½–3 months
Soon he will try to do something about the object you show him. His first deliberate action will probably be to swipe at it . . .

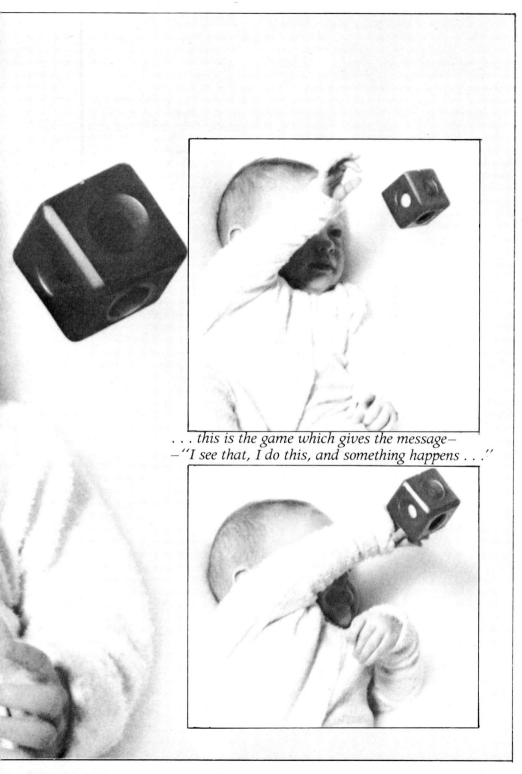

. . . this is the game which gives the message—
—"I see that, I do this, and something happens . . ."

3–4 months
Getting hold of things is still a problem.
He lifts his hands towards the object,
measuring the distance between the two . . .

. . . he looks at his hand

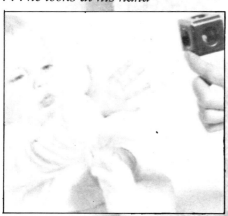

. . . he looks at the object

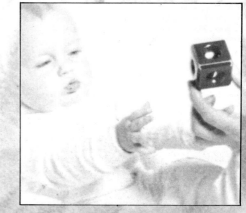

. . . and only then can he bring them together.

4–6 months
By her half birthday she can focus on an object at almost any distance and lift her arm and hand straight to it. She can get hold of things too, even adjusting her hand to suit the size.

3–4 months The baby may still swipe at things, but most typically he looks at an object, looks at his own nearest hand, lifts the hand towards it, "measures" the distance by eye again and then goes on repeating this until he actually manages to touch the toy. He does not manage to get hold of it, though. He almost always closes his hand before it gets there.

What you can do to help. Swinging objects are not suitable now: the baby is no longer happy just to hit things, he wants to touch them. If they swing away, he will be very frustrated. The ideal toy, while he is alone, is a "cradle gym" fixed across his cot or pram within his eye-line and within easy reach of his hands. There are "stabiles" which fix on, too. Left with these the baby will spend long periods getting his hands to within touching distance.

Adults who hold toys out to babies at this stage often spoil their practice by mistake. The glancing backwards and forwards from toy to hand to toy takes so long that the adult gets sorry for the baby and puts it in his hand. Have patience. Don't help him until he has actually touched the object he wants. *Then* he needs to have it put in his hand so that his pleasure in having touched the toy can be increased by having actually *got* it.

This kind of careful, slow reaching out is easiest for the baby if he is in sitting position, so that his body is supported and his hands and arms are free to move. He will enjoy having toys on the tray of his chair, now. He will also like touching things as he sits on your lap – wearing beads or a medallion around your neck is a good way to keep him happy on a bus or at an adult gathering.

4–6 months The baby can now focus on objects at almost any distance, and follow them with his eyes in any direction. Gradually he stops needing to look backwards and forwards between the object he wants and his own hand. He knows where his hand is. He only needs to keep his eyes on the object. By six months, he will lift his arm and hand straight to the thing he wants. During this period he also learns to get hold of what he touches. He will keep his hand open until it makes contact, and then close it around the toy. Or he will go for a large object with both arms open, and clutch it to himself.

What you can do to help. The more interesting things the baby is given to look at and to reach out for, the more quickly he will learn to reach straight out without looking at his hand and to get hold of the thing he is touching. He needs (and enjoys) lots of practice. But be careful about the objects you allow within his range: once he *can* get hold of things he will, and everything he gets hold of will go into his mouth – cigarettes and scissors as well as rattles and rusks.

Toys for hand and eye

There are plenty of toys available which will give your baby good practice in using her hands and eyes together. But at this stage she needs constant variety rather than well-made toys that will last. A bit of improvisation with ordinary household objects will give her extra fun and learning while saving you money and storage space.

Things for looking at

Until she can touch, your baby learns by looking. She will soon know all about the string of plastic ducks across her pram or the mobile hung low over her cot. Here are two variations that are easy to set up.

Buy 1 yard (1m) of ½in. (12mm) wide elastic and 6–8 bulldog clips.

Thread the elastic through the rings on the clips, taking a turn round each so that they stay evenly spaced out.

Stretch the elastic tightly across the elbow hinges of the pram hood or the top bars of the cot, and tie it.

Now clip up objects of various shapes and colours; a sock, sieve, ball, tassel, rag doll . . . change them often.

Put a small hook in the ceiling above her cot. and attach a long string to it for lots of different "mobiles".

Anything light will move in the air currents. Try various balloons, foil plates, paper streamers or toy windmills.

A coathanger on that string is the basis for a more elaborate mobile. It will do for Christmas decorations.

If you don't want to make a hole in the ceiling. an old-fashioned hat stand by the cot is a good substitute.

Toys for trying to touch

Soon your baby will try to touch the things she looks at. Objects that are in range must be safe to handle as well as firmly attached in case she makes a lucky grab and pulls one off.

Stabile

A cot stabile like this is safe and interesting. especially if you add some extra objects. A more adaptable stabile can easily be made at home.

Making your own

Take one 18in. (460mm) and one 12in. (300mm) length of 1in. × 1in. (25 × 25mm) wood. and screw them together to make a "gallows". Into the short side screw 4–6 cup hooks. Screw 3 spring clips to the fixed side of the cot. Clip the long side of the "gallows" into them.

The hooks are out of your baby's reach. but from them you can hang light, safe objects she can look at and practise touching–a woolly ball. a rattle. milk scoops. cotton reels. . . .

Toys for swiping

Her first successful touching will be swiping. Just swiping is fun but you can help her discover that her actions have results by choosing objects and places carefully.

Hang a woolly ball. rag doll or plastic ring from a handy twig over her pram. When she swipes it she will make the whole bush move.

Her stabile will still be useful when she is in her cot. A rattle. chiming ball or string of bells will sound as she swings them.

Faces cut from foil plates or drawn on balloons look different as she moves them.

Toys for getting hold of

Practised swiping leads to grabbing. This will mostly happen when she is sitting up, but she can practise in her cot if you provide an appropriate toy. It needs to be secure, her stabile is not strong enough.

Cradle gym

You can buy a "cradle gym" to stretch across her cot. Its own safe-to-handle objects will take her weight even if she uses them to pull herself up.

Making your own

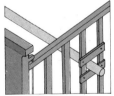

You need: a piece of 1½in. (38mm) round dowelling long enough to span the cot with a safe 3in. (76mm) overlap; small wood battens to screw to the cot bars to slip it through as shown; strong curtain rings big enough to slip over the dowelling; strong adhesive to fix them to it, and thread so strong you cannot break it yourself (cobbler's or carpet thread) to sew objects to the rings.

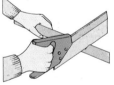

Saw a slot in the dowelling for each ring to sit in.

Glue each ring into its slot.

Use the thread to sew objects tightly to each ring. Remember these are for her to get hold of, so they must be held firmly without swinging. Vary their size, texture and colour. Remember that one day she will use them to pull herself to sitting. They must take her weight and they must be safe to suck.

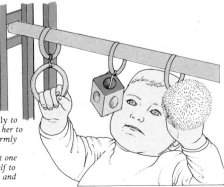

Hearing and making sounds

By the time babies are around four or five weeks old they will be beginning to link up their listening with their looking. One day your baby lies on a changing mat gazing absently towards the ceiling while listening intently to your pleasant chat. The next day the baby listens just as intently, but stops gazing at the ceiling, beginning instead to search visually for the source of your voice.

If you watch carefully at this stage you may see your baby's first social smile. This first one is not produced as a reaction to your smiling face or even to your smiling *talking* face. The baby smiles to your voice alone. Once your talking face is discovered, the baby will smile to the sound *and* the sight. Only two or three weeks later still will your smiling face, without that vital voice, be enough to evoke smiles.

During the second month, the baby begins to react to a wider variety of sounds than before. A crash will still make him jump, music will still soothe him, but sounds in the neutral middle range become important too. His reaction to any particular sound will usually depend on the mood and state he is in when it begins. If you switch on the vacuum cleaner while he is feeling grumbly and on the verge of crying, the sound will act as the last straw; he will cry. But if you switch that same cleaner on when he is feeling happy and playful, it will probably make him smile and kick. It is as if these medium-range sounds act as a general stimulus, making the baby feel more strongly whatever it was he was feeling before the sound began. Only voices seem to please him consistently, whatever the circumstances and whatever his mood.

First deliberate sounds

Because a baby has a built-in interest in listening to people's voices, it is not surprising that his own first deliberate sounds usually happen in a social situation – while he is being held and played with by an adult. He will have made a few sounds that were not crying from soon after birth, but those contented gurgles after feeds and little whimpers before crying are not deliberate sounds. They are the result of his physical state. A full stomach, a totally relaxed throat and a half open mouth lead to "contented" gurgles. A tense throat and faster breathing lead to whimpering.

By around six weeks, a baby responds to being smiled at and talked to by smiling and kicking and general signs of pleasure. By around two months, he adds some sounds of his own to his smiling. He grins and kicks, watching your face and producing small explosions of liquid sound. A couple of weeks later, he has sorted out smiling from talking. Now, if you smile, he smiles back. If you talk, he talks back.

Babies who are talked to a great deal are talkative. Babies who are usually cared for in silence, are not handled much at all or who are usually handled while you carry on a conversation over your shoulder with an older child, talk much less. Of course babies do not *only* talk when they are talked to. They also talk when they are on their own in their cots or prams. But on the whole the more social talking a baby experiences, the more of this "practice talking" he will do when he is alone, too.

These early vocalizations are not "talk" in the sense that the baby is trying to say something specific, but they are "talk" in the sense that he is deliberately trying to join in communication with you. He is using his voice as a means of interacting with you. You say something to the baby, he says something back and then pauses, as if waiting for your reply. When you say something more, he waits until you stop and then makes some more noises. His "social intentions" are made even clearer by the fact that only a *voice* makes him behave like this. Other sounds have no effect. Some research workers experimented by following each sound made by babies with the tinkling of a little bell. That did not make any of them "answer", nor did it affect how much the babies talked overall. Your baby "answers" because *somebody is talking to him*, not just because he *hears a sound*.

Even when the baby is alone, his sound making has a conversational rhythm. You will hear him make a sound and then pause, as if he were listening to the sound he had just made. Then he makes it again and pauses again. This kind of "practice", combined with playing with his hands, is often a baby's best solitary entertainment at this age. In fact babies who talk a lot (both to adults and to themselves) are likely to be more contented when alone than less chatty babies. This is yet another reason why babies who are given plenty of attention by adults tend to be more contented and less demanding than babies whose parents ration the attention they give for fear of spoiling (see p. 193).

Babbling

The second three months of a baby's life typically produce a positive spate of what is technically called "babbling". He has reached a stage of overall development which makes life very stimulating and exciting for him. As he kicks and rolls, plays with his hands, swipes at objects and triumphantly touches them, he celebrates and comments with streams of talk. He will still talk most of all when you talk to him, but he will seldom stay silent for long even if he is occupying himself alone.

At three to four months most of the baby's sounds are open vowels. He says "Aaah" and "Oooh". This stage is often called "cooing" and the name is accurate: he sounds very like a dove. The first consonants which he adds to his cooing are P, B and M. These turn his cooing sounds into noises which sound much more like words. The one parents usually notice most is "Maaaa". Unwary mothers assume that their babies are trying to name them. They may even worry because the baby says "Maaa" but does not say "Daaa". . . . In fact this is nothing whatsoever to do with naming or not naming anybody. The baby says "Maaa" because the M sound comes first in his speech development. He does not say "Daaa" because the D sound is always learned later.

Learning to make more and more complicated babble-sounds by going through these stages in sound making is built in to a baby's development. He will babble more fluently if he is talked to a great deal but he will babble to some extent even if he is badly neglected or hears no sounds from outside because he is deaf.

You cannot assume that the hearing of a baby under six months is normal just because he babbles and makes sounds. Deafness will not show itself in his voice until the second half of his first year. You can only spot hearing-loss early by watching the baby's reaction (or lack of reaction) to sounds from outside himself. If he never turns his head to look for the source of your voice and does not jump when you drop a saucepan just behind him, consult your doctor however much he talks.

Listening By the time your baby is four or five months old, being talked to will not only make him talk more, it will also help to speed up the rate at which he learns to make more and more complex sounds. Whenever you speak to him he will listen intently, watching your face. When you leave a space in the flow of words he will answer you. When he is alone he will practise running through his repertoire of sounds.

Many parents assume, all through the language-learning period, that their children learn to talk by copying. They simplify the things they say to their children and they emphasize particular words, thinking that they are making the job of imitation easier. But, as we shall see, (see p. 260), babies do not learn to speak by imitation and attempts to make them respond parrot-fashion are both ineffectual and valueless. When you talk to your baby you provide something much more important than a model to copy: you provide him with pleasurable social stimulation to make every sound that he already can make and to achieve new ones.

Babbling sounds are identical for all human babies, whatever their nationality and whatever the language or accent used in talking to them. Because the sounds are universal, they naturally include noises which sound like attempts at words, but words in whose language? If listening parents speak English, they select the English-sounding noises, label them attempts at words and dismiss the rest as "mere babble". Italian parents pick the Italian-sounding noises, Japanese parents select the Japanese sounds.... But in truth your baby is not trying out words in any particular language; he is not trying for words at all. He is just babbling. His sounds will not become different from those of his foreign friends until he starts to make real words at about a year.

Although the listening baby is not trying to imitate you he is learning your voice. Just as he learns, during this age period, to distinguish familiar people from strangers by looking at them (see p. 165), so he learns to distinguish them by listening, too. By the time he is six months old he will show you, by his excitement, that he has heard a friend talking in the front hall. If you go into his room talking, he will begin to smile even before he has disentangled himself from the bedding enough to look at you. But if a stranger should go in and talk to him, the face he lifts from his cot will be a watchful and suspicious one.

Helping your baby to "talk" The ease, fluency and complexity with which your baby babbles now is closely related to the ease and speed with which he will learn to use real language later on. His talkativeness now is at least partly dependent on his getting lots of stimulation from you, and his talkativeness later will dictate his readiness for many kinds of learning. Providing the talk which will stimulate him is therefore a very major parental responsibility.

Talking to their babies is easier for some people than for others. Some parents are natural talkers: they chat to anyone who is around and if the person who happens to be around is the baby, he gets the benefit. Some have a real sense of their baby being a person from his earliest weeks. To them, it would be as rude to ignore an idle baby while reading a book or gazing into the middle distance as it would be to ignore another adult. But other parents are naturally quiet people who do not talk very much even to each other. Talking to a baby who cannot even answer in words may make them feel silly – as if they were talking out loud to themselves.

It is no good trying to force yourself to behave in a way that feels unnatural to you. You cannot just decide to turn yourself into a talkative person. But you can deliberately set up a few situations which help you to talk to your baby; if you do, you may find that his responsiveness to your conversation inspires you to talk to him more and more.

Show your baby a picture book, point to and name the things in it and tell him, just as you would tell a three year old, what they are doing. He will enjoy the pictures and the talk even without understanding them.

Tell the baby what you are doing whenever you are handling him. As you undress him, tell him which garments you are taking off which parts of his body. As you bath him, tell him which part you are soaping or what you are reaching out for. As you give him a meal, tell him what is in it and what is coming next.

Ask questions. He will not answer you in words but he may do so in expressions, intonations and gestures: "Is that nice?" "Where's it gone?" "Is it too cold?"....

Talk naturally, without over-simplifying what you say. At this stage it is your fluent, interesting sounding talk that he needs to stimulate him. If you try to keep your words simple, the pace slow and the subject matter comprehensible, you will sound stilted and unnatural. Your baby will respond just as gleefully to your comments on the latest political developments or the price of cheese as he will to a carefully chosen sentence about the family dog. If baby talk comes naturally to you, use it. If it is false to you, don't use it. It does not matter, at this stage, either way.

Make a point of having some play-talk time alone with your baby. This is especially important if chatting to him in front of other people makes you feel silly, or if you have an older child around who also needs lots of conversation and is infinitely better at making sure that she gets it!

Most important of all, listen to the baby and try to answer him, in words, every time he makes noises at you. He does not want a running commentary or monologue from you every moment of the day, he wants conversation. If you are not a person who finds it easy to start many conversations yourself, you can at least discipline yourself to reply whenever he tries to start one.

Playing and learning

Play is more than "just fun" to babies. Play is learning and practising what they have learned. It is finding things out and exploring what they find. It is anything which stimulates them to use their bodies and their senses and to develop their thinking and their intelligence. So while play must be fun (or the baby will not go on with it), not all play has to be *deliberate* fun. Your baby will get some play value out of every single ordinarily pleasant thing you do with him or her, from changing a nappy to feeding a meal.

But when you do play deliberately with your baby you are doing a very important job: you are teaching him. The toys you offer him are as valuable to him now as educational equipment will be when he is a five year old. The games you play with him are as important as the projects his teacher will work on with him when he goes to infant school. Although the baby would probably like you to play with him almost whenever he is awake, the time that you can devote to deliberate play is almost certainly limited. So it is worth making sure that it is spent in offering him the most appropriate, and therefore interesting and enjoyable, experiences you can possibly think up.

Making the most of play time

Adjust kinds of play to your baby's moods. Like everybody else he enjoys different things when he is in different moods. When he is feeling tough and good, he enjoys rough and tumble play. It makes him triumph in his body and, gradually, in his own control and power over it. But when he is feeling tired or unwell, the same games frighten and upset him. He does not feel controlled and powerful now; he feels manhandled.

When he is feeling quiet and affectionate, he revels in being cuddled and crooned to. But when he is feeling restless and energetic, the same games make him feel imprisoned.

When he is tired or hungry or miserable, no game is any good. He does not want your play, he wants bed or food or comfort.

When you are being a playmate, adjust your timing to the baby's. Your baby's reactions are much slower than yours, especially when the play that you are offering stretches new abilities to their limits. If he is to take his full share in the "game", you must train yourself to play at his pace. If you speak to him, for example, wait five seconds for him to answer and then get impatient and say something else, you have done him out of his turn. Wait. It may take him fifteen seconds to find his answering sound.

If you hold out a toy for him to take, wait while he starts the painstaking process of reaching out for it, but then lose your patience and put it into his hand after all, you have done him out of his part. Wait. Give him time to get his hand there; time to succeed in the play-task you have set him.

If you smile down at him for a few seconds, blow him a kiss and then turn away, you have left him yet again with no part in the game. He was probably going to smile back at you but you did not give him time. Now he is smiling, puzzled, at your back.

Play means learning and finding things out—like where "me" ends and "not me" begins . . .

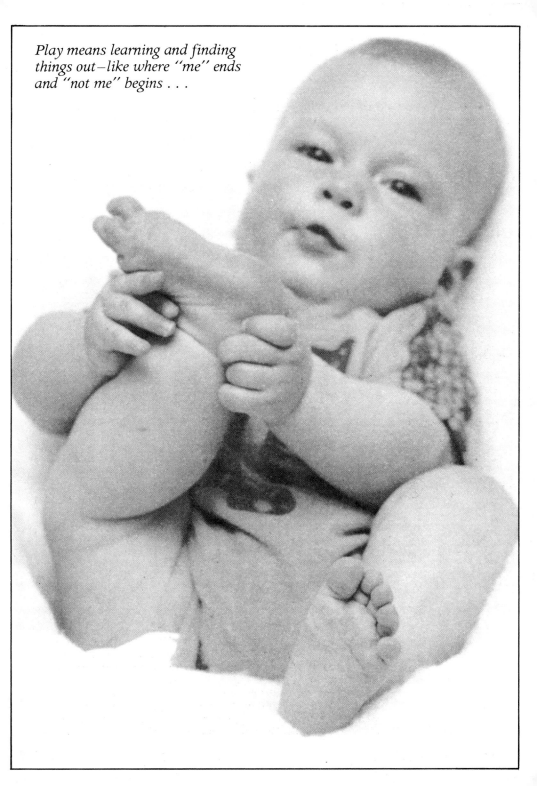

Play means using all the senses—like hearing a message and feeling it too . . .

Play means endless investigation
–of the way things feel
and the way they move . . .

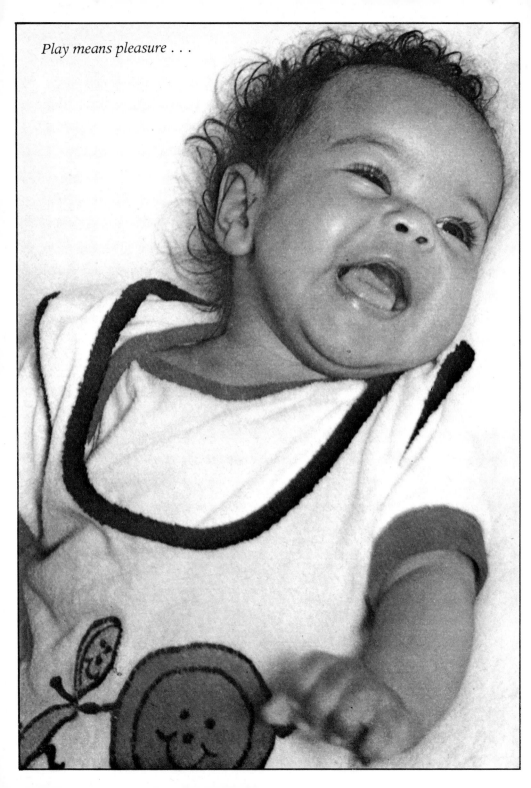

Play means pleasure . . .

Some like it rough . . .

some like it gentle . . .

. . . most like a bit of each.

Adjust your games to your baby's temperament. There is a "right" intensity of stimulation for every baby – enough to interest him and make him notice, but not enough to overwhelm him and make him withdraw. The swinging game that makes one five month baby crow with delight will really frighten another. The gentle lullaby that makes one smile and try to sing will pass unnoticed by another. You know your own baby best; by being alert to his reactions you will be able to get your play just right for him.

Does he hate loud noises? Then don't give him a metal spoon to bang on that saucepan, give him a plastic spatula instead. Don't give him a rubber duck with a loud squeak either, put sticky tape over the squeaker hole until he has got acquainted with it.

Is he physically timid? Then don't play "This is the way the farmer rides", bouncing him on your knee. Play "This little piggy went to market" instead, playing with his toes.

Is he physically very active? Then don't confine him in his chair with a rattle, put him on the floor instead and help him to "bicycle" his legs and learn to roll over.

Provide the "right" amount of novelty. Between about three and six months babies are most alert to and interested in things which are familiar enough to be manageable to them but yet slightly novel. Entirely familiar objects bore them – they have found out all they can about them, there are no more discoveries to be made. What your baby will like best is another rattle, rather like the last one but a bit bigger, perhaps, and a different colour. A piece of paper like the one he had yesterday, but tissue this time so that it feels different and makes a new kind of rustle. A music box like the first one but with a new tune; a mobile as before but with different shapes; a long balloon instead of a round one, or a plastic bottle instead of that plastic jar. . . .

Give your baby the chance to play naked. By two to three months most babies take a tremendous pleasure in being naked, in striking contrast to their fear of nakedness earlier on (see p. 97). Naked playtimes have everything to recommend them. The baby has the chance to discover and practise new physical skills, un-hampered by clothes and coverings, and he has the chance to "find" all the parts of himself that are usually hidden from view and from touch under nappies and vests. He also experiences a complete change in the texture of his world, as air or sunlight finger his skin while he rolls and chortles. Physical play and cuddles with you take on a new dimension, too. You will probably find his bare dimpled back irresistible.

But he needs to be warm and he needs to be safe. The centre of a double bed with a towel spread over it is an ideal playground – at least until he learns to roll right over. A rug on the grass under a tree is an idyllic place for him to play when the weather is warm.

Playthings   Throughout this age period you are your baby's best plaything. Your body is his gymnastic equipment; your muscles supplement his so that with you he can do a thousand things he cannot yet do alone. Your face and voice together are entrancing to him; the things that you do and the things that you use all fascinate him. If you will give him your attention, your affection and your help, you give him the best kind of play there is.

But gradually the baby needs and wants to learn about his world and the things as well as the people that are in it. He needs objects. Toys for this age-group are designed to be safe, colourful and easy for the baby to hold. The better ones are also intended to provide him with a wide variety of experiences of different shapes, weights and textures. So there is a lot to be said for buying rattles and rings, cuddly toys and mobiles, squeaky toys and balls.

But these bought toys alone will not be enough for the baby at this stage. Whatever you give him to play with, he will do very little with it. His main interest in objects is in getting hold of them; looking at them, feeling them and exploring them with his mouth. Once he has thoroughly examined an object in this way he is ready for a different one. To buy enough toys to satisfy his in-satiable curiosity about different objects you would have to be a millionaire with unlimited storage space. The answer lies in lending him a wide range of ordinary household objects to supple-ment his own possessions.

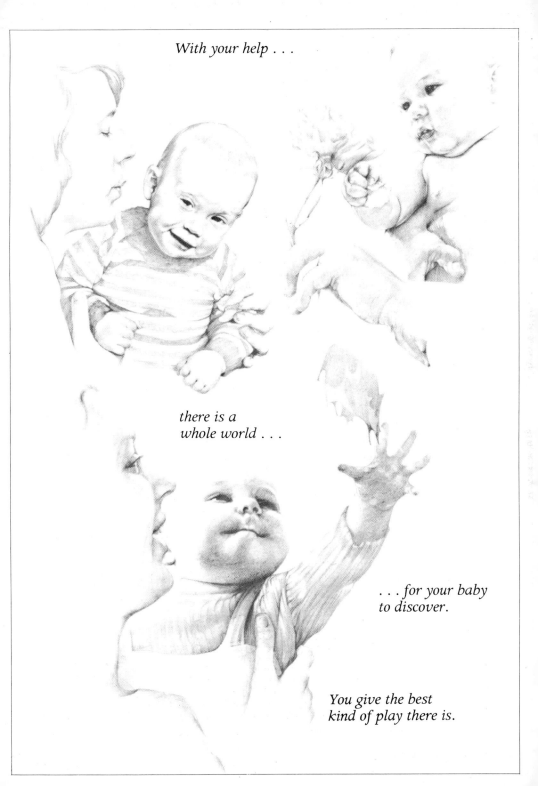

With your help . . .

there is a
whole world . . .

. . . for your baby
to discover.

You give the best
kind of play there is.

Everyday objects for play

All objects are new to new babies so they will enjoy anything you are prepared to lend. It does not matter what the object is *for* as your baby will not be able to make it work. Colour, shape, weight and feel are what matter. This list includes items available in every home: you can probably add many more:

Caution. Your baby will suck everything. Things that are safe when whole can become dangerous when broken; yoghurt pots, for example, are sharp once they have cracked. Play needs supervision; "toys" need regular inspection. The baby will learn to take things apart; make sure the contents of a home-made "rattle" cannot be swallowed or cause choking. The baby will drop things; avoid anything heavy enough to hurt. Sucking sometimes means swallowing; watch out for poisons such as newsprint or a remaining drop of bleach in a plastic bottle.

Plastic cups, spoons, plates etc.
Wooden spoons of various sizes.
Small saucepans and their lids.
Empty plastic bottles (add water for a change of weight and feel).
Plastic jars with lids (put in a couple of harmless sugar cubes for a different kind of rattle).
Various types and textures of paper to crumple and tear.
Different colours/textures of material to handle.
Small boxes with and without lids.
Foil freezer containers of every size and shape.
Every possible variety of "ball" – from ping-pong and tennis to apples, oranges or balls of string or wool.

Things to put hands through –rolls of sticky tape, a napkin ring.
Stretchy things – a garter or the rubber ring from a preserving jar.
Things that roll but are not spherical – cotton reels, or toilet paper tubes.
Flat, hard things – a ruler or sandpapered strip of wood.
Things that are surprisingly light – balloons, polystyrene.
Things that are surprisingly squashy – foam rubber or a sponge.
Things with holes – a fish slice or sieve.
Things with lumps and dips – an egg carton or bun tin.
Something big, heavy but safe – a loaf of bread or a cushion.

Helping your baby to explore objects

Although the baby learns, during these months, to stretch out and touch objects very efficiently (see p. 177) he will find it easiest to get hold of them if he can use a two-handed approach, trapping the object between his wrists and scooping it up with his palms. This kind of play is easiest for him if he is firmly supported in sitting position with both arms free and with the object on a table or tray in front of him. Your lap as you sit up to table is an ideal support. Failing that he needs to be put into his infant seat or high chair with its own table.

At this stage he can only attend to one object at a time, so a trayful of toys will only confuse him. He plays best if you put one or two objects on his table at a time and replace them with others when he is clearly bored with the first lot.

If the baby is playing with one of your kitchen toys and you want it back, offering another object is the only way you can get it without a fuss. He cannot yet release it on purpose and he will bitterly resent having it removed by force. So make use of his inability to do two things at the same time – offer him a spoon and he will drop the saucepan you are waiting for.

Loving and spoiling

Loving and playing, putting yourself in your baby's place, thinking about needs and moods, noticing every gesture and sound all add up to a lot of attention. Should your baby have so much? Will he or she not get spoiled?

Older children and adults who are selfish, thinking only of their own gratification and giving no thought to other people's needs, are spoilers of everyone's pleasure. When a four year old hurtfully rejects a present which was the best her granny could afford, or bawls for a third ice cream with her second still melting in her fist, watching adults agree that she is "spoiled rotten". So horrid is the prospect of being responsible for a spoiled child that many parents start trying to prevent it almost from the moment of their baby's birth. "She must learn that she isn't the only pebble on the beach", they declare. "Life is tough and he'd better get used to it" and even "Mummy only likes *good* little girls. . . ."

But these phrases, echoing down the years from our own childhoods and applied without much thought to our new children, have no sense or meaning in the life of a baby. In order to become spoiled (or indeed to become the opposite, a paragon of unselfishness and thought for others), a child has to be able to *want* things as well as to *need* them. He has to be able to see himself as a being who is separate from everyone else. He has to appreciate other people's rights as well as his own and he has to be able to plan to assert his own over theirs. A baby can do none of these things. He feels a need and he expresses it. He is not intellectually capable of working out involved plans and ideas like "Can I make her give me . . . ?"; "If I make enough fuss will he . . . ?"; "They let me do . . . yesterday and I want to do it again today so I'll . . .". So when I say that babies cannot be spoiled, I am not saying that they are naturally "good". I am saying that **they are not grown up or clever enough to be spoiled.**

Meeting a baby's needs is a tough job at times. Every baby has phases when because his needs are changing he has to express a good many. As soon as you learn what the new needs are so that you can meet them more quickly or even anticipate them, your baby will stop needing to express them so loudly and so often. But if you allow the idea that he may be getting spoiled to edge its way into your mind, you may not set yourself to understanding and meeting his needs. You may decide that he is becoming too "demanding" and set yourself instead to resist those needs, following the disastrous policy of "the more he demands the less we will give him". Often this happens at around four months when the baby begins to cut down his daytime sleeping hours (see p. 146). You have become accustomed to periods of peace between feeds, but now the baby begins to wake and cry hours before the "proper" time. The easy answer is to pick him up and help him play, but the fear-of-spoiling answer is the direct opposite. You had intended to pick him up at 2pm but because he cries for you at 1pm you not only refuse to pick him up right away, you even delay until 2.15pm because "he has got to learn".

What could a baby learn from this? What message could your disciplinary behaviour convey to him? "Don't bother to call me because I will not come until I am ready."? "Don't tell me when you are unhappy because I am not interested."? "The more you tell me what you need the less likely I am to give it to you."? "I will only do things for you if you do not ask."?

In this situation everybody loses.

The baby loses because his needs are not met, or they are met only after so much delay that he loses his vital confidence that they *will be* met. He becomes anxious; quicker to cry and fuss and slower to accept comfort. Where earlier he might have been happy to play alone in his cot when he woke, now the experience of being left has taught him to associate the cot with loneliness and boredom. Soon he starts to cry the moment he opens his eyes.

You lose because the less you meet the baby's needs the more demanding he becomes. As your determination to resist him hardens, so his natural demands turn into anxious ones. You get caught in a vicious spiral which is actually creating the thing you sought to avoid: an unreasonably demanding and whiny baby.

The rest of the family loses because resentful parents are not good company and an anxiously demanding baby is not much fun to live with either.

If you are already feeling "put upon" and over-burdened by the job of caring for your baby, it is difficult to believe that offering even more will make things easier for both of you. If you are run off your feet while rationing your attention, you probably feel that, without rationing, the baby's demands would simply exceed the time and energy you have available. But it is not so. Bringing up a baby is undeniably hard work, but parents who always meet their baby's demands fully and without unnecessary delay have *less* work, *less* drudgery and *less* stress.

An actual example may prove the point most easily. The chart opposite describes a single night in the lives of two mothers of three month babies. Mother A believes that she can and should save time and energy by rationing her attention to her baby. Mother B is not haunted by the spoiling spectre; she finds it easiest just to do for her baby whatever the baby seems to want.

Whichever mother you are inclined to agree with, you will see that in this real situation Mother A was clearly the loser. She spent more of her night awake and she spent the time less pleasantly too. By keeping her baby waiting for his feed Mrs A induced a long period of frustrated and miserable crying so that when she finally went to her baby he could not be pleased to see her. He was much too upset to greet her with a rewarding smile. Even when she offered him the feed, he was too distressed to settle to it with pleasure, so Mrs A did not get the satisfaction of watching him luxuriate under her ministrations. Giving the feed was tiresome and frustrating for her; it took much longer than it would have taken had he been calm, and once he had sucked a couple of ounces, exhaustion and indigestion overtook him. Because he had not managed a full feed, Mrs A faced the possibility that he would wake again in a couple of hours. . . .

Time is 3am. Both babies wake and cry.	Mother A (who worries about spoiling)	Mother B (who is not concerned about spoiling)
	Wakes; listens; checks time; finds baby has only slept 3hrs since last feeding. Puts head under pillow and tries to go back to sleep. Cannot sleep through noise. Gets up after 20mins, feeling cross and disgruntled.	*Wakes. Listens to make sure crying persists, gets up sleepy but resigned.*
Time awake before reaching baby	**22mins**	**2mins**
	Baby is in lather of misery. Too upset to smile at mother. Sobs shakily as she prepares to feed him. Cannot settle easily to feeding. Needs frequent burping as has swallowed so much air in crying. Takes 30mins to get through 3ozs (85ml) of milk.	*Baby stops crying as mother enters room. Smiles at her as she is lifted. Settles at once to lusty sucking. Needs burping in the middle of feed. Takes 20mins over full feed.*
Feeding time	**30mins**	**20mins**
	Still needs more burping and has to be re-settled twice before he finally drops off.	*Sucks self to sleep at end of feed. Burps as she is lifted back into her cot, then goes instantly to sleep.*
Time to resettle baby	**15mins**	**2mins**
	Mother is free to get back into bed and go to sleep herself.	*Mother is free to get back into bed and go to sleep herself.*
Time from first being woken	**1hr 7mins**	**24mins**

Nobody *likes* giving nightfeeds, but where Mrs B could go back to sleep feeling that she had done a satisfactory job pleasantly, Mrs A was bound to feel that Babies are Hell and Nightfeeds a Torment. When the 5am summons racketed through the house she was all set to start another day feeling resentfully at odds with her baby.

Even if you feel that this proves the point where meeting your baby's *physical* needs is at issue, you may still feel that you should resist his demands when "he doesn't really *need* anything, he just wants attention." But your baby is not yet old enough to want anything that is not also a need. Attention from adults *is* a real need; just as real as his physical needs. Without food or warmth he will die; without social attention from adults he will not be able to become a full human being.

Your baby needs you not only to provide for his bodily needs but for comfort and reassurance. He needs you to interpret the world for him, to demonstrate and help him practise all the thousands of skills he must acquire. He needs you to do for him all the things which neither his brain nor his muscles can yet manage. He needs you to be his special person; to talk to him and to love him so that he too can learn to be a special individual person who can talk and who can love.

Be glad and honoured that your baby needs you so much. He is probably the only person in the world who will love you 100 per cent without criticism or reservation. Enjoy his company; he is probably the only person in the world who always wants to be with you and would never prefer anyone else. Make him feel good and let him make you feel good, too. You have everything to gain and nothing to lose.

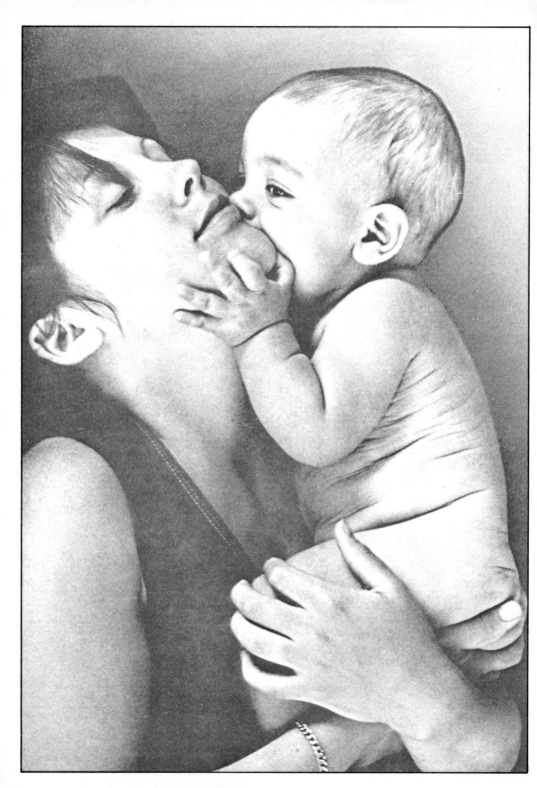

CHAPTER FOUR

THE OLDER BABY

From six months to one year

In this half of his first year your baby will be ready to use the control over his body for which he has worked so hard. He will sit alone, crawl about, and get hold of anything that is left within his reach. He will discover fascinating things to do with those objects too. He will find a wastepaper basket and empty it, find a book and scrumple it, find the record player and open it, find the cat's food and eat it. . . . He will no longer have to be content with the places you put him and the things that you bring him. He will need your constant vigilance. But it is not only for safety reasons that he will need your continual attention; he needs it for emotional reasons too. There is nothing more devoted than a six month baby who has been allowed to attach himself to his mother – except that same baby, three months later!

During these months, the attachment to you which began as soon as the baby could distinguish his "special people" from people in general, turns into a love affair from his point of view. He has learned to know and love you better than anyone else and now he wants you all the time and all to himself. He does not want to share you or to have you give your time and attention to anyone or anything else. His ideal would be your continual presence and constant attention. He feels passionately for you physically. He will sit on you, play with you, stroke and pull you, pop food (and worse) in your mouth and generally behave as if your body belonged to him.

The possessive demands of a lover are delightful if you love him or her but irritating if you do not. In the same way, the physical and emotional relationship which babies in this age-group demand of their mothers tends to please and flatter those who have enjoyed mother-hood so far. But it can be too much for those who are already finding their babies over-demanding, and who fear, as the clinginess increases, that they may be getting spoiled. Such a mother may find her baby's physical demonstrativeness positively embarrassing. Taught, all her life, to keep her own feelings under control, neither displaying nor giving way to them, she is faced with a baby who is simply demanding to be cuddled and kissed, patted and stroked. He holds out his arms for more, laughing with glee when he is tickled, sucking his mother's nose if it happens to come within range and stretching and purring like a sensuous kitten when it is time for a bath or a change of nappy.

If you can persuade yourself to accept and be proud of your own prime importance to your baby, you may find that you can revel with him in the relationship. Look at yourself through your baby's eyes and you will see yourself as good and warm and loving; worthy of all this devotion and with plenty of your own to offer. If you can, you should. The baby is practising loving for life. The more he can love, now, and feel himself loved back, the more generous with, and accepting of, all kinds of love he will be, right through his life. He will find it easy to respond to the emotional needs of your grandchildren when his turn comes for parenthood. You will help yourself, too. Finding your baby irresistibly delicious will help you, more than anything else, to ride comfortably through the hardworking and sometimes stressful months ahead.

At six or seven months all the signs of your baby's devotion are positive ones. He is nice to everybody but he is nicest of all to you. His swiftest, widest grins, his longest "conversations", his earliest laughter and very first "songs" are all saved for you. But soon you will see a negative side to all this joy. If he so much likes to have you with him, it is natural that he should come to dislike having you leave him. He will probably reach a point, at around eight months, when he tries to keep you in sight every moment of his waking day; when he cannot, he will be uneasy, tearful or even panic-stricken.

Psychologists call this reaction "separation anxiety", but whether or not you see anything worthy of such a name in your baby depends both on his physical development and on his exact home circumstances. If he can already crawl when the uneasiness first strikes him, he will keep you in sight simply by crawling after you wherever you go. If you happen to spend your days in an open-plan single-storey space, he may hardly ever have to watch you vanishing. But if he gets anxious about you before he gets mobile, he will be in quite a different situation. He cannot follow you so he will keep an eagle eye on you instead, starting to whimper whenever you move from his immediate vicinity.

On a good day you probably will not find it difficult to help your baby keep you in sight. You arrange life so that you can do your things while he does his close by. You get into the habit of chatting to him while you work, commenting on his activities without interrupting your own. When you must leave the room, you either wait for him to follow or you scoop him up and take him with you to the front door or to the clothes line. . . . But on another day and in another mood you may find yourself resenting his minute-by minute dependence. You are being loved more than you can stand. Once irritation begins to grow inside you, his behaviour feeds it with each successive half hour. You leave the room and he howls. You come back, comfort him and start to iron. He rolls and crawls beneath your feet, almost pulling the iron on to himself by its flex. A friend comes for coffee and, determined not to lose your attention completely, the baby insists on sitting on your lap, using all his new sounds to join, or interrupt, the conversation. To crown it all, when your friend leaves you go to the lavatory, only to find your little burden thundering piteously on the door. . . . Every mother has days like that sometimes. But they are no fun. You can keep them as few and as brief as possible if you look at the baby's feelings from his, rather than your, point of view.

To you, it seems totally unnecessary for the baby to cry just because you have gone to the clothes line. But when the baby loses sight of you, he *minds*. You are the centre of his world; the mirror in which he sees himself and everything else; his manager, who copes with him and helps him cope with other things. When you go away from him *you* know where you are going and how short a time you will be gone, but *he* does not. This kind of thinking is much too difficult for him. Over months and years he will learn that wherever you have gone you will always return. But right now he only knows that you have vanished and that he feels bereft.

If you try to override his feelings, ignoring his cries, prising off his clinging arms or shutting him in a playpen to stop him following, he will get more and more anxious. The more anxious he feels the more determinedly he will cling to you. If you try stealth, sneaking out of the room when he is busily occupied, he will occupy himself less and less because he will keep an ever-closer eye on your movements. Once you can accept that his feelings are real and, in terms of his stage of thought-development, reasonable, separation anxiety becomes much easier to live with. Take him around the house with you whenever you can and let him follow when he is able. When you must leave him, find a phrase that you always use to signal your departure, such as "bye-bye for now". This will give him fair warning, so that he does not feel deserted or betrayed. Another phrase – a "here I am again" – can mark a definite ending to the separation, something that he will gradually come to recognize and expect after any parting.
Obviously you will not want to leave your baby, during this especially clingy phase, more often or for longer than you need. But everyone needs a break sometimes, and there is always the possibility that illness or some other drama will make a short absence from home a necessity. So try, from the beginning of this age period, to get the baby accustomed to being looked after by at least one other person. If he has a close relationship with his father, a relative or a neigh-bour, you will leave him, when you must, with somebody he can use as his "completing half" while you are away. He will not be quite

happy nor feel quite himself until he has you again. But at least you will have left him on a life-raft rather than struggling in a sea of complete despair.

Towards the end of this first year your baby may seem to add anxiety about contact with people he does not know to his anxiety about being apart from you. Usually the two kinds of fear are mixed together because the occasions when you notice that he is extremely shy with strangers are the ones when you want to detach him from yourself. Perhaps you want to hand him to an admirer who asks for a cuddle; perhaps the clinic nurse tries to undress him for examination or a stranger stops to chat with him as he sits in his pram outside the shop into which you have vanished. . . .

Usually it is not the strangers themselves who distress your baby; it is what they *do*. He is happy to smile and talk to people he does not know provided they behave discreetly and keep their distance, but if they try to make physical contact with him he objects. It is reasonable enough. Some adults are shyer than others but even the least shy would be disconcerted if a stranger rushed up in the street and kissed and hugged him or her. We like to know people a little before we accept physical affection from them; babies feel the same.

If the baby is allowed to peep over your shoulder at the people in shops and buses, to play peek-a-boo with visitors around your legs and to go voluntarily towards them when curiosity overcomes shyness, he is far more likely to feel like making friends with people who are at present strangers. Letting him make the social running now will produce a toddler who is confident and interested in new people.

Anxieties over being away from you and being with people who are neither you nor known friends, are real fears. Like other fears they will die down most quickly in babies who are given least cause to feel them. At present your baby is too newly in love with you to take you for granted. But if you can ride him through this period of intense and anxious attachment on a wave of securely returned and protective adoration, he will come to take your love and your safety for granted in the end. Only when he has had a full measure of you will he be ready for other adults and for other children. Only a ground-base of confidence in his home relationships will make him free and ready to turn his attention outwards as he gets older.

Feeding and growing

Just as babies' ideal rate of weight gain slows down in their second three months from about 6–8ozs (170–227g) per week to around 4–5ozs (114–142g) per week, so it now slows down even further. From around six months to the first birthday a weekly gain of 2–3ozs (57–85g) with an overall height increase of 3–4 inches (8–10cm) is perfectly adequate.

Although the increasing growth of all babies will still follow the "average" curves given on the chart (see p. 506) you can expect more wiggles in the record that you keep for your own growing baby. Illness may mean no weight gain at all for a couple of weeks. A high gain will then catch the baby up. Once you have really embarked on solid feeding, food preferences will make the weight gain more variable too. If your baby gets a passion for some very nourishing dish such as baked cheese custard, and eats it for supper every night for a week more weight will be gained than during the week when the preferred food was vegetable soup.

Unless you or your doctor are worried about the baby's weight gain or general health, there is no longer any point in weekly weighing. Monthly is ample.

Type of milk

By six months, a bottle-fed baby can safely give up drinking special formula and change to ordinary cow's milk – as long as it is pasteurized or sterilized. A breast-fed baby can have cow's milk mixed with cereals, or for drinking from a cup. Never give a baby milk that is untreated and direct from a cow. The cow's health or the hygiene of the milking arrangements may leave a great deal to be desired. If you are in doubt, boil the milk you use for the baby. Remember that as long as your baby uses a bottle, it needs sterilizing whatever kind of milk he has.

Here again are the heights and weights for the babies you first met on p. 37. All three slow their growth rate now. All grow at similar rates while maintaining their differences from one another. Their curves are therefore like those on p. 506, even though, being individual children, their actual measurements differ from the average.

HEIGHT

LONG
AVERAGE
SHORT

WEIGHT

HEAVY
AVERAGE
LIGHT

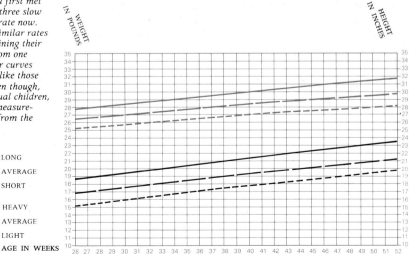

Effect of changing to ordinary milk

The changeover from formula means less expense and less trouble for you. But it also means that your baby's milk will be a slightly less perfect food than before. Ordinary cow's milk is not fortified with extra vitamins and iron, as baby formulae are, and it is not as well balanced for a human baby's needs as breast milk. So once you have made the change, you need to take a little more trouble about the solid foods that you give your baby (see p. 209). Above all, babies on cow's milk should have multivitamin drops every day.

Weaning

As long as your baby goes on having four feeds every day, and drinking 6–8ozs (170–227ml) of milk from the breast or from a bottle at each one, he will still be getting most of the food he needs from milk alone. You can assume that around 30ozs (852ml) of milk each day give him most of the calories and all of the protein he needs. So his solid foods are still only necessary to fill in the gap between the calories in his milk and the calories his appetite demands.

Soon after six months most babies will be ready to abandon their fourth feed – whether they have been having it early in the morning or late at night – and to settle down to a regular pattern of three meals per day. This at once does your baby out of 6–8ozs (170–227ml) of milk each day and puts his need for solid foods up.

A gradual start to weaning is likely to reduce his milk intake too. Although your baby will probably be perfectly content to abandon sucking at lunchtime and have a drink of milk from a cup instead, he will not get through as many ounces by this new drinking method. Determined efforts to wean him away from sucking altogether will undoubtedly cut his milk consumption right down, so you need to go at weaning very gently, making due allowance for the fact that if your baby can no longer have his milk by sucking breast or bottle he may well refuse to have it at all.

Weaning breast-fed babies

Breast-fed babies can go on having all their milk from their mothers until they are ready to have all of it from a cup. There is no reason why bottles should ever be introduced for milk, although you may already be using them for water and juice.

Exactly when you make the changeover will obviously depend on how anxious you are to stop from your own point of view, and how luxuriously attached your baby is to the breast. You can leave it to the baby to run your milk supplies down just as he built them up when he was newborn. If, for example, you cut out his lunchtime breast-feed in favour of milk from a cup, your breasts will get less stimulation. Although you may feel uncomfortably full in the middle of the day on the first few occasions, your breasts will adjust and make less milk within two or three days. If you also offer your baby milk from a cup as well as solid food at his other meals, and then let him suck as much as he wants at the end of the meal, he will gradually take less and less from the breast so that you will make less. Over a few weeks he will probably reach a point where he is taking only a token few sucks in the morning and a small "comfort feed" at his bedtime. That last night-time session will be the last to be given up, but many babies will abandon it of their own accord by the time they are a year old.

If you do not want to go on being even partly committed to breast-feeding for this long you will probably be wise to introduce a bottle after all. Although your baby can be adequately nourished by solid foods and whatever milk he will drink from a cup, he may miss sucking badly, especially at bedtime.

Weaning bottle-fed babies

Some parents take a very easy-going attitude to weaning babies from their bottles. They are happy to let them move on gradually from taking all their food as milk from a bottle, to part by bottle and part by spoon, and then to taking most of their food off a spoon while still using the bottle for comfort-sucking.

Other parents feel quite differently. They regard bottles as a necessary evil and can hardly wait until the baby is capable of eating from a spoon and drinking from a cup.

There are advantages and disadvantages to both attitudes. The essential point is that you need to decide now, at around six months, what your attitude is going to be. Changing your minds half-way through the weaning period will not work very well. Let us look at some of the pros and cons of definite weaning and of leaving it up to the baby.

Leaving weaning to the baby

Advantages	Disadvantages
Sucking gives your baby a great deal of pleasure and security, so as well as being a way of feeding, sucking is a good way of soothing himself or of relaxing when he is tired or stressed. *Being allowed to suck milk for as long as he likes may make thumb or finger-sucking unnecessary. It may even modify his development of other comfort habits (see p. 216).*	*Babies become increasingly attached to their bottles, especially after about eight to nine months. If he goes on with it for much longer than this he may never spontaneously "wean himself", but may go on asking for his bottle right up to school age, giving it up finally as a positive decision when he decides that bottles are too babyish for his new school-boy self.*
A bottle-feed at bedtime usually means less fuss over settling for the night.	*Bottles at bedtime tend to turn into bottles in bed, because the toddler insists on taking it with him. While the habit certainly makes for peaceful evenings it also makes for decayed teeth (even unsweetened milk is extremely bad for teeth if they are constantly bathed in it). It is also risky in that the baby who goes to sleep with milk still dripping into his mouth could choke.*
	The baby may become so attached to his bottle that he turns to it whenever he is tired or upset. This often means that half-drunk bottles are left standing around wherever he has abandoned them, and then sucked again later when he discovers them again. Milk treated in this way is an ideal breeding ground for germs.
Sucking means that he will take plenty of milk, and this is a major help in providing him with a good diet.	*As he gets older and eats a normal mixed diet, a very great deal of milk, drunk primarily because he enjoys sucking his bottle, will make him fat.*

Weaning the baby	Advantages	Disadvantages
	If the bottle is gradually phased out of the baby's life by the time he is about nine months or one year old, he will miss it much less than if it is taken away from him forcibly later on.	*The baby may miss his sucking and search for other forms of comfort like sucking his thumb.*
	Weaning means an end to sterilizing bottles and to carrying feeding equipment with you wherever you go.	*His milk intake may drop so that it is difficult to make sure he gets enough of the right kinds of food.*
		You may be tempted to put pressure on him to eat more solid foods or to drink more from a cup than he takes willingly. This kind of pressure can start feeding problems.
		Bedtime troubles may begin.

A compromise weaning policy

If you start weaning your baby by around six months old and take about six months over gradually reducing dependence on the bottle, you will almost certainly find that you can get the best of both extremes. Take the process in very gradual stages:

Introduce a cup at 4–5 months and gradually get your baby accustomed to the idea that milk, pleasant tasting fruit juices and water can all come out of this as well as out of a bottle. By six months the baby will probably be willing to take all extra drinks from a cup so that juice and water never come from a bottle.

Abandon the lunchtime bottle in favour of solid foods, with milk from a cup, at around six months.

Abandon the late night bottle (or early morning one) as soon as the baby shows you, by sleeping right through the night, that three meals a day is now enough. But until the baby can manage this regularly, offer drinks from a cup together with hard finger-foods (see p. 145) as snacks to bridge the gap until the next meal.

If all goes smoothly, the baby will now only be having two bottles per day: one after the solid part of breakfast and the other after the solid part of supper, before bed-time.

Let the baby go on with these two bottles as long as they are drunk sitting on your lap. Somewhere around the first birthday the baby's drive to move around the room and to be independent will become so strong that he or she will hate sitting still. This is where you can practise a bit of parent-upmanship: if you *never*, even *once*, let the baby discover that a bottle can be taken around the room on crawling adventures, the baby will eventually want to move about more than to suck. Your baby's feelings will not be hurt because the bottle will be right there if it is wanted, but sucking will gradually be given up in favour of moving.

Don't weaken. Once this point has been reached it is important not to be trapped into letting the baby carry the bottle off "just this once". If you do – perhaps because you are visiting friends and you want them to see your relationship with the baby at its smoothest – he or she is bound to demand to carry it off again the next night and the one after.

Food and bliss in one.
Don't hurry to wean your baby
from "her" beloved breast . . .

. . . but when your baby is ready for other foods, fingers are the natural tools for eating. Make it easy with cubes and slices . . .

. . . it doesn't matter how the food gets there

. . . as long as it does, and he enjoys it

. . . spoons are fun too—fun to wave, to bang,
to bite, and fun to eat off—sometimes.

Don't use the bottle for anything other than milk. If you suddenly decide to give juice, or water from the bottle again – perhaps because it is the easiest way to carry it on a picnic – the baby is almost certain to fuss next time a drink is given from a cup.

Buy the baby a cup with a lid and a spout. Few babies can manage an ordinary cup without any help before they are a year old. Even babies who can drink from them before this will spill as they put the beaker down. But managing alone is important to your baby. The changeover from bottle to cup is likely to be greeted with far more enthusiasm if you do not have to insist on holding it. A spouted "teacher-beaker" will only drip milk if the baby up-ends it and it will not actually spill even when it is dropped. Furthermore drinking from the spout is a compromise between ordinary drinking and sucking and it is therefore a less abrupt change for the baby.

Solid foods

Quantities and qualities of solid foods

The average six month old baby needs about 800 calories every day (see Enc Diet). There are 280 calories in every pint of ordinary cow's milk, so as long as he is drinking, say, four 8oz (227ml) bottles each day he will be getting just over 575 calories from his milk alone. He will only need about 200 calories from solid foods. Two cans or jars of commercially prepared babyfood, or one of these and one helping of baby cereal will provide that amount of energy. If you expect him to eat three meals a day while drinking this much milk he is bound to get either fat or fussy or both.

As weaning progresses, your baby will drink less milk and therefore need more solid food to fill the calorie gap and give him energy for activity and growth. As long as he drinks one pint of milk every day he will continue to get plenty of first class protein, ample calcium and plenty of vitamins of the "B" group. He will not get enough iron or enough vitamin A, D or C. So when you are planning which solid foods to give him, it is sensible to make sure that they are rich in these particular nutrients. Detailed information is in Diet in the Encyclopedia, but a helping of fortified baby cereal will give him the iron he needs, while daily multi-vitamin drops will make certain that he gets the vitamins.

You do not have to try to persuade him to eat expensive high protein foods like meat and fish if he does not like them. His milk takes care of his protein requirements. There is no point, either, in going out of your way to buy the commercially prepared foods that use "high protein" as an advertising point. He cannot use protein over and above his body's needs. Give him whatever he likes to eat and whatever it is convenient for you to serve.

If your baby refuses milk altogether – perhaps because you have taken away his bottle and he resents being offered milk from a cup – then he must have a complete mixed diet (see Enc/Diet). But you will still find that milk is an excellent help in providing that diet because a good deal of milk can be "lost" in food preparation. It takes at least 2ozs (57ml) of milk, for example, to mix a helping of baby cereal to the soft texture babies usually prefer. It takes 1oz (28ml) to cream a small potato or to scramble an egg, and you can easily use 2ozs (57ml) in an egg custard.

What solid foods should your baby have?

As we saw in a previous chapter (see p. 141), ideas of which particular foods are suitable or unsuitable for babies vary dramatically from country to country. If few British babies like spaghetti with tomato sauce it is because they are seldom offered it until they are toddlers and have become accustomed to "British food". An Italian baby will have been given pasta dishes since weaning began. He will probably loathe mashed potatoes because he is not used to them.

There are very few foods which you normally serve to your family which the baby should not have. As long as you avoid much salt, hot spices, alcohol, coffee and tea, the baby can try anything you are cooking. You will soon find out whether he likes it and whether his digestion copes with it or not. But stick to the policies outlined earlier (see p. 141) of introducing new foods one at a time and in tiny amounts. If there is a digestive upset you will know what has caused it. If the baby is allergic to the food the reaction will be slight.

Many babies between 6 months and about 18 months are fed almost entirely on ready-prepared babyfoods. Surveys have shown that many families use no fresh foods at all in their babies' meals, with the possible exception of eggs.

Ready-prepared baby *cereals* are excellent foods. They are fortified with iron and with vitamins; they use milk for mixing. Your baby could benefit by going on having these once a day right through toddlerhood or until he gets fed up with them. You would have a hard job to duplicate them in your own kitchen and the ordinary breakfast cereals you serve to older children and adults are far less nutritious.

The commercially prepared cans and jars are a different matter. People who use these foods tend to swear by them while people who do not use them tend to scoff at them. Let us compare a commercially prepared "dinner" and "supper" variety with their home-cooked equivalents:

Canned "Beef dinner"	Home-cooked equivalent
	1 oz cooked lean minced beef
	1 tablespoon mashed potato
	1 dessertspoon mashed carrot
	1 tablespoon stock gravy
Quantity: 3 tablespoons	3 tablespoons
Protein: 7 grams	7½ grams
Calories: 123	130

Canned "Cheese & egg supper"	**Home-cooked equivalent**
	½ an egg
	¼oz cheddar cheese
	2ozs milk
	(baked to make a custard)
Quantity: 3 tablespoons	3 tablespoons
Protein: 4 grams	6½ grams
Calories: 75	110

As you can see, the first meal gives the baby almost exactly the same food value whether it comes out of a bought jar or can or one of your casseroles. The second home-cooked meal looks slightly different from the bought one but is merely a more concentrated food. Both home-cooked and commercial versions give the baby about 2 grams of protein for every 35 calories, but the home-cooked version provides more calories per tablespoon so the baby would get the same food value from a smaller quantity.

Clearly there is no significant nutritional difference between these dishes. But there are other differences between home-prepared and commercially prepared foods which may make one or the other form of food seem more desirable for your baby.

	Home-prepared foods	Commercially prepared foods
Convenience for you	*Can be a nuisance to prepare for the baby alone, although are no trouble if you are cooking for others and can adapt the meal.*	*Are never any trouble to prepare.*
	Awkward to carry hygienically or to find in strange places.	*Easy to carry with you and serve anywhere.*
Food value	*Variable. Freshly cooked and quickly served food will be excellent; leftovers may not be as good.*	*Always excellent and always the same, although different varieties have unexpected differences in calorie value, etc.*
Adaptability	*Can be adapted to suit your baby's individual appetite, taste and digestion. Can also be served in different ways to make a change in appearance or texture. Different kinds of food can be served separately so that the baby can discover what food he or she likes and dislikes and choose what to eat and what to leave.*	*Cannot be adapted at all. A meal is a meal, with everything mixed together so that a fat baby must have all the carbohydrate if he or she is to have the meat; a bored baby must see a dish that always looks the same, and a baby of taste cannot separate peas from carrots.*
	Familiar foods can be made suitable for finger-feeding as the baby gets older, with cubed or grated, rather than pureed, vegetables, cheeses, etc.	*Finger-feeding is impossible. "Lumpy" varieties made for older babies are often disliked.*

Preparation for family meals	*Excellent; the baby will become accustomed to various tastes and textures and eventually see that he or she is eating the same as you.*	*Not good. All tend to be bland, so that "apple variety" is no preparation for the tartness of fresh stewed apple. The baby may become so used to consistently smooth textures that food that needs chewing is rejected. The baby's food does not even look like yours.*

A mixture of home-prepared and commercially prepared foods will probably suit you best. Your baby could share family meals whenever you are cooking something which he likes and which it is easy to make suitable for him – by withholding seasonings until his portion has been served, and by sieving or liquidizing.

When the main dish of a family meal consists of something he dislikes, which disagrees with him or which you consider unsuitable, it could be replaced with an egg, some cheese or a can or jar of commercially prepared babyfood; he could still share the accompanying vegetables.

When only the baby is to have a cooked meal, serving commercially prepared food will save you time and be better for him than a meal made-up of leftovers. While fresh fruits are ideal for his sweet courses, using cans or jars of fruit will save you stewing tiny portions, while other sweet varieties can be used to make a second course for him when other members of the family are not having one.

When you are going out, commercially prepared foods make it easy to give him a meal which is adequate both nutritionally and from the point of view of hygiene.

Self-feeding

Problems over a baby's eating often dominate the lives of whole families for months on end, as we shall see (see p. 287). You can do a great deal to avoid them by cultivating a relaxed and accepting attitude now. Ideally your baby should feel that eating is something pleasurable which he himself does because *he wants and enjoys the food*. He should not be made to feel that eating is a duty and something which is done to him because *you want him to have the food*.

At six to eight months, your baby is bound to be fairly passive during eating, because he has to be fed: he cannot yet manage to feed himself. But being fed is an uncomfortable business. Try exchanging a few spoonfuls with your partner and you will find that the food never comes at exactly the rate or in exactly the combinations you would have chosen and that the whole business makes you feel extraordinarily helpless. Keep the months when your baby must put up with this to a minimum by encouraging him to take part in the process himself and by handing it over completely to him as soon as he can get the food from plate to mouth by any means he chooses and no matter how much mess results.

Give your baby a spoon as soon as he will take one from you, even if he merely bites and waves it. Let him do what he likes with the spoon – by around eight months he will sometimes manage to dip and lick it. A few weeks later he will actually eat off it – sometimes. In the meantime use a second spoon yourself and be prepared to swap your loaded one for his empty one whenever he gestures towards it.

Positively encourage your baby to eat with fingers. If you let him dabble in his food and then suck his fists at six months, he will soon learn to do it on purpose. You will be able to slow down your spoon-work to let him get as much food for himself as he can.

A spoon for
messy fun . . .

. . . soon becomes
an efficient tool
for eating.

Give your baby some easy finger-foods. While dipping and sucking are fun, picking up cubes of bread and butter or diced cooked carrots or pinches of grated cheese is much more satisfactory. At six months these finger-foods will keep him actively involved in his meal while you feed him the mushy food. By nine months to a year he will hardly need any mushy food at all. He will eat with his fingers and sometimes with a spoon, and your help will be limited to helping him get the last bits of food that fingers cannot cope with, like custard and gravy.

Don't impose your ideas of suitable combinations. If he wants to dip cheese in chocolate pudding or stir bread into his jelly, why should you care? Every society has its own conventions about what goes with what. He will adopt yours in the end.

Don't try to make your baby eat anything without eagerness. Many foods are good for him but none are irreplaceable or worth the dangers of persuasion or force. When he has had enough food it is actually better for him to stop eating, so don't keep him sitting there hoping he will eat a bit more.

Don't make the baby eat different courses in their "proper" order. If you will not produce his sweet course until he has eaten the main course, he will often miss the pudding altogether because the thought of it will not encourage him to finish meat that he does not want. Later on, when he understands what you are doing, it will only make him want the forbidden sweet more.

Expect a mess and arrange to cope with it. A really efficient bib (perhaps the kind with an ever-open pocket at the bottom to catch his dribbles and misses) will keep his clothes clean. A thick layer of newspaper under his chair will catch the rest and can simply be thrown away afterwards. If you simply cannot feed him in a public place without finding yourself holding his hands out of the way while you pop neat spoonfuls in his mouth, feed him in private. Trying to make him eat tidily is the best possible way of putting him off the whole business.

If you think your baby eats too little

Beware! You are almost certainly wrong because babies are designed for survival and will not, under any circumstances, starve themselves if they are offered milk and manageable solid foods. Worrying about the amount your child eats may create real problems for all of you later on (see p. 287), so cultivate the habit of trusting the baby to know how much is enough. If this trust eludes you:

Look at the baby's growth. If the upward curve on his weight and length chart is steady, he is getting enough to eat.

Look at the baby's energy and vitality. If he is lively and active, he is not going short of food.

Consider the baby's milk intake and remind yourself that milk is food. He may be drinking almost everything he needs.

If you are still tempted to push food at him, have him checked by your doctor. Even if he can see at a glance that your baby is well-nourished, he will be happy to give you the time necessary for reassurance. He will know how important it is for you to relax about your baby's eating before he enters toddlerhood.

Sleeping

Just as parents often expect babies to eat more than they need, thus starting feeding problems, so they often expect them to sleep more than they need, thus inventing sleeping problems.

Babies' need for sleep varies widely. Your baby's need in the second half of this first year will probably be consistent with the first. A baby who has always slept comparatively long hours will continue to do so. One who has always been comparatively wakeful will continue this pattern. But, overall, the number of hours per day which the baby spends sleeping will drop. Although it is often said that babies in this age-group will, and "should", sleep for 14–16 hours out of every 24, research has shown that the average number of hours slept is around 13 and the range around that average runs from as few as 9 to as many as 18 per day.

Although there is still some connection between the baby's eating and his sleeping, so that a good meal still makes him inclined to feel sleepy, the connection is not nearly as strong as it was. He will not necessarily fall asleep after each meal; intriguing activities may be enough to keep him interested and awake. His pattern of sleep during this half year is likely to consist of a 12 hour night, which may or may not be broken by brief awakenings, and two separate "naps" during the day, which may be anything from twenty minutes to three hours long.

At six months the baby will still fall asleep when he needs to. Nothing except acute hunger, illness or pain will keep him awake. So if you put him comfortably to bed at night and settle him for naps during the day, you can assume that he will sleep if he needs to and that if he does not sleep, he does not need to.

After about nine months this changes. The baby becomes able to keep himself awake, or to be kept awake, by excitement, tension or a reluctance to release himself from the world, or from you, by falling asleep.

Difficulty over going to sleep

This is one of the most common and most disruptive of all child-rearing problems. You are almost certain to suffer from it with at least one of your children, so do not add to your misery, when it first strikes, by assuming that everybody else's child goes to bed like an angel, and that your child's behaviour is your fault.

Trouble when the baby is put to bed at night becomes common at around nine months, the first age at which children are able to keep themselves awake on purpose. After this time you cannot assume that your baby will sleep if he is tired and that if he does not sleep he is not tired. The reverse can be true. The baby can get over-tired; if this happens he becomes so strung up and tense that he cannot relax enough to go to sleep.

The first signs of trouble sometimes follow an obvious upset. For example, research has shown that many babies who have been admitted to hospital, even for a few days, have trouble settling to sleep once they return home. But the disturbance that starts night-time trouble need not be a traumatic one. A holiday away from home can break the baby's routines so that problems begin when the family returns home. A new room can disturb him in the same way; even a turn around of the furniture in his old room can leave him feeling disorientated and unable to drop easily into sleep. So since bedtime trouble is a great deal easier to prevent than it is to cure, it is worth being extra careful about introducing major changes into your baby's surroundings during this age period. Even the most glorious holiday abroad may in the end cause more trouble than it was worth.

It is more usual, though, for trouble over going to sleep at night to start gradually without any obvious cause. The basic factor that lies beneath it is your baby's passionate attachment to you. If he allows himself to go to sleep, he allows himself to go away from you altogether. Rather than do this he will scream and cry when you leave him; greet your return with delight and scream again as soon as you leave. If you sit with him, he will lie quietly; but as soon as you move towards the door, he will snap fully awake again. His ability to keep himself awake will certainly outlast your patience. After all he has nothing else to do all evening; you have plenty.

Preventing difficulty over going to sleep The answer lies in making it possible for your baby to release you gradually at night. Your aim is to narrow the gap, for the baby, between the state of being awake and with you and the state of being asleep and without you. If he is suddenly carried away from the warm, bright living room, full of the pleasant and familiar sounds of people, up three flights of stairs to a cool, dim, silent room on the top floor, put to bed and then left to listen to your footsteps receding, he is likely to panic. Exactly what he thinks we cannot know, but his sobs seem to say "you are going, you are gone, I have lost you, I am alone forever...."

Re-organizing his bedtime routine and his sleeping arrangements may enable you to soften this situation for him. If he is bathed, taken down to the family for supper, played with by an adult for a few minutes, and then taken to a nearby room with the lights on, the door open and all those family sounds still audible, he will feel far less cut off. If, instead of instantly going right away, you spend the next ten minutes or so tidying away dirty clothes, readying things for the next morning and generally pottering around near his open door, he can settle himself and begin to drift towards sleep in the comfortable knowledge of your presence. But eventually you have to leave. If you have managed to prevent your child feeling panic-stricken and bereft by your departure, these are months during which he will develop ways of giving *himself* security and comfort. He will use these to help himself cope with being without you.

Comfort habits A baby's comfort habits are under his own control in a way which the comfort which he gets from other people is not. He cannot force you to stay with him or to go on cuddling him; the amount of comfort you will give him is up to you. But he can rely on as much comfort as he wants if it comes from himself.

This is both the strength and the weakness of all comfort habits. They are good for the baby because they give him an independent and autonomous source of security; make him more able to rely on himself and leave him less at the mercy of the adult world. But they can be bad for the baby if he relies on them so much that he cuts himself off from the kinds of comfort which do come from other people. In general, then, a baby who uses a comfort habit to keep himself calm and relaxed while his mother leaves him to fall asleep at night is doing himself nothing but good. But a baby who often uses that comfort habit during the day, when his mother is present and the world of toys, play and exploration is open to him, is showing signs that all is not well. Of course an occasional incident need not worry you. His desire to rock in a corner instead of playing, today, probably means nothing more than that he is particularly tired or is feeling unwell. But if this kind of behaviour were usual for him it could mean that he needed to give himself a lot of comforting because he was not getting enough from you. At the furthest extreme, a child who is totally withdrawn into a world of rhythmic rocking is usually showing us that he cannot manage or get satisfaction from the world of people and activity.

Sucking is the most basic of all comfort habits. Your baby may have been sucking his fingers, thumb or a dummy for months. But now the sucking takes on a new significance for him. He may be able to let you leave him calmly provided he is sucking, but not otherwise. As you leave, he sucks harder. He sucks instead of crying; uses the comfort of the sucking instead of the comfort of you. Sucking is so basic that your baby may combine it, now, with other forms of comfort.

Cuddlies. Dignified by psychologists with the name of "transitional comfort objects", these are soft things, ranging from gauze nappies through old cot blankets to more conventional soft toys, which many children adopt with passion at about this time and use either with, or instead of, sucking. A baby's cuddly takes on a very real emotional importance for him. It is his familiar; the thing that spells safety and security, wards off evil and promises your return. He may simply hold and finger it or he may use it in all kinds of elaborate ways. A scarf, for example, may be wound round his head with one end looped across his face so that he can suck his thumb through it.

If your baby has adopted something in this way it will be his most important possession; the thing that must not be forgotten when you go on holiday nor left behind if he has to go to hospital. You probably will not even be able to wash it as often as you would like. Hygiene will lead to protests because you have ruined its precious familiar smell! Parents with foresight will quickly realize that, with years of use ahead of it, the child's cuddly had better be duplicated in case of disaster. If it is something simple like a gauze nappy, you can put two or three away for emergencies. If it is a soft toy, it would be wise to buy a second and put that somewhere safe. If it is a piece of blanket or rag, you may be able to cut it in half without the baby noticing and keep the second half against the dreadful day when the first falls to pieces or gets thrown away. Such a "second" will not entirely prevent misery, because the new object will not look or feel or smell quite the same as the one that has shared your baby's cot for months or years. But it will be very much better than nothing.

Rhythmical movements. Whether he sucks and/or has a cuddly or not, your baby may adopt other ways of relaxing himself for sleep. He may twist his ear, twiddle his hair, rock on hands and knees so that his cot thunders across the floor, bang his head against the cot bars. Any particular habit he takes to will be rhythmical.

Head banging is a slightly worrying habit even if the baby only does it in his cot at night. Some babies do it hard enough to hurt, and seem displeased when their parents pad the end of the cot so that it does not hurt any more. If your baby should be one of these, ask yourself why he should want to cause himself pain. It may be that he is generally upset or disturbed (see Enc/Head banging).

Rituals. These are comfort habits which your baby will build with your help. They are really part of making the process of releasing you a gradual one. A baby who is building bedtime rituals will insist that you do exactly the same thing tonight as you did last night; tomorrow he will want the same again. The only "risk" is that once the two of you have begun to formalize his going-to-bed routines in this way, he may build the ritual up so that what took three minutes each night when he was nine months old takes thirty-five minutes when he is three!

Your personal rituals will depend on your own routines, but a very normal bedtime process might go something like this: you carry the baby into his room and around it so that he can say "goodnight" to three favourite pictures. Then you hold him up to get two soft toys off the shelf. Next, baby and toys are put into the cot, each gets a kiss in turn and the baby gets an extra one. You then cover him up, turn down the lights, kiss him one more time, sing a lullaby, spin his mobile and leave, adjusting the door to an exact six inches open.

If your baby does take to a ritual of this kind, he will come to expect every bit of it every night. Boring for you perhaps, but infinitely better than enduring anxious screams. Do make sure that anyone who is ever going to put your baby to bed knows the details of his chosen ritual. His grandmother cannot be expected to cope successfully while you have an evening out if she is not equipped with the same tools for peace that you use yourself.

If bedtime still upsets your baby . . . Sometimes, despite all your attempts to make it easy for your child to let you go, with plenty of encouragement of comfort habits and lots of cooperation in making gentle rituals, a baby does still become really upset about going to bed. If this happens to you, the basic principle is this: don't ever leave him crying alone, but don't ever get him up again either. If you leave him crying, you will increase his feeling that it is not safe to let you go because you may never come back. But if you get him up again, you make him believe that you agree with him that to be left alone in his cot is intolerable. So the idea is: *visit often but pick up never.*

Try to keep the pre-bedtime hour affectionate and enjoyable. A squabble over supper or a jealous tussle for father's attention will be enough to increase his uncertainty about how much he loves and is loved, and therefore how safe it is to let you leave him. This is not the time of day for sudden discipline.

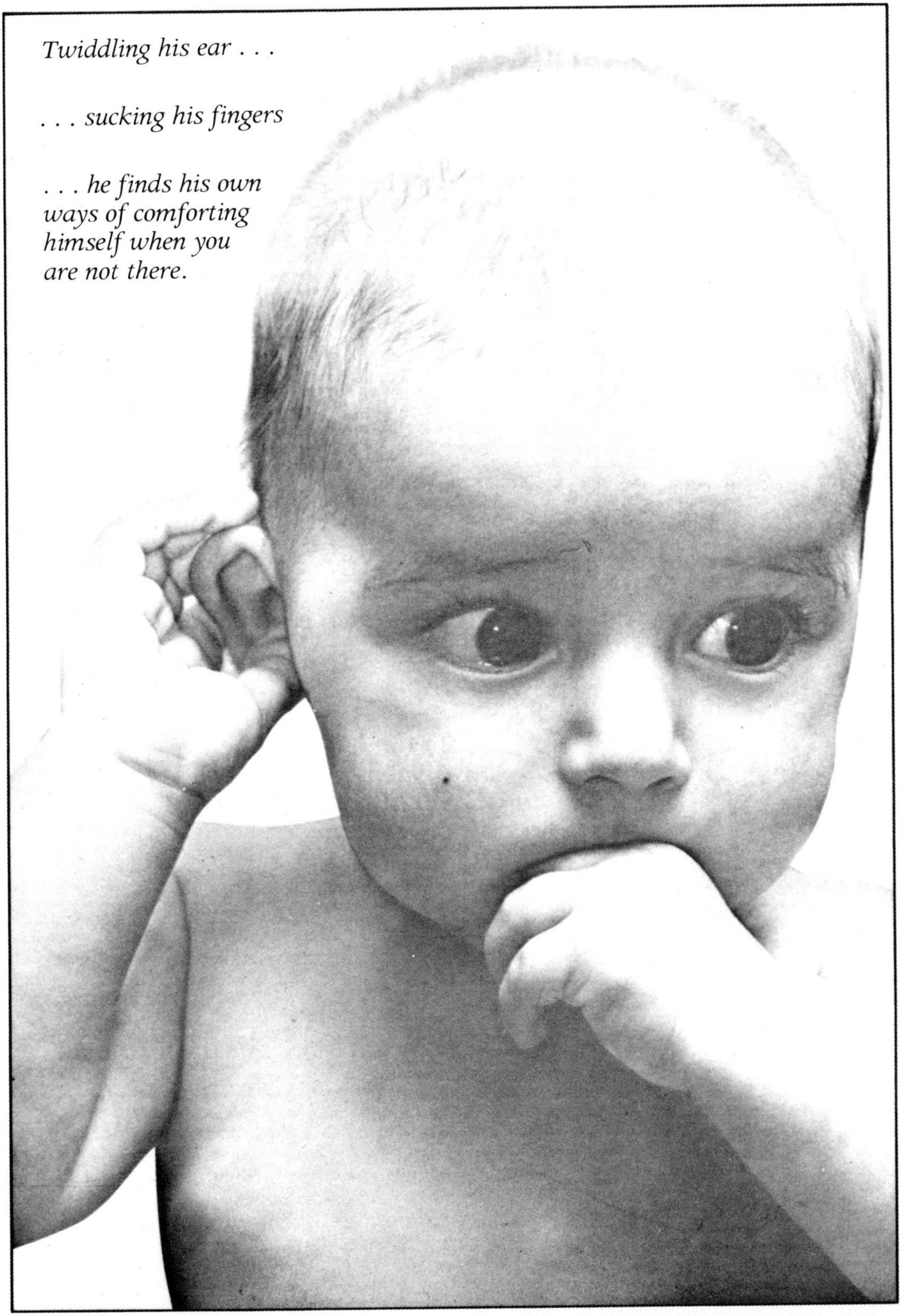

Twiddling his ear . . .

. . . sucking his fingers

. . . he finds his own
ways of comforting
himself when you
are not there.

Always make sure that the baby knows bedtime is coming up, by following the same evening routine of, for example, bath, play, supper, bed.

Keep to going-to-bed rituals, or even invent some for your baby. Getting a teddy settled into bed, for example, can be a good lead in to getting him settled too.

If, after all this, your baby cries when you leave, go back. Reassure him that you are still close by; kiss him again and leave. You may have to repeat this over and over again, but it is the only sure way eventually to convince him both that you *will* come and that you *will not* get him up.

If repeated visits are necessary, try using your voice alone. It may be enough reassurance for the baby if you simply call pleasantly to him. If so, you can at least keep him calm while simultaneously cooking supper and saving your own legs.

Waking in the night

Although babies can, and often do, sleep solidly for a 12 hour period, some wake frequently, even if only briefly. This kind of waking used to be called a "bad habit": babies were ignored when they woke or even scolded or smacked for awakening, the argument being that this would "break the habit". But the baby cannot wake himself on purpose. If something disturbs him before he has had enough sleep, leaving him to cry is not going to prevent the same thing (or something different) from awakening him the next night. "He will soon learn not to do it", people say. But how can your baby learn not to do something which is outside his conscious control?

The baby is at an age and stage where his daytime care is extremely demanding. A continuance of disturbed nights can be very exhausting for you. So if something external (see below) is disturbing him, it will be worth almost any amount of trouble to prevent it. If the trouble is internal (see opposite), so that you cannot actually stop the waking up, it may help, now that feeding is not part of the night waking pattern, if you decide between you to take responsibility for the baby on alternate nights. The "off-duty" partner may still be awakened by the baby but at least he or she need not get out of bed.

Outside disturbances

Some of the night waking of this age group is due to the baby being woken up by external events. He no longer sleeps as deeply as he did when he was younger. You cannot necessarily assume that once he is asleep, almost nothing will wake him.

Noises which blur into the general level of background noise during the day can become disturbingly sharp in the comparative silence of the night. Heavy traffic on the road outside his room, low flying aircraft or trains on a nearby line may all disturb him.

He may also sense comings and goings around him even if they are not very noisy. Admiring visitors peeping into his room may wake him. If he shares your room, your movements, your whispered conversations and your sleeping noises may all tend to disturb him, too.

Getting cold will make him more likely to wake up. A very cool room is much less dangerous to him than it was when he was younger because he will not pass straight from deep sleep into a chilled state, but if he kicks his covers off and begins to cool, he will also begin to wake. If nothing happens to warm him again, he will wake right up and cry.

A very sore bottom, due to nappy rash, sometimes means a lot of night waking because the urine stings when he wets himself.

Reorganize the baby's sleeping arrangements so that noises are less likely to disturb him. If the room he is in is the only one available, you could double-glaze its windows. Even heavy curtains help.

Don't let visitors go into your baby's bedroom and don't go in yourself unless you have reason to believe he needs you. Leave his door ajar so you can take a reassuring peep from a distance.

Make sure the baby stays snugly warm. A baby bag or blanket sleeper will keep his own warmth insulated in even if he does kick off the blankets. More overnight heating in his room may be needed too.

Protect a sore bottom with a thick coating of a silicone-based protective cream at night and by using a one-way nappy.

Internal disturbances Unfortunately most of the night waking in this age group is due to disturbances that come from within the baby. Some kind of nightmare, or nightfright, is common. Of course there is no way that we can know what form it takes because the baby cannot tell us, but he wakes, usually, with a sudden terrified scream. He appears afraid, is completely reassured the moment one of his parents appears, and often goes back to sleep even as he is comforted. The baby may repeat this behaviour several times each night and every night for months. The pattern seems to be most common in those babies whose parents are afraid of spoiling them and therefore do not pick them up readily when they cry by day. It is almost as if the subconscious part of the baby's mind is making up at night for too little loving attention by day; making sure, during sleeping hours, of a love he feels uncertain of when he is awake. If your baby seems to be falling into this pattern try to put yourself into his place and see whether he might feel that he has to fight for your affectionate attention.

Slow up on anything that seems to be putting a strain on the baby. If you are trying to wean him from his bottle, for example (see p. 203), you may be going faster than he can easily bear. A return to some sucking could bring you more peace.

Make sure that bedtime is relaxed and enjoyable. Going to sleep feeling warmly loved and protected may help him to stay comfortably asleep all night.

If a pattern of waking is set . . . If a night waking pattern has been set, there is little that you can do but endure it, remembering that the faster you meet the baby's needs now, the shorter will be the time during which he needs you so often. Go to him immediately when he cries. The disturbance will cease as soon as he sees you, hears your voice or feels your stroking hand. With practice you can give this kind of instant comfort half asleep and roll straight back into bed.

*Awake early, with light and toys
and perhaps her own face for company,
she may keep herself happy . . .*

. . . at least for a while.

Waking early in the morning

The baby does not know what time it is. He wakes because he has had enough sleep. Once you have finally abandoned the idea of an early-morning bottle or breast-feed it is not very likely that you will be able to persuade him to go back to sleep again.

If he cries or shouts for you there is no point in trying to ignore him. You will have to go in the end so you might as well go at once. But you need not let him get up and start his day.

Make sure the baby has light to see by and toys to play with. If his room is dark in the early morning, leave a low wattage night-light burning. Put a selection of toys in or beside his cot and he may occupy himself, at least for a while.

Be prepared to make the baby comfortable by changing his nappy, removing his sleeping bag and offering him a drink. Ten minutes spent in this way may earn you another hour in bed.

Consider offering the baby the company of an older child if you have one. If the older child sleeps with the baby or is allowed to go to him when he wakes in the morning, they may entertain each other beautifully. There are no grown ups around to create jealousy; the baby is safely imprisoned in his cot so he cannot pull hair or steal toys; he has nobody to appeal to except the older child so he offers all the charm he normally reserves for adults. These early-morning play sessions sometimes create and often cement a close and affectionate relationship.

Wakeful babies and daytime sleep

As we saw earlier, babies who need much less daytime sleep than the average are harder work for their parents to look after, but get considerable advantages because of the extra hours they spend in looking, learning and interacting with adults.

Even if your baby only sleeps for twenty minutes on two occasions during each day, he may well be happy to spend much longer than this comfortably settled in his cot or pram with toys to play with and interesting things to look at (see p. 178). So don't be too quick to decide that because he does not actually sleep during each nap, he should not be put down to rest at all.

Stick to the routine of a morning and an afternoon rest. Ignore a brief protest on being left – any sensible well-attached baby is bound to announce that he would prefer you to stay with him. If after a couple of minutes he is happily playing or talking and looking at things, leave him. He may be enjoying a rest from his demanding life just as you are enjoying a rest from him.

Go to the baby quickly if he grumbles because of boredom. If you leave him he is bound to begin to feel that his pram is a prison. He will not go happily into it next time.

A wakeful baby is living a much fuller life than one who sleeps for several hours each day. You will have to find ways of getting on with your life while sharing it with your baby, rather than dividing it into periods of babycare and adult activity. The sections on pp. 267 and 272 should help you. So too should the thought that your baby is probably intelligent (most very wakeful babies are) and, with plenty of waking time spent with you, will probably turn into an extremely sociable and competent toddler.

Excreting

Once solid foods and/or cow's milk are added to breast milk or formula, the baby's digestion has to cope with food that moves more slowly through the intestines and contains more waste. The result is less frequent and bulkier stools which look and smell more like those of an older person.

Constipation

Babies vary in the frequency with which their bodies need to evacuate waste. A daily motion is not a prescription for, nor a sign of, good health. Your baby is only constipated if, when a motion is finally passed, it is dry and hard enough to make its passage difficult or painful.

If your baby does have hard motions, offer lots of extra drinks. Fruit juice or vegetable juice is good as the small amount of extra sugar has a mildly laxative effect.

Don't give any form of laxative without instructions from your doctor. They are practically never needed and it is a great mistake to try and override the body's natural rhythms.

Don't use soap sticks or suppositories without instructions from a doctor. The baby's bowels will open when they need to.

Diarrhoea

As we saw in an earlier chapter, new foods may prove difficult for a baby to digest at first. Undigested particles are a signal to go slow with that particular food. A lot of mucus usually means that the food was too coarse and needs sieving.

A sudden increase in his intake of sugar can also cause very loose stools, but on its own this will not make him ill. If, in addition to loose stools, he seems unwell, goes off his food, runs a fever and/or vomits, you should take him to your doctor on the same day. He may have gastro-enteritis. While this is not quite such a serious threat in this age group as to younger babies, the loss of fluid can still rapidly make them exceedingly ill. So get medical help quickly and, while you are waiting for it, offer him as much cool boiled water as he will drink. At this time, contrary to all other times, extra salt will be good for him. A quarter of a teaspoon dissolved in each pint of water you offer him will help his body retain the vital fluid.

Sensible precautions will help you avoid gastro-enteritis. The hygiene "rules" are the same as for younger babies (see p. 65) but in addition:

Don't stop sterilizing bottles, teats etc just because he now drinks ordinary milk. Add his teacher-beaker; that spout can trap bacteria-breeding drops.

Don't use the family milk bottle if it has been standing around the kitchen. Keep his milk covered and refrigerated.

Don't carry warm milk in a vacuum flask. Carry it cold and warm it when it is needed.

Don't buy dairy produce from a shop with no chiller. Cream buns, milkshakes etc. are not safe unless kept very cool.

Don't buy cream ices for the baby from ice cream vans. The ice cream itself is cold enough to be safe but the scoops and spillage may be contaminated. A wrapped water ice lolly is far safer.

"Potting" Late in the first year most babies have learned to sit up by themselves and some have adopted quite regular times of day for passing bowel movements. Some parents decide that they might as well sit their baby on a pot at these times. They call this "toilet training" but it is important to realize that there is no *training* in it at all. The baby is simply being put in the right place at the right time for the movement to be caught in a pot instead of a nappy. The baby can neither understand nor cooperate.

True toilet training means helping a child to recognize his own full bowel or bladder and then to do something about it – like telling his mother or going to find his pot. He cannot begin to be trained until he can recognize his own "need to go". Children are not capable of this recognition until they are *at least* a year old and often not until well into the second year.

Catching a baby's motions in a pot may seem harmless even if it is not doing anything towards eventual toilet training. But it is a mistake. If you start doing it when he is seven months old he probably will not object: the pot will seem no odder to him than some of the other places that you sit him down. But two months later he is likely to hate it. He has learned to crawl; he does not want to sit still anywhere for a minute longer than he need, and sitting on a pot seems to him the most pointless kind of sitting of all. When you sit him in his chair he gets a meal; when you sit him in his pushchair he gets a walk; when you sit him on his pot he gets nothing – except the movement which he was going to have anyway. So if you go along with his wishes, the pot that you introduce early will be abandoned again within a very few weeks. If you do not go along with his wishes you run a real risk of starting a pot-battle long before your child is physically ready to learn to use it properly.

There are other reasons for avoiding early "training" too. A little frivolous arithmetic will show that however successful you might be at catching your baby's motions, you will not save yourself any time and effort by doing so. Research has shown that no matter when you begin to introduce a baby to a pot, he will, on average, become reliably clean and dry by the middle of his third year. Suppose that you start putting him on a pot at six months, six times per day: you will have done so 4380 times before you reach your objective – a fully "trained" child. You will have had to undress and redress him on each occasion and you will have failed to catch the motion a good many times too so that there will still have been soiled nappies to launder. If you leave out this "catching" stage altogether and start proper toilet training at, say, eighteen months you will only have to pot your baby about 2000 times for the same effect. Since changing him is quicker than potting him, you have everything to gain by waiting from your own point of view as well as his. Don't buy a pot at all this year.

Everyday care

Now that your baby is older...

As babies get older they spend more and more time on the floor. Once they can crawl they get exceedingly dirty. Washing them is by no means as easy as with the younger age group who kept (more or less) still.

You will need to develop techniques for washing the face of a person who sucks the flannel whenever it comes near and for changing nappies while toes are being chewed. It is not easy but if your sense of humour stays intact, it can be fun.

Your baby's skin will have toughened up by now so you need not be so careful about patting dry instead of rubbing, or using unscented soap. Your child will enjoy a good rub. In fact he or she will probably enjoy being handled and physically fussed over altogether. If you want to try out trendy clothes or the latest babycare gadgets, now is the time....

Bathing

An evening bath is probably a "must" now. In the morning she only needs her bottom cleaned and her face and hands sponged, but by the evening she will be grubby from top to toe. Your baby will probably love being bathed. But it is a back-breaking job for you. Don't try to lean down to her, kneel on the floor so you are at her level. At six months she will try to do gymnastics all around the bath, making tidal waves and turning in your hands like a dolphin. Later she will struggle to sit up, her uncertain balance making a dowsing all too likely. By about eight months it may be easier to keep her safe in the bath if you put her into it in sitting position and hold her there. Keep hold of her every moment – she is slippery and so is the bath.

Kneel by the bath with an arm round her shoulders, holding her arm. Steady her with your other hand on her thigh.

Choose a moment when she is well-balanced to grab for what you need with the hand from her thigh. Have everything on the floor.

She will enjoy floating and pouring toys. Help her with that same hand. Don't remove the one that is around her.

Watch out for the soap; if it is within reach she will grab for it. Nasty to eat and painful if she then rubs her eyes....

A shiny tap will attract her attention too. If it is hot, wrap it in a washcloth, in case she wriggles near it even as you hold her.

At 9 or 10 months she may try to pull herself out of your grasp and stand up. Don't let her. The bath is too slippery to be safe.

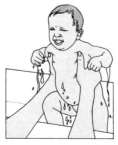

To lift her out, hold her firmly under both armpits. She is heavy, slippery and probably protesting....

Don't try to stand up with her until you have dried her on the floor.

Making bath time happy and safe

Do	Don't
Collect up everything you might need before you begin, and put it all where you can reach with one hand.	Even turn round to reach for something once she is in the water. It does not take her even one second to slide her head under.
Put a good warm bath mat beside the bath and reckon to kneel on it with your things.	Try to bath her from standing position, even from sitting on a stool; you can only hold her at her level.
Run all the water before you put her in. Wrap a washcloth round the hot tap if it still feels very hot to touch.	Risk even a trickle of extra hot water while she is in the bath; she could get a kicking toe under it.
Let her sit up if she wants to, keeping one arm round her. Keep your other hand free for washing and playing.	Let her practise her independent sitting balance in the water; a tumble could put her off her bath for months.
Give her suitable things to play with in the water.	Make bathing a question of washing and no fun.
Bath toddlers or older children separately just for these few months when the baby is nearly sitting or just sitting but not yet able to cope safely with the slippery surface.	Have a child in the water with her; a by-accident-on-purpose push or splash is all too easy. Don't even have another in the room if you can arrange occupation elsewhere. The baby needs your full attention.

Frightened babies

As at earlier ages the immediate answer to bathing a baby who is frightened is *don't*. Wash her as best you can right away from the bathroom. At the same time use her new mobility and her desire to explore to get her gradually used to thinking of water as fun. Sit her on a big towel on the floor beside a washing up bowl. Help her to splash and call her attention to the ripples. Once she will put her hands in she will probably play. Give her a beaker and a duck, and encourage "water play" at the end of every sponge bath. As soon as she has accepted that water is fun, she will probably enjoy putting her feet in and splashing, so spread newspaper under the bowl.

Once she enjoys splashing she needs a larger container. Her old baby bath is ideal. Don't put her in yet. She will soon try herself. . . .

When she tries to crawl in you will have dealt with the worst of her fear. A couple of hip-baths and you can . . .

. . . transfer the full baby bath from the floor to the empty big bath, and let her crawl in there too.

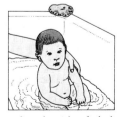

After a few nights of a bath in a bath she will happily accept the same three inches of water run directly into the tub.

Hairwashing

Whatever they feel about baths many babies develop an acute dislike of having their hair washed at around eight to nine months. This often remains a problem right through early childhood so it is worth doing what you can to get it right from the beginning.

The baby is usually afraid of getting *water* in her eyes. Don't make the mistake of thinking that she is crying because there is soap in her eyes and that splashing water in her face will make it better. Water was probably the trouble in the first place; if you add more and more she will think you are deliberately tormenting her. If it is clear that she is afraid of having water poured on her head, do not try to show her, by force, that there is nothing to be afraid of. If you try to wash or rinse her hair while she screams and struggles, you are bound to get water if not soap in her eyes. Her fears will be confirmed.

If a struggle has begun, give up. The baby's short memory is still on your side. Don't try to shampoo her hair again for at least a month. In the meantime sponge bits of food out of her hair and brush it with a soft damp brush to stop it looking lank and greasy. When you do try to shampoo again there are a few tricks you might find useful:

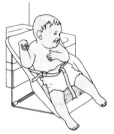
Sit her backwards on to the basin so that she cannot even see any water. Use her chair on a chair, or sit her on your lap.

Have the basin full of warm water, wet her hair by wiping over it with a wet flannel.

Pour "non-sting" shampoo into your hand and rub it over her head. She will not be frightened: all she feels is your familiar hand.

Rinse her hair by dipping the flannel repeatedly into the basin. She need never feel water pouring or dripping on her.

If the baby is still frightened

There are a few other tricks you can try, although none of them is a sure prescription for peace. It may be a matter of finding what your child dislikes least. Don't wash her hair in the bath. If you do, she will be aware of a great deal of water all around her, and her dislike of hair-washing will probably spill over into a dislike of being bathed at all.

Eye infections
If an eye infection ever requires treatment, ask your doctor for ointment, not drops. Most babies loathe having drops put in their eyes. Such treatment will start hairwashing troubles all over again.

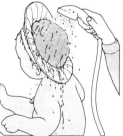

Lots of water play will help her to get used to putting water on her own face. A hand-shower is a good toy for this if the thermostat is safely accurate . . .

A rather small big brother can be a good example. Even if he is not keen himself he may put up with it to help reassure the baby, whose fears he can well understand.

A headband, bought or made by cutting the crown from a bathing cap, stops water crossing her hairline. Swimming goggles keep it out of her eyes. Once she believes you, the problem may be solved.

Nappy rash

The general toughening up of the baby's skin usually means that nappy rash is less of a problem than it was earlier in her life. But for some babies new maturity brings new problems. . . .

Protecting the baby's bottom at night

Sleeping through the night can lead to a sore bottom. The baby probably now goes for eight to twelve hours without a change of nappy and during that time she passes a great deal of urine. If she wears plastic pants, which efficiently keep moisture off her clothes and bedding, air is unable to circulate around her sodden skin. Her bottom is kept warm, wet and airless all night and is likely to get sore. If she does not wear plastic pants, her clothes and bedding will get wet which means that she will get cold and uncomfortable and you will have a heavy laundry load.

The answer usually lies in using comparatively *inefficient* plastic pants, which keep most of the moisture in but still allow some air to circulate. Use a one-way nappy next to her skin, and, if she wears towelling nappies, insert a disposable one between the one-way and the towelling nappies to provide extra padding. If she usually wears disposable nappies, she will need at least a double thickness by now. Whether you are using all disposable nappies or only using them as extra padding inside towelling ones, you can save money by buying them in rolls and cutting off the size you really need.

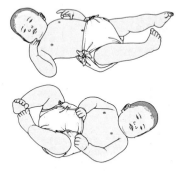

Tie-on plastic pants have just the right balance of efficiency and air circulation. They will not keep her bed perfectly dry but they will allow some evaporation. If you use popper-pants, leave the bottom snaps undone so the elastic legs are not pulled perfectly tight.

Protecting the baby's bottom by day

As we have seen (p. 190), it is very good for babies to play with no nappies on, or no clothes at all if the weather if hot enough. But once your baby can sit alone, and especially once she starts to roll over and crawl, her bottom will get rubbed against the carpet or the lawn and the friction will tend to make her skin sore. In the same way, sand on a beach may feel lovely at the time, but the grit will rub those soft creases. Once this has happened, urine and faeces are much more likely to sting and set up nappy rash. You may find that a pair of soft cotton underpants gives her most of the freedom of nakedness while protecting her skin.

Her bottom is less accustomed to sunlight than the rest of her. She will enjoy crawling around naked in the sunshine with her bottom up in the air, but twenty minutes of this will be enough to produce a burned bottom. Once again, use soft cotton pants to protect her. If her bottom does get burned a silicone-based cream will keep urine off it.

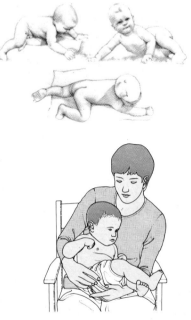

Cleanliness and hygiene

Once your baby can get around a room alone, picking things up to explore them by mouth as well as by hand, it is important to distinguish between cleanliness and hygiene. Cleanliness is anathema to an exploring baby who cannot learn and have fun while staying clean. But hygiene is vital to health. You will get the balance between the two about right if you are exceedingly fussy about food and excreta but not very fussy about the cleanliness of anything else.

Protecting your baby from bacteria

Good hygiene is a matter of protecting your baby from an overdose of harmful bacteria. There are bacteria everywhere but very few of them are harmful and the body's defences can cope adequately even with the harmful ones provided it gets them in small amounts. A potentially dangerous build up of bacteria is only likely to be present on an object which provides them with a breeding ground.

An object is *safe* when it is dry and free from food, even if it is dusty or generally grubby. The piece of paper your baby extracts from the waste-paper basket may not look *clean*, but it will not be a breeding ground for dangerous bacteria.

An object is *unsafe* when it has been in contact with food (especially milk) and then left at room temperature. The tiny piece of cream cake you dropped yesterday may still look quite edible, but it is likely to be teeming with bacteria. The rate at which they multiply is enormously fast.

If your kitchen hygiene is good, with adequate sterilization, refrigeration, and care about keeping cooked foods covered and cold *or* hot but never warm, you need not take any extra care about the rest of your house. Normal cleanliness is enough. There are, however, one or two traps for the unwary:

Bacteria regard excreted food as food, so lavatory hygiene and hand-washing are important. We all excrete bacteria in our faeces and even an invisible trace of faecal material will provide a bacterial breeding ground. So wash your hands after attending to your own or the baby's toilet needs, and wash the baby if he or she has been exploring while you changed a nappy. Be scrupulous, too, about mopping up any "accidents" or cleaning up after a baby who has burped up some milk.

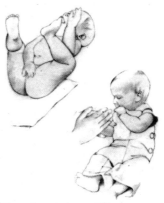

Bacteria regard animal food or excretions as food, so if you have pets as well as a baby, keep their food dishes out of reach and deal immediately and thoroughly with any animal "accident". Don't let the baby finger the dog or cat all over and then suck his or her hands: most animals keep themselves scrupulously clean, but some do not. When your baby is crawling in parks or gardens, you will obviously have to watch out for animal excreta.

Keeping poisons out of reach

Don't let concern about bacteria blind you to the much more likely hazard of poisonous substances (see Enc/Poisoning). A full ashtray will not give your baby gastro-enteritis but if he eats cigarette ends he will be exceedingly ill. That bottle of sherry will not give him gastro-enteritis either but the alcohol could kill him. It is not the grubbiness of that box that need worry you but the possibility that its paint contains lead. . . .

Teething

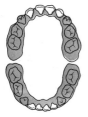

Teeth appear fast and furiously during this half year. First lower incisors, cut at around six months, are closely followed by their next door neighbours. At around seven months most babies produce a top incisor and by eight months all four of these top front teeth are often through. By nine to ten months the remaining two lower incisors appear so that babies have achieved a row of four top and four bottom teeth. There is usually a pause before the first molars. Some babies produce one of these by the first birthday, others not until a month or so after it. Few babies suffer anything but the most fleeting and trivial discomfort while cutting their front teeth. Their sharp, flat shape helps them to come through easily, more easily than the larger, broader molars which are to come. Make sure that your baby has plenty of things to bite. Fingers and toys are fine, but any hard (reasonably clean) smooth object will both help and provide an interesting change. Once the baby has two or three teeth, chewing on a variety of objects will also help to "file down" their exceedingly sharp points.

Teeth and weaning

As we said in a previous chapter (see p. 154), these first teeth are not chewing teeth and their appearance should not therefore speed up the process of weaning. But occasionally once a baby has a pair of bottom teeth and two or more top ones, he will try to chew the teat of his bottle or to nip your nipple. Don't decide that he is forcing you to wean him. As long as the teat or nipple is well back in his mouth in the proper position for sucking (see p. 71), he cannot bite: the position of his jaws prevents it. Biting is therefore only a problem when he has temporarily stopped sucking and is playing instead. Remove the teat or nipple from his mouth with a firm "no"; give it back if he wants to suck some more, but don't let him play with it in the front of his mouth. Many breast-fed babies actually learn not to bite after a week of this handling.

Looking after your baby's teeth

Once he has two or more teeth side by side, try to make sure that bits of his finger-foods do not get caught between them and stay in his mouth for hours. If you can see a piece of carrot or a shred of apple, remove it. Encourage him to like plain water to drink. As long as he is getting all the vitamin C he needs, plain water is better for his teeth than endless sweet drinks and it helps to rinse milk and other foods out of his mouth too.

As well as looking after the teeth that he now has, you should be thinking about the strength and health of his second teeth. Calcium and vitamin D are especially important for them, but you should also find out (from your doctor or local pharmacist) whether or not the drinking water contains adequate fluoride. If it does not, your doctor or your dentist can advise you about giving the baby extra fluoride in the form of tablets dissolved in his drinking water.

Crying and comforting

Most babies cry much less in the second half of this year than they did earlier in their lives. They cope more robustly with the hurly burly of ordinary daily life. The sudden loud noises and quick movements which used to make them startle and cry often now make them laugh. When things do displease them they will often express worry or alarm with facial expressions and whimpery sounds, only embarking on full-fledged crying if nobody comes and offers reassurance.

But although babies tend to cry less readily and less often than before, there are various aspects of their development in this half year which will lead to considerable crying if they are not understood. Learning to understand them in your baby is important because they are all developments which will continue into toddlerhood. Sensitive handling, which is well-tuned to your son's or daughter's needs and emotions now, will certainly make life easier for all of you later on.

Crying from fear

When your baby was younger he may have given the impression of being afraid of a great many things. Now he is much more confident about life in general but he is likely to develop intense fears about one or two particular things. He may, for example, be quite unworried by most loud noises, but appear terrified by the sound of the vacuum cleaner. He may enjoy every kind of rough and tumble play but intensely dislike having clothes pulled on or off over his head. He may love his bath and everything to do with water, but then panic if he sees the water running out of the plughole.

Fears of this kind often seem completely irrational. You may be quite unable to see why the vacuum cleaner's sound should worry him when the noise of the washing machine does not. But irrational or not, the baby's fears have to be accepted and respected. It may help if you think about some of your own irrational anxieties. We all have them. Why, for example, do you mind spiders when you are not afraid of flies?

The best way to handle these quirky fears is by avoidance whenever possible. Use the vacuum cleaner during the baby's nap times or while he is in his pram in another room. Don't empty his bathwater until he is well out of the way; avoid buying clothes with tight necks and no fastenings. The less you frighten your baby the faster his fear will die down. You will only make it more intense if you try to force him to face it.

Crying at the unexpected

During these months your baby is beginning to build up a lot of expectations about people and about his daily life. He is also making patterns in his mind; learning routines, rhythms and rituals. When these strong, new expectations are contradicted he is afraid. For example, the baby has learned that when he has been awake for a little while in the morning, either his mother or his father will come to greet him and get him up. If a total stranger were to walk in instead of the familiar parent, his expectations would be shattered and he would cry in fear. Yet that same stranger walking into the house to join the family for tea might well get brilliant smiles. It is not the stranger the baby minds but the unexpected context in which she appears. In a similar way the baby has built up expectations about feeding from a bottle. If he is accustomed to milk which is warm and you suddenly feed him milk which is icy cold he will probably cry from the shock. It is not that he dislikes cold milk, it is just that it is not what he was expecting.

Experiences which are totally new to the baby may affect him in the same way as experiences which contradict his expectations. His very first ride on a swing, his very first taste of ice cream, or his very first meeting with a horse may all make him cry. They are all experiences which are potentially enjoyable but he needs time to get used to them.

Supporting your baby through unexpected or novel experiences is an important skill. As he gets older his horizons will broaden. It is novel experiences which will gradually make the fabric of his life richer. Even at six months you will probably find that you can warn him, by word, touch and gesture, when something unexpected or new is coming up. You can foresee the things that may be going to alarm him and turn his attention to your own calm presence so that he receives the experience with and through you. If he has that first swing sitting on your lap, with your interested reassuring voice telling him about this new sensation and your familiar arms holding him steady, he will probably enjoy it from the beginning.

Crying from helplessness

Babies have strong emotions but very little power. As far as we know, their loves and hates, their wishes and wants are as strong as ours, but because they are still physically incompetent and unable to use language, there is much less that they can do about them. A lot of your baby's crying is in place of action. He cries because a situation has arisen in which he can do nothing to help himself. His crying is a signal to you to take action for him.

You go out of the room. The baby wants to go with you. He cannot follow, either because he is not yet mobile or because he is trapped in his pram or his playpen. He cannot ask you to take him with you. So he cries. Another time he is playing happily in his cot when the toy which he was enjoying drops through the bars. He cannot get it for himself. He cannot call to you to pick it up for him. So he cries. Out on a walk, a friend of yours whom the baby does not know stops to chat. She holds out her arms to the baby saying "You'll come to me for a cuddle won't you, darling?" The baby feels your arms starting to hold him out. He cannot answer the stranger's rhetorical question with words; he can only cry his "no!"

If you are sensitive to cues from your baby that are more subtle than crying he will not need to cry so often. If, for example, you make a point of indicating to him that you are intending to leave the room, he can hold up his arms to ask you to take him too. If you are half-listening to his contented play in his cot, his dismayed silence will alert you to the dropped toy. He will not then need to cry. At the same time the growing independence that mobility gives him will help to counteract his feelings of helplessness. The crawling stage may be exhausting for you but it often brings great relief to your baby. At last he can go where he wishes and get what he needs – at least within the limits of the freedom that you are prepared to allow him.

Crying from anger and frustration   Crying from helplessness usually diminishes as mobility increases in the first year. But crying from frustration and anger tends to build up in its place. By your baby's first birthday these emotions may lie behind most of the crying that takes place in any single day.

The crawling, exploring baby gets himself into continual trouble. He has to be constantly checked both for the sake of his own safety and the safety of other people's possessions. Removing

She cannot understand why you keep interfering . . .

him from the refrigerator door eight times in ten minutes may drive you mad but it drives him mad too. He wants to open that door and he is months away from understanding why he may not, or even from remembering that you will not let him. The more he grows up and discovers things he wants to explore and do, the angrier it will make him when he is prevented from doing them, either by you or by his own incompetence.

It is not always possible or desirable to prevent this kind of crying. You have to frustrate the baby when his intentions are unsafe or destructive. And he must attempt difficult and frustrating tasks if he is to learn. So a certain amount of angry, frustrated crying is inevitable. But a baby who feels continually beset by restricting adults or continually defeated by his own immaturity will not forge ahead in his development. There is a balance to be struck between too much frustration and too little.

When you must frustrate the baby, because what he wants to do is dangerous or damaging, you can make use of the fact that "out of sight is out of mind" and will be so for months to come. There is no need to have a long drawn out tussle about that refrigerator. Take the baby right out of the room and, after a brief burst of fury, he will forget the whole issue. Fortunately he is still infinitely distractible.

When the baby frustrates himself, it is for you to judge whether he can learn by the situation he has got himself into or whether he can only fight himself into a fury of frustrated crying. If he is struggling to get the lid off the toy box and there is a good chance that he will succeed, leave him to it. The success will be worth the effort. But if you can see that he is not going to be able to manage alone, help him. You will not offend his dignity by interfering. Managing alone is not yet important to him for its own sake. He just wants that lid off, no matter how.

Just as some very young babies cry more readily and more persistently than others, so older babies vary too. Some seem to have a far greater tolerance of frustration than others; a setback that makes one howl leaves the next still smiling. Parents cannot do very much about these inbuilt differences so there is no point in worrying about them. If you stay tuned-in to your baby and handle him in the way his cues to you suggest, you are doing the best you can. Don't decide, even during this half year, that your baby's temperament is set for life. He may be a real trier later on even if he is easily frustrated now. On the other hand, being placid now may not stop him taking life hard later on.

But even though some of these kinds of crying are bound to occur and some babies do cry more readily than others, the overall amount that your baby cries is some kind of index of how contented he is with life. If nothing ever seems to go right for him for more than five minutes at a time, it is worth sitting down and thinking about what it is that most often upsets him. Apart from pain, illness or hunger, crying is either a reaction to fear, a signal to you to take action, or an explosion of frustration and rage. If you can work out which emotion is causing most of your baby's crying you may be able to offer the extra security, the quicker response or the greater freedom which will transform him into a happier baby.

Using his or her body

Six month babies usually give a distinct impression of being happy and at ease in their bodies. They use all four limbs smoothly and rhythmically. They enjoy physical movement for its own sake and they continually test the limits of their own strength as they struggle to roll right over or to lift their heads and shoulders even further from the floor. They have understood, now, that their bodies are single, complete units. They have come to terms with them.

As we have seen, muscular control starts at the top and moves downwards. So at this stage the baby's use of his upper half, his head, shoulders, arms and hands, is well ahead of his use of his lower half. He can use his arms and hands for accurate reaching out, and he can use his head to track moving objects with his eyes. He does not yet have similar control over his hips, knees and feet. It is the struggle for control over these muscle groups that the baby is now entering. The fight to stop lying around and become a sitter, a crawling quadruped and a walking biped is on.

Sitting If you put your six month old baby squarely on his bottom on the floor, spread his legs apart, get him balanced and then slowly remove your hands, he will probably stay "sitting" for three or four seconds. His muscular control has already progressed downwards to a point where he can hold himself straight from the top of his head to his bent hips. But it has not yet reached a point where he can balance himself in this position.

By seven to eight months some babies will have solved this balance problem for themselves by leaning forward and supporting themselves with both hands flat on the floor in front of them. If your baby takes up this position he will be comparatively stable and he will certainly be sitting, but you cannot yet describe him as being "able to sit alone" because this form of sitting is not developmentally useful to him. Both his hands are occupied in providing balance, so he cannot play or even suck his thumb. And because he has to lean forward to get his hands securely on the floor, he cannot look around or see anything very interesting.

By eight to nine months, independent balance, without support from an adult or his own hands, is really coming. Now the baby can balance in a sitting position for as much as a minute at a time. But even now his sitting is more for practice than for use; his balance is still so precarious that he topples over as soon as he turns his head or reaches out a hand. It will take him another month of constant practice before his sitting becomes a position in which he can carry on with his life.

Helping your baby to sit alone The drive to sit is built-in to your baby's development. You do not have to do anything to make him *want* to sit.

As we have seen, he will be ready to practise balancing in sitting position at six or seven months but he will not be able to *get himself* into sitting position without help until he is around nine months. Giving him the opportunity to practise, by getting him into position, is therefore up to you.

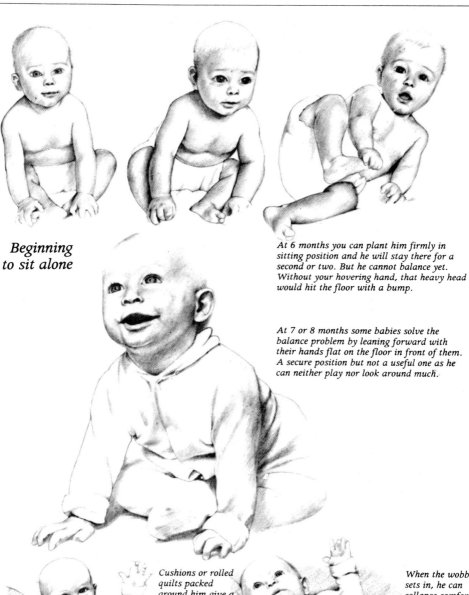

Beginning to sit alone

At 6 months you can plant him firmly in sitting position and he will stay there for a second or two. But he cannot balance yet. Without your hovering hand, that heavy head would hit the floor with a bump.

At 7 or 8 months some babies solve the balance problem by leaning forward with their hands flat on the floor in front of them. A secure position but not a useful one as he can neither play nor look around much.

Cushions or rolled quilts packed around him give a little support at hip level and let him balance for a minute.

When the wobble sets in, he can collapse comfortably. This is the ideal arrangement for sitting practice.

He will make it clear that he wants you to sit him up. While he lies on his back on the floor he will sometimes crane his head and shoulders up in a desperate but unavailing effort. If you kneel beside him, he will instantly grab for your hands and use them as levers to pull up by. Whenever you go to him as he lies in his cot or pram, he will offer you his hands, hoping for another session of the pull-me-up-to-sitting game.

You cannot play the sitting game all the time, so you have to find ways to help him practise balancing alone, too. Where and how you do this is important. Sitting, as he is accustomed to do, propped in his pram or strapped in a chair is no longer enough for the baby. It is still a good position for play but he cannot really practise balancing alone with that amount of back support available. On the other hand, sitting completely unsupported is not yet possible for him. He needs a compromise between the two.

The best compromise is to put your baby on the floor, surround him with cushions or with rolled blankets or quilts, and then sit him amongst them. When he is six or seven months you can wedge the protective padding under his buttocks so that he has just enough support at the base of his spine to sit for a minute or two. When he goes over backwards or tips himself forward into crawling position the padding gives him a soft landing.

Experience of this sort of protection may mean that your baby never bothers to balance himself with his hands on the floor. Even if he does go through this stage it will be over quickly because he will be confident that he will not hurt himself. When he is around eight months, or when you can see that his balance is improving, you can arrange his padding so that it surrounds but does not actually support him. It will still make his fall comfortable when he waves both hands in the air in triumph at finding himself sitting alone.

A month or so later the baby will be sitting steadily as long as he keeps perfectly still and concentrates on his balance. But sitting *still* is not his idea of fun. That padding will still be invaluable whenever he stretches forward just too far or falls over backward because he makes a wild gesture with his arms.

Safety while your baby learns to sit steadily

Once your baby has really started to practise sitting alone he will try to get himself into sitting position by any "handle" he can get hold of, and he will try to balance himself wherever you put him to sit. This means that some of the equipment which was safe for him in the early months may now be dangerous.

Beware of lightweight prams. If the baby wakes from a nap in a lightweight pram, finds himself wedged against the side of it, gets hold of the edge and manages to get himself almost to sitting position, he may tip the whole thing over. If he is left propped sitting in such a pram while you are in a shop, he may work his way forward and try to balance without support. When his balance fails and he flops forward with a thump, both the brakes and the chassis will be put under considerable strain.

Once he reaches this stage a lightweight pram is best used only for transport, or it can be replaced for this purpose by a pushchair. If you want the baby to go on sleeping in a pram, perhaps so that he can nap in the garden, you may be able to buy a second-hand, heavy, coachbuilt pram extremely cheaply. Few families want this type of pram any more as it does not fit in a car or easily go up steps. Its cumbersome weight and solidity make it an ideal outdoor bed which the baby will safely be able to use into his second year.

Another possible solution is a canvas camping cot for the garden. Although expensive, the purchase may well be sensible if you plan to camp or go away for weekends. It is easy to transport and it can be used, temporarily, instead of a dropside cot. On the other hand it will be less useful at home than a big pram as the baby will not be able to sleep out in it in cold or wet weather.

Beware of lightweight chairs. A younger baby keeps up a steady pressure on the back of his chair (see p. 163). When he cranes forward he moves his head and shoulders but leaves his bottom and most of his weight squarely in the base of the seat. Now, he struggles to get right forward; he balances for a few seconds and then relaxes his muscles and hits the back of the chair with a thud that can make it tip. If the chair is on the floor, the fall will be frightening and painful. If the chair is on a table, it may be a serious matter.

If you want to go on using the infant seat you will have to acquire its own stand (see p. 144). This turns it into a safe, steady high chair which can be used into toddlerhood. The seat alone should no longer be used for anything except perhaps picnic meals where you are constantly present. If you do not want to buy the stand, the baby must now have either a steady, safe high chair or a low chair-table combination.

Use a safety-harness always. The hazard of the baby falling right out of a pram or chair is almost as great as that of his tipping it over. He should wear a safety-harness, as a matter of course, whenever you put him into anything that is meant to restrain him, such as a chair, pram, pushchair or car seat. The exceptions, of course, are his cot and playpen. It will be a long time before he can climb out of those and their design is intended to provide safe freedom. Using a safety-harness, always, is much less irksome if you have a separate one for each regularly-used item of equipment. If you have to go into the garden and get the harness off the pram in order to put it on the baby and his high chair, the day will almost certainly come when you will not bother. That will be the day your baby discovers how to tip himself out.

Stop putting your baby to sit in armchairs or on beds. Constant sitting practice means constant tumbles, but the best kind of tumble is from the floor to the floor. If your baby tumbles from a chair or sofa he is unlikely to do himself real physical damage, but damage to his nerves, morale and confidence can easily delay both his progress and his pleasure in sitting up.

Don't leave your baby alone on the floor, especially if he is surrounded by cushions while he practises sitting. If he fell face down into them, he would almost certainly lift his head and roll free, but he could fall with his arms awkwardly trapped; he could smother. Padded or not, your almost-sitting baby is also almost crawling. He should never be left free and alone in a room.

Crawling   Many babies learn to crawl at the same time that they learn to sit alone. The two developments may parallel each other closely. At six months the baby can sit alone for a second but cannot balance, and can get into crawling position but cannot progress. At nine or ten months the baby can sit steadily and play at the same time, and can also crawl anywhere.

Babies who do not make these advances simultaneously will almost certainly learn to sit alone before they learn to crawl. Perfectly normal babies may still be immobile sitters on their first birthdays. Delayed crawling is nothing to worry about, especially if your sitting baby also shows signs of being interested in pulling up to standing position (see p. 243).

Although "crawling" is usually taken to mean progress across a room on hands and knees, quite a lot of babies adopt other manoeuvres, either before, or instead of, a conventional crawl. Early mobility, for example, may come from skilful rolling over and over, with a slither to take the baby the last three feet to his objective. A slippery floor may help your baby learn to get about by pulling himself along on his elbows, with his legs straight out behind him. If he finds this satisfactory, he may be late in learning to pull his legs up and push with his knees.

Babies who learn to sit steadily comparatively early sometimes adopt a "bottom shuffle" instead of a crawl. The baby pushes himself around on his bottom using one hand to propel himself. From his point of view this method has a lot to recommend it. He saves himself the effort of going from sitting position to crawling

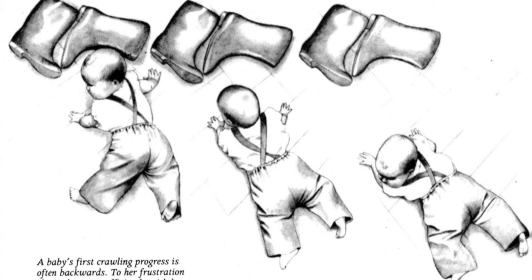

A baby's first crawling progress is often backwards. To her frustration she pushes more efficiently with her arms and hands than with her feet and legs. But once she can move along at all, she will soon get her direction right.

position and back again, and he keeps one hand free even while he moves. He can see what is going on better than a conventionally crawling baby, too. Bottom shuffling babies often leave out conventional crawling altogether and go straight on to pulling themselves into standing position and cruising around furniture.

Some babies learn to crawl in the ordinary way but then discover that they can move faster on hands and feet than they can on hands and knees. A few leave hands and knees out altogether and "walk like bears" right away.

So while the following paragraphs describe average progress towards ordinary crawling, different rates of development or idiosyncratic methods of getting around do not suggest that there is anything amiss with your baby. He must learn to sit alone and he must eventually learn to stand and walk alone. How or whether he gets around the room in between is far less important in his development.

If a desirable toy is put just out of the reach of a six month old baby who is lying on the floor on his tummy, he will pull his knees up under him, push up with his hands, and often manage to get his tummy right off the floor. For a moment he is in true crawling position but he will not get anywhere. Just as he still has a problem with balance when he is trying to sit, so he has a problem with actually moving *forward* when he is trying to crawl.

During the seventh and eighth month most babies clearly show their desire to crawl. If you watch carefully you can see the effort that is being made; see that the baby is "thinking forwards". But very few will manage to cover any ground at this age.

Towards the end of the eighth month the baby will probably give up lying on his tummy altogether. As soon as he is placed face down, turns over or collapses from one of his sitting adventures, he gets himself on to hands and knees. He learns to do everything but move along. He rocks backwards and forwards and he swivels himself around and around, following your progress around the room or the cat's escape from his attentions. It is at this stage that he may be so desperate to get moving that he develops all kinds of peculiar ways of getting around, none of which is a true crawl. He may rock, swivel, roll over and squirm on his tummy, so that one way or another he does actually get from one side of the room to the other. But this is not useful progress any more than sitting, using his hands for balance is useful sitting. He still cannot choose to go in a particular direction, and if he sets off because he has caught sight of something he wants, he will have lost track of it by the time he has finished playing acrobats and come to rest again.

It is during the ninth month that most babies actually begin to make progress. To their fury it is often backwards! The baby fixes his eyes on something he wants and makes a mighty effort. Because his control of his upper body is more developed than his control of his legs, he tends to push harder with his hands and arms than with his knees. Instead of finding himself closer to the thing he wants he finds himself moving backwards away from it. Furious though the baby may be, this is a short lived phase. Once he can crawl backwards he will soon get his direction and the power of his pushing right.

Helping your baby to crawl A baby does not need help in getting into crawling position. He can get there himself either from lying on his tummy or by going forward from sitting. All he needs from you is opportunity. He will get plenty of that provided he spends a good part of his waking day on the floor. There are, however, a few things which you can do to encourage early crawling by making it enjoyable and safe for him:

Protect your baby's knees. Their skin is still soft and easily chafed. Even in summer he will be more comfortable if he wears cotton dungarees or light trousers when he is trying to crawl on grass or rough textured carpet.

Foresee possible dangers. He will learn to crawl without learning any extra good sense to go with his mobility. Steps between rooms, staircases, splintery floors, and unsuitable objects left lying around can all cause accidents.

Watch out for unexpected spurts in ability. Even before he can actually crawl across a room the baby may roll and squirm himself out of the safe corner where you left him and into danger. Take action to child-proof the rooms he will use before he is fully mobile (see Enc/Safety).

Remember that part of the desire to crawl is a desire to get hold of things. Something that looks really entrancing may give him just the extra surge of motivation he needs to get moving. Make very sure that when this happens it is not a box of cigarettes or a pin cushion that has caught his eye.

Don't leave your baby free, alone, in a room, but don't keep him imprisoned in a playpen either. Being alone may mean that he gets into danger; being enclosed will frustrate him desperately because it will take away all the fun of crawling and much of the point of the tremendous efforts he is making. He needs a safe floor, safe interesting objects and constant supervision.

Don't try to keep your baby clean. Fussiness about hygiene is essential in the kitchen and the lavatory but out of place when your baby is playing on the floor (see p. 230). Ordinary household dust will not harm him and skin is the most washable of all materials. Don't dress him nicely if you are going to mind when his clothes get grubby. Treat him like a manual labourer; let him wear workclothes all day and be changed into party gear only on special occasions.

Once she can crawl she needs space – as much as you can make safe for her – and the freedom to explore it.

Standing

While learning to sit up and to crawl often go together, both being accomplished at around nine to ten months, standing and walking are definitely later accomplishments.

At six months most babies love to be held standing on a lap, and behave as if they were on a trampoline, "jumping" by bending and straightening both knees together.

During the seventh month they begin to use alternate feet instead of both together. They "dance" rather than "jump", and they often put one foot down on top of the other, pulling out the underneath one and then doing it all over again.

At this stage, the baby cannot bear anything like his full weight. Nor is he yet "thinking forward" as he does at this age when he tries to crawl. It is not usually until around nine months that he begins to get the idea of using his feet to go forwards. Now his dancing movements and the placing of one foot on top of the other give way to a definite placing of one foot in front of the other. The baby "walks" two steps to the end of your knee and then collapses, giggling. If he is held securely, with his feet on the floor and with you taking most of his weight, he may now enjoy making a few wobbling steps.

By ten months the baby's control of his muscles has moved downwards to his knees and feet. At last he can take his whole weight, standing squarely on his flat feet, keeping his knees braced though still sagging forward a little at hip level. He has reached the same point in standing that he reached at six months in sitting. He can stand, but he cannot balance.

Once the baby can take his full weight and stand square on the floor provided somebody balances him, he will soon learn to pull himself up to a holding-on standing position. Most babies will do this at around eleven months, starting by pulling themselves, hand over hand, up the bars of a cot or playpen. Your baby may use you, crawling up to you as you sit on the floor, and then hauling himself up by your clothes to stand triumphantly balancing by your hair.

Just as newly crawling babies are often flummoxed by their inability to crawl forwards rather than backwards, so newly standing ones often find it impossible to sit down again. For two or three weeks on end the baby may find something to pull himself up by as soon as he is set free on the floor, but shout piteously for help as soon as he reaches standing position because he cannot let go and sit down again. As soon as you come to the rescue and sit him down, he repeats the performance. It can be a tiresome phase because you have to go to his assistance every couple of minutes and both of you get tired and frustrated. Luckily it does not last for long. Don't just pluck him from his hold and dump him in sitting position. Lower him gradually to the floor. He will soon acquire the confidence either to let go with his hands and sit down with a plop or to lower himself by sliding his hands down his support, not releasing it until his bottom reaches the floor. In the meantime, if you are both getting fed up, extra rides in his pram or pushchair may help. He has not yet got to the stage where he will even think about walking when he is out on an expedition. He will happily sit and look at the world, resting both his muscles and your nerves.

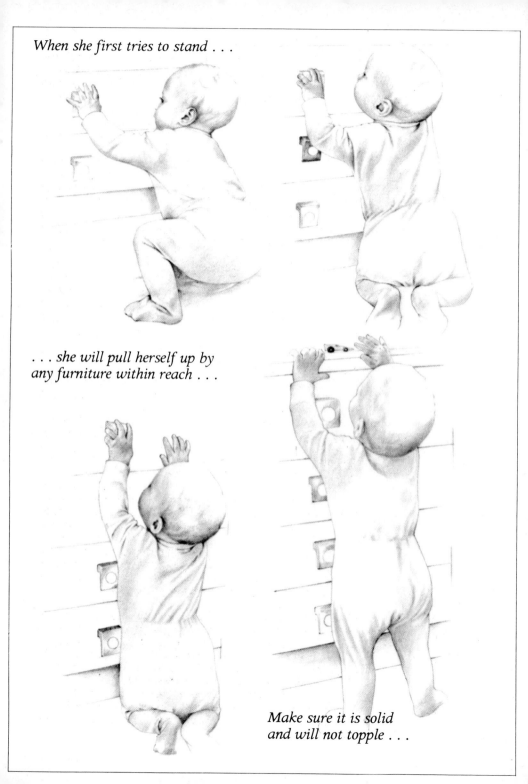

When she first tries to stand . . .

. . . she will pull herself up by any furniture within reach . . .

Make sure it is solid and will not topple . . .

About a month after first pulling himself up to standing position the baby will learn the assisted walking we call "cruising". He pulls himself up as usual so that he is standing facing the back of the sofa or the bars of his playpen. Gradually he inches both hands together along the support and then follows them by stepping sideways with one foot. Left straddle-legged, he will usually sit down, looking dumbfounded by his own achievement. It is a major one. That shuffle was his first step. Never again will he be a baby who cannot walk.

As long as the baby feels that he needs to take some of his weight on the hands that cling to his support, he will have to move those hands together. But practice brings confidence; within a few days or weeks of that first shuffling sideways movement he will have become convinced that his legs will bear his whole weight. He will then be able to stand further back from his support and pass himself hand over hand along it. Every time he moves a hand he moves his leading foot one step sideways and then brings the other foot up to join it. If you watch him carefully you can see that it is the moment when one foot is actually moving, leaving all his weight on the other one, which still worries him. Gradually his balance improves. By the end of the year you will probably see him standing right back, holding on to his support at arms length, using it only for balance. Very soon now he will be ready to let go altogether and stand quite alone.

Helping your baby to stand

You cannot help your baby learn to stand by putting him in standing position as you sat him up to practise sitting. Given the opportunity and some careful attention to his safety, he will pull himself upright as soon as he feels ready to do so.

Giving him the opportunity is not difficult. If he is free in a room with furniture, he will hold on to that; if he is in his cot or playpen, he will pull himself up by the bars; if nothing better presents itself, he will grasp your hair or the family dog's neck. The problem is that many of these adventures will lead to falls and while some are inevitable at this stage of a baby's development, too many, especially when they take place from standing up, can hurt his confidence as well as his head. Later on, when he is walking freely, he will learn to put his hands out as soon as he feels himself falling. Toddler tumbles are usually no worse than grazed knees and palms. But at this early stage he is not good at protecting himself, because his hands are taken up with trying to hold on and his balance is so precarious that he is likely to fall awkwardly. It is worth planning protection for him.

Consider the furnishings in the room. Flimsy pieces are dangerous because they will support him as he first grasps them and begins the leverage part of his getting up, but they will topple over as his hands and his weight move upwards and he pulls. He will then fall from his most unbalanced position – neither sitting down nor standing up, but halfway between the two.

High flimsy furniture – such as a small round side table or wicker plant stand – is the worst of all; it will not only topple over but, because of its height, will almost certainly fall on the baby. Even if it is light, it can hurt him.

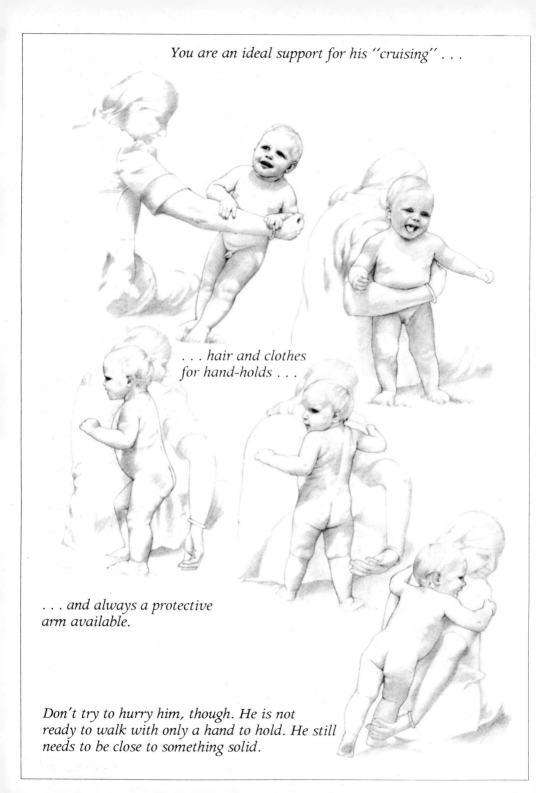

You are an ideal support for his "cruising" . . .

. . . hair and clothes
for hand-holds . . .

. . . and always a protective
arm available.

Don't try to hurry him, though. He is not
ready to walk with only a hand to hold. He still
needs to be close to something solid.

Some obviously hazardous pieces can be wedged in place; others can be positioned in such a way that they are inaccessible to the baby. A few would be better removed to another room for a few months.

Watch out, too, for dangers above the baby as he pulls himself up. He will not be able to reach out for things while standing until he can spare a hand from holding on (probably at around a year), but he may try to pull himself up by a hanging tablecloth or dangling electric cable. Neither a coffee pot nor a table lamp will do his skull any good.

Don't start using a sleeping bag at this stage if your baby has not been accustomed to one. He will try to stand up while he is in it, will certainly fall and probably bang his head on the bars of his cot. But if he is accustomed to a sleeping bag don't give it up now either. He will not attempt to stand in it if he has always worn one and this simple fact may keep him happily in his cot later on when your friends' babies are driving them mad by climbing out! (See p. 303.)

Don't put shoes on your newly-standing baby. He only needs shoes to protect his feet once he is really walking and doing so outdoors. Shoes at this stage will make it far more difficult for him to balance because they will cut down the sensations his feet receive from the floor. They can be slippery too and may cause an accident.

Don't put socks on your baby without shoes unless your floors are carpeted. Socks turn hard floors into skating rinks; your baby may fall and even if he does not, the difficulty of standing under these conditions will badly shake his confidence. He is safest in bare feet. If cold is a problem, use slipper socks which have a light non-slip sole and a knitted sock instead of an upper (see p. 315).

Don't try to make the baby walk holding your hands. At this stage he will not like walking with all that empty space around him and only wobbly hands to hold on to. He feels safer doing his cruising around something solid. If you want to give him the chance to practise pulling himself up when you are out in the park where there is no furniture, kneel or sit on the ground and let him use your body as if it were inanimate.

Don't try to hurry your baby on towards independent standing and/or walking. Standing, cruising and eventually walking alone are all dependent on the baby's confidence and his motivation as well as on his muscles and coordination. If you try to hurry him you may slow up his development by causing falls that make him afraid. If he seems to have managed one stage, such as learning to pull himself upright, but does not seem to be moving on towards cruising or standing alone, it may be because he does not actually want to go further with the walking game at present. Pleasure in crawling all over the place at will may mean that he has no motive for learning to walk just yet.

Although most babies will pull themselves up and cruise before their first birthday, a large minority will not get on to two feet until their second year.

Using his or her hands

Your baby spent much of his first six months in discovering that his hands were part of himself; that they were always there even when he could not see them and that by conscious effort he could make them reach out and get hold of things (see p. 165).

By around six months he has completed this stage of development. He has "found" his hands once and for all and he can wave them, reach out with them or grab with them as directly and immediately as you or I.

But the baby still has a great deal to learn about using his hands. Efficiency at reaching out and grabbing is not enough. He has to learn to make his hands perform complicated manoeuvres and he has to learn to use different bits of them separately.

These developments are difficult to catalogue because the changes which take place in your baby's day-to-day use of his hands are minute, even though the overall change between six months and one year is enormous. Furthermore, the exact ways in which he learns his increasingly fine hand control will depend on the kinds of objects and opportunities he is given for practice.

Using hands for touching as well as grabbing

At six to seven months the baby begins to understand that he can use his hands to explore things by other means than grabbing hold of them and putting them in his mouth. While his most usual reaction to a toy will still be to reach out, grasp it, put it in his mouth and then look at it, he will sometimes simply use his hands to touch, stroke or pat. This small development is important because it enables the baby to find out something about things which are not graspable. As he lies on the carpet, for example, he will stroke it, exploring its texture. Even three or four weeks earlier he would have concentrated his energy on trying to pick up those bafflingly flat flowers in its pattern. The flowers would have defeated him by being ungraspable and the rest of the carpet would have gone unexplored.

Once your baby has discovered that simply feeling things with his hands can give him some information about them, you will probably notice him becoming increasingly interested in different textures and sensations through his fingers. He will stroke the tray of his high chair; feel the window pane and pat his blankets. You may even get your hair stroked rather than having it grabbed by the handful!

Differentiating hands from arms, and fingers from hands

At six months your baby still usually behaves as if he thinks his arms and hands are single units. If he wants to call your attention to something, for example, he gestures in its direction with a broad sweep from the shoulder.

Although expansive gestures will continue, because your baby characteristically reacts in a very physical way to things which interest him, he will gradually learn to use his lower arm, from the elbow, and his hand alone, from the wrist. By eight or nine months he will be able to wave goodbye with a royal gesture from the wrist only.

*Hands are for touching and exploring,
but life can be baffling
—those flowers look pickable . . .*

Hands are for getting hold of things, and sucking is a way of finding out about them . . .

. . . but your baby can still only attend to one thing at a time

. . . if you offer another, the first will drop, forgotten

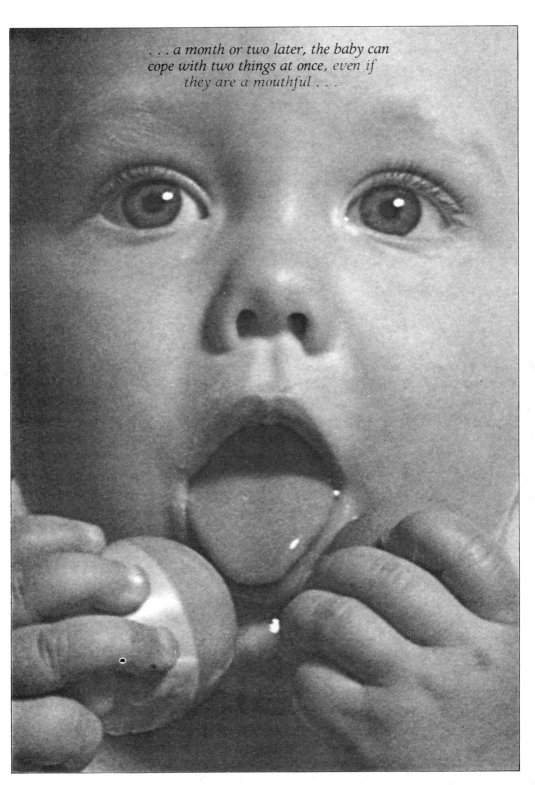

*. . . a month or two later, the baby can
cope with two things at once, even if
they are a mouthful . . .*

As manual skills develop, containers can be emptied and filled quite deliberately . . .

*. . . though they may empty themselves
at quite unexpected moments.*

As she gets control over her hands, she imitates what you do with yours. If you draw on the paper and give her a crayon, she will try too . . .

As she gets control over her separate fingers, she can use just one to point things out . . .

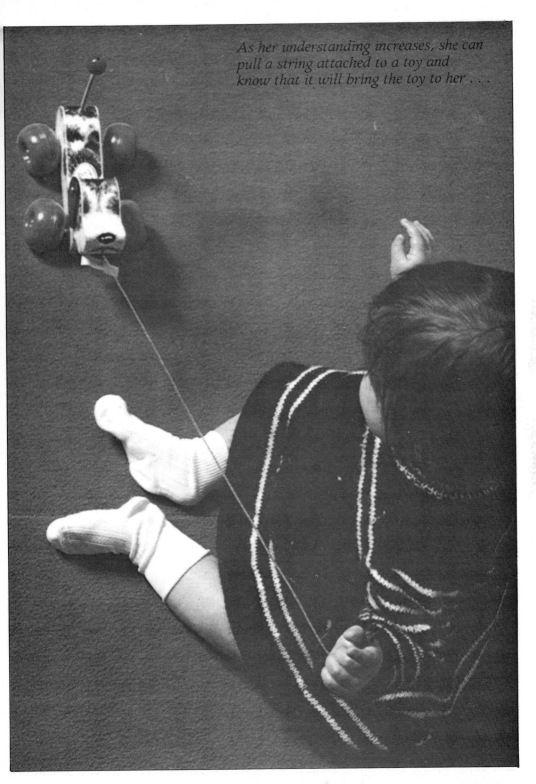

As her understanding increases, she can pull a string attached to a toy and know that it will bring the toy to her . . .

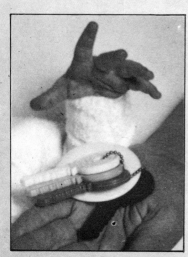

Letting go of objects is
another skill . . . you can
help him "undo" his fingers
by holding your hand
flat underneath . . .

. . . eventually his control of his hands will be so fine
that he can pick things up with his thumb and forefinger alone.
By his first birthday he may well be able to retrieve the
tiniest currant or the smallest crumb . . .

While your baby is learning to use different parts of his arms separately he is also learning to separate out the various sections of his hands. At six months he grasps objects with his whole hand and picks things up by using his cupped hand as a scoop. Large objects are tackled by using both hands together as if they were a pair of tongs. During the seventh and eighth months he begins to make use of his fingers and thumbs for grasping and for holding on to objects; by nine months he will probably have such fine control over his separate fingers that he can use an index finger to point or to poke.

Opposing thumbs and learning to release objects

During the last three months of the first year the baby's new ability to use different parts of his hands separately from each other leads to the gradual development of a more mature grasp and grip. Instead of trying to pick up small objects by using his whole hand adjusted to a small cup or scoop, the baby learns to approach them with his forefinger and thumb using a pincer grip. This change may not seem to make much difference to his daily life and play, but it is interesting to realize that it is the ability of human beings to "oppose" their fingers and thumbs for pincer gripping which makes them so much more dexterous than other mammals. By the end of the year your baby will probably be capable of delicately retrieving the smallest crumb using this grip.

Simultaneously with acquiring these new and delicate finger abilities the baby also tackles the difficult problem of learning to let go of things he is grasping. At nine months most babies understand the idea of letting go. If you hold out your hand and say "give it to me", he will hold the toy out to you, clearly realizing that you want him to release it. But the actual process of uncurling his fingers in order to release what he is grasping is still very difficult for him. If he sits there holding out the toy but with his fingers still curled around it, don't assume he is teasing you. He probably does not yet know how to proceed. Releasing objects is no problem to the baby if he happens to be playing at a table. When he feels his hand and the object on a flat surface, he can relax his fingers easily.

Most babies will have discovered how to uncurl their fingers by the tenth or eleventh month. Once he has discovered how to let go of things the baby will practise at every opportunity. You may face weeks of toys being dropped from his cot; food being dropped from the high chair, flannels and soap flopping over the edge of the bath and trails of shopping left behind his pushchair.

Letting go

By 9 months, a baby knows when you want her to let something go, but deliberately relaxing the finger-muscles is still a complicated manoeuvre. She will manage best if her hand and the object are both resting on a firm surface.

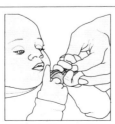
Don't uncurl her grasping fist by force...

Place your palm so her hand and the object rest on it.

She will be able to open her fingers and let go of the toy.

Helping your baby to use his or her hands

Until he becomes mobile at around nine months, a baby has to rely on you to bring the world to him. He cannot go and get things for himself so he has to wait for you to bring things to him. Bring him plenty. Even while he is too young to *do* anything much with objects, he is ready to learn about them. If you provide him only with rattles, rings and woolly balls, while keeping all those interesting household objects out of range, you deprive him of endless fun and learning.

As he gets more competent with his hands, you can really help him by encouraging him to use his skills all the time. You can let him have a spoon at mealtimes and a flannel at bathtime. You can show him how to pull off his socks and turn the pages of his board-books. He can put the potatoes in the vegetable rack as well as bricks in a box; bang the piano as well as his tambourine and throw a ball for the dog when you do. All these things, and thousands more, are new experiences for a baby. They are fun and learning and what is more they mean that he will feel properly involved with you and the things that you do. He does not really want to be kept separate from the rest of the household, with special toys and special games that are only for him. He wants to join in, and the more you can slow your pace down to his and put up with his messes, the faster and more happily he will learn.

Give your baby plenty of objects to explore. At six months your baby will not do more with a plaything than grasp, suck and inspect it. But he is learning about the objects you give him even though he is not using them. Let him handle as wide a range of objects as possible (see p. 192) but give them to him one at a time. A single toy takes up his whole attention. He literally cannot think about two things at the same time, even if they are two identical things like two little red bricks. If he is holding one of these in his left hand and you offer him another, he will not take it with his free right hand and hold them both. His attention will turn to the new brick and the one he was holding will simply drop out of his hand and mind.

Encourage interest in touching and stroking as it develops in the seventh month. Let him play on grass, carpet, matting, wooden floors; let him discover with his hands the fascinating differences. Now that he need not grab and mouth everything he touches you can bring him the pet rabbit to stroke and hold him up to pat the window, too.

Give the baby more complicated objects as he begins to use his fingers and thumbs separately. In the seventh and eighth month he will practise threading separate fingers through rings and handles; poking his index finger into indentations and using it to trace out the squirly patterns of well designed toys. Once he uses his hands in this way he will also be able to cope with two things at the same time. If you give him two rattles or two bricks, for example, he will probably hold one in each hand, which is good practice for him. He will still treat the two toys separately, though. It has not yet occurred to him that he could make each more interesting by combining the two. It will be a few weeks yet before he bangs those two rattles together to increase their noise.

Give your baby lots of opportunities to watch adults using their hands. The baby learns the properties of many different objects by handling them. He will learn how to use some of them by fortunate chance: his rattles sound when his arm waves so he learns to wave the arm deliberately to make the sound. But he also learns how to use objects by watching you. By late in the eighth month he may be ready to copy actual demonstrations. If you now give him a thick stumpy crayon and a piece of paper, for example, and then take a similar crayon yourself and scribble on the paper with it, he will try to do the same. He may not manage to make a mark, but his actions will imitate yours. Next time he gets a crayon he will try again, so beware of scribbles on walls.

Toys on strings also often produce a miracle of understanding for the baby. At seven months, if you give him the string attached to a toy car he will probably pull it more or less by mistake. Even when the car moves towards him he will show no understanding of what he has done. But only six weeks later his face will light up with amazement, and he will pull that car towards him as often as you are prepared to move it away from him again.

His willingness to copy what you do will increase steadily from now on. You can use it both for his benefit and for your own. If you will show him how to unscrew lids, thread rings on a rod, push toy cars and pour water, he will try to copy you. You will be giving him good ideas for things to try to do and he will be trying to do them. Because he is given the ideas and because he tries, his manual development will proceed as fast as it can.

As his manual skills increase, you can show him how to do things that will help you, like feeding himself, washing his own hands and pulling off his clothes. If you start him off on self-care at this early stage by learning-by-imitation, your baby will see no difference between these "tasks" and "play" with toys. You may avoid the usual battles that take place over teaching three year olds to wash their own faces when they would rather play.

Help the baby to learn to release objects by making sure that most of his play with small toys takes place at a table or other firm surface; by helping him to release things into your flat hand; and by providing toys he can practise on when he has finally got the idea at around ten months.

The phase when the baby throws everything out of his cot or pram can be made educational for him as well as less tiresome for you if his small toys are fastened on with pieces of wool. He will throw them out and then discover, with joy, that he can fish them up again by pulling the wool. Don't use string or tape for this in case he gets himself entangled in it. Knitting wool is safe because it breaks well before strangling-point, but watch out for acrylics and other synthetics which might not. Just make sure that anything used will break under minimal pressure.

Towards the end of the year just dropping things will give way to a deliberate throwing and to an equally deliberate placing of objects. The baby needs a light ball to throw and he needs collections of bricks or other small toys which he can practise putting into a container and emptying out again.

Listening and talking

This half year is crucial to babies' language development despite the fact that many will not produce a single recognizable word before their birthday. Babies learn language long before they can speak it. First they must listen to other people's words and learn to understand what they mean. Only then will they be able to produce meaningful words of their own.

The importance of a baby's listening and understanding is often underestimated because we tend to overestimate the importance of babies' own word production and try to force babies to produce word-sounds by imitation. But just saying a word or two is not useful language; we are trying to bring up a person, not a parrot. So try not to confine your interest to listening for sounds which sound like words, saying words for your baby to imitate, and identifying his or her first real words. Concentrate instead on giving the baby lots of talk to listen to; plenty of opportunities for grasping the meaning of the words he or she hears and an immediate and pleasant social response to the sounds he or she makes.

Why babies learn to speak
Most people assume that babies learn to speak because they must communicate in order to get what they want or need. The facts do not support this simple idea. Babies manage to communicate with their caretakers for the whole of their first year without using words. So why should they suddenly feel a need for them? When they do produce some words they are very seldom words which have anything to do with the baby's needs. He will not first learn to say "biscuit" or "come" or "up", he will learn instead the name-labels of people or things which are emotionally important or pleasurably exciting to him.

Pleasant emotions may be the key to the development of speech. Babies are born with a built-in interest in listening to human voices and a built-in tendency to produce babbling sounds of their own (see p. 181). During the first six months, the baby comes to associate the gentle, pleasant speech sounds he hears from you with pleasure and with having his needs fulfilled. When he babbles, he hears his own noises as similar to your voice and so those sounds are associated with pleasure too. His own sounds make him feel pleased and happy because of their association with your sounds and you, so the baby is motivated to go on making more and more sounds, to elaborate his babbling into the more complicated form we call "jargon" (see p. 263) and eventually to develop actual speech (see p. 355).

This is only a theory, of course, but it is a theory which fits many observable facts. Deaf babies, for example, babble normally until around the middle of the first year (see p. 182) but instead of increasing in amount and elaboration, their sound making then dies away. It may well be that they stop making sounds because they are not receiving the affectionate feedback which motivates normal babies to go on. There are less extreme examples which support this theory too. One little girl who was born partially deaf also failed to develop sounds beyond the babbling stage. Examination later showed that her hearing loss was sufficient to cut her off from gentle speech sounds but was not great enough to cut out loud, angry talk or the sounds of her own crying. She could hear when her parents were cross with her or when she herself was miserable, but she could not hear when they were affectionate or she herself was happy. As soon as a hearing-aid restored the gentle sounds to her she developed normal speech.

If you listen to the development of your own baby you may well feel that his behaviour also fits this theory. Throughout this half year he will do all his talking, whether it is to an adult or to himself, when he is pleased and excited or at least happy and content. When he is cross and unhappy he will not talk; he will cry. Whenever you hear him carrying on a "conversation" with himself, making a sound, pausing as if for an answer and then speaking again, you will find that his noises sound like pleasant, friendly or joyful speech, but never like cross or irritable speech. When the time finally comes for your baby to produce real words they too will be in a pleasant context. If "ball" is to be his first word it will not be spoken in angry demand but in pleased comment. If your name is his first word, he will not use it first as a reproving whine but as a delighted greeting.

The development of speech sounds

In the middle of this first year most babies will carry on long babble conversations with an adult, making a sound, pausing while the other person replies and then answering back again. The baby will continue for as long as you will go on looking and speaking directly to him. He cannot yet talk to you if he cannot see you nor even respond vocally if you call across the room.

Most of the sounds are still single syllable cooing noises (see p. 181). He says "Paaa" and "Maaaa" and "Boooo". He intersperses them with laughter and gurgles and hiccups of delight. His conversations are all joy. If he is cross he will not talk; conversely, if he will talk to you he is not miserable.

During the seventh month the baby becomes increasingly on the alert for speech sounds. He begins to search the room with his eyes if you call him when you are out of sight. He will look for the source of the voice on the radio, too, ready to respond with conversation as soon as he can discover who is talking.

Towards the end of the seventh month you will hear elaborations of his own sounds. The first change is that he turns his cooing noises into two syllable "words" by repeating them. He says "Ala" and "Amam", "Mumum" and "Booboo". Gradually these "words" becomes more separate from each other, with less musical cooing between them. Once this happens, usually by the end of the seventh month, there are new sounds on the way. This batch is more exclamatory and less dove-like: he says "Imi!", "Aja!" "Ippi".... These new two syllable "words" seem to make the baby increasingly excited by his own sound making. Once they are in his repertoire, he will probably wake you each morning with a dawn chorus of delighted talk in which he behaves exactly as if you were in the room and talking to him. He will exclaim, pause, speak again, pause and then say some more, and he will go on for minutes at a time, entertaining himself until you choose to go and join in.

During the eighth month most babies begin to take an interest in adult conversation, even when it is not directly aimed at them. If your baby happens to be sitting between you as you talk over his head, that head will turn from one of you to the other as each speaks. He behaves as if your conversation were a tennis match he was closely following. But the talking game is too good for the baby to let himself be left out for long. Soon he learns to shout for attention. It is not a yell that he produces nor a squeal nor a cry: it is a definite and intentional shout. It is often the very first time that the baby uses a speech sound with a specific communicative purpose in mind.

At 8 to 9 months the baby can take an active interest in conversation even when it is not addressed to her. But she will not let you leave her as passive audience for long: within the month she will learn to shout for your attention.

Soon after the shout, many babies learn to sing. Of course the song is not elaborate: four notes up or down a scale is about average. But it is quite definitely musical and usually set off by your singing, by music on the radio or "theme tunes" on television.

The ninth month usually produces exciting speech developments which all happen at once. The baby's forms of speech suddenly become much more elaborate, with long drawn out series of syllables being produced such as "Loo-loo-loo-loo". At the same time he begins to inflect and change the emphasis of his sounds, so that listening parents hear varied sounds suggesting questions, exclamations and even jokes among the babble. Then the forms of speech change yet again. This time the baby does not just add more and more of the same syllables to what he says; instead he combines all the syllables that he knows into long complicated "sentences" such as: "Ah-dee-dah-boo-maa". Once this kind of combination, which is technically called "jargoning", is heard, the baby is on the verge of producing real words.

For another month or so you may not be able to identify any words, but the baby's speech sounds become so clearly inflected, so varied and so expressive that he sounds exactly as if he were speaking, fluently, but in a foreign language. The jargon sounds so realistic that sometimes, if your mind is on something else when he starts to talk, you may find yourself saying "what did you say, darling?", forgetting for the moment that he cannot really have "said" anything!

Most babies produce their first "real" word during the tenth or eleventh month. We cannot be exact, because first words are surprisingly difficult to identify. "Mummy" is a good example. When a seven month old baby says "mum", few parents will be fooled into thinking it is a real word because they do not expect a seven month old baby to talk. But when that same baby makes the same sound at ten months, it is easy to be fooled. You are expecting words now so you tend to find them among all that babble, and to forget that the actual noises you are now considering for word-status are sounds he has been making for months.

Identifying first words

There is no particular point in trying hard to identify your baby's first words. It does not matter whether he uses any or not at this stage. His expressive, fluent, varied jargon is an absolute assurance that he is going to speak when he is ready.

But the stages the baby goes through in getting to words are interesting developments and if you find them so you will help the baby's language development along. Interest will make you listen carefully to what he says. Listening carefully will probably make you answer him with more adult talk. Being listened and replied to is what he most needs for his speech development.

In the tenth or eleventh month the baby is likely to get the idea of *using* a particular sound to refer to a particular object, but he may still take a while to "decide" *what* sound to use as a name for the object he has chosen. One child, for example, used the word "bon-bon" when asking for her ball. Later she used the word "dan" about the same ball. On each occasion it was clear that she meant that ball and did not mean anything else, but she behaved as if all that mattered was to use a word – any old word would do.

After a week or two of this kind of confusion, the baby moves on a stage and starts to use one sound, and only one sound, to refer to one and only one object. But the sound he uses may still not be a "word" in the adult sense. It may be an "own-word"; a sound that the baby has invented, and attached to a particular thing or a particular person. But even if the "own-word" has not the slightest similarity to the "proper" one, it should be counted as a word *if you know what he means by it*. After all, the whole point of speech is communication between people. If you know that your child means "bus" when he says "gig", then he is talking to you.

How babies learn their early words

Babies of eight to twelve months are highly imitative. As well as imitating actions they will often imitate word sounds. Because of this, many parents spend a great deal of time during these months holding objects up in front of their babies and saying "Say shoe; shoe; say shoe, darling", and so on. This kind of thing probably does not do babies any harm. They may enjoy the long "conversations" it gives them and they may enjoy the imitating game for its own sake. But they will not learn to talk that way. As we said at the beginning of the section (see p. 260), learning to talk is not a matter of learning to imitate sounds for their own sake.

A baby hears a word like "shoe" over and over again in daily life as the one constant sound in a large variety of statements. In one day you may say to him "Where are your shoes?"; "Oh, what dirty shoes!" "Let's take your shoes off"; "I'll put your shoes on"; "Look what nice new shoes". That word "shoes" is the one sound which occurs in all those sentences and it is always associated with those things that go on his feet. Over days and weeks he will come to associate the sound with the shoes. When he has made the association "shoes" = what are put on his feet, he will know what the word means.

Your baby will probably learn the meanings of dozens of words before he actually says more than one or two. He will first use words which mean something joyful or exciting to him. Perhaps he has in fact understood that word "shoe" for several weeks but has never said it. When you take him to a shoe shop and buy him a pair of bright red slippers, his pride in them as they glow on his feet may be what stimulates him at last to say "SHOES!". He may have known that the recurring word "Toby" referred to the family dog; a sudden rush of affection for him, as he plonks himself down beside him, may stimulate the first use of his name.

First words come slowly but understanding of words goes on apace. If your baby has only used a word or two by his first birthday, don't assume that he is not learning language. He is listening and learning to understand.

Helping your baby to listen and to talk

Lots of loving talk is the best overall help that you can give to your baby's language development, but there is talk which is positively useful and talk which is less useful:

Talk directly to your baby. A baby cannot pay attention and listen carefully to general conversation. If he is in a room with his whole family and everybody is talking, he will be lost in a sea of sound. You say something and he looks at you, only to find that your face is turned away to his brother. Brother replies, sister interrupts with a half-finished sentence that ends in an expressive shrug, and meanwhile somebody else has started a side conversation and the television has been switched on. Third or fourth children, especially in families where the children are born close together, are often actually delayed in their language development because they get so little opportunity for uninterrupted one-to-one conversation with adults. Even if you are coping with a baby, a toddler and a four year old who never stops asking "why?" try to find at least some times when you can talk to the baby alone.

Don't expect him to learn as much language from strangers, or from a succession of caretakers, as he will from you. The baby learns the meanings of words by hearing them over and over again in different sentences and with varying tones of voice, facial expressions and body language from the speaker. The more familiar he is with the person who is talking, the more likely he is to understand. Talk from you will mean much more to him than talk from a stranger. Indeed, even at the toddler stage (see p. 356) he may be quite unable to understand a stranger's *words* because the accompanying expressions and tones of voice are strange to him.

Make sure that you actually use the key labelling words when you talk. The baby is going to single out label-words which continually recur in different sentences, like that label-word "shoe". So when the two of you are hunting under the bed, make sure that you say "Oh, where are your shoes?" rather than "Oh, where are they?" When the door needs shutting, make sure you say "I'll go and shut the door" rather than "I'll go and shut it". The child's own name is a vital label for him to learn. He will not think of himself as "me" or "I"; indeed as we shall see (see p. 416), English grammar makes this kind of word extremely difficult for a child to learn because the correct word depends on who is speaking. I am "me" to myself, but I am "you" to you. So at this stage, you use his name-label, too. Don't feel embarrassed because it is "baby talk". "Where's a biscuit for John?" you can say as you rummage in the biscuit tin. It will mean much more to him than "where's one for you?"

Talk to the baby about things which are physically present so that he can *see* what you are talking about and make an immediate connection between the object and the recurring key word. "Wasn't it funny when that cat we saw ran up the tree?" will not mean nearly as much to him as "Look at that cat. Do you see her? The cat is going to run up that tree. There! A cat in a tree. . . ."

Talk about things which interest your baby. Not all your conversation can be about immediately visible things, but you can make sure that the subject means something to him. A long story about his sister's day at school will mean very little but the story of the squirrel he saw in the park that evening may rivet his attention. Even if he does not understand everything you say, he will pick up the subject matter and, perhaps, the labels for the things he learned while they were visible, like "squirrel" or "nut".

Overact. Use lots of gestures and expressions. You can make your meaning much clearer to the baby if you point to the things you are talking about, indicate the thing you want him to crawl over and get, and generally "ham" your message a bit. Babies with vocal, outgoing parents often learn to understand and use exclamations first of all because they hear them used over and over again and with exaggerated inflections and infectious excitement: "Oh dear!" you may say when he falls down and "Up you come!" as you lift him from his cot.

Try to understand your baby's words or invented words. You will help to motivate him towards ever-increasing efforts at speech if you can make it clear to him, by your reaction to his sounds, that you care what he says; that it matters to your understanding whether he uses the right word or not; and that you will try to understand any attempt at communication that he does make. Of course this is a subtle message to try to convey to a ten or eleven month baby, but the general idea will get across to him if he sees you taking trouble. For example, if he makes a sound and gestures towards something when he is sitting in his high chair, you might look to where he is pointing, and list for him all the things that you can see which he might have meant. If you hit the right one his pleasure as he repeats his "own-word" will be immense.

If you see him crawling around looking for something, using a word questioningly, join the hunt for the nameless object. Once again, when it is found, the baby's pleasure in your understanding will repay the trouble you have taken.

Help your baby to use those few words in obviously useful situations. If you are playing together and you can both see where the ball has rolled to, ask him to get it for you. When he crawls back with it you can confirm that he understood you correctly by thanking him, using the word again: "Good boy, you've brought your ball". If you then play ball with him the whole transaction of words and actions will have an obvious and pleasurable point for him.

Don't correct or pretend not to understand "own-words". Correcting him, or trying to make him say the word again "properly", will only bore the baby. He does not want to say the same thing again better, he wants to say something else now. Your corrections will not have any effect anyway because, as we have seen, he is not imitating language but developing it. His "own-word" will evolve into something more correct in its own good time but not at your command. If you pretend not to understand the baby unless he says something "properly", you are cheating him. He has communicated with you, made you understand his meaning. He has therefore used a piece of language. If you refuse to acknowledge it, you spoil the flow of his language development. He cannot instantly produce the "correct" word, because that word has not evolved for him yet. His "own-word" is the best that he has to offer. Remember, too, that it is pleasure, affection and excitement that motivate early speech. Refusing to hand him his bottle until he says "milk" instead of "bah-boo" will make him frustrated and cross. You are more likely to get tears than words.

Playing and learning

This is a very physical half-year. During it babies are learning to sit up alone, to get across the room on their own and to get up on their own two legs (see p. 236). Achieving these things takes enormous physical effort, and each has to be practised endlessly before the baby is ready to pass on to the next. Luckily for children's continuing development, all babies have a tremendous inbuilt drive to succeed. A baby who can crawl, will crawl. Nothing but actual confinement will prevent it. A baby who can pull up to standing position will do so and the persistence with which he or she will go on trying to stand alone, despite endless wobbling, falling and getting up again, is remarkable. We adults would send for a wheelchair after two days of it but the drive in your baby ensures that he or she will press on.

These new physical achievements earn babies a large new measure of independence. They no longer have to rely on adults to bring them bits of the world to handle and explore. They can go and find things for themselves. They need no longer accept passively whatever is offered to them but can begin to have their own ideas about what they want to do, what they will play with.

Yet along with this new physical independence goes an increasing emotional dependence. Your baby wants and needs constant emotional support and encouragement as he or she learns the difficult lessons of growing up, through play.

Safe physical freedom

Sitting, crawling and standing are occupations in themselves for a baby. At this stage he is just as keen to practise crawling for its own sake as he is to crawl so as to get to somewhere else.

So the main thing he needs for his play is a floor and freedom to use it. If the household has not yet set up a playspace for him, it will need to now. He must have some area of floor which is suitable and acceptable for his constant use. The ideal floor is large, uncluttered (especially by delicate, breakable or tippable furniture), reasonably soft and warm, easily cleaned and near to wherever you are likely to spend most of your time.

A few families will be lucky enough to have such a floor, perhaps in an already established playroom, perhaps in the family living room or even perhaps in a large open-plan kitchen. Others will have to compromise and invent.

A hard, cold, stone or tiled floor can be partly covered with carpet tiles or even with cheap coconut matting, which is hard on knees but not bad for heads.

A dining room opening out of the kitchen can often be made suitable for the baby, without losing its basic use, if the door between the two rooms is left open with a stair gate fixed across. This gives the baby a view of his mother without giving him access to a small and dangerous kitchen. With thought, a large kitchen can itself be made safe. Dangerous knives, cleaning fluids etc can live on wall racks or high shelves; electric appliances can be guarded and most cooking can be confined to the back burners.

If living space is very short, a corridor or hall is often usable by the baby if stairs are properly gated. And any kind of garden, porch or yard can be made safe for him with a little do-it-yourself (see Enc/Safety).

If the baby has suitable floorspace close to you, he will occupy himself on it and around you for a great deal of his waking time. It is worth putting thought and effort into this space both because it will be basic to your lives together for many months and because some obvious-seeming solutions will not work well for any of you.

A special playroom in some out-of-the-way part of the house will not work, however beautiful it is. If you make him play there, he will be extremely lonely and bored as well as at risk without your constant presence. You will find that you either abandon it and let him play in the (unprepared) kitchen or that you take all your jobs from their natural places in order to do them companionably in the playroom. The same applies to making his upper-floor bedroom into a bed-playroom. On the other hand he should not be expected to play in a crowded family living room unless it has been carefully adapted for him. He will inevitably damage and break things like books, records, ornaments and pot-plants. The damage is not fair to you and your recurrent irritation because of it is not fair to him. Nor is a playpen, in that living room, the answer. Even a baby who willingly goes in it cannot learn all that he should if he is constantly confined. An unwilling baby should not be imprisoned at all.

Of course the baby needs other kinds of play too, but these can be saved for times when you can pay him your full attention, protect him from dangers and keep other people's possessions from his clutches. Changes of scene and associated changes of activity are important. They broaden the play possibilities which are available to the baby, and stop him from getting bored. Changes can range from a simple move to another room, to an elaborate expedition. For example, a romp on a double bed is a marvellous game for a baby of this age. Play with toys on the carpeted floor of the sitting room makes a welcome change from the hard floor of the kitchen. Trips outdoors combining pushchair riding with, perhaps, a crawl on the nearest available grass, are vital. The more you can take him out with you the better. A 20-minute shopping trip which seems boring to you is full of new experiences for him.

Playthings Actual toys are less important to babies during this age period than freedom to get moving and eventually to start exploring. Many of the playthings suggested for younger babies (see p. 192) will still please this age-group and they will seem different to them too, once they can sit up alone to manipulate them and crawl across the floor to find them. But a few new things will give your baby particular pleasure because they are especially appropriate to this particular stage of development.

Once he can crawl, he will much enjoy things that roll along, whether they are actual balls or wheeled toys. He will crawl after them, learn to push them and then give chase. Choose large objects and be sure that wooden toys have no sharp or protruding bits.

Once he learns voluntarily to let go of objects, two kinds of "game" become possible. He will enjoy actually throwing things.

He can have small cushions, beanbags, or balloons which are not blown hard enough to pop. He will also begin to enjoy putting things into containers and emptying them out again. Small bricks and a box or oranges and a paper bag are ideal.

As he learns about cause and effect and discovers his own power over objects, he will begin to enjoy simple musical instruments such as a drum, tambourine, maracas and xylophone. He will enjoy the noise itself (even if you do not) and he will revel in the realization that it was his own action that produced the sound and that he can produce it again whenever he pleases.

He will feel the same joyous sense of power if he is given toys which do something when a string is pulled or a lever is pushed, such as a jointed "dancing man" or a duck that quacks when he pushes it.

Organizing toys   The baby will not remember what toys he owns during these months except that he will notice if special things (like his "cuddly") are missing. If you keep toys put away out of sight, they will be out of mind too. You cannot leave it to him to go searching for what is not immediately available. On the other hand, if everything he owns is permanently strewn on "his" floor, he will get bored of all his toys just because he has seen them all so often. Some toys actually age without ever being used because the baby comes to regard them as totally familiar.

At this stage a very large shallow basket – such as the old-fashioned baker's basket – or a large smooth plastic tray, provides a good toy hold-all. If everything lives in there, and it is kept in a corner of "his" floor, the baby will quickly learn where to go when he wants something, and you will be able to do a quick clear up in between play sessions.

A baby who cannot yet crawl needs to be given a few toys at a time as he sits in his chair, his pram or on the floor. Once he is mobile he can help himself from a small selection. When he is first put down on the floor, after breakfast or after a nap, get out a small number of toys for him, and just put them on the floor. Then, when he begins to get bored, pick those toys up and get him out a new batch, encouraging him to add to them from the hold-all.

Keep a few items on a high shelf or in a cupboard, to be produced occasionally. They might be toys that need close supervision, or toys that make so much noise you cannot stand them all the time. Either way they will keep their play value for longer by being produced only on special occasions.

Keep a box or basket into which you put things the baby might like as you come across them. Each shopping trip will produce some. Christmas will bring bright papers and labels and ribbons. Clearing out a kitchen cupboard might produce a plastic pot with a lid that can be filled with something rattly or a plastic scoop you don't want any more; you might save a cardboard box or cereal packet or an empty squeeze bottle he will enjoy in the bath. If you are clever about this, you will always have a "new toy" for the baby, ready to be produced on a grumbly day or when the weather keeps him in or a visitor comes and takes your attention from him. No "toy" will do *instead* of you, but a new one might allow you a few minutes conversation!

By around eight months your baby will be into a highly imitative phase. This, combined with attachment to you and growing mobility (see p. 236), will make him or her want to use the things you use, do the things you do and generally join in your life.

While the baby clearly cannot "help" you to practise the violin, type your novel or do your research, almost every form of domestic activity lends itself admirably to being companionable and educational fun for the baby while getting itself accomplished. However tedious daily housework chores, like cleaning the bath, may seem to you, they are neither tedious nor chores to your child. You are playing with water and he or she would like to play with water too. The baby has no idea that there is a hygienic purpose behind your "game", much less that you "play" it out of duty rather than pleasure and want to get it over as fast as possible.

Your baby's "help" will certainly slow you up. The pie you might have made in twenty minutes may take an hour if he is to have some pastry to play with, dabble in the flour and do the washing up. But if you refuse to let him join in, trying to get an efficient minimum of chores done at your usual high speed despite the baby's presence, he will be unhappy and you will be irritated. The trick is to select those aspects of domestic life which you quite enjoy and slow your pace for them right down so that there is room and time for him. The chores you really dislike, and could not bear to have spun out over unnecessary hours, can be saved to be efficiently polished off while he is napping.

Cooking will delight the baby, who will see it as "messy play" or as "water play". You will probably be able to work most safely if you put him in his high chair in the kitchen and hand him odds and ends to mix, pummel and taste.

Housework can seem like a pleasant play all over the house if you are prepared to take the baby with you and bounce him on the bed you are making, play peek-a-boo around the furniture and give him a duster to wave. Watch out for cleaning chemicals, though. Almost all will be dangerous if he tries to drink them, while spray polishes are dangerous to his eyes as well.

Gardening is also a good game, especially if there is earth he can scrabble in and grass to crawl on. Once again there may be danger from sharp implements or chemicals; an apron or coat with capacious pockets to secrete them in as you move from one job to another may be a good idea.

Laundry and ironing are neither much fun nor safe "games" for the baby. They are probably best saved for nap-time.

Shopping, whether it involves a saunter to a shop nearby for two items or a major supermarket expedition, can be a treat. He will enjoy riding in a trolley, helping himself to things off the shelves, opening the packets and sampling the contents. . . . Accept the inevitable and let him help himself to something innocuous, like a small packet of biscuits, right at the beginning. Getting them open and eating a couple will distract him from destroying every shelf display and opening every purchase!

Unpacking shopping is almost the best game of all. If you can deftly remove the eggs, tomatoes, and any other squashy or dangerous purchases, he will unpack the cans and the oranges for you and roll them all over the floor. . . .

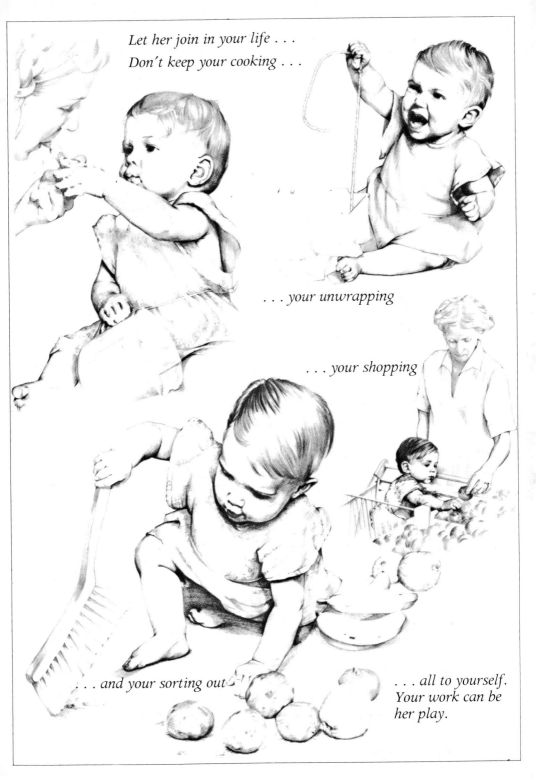

Let her join in your life . . .
Don't keep your cooking . . .

. . . your unwrapping

. . . your shopping

. . . and your sorting out

. . . all to yourself.
Your work can be
her play.

Enjoying the mobile baby

Newly mobile babies are not always easy to live with. Being able to get around a room enormously increases their ability to get themselves into danger or to break and destroy things; yet the mobility does not bring even the smallest amount of extra commonsense with it. You have to watch your baby, every minute that he or she is awake. You have to prevent what you cannot allow as well as helping with the activities you approve of, and somehow you have to make space for the baby to do baby things while you preserve the space that rightly belongs to other members of the family. Many mothers find this the most difficult of all stages in child-rearing. Anything that you can do to make daily life easier for yourselves will be worthwhile. After all you are aiming to enjoy these months, not merely to survive them.

Making life easier for all of you

Try to arrange the easiest possible physical circumstances for yourselves and the baby. Even if it takes a whole week-end of hard work to reorganize the living room so that breakables and books are out of reach, it will be worth it. If you don't, you will spend literally *hours* taking things away from the baby and the baby away from things, day after day.

Where one particular issue continually makes trouble between you, take action to make it totally impossible for the baby. If, for example, he is always escaping from you and trying to climb the stairs, put up a stair gate and leave it there permanently. The danger and the trouble are both removed together. If he insists on messing around with the magazine rack, remove it out of reach. Once it has gone it cannot cause trouble. Sometimes this kind of action takes a bit of thought. If trouble arises over something like opening the refrigerator door, you may have to tie it shut until the craze wears off. It is a bore for you but better than endless rows.

Arrange basic safety precautions (see Enc/Safety). Your nerves will stay in better shape if you know he cannot fall downstairs, electrocute or burn himself.

Be positive with your baby. Try and provide a permitted equivalent to every action you have to forbid. If he may not empty out that drawer, which may he empty? The answer "none" is bound to lead to trouble once he has got the drawer-emptying idea; the answer "this one" will satisfy you both.

Use the distractibility of this age-group. If he insists on playing with the wastepaper basket, remove it out of sight and give him something else. He will have forgotten in two minutes. If you can't move the object, move the baby. Five minutes in another room and he will have forgotten any but the most entrancing games.

Put fun for everybody before pride in your home. If you try to sweep every crumb and tidy each muddle *as it occurs* you will go mad. Decide when you really want the place cleaned up (whether that is twice a day or once a week...); do it all in one almighty blitz and then don't worry until the next blitz is due.

Anger and punishment

However well you get yourself organized, life will not always run smoothly. You will have days when everything the baby does seems irritating. You will get angry. Don't be too upset if you find you have yelled at him. It is often easier for a baby or small child to cope with a parent who loses his or her temper from time to time than with one who bottles the irritation up and becomes silent and withdrawn. Your baby needs your cheerful companionship. If you withhold it from him he will be bewildered and lonely. He cannot flourish in an emotional vacuum. If you yell at him he will certainly be frightened but at least it will be quickly over. With your pent-up feelings relieved he will be able to see that you are ready to talk and to play again.

But try to remember that he will not have the least idea *why* you yelled and that your anger will therefore seem to strike out of the blue, like a thunderbolt. He has no way of knowing that just one more minor disaster was a "last straw" for you. He knows very little of your feelings which are not yet his concern. If you actually punish him physically, shaking him, smacking him or dumping him in his cot, he will be as amazed and horrified as you would be if the family dog suddenly turned on you and took a chunk out of your leg. Whatever you do to him in anger, he will not understand *why*.

Suppose he breaks an ashtray. You will probably justify your anger by saying that you have told him many times not to touch it and anyway he should have been more careful. But think a minute. He touched it because his vital curiosity told him to examine it and his memory and understanding are not yet good enough to tell him it was forbidden. He broke it because his manual dexterity is not yet adequate for handling delicate things gently. So was the accident really his *fault*? If the ashtray was really valuable, what was it doing left within his reach? He is being punished for being what he is. A baby.

Suppose he tips food out of his dish on to the freshly-washed floor. In fury you say that "he ought to know better". But ought he? A few minutes earlier you helped him to tip bricks out on the floor. Is he supposed to share your ideas about what is a "toy" and what is not? As to the clean floor, he probably watched you sloshing bubbly water over it. Is he supposed to understand that soapy water cleans things, but gravy dirties them? Once again you are being angry with him for being the age he is and for behaving as people in his age bracket are meant to behave.

Staying on your baby's side

Somehow, as parents, you have to find ways of staying on the same side as your baby, making the most of the good bits of each day and laughing at the misfortunes. An absolute determination to enjoy yourselves is what makes this possible. Find pleasure in being clever enough to guide him without his noticing, distract him before there is a clash and save him before there is an accident. Teach yourselves to look at life from his point of view as well as your own. Be intent, above all, on loving him and enjoying his passionate love for you. The last thing he wants is to displease you. You are his Gods. But it will be a long time yet before he can understand what *does* please you. Your pleasures are not the same as his. You don't *like* gravy on the floor. . . .

CHAPTER FIVE

THE TODDLER

From one year to two and a half

Your toddler is no longer a baby feeling himself as part of you, using you as his controller, facilitator, his mirror for himself and the world. But he is not yet a child either; ready to see you as a person in your own right and to take responsibility for himself and his own actions in relation to you. He has begun to be aware that you and he are separate people. Some of the time he asserts this new-found individuality, crying "No!" and "Let me!", fighting your control and help each time an issue presents itself. But some of the time he clings to you, crying when you leave the room, holding up his arms to be carried, demanding with open mouth that you should feed him.

His in-between behaviour is confusing for you but it is painful for him. He has to become a person in his own right but it feels safer to remain your possession. He has to begin to reject your total control over him yet it is easier to accept it. He has to develop likes and dislikes of his own and to pursue his own ends even when they conflict with yours, yet the conflict feels desperately dangerous to him. He still loves you with an unrivalled passion; depending on you totally for emotional support. The developmental imperative of independence conflicts with the emotional imperative of love.

If you expect your toddler to remain what he was – a comparatively biddable baby – he will have to clash with you directly. He needs your love and approval but his drive to grow up will not allow him to accept them at the price of too much dependence. But if you expect him to change overnight into what he will be – a sensible child – he will feel himself inadequate. He needs your help and comfort and if they are withheld from him, he cannot manage. Babied, he is bolshy. Pushed on, he is whiney.

There is a middle road which allows him to adventure but ensures him against disaster; helps him to try but cushions his failures; gives him a firm framework for acceptable behaviour yet pads it so that it does not bruise his dawning sense of being his own boss. It depends on understanding and on a refusal to be fooled by appearances. In many ways he seems much more grown up than he feels. His walking, his talking and his play develop to a point where he seems little different from a three year old, but his understanding and his experience do not match up to them. If you treat him as a baby, you will hold him back. He must learn to understand. He must have experience. But if you treat him as you would treat a pre-school child, you put him under intolerable pressure. He has to be taught to understand. He must have experience made manageable.

The key to understanding him lies in understanding the development of his thought processes. It is only as these mature that those conflicting emotions and misleading abilities can come together to form the reasonable and manageable whole we call a child.

The toddler has a memory, but it is still very short. When he was a baby, doing baby things, this was neither very important nor very obvious. But now he is trying to do more grown up things it is both vital and conspicuous. Day after day he trips and tumbles over the step between kitchen and living room. Wild with irritation and plagued by worry over the bumps on his head, you wonder whether he will ever learn. He will, but it will take time. He cannot "bear that step in mind" until repeated experience has finally given it a permanent place in his memory. When he was a baby it would have been your job to prevent him tumbling. When he is a child it will be your job to point the step out to him. But right now your job is to modify the painful results of that series of experiences and to jog that memory. You may need to pad the step and issue endless reminders.

With little memory of events in the past the child is almost without forethought. If he can climb that step-ladder, he will do so. He cannot think ahead to the problem of how to get down again. Often lack of memory and of forethought combine to get him into trouble. He has been scolded again and again for twiddling the knobs of the television set, but as he approaches it again today he neither remembers past scoldings nor foresees the new one that is coming. Those knobs draw him like a magnet.

Because he cannot think ahead, he cannot wait a second for anything. If he wants it at all, he wants it *now* and the clamouring begins even as he watches you remove the wrapper from the longed-for lolly. Unable to wait for things he likes, he cannot put up with even minor discomfort now, in order to be more comfortable later. Wailing with misery because the lolly has made him so sticky, he will still fight off the washcloth that brings relief. He is a creature of this moment only.

Similar immaturities in his thinking get him into trouble in his relationships with people, too. He loves you. Everyone tells you that he loves you. He tells you that he loves you. Yet he cannot behave in the ways we adults think of as "loving". He cannot put himself in

*No longer a baby, not yet a child, a toddler
can swing in a moment from happiness to misery...*

your place or see things through your eyes. He will hate it if you cry but it will be the feelings your tears arouse in *him* which he dislikes, not the feelings the tears represent in you. It is not his job yet to consider other people's feelings, he has to come to terms with his own first. If he hits you and you hit him back to "show him what it feels like", you will have given a lesson he is not ready to learn. He will wail as if hitting was a totally new idea to him. He makes no connection between what he did to you and what you then did to him; between your feelings and his own.

Even his own feelings are often still a mystery to him. He does not know what he feels now, and this, combined with being unable to remember what he felt last time or predict what he will feel later, makes decisions impossibly difficult for him. "Do you want to stay with me or go to the shop with Daddy?" seems a simple and insignificant choice. But it is neither straightforward nor unimportant to the toddler. Which will he enjoy more? Which did he enjoy last time? Which does he feel like doing now? He does not and cannot know. He dithers and, whichever is finally chosen for him, he is miserable. He will have to learn to make his own decisions. Nobody can be mature who has everything decided for him. But practice-decisions should be ones where he has nothing to lose. If he has two sweets, "which are you going to eat first?" is a question he can consider without stress. He has got them both. Nobody is going to take away the one he decides against. He can change his mind six sticky times if he pleases.

The child's language may get him into trouble by suggesting that his understanding is greater than it is. He learns new words and he uses them more and more freely, but many of them still lack for him the subtler meanings. He cannot possibly understand, much less keep, a promise. Yet he may well use the word. If you offer him five minutes more play if he will promise to come straight to bed afterwards, he will happily say "I promise". The word is an agreement label. But after that five minutes he wants a further five. He cannot understand the reproach in your voice as you say "but you *promised.....*"

Words make trouble over truth too. He may talk fluently enough to issue frequent accusations and denials while their accuracy still means nothing to him. He talks as he feels. It might have been the dog that made that puddle. He wishes it had been and says that it was. When in the course of a quarrel with his sister, he falls and hurts his knee, he says that she pushed him. She did not hurt his knee but she did hurt his feelings. He is telling a kind of feeling-truth which just happens to be different from adult truth.

Later on you will be able to demonstrate the value of promises thoughtfully made and reliably kept; of truth told and lies avoided. But it is too soon yet. Don't corner him with concepts he cannot understand. He is doing his best to please, but if nothing less than child-standards will please you, he will fail.

. . . your role is to keep a balance
between her need for independence as she jumps in
and her need to be protected from going right under water

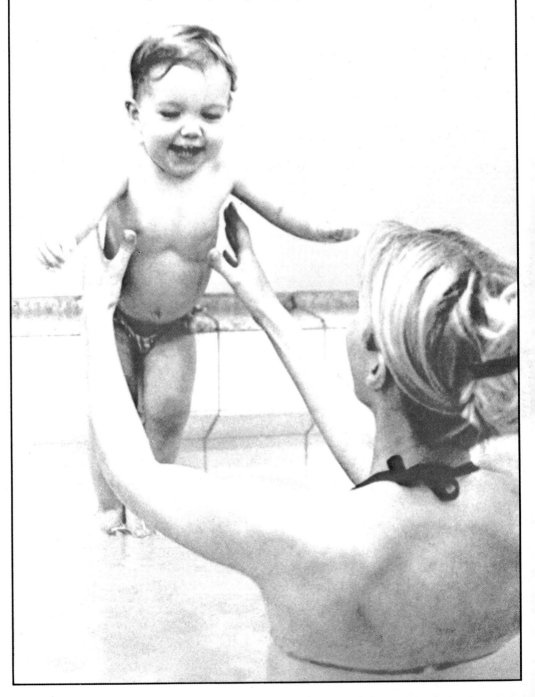

Your child's developmental clock has told him that it is time to stop being a baby and move towards being a separate person. If you treat him as a baby, he will fight you every step of the way and, in the end, he will win his independence because he must. But he will win it at a terrible price paid in lost love.

That clock does not yet read "childhood", so attempts to discipline him as you discipline a child will not work either. You will be faced with a lack of comprehension that looks like defiance, and every battle you join will end with love lost. So don't try for absolute control and don't join moral battles. Your toddler will be "good" if he feels like doing what you happen to want him to do and does not happen to feel like doing anything you would dislike. With a little cleverness you can organize life as a whole, and issues in particular, so that you both want the same thing most of the time. Your toddler has his bricks all over the floor and you want the room tidy. If you tell him to pick them up, he will probably refuse. If you insist, a fight will be on and you cannot win it. You can scream at him, punish him, reduce him to a jelly of misery but none of that will get those bricks off the floor. But if you say, "I bet you can't put those bricks in their bag before I've peeled these potatoes", you turn the whole issue into a game. Now he wants to do what you want him to do, so he will. He did not do it "for Mummy"; he did not do it because he is a "good boy". He did it because you made him want to. And that is the trick. You conduct his life by foreseeing the rocks and steering around them, avoiding absolute orders that will be absolutely refused, leading and guiding the toddler into behaving as you want him to behave because nothing has made him want to behave otherwise.

The payoff now is fun instead of strife for you all. But the payoff later is even more important. This toddler, who does not know right from wrong and cannot choose to behave well or badly, is growing up. The time will come when he does understand your feelings and your rights; does remember your instructions and foresee the results of his actions. When that time comes he *will* be able to be "good' or "naughty" on purpose. Which he chooses will depend largely on how he feels about you. If he reaches that next stage of growing up feeling that you are basically loving, approving and on his side, he will want (most of the time) to please you. So, with many lapses, he will behave as you wish. But if he reaches that stage feeling that you are overpowering, incomprehensible and against him, he may have decided that it is no use trying to please you because you are never pleased; no use minding when you are cross because you are cross so often, and too dangerous to let himself love you because you have so often seemed not to love him. If he reaches pre-school age not wanting approval, not feeling cooperative, not confident that he loves and is loved, you will have lost the whole basis for good and easy "discipline" right through childhood. At this age, a happy child is an easy child and a child kept easy now will be easy to handle later.

Feeding and growing

Once past the first birthday your baby's weight gain will probably slow down to around 1–2ozs (28–57g) a week. A faster or slower rate of gain may, of course, be perfectly right for your baby because, as we have said, there is a wide variation around the "average" at all ages.

Unless the baby has been ill or has had major feeding troubles during the first year, there is not much point in going on with regular weighing now. To weigh every week would be absurd as the scales may not be accurate enough to weigh to the nearest ounce and simple things like passing a motion before or after the weighing will be enough to produce a false gain or loss. It is probably best to weigh and measure every three months, so that you can see your baby getting heavier and taller both at the same time.

Changing proportions

We have already seen that the proportions of a newborn baby's body are quite different from those of an older baby (see p. 160). During this year they change even more. When a baby of around a year first gets up on his own two feet parents are often very worried by his appearance. His head is still large in relation to the rest of him and his neck seems non-existent. His shoulders and chest are thin, his belly sticks out, his legs seem bowed and his feet have no arches. But in the course of a year, all that will change. The year old baby is still the right shape for life on all fours. By the time he is two his proportions will have changed so that he is much better suited for life on his hind legs. A year later still he will probably have slimmed down and elongated, so that he has the lithe and leggy elegance typical of an active pre-school child.

Here again are the heights and weights for the babies you first met on p. 37. All three slow their growth rate now. All grow at similar rates while maintaining their differences from one another. Their curves are therefore like those on p. 508, even though, being individual children, their actual measurements differ from the average.

HEIGHT — TALL / AVERAGE / SHORT

WEIGHT — HEAVY / AVERAGE / LIGHT

AGE IN YEARS

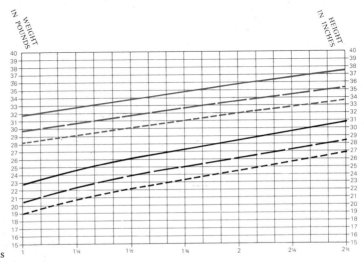

Feeding By the beginning of the second year your baby will be ready to share many of the foods which you serve to the rest of the family and ready to have meals at the times which suit the rest of you.

If you are cooking fresh foods, you can make almost all of them suitable for a baby by a little last-minute adaptation. Any form of meat or fish, for example, can be cut into small pieces while you are serving. Vegetables can be puréed or cut into finger-sized cubes. Cooked fruits can be mashed, or sieved if they are pippy. Fried foods which might be too fatty for him can be grilled or dry-fried in a non-stick pan, while rich sauces can be replaced at the last minute with plain stock.

If you are not doing much cooking for the rest of the family, you may find that some of the commercially prepared babyfoods are still useful. For example, if you do not provide a cooked breakfast for anyone else, a helping of baby cereal (see p. 210) will provide your baby with much more nourishment than a similar sized helping of adult breakfast cereal. If you do not usually provide puddings, "Toddler desserts" or "Fruit varieties" will save you stewing half an apple or cooking a minute rice pudding just for the baby.

Adult convenience foods need to be used with some care. Although most frozen foods have the same nutritional quality as fresh food, canned and dehydrated foods are often nutritionally poor. A bowl of canned tomato soup, for example, may fill your baby's tummy but it will not provide many calories nor many useful vitamins. Dehydrated meals, soups and sauces usually contain a great deal of salt. Although the baby's ability to cope with salt does improve with age, too much will still place a strain on the kidneys. Furthermore these foods also usually contain a variety of preservatives, colourings and artificial flavouring agents such as the ubiquitous monosodium glutamate. Although most countries have stringent regulations to control the use of chemicals in food, many people believe that we should all be better off with eating fewer of them. So while there is no need to go to extremes – the occasional gravy made with a stock cube will not hurt your baby – it is not a good idea to feed a steady diet of these manufactured foods.

The same caution applies to adult soft drinks. If you read the small print on a bottle of fruit squash, you will probably find that it contains a variety of sweeteners, flavourings and colouring agents and very little real fruit. An occasional drink of one of these products will not do your baby any harm but for regular consumption and plenty of vitamin C, stick to fresh orange juice or to one of the vitamin C enriched fruit syrups. Of course if the toddler is simply thirsty, there is no drink to beat plain water.

Worries about feeding After being bombarded with detailed advice about feeding a baby, parents who seek help at the toddler stage usually find themselves fobbed off with the magical phrase "a good mixed diet". When they enquire what such a diet consists of they are told to "give plenty of meat and fish; eggs; cheese; milk and fresh green vegetables...". Realizing that their toddler dislikes and refuses almost every one of those items, they wonder whether their child can be eating properly. The seeds of anxiety (and therefore of feeding problems) are sown. So let us look a little more deeply into that good mixed diet.

<table>
<tr><td>

What is a "good mixed diet"?

</td><td>

A mixed diet is one which contains some of each of a wide variety of foods, eaten in different combinations, every day. Its virtue lies in the fact that a person who eats it will quite certainly get everything his or her body requires under all circumstances (see Enc/Diet). If what you need is not in one food, it will be in another. If you do not eat enough of one nutrient at breakfast, the deficiency will be made good at lunchtime. So if your child *does* eat a good mixed diet, you do not have to think about it. You need not even try to work out what your child needs or is getting because day by day and week by week the two will match up.

</td></tr>
</table>

This is a major advantage because working these things out is complicated. Total food needs and requirements for specific nutrients vary both from person to person and in the same person from one day to the next. Your own entirely adequate diet, for example, may suddenly fall short of the exceptional need for iron brought on by a series of heavy menstrual periods. Working out what you are getting from specific portions of food is even more complex. We know, for example, how much protein is in 6ozs (170g) of lean beef. But how lean is lean? We know how much vitamin C is in 4ozs (114g) of freshly picked raw spring cabbage. But how much reaches your stomach after the cabbage has been picked, transported, stored, cooked and kept warm? On a mixed diet these vexed questions need not concern you. If you have some meat or fish, some cheese, eggs and milk you will be getting adequate protein. And if that cabbage does not contain much vitamin C, it does not matter; there will be plenty in your potatoes and fruit.

So wide variety, that "good mixed diet", is the safe and easy way to feed any child well. Aim at it, by all means, as you gradually accustom yours to ordinary family meals, but don't feel that without it he or she must be poorly nourished.

Your child's diet can be both good and mixed enough without having to include normal quantities of all the foods that are conventionally considered "good for him". The value of any one food lies in the use which the body can make of its constituents. No food is magically good-in-itself; it is only as good as the sum total of what is in it. There is therefore no single food which is absolutely necessary, because anything which is in one food will also be in some others. Milk is an excellent example because it is often described as "necessary" for children. This is nonsense. Milk is an exceedingly valuable food and a very convenient package of nutrients children need in an easy-to-take form. But even milk is not unique. The valuable proteins, minerals and vitamins it contains are in other foods too.

This argument carries over into the way in which you present foods to your child. Eggs are good for children. But they do not have to be presented in the shell, or gazing one-eyed off a plate, in order to be nourishing. The egg in the pancake your child enjoys is just as nourishing as that breakfast egg would be if it was eaten!

So if your child does indeed eat a conventional good mixed diet, you are fortunate. He will certainly be getting everything he needs and you need not think any further about his food. Don't even bother with the rest of this chapter. But if he does not, don't worry. If you read on, you will almost certainly find that, whatever individual foods he rejects, he is getting enough of everything important from the combinations he likes.

Calories Whatever foods you offer your child they will contain calories. He needs calories for growth, to keep his body's functions ticking over and to fuel his activities. However much or little he chooses to eat, you can be quite sure that it is enough if he is well, energetic and growing.

Foods vary in the concentration of calories which they contain. Those rich in fats contain most of all. One slice of bread thickly spread with butter gives the child more energy than two slices eaten plain, one French fried potato yields as much as three boiled ones. A child who seems to eat very little food may be eating it in a high-calorie form.

Carbohydrates Sugar is pure carbohydrate, but most of the carbohydrate foods are bulky ones like bread (and other flour products) and potatoes and other root vegetables. We get most of our energy from carbohydrate foods because we eat a lot of them.

If your child is eating at all, his appetite will see to it that he gets all the carbohydrate foods he needs for energy and bulk. Although too many sweet foods might be bad for his teeth and/or his figure, don't dismiss all these starchy foods as "just fattening". Potatoes and bread, for example, are excellent items of diet.

Fats It does not matter if your child does not appear to eat any fat at all in any form. His body needs minute traces of three specific "fatty acids", but these occur in all animal and vegetable fats and he will get enough from invisible sources like greased cooking pans or commercial biscuits.

Protein Protein is important in your child's diet as his body needs it to build new tissues. But the amount needed and the difficulty of providing it have both been overplayed by food manufacturers. "High protein" has become an advertising point. In fact a shortage of protein in a child who is offered as much food as he wants to eat is extremely rare.

The use of the terms "first class" and "second class" protein is partly responsible for this confusion. Protein is made up of a number of amino acids. Your child has to eat some of these in ready-made form because his body cannot manufacture them out of the others. These vital amino acids are present in the correct balance in animal foods like meat, fish, milk and other dairy produce and these have therefore been termed "first class" proteins. But there are amino acids in other foods too. The vegetable proteins in bread, potatoes, beans, nuts, etc., are not complete in themselves but they can complete each other. If your child eats a mixture of these, the specific amino acids lacking in one will be balanced by the other and the nett result will be a complete protein intake. The imbalance in the amino acid composition of these "second class" proteins can also be corrected by the addition of very small quantities of animal protein. Bread (which contains vegetable protein) with a hot dog inside (which contains animal protein) would provide the child with a protein intake just as "first class" as that highly recommended, much-disliked slice of meat.

On this basis most toddlers get an ample supply of protein. They may refuse eggs, but they eat puddings and cakes with egg in them. They may refuse meat but they eat luncheon meat or ham, bacon or sausages, fishcakes or hamburgers. The protein they are getting is not as concentrated as it would be in butcher's meat, but balancing the vegetable proteins it is ample.

If your child does not eat enough foods to make a good mixture of vegetable proteins nor like any of the less concentrated forms of animal protein, don't forget milk. As long as he gets as much as one pint of milk per day, either as a drink or in cooking, he will not go short of protein whatever else he does or does not eat.

Calcium
Your child needs an adequate calcium intake both for the proper development of growing bones and teeth and for the correct functioning of muscles and blood clotting. There is a useful amount in bread, flour and other cereals, but a more concentrated source than this is needed. The obvious source is milk. A pint a day will ensure calcium intake. Even if your baby does not appear to *drink* that much milk, you can (and probably do) "lose" it in ordinary cooking, as shown in the following examples.

1oz (28ml) milk per toddler serving	2–3ozs (57–85ml) milk per toddler serving	4ozs (114ml) milk per toddler serving
Creamed/mashed potatoes	Baby cereal	Creamed soup
Scrambled egg	Breakfast cereal	Milkshake
Omelette	Cheese sauce	Cocoa/drinking
Pancake	Custard	chocolate
White sauce for veg	Blancmange	Yoghurt
Batter pudding	Milk jelly	
Creamed fish	Rice pudding	
	Ice cream	

Try cheese too, remembering that this is also a superb source of protein. Given the chance many small children develop a passion for cheese; in cubes to eat in the fingers, grated over vegetables, in sauces, or spread on bread.

Other minerals
The other minerals your child needs are either so widely distributed (like phosphorus) that he is bound to get plenty, or, like iron, they are used and re-used by the body so that daily supplies are unnecessary, provided his stores are adequate.

Vitamins
Most vitamins are widely distributed so that your child automatically gets plenty. Giving the three vital ones as daily multi-vitamin drops or tablets ensures adequate intake, however peculiar the child's eating habits.

Vitamin A. The main sources in the diet are liver, then milk, butter or fortified margarine. Carrots yield "carotene" from which our bodies can make their own vitamin A. A child will probably get enough from these sources but a supplement is a safety measure.

Vitamin D. The only concentrated food sources are egg yolk and fatty fishes. Our bodies can make their own in response to sunlight on bare skin; but a supplement is essential, especially in winter.

Vitamin C. Widely available in fruits and green vegetables, this vital vitamin is nevertheless quite difficult to provide in adequate daily quantities because it is destroyed by both light and heat. Green vegetables displayed outside the greengrocer's in the sunlight, cut up ahead and then boiled in water will have lost most of their vitamin C by the time they are eaten. Quick cooking, instant serving and use of the cooking water, with its dissolved vitamin content, in soups or gravies, help, but it is still difficult to know how much he has had. Potatoes have plenty of vitamin C just under the skin. Served in their jackets some is lost because of heat; peeled and then boiled, even more vanishes.

Fruit is a better source because it is either eaten raw or with its cooking water served as juice. Citrus fruits, which are naturally packaged against light and always served raw, are an ideal source. One orange or its juice will give your child all the daily vitamin C which is needed. A daily serving of one of the commercially prepared vitamin C enriched fruit syrups serves the same purpose. There is no harm in giving this as well as the dosage of vitamin C which is in the multivitamins.

Mealtime behaviour

If your have done everything you can to set your minds at rest about your toddler's diet but you still find yourselves worrying, you may be worrying more about eating *behaviour* than about actual food intake. Refusal of food, which has cost money and which has been prepared with care and love, is hurtful. The mess he makes as he plays with food he is not going to eat seems wasteful and goes against everything adults have been taught about "good manners". His anxiety to get down and get on with life after a few mouthfuls disrupts the family meal and prevents it from being a peaceful social occasion. But understandable though these feelings are, it is a great mistake to get them mixed up with worries about the child's actual *diet*. You are trying to feed him so that he can grow and be healthy. You are also trying to teach him to behave in socially acceptable ways. These are separate tasks: both important, but totally different.

When you say that your child "ought" to eat cabbage, are you thinking of vitamin C or of discipline? As we have seen there are many sources of vitamin C: cabbage is not even a very good one. There are better issues for discipline too.

When you say that he "ought" to eat everything on his plate, are you thinking of him having enough to eat or of "not wasting good food"? As we have seen, he is the one who knows whether he has had enough or not. As to wasting food, isn't it just as much of a waste to force it down a reluctant child as to feed it to the cat?

When you say that he "ought" to eat his main course before

he can have any pudding, is it because you really think the first course contains more important foods, or is it because you know he likes sweet things better and you think he ought to pay for them by ploughing through his meat and vegetables?

Of course it is up to parents to choose how and when to discipline their own children, but if you choose mealtimes you may pay a high price. I have talked to families who had got themselves into such a vicious circle over their toddlers' meals that the whole family's life was ruined by it, often for months at a time. Some families banned all mealtime conversation except stories and nursery rhymes designed to distract the toddler while mother ladled in some food. Others refused all invitations to visit friends for meals because the toddler would only eat at home. Some mothers regularly spent two hours over every meal and a great deal of time in between devising tempting little dishes for the next battle.

It is curious that we get ourselves into this situation, because toddlers get hungry just like everybody else. When they feel hungry their bodies are telling them to eat, and eat they do. Most toddlers with serious "eating problems" are actually rather fat. Very few are thin. But trouble begins because the child does not eat what you offer, when you say or in the way that you approve. The more you try to impose rules and regulations on eating and table manners, the clearer it becomes to the toddler that the mealtable is a marvellous place for a fight. Soon your child knows that it is one place where he or she can always get your attention and concern. That situation is irresistible to the child's growing sense of his or her own power and independence.

Avoiding feeding problems

You are much cleverer than your toddler. If you foresee the possibility of mealtimes becoming a battleground, you can stay one jump ahead by resolutely refusing to become involved. It takes two to make a quarrel. The first steps are to do with you and your own feelings:

Believe that your child will never starve, if he is offered adequate food. This statement is not a careless generalization. It applies to all children and that includes yours. Somehow you have to persuade yourselves to believe it or you will not be able to follow the rest of the programme for avoiding problems.

It might help to check your child's weight so that you can see that it is still following a steady upward curve. If that does not convince you, it might be wise to have the child checked over by your doctor so that you can be authoritatively assured that he is healthy and well-nourished. Finally, you could compare what your child actually eats and drinks with the average "needs" set out in the Encyclopedia (see Diet). Go on seeking reassurance until you honestly believe that your job is only to offer good food, not to force it down your child. A long time ago a research study showed that year old babies who were offered a wide range of foods three times each day selected for themselves, with no adult assistance, persuasion or instruction, diets which, while they were wildly unbalanced day by day, were perfectly balanced in the longer term. Like them, your child may have a bread jag and then a meat passion and then may eat almost nothing but fruit for a day or two without doing himself any harm at all. Trust him to know best. Once you have got yourself to this point the rest of the prevention programme follows naturally:

Encourage your toddler's independence in all areas, especially at meals. Present his food in a form that is reasonably easy to manage, and don't help him unless he asks or gestures for help. If he does, don't scoop food straight from the plate into his mouth. Load the spoon for him and let him take it in his hand and put it in his mouth. Let him feel, always, that eating is something active which he does because he wants the food, not that being fed is something he accepts, passively, from you.

Let the child eat by any method. You want him to feel that getting the food he wants is the important thing, not getting it by tidy use of a spoon. If fingers are easiest for him, let him use them.

Let the child eat in any order or combination. If you will not give him pudding until he has eaten his meat, he will quickly realize that you care more about the main course than the dessert. By the laws of toddler contra-suggestiveness that will instantly make the pudding seem even more desirable. If you will not let him dip bacon in his cereal, he may well decide that he will not eat either of them. Just don't watch if you cannot stand the idea of the combination.

Let the meal end when the child has had enough. If you have accepted that what he eats and how he eats it is up to him, it follows that not eating any more or not eating anything at all is up to him too. You will ruin the effect of your whole campaign if you weaken at the last moment and try to feed him just a few mouthfuls to finish his meal.

Try to keep mealtimes enjoyable. Remember that sitting still is his least favourite occupation and that he still finds it difficult to join in a general family conversation which is not especially directed at him or his interests. Trying to make him sit up to table for a whole family mealtime is bound to lead to trouble.

If you want him to feel part of a family group at table, let him sit up with you, eat what he wants and then get down to play. For a while he may keep coming back for one more mouthful but he will soon learn that once he has got down his meal is over.

If you do not feel able to allow him to leave before others have finished, feed him on his own. At three or thereabouts (see p. 370), he will be delighted to join you and will be able to "behave nicely" in order to earn the honour.

Many families will find that a compromise between these two positions works best. Perhaps you all have breakfast informally together before members of the family leave for work or school; lunch might be with mother and/or older brothers or sisters, while supper might be served separately to the toddler so that the older members of the family can enjoy a peaceful meal once he has been put to bed.

Let him enjoy eating in his own way. Green beans dipped in ice cream may be unconventional, but if that is what he likes . . .

Don't take an unreasonable amount of trouble over your child's food. Of course it is vitally important that he should be offered that "good mixed diet" (see p. 283) but the more money, time and trouble you take buying and preparing attractive and delicious food for the child, the more maddening you will find it when he is unappreciative. Keeping the child's meals simple often helps to keep the emotional temperature down. Why cook minced liver, three vegetables and a rice pudding when you know he will not eat them? Think what he is likely to eat. If the answer is "bread and butter and ham – again", give him that. It is perfectly adequate food; if he eats it, fine. If not, you will not have wasted much.

Don't use food as reward, punishment, bribe or threat. Remember that you are trying to keep the child's eating completely separate from his discipline. If he is hungry, he should eat as much as he wants of whatever is available. If he is not hungry, he should not eat. Food should be neither a treat nor a duty, and it should never be offered as a bribe nor kept from him as a punishment. If he has ice cream, it should be because that is the pudding on today's menu, not because he has been a good boy. If he cannot have ice cream, it should be because it is not on today's menu, not because he has been naughty.

Sweets   If you do not eat sweets yourselves and your child has few older friends, you may be able to prevent him or her from even finding out what a sweet is until around the second birthday. It is probably worth trying. If the rest of the child's diet is sensible, even this period without sweets will help those first teeth to get a good start.

But however careful you are, you are bound to meet the sweet problem by the time of that second birthday. Children see the pretty packets in shops, see the advertisements so cleverly aimed at them on television, see other children munching and sharing. Your child will want to know what they have got. Once sweets are known and recognized, he or she will demand to have some too.

There is no doubt that sweets are bad for your child's teeth. But carefully selected, they do not have to be worse than many other foods; sensibly handled, sweets do not have to become a major issue. Highly refined sugar makes enamel-attacking acid in the child's mouth. Every time sugar is eaten teeth are at risk; the more times per day they are put under attack and the longer the sugar remains in the mouth, the more holes there will eventually be for the dentist's attention. But this applies to *all* sources of refined sugar, not only to sweets. A dinky feeder filled with fruit syrup and sucked over a long period will do just as much harm as the worst kind of sweet while a slice of cake will do as much harm as the least deplorable kind of sweet. So to try and ban all sweets while feeding the child the rest of a normal Western diet is foolish. It is much more sensible to take reasonable care over all sweet foods.

Sweet food which is eaten quickly will do little harm because the acid which is produced is gone from the mouth before it has time to eat into the tooth enamel. A slice of cake or a piece of chocolate are therefore much less harmful than a lollipop which the child sucks all afternoon. Chewy cakes and sweets are usually

worst of all since fragments tend to stick between the teeth and stay there until the next thorough brushing. This may also apply to many of the "healthy" foods which are often suggested as alternatives to sweets; raisins, dates and other dried fruits can cling tenaciously, and although their sugar is not refined, it can do considerable harm. Some dentists even now believe that finishing every meal with an apple is bad advice as small pieces of sweet apple skin wedged between the teeth can do as much harm as the sugary film the apple was intended to remove.

So, when your child reaches the stage when he must have sweets or feel conspicuously different from other children, select the particular sweets carefully and control the manner in which he eats them. Choose types which dissolve quickly, such as chocolate or boiled sweets. Encourage him to eat all that you are going to give him in one short session, so that he eats a ration of six sweets in a quarter of an hour rather than one every half hour throughout the afternoon. Try to arrange for him to have a drink of water as soon as possible after he has finished them, and make sure that his next tooth cleaning session is thorough.

Along with this kind of practical approach it is important to monitor your emotional approach to sweets too because it is the emotional aspects of sweet-eating which tend to make so many problems later on. Almost every human being likes sweet things. Research has shown that even newborn babies can distinguish between plain and sweetened water and that most of them suck longer on the sugared bottles. But instead of calmly accepting that sweet foods are pleasant, we, with our copious supplies of cheap refined sugar, have made the buying and eating of actual sweets part of our pleasure *rituals*. In many families boxes of chocolates are an accepted part of any outing and an expected purchase on any feast day. Sweets are bought as presents, sent as "thank you's", hidden as surprises, given to make banged knees better or disappointments bearable. They are used to convey or to stand in for love, and it is in this light that children yearn, whine and badger for them.

If you use sweets as rewards and treats during the toddler period, your pre-school child is bound to place an emotional value on them as well as liking the taste. If, when he grazes his knee, he gets a chocolate drop along with your hug, that chocolate drop will come to seem comforting to him. He will want sweets whenever he is miserable or hurt and tired. If, when you are especially pleased with him, you buy him sweets, he is bound to see those sweets as being part of your loving feelings. He will want you to buy him sweets to show that you love him. If, when he has to face something unpleasant like an injection, you pay him with a sweet, he is bound to see those sweets as something he is owed whenever anything nasty happens. He will want payment in sweets every time you make him do something he dislikes. If you can keep sweets out of the emotional arena and treat them as coolly and calmly as you treat other particularly nice-tasting things such as strawberries or coca-cola, none of this trouble will arise. Many children passionately enjoy strawberries and will eat as many as they can get during their short season. But how many of those children whine and cry and throw tantrums for strawberries?

Snacks   Many toddlers genuinely need to eat between the day's main meals. A mid-morning and/or a mid-afternoon snack may improve your child's temper as well as giving a welcome structure to the passing hours. Something to take the edge off hunger may prevent a late meal from becoming a major disaster. So try not to take a moralistic attitude to snacks. Food is food and there is no dietary law which says that it is better to eat three times a day than twice or six times. It is all a matter of commonsense and convenience mixed with social convention.

Part of the trouble over snacks arises from the vast market in fun-foods which has grown up during the last ten years. Like sweets, fun-foods are heavily advertised and attractively packaged. Many families react against them in ways which are really quite irrational.

Snack foods are said to be "all rubbish; no goodness in them". In fact these foods are neither more nor less likely to be nutritionally valueless than any of the manufactured foods you serve at table. A hot dog, for example, is a nicely balanced item of diet (see Enc). Dairy ice cream from a reputable manufacturer is an excellent food, at least as good for your child as a home-made custard or milk pudding. Even the lowly potato crisp (although too salty to be good for babies) is only potato, with the water removed, fried in vegetable oil. As such it is a surprisingly good source of vegetable protein and in no way worse for a child than a helping of french fries.

Snack foods are said to be "fattening". Of course all food is fattening if it is food in excess of the amount the child needs. A child who eats adequate meals *and* a lot of snacks will certainly get fat but a child who eats snacks *instead* of part of his meals will not. There is nothing devilish about snack foods which makes them more fattening, calorie for calorie, than food which is served on a plate.

Snacks are said to fill children up so that they "cannot eat 'real' food". Again, this can happen, but it need not. If a child eats a non-nutritious snack when he was not really very hungry, he may well refuse that "good dinner" and indeed he ought to refuse it or he risks obesity. But the child who eats a nutritious snack and then refuses his meal may not be losing anything. It depends what the snack and the meal consisted of. So don't tar all snack foods with the same moralistic brush. As with sweets, the real problem with snacks is an emotional one.

Snacks are almost always foods which, by definition, are bought because the child is hungry, are chosen by him and eaten because he wants to eat them rather than because anyone else cares one way or the other. They therefore escape the pressures to eat which, as we have seen (see p. 287), are so common with toddlers. This alone is enough to make them seem more desirable than "ordinary food". Snack foods are usually eaten under circumstances which are enjoyably different from sitting up to table. Even the process of buying them is more fun for the toddler than the complex processes of supermarket shopping and kitchen food preparation. It is not surprising that many children would rather have that packet of peanuts than their lunch, even if both are available simultaneously.

The answer is to treat snack foods as *food* (which is what they really are) rather than as *treats* (which is what will make trouble). A child should not get potato crisps because he has been good any more than you would offer him cabbage for this reason. His ice cream should not be withheld because he has been tiresome any more than you would refuse to serve him meat. As with sweets, if you keep the emotional temperature down in this way, remaining problems over snacks should be easy to handle.

The trick is to make sure that you offer the child the kinds of food he likes best as occasional parts of his regular meals, while keeping simpler foods freely available for eating between meals when he is genuinely hungry. Instead of waiting for him to nag you for chocolate while you are out shopping, serve him a couple of squares, with an apple, as a sweet course at lunch. Instead of taking a moralistic attitude to pleas for potato crisps, serve them occasionally in place of that boring mashed potato.

Your child will still get hungry between meals from time to time. When he does, offer him something plain like bread and butter. If he is hungry enough to accept it, he is hungry enough for a snack to be sensible. He will not eat bread and butter from greed, and the sweet biscuits he might have eaten from gluttony are coming up on the supper table to be eaten or left as he thinks fit. The whole situation is emotionally de-fused.

Fat toddlers

A toddler can be plump without being fat. A lot of children are meant to be big; they are big babies, big toddlers, big children and eventually big adults. You cannot always judge whether your toddler is getting too fat just by looking. At this age faces are often very round and tummies almost always stick out.

If you think your child is getting too fat, look at the upper arms and at the thighs. If there are rolls of fat in those areas, so that the sleeves and the legs of the clothes strain tightly around them, then the child probably is too fat.

If you have been keeping up the weight and height chart, you can make sure by looking at that. Your child's ideal weight will go up in strict relation to height. If weight is being gained much faster than height, the child is bound to get fat.

What to do

Growing children should never be put on a diet which is designed to make them *lose* weight. You should aim to slow down your child's weight gain so that his height can catch up with his weight. If you try to diet a toddler more actively than this, you may actually distort his growth.

The fat toddler is almost certainly eating a diet which is high in carbohydrates. But that does not mean that the answer is to put him on the kind of low carbohydrate/high protein diet you might adopt if you were slimming. He needs his carbohydrate foods to satisfy his appetite and give him energy. He also needs the useful range of proteins, vitamins and minerals they contain.

Look first at your child's consumption of fats. You can cut a small child's calories very substantially without him noticing the difference at all or going without anything useful, if you just cut down his table fats and fried foods. A one oz (28g) slice of bread contains about 70 calories. If you add a normal spreading of butter you add another 70 calories with no extra value except some vitamin A which he is having in his multivitamins anyway. Roast potatoes have about twice and chipped potatoes about three times the calorie value of boiled ones.

Look at your child's consumption of snacks. You don't want to make him unhappy by suddenly forbidding all food between meals, but if he eats high calorie snacks all day he may actually be getting as many calories in the form of extras as he is getting from a complete diet of meals. See whether you can substitute dried or fresh fruit for sweets, jelly for ice cream, plain rusks or water biscuits for sweet ones, bread for cake or buns.

Look at your child's sugar consumption. If he is a thirsty child who gets through a large bottle of concentrated vitamin C fruit syrup in a week, he will be getting far more vitamin C than he needs and the sugar in those drinks alone will be giving him a lot of extra calories. Fresh orange juice, even with a reasonable amount of sugar added, will be better for him. Provided he gets enough vitamin C from multivitamin drops or tablets, an ordinary fruit squash will be less fattening still, while water is the best of all drinks for fat children.

Does he have a lot of convenience baby fruits and sweets? Many of them are made extremely sweet; home-cooked or raw fresh fruit would be less fattening.

Does he eat a lot of sweets? If so, try giving them to him as part of his meals (an apple with some chocolate or a few Smarties, as a sweet course for example) and then just not having any available between meals. If you want him to have some sweets but he always insists on having a whole packet rather than just a few at a time, you can fool him by taking the trouble to split a $\frac{1}{4}$lb (113g) packet into eight tiny cellophane bags. Once he has eaten the contents of one he will accept that they are "all gone".

Look at your child's milk consumption. If he is still drinking more than, say, $1\frac{1}{2}$ pints (0.85 litres), it is worth trying to cut him gently back to somewhere nearer a pint (0.57 litres) – though not below this. If he is still having bottles, put a couple of ounces less in each. If he drinks milk from a cup just give him a bit less each time but remember to offer him plain water to make up the fluid.

Most of the calories in milk are in the fat of the cream while the valuable protein and calcium are in the milk. If you pour a pint of milk into a flat bowl and put it in the refrigerator for a couple of hours, you will be able to skim off the creamiest and most fattening two ounces and use it for the family's breakfast cereal. Your toddler will never notice the difference.

Look at your child's daily life. Does he get the opportunity for all the exercise he wants? Is there somewhere for him to play actively? Do you let him push the pushchair some of the way when you go shopping, or does he just sit in it? Is he free on the floor when he is at home and awake, or does he spend a lot of time in his pram or playpen? Given the chance he will be constantly on the go, and the more exercise he takes the less chance food will have to settle down in his fat cells: it will be needed to give him energy.

Sleeping

Once your child is too big to sleep in a carry cot and too alert and mature to drop off to sleep while the outside world is offering entertainment, meeting sleep needs inevitably imposes some restrictions on your freedom. Keeping these restrictions to a minimum means making some decisions, now.

The happy-go-lucky approach

If you want to be able to take the baby with you wherever and whenever you go, you can. Your child will be happy to accompany you out to supper with friends, to be taken away for weekends or long day trips, even to sit on your lap in a cinema. But you will have a price to pay. A baby who is kept up on occasion to suit your convenience is very unlikely to go happily to bed at a conventional hour just because that is what would suit you tonight. He or she will probably be the kind of toddler who is around until all hours most nights of the week, and whose daytime sleep pattern is also irregular because it depends on how tiring those nightly junketings have been.

The regular routine approach

If you want to be fairly sure of adult peace and privacy in the evenings and of a break from the baby's demanding company during the day, you can. A regular routine of naps and bedtimes will be accepted, but you, too, will have to pay a price. The routine approach only works if it is kept to almost all the time. That means arranging your evenings out so that you put the baby to bed before you go and have a baby-sitter. It means keeping as close to the normal pattern as you can even when you are on holiday, and it means arranging most of your trips and expeditions to fit in with that routine.

Sleep needs

As we saw earlier (see p. 215), babies vary widely in the number of hours they need to sleep in each twenty four hours. If your baby has always needed plenty of sleep, he will still need it. If your baby has never slept for more than ten hours a day, he will not suddenly get sleepier.

The overall number of hours slept will only drop very gradually during this age period. By the second birthday the baby will only have reduced his total sleeping time by about one hour.

Sleeping patterns

Almost every toddler will sleep through an eleven or twelve hour night. The difference between those hours and total sleep needs will be made up in daytime naps. A wakeful child may only sleep for twenty minutes in the daytime, a sleepier one may sleep for four more hours.

At the beginning of this age period toddlers will almost all need two naps in each day, arranged so that they break up their waking hours fairly evenly. A baby who regularly wakes at 6:30am, for example, might rest from 9:30 to 11am and then rest again from 2 to 3:30pm being put to bed for the night at around 7pm.

Somewhere around 15–18 months most toddlers go through an awkward phase. Two naps are too many and one nap is not enough.

The baby makes it clear that he is not ready to be put to bed after the family breakfast. But if you let him stay up, he cannot last through the morning. By midday, just when his meal is cooking, he is exhausted, whiney and impossible.

If you realize that in this state he will not eat any lunch anyway and put him to bed at 11:30, he will go to sleep at once but exactly the same thing happens in the afternoon: he has his late lunch, does not want to go back to bed during the afternoon, but cannot stay comfortably awake until bedtime.

By the end of the second year this awkwardness usually resolves itself into a single nap taken either at the end of the morning before a late lunch, or at the very beginning of the afternoon after an early lunch. In the meantime you may find yourself serving your child lunch at 11:15 or putting him to bed for the night at 5:30!

Waking from naps

If you are to keep any kind of pattern to your own and your toddler's day, you will often have to wake him from his naps. A nap that begins at 11:30am might go on until 3:30pm if you left it to him. He has had no midday meal; you have not been able to go out shopping; and there may be an older child who needs meeting from school. Even if it suits you to let him sleep all afternoon, it probably would not be wise. After such a long daytime sleep he will not be ready for his ordinary bedtime.

Waking your toddler from a nap takes tact. He will probably bitterly resent being disturbed, and need at least half an hour of peaceful cuddling and conversation before he feels ready to face the world. If you try to wash or dress him, he will howl. If you hurry him to a meal, he will not eat it. If you rush him off to meet another child from school, he will whine and moan and make it impossible for you to pay proper attention to the schoolchild.

So, wake him gently while you still have plenty of time in hand and let him make a gradual transition from being asleep to being awake, from being cocooned in his cot to being loose on the floor.

Getting overtired

This is a very common toddler problem especially during the middle of the second year when the child really needs one and a half naps per day!

Your toddler is working extremely hard. As he learns to walk and to climb he pushes himself to the limits of his physical strength. Because he is learning he falls down, bumps himself, surprises and hurts himself many times each day. His daily life at this stage must be something like an afternoon spent by an adult learning to water ski or to skate.

Like the rest of us, the toddler manages his body less and less well as he tires. Getting tired makes his physical coordination less efficient, so that he has to put more and more effort into everything he does. The more effort he has to make the more tired he becomes. If you watch a toddler in a public playground, you can see this happening before your eyes. When he arrives, keen and fresh from a rest, the child rushes around managing everything beautifully. The sand that he digs goes into his bucket and he can get three rungs up the climbing frame. An hour later it takes him ten minutes to fill that bucket; all his sand pies break and his hands slip every time he tries to climb.

When you wake her from her naps, be tactful; give her time to re-adjust to the wakeful world.

Along with physical efforts the child is also making enormous efforts to understand and to manage the world. That playground is noisy; there are lots of other children; it may frighten him or it may excite him, but it certainly will not relax him.

Physical tiredness, excitement and tension can build up in a toddler to a point where he no longer knows that he is tired, does not see how to stop and rest, and cannot relax anyway. He needs rescuing before he reaches this point. Don't assume that a child who is still rushing around is not tired: look at what he is doing and see whether he is finding it more difficult than he was finding it half an hour ago. If he is, then he needs a rest. Don't assume that a child who has difficulty in getting to sleep at night (see opposite) is not getting tired during the day: he may be getting overtired, and it may be the resulting tension which is keeping him awake. The answer is not necessarily more sleep, but it is probably more rest.

Resting without sleep Try to find some ways of giving your toddler both physical rest and relaxation from stress without actually putting him to bed. Quiet occupations that he enjoys now, between bouts of energetic and effortful play, will be useful for years to come. You will be able to build on them ways of keeping him occupied whenever circumstances make it desirable that he should keep still, whether it is because you are travelling, sitting in the dentist's waiting room or because the child himself is unwell.

Different families will select their own "resting occupations", but during this age period they will almost certainly depend on your doing something *with* the child. No self-respecting toddler will sit down alone to anything for more than five minutes.

"Magic" a horse, read her a story, play her a record or settle to a puzzle

. . .with your help, she can rest even without sleeping.

Sleeping problems

Trouble in going to sleep at night

Many parents believe that every toddler except their own goes peacefully to bed at the right time every night. There is a general belief that if you are kind but firm no fuss should ever happen. It is a myth. When research workers give parents a chance to describe what actually happens in their houses, it becomes clear that at *least* 50% of all children between the ages of 1 and 2 make a major fuss about being put to bed. Night after night toddlers are rocked and sat with, cuddled, taken back downstairs, nursed to sleep on the parents' bed, fed, slapped, scolded and fed again.

So let us not pretend that it is easy. Let us think about the reality not the myth. The reality is that a fuss at bedtime wrecks the evening for the whole family. There is a meal to be prepared and eaten; there may be older children needing attention; there is news to exchange and everyone is tired. Most parents will do almost anything to get that toddler to settle down quietly. They know that bringing the child downstairs again is not really a solution but if it works for tonight, that is good enough – until tomorrow brings a new commotion.

Leaving your toddler to cry

The most usual advice is to settle the baby down, leave and then refuse to go back into the room however much he cries. Parents are told that if they can only survive two hours of crying tonight it will be one hour tomorrow, half an hour the next day and peace after that.

Many families do not find that this works and indeed if you look at it from the toddler's point of view it is difficult to see why it should. What message does staying away convey to him? He is crying because he cannot bear you going away. So if you stay away you must seem to be saying "It's no good you crying because I'm not going to come back no matter how sad you are". If that is the message the toddler receives, it is hardly likely to make him feel safer about bedtime tomorrow. It can only make him more sure that it is dangerous to let you go at all.

If you did persist with this policy to a point where your child actually gave up crying when you left him, you would have won your battle at a very high price. You would have convinced the child that you did not care enough about him or understand him well enough to take any notice of what he was trying to communicate to you. How can he feel like an important, independent person in a world full of other important independent people if nobody listens to what he "says"?

In fact very few families do pursue this policy. A determined toddler can keep himself awake and crying for much longer than his parents or the neighbours can stand. If you are going to have to go to him in two hours time when he is convinced that you have abandoned him forever, you had much better go now.

Staying with your toddler

The opposite approach is to give the toddler what he wants, by staying with him or taking him back downstairs. Although it is kinder than leaving him to cry, it is not really any more sensible if you think again about the message your behaviour will convey to him. "You're scared of being left and you're right, it is worrying

to be left all alone so I'll stay with you/take you with me"....
Once again this is not a message likely to make for easier bedtimes later on. How can the child come to believe that it is perfectly
all right to be left to go to sleep if you suggest that he is right to
mind? And how can he be expected to accept that bedtime is the
end of his day if he has nightly proof that his day will go on if
he cries?

The middle path There is a compromise which neither leaves the child desperately
alone nor gives him victory in getting some more day. The message
it is supposed to convey is something like this:

"There is no need to cry. You aren't deserted. We will always
come if you need us. But it is the end of today and time for you to
go to sleep."

You settle the child down cheerfully, going through whatever
rituals are usual and finishing up with your usual "goodnight"
(see p. 218). If, when you leave, the child cries, wait to see whether
it is just a "testing cry". The minute the crying starts to build up,
you go back into the room and repeat just that last "goodnight".
Then you leave again.

Between the two of you and the burning potatoes, you repeat
this performance for as long as it takes the toddler to settle down.
As long as the crying lasts you visit every five minutes, but on
each visit you only stay for that 30 second "goodnight". "I am
still here" you are saying, "but there's no more of today."

Don't get the toddler out of the cot, or stay in the room, or stay
away for more than five minutes at a time.

Do try and get the toddler to see that you are there always, but
that at this time of day you are completely boring.

I have known it take a week for this policy to work. I have never
known it to take longer except when the parents weakened. If you
get so fed up one night that you decide to leave your toddler crying
alone after all, you will have the whole job to do again. Equally if
you cannot stand going up and down any longer and decide to take
your child downstairs with you, the whole thing will start again.

Waking in the Although the child is now old enough to keep himself awake on
night purpose he still cannot (and never will be able to) wake himself
on purpose. Waking up in the night is not a "habit". You cannot
teach your child not to do it, either by ignoring him when he
wakes or by scolding him for it. In fact, night waking has nothing
to do with discipline, and any parents who tell you, smugly, that
their children know better, are fooling themselves.

Waking without All children wake several times each night as they turn over. If
fear nothing interests or disturbs them, they drop straight down into
sleep again without anyone ever knowing that they have woken.
If your child insists that you know about all his wakings, check
some of the following:

Do you go into the room whenever you hear a movement?
You may be disturbing *him*. If he wants you, he will let you know.

Does your toddler go to sleep on top of the bedclothes and then get cold in the small hours? If so, either put him in a sleeping bag or blanket sleeper or keep a separate cot blanket to drape over him and his toys at your own bedtime.

Is your toddler afraid of the dark? If so, give him a 15 watt nightlight. It will not stop him waking, but it may stop him needing to call you when he does wake.

Does the toddler use a dummy or a cuddly? If so, tie it on to the cot bars when you go to bed. If he can always easily find it when he wakes, he may not need to wake you.

Is the toddler being disturbed by outside noises? As with a younger child (see p. 220) you may have to do something about traffic etc.

Does your toddler get hungry in the night? Some toddlers are so tired by bedtime that they cannot eat much supper. Breakfast then seems a long way off. An earlier supper with a drink of milk at bedtime may be a better pattern in these months.

Does your toddler get thirsty? A few parents, even at this early age, believe that restricting evening drinks will mean fewer wet beds. It will not. The child must drink as much as he wants right up until bedtime or thirst is very likely to wake him in the night.

Waking up afraid

This is the more usual kind of night waking. Nearly half of every group of toddlers studied by research workers suffers from it. The waking is due to some form of nightmare, but of course we don't know what the child dreams, thinks of or sees while asleep.

Some children wake up terrified several times each night for a while and then not at all for months. Others wake three or four times a week for months on end.

The waking may take the form of instant panic, so that you find the child sitting bolt upright in the cot, clearly terrified. On other occasions it takes the form of terrible grief, so that you find the child lying down, crying as if something dreadful had happened. Either way, if you arrive quickly the drama is usually over in 30 seconds. One glimpse of your familiar figure, one soothing pat and the child is asleep again. He remembers nothing about it in the morning. But if you don't arrive quickly, things tend to be very different. The toddler becomes more and more afraid as he listens to his own frightened voice crying in the night-quiet. When you do come to him he is shaky, tense and sobbing. Instead of being reassured by a glimpse and a pat, he may need 15 or even 30 minutes cuddling and talk before he can settle into sleep again.

Dealing with nightmares

Dealing with the nightmares is simple: you just get to the child as fast as you can the moment you hear him crying. But preventing them is much more difficult; and it is prevention you will want when you have had to haul yourself out of bed in the small hours eight nights in a row.

Specific suggestions such as tiring the child out during the day or giving him more to eat at suppertime seldom work. An over-tired child or one who has had an extra large meal forced upon him is likely to sleep less, rather than more, peacefully. But sometimes a more general approach to the child-as-a-whole does seem effective. We do not know exactly what causes nightmares either in toddlers or in older people. But we do know that they are associated with anxiety and stress. If your toddler is finding life a strain and you can relieve that strain a little, the nightmares may become less frequent.

Is there a new baby present or imminent? Have you recently taken a job so that the child is being cared for by someone else? Is his father away from home a great deal at present? Any radical change in his small world is liable to have made him anxious whether he shows it during the day or not. Even when you cannot remove the cause of his stress you may be able to help him, both by being extra-loving and tolerant and, perhaps, by talking to him about what is happening. Even a child who does not yet use many words can often be reassured by a simple acknowledgment from his parents that they know he is upset and understand why.

Are you in the thick of battles about eating, toilet training or his general desire for independence? However hard he fights you while he is awake, a baby-bit of him is liable to be worried about these battles. He is not sure that he can really afford to risk your displeasure. You may find it possible to relax the demands you are making on him for a while. This, together with lots of assurance that you love him, just as he is, may relieve the stress.

Have you just returned from a holiday? Has he been in hospital or ill for a long time at home? Happenings which temporarily take him away from home or break up his accustomed routine can have a disturbing effect. Sticking carefully to a more than usually rigid nursery-type routine for a few weeks will give him back a feeling of structured security.

All these suggestions really add up to the same idea: that a toddler who is having a lot of nightmares may benefit from being treated, for a while, as if he were a little younger than he really is. Something is making him feel worried and unable to cope with the demands made by his life. Baby him a little so that he can meet all demands with ease, and the nightmares will probably stop.

Night wandering
Late in the second year a new reason for not leaving your toddler to cry alone at night often emerges: if you will not go to him, he will learn to come to you.

Climbing out of his cot at night is a development to be avoided at all costs. It is dangerous. Cot sides are high for a toddler who is only just learning to climb. If he gets out safely without you hearing, he is loose and unsupervised around the house. Even if no real disaster occurs, a child who discovers that he *can* get out of bed, and come to find you, will do so night after night. Thousands of families are driven mad by their toddlers appearing in the living room or, worse, in the bedroom, several times each night.

Preventing night wandering
Prevention does not just mean physically preventing the child from getting out of bed, it means stopping him from ever thinking about getting out of bed alone. If it occurs to him to try to climb out of his cot, typical toddler persistence will probably keep him trying until he succeeds, so you have to make it seem completely impossible *and* make sure that he has no strong motive.

*Climbing out of the cot
is a habit to be discouraged . . .*

*a sleeping bag will keep her
safely in her cot, and warm as well.*

It is at this stage that a sleeping bag, started during the first year (see p. 148), proves itself valuable for more than keeping him warm. If he has worn such a bag, all night and every night for as long as he can remember, he will know that he cannot walk about until you have taken it off. A simple piece of parent-upmanship but a very effective one. But it only works if you start using a bag before he shows the least sign of trying to climb. If you put him in one after that he will either regard it as a trap and refuse to wear it, or he will try to climb despite it and then he really will fall. Once he is used to wearing a bag, don't abandon the idea just because the weather gets warm. A "Viyella" or cotton bag will keep him in bed without making him uncomfortably hot.

If he is always visited when he cries, whether it is before he has fallen asleep or during the night, he will not have an urgent and desperate reason for trying to get out. The times when he is most likely to try to come to you are the times when you have refused to come to him.

If he has never been taken downstairs again during the evening, or into your bed during the night, he will not have an alluring picture in his mind of the companionable pleasures he is missing by being in his cot. It is the toddlers who can envisage a cosy family group, or an even cosier sleeping couple, from which they are excluded, who try hardest to get out of bed.

Dealing with night wandering

If the night wandering habit does start, it is extremely difficult to break. Nothing short of physical restraint will keep the toddler in. But physical restraints, such as locking the bedroom door, stretching netting over the top of the cot, or putting him to sleep in a safety-harness, are all potentially dangerous. Worse, keeping your toddler in by force makes it certain that he will regard going to bed as imprisonment. Once this happens there is little hope of contented bedtimes and peaceful nights.

Clever do-it-yourself parents may be able to solve the whole problem by taking the base of the cot out and putting it back several inches lower down the frame. The toddler will never notice the difference. He will just be surprised to find that he cannot reach to climb out tonight even though he managed to do so yesterday.

Failing that, the best way of teaching him not to get out is probably to make absolutely sure that he gains nothing by his exploits that he cannot get by calling. If you can get hold of a "baby alarm" so that you can hear over the loudspeaker when the child starts to climb, you can meet him before he so much as reaches his bedroom door. If he is always put instantly back to bed again, he will probably give up.

Even without quite such a quick response you can make sure that night wandering does not get him anywhere. If he appears in the living room, hustle him straight back to bed; do not give him even two seconds to be charming. If he appears in your bedroom, take him straight back to his own. Letting him cuddle in beside you is asking for nightly repeat performances.

A sleeping bag, a cot and parents who come when he calls are likely to keep a toddler in bed. It follows that this is not the time to promote him to a "big bed". There is plenty of time for that later on (see p. 375). If there is a new baby on the way, plan to buy or to borrow a second cot.

Early waking While early morning waking is even more common in toddlers than in younger babies, it is usually easier to live with. The toddler is at his best and most cheerful first thing in the morning. He may wake you up at 6am but it is more likely to be with loud singing than with crying or grumbling.

Some toddlers simply occupy themselves with talk and song and with bouncing their cot around and bossing their teddy bears. Others welcome older children, swapping charm for service until the grown up world appears. If your toddler insists on you coming to him, try one of the following:

Leave a small cardboard box of selected toys and books beside his cot when you go to bed. Simply unpacking them will occupy him for a long time. And with any luck you will have chosen at least one object that he would actually like to play with.

Leave a drink in a teacher-beaker and a biscuit or two. Helping himself is half the fun and his cot will need changing anyway so the mess does not matter.

Make sure there is enough light. In summer thin curtains will let enough light through; in winter leave on a low wattage bulb.

Teach the toddler how to know when it is really morning. He will learn to recognize a signal which means it is time for you to get up and come to him. It might be your alarm clock going off or the radio being switched on.

Toilet training

Learning acceptable toilet behaviour is much more difficult for children than learning sensible eating or even sleeping habits, because the toilet behaviour that is asked of them has no obvious reward. Children who are sat in high chairs get food for which they are hungry. Children who are put to bed get rest that their bodies are demanding. But children who are put on pots just have bowel movements that they were going to have anyway. It is parents who care where the movements go. Eventually a toddler will get the reward of pleasing you and of feeling "grown up". But these are vague pleasures; behaving nicely on purpose is not your toddler's strong point.

Do not be in a hurry to start. If you begin before your child is physically ready you will be asking something of the toddler which he or she is simply not mature enough to give. There is bound to be stress. If you try to insist on cooperation before your child is emotionally ready, you will be trying to impose your will on the toddler's in an area where you cannot win. You cannot *make* him or her use that pot; attempts to force training invite the child to experience successful defiance.

Remember that no matter when you start "training", your child is unlikely to be entirely reliable, even in the daytime, before the third year. An early start means that the learning process takes longer; if you start later he or she will learn faster and reach the same point at the same time. However late your child seems to be in acquiring control, he or she will not set off for big school in nappies. . . .

Judging the right moment to introduce a pot

Until around fifteen months old your child still moves his bowels or passes water quite automatically. He neither knows when he is going to, nor does he realize when he has done so. Watch him if he happens to pee while he is naked: he does not even look at the puddle he produces because he does not realize that it is anything to do with him. He is not yet ready for a pot.

Somewhere around the middle of the year he makes that vital connection. Now he looks at the puddle and clutches himself. He has connected the feeling of urination or passing a motion with what is produced. He knows when he *has* performed but he still does not know when he is going to do so. At this stage the child is not ready to use a pot but he is ready to meet one.

What kind of pot?

The child's pot needs to be comfortable to sit down on and feel perfectly secure even if he wriggles while he is sitting. It must be virtually untippable and, or course, easy to clean. A boy needs a shield in the front.

A "pot-chair" is a good buy. Sitting down and getting up are easy for him and he has good back support. The actual pot lifts out for cleaning and taking on trips.

Gimmicky pots, such as those that play a tune, may amuse him or you. But the child will soon learn that a thrown toy produces the tune just as readily as a movement does.

Introducing the pot At this stage you only want to make sure that the child knows what the pot is for. Its use is obvious to you and, if he has older brothers or sisters, may be obvious to him too. But an only child may be totally mystified. After all he is accustomed to seeing you use a lavatory, not a pot. The two items do not look at all alike.

Show him the pot, tell him that it is for putting urine and faeces in when he is big enough to stop wearing nappies. Then put it in a corner of his usual playroom. Don't actually encourage him to use it as a hat, but let him make friends with it. If he is ready to be interested at all he may sit his teddy bear on it. Eventually he will want to sit on it himself. When he does, don't insist on taking his nappies off. He only wants to see what sitting on that pot feels like. He is not ready to use it yet.

Judging when your child is ready to start using the pot The right moment is the one at which your child becomes aware that he is *about to* produce urine or a motion rather than only being aware after the event. This awareness starts with advance warning of a coming bowel motion. The child may stand stock still, clutching himself and going red in the face. He may look at you and make sounds of anticipation. Now, if he chooses, he can put that motion in the pot instead of in his nappies. But remember that we are talking only about *bowel* training and that the choice is the child's.

Bowel training Becoming "clean" is far easier for a child than becoming "dry". Most children only move their bowels once or twice a day and many do not move them that often. Many children (especially if they have not been involved in too-early attempts at "training") are naturally regular in their timing. The signs of an imminent motion are quite clear to a watching adult, and the interval between the child first feeling the need and actually moving the bowels is quite long. If the toddler is emotionally ready to cooperate in using that pot, it is easy for you to help.

If you know that he is likely to move his bowels immediately after breakfast or on waking from a nap, delay putting on nappies, plastic pants, trousers or any other encumbrances, so that the whole matter is quick and easy. Make sure that the pot is in its usual place. Wait until the child tells or signals that a motion is on the way and then casually suggest that he might like to sit on the pot so that it goes in there.

If the child says "no" do not push it. If he does not seem to care either way or seems to like the idea, produce the pot, stay while he performs and be calmly congratulatory.

Many children who are introduced to the idea in this casual way and at just the right moment, will bowel train themselves completely within a couple of weeks. But if your child does not take so readily to the idea, be cautious:

Don't try to force the child to sit on the pot even if you can see that he is about to have a bowel movement. Toddlers are extremely contra-suggestive. The clearer you make it that you really want him to sit there, the less likely he is to want to. Since toilet training can only succeed through his voluntary cooperation, battles will mean certain failure.

Tone your reactions right down. If you are thrilled when he "succeeds" and disappointed when he "fails", keep your feelings off your face and out of your voice. Above all don't make his use of the pot a moral issue by calling him "good" for using it or "naughty" for not doing so. Using a pot instead of nappies is just a new skill which he is learning. Faeces in the pot deserve a quiet word about how grown up he is getting. Faeces in his nappy or on the floor need an equally quiet word about the possibility that he might choose to put them in the pot tomorrow.

Don't try to make the child share your adult disgust at faeces. He has just discovered that they come out of him. He sees them as an interesting production belonging to him. If you rush to empty the pot; change him with fastidious fingertips and wrinkled nose and are angry when he examines or smears the contents of his pot, you will hurt his feelings. You don't have to pretend to share his pleasurable interest – discovering that adults don't play with faeces is part of growing up – but don't try to make him feel they are dirty and disgusting. If he knows his faeces are disgusting to you, he will feel that you think he is disgusting too.

Don't try to tamper with the natural bowel pattern. Laxatives to make it "easier" or soap sticks to induce a motion at a convenient moment are totally wrong. It is his body. If you forcibly tamper with it, he really will feel that you are trying to overwhelm him.

Help your toddler towards toilet independence. If you have delayed introducing the pot until late in his second year, he will be able to go to it himself, manage his clothes with minimal help and get on and off the pot alone. The more he feels that the whole business is within his own control, the less likely he is to resent it.

Bladder training Although your child will learn to recognize the feelings which mean imminent urination at about the same age that he recognizes a coming bowel movement, doing something about those feelings comes considerably later.

Between noticing the sensations of a loaded rectum and actually passing the motion he has plenty of time to get to the pot and sit down. But there is no time at all between noticing a coming pee and producing a flood. The exclamation that means "I'm going to" is simultaneous with the puddle. It is too soon for training.

But your child will learn that urine can go in a pot as well as in a nappy because urine will often be passed while the pot is being used for a bowel movement. If bowel training is going smoothly, the toddler may be very ready to cooperate in urine training just as soon as he is physically capable of it.

Judging when your child is ready for bladder training The first sign of readiness is your child's learning of the momentary control over coming urine which older children call "clenching your bottom". The child realizes, just in time, that urine is coming. He or she clenches the muscles around the urethra and the anus and stops it. But these muscles are too low down for efficient control; the pressure in the child's abdomen is already high; the urgency is extreme; the child can hold on only for a few seconds and only while standing stock still with legs crossed. While any control at all is a sign of progress this is not yet useful control because if the child moves towards the pot he or she will urinate.

Somewhere around the second birthday the child will learn to take charge of the coming urination at an earlier stage, by recognizing a full bladder and tightening the muscles of the abdomen. Now he or she can delay the flow for several minutes and can walk without losing control. The toddler is therefore ready to make for the pot – if he or she wants to.

Helping your child to manage urination

Even when your child can recognize a need to urinate while there is still time to get to the pot, becoming "dry" will probably be a long, slow process. Children urinate so many times in the day that many failures are inevitable, especially when they are absorbed in play and therefore do not notice their need in time. They still cannot wake themselves to pee so they go on being accustomed to wet night-time nappies and perhaps to nap-time ones as well. Unless you can be extremely tactful and gentle, your toddler may get very bored and discouraged about the whole matter.

Your first aim is to help him experience some "successes". Once you know that he can wait a few minutes after realizing that he needs to go, pick a day when he wakes up from a nap dry, and delay dressing him. Suggest that he sits on his pot but if he does not want to, or sits for a moment and gets up without doing anything, make no comment. Just leave him bare-bottomed, pot to hand, and encourage him to sit there when he feels the need. If he succeeds, be gently congratulatory and then put his nappies on as usual. If he gets absorbed in play and makes a puddle, mop it up without comment and dress him as usual. If the weather is warm and you can leave him naked in the garden, so much the better. Each experience of feeling and seeing himself urinate will help to clinch the connection between the feeling and what happens next.

After a few days or weeks of occasional casual successes, take the child out of nappies when he is *at home and awake*. Don't make a big thing of it or he may feel demeaned by having the nappies back on for outings, naps and the night. Just suggest casually that he would be more comfortable without them while he plays and that if he needs to pee, his pot is close by. Do realize that this is a puddly stage. Be actually sympathetic about his frequent accidents: "Bad luck, you left it a bit late, didn't you? Let's mop it up...."

Once he manages to use his pot about half the time, buy him some plastic coated terry-towelling training pants. They will not absorb a whole urination but they will reduce flood-damage in the home; they are comfortable for the child and they are easy for him to take down and pull up. Go on using nappies for naps, nights and trips. You are still trying to prevent him from experiencing too many discouraging "failures".

During this stage it is a good idea to introduce the child to the lavatory as well as the pot. If he will happily use that too, you will not have to spend the next six months carrying a pot with you whenever you go out! He will probably like the idea of peeing where you do, but he will need a firm stool or box to

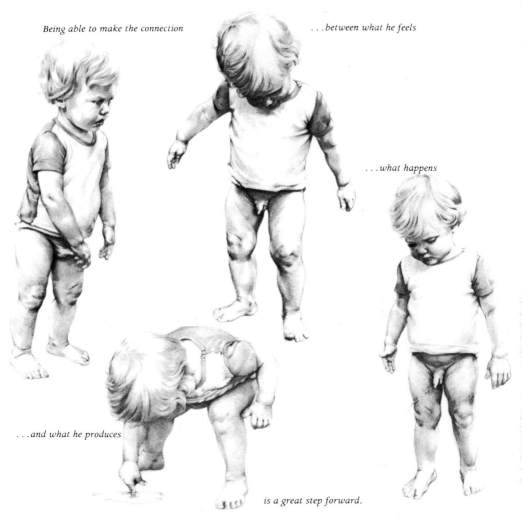

Being able to make the connection

...between what he feels

...what happens

...and what he produces

is a great step forward.

help him climb on and off, and a small seat clipped over the large one so that he does not feel that he is going to fall in. Be tactful about flushing the lavatory. Many children hate the noise and are frightened of the idea of things being sucked away. They have so little idea of the relative sizes of things that they may actually think that they might be flushed away too. So let your child pull the handle himself if he enjoys doing so. If not, leave it until he is out of the bathroom.

If your child seems relaxed and cheerful about the whole peeing-business, you may like to show him or her how easy it is to go behind a bush in the garden. It is excellent practice for the inevitable day when you get caught out in the middle of the park with a newly trained child and no pot.

Once he is more or less reliable at home in the daytime, abandon nappies as part of his regular clothes. He can have them on for naps if he prefers and he should still wear them at night, but that is all. Although you will still get a fair number of pools, giving up nappies is important. While he still wears them sometimes, the child cannot finally learn that *every* feeling of bladder fullness means a trip to his pot. You cannot expect him to think "I'm going to pee in a minute; am I wearing nappies or not?"

With many children, urine training will go smoothly from this point on. You will get fewer and fewer accidents until you suddenly realize that you have stopped taking mopping up for granted as one of your daily tasks. But there are some pitfalls:

Don't continually nag and remind your child to sit on the pot. You want him to feel that pants are more comfortable than nappies and that using a pot is quicker and easier than being changed. If you keep nagging, you will make him feel that life was easier when he had those safe old nappies on and that being put into pants has spoiled it all. Reminders ruin training anyway. You are trying to help him recognize his own need to go and do something about it for himself. If you keep reminding him, you are doing his thinking for him. You may actually delay the moment when he is fully reliable.

Don't expect a toddler to be able to urinate without feeling the need. Until he is around three years old he will not discover how to urinate when his need is not urgent and therefore recognizable. So it is useless to send him to the lavatory before an outing "so that you won't need to go later", and it is bitterly unfair to be cross with him for an accident in the supermarket "because you ought to have gone before we came out...."

Cultivate your skill as a lavatory-finder. Once your child wants to stay dry he must be able to rely on you to find him somewhere to pee, quickly, wherever you find yourselves when the need strikes. Get into the habit of carrying a pot when you go out for long periods and of noting the whereabouts of the facilities in shops and on the street. Be patient if you have to get off a bus or come home in a hurry. You are the one who wanted the child to stop wetting himself. Once he has stopped he will be really upset if too long a wait forces him to wet his pants after all.

Lavatory talk   Our language is full of euphemisms for lavatories and the functions we perform in them. Adults find it easy to adapt their language to the company they are in, but children will accept whatever words you use when you first invite them to perform on a pot, and they will go on using the same words for years no matter where they are. So it is worth giving those words a bit of thought. An invented baby-name for a bowel movement may seem perfectly appropriate for a two year old but turn you up when your child uses it at four and be incomprehensible to the school teacher a year later. Correct medical terminology from the beginning may seem the answer, but unfortunately both teachers and classmates will be amused and incredulous if he announces "I need to urinate".

There is no general answer to this minor problem because acceptable terminology will vary from place to place. Wherever you live there will be a fine line between the over-medical and the vernacular, the acceptable and the rude. It may help to listen in your local playground for the words toddlers use among themselves.

Everyday care

Caring without bossing

Physical care involves looking after your child's body. Because toddlers are increasingly conscious of their own ownership of their bodies, it takes a lot of tact. They cannot do everything for themselves yet they bitterly resent being handled like objects or possessions. Take plenty of time and use lots of imagination. If you have time you will not be tempted to do things by force. If you use imagination, almost everything you have to do for your child can either be turned into a game or into something he or she can do with your help.

It is worth taking trouble. This is a very contra-suggestive and bolshy stage. If you let yourself get drawn into battles over face-washing or clothes, your child may use these issues as good excuses for thrice daily quarrels. The quarrels will cost you far more time and effort than the tact!

Toddlers get incredibly dirty and they should. Clean clothes, hands, face and knees at the end of the day either mean a swimming expedition or boredom. Of course a clean neat child with shining hair and pretty clothes is a pleasure to you, but save this as an occasional treat for yourself.

As long as your child is kept clean enough for health and comfort, it does not matter what he or she looks like between washes. The toddler is a labourer, working at the job of growing up. Like any other labourer he or she can start and end the day clean, but in between needs sensible clothes and freedom to get on with the job. If outsiders should look askance at your ragamuffin, don't make furtive attempts to clean that face with spit and comb hair with your fingers: just tell yourself that they don't know how a toddler needs to live....

Getting up in the morning

The toddler is a sopping wet bundle of energy. You cannot let her loose until you have changed those nappies but she is certainly not going to keep still while you "top and tail" her. Strip the wet things off as she stands in her cot: the bedding will need changing anyway. Then let her go naked to the bathroom and stand on a bathmat looking in the mirror while you wash her bottom, face and hands. If she prefers to do so, she can stand on a rubber mat in the empty bath while you help her use a hand-shower.

Dressing

Dressing her top half is easier than when she was younger because you can pull things over her head while she sits or stands, and if you get sleeves at the right angle she will push her own hands through. It may be a mobile business though. She will probably toddle off, laughing, leaving you to pursue her, jersey at the ready, and pop it on when you catch up.

Getting nappies on is more of a problem as captured and laid on her back, she will probably roll away from you and suck her toes....

Nappies

With washable nappies, distraction is the answer: lie her on the ready-folded nappy and then hand her a really interesting toy, kept specially for the occasion. She will become still at least for the few moments it takes her to examine it. Watch out for pins though when delight produces a sudden wriggle! Disposables are easier to manage on your lap. Popper them up first and put them on as if they were pants. You can make final adjustments with the child standing down.

Bathing

An evening bath is much the easiest way to remove the day's embedded grime. The toddler will probably object to being scrubbed with a washcloth, so try some children's bubble bath in the water. It will loosen the dirt and save you cleaning a grimy ring off the bath afterwards. You need not hold the child in the water any longer, but don't move out of arm's reach or leave the room. A one year old may fall if he or she pulls up to stand holding the slippery bath edge. A two year old may turn on the hot water. Either could drown in 3 inches (8cm) of water because the reflex which makes us hold our breaths when our faces submerge is not fully functional during this age period. If your child slips and gets that face in the water, he or she will take a big breath, ready to yell. But it will not be air that is drawn in, it will be water. If the bath bottom is very slippery, use a rubber mat. If the hot tap stays burning, wrap a washcloth around it.

With all safe, provide lots of floating toys and plastic beakers and let your child have fun while getting clean.

A double bath can be fun and save you time, but watch out for jealousy and those by-accident-on-purpose pushes....

It is your child's face, so don't wash it as if it belonged to you. Hand over a flannel and let him or her have a go. You can touch up the edges with another one.

Frightened toddlers

Although most toddlers love baths, treating them as warm water play, a few are frightened. Don't try to force her. Use the methods suggested on p. 227 to re-introduce her to enjoyable bathing gradually. In the meantime you have to get the dirt off somehow and she certainly will not lie still for a blanket bath!

Try to work out what it is that frightens her. If it is the big bath itself, then water in any other container and room will do. If it is the amount of water, a smaller container or a hand-shower may put things right.

If only water scares her, stand her in the bath, wash her and let her shower off the bubbles.

If the bath scares her, try sitting her on a towel on the draining board. She associates the sink with washing up, so she will probably enjoy dabbling her grubby feet.

Hairwashing

Many small children loathe having their hair washed. You may not find the answer here because there may not *be* a complete solution. Any of the tricks suggested for younger babies on p. 228 may still work, but there are a few extra ones to consider now that your child is older. If hairwashing (and indeed brushing and combing too) makes real misery, are those budding plaits or "with it" locks really worth it? A short style can be *sponged* clean, is easily cared for and encourages thick, healthy hair growth too.

Taking your child swimming will get him or her used to water on the face and pay off at hairwashing time as well as being fun and good for the child too. If you go to a swimming pool, the hot showers provided for bathers can make an ideal setting for a quick rub with non-sting shampoo. The child is wet already; wants to get warm and has you in there too.

If the child enjoys coming with you to the hairdresser, you can use the new passion for "let's pretend" games to set up a weekly hairdressers at home. With a little ingenuity, you can set up a "backwash". Provide "madam" or "sir" with a plastic bib, a choice of shampoos and much chat

about hair styles and water temperature and he or she will probably let you do the whole job with a hand-shower. If the game goes well, this is the moment to snip any straggly ends too.

If the child happens to have seen you having a manicure, coping with fingernails will follow naturally; the whole thing can turn into a pleasant weekly spring-clean. Don't push your luck by insisting on blow-drying the hair if, like many toddlers, yours is scared of the dryer. Once rubbed, the hair will dry quite fast enough if you just settle him or her in a warm corner for a story.

Hands and nails

Short fingernails are important to hygiene, and hands really do need washing before meals and after the child has used the pot or "helped" you change nappies.

Don't bite the nails any more; you don't want to give your child the idea of biting his or her own. Try cutting them with small, curved nail-scissors, keeping interest and cooperation by letting the child say which should be done next and how long each should be. Don't cut them uncomfortably short: you should leave just enough nail to stand proud of the fingertip following its natural curve. If scissors are difficult, try nail clippers. If your child will not cooperate, demonstrate a nail file or emery board; he or she can dab at one finger while you cope with another.

A young toddler will like the feeling of handwashing if you get your own hands soapy first and then take the child's hands between them. Soon he or she will get the idea of making bubbles by soaping hands. You will have to give a bit of help and watch that soapy fingers don't go near eyes. But by the third year

the child will make a good job of doing it alone. You can give the child extra independence with a box or stool like that used at the lavatory, to stand on to reach the basin. Do guard that hot tap though. If the child can turn it on alone, you may need to reduce the temperature of the whole supply. 120–130°F (50–55°C) is safe, 150–160°F (65–70°C) is not.

Clothes

Don't let clothes make trouble between you and your toddler. He or she will feel very strongly about them. The main concern will (and should) be comfort, but, boy or girl, the child may surprise you with strong feelings about what he or she looks like, too.

Clothes should protect the skin and keep the child warm and/or dry. They should never be stiff, heavy or physically restricting. They should not have to be "looked after" either; ban anything which is not easy-wash and minimum (or non)-iron.

Don't try to save money by buying clothes too big; they will not look or feel nice while new and by the time they fit they will be shabby. Buy cheap clothes; they will not last but the child will grow faster than they disintegrate.

Top clothes

Don't spend money on a "good" winter coat. The child will grow out of it in one season; it will need dry cleaning; it will restrict movements and it will not do for all weathers.

Instead, buy a cheap, colourful shower-proof anorak with a hood. It is light, comfortable and warm, and extra layers underneath can make it warmer. You can wash it in a washing machine, dry it overnight and replace it when it gets shabby.

Mud-puddling demands special gear. Most children loathe stiff oilskins. A waterproof suit or waterproof over-trousers with the anorak plus ankle length rubber boots will ready your toddler for anything.

Main clothes

Stretch materials – lightweight terry or synthetic mixtures – are ideal for you and your child. They are comfortable, they save you money (because stretch means a little more growth room) and they save time because they need no ironing. They are also available in a vast range of exciting colours but stick to fairly dirt-concealing ones.

Both sexes will be least restricted and best protected in long trousers while they spend their time crawling and falling. Dungarees or overalls avoid tight waistbands and chilly gaps when tops separate from bottoms. You can buy these with poppers at the crotch. You will need elastic waisted trews once your child uses a pot independently; all-in-one garments or zip flies are too difficult. If a girl positively wants to wear dresses, buy short "angel top" types to put over stretchy tights. Longer skirts will hamper her movements. Avoid thick sweaters especially tickly polo necks. Add extra, light layers when it is cold.

Don't buy lots of different clothes for different occasions. Many will be outgrown after a couple of wearings.

Instead buy clothes which double up for many activities and can be gradually relegated down the grandeur-scale as they get shabby. A boiler suit could start as a "best" outfit, give good service for everyday wear and finish life, too small and well-worn, as coveralls for painting. Consider before buying *anything* which needs separate treatment from the rest of your washing machine load. That hand-knit jersey may get handwashed the first few times, but you will then probably shove it in with the rest and ruin it.

Underclothes

Conventionally, children wear vests and, when they abandon nappies, underpants. Man-made fibres prevent sweat evaporating from the skin; the child may well be less hot and clammy in cotton mixtures even though these are less easy to launder.

But you might like to abandon these items altogether and replace them with brightly coloured stretch cotton tee-shirts and play-pants. Your child's innermost layer is then as pretty and serviceable as what goes on top and you can simply strip off or add layers as the weather dictates. You will not have to buy special "romper suits", "sun-suits" or "bathing trunks" either; the underclothes serve all these purposes and the money you save can be used to replace them as soon as they start to look washed-out.

Shoes and socks

Don't make your child wear shoes at all until he or she is walking out of doors. Bare feet are safer as the child uses the toes to help balance. They are more comfortable too unless floors are cold. If cold is a problem, find some "slipper socks" which are heavy woollen socks with a non-slip sole attached. Don't let the child wear ordinary socks without shoes: they are very slippery on a hard floor.

Once shoes are needed proper fitting and regular checking are vital. Your child cannot tell you if shoes are too short or narrow: the bones of the feet are still so pliable that they can be squashed up without causing pain even though damage is being done. Use a proper shoe shop or specialist children's department and make sure the feet are measured for width as well as length. Have the size of those same shoes re-checked at least every 3 months; check wellington boots too. Provided shoes fit properly they need not be grand leather ones with "good support". It is muscles that support feet. Canvas play shoes are fine provided they neither squash nor chafe the feet.

Once hard shoes are worn your child will need socks to prevent rubbing and absorb sweat. The fit matters; socks which are too tight will soon distort toes. Watch out for shrinkage in cotton socks. When the child is standing, there should be at least $\frac{1}{8}$in. (3.2mm) spare material over the longest toe. Buy socks according to your child's shoe size.

Both length and width must be measured with the child's weight on the foot. If the shoe is not available in his or her fitting, don't buy it however pretty the colour.

If it is a stretch sock designed to fit a range of three sizes, don't buy it if your child already needs the largest size: buy the next size-grouping up.

When you buy new socks which are bigger than the last ones, be sure to clear all the old ones out of drawers. It is no good having two pairs the right size and four more which are too small....

Teething

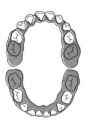

The toddler will be "teething" throughout almost the whole of the second year. The teeth which are most likely to cause discomfort are the first molars, cut between 12 and 15 months, and the second molars, cut between 20 and 24 months.

While teething will not make a child ill, this second year teething will sometimes make him or her miserable and irritable. The cheek may be red and warm on the affected side, and the very things that give comfort (such as sucking or biting) may also cause pain. There is not a great deal you can do to help, and the trouble will only last a few days with any one tooth, but in the meantime:

Something cold to bite on may be comforting. There is a type of teething ring available containing a special gel which can be cooled in the refrigerator. It can be very soothing, but watch out that the child (who is, after all, older than the age for which teething rings are designed) does not bite through the plastic.

Rubbing the affected gum with your finger sometimes helps; at least it makes the child feel that you are doing something.

Sucking a bottle may make the gums hurt intolerably. Give a bottle if that is what the child is used to, but offer drinks from a cup as well so that if sucking stops after a couple of painful minutes he or she will still get enough to drink.

Cold winds often seem to make "toothache" worse. If it is winter, keep the child in for a day or two or make sure that a hood or a scarf is worn.

If the child seems to be in real pain, teeth may not be the cause. At this age earache sometimes gets confused with teething pain. A child who keeps putting a hand up to the side of the face and/or cannot eat or sleep, should be checked by a doctor.

Caring for teeth

The formation of strong teeth which will resist decay depends on diet. The baby's first teeth formed during your pregnancy, so they depended on your diet then. But you can still do a great deal to ensure the strength of later teeth as well as to look after the ones the child already has.

Make sure that your child gets plenty of calcium and of the vitamin D which enables the body to use it for laying down bones and teeth (see pp. 285/286).

Find out whether your local water supply contains adequate fluoride. This trace mineral does more than anything else to strengthen tooth enamel and help it to resist decay. If there is an inadequate amount in the local water, ask your doctor or your dentist about giving extra fluoride in tablet form.

Brush the teeth regularly especially once the molars, which have irregular surfaces to which food can easily stick, have been cut. Your aim is to clear all food debris from on or between the teeth. You can do it with a small, soft toothbrush which should be used with an up and down motion rather than from side to side. Clean the teeth at least twice every day and make sure that the last time is after supper so that food debris do not stay in the mouth all night.

Sticky sugary foods which stay on the teeth for a long time are the most likely to cause the acids which lead to decay. If you are not going to clean your toddler's teeth after a meal, try not to let it finish with this kind of food. Even an apple may not protect teeth (see p. 291). A drink of water is probably better.

Don't give sweetened dummies or bottles of milk or sweet drinks to take to bed. Dummies dipped in sugar are responsible for a horrifying number of decayed teeth in children under three. There is no need to start this pernicious habit; it is not one that will enter a child's head unless you offer it.

Giving a toddler a bottle to take to bed is a temptation if he or she is difficult about settling to sleep (see p. 204) but even plain milk contains enough sugar to cause dental trouble if it washes around the teeth over a long period, while sugary drinks from a bottle are just as bad as sweetened dummies. If you must give something to suck, make it a plain dummy or a bottle of plain water.

Take your child to the dentist sometime before the second birthday. The baby is having so many new experiences now that such a visit will be accepted as just one more adventure – especially if several visits pass before there is any question of treatment.

Such appointments may seem rather a waste of time, but they are not. Even though the child is going to shed all these teeth and acquire a second set, the first ones are vitally important. Healthy first teeth keep the proper spaces open for the second ones and they also allow the child's jaw to grow in its proper shape. Regular dental supervision now, with treatment as soon as it is necessary, may save months of orthodontic work later on: and school-children hate wearing braces.

Even though these first teeth will all be replaced, early dental supervision can still save time, trouble and agony later on . . .

Crying and comforting

Toddlers tend to live on an emotional see-saw with anxiety and tears on one end and frustration and tantrums on the other. Their feelings are as powerful at this age as they will ever be but they are very new. Children have not yet had time to grow a protective skin over them: they have not had enough experience to know how to cope with them; they cannot control themselves. It is the violent emotions of this age period which so often lead parents to talk despairingly of "the terrible twos".

Most of the toddler's troubles, tears and tantrums arise from a basic contradiction in what he or she wants from you, the parents. The desire to be independent, to shake off the absolute control adults have and to become a person in his or her own right, weighs down one end of the emotional see-saw. The contradictory desire to stay a baby, who can depend absolutely on continual protection from the adult world, weighs down the other end. Day by day, hour by hour, even minute by minute that see-saw tips. One moment the toddler demands that independence: "Let me" and "Go 'way!" the shouts resound. The next moment you do go away and the toddler turns back into a baby again, weeping bitterly because you have left the room.

That see-saw can only be kept in balance if you stand in the middle, adjusting to these rapidly changing emotional needs. If you surround your toddler with too much close care and protection, the need for independence will break out in anger and frustration. If you give too much personal autonomy, too much responsibility for self-care, the need to be close and protected will break out in separation anxiety. Keeping the balance between the two is the essence of your job as a parent.

Anxiety and fears

Anxiety and fear are normal human emotions but they are not comfortable ones. Most adults learn to cope with situations which make them anxious or to avoid things which make them afraid. But toddlers have neither the experience nor the power to do this for themselves or to force adults to do it for them.

If your toddler is anxious when you leave him at night, he will probably have developed some defences against those uncomfortable feelings like sucking his teddy bear's arm or wrapping his cuddly around his head (see p. 216). But even these simple defences are not truly in his own power. If a jealous older sister hides that teddy bear or the cuddly gets lost at the supermarket, there is nothing he can do about it – except cry.

If he is anxious when you leave the room without him during the day, he can keep his anxiety down to a tolerable level by following you. But if you go into the lavatory and lock the door between you, he is powerless. He can never be quite sure of being allowed to feel safe.

Your toddler probably begins to feel anxious whenever his own feelings begin to get out of control. Anger, which he intended to frighten you, frightens him as it builds up. If you will change the mood, the anger and the anxiety will die down, but he cannot make you. There is nothing he can do to stop you answering his anger with your own until he is driven into a frenzy of furious fear. So the toddler is very much exposed to his own feelings and only you can see to it that he gets help in managing them.

The very first step in giving a toddler this kind of emotional help is to watch and listen closely to him so that you pick up all the clues to his feelings that he can give out. It will be a long time yet before he can take you by the hand and say "Daddy, I'm scared of the thunder." In the meantime you have to notice without being told. Not all parents take notice of even the most obvious clues. Recently I spent an afternoon in a public playground, watching and listening. I saw 38 separate instances of children crying, screaming or shouting their fears of the various pieces of equipment, while their parents blandly assured them that: "You aren't scared of that"; "This one isn't too high for you"; "You like it really, you know you do...". Of course these phrases are only a "manner of speaking". Of course those adults did not really mean to suggest that they knew what their children felt better than the children knew themselves. But toddlers do not know about our strange "manners of speaking"; to them it must have seemed that the adult world refused to understand their feelings.

Clues to general anxiety If your toddler is feeling rather anxious about life, a little pressured, perhaps, to grow up faster than he feels he easily can, you will be able to spot the signs:

The toddler will probably be more clingy than usual, choosing to go with you rather than to stay in the room alone; choosing to hold your hand rather than to run ahead; choosing to sit on your lap or your hip rather than on a chair or the floor.

The toddler will probably seem less naughty than usual. He is feeling extra-dependent on you so whenever he can remember what it is that you like him to do, he tries to do it. He does not feel very adventurous either so he does not think up much new mischief.

The toddler will probably seem worried by strange places and people. If you take him out to tea, he will turn shy and spend all afternoon with his head in your lap. If you take him to a new park he will be too busy keeping close to you to explore.

If you pick up this kind of cue from your toddler and offer a large extra ration of affection, attention and protection for a few days or weeks, the see-saw will swing back to the level again. If you miss the cues, it may tip further into anxiety:

The toddler may have new or extra difficulty in going to sleep. He may build up his bedtime rituals; add new members to the family of comfort creatures in his cot; cry piteously to have the light left on and call you, endlessly, after you have left him.

The toddler may enter a phase of nightmares (see p. 301).

The toddler may seem to lose enthusiasm for food, preferring the more "babyish" items in his diet and refusing to feed himself as independently as before.

Once a toddler's general anxiety is at a high enough level for it to affect sleeping and eating, he is very likely to produce sudden fears of specific things. It is as if all that general anxiety bottled up inside were looking for a means of expressing itself.

Handling
specific fears

If a toddler is afraid of something which parents feel is "reasonable" he will usually be handled gently. Nightmares, for example, frighten us all, so the child who wakes screaming, sweating and shaky will usually receive instant sympathy and comfort. But many toddler fears do not seem "reasonable" to adults. Instead of sympathy and respect for genuine feelings, the toddler may get nothing but exhortations not to be "silly".

...and does not want to stroke

To you it may be a dear, gentle, harmless tortoise. To him it is something strange and horrible that he has never seen before...

...or even look at.

And if you tell him that he is silly to be frightened, you are doing nothing to help him conquer his fear.

If your child shows fear, accept that fear. It may not seem reasonable to you, but you are not the one who is feeling it. If you find yourself tempted to scoff, think over your own private fears and ask yourself whether they are all "reasonable" and how you would feel if you were not allowed to avoid them. Do you, for example, like large, harmless spiders?

Tell your child when there is nothing to fear, but don't tell him not to be afraid. If you say "It will not hurt you, but I can see it frightens you so we won't go any closer", your child will feel that you are on his side; but if you say "Don't be frightened, you silly boy," you offer neither reassurance nor support.

Most toddler fears are based on a natural and self-protective fear of things that are strange. Your child tends to be wary of new things until they have proved themselves harmless. Since most things in the environment either provide this proof or go away, the fears often pass as suddenly as they appeared. But some fears do not vanish so easily especially if they are not handled tactfully. Instead of coming to terms with the strange thing, making it part of the familiar world and accepting it, the toddler focuses more and more fear on it until the kind of fear which is technically called a phobia develops.

Phobias   Phobias in small children are very common and do not suggest that there is anything unusually amiss. The world *is* a frightening place to a toddler. There are a great many things which he cannot yet understand or cope with. It is not surprising that sometimes general fears should become focused in this way. More than half of all children develop at least one phobia during their second and third years. A large number of them fear the same things. The most frequent objects of these phobias are dogs. Darkness and the wide variety of bogeys that flourish there come a close second. Insects and reptiles, especially snakes, come next, while loud noises like fire-alarm bells and ambulance sirens come last.

A phobia works differently on the child from an ordinary fear. Since dogs head the phobia list let us take them as an example: A child who is simply afraid of dogs will show his fear when, and only when, he meets one. The rest of the time his life is unaffected by his fear. Out of sight is out of mind. A fear like this will usually vanish when (and if) the child discovers that dogs are not hurtful. If he does not make this discovery spontaneously, you may be able to help by, for example, casually showing him the tiny puppies in the pet shop window or your neighbour's furry poodle safely on a lead.

A phobia of dogs works on the child through his new imagination. He is not only afraid when he meets a dog, he is afraid when he sees one in the distance, looks at a picture of a dog or even thinks about one. He not only tries to avoid going where he knows there are dogs, he tries to avoid going where dogs might be. If the phobia becomes very acute he may have to ride in his pushchair in the street in case a dog should come by; keep out of the park because dogs play there; abandon a beloved picture book because there is a dog on page four and throw his toy monkey out of his cot because at night it reminds him of a dog.

Handling
phobias

Phobias are not open to rational explanations. You cannot help your child to get over this particular kind of fear by trying to show him that the thing he fears is harmless. If you try to do this, perhaps by taking him to visit that charming poodle, you provoke in him such horrible fear sensations that he is only confirmed in his phobia. It is not the actual dog-in-reality that is causing the trouble, it is the dog-in-his-mind.

Because it is his own sensations of fear which upset the child so much, you have to tackle phobias indirectly; by trying to lower his general level of anxiety to a point where he no longer has so much fear inside him that he needs to focus it on something:

Help the toddler to avoid the fearful thing but be careful not to let your behaviour suggest to him that you are also frightened of it. If he wants to climb into his pushchair in case there should be a dog in the street, let him do so, but make it clear that you are only giving him a ride because you understand that *he* is frightened, not because you feel there is any genuine danger. Fear is very infectious. If you yourself have an insect phobia, for example, do your very best to conceal it from the child. If the arrival of an earwig leads you to snatch him up and rush from the room he will certainly feel that earwigs are trebly alarming because they even frighten you, his calm protector.

Look for specific causes of stress in his life (see p. 302) and see what can be done to lessen the strain. You obviously cannot get rid of that new baby but you may be able to help the toddler with his feelings about her (see p. 400).

If you can find no specific cause, baby the toddler for a while. It may well be that he has forged ahead in growing up and becoming independent faster than is really comfortable for him. That emotional see-saw has hit the ground on the anxiety/fear side and you will have to work at making him feel safe again.

If the phobia is taking over life, limiting his play and making it impossible for him to go to places he used to like or to do things that he used to enjoy, seek help through your local clinic or through your doctor.

Bravery and
fearlessness

Sometimes parents find it difficult to handle anxiety, fears and phobias sensitively because they cannot accept that it is normal for a toddler to have any at all. They may even be ashamed of the child for being a "cry-baby" or a "coward". Little boys especially may suffer because their parents are afraid of them being "sissies".

It sometimes helps if you sort out in your mind the very real difference between being *brave* and being *fearless*. Being brave means doing or facing something frightening. You may ask your child to be brave about an injection or a thunderstorm. If you demand bravery, the least you can do is to acknowledge that he is afraid, show that you understand the feelings and make it clear that you recognize and appreciate the effort your toddler is making to control them. You will not help your child to behave bravely if you refuse to allow expressions of fear. You will not help your child to behave bravely next time if you deny that there was anything to be brave about in the first place.

Being fearless means being without fear. It follows that the less a child is frightened the more fearless he or she will be. To try and make a child adventurous and fearless by forcing him into the things that frighten him is a contradiction. When you carry your son, screaming, into the swimming pool because you want him to be fearless in water, you are really asking him to be brave. The more you demand the effort of brave behaviour from your toddler, the more frightened he will become and the more effort it will cost him to behave as you wish. Continual fear and anxiety tip that emotional see-saw further and further towards the dependent end and away from the independence you are trying to encourage. Things can reach such a pitch that he cannot become the fearless adventurous child you yearn for because your demands for bravery keep him so busy trying to get your protection and support.

Independence and frustration

Your toddler is rapidly developing a sense of being a separate independent person with personal rights, preferences and ploys. He no longer sees himself as part of you, so he no longer easily accepts your total control over his life. He wants to assert himself and it is right that he should do so. His "wilfulness" is a sign that he is growing up and that he feels secure enough at present to try to manage things for himself.

But life is very difficult for a toddler to manage. He does not understand things very well yet; he often wants to do things which the adult world cannot allow and he is still very small and physically incompetent. His efforts at independence inevitably lead to frustration. While some frustration is inevitable, too much can damage the toddler's self-esteem and make him waste time and energy in fury which he could better spend in learning.

Frustration by parents

Parents can easily frustrate the toddler's new sense of independence, his feelings about himself as a separate person and his sense of dignity.

As soon as he feels himself harried, bullied, pressured, he digs his heels in. Any issue will do for a row. It can be his pot or his clothes, his food or his bed. If he feels you insisting, he will resent it. But if he feels he is being allowed to control his own life he will use that pot, eat the food, stay in bed, come when he is called, leave when he is told and love it.

Since there will be innumerable occasions when you must stop your child doing things for his own safety or the safety of other people's possessions, you will need all the obvious virtues of tact, humour and patience, but you will need talent as an actor too. Are you in a hurry to get home? If you swoop the toddler into his pushchair when he wanted to walk all hell will be let loose. Act as if you had all the time in the world, offer to be a horse and pull him home and you will get there as fast as your legs will take the two of you.

Frustration by objects

The objects your toddler tries to use often refuse to behave as he wishes because he is not yet very strong and his muscular co-ordination is still not always accurate. Battles with objects or with frustrating toys are often educational. The toddler is finding out what things will and will not do and this is essential information for him (see p. 345). He may be frustrated, for example, because he cannot force his square bricks into the round holes of a hammer-peg toy. But the fact that they will not fit into the round holes is something he must learn; there is no point in concealing such facts from him.

A little frustration of this kind will keep your toddler trying and it will keep him learning. But too much works the opposite way. If he faces impossible tasks all alone and therefore faces continual failure, he will give up. Be ready to step in and help when you can see (and hear!) that your toddler is getting more and more frustrated and therefore less and less efficient. Try to see what his problem is and to offer the minimum help that will enable him to succeed; just doing it for him is not helpful.

Frustration by his or her own body and size
When a toddler understands what objects are supposed to do, understands how to make them do it, but cannot manage because he is too little or too weak, then he needs help. There is no pleasure or learning in such a situation, only grief and giving up. Children do not need rooms full of expensive toys, either for their pleasure or for their development. But any equipment they do have must be tailored to them physically. The toddler may long to push his sister's doll's pram but be too small to reach the handle. He may long to throw his brother's football but be too light to manage its weight. If he cannot have a babywalker or a small push cart and an inflatable beach ball or plastic "football", he is better off with none at all until he is bigger. We want him to feel as big and strong and competent to manage his world as possible. So we must keep at least his own possessions in scale with him.

Tantrums
You will not always manage to strike the right balance between the amount of frustration which is useful to your child's learning and the amount which is too much. When acutely frustrated the toddler is as liable to extremes of rage as to extremes of fear. Temper tantrums are the result of too much frustration just as phobias result from too much anxiety. More than half of all two year olds will have tantrums at least once or twice a week while very few children will reach their third birthday without ever having experienced one. Toddlers who have a lot of tantrums are usually lively children who may be highly intelligent. They know what they want to do; they want to do a great many things and they mind a great deal when someone or something prevents them.

A tantrum is like an emotional blown fuse; it is not something which the toddler can prevent. The load of frustration builds up inside him until he is so full of tension that only an explosion can release it. While the tantrum lasts, the toddler is lost to the world, overwhelmed by his own internal rage and terrified by the violent feelings which he cannot control. However unpleasant your toddler's tantrums are for you, they are much worse for him.

Children's behaviour during a tantrum varies, but your particular child will probably behave similarly each time:
He may rush around the room, wild and screaming. Remember that he is out of control so anything movable that happens to be in his path will be knocked flying. If you do not protect him he may bang into solid walls and heavy furniture. He may fling

himself on the floor, writhing, kicking and screaming as if he were fighting with demons. He may scream and scream until he makes himself sick. He may scream and turn blue in the face because he has breathed out so far that, for the moment, he cannot breathe in again. Breath-holding tantrums are the most alarming of all for parents to watch. The child may go without breathing for so long that his face looks greyish and he almost loses consciousness. It is quite impossible for him actually to damage himself in this way. His body's reflexes will reassert themselves and force air back into his lungs long before he is in any danger.

If she will let you hold her through her tantrum, your arms will help her to be comforted when the monstrous rage within her drains away...

Handling tantrums You can prevent many tantrums by organizing your toddler's life so that frustration stays within the limits of his or her tolerance most of the time. Tantrums do no positive good to either of you: when you must force your child to do something unpleasant or forbid something he or she enjoys, do it as tactfully as you can. There is no virtue in facing children with absolute "dos" and "don'ts" or in backing them into corners from which they can only explode in rage. Leave an escape route.

Prevent the child from getting hurt or hurting anyone or anything else. His overwhelming rage already terrifies him. If he comes out of a tantrum to discover that he has banged his head, scratched your face or broken a vase, he will see the damage as proof of his own horrible power, and evidence that when he cannot control himself you do not have the power to control him and keep him safe either.

It may be easiest to keep him safe if you hold him, gently, on the floor. As he calms down he finds himself close to you and he finds, to his amazement, that everything is quite unchanged by the storm. Slowly he relaxes and cuddles into your arms. His screams subside into sobs; the furious monster becomes a pathetic baby who has screamed himself sick and frightened himself silly. It is comfort time.

A few toddlers cannot bear to be held while they are having tantrums. The physical restriction drives them to fresh heights of anger and makes the whole affair worse. If your child reacts like this, don't insist on overpowering him. Remove anything he is obviously going to break and try to fend him off from physically hurting himself.

Don't try to argue or remonstrate with the child. While the tantrum lasts, he is beyond reason.

Don't scream back if you can possibly help it. Anger is very infectious and you may well find yourself becoming angrier with every yell he utters, but try not to join in. If you do, you are likely to prolong the outburst because just as the toddler was about to calm down he will become aware of your angry voice and it will start him off again.

Don't ever let the child feel rewarded or punished for a tantrum. You want him to see that tantrums are horrible for him and that they change nothing either for or against him. If he threw the tantrum because you would not let him go out into the garden, don't let him out now. Equally, if you had been going to take him for a walk before he had the tantrum, you should take him all the same.

Don't let tantrums embarrass you into kid-glove handling in public. Many parents dread tantrums in public places but you must not let your toddler sense your concern. If you are reluctant to take him into the corner shop in case he throws a tantrum for sweets, or if you treat him with saccharin sweetness whenever visitors are present in case ordinary handling should provoke an outburst, he will soon realize what is going on. Once he realizes that his genuinely uncontrollable tantrums are having an effect on your behaviour towards him, he is bound to learn to use them and to work himself up into the semi-deliberate tantrums which are typical of badly handled three and four year olds (see p. 443).

Assume that your child will not have a tantrum; behave as if you had never heard of the things and then treat them, when they occur, as unpleasant but completely irrelevant interludes in the day's ordinary events. It sounds easy, but it is not. I recently visited a friend whose twenty month boy asked her to take the cover off his sandpit. She said "Not now, nearly time for your bath," and returned to our conversation. The child tugged her arm to ask again but got no response. He then went to the sandpit and tried in vain to open it himself. He was tired and the frustration was too much for him. He exploded into a tantrum. When it was over and his mother had comforted him, she said to me "I do feel like a beast, I didn't know he wanted to play in the sand that badly." She took the cover off for him after all.

That mother's behaviour was easy to understand but also an excellent example of how not to handle tantrums! She said "no" to the child when he first asked for help without giving any real thought to his request. The child's own efforts to uncover the sand did not show her how passionately he wanted to play there because she was not paying attention to him. Only when he threw a tantrum did she realize that he really did want that sand and that there was no very good reason for forbidding it. She meant to make it up to him by giving in after all but she had her second thoughts too late. Hasty or not, she should have stuck to her original "no" because by changing it to "yes" after the tantrum she must have made her child feel that his explosion had had a most desirable effect. It would have been better for both of them if she had listened when he asked for help rather than giving in when he screamed.

It is not easy being a toddler rocking wildly between those anxious and angry feelings. It is not easy being a toddler's parent, either, striving to stay on the centre of that emotional see-saw and to hold it in equilibrium. But time is on your side. The worst of the emotional turbulence will be over by the time you discover that you now have a pre-school child.

He will get bigger, stronger and more competent. As he does so he will learn to manage things better so that he meets less extreme frustration in his everyday life. He will get to know and understand things better, too, so that his life contains fewer frightening unknowns. As he becomes more fearless he will stop needing quite so much reassurance from you. Gradually he will learn to talk freely not only about the things that he can see in front of him but about things he is thinking and imagining. Once he can talk in this way he will sometimes be able to accept reassuring words in place of your continual physical comfort. With the help of language (see p. 355) he will also learn to distinguish between fantasy and reality. Once he reaches this point he will at last be able to see both the unreality of most of his worst fears and the reasonableness of most of the demands and restrictions which you place on him. He will turn into a reasonable and communicative human being. Just give him time.

Using his or her body

Walking   Learning to walk alone is a major landmark in human development. Those first staggery steps across open space mean that a new
person has achieved one of the outstanding abilities of being
human: walking on the back legs with the front "legs" free to do
other things.

Babies go through several distinct phases between the day
when they first haul themselves into standing position and the day
when they first set off across open space. As we have seen (see
p. 243) there is wide variation in the ages at which different
children learn to stand and walk, so your baby may have reached
any one of these phases on his or her first birthday. Whichever
point has been reached, don't try to hurry your child into by-
passing the next phase. Each one has to be gone through even
though one child may spend only a few days, while another spends
several months, on each one.

Phase 1. In the first phase the baby, who has already learned to
pull himself up to standing position by cot bars or heavy furniture, learns to "cruise" along the support by sliding both hands to
one side so that he is off-balance and then sliding his feet along one
at a time until he is standing straight again. He does not trust all his
weight to his feet nor even to his feet supported by one hand.

Phase 2. The second phase ushers in a much more efficient and
confident kind of "cruising". The baby stands back a little from
his support so that all his weight is on his feet and he is using
his hands only for balance. Instead of sliding both hands along
together when he wants to move he moves hand-over-hand. By
the end of this phase he is moving hands and feet in rhythm so
that at critical moments he is relying only on one foot and one
hand for support, the other member of each pair being in motion.

Phase 3. The third phase gives the baby an increased range of
mobility because he learns to cross small gaps between one support and the next. If the furniture is conveniently arranged, he
will now be able to get around the room, moving along the sofa
back, crossing to the window sill and then to a chair.... He
will cross any gap that can be spanned by his two arms, but he
will still not release one hand until the other hand has caught hold
of something else.

Phase 4. The fourth phase brings the child's first unsupported
step. Now he will face a gap between supports that is just too
great for his arm span. He will hold on to the first support, move
his feet out into the centre of the gap, release his hand and then
lurch a single step to grab his new support with the other hand.
Once the child can cross a small gap in this way he will also be
able to stand alone. Often he will discover this by mistake.
Perhaps he is standing up holding on to the back of a chair when
you cross the room towards him carrying his mug. Without
thinking about gravity, he lets go of the chair to hold up his arms
for the drink; he probably does not even notice that he has let
go of his support.

Helping your child towards those first steps

Phase 5. Once your toddler can take a single step to get from one support to another he will soon be ready for the fifth stage. He will still do most of his walking with support, but he will toddle two or three steps to get where he is going if there is no convenient supporting furniture between him and his objective.

Phase 6. The sixth phase brings him to fully independent walking. He may not yet walk very far without a supported rest, but when he sets off to cross a room he moves in a straight line irrespective of whether or not there is anything to hold on to along his way.

Don't try to hurry him. Once he has got on to his own two feet (Phase 1) you can be quite sure that he will eventually walk. If there were anything the matter with his legs, his muscular co-ordination, or his balance, he would have stayed at the sitting/crawling stage and never become a biped. Let him take his time.

Offer opportunities to practise the phase already reached. You can give him great pleasure in phase three, for example, by sometimes arranging the furniture so that he finds he can get himself all the way around the room or even from one room into an adjoining one. At phases four and five he will enjoy the "walk to mummy" game where you position yourself as a support and invite him to toddle two steps into your arms.

Remember that the child is learning other things too. Your baby is learning to walk during the same period that brings a spurt of learning about objects (see p. 344) and learning words (see p. 355). He has only a limited number of hours awake each day and he may have periods when he wants to use more of them on play than on trying to walk. If his walking does not seem to be progressing, ask yourself whether he is not making a spurt in some other aspect of his development.

Protect your child from falls and the fear that they can bring. Even though he is used to the kind of bump he gets when he topples over from sitting position, falling down from standing may frighten him, especially if he bangs his head. Several frights in a row may put him off the whole walking business for weeks, so protect him:

Slippery floors make independent walking seem as difficult to him as walking on ice seems to us. Never let him wear socks alone on a hard floor. Bare feet are safest because he can feel the floor and use his toes for balance. If it is too cold for bare feet, buy him slipper socks (see p. 315). He is not ready for real shoes yet.

Rowdy older children playing around him make the middle of the floor seem a very dangerous place. Make sure that he gets the chance to practise walking when there are no human trains around to knock him down.

Don't worry about brief setbacks. Once your child has got through phase one he will progress gradually towards independent walking. But as well as weeks or months when progress seems to halt while he concentrates on something else or gets over temporary nervousness, he may also have brief periods when his ability to walk seems to have gone backwards.

A brief but acute illness, such as measles or bronchitis, can mean several days of high fever and little food or exercise. At this stage of his life the combination can reduce his muscle tone and his energy to such an extent that he reverts a phase or two for a few days. If he was cruising confidently before the illness, he may go back to crawling and pulling himself to standing. If he was walking two steps between supports, he may go back to cruising. There is no need to worry. He will repeat all the learning phases again but in a few days instead of months.

Even an emotional shock can cause your baby to abandon his newly acquired walking ability. If a separation from you or the arrival of a new baby causes him to go back to a bottle, it may also cause him to go back to crawling for a while. As soon as he feels safe again he will spurt ahead once more.

Getting moving   Most babies will reach phases five and six between 14 and 16 months. The child can now toddle at least a few steps and once he can do this his progress will almost invariably be very rapid. But he still cannot abandon crawling as his usual means of getting around because he still cannot get himself into standing position without first crawling to a support and pulling himself up. He will probably not be able to get from sitting to standing position without help until he is 16–18 months old.

He can be helped, at this stage, by a specially designed push-truck, usually known as a "babywalker". The point of this "toy" is that it is balanced in such a way that the child can safely pull himself up by its handle without it tipping. Having got to standing with its help, he can then push it along without it running away from him. Obviously the design is vital. A push-cart or doll's pram meant for older children will tip when he pulls up and rush away when he tries to walk. This vehicle allows him to take his pullup help and his walking support around with him. Used in the house or the garden or the park, it enormously increases the toddler's mobility. With years of use ahead as a brick cart, first doll's pram or wheelbarrow, it is a real best buy.

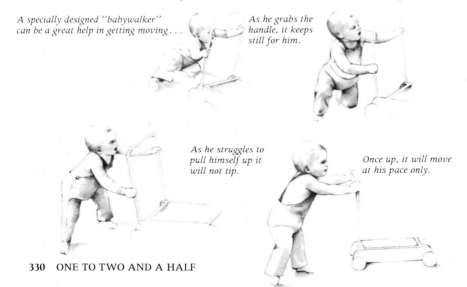

A specially designed "babywalker" can be a great help in getting moving . . .

As he grabs the handle, it keeps still for him.

As he struggles to pull himself up it will not tip.

Once up, it will move at his pace only.

Toddling at first is very uncontrolled. The child has no brakes and no steering. Once he has got up speed he cannot stop quickly enough to avoid falling down the steps nor steer accurately enough to avoid the lamp-post. Indoors he may be reasonably safe because a restricted space does not allow him much acceleration. Out of doors, a big open space, such as a park, will delight him, but practising his walking in busy streets or crowded shops is liable to be dangerous. If he sits in his pushchair while you shop and saves his walking practice for a visit to the park on the way home, that is fine. But if most of his outdoor life has to be passed in streets, he will have to be held. Holding hands will be extremely uncomfortable for both of you. Your arm is not long enough to allow you to hold his hand at a comfortable angle so his shoulder will be continually wrenched upwards and he will not be able to follow his natural inclination to stop and look at things and then to dash ahead. You will both be far more comfortable if you use reins. These useful inventions have been unfairly maligned on the grounds that they restrict the child's freedom and keep him a prisoner. In fact they give freedom to children in this age group.

By his second birthday the child's brakes, steering and general control over his legs will have improved a great deal. He will be able to walk steadily over quite long distances (although children vary, at all ages, in the distances they are *willing* to walk!) and he will be able to start and stop without needing support.

Doing other things while walking

When a child first learns to walk a few steps alone, the business of moving along on his own two feet takes up all his energy and concentration so that he cannot do anything else at the same time. If he wants a toy he will have to stop, sit down, get the toy and then find something by which he can pull himself up again. If he wants to listen to something you are saying, he will stop, and probably sit down, to do so.

But once walking has really begun, constant practice soon makes it easier for the baby. By 17 months or thereabouts he will have learned to get up without pulling himself to his feet and he will have become so steady that he can pay attention to other things at the same time as walking. He will learn to stoop down, pick up a toy and walk along while he carries it. He will learn to turn his head so that he can look at things while he walks and listen to you when you talk to him. He will learn to glance back over his shoulder, too, and once he can do that, a pull-toy to take along with him will be very popular.

A few months later the toddler will have discovered that he can walk backwards as well as forwards and that he can actually run rather than simply toddling fast. Once he can run, he will soon be able to jump so that both his feet leave the ground at the same time.

By the time he is two years old, your child will probably be so dexterous and sure on his feet that you will almost have forgotten those staggery steps he took only six months or so earlier. He will like to play running-away games, dashing off, glancing back at his pursuer, dodging to avoid your catching hand. He will be able to play games that mean sudden starting and stopping, like

At first she must hold on to reach down, but soon she can stoop, carry things and even kick a ball...

"grandmother's footsteps" and "statues". He will be so pleased with his new agility at getting up and down off the floor that "musical bumps" and "ring-a-roses" will be among his favourite games. He will even be able to kick a ball after a fashion but because he cannot yet balance on one leg for more than an instant, it will be a shuffling kind of kick.

Using his or her mobility

Adults think of walking as a means of getting from one place to another. Toddlers do not. It is no use expecting your child to use walking in the same way as an older child. He will not because he cannot. Understanding the limitations and the peculiarities of his walking can save you a lot of irritation and friction.

Mother or father as home-base

For a toddler walking is not a going-along activity but a coming-and-going around a central adult. The toddler will do most walking when you are still and least if you are moving around. Mothers often say "he makes me wild; this morning I was busy doing the chores and he kept whining and clinging around me until I thought I'd go mad. Now I've sat down all ready to play with him and he's rushing around all over the place as busy as a bee". That is being a toddler. In the morning the child had to keep a close eye on you because he never quite knew where you were going to be next. Now you have fixed yourself and he can go adventuring, come back and go again safely. He knows you are there. He knows he can get back to you in a hurry if he should need to.

Distance limits

If you do fix yourself, perhaps on a park bench, the toddler will at once go away from you. He will toddle off in a straight line in any direction. He will not go further away than about 200 feet. There is no need for you to get up and follow him. He knows exactly where you are. When his outward journey reaches his own personal distance limit, he will start back again, often making several stops along the way but always getting closer. The home-ward journey may end before the child actually comes into contact with you. He may stop several feet away, closely examine a twig or a leaf and then set off again without ever looking at you. He will go on like that all afternoon.

The "come to mother" problem

The toddler's coming-and-going pattern is built in to him. It has a logic of its own which is very different from your logic. If you move to a different bench or a new patch of sun, you disrupt the toddler's pattern. Although he can see where you have moved to and although there is no logical reason against him using this new base as easily as the old one, he simply cannot. His built-in rails lead back to where you *were* not to where you *are*. So he freezes where he finds himself; he may even cry. You can call, you can wave, but whatever you do the toddler will not come. You will have to go and get him, bring him to your new base and let him start out all over again on a new set of rails.

The "walk nicely" problem

A toddler does not learn to follow or to stay with a moving adult until he is around three years old. Until that time he will ask for transport as soon as you signal your intention of moving off. Unfortunately very few people understand that the toddler, who plants himself squarely in mother's path and holds up his arms to be carried, is not being lazy or tiresome but is simply following his natural instinct. He knows that once you walk off he will be unable to stay close to you. If you watch the apes at the zoo, the moment an ape-mother moves purposefully away, her baby will become motionless and cry. Sometimes the mother will call angrily to the baby. But it will not move until she fetches it and it will not accompany her without riding on her back.

Many a pleasant afternoon in the park has its ending ruined by a toddler's apparently wilful refusal to walk home. You know that he is not too tired to walk; he has been rushing to and fro for the past hour and could clearly go on rushing towards home. But attempts to make him do so will cause sad trouble.

If you have no pushchair with you and you do not want to carry the toddler, you will probably take his hand. Being physically joined on to you helps him to stay close, so for a few yards he will manage. But holding hands is not enough. Progress will be slow and jerky. The child will keep stopping, be yanked on again, will steer off in the wrong direction and be pulled back. A few minutes of this will probably be enough for both of you. The toddler will keep getting in front of you, holding up his arms, begging for a lift. You may lose patience and drag him along by the hand or you may decide to let go and leave him to follow at his own pace. He will not because he cannot.

Left to his own devices while you move slowly on, the toddler will lag, stop, go off on side tracks and probably sit down. His behaviour looks like teasing and most people would describe it that way and tell you to keep moving because "he'll follow soon enough when he sees that you mean it". But although he will try, he does not know how to follow you. If you really move off purposefully, you will lose him. If you go slowly, you will have to keep going back, retrieving him and setting him on the right course again. It would save time if you carried him from the beginning. It would save time, effort and irritation if you took the pushchair with you on these expeditions and let him ride whenever you wanted to move on. He does not want to get separated from you; to lose you is his dread. He is only asking you to help him stay where you both want him to be: close.

Playing and thinking

For a small child there is no division between playing and learning; between the things that he or she does "just for fun" and things that are "educational". The child learns while living and any part of living that is enjoyable is also play.

Toys and other playthings are fun – if they were not, children would not use them and so they would learn nothing from them – but they are also tools for finding out about the world and for gradually acquiring the hundreds of skills which will be expected from the child when he or she becomes an adult member of society. While all children enjoy and learn from toys, they have a particular importance for children who live in highly mechanized, urban societies. Selected playthings can reveal to such children many aspects of their world which life in a city apartment conceals.

A century ago a country child was part of a family who worked and played around him at activities whose point he could clearly see. Cows were milked so that everyone (including the toddler) could have milk to drink; musical instruments were played so that everyone (including him) could dance. He could see, and soon understand, adult concerns – the corn flattened by unseasonal weather, or water coming through the roof – and he could "use" most of the adults' tools, from spades to washtubs. But, in contrast, a modern urban toddler is cut off from most of the meaningful basics of life. Productive work goes on away from home in a mysterious place called "the office", or even more mysteriously "up town". Instead of producing obviously useful stuff like milk, it produces incomprehensible stuff called money. Adult play is usually equally mysterious – evening classes, or meetings or the drinking of special drinks – while adult worries are inexplicable, concerned perhaps with redundancy, promotion or the landlord. Activities which do go on at home mostly involve gadgets which are too complex for him to understand or too delicate or dangerous for him to handle. He can neither comprehend nor may he touch the record player or the washing machine.

While nothing you can do will make an urban apartment the ideal environment for a new human being, a wide range of playthings can do a great deal to ensure that your toddler understands the natural world which is concealed under concrete, and the principles of how things work which are hidden in all those gadgets. By giving your child things to play with you can give him or her the opportunity to practise the many skills which are not made familiar by being used at home. By providing the child with his or her own possessions you can make sure that your toddler's development does not suffer because your possessions are forbidden.

There are thousands of toys on the market and there are many playthings available at the cost of only a little imagination. Making good choices depends on taking a thoughtful look at what the child already has, but it also depends on an understanding of how your child's thinking is developing and the stage he or she is reaching, as well as on observation of what is already being enjoyed.

The world of the one year old

The one year old's world is a world of reality taking place in the here-and-now. He is not yet interested in the worlds of imagination; he is too busy making sense of what *is*, to be ready for what *might be*. He cannot cope with the past or future. He cannot yet remember yesterday nor plan for tomorrow; his job is to come to terms with real people and real things as they come before his eyes.

He has already learned an enormous amount about the real world as it is revealed to him by his five senses. He can recognize familiar objects even when he sees them at peculiar angles, like his bottle, presented endways on so that all he sees is a white disc. He can recognize familiar sounds so that he knows his father's voice even while he is still out of sight. His sense of touch is well-developed: if his hand touches his cuddly, he knows it by feel alone and gathers it to him without bothering to open his eyes. The good smell of baking is enough to tell him that something nice to eat is coming up and his sense of taste will differentiate the chocolate buns from the plain ones.

But his interpretations of the world are by no means always accurate. The world is an unpredictable place and he can still be fooled by people and things which do not appear as he has learned to expect. He has clear expectations of your appearance, for example. If you come home from the hairdresser with a new style, or emerge from the swimming pool changing rooms in a bathing cap, you will contradict those expectations. He may not know you. He may even be alarmed by your combination of strangeness and familiarity. He may expect his father's home-coming around that corner and on foot. If his father emerges from a friend's car, the child may go on gazing up the road for him. Even as his father greets him, the child may glance puzzledly from his face to the point where he expected him to appear. But he is ready now to learn to cope with these inconstants in his world.

One year to eighteen months – being an explorer

Somewhere around the first half of his second year all the child's new abilities come together to make it easy for him to learn. He is mobile. He can go and find things and angles on things which you could not bring to him as he sat. He has seen that table many times but now he can view it from underneath.

His reaching out, grasping and letting go are competent. He can get hold of the things he wants to find out about. His "jargoning" is highly expressive. He can question and exclaim, even without words, and you will answer him; tell him things, show and help him. Soon he will use real words himself and they will both help him to understand and help him to remember what he finds out.

His need for sleep is diminishing a little and, when something really interests him, he can keep himself awake. So he has more hours for finding out, for learning. He learns by exploring. When you set him free in an interesting room he moves around from object to object, looking, touching, tasting, smelling and listening. He has no particular purpose in view. He examines an object as a mountaineer climbs a mountain: because it is there. But he may examine a hundred things in an hour.

Because almost everything is new to him, he does not easily get bored. Tiny changes in that interesting room start him exploring it all over again. The dining table was bare this morning; now it is laid for a meal. The ashtray was full but it has been emptied and moved; the wastepaper basket he emptied has been (wisely) hidden; his spread out bricks have been piled up and it takes him quite a while to recognize his lorry which is upside down and looking quite different.

He cannot have too much exploring time or too much variety to explore. As he picks things up for the sake of picking them up, drops them because dropping things is fun, puts them in his mouth to understand them better, he is playing and learning.

The explorer turns research scientist

After months of pure exploring, the toddler begins to experiment too. He still picks things up and puts things in his mouth, but now he is trying to find out what he can do with them, what they taste like. He fingers, drops and squeezes things *to see what will happen*. He is carrying out an endless series of basic experiments.

His experiments gradually teach him the rules which govern the behaviour of objects in our world. It is not fanciful to call him a "scientist" because most of these rules are ones which real scientists examined and explained to us generations ago. The toddler does not understand them but nevertheless he discovers them for himself.

When he drops something, it falls down. Always down, never up. He does not understand the idea of gravity, but he discovers its effects. When he pushes a ball or an apple, it rolls – always; but when he pushes a brick it does not roll – ever. The ideas of solid geometry mean nothing to him either but once again he is discovering its rules.

When he tips a beaker of water, he gets wet; when he tips a beaker of sand, he does not. The water soaks into his clothes but the sand cascades off when he stands up. He could not describe to you the different properties of liquids and solids but he is finding them out all the same.

Discovering group identities

As he discovers how different objects behave, the toddler also begins to realize similarities and differences in what he can do with them as well as in how they look. He may have bricks in several different colours and shapes, but he comes to realize that all those various bricks are more like each other than any of them is like any other object. Foods look very different from each other, yet that slice of bread has a greater similarity to a strip of bacon than to a sponge or a sheet of paper. Gradually he will learn to make more and more differentiations and if you watch carefully you can see him doing so. When he was newly crawling, he tried to treat the family dog or cat as if they were toys. He rushed at them and tried to grab as he grabbed a ball or a toy car. You could see his surprise when the animals failed to behave like toys but instead did a bit of rushing themselves and escaped him. Now he knows those pets are not toys. He treats them differently.

Forming mental "concepts" at around two years old

Once your toddler is able to recognize similarities and differences in things and to make them into groups in his mind, he is on the way to making a vital intellectual stride. Adult human beings organize their perceptions of an extremely complex world by using a more sophisticated version of the same sorting technique.

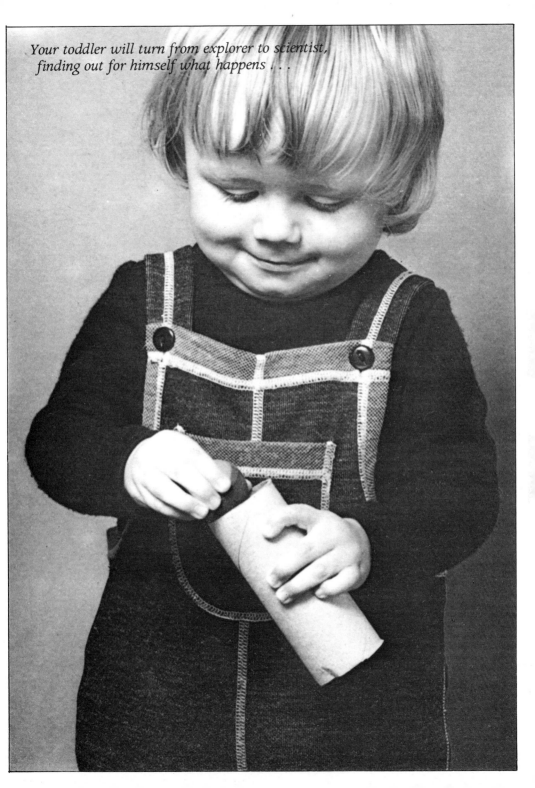

*Your toddler will turn from explorer to scientist,
finding out for himself what happens . . .*

. . . the way natural
materials behave – like
clay, which squishes

. . . and water,
which can be
seen and felt
but not held

. . . and the various weights and textures of things, and how they change shape as they move.

She becomes an engineer too . . .   *. . . discovering how to build at the top*

. . . and what happens if you take from the bottom.

Each one of us sorts, compares, contrasts and groups innumerable objects, facts, people, feelings and ideas. Having "sorted through" what we know of the world, we form complex "concepts" in our minds which allow us to join new information up with what we already know and allow us to communicate freely with each other on the basis of shared knowledge. If I speak to you about an "insect", for example, you will know at once what class of creature I am talking about. I shall not have to spend the first minutes of the conversation explaining to you that an insect is a living creature rather than a man-made one or that it is smaller than an elephant. We share a concept of insects and we can start talking from that basis. In the same way if you want to talk to me of "jealousy" I shall know that our discussion is in the area of uncomfortable feelings of envy and loss. You need not explain the concept of jealousy to me because we already share it.

Because we label our concepts with words, it is difficult to see how your toddler's concept-formation is progressing until or unless he uses at least some language. If you watch and listen carefully, you will see that while he is learning to differentiate "dogs" from all other objects he is also learning name-labels (see p. 356). Eventually he may learn the name-label "dog" and attach it to the family pet. Has he therefore acquired a "concept" of dogs? Not necessarily. His use of the word starts as a simple label for one particular thing – that individual dog. To make a concept of dogs he has to put *all* dogs, your own, the ones he sees in the park, picture book dogs and toy dogs, into one single category in his mind and use that label "dog" for the whole group. He has to recognize that although each member of that mental group is different, they are all more like each other than they are like anything else. You may suspect that he has reached this stage

Early concepts can thrill; these are quite different yet they are both "DOG!"

when he turns from the family dog to his picture book and points out all the dogs on a page of mixed animals. Later, you can be sure he has got there if he says something like: "Dog, Bow-wow! Horse go Neieieigh!" He will have picked out one of the characteristics that differentiate dogs and horses (the sounds that they make); generalized them to all members of each group (all dogs bark, all horses neigh), and contrasted the two groups (dogs don't neigh, horses don't bark).

Once his thinking has reached this stage the toddler will spend a great deal of time sorting and classifying in play. But his concepts are still firmly attached to the real, visible, here-and-now world. If you show him a page of mixed pictures or a box of mixed toys, he will find you all the dogs or all the cars, but he will not find you all the "nice" or "heavy" or "round" things. These are *abstract* ideas and they come slowly.

The beginning of abstract ideas in the third year

Abstract concepts, which describe things which are not real or visible, are still impossible for the two year old. He may, for example, have a vague understanding of the meaning of "more" and "less", but actual numbers defeat him. Any number of objects which is more than one is likely to be "lots"! He may vaguely understand "soon", but any more distant time concept like "next week" is impossible for him. Even ideas like "food" are beyond him although he will know what you mean if you re-phrase the idea in terms of known reality: "things you like to eat".

But as he feels his way towards abstract concepts he begins to be able to think and play in a way which is further removed from real objects in his hand or in front of his eyes. He begins to be able to think about familiar objects when they are not there; to remember them and to make future plans for them. Out of sight is no longer always out of mind. Called in for lunch from a game in the garden, he can leave the game, eat the meal, and return to the game afterwards. It may not sound very clever but it demonstrates remarkable advances in his thinking. He had a picture of that game in his mind. He remembered it through the meal; he planned to go on with it in the future and he was able to do so without prompting.

Being an inventor in the third year

Once your child can think like this, he will begin to imagine and invent; you will see the beginnings of imaginative play. Don't belittle the original ideas that he now produces. A saucepan used for a hat does not look brilliantly original to you because you have often seen children wearing saucepans on their heads. But your child has not. He invented that hat out of and for his own head.

Early imaginative play sometimes looks like the kind of imitative play which has been going on for months, but if you watch carefully you will see the difference. At eighteen months a little boy loved to be given a cloth so that he could help his father clean the family car. A year later he took a pair of underpants off the clothes-rack, dipped it in the dog's water bowl and cleaned his pedal-car with it. He was not imitating a present father; he was being the absent one in his mind. He was *inventing* his cloth and his bucket, *pretending* that the toy car was a real one, and *imagining* that he was his father.

Learning about his or her world

Children will play with whatever is available to them. They need raw material to explore and experiment with but they do not care whether it comes from a toyshop, is passed on by a friend or is assembled from junk materials.

It is impossible to generalize about which of the thousands of available toys a child should have. It depends what yours already has, and chooses to spend time on. This list will show you the types of plaything every child will enjoy and learn from during this age period.

A real understanding of the world and how it works must be founded on a knowledge of natural materials. Country life or a garden and a tolerance for mud mean that a child acquires this automatically. But if you live in a city apartment, it could take your child years to discover that concrete is man-made and that not all water comes out of taps....

The materials a toddler needs	What they are needed for	Ways of providing them
Water: Plain, bubbly, coloured, warm, ice. 	*It pours, splashes, runs, soaks; it feels warm, cold or icy. If you blow, it bubbles. Some things float, some sink, some dissolve in it. It can be carried in things with no holes but it leaks through a sieve or cupped hands....* 	*The child will play in scale with the quantity you provide, so while a paddling pool is glorious and a bath is obvious, a washing up bowl on lots of newspaper, with small containers to fill and empty provides a lot of fun. Emphasize the changes with ice cubes, food colouring, a whisk....*
Earth: Mud, clay or a practical dough. 	*It squidges gloriously in the hands; it can be rolled and pounded, shaped and moulded. More water makes it sticky; less makes it powdery. When it dries it changes; it sticks to hands and hair; water removes it....*	*Clay is hard to handle and almost as messy as real mud. Commercial doughs and plasticines are expensive and the colours soon get reduced to overall brown. Make your own dough (see Enc p. 504); provide an apron, protect the table and let your child explore.*
Sand: "Washed" or "silver sand". Avoid cement or chemicals.	*Wet sand behaves rather like dough but with interesting differences; dry sand behaves like water but is different again. A solid that is not solid and a liquid-like substance that is not liquid.*	*While a beach is heaven and a sandpit is an excellent buy for the garden, a child can have a couple of pounds of sand on a tray in the kitchen even in mid-winter. Failing sand, a couple of pounds of sugar is a worthwhile extravagance. Don't use salt; it will get in the eyes.*
Stones, shells, leaves, twigs... 	*The toddler is not ready for formal botany, but shiny stones dull as they dry; green twigs bend but later snap, and the world is full of fascinating shapes and textures....*	*Let toddlers find things for themselves and bring them home to be kept while interest lasts, not thrown out as "rubbish".*

Basic engineering

The child has to learn both *how* things work and how to *make* them work. He or she must discover the principles and perfect the fine manipulations. The toddler needs some bought toys here because materials must be light, smooth and unbreakable, even when they are subjected to the forces of many mistakes. Make sure that everything is well-designed so that once he or she discovers how two objects fit together, they do actually fit....

The materials a toddler needs	The kind of thing learned from them	Ways of providing them
Bricks 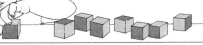	*Tip them and they are higgledy-piggledy; put them end to end and make a line; pile them with the smallest underneath and they fall, build on the largest and they stand....*	*Bricks make one of the most valuable and longest-lasting "toys" and the child needs at least 60. Different colours are fun but different shapes are more important. They must all be in scale so that tiny ones are quarters and small ones are halves. If you make your own, sandpaper them very carefully. If you paint them, use safe, lead-free paint.*
Fitting toys of every kind 	*Round balls will not go into square holes; big things will not fit smaller ones; complex shapes only fit if the angle is right.*	*There is scope for making and for buying here. Make a first "posting box" by cutting brick-and-ball-sized holes in a cardboard carton; follow up with a more complicated bought one. Find some plastic beakers that will build up as well as being used in the bath, or buy a "nesting doll". "Play people" that fit into holes on a range of vehicles etc. have a long and varied play life. Simple "formboards" are the first step to jigsaw puzzles. Make your own by cutting squares, triangles and so on out of cardboard and helping to put them back in the holes. Later the child will like the kind of jigsaw where whole figures lift out by a knob, leaving their self-shaped holes for re-fitting. Putting a key in the lock is fun, too.*
Hook-together toys 	*Any hook and ring will join together; two hooks will too but two rings will not. Why?*	*The toddler will hook a quoit with your umbrella or experiment with a train with simple couplings. There are plastic chains whose links join and come apart and one of your doors may fasten with a "hook and eye". Stick to a large scale for those small hands....*
Threading toys	*Closed circles have all kinds of interesting properties, such as the way they can be threaded on to anything longer and thinner than the hole.*	*Start with rigid rings to thread on a rod. The child can have a cucumber and the rings from your preserving jars, or a toy which builds up into a pyramid when (at last) the right threading order is learnt. He or she will learn to put the dog's lead over the fence and the toothbrush into its holder. Eventually your child will enjoy threading curtain rings or big beads on to a piece of string or a shoelace. Both sexes will enjoy wearing the results, too.*

Beginning to classify

One of the toddler's most important thinking-tasks is noticing the similarities and the differences between things and gradually learning to group them mentally. Doing it with hands as well as brain will help, as well as being fun. If you watch carefully you will see your child beginning to classify things in obvious ways like "my cars versus everything else". Later you will see oranges separated from potatoes. Later still you may watch the child consider universal dilemmas such as whether the apple goes with the ball, because they are both round, or with the biscuit, because they are both edible.

Things to sort and group

All your child needs for sorting and grouping play are collections of objects which are safe and of a manageable size. These can be coloured bricks, big counters, little cars, miniature farm animals. But the child will be just as happy and absorbed with more mundane objects like cotton reels, or big buttons. Natural objects with less definite differences, such as stones or shells, make a change. A grocery bag (with the eggs removed!) is best of all.

Things to fill and empty

Apart from the skill involved, there are all kinds of lessons to be learned about how much water will fill that mug; how many bricks will fit into that box and what happens to them all when the containers are overturned. The child will discover interesting things about weight and about what can be carried, too. You will see it happen: see the toddler set off with half a pail of sand, having found a full one too heavy....

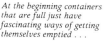

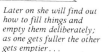

At the beginning containers that are full just have fascinating ways of getting themselves emptied . . .

Later on she will find out how to fill things and empty them deliberately; as one gets fuller the other gets emptier...

With practice she can discover all kinds of sophisticated methods of getting things out of one container and into another.

Miniature worlds

At the same time that the toddler is learning to sort and group objects, to understand their behaviour and to manipulate them by hand, he or she is also becoming able to *imagine* the objects and to *pretend* their behaviour. Although much of this kind of play will take place with the child as the main actor, a miniature world in which to play God is also valuable. If you give little cars, farm animals, etc., your toddler will start by sorting them, but eventually will move through that to creating situations and disasters. Lambs will frisk in fields in his head and cars will crash on the roads of his mind.

Domestic play

Domestic chores may bore you, but they are among the few adult activities whose point the toddler can easily understand and in which both sexes can join you. At first your child will simply want to be given a duster like yours so as to dust too. Later the child will want to pretend that he or she *is* you, and will need a "house" in which to do his or her own "washing up"....If you buy domestic toys rather than sharing your tools with your child, don't go for the gaudiest versions. Choose toys that are most like the real tools you use yourself.

Dressing up

Around the second birthday, your child will increasingly experiment with "being other people". The roles of bus conductor or builder's labourer will be tried out just as the child tries out your domestic roles.

At this stage elaborate clothes are seldom the point. The toddler neither wants nor needs an accurate cowboy outfit. Needed instead are the "props" which, for the child, identify the character. Hats are often the key item. A good buy is a collection of plastic helmets, hats, caps and headdresses, as supplied to nursery schools. Otherwise the toddler needs the use of your handbag or shopping basket, your tie or your running shoes, together with a collection of adaptable cast-offs. An old night-dress makes a bride or a queen. A jacket that is no longer even good for gardening automatically makes its wearer into a large man.

Dolls and soft toys

Don't reject soft toys as too babyish or dolls as too girlish for either sex. Apart from the familiars who guard the cot at night a large family will be well-used for a long time. The toys will people imaginary games from tea-parties to rides on chair-trains. They will receive and relieve a lot of uncomfortable feelings as your child inflicts on them some of the bites and pinches he or she is learning not to give to real people. Don't be surprised if your child subjects them to harsh discipline, shouting and smacking them; children try out the exasperated as well as the loving aspects of parenthood as they think about themselves in relation to you.

If there is a new baby on the way, a realistic baby doll can be useful to bath or drown, love or hate.

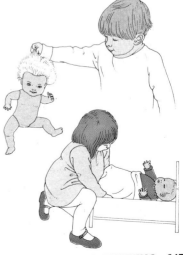

Physical play

Your toddler must run, climb, jump, swing, push, pull, roll and generally leap about. It is only by using their whole bodies to their physical limits that children can learn to control and manage them. The more practice your child gets at this stage the more agile, well-coordinated and safe he or she will be as a pre-school child. And using up energy in physical play is relaxation from the stress of new thinking and the efforts at control which must be made when play uses hands without the rest of the body.

Your child will find plenty of opportunities for physical play in ordinary daily life, but furniture is not really made for daily gymnastics. The child and your possessions will be damaged less if there are some special facilities and equipment. While no one family could buy or house all the suggestions listed below, you can select what is possible and desirable for your child. A friendly apple tree is the best thing for climbing, but it is easier to magic a frame into your garden than to produce a tree where there is not one.

Climbing frames *These give most children a great deal of pleasure and valuable varied play over many years. A fold-away version making a 4ft (1.2m) cube can be used indoors and out. Larger models need permanent installation in the garden. Tubular metal has a long life but tends to get rusty when the paint chips and to feel unfriendly on wet cold days. Wooden frames need occasional weatherproofing. Both need an annual safety inspection.*

Once you decide to invest this much money it is sensible to think ahead to your child as an eleven year old. Buy the biggest frame possible. You will be able to add all kinds of swinging gear, slides and scrambling nets when he or she is older. You can transform it into a tent or a house now by throwing an old sheet over it. Unless teased or pushed, your toddler will be safe on a climbing frame. Let the child do whatever he or she feels able to do, but pander to your own nerves by siting it on grass or earth, not concrete.

Stairs *Stair climbing "lessons" are important to your child's safety. They are fun, too. Teach your toddler to turn around at the top and come down backwards on his or her stomach. When that becomes too easy, teach him or her to come down on his or her bottom. Adult stairs will be too high for a toddler to walk down during this age period.*

If there are no stairs in your child's life, make a point of going to find *some occasionally. If you don't, the toddler may come a cropper when you visit two-storey friends.*

A bought or home-made set of double-sided steps, three to four high and with a small platform at the top, makes a surprisingly adaptable plaything if you have the space. You can use it to support a slide, a see-saw plank or a balancing bar and it serves well as a ship's bridge, too.

Balancing *Putting one foot directly in front of the other instead of in front-but-to-the-side is difficult for a toddler. He or she can have fun practising trying to walk along the lines of your floor tiles or the paving stones.*

A board about 8in. (20cm) wide and 6ft (2m) long, put flat on the floor, is fun to walk along and can be made more exciting later if it is put across two piles of magazines. It is worth getting hold of such a board as it will stay in use for years. By the time your *child is two he or she will walk up it with one end planted on a chair, and across it with both ends on chairs and your hand to hold. Children can learn to jump off it, too.*

A see-saw gives a different kind of balancing play. That same board placed across a sturdy box will do to begin with, but supervise it closely or it will work its way off.

Once children have got the idea of balancing along things they sometimes want to walk every wall they meet. For safety's sake don't *help much. Staggering along, clutching your hand, the child uses your balance instead of finding his or her own. Walking it with only your fingertip to lend confidence, the child finds personal balance and will probably be safe.*

Swinging

Swinging gives children a glorious sense of power and freedom as well as appealing to their innate desire for rhythm. While loving it, they learn a lot about weight, balance and gravity.

An ordinary garden swing is a passive toy which children can only use when you will push. Later on it is hazardous when more than one child is in the garden: flying feet are the cause of many bashed-in milk teeth. Outdoors, a convenient tree branch or the central rung of a climbing frame

will take much easily-available swinging equipment. An old car tire on a rope is among the most popular. Indoors, a couple of stout hooks in the rafters above the usual play-space give a vast potential for physical play which can grow up with the child. Such hooks can take a baby bouncer to start with. Later there can be a thick, soft rope with a big knot on the end to hold on to and try to straddle. Later still there are rope ladders, a monkey swing, a climbing rope....

Push/pull toys

Large scale toys to push or pull are a "must". That babywalker (see p. 330) is still a good buy – usable indoors or out, for dolls, sand or a friend.

The toddler will enjoy pulling something while walking. You can choose from a vast range of toys including a realistic dog on a lead!

Don't buy doll's prams or other free-wheeling and lightweight toys until your child walks absolutely steadily. Tipping and running away are both vices in toddler equipment.

Ride-on toys

All toddlers love to ride on things. In the second year the best buy is a low stable toy on swivel castors which he or she can sit on and push along with the feet. This is preparation for the tricycle for which many children are

ready by the time they are $2\frac{1}{2}$. Do watch out, though, if he or she rides on a toy with ordinary wheels. Because the wheels cannot swivel the toddler can easily tip these horses etc. over as he or she pushes sideways on corners.

Throwing and catching

Few toddlers can manage a game of ball, but all enjoy and need big, light, inflatable balls to chuck around, capture and practise catching. Balloons, kept fairly soft, are fun too. Bean bags, easily made at home and filled with rice or lentils, make an interesting change because they neither roll nor float.

Acrobatics

Toddlers fall down all the time and it usually hurts. A situation where falls are fun instead of being painful is bliss.

A double divan is a fabulous playground. Toddlers learn to turn head-over-heels, to look between their legs, to roll over and over and to bite their toes.... It may not sound grand and educational but it all helps to give knowledge of and confidence in his or her body as well as to relax and get rid of tensions. If you are one of the fathers who has the knack of throwing your child around without anyone getting hurt, this kind of roughhousing will probably become one of your child's very favourite games.

If you cannot stand the idea of the child on your bed, even without

shoes and its cover, a couple of bean bags or giant floor cushions are almost as good. When opportunity offers, don't forget the bliss of throwing oneself into a giant pile of leaves or even a haystack....

Watching and listening

Although your toddler will seem to be on the go all day and every day, quiet play is important, too. This is the time to introduce the peaceful joys of books and music. They are things that will be more obviously important later, but the child can get great pleasure and benefit from them now if you will help. Watching and listening activities need your participation to help understanding and concentration.

Books

Books are going to be vital to your child's education. Help him or her make friends with them and learn to value them. Picture books with big, detailed illustrations of familiar scenes will hold the attention even if a toddler is alone if you give them when circumstances (such as being in a cot!) mean that he or she is forced to keep still.

Being read to is a lasting pleasure for every child. Take it slowly; teach yourself to adapt difficult words or put in explanations as you go. Show the pictures and encourage talk about what is happening.

Drawing

Drawing is the first step to writing. Let your child watch you "magic" a cat on paper or a blackboard, or with felt-tip pens on a piece of plastic laminate. Toddlers will want to try scribbling for themselves, but most of all they will probably enjoy finger painting, with no instrument to form a barrier between themselves and those glorious colours and textures.

Music

A sense of rhythm seems inborn in every child but musical sense can also be taught. Listen with your toddler to records of whatever music you prefer as well as to children's songs and nursery rhymes. Encourage dancing or marching or clapping. Help the child to hear how the melody rises and falls and to feel its meaning through the body. Help him or her to make music too.

Percussion instruments range from saucepan lids to tambourines, but the child will need something accurately tuneful, too. This is only a toy but a good xylophone (from a music shop) will be used spasmodically for years. You will hear the difference between "just banging" and "making a tune" during this age period.

Professional entertainment

Toddlers are barely ready to enjoy television, cinema or live entertainment because instead of moving at their pace, waiting while they take it in, it moves on without them and they get lost. But there are a few special TV programmes directed at the end of this age-group which your child will enjoy and get new ideas and words from, especially if you will watch too.

If your local park or playground offers summer children's shows, with puppets or the simplest comic magic, a toddler will probably enjoy them, especially if they involve shouted participation: they are the first experience of the magic of being part of an audience....

Helping your child to play and think

If you provide the space, equipment and time for your child's play, he will see to the development of his thinking for himself. He is the scientist and inventor; your job is merely to provide the laboratories, the facilities and a research assistant – you – when he needs one. What he actually does with the play materials you provide or allow is his business. He needs the true scientist's independence to work as he pleases, involving you or showing you results only as and when he thinks fit.

Make sure the toddler has basic play-space which is close to you. He is still better off with a suitable corner in the kitchen or living room than with a special room that is tucked away (see p. 268).

If you, or other children, share that space, you must make sure that he can play freely without driving you mad. His relationship with a four year old sister will be loudly ruined if the toddler snatches her pencils whenever she tries to draw. If you have space, a playpen can protect her (inside) from the roving toddler (outside). You and your typewriter or sewing machine would be sociably safe in there too. If space is short, a clothes-rack opened out can be used to toddler-proof a corner.

He will need changes of scene, especially if he does not go out often. Make use of the kitchen or bathroom for messy play and break the day up with sessions in a different room, perhaps listening to music in the sitting room or romping on your big bed.

Outdoors is important. Make use of any outside space you have. Making a balcony safe is a problem, but it can usually be done by stretching strong nylon mesh from the railing to hooks set into the masonry, thus encaging the balcony completely. If the resulting cage will take your weight, you can be certain it will take his, even if he tries to monkey-climb it. Backyards and gardens can usually be made safe with a little thought, but they will not be much use if your home is several floors up. He will not want to be far away from you. If you live on the ground floor, you may be able to make it possible for him to move freely in and out through a window. A stool on the inside and a slide down the outside give him a route that is also a plaything. Parks and meadows give him a completely different range of experiences from those he can get indoors or in the streets. He needs to know about wind and rain and sunshine, about grass and mud and twigs, about puddles to splash in, banks he can climb and the half-frightening freedom of wide open spaces.

A toddlers' club or playground set aside for children under five will probably be a favourite place for your toddler, but think carefully before you take him to ordinary playgrounds intended for older children. The crowds and the noise may be too much for him, the equipment will be too big and fierce and he will find no peace for his small experiments. He is only just discovering how to make a sandpie; he will learn nothing useful from having his early efforts trampled on.

Even routine outings can be fun. He is at the age and stage where the combination of familiar routes with the novelty of the small changes that take place day-by-day is ideal. He will not get bored with local shopping expeditions even if you do. Yesterday he saw a bus, a dog, Mrs. Jones and a tramp. Today he sees a motor bike, two cats, Mr. Smith and a milkman. Let him join in with this ever-changing world: let him speak to Mr. Smith, load the clothes at the launderette and feed the end of his bun to a pigeon. If you do, he will enjoy and learn from that ordinary little walk as much as from an elaborately arranged trip to the zoo.

Use local facilities and your imagination to prevent winter boredom. Unless you live in a very fierce climate, wintry weather is an ordinary part of his world and he needs to discover it. A waterproof suit and boots for him and enough clothes and courage for you can make howling winds, rain and puddles into adventures.

When you want to stay dry there are all kinds of improbable public places which will give your toddler new and exciting experiences. Riding on buses and trains is always popular and so is watching them at their terminals. Stations have escalators too. . . . Large department stores can seem like fairyland to a child; they are warm, bright, full of people and fascinating objects and the shopping expedition can finish with a ride in the lift. Museums and art galleries are usually empty on weekdays. They can give your child a quarter of a mile of warm carpeted running space and you a chance to look at the exhibits. He may even surprise you by wanting to look too.

But if winter palls, what about sharing the load by starting an informal house-swap system with one or two neighbours? If they and their children come to your home one afternoon, you will have fun and a mess to clear up. If you then go to each of their houses that is two more afternoons of fun and *no* mess. . . .

Organize play materials. He cannot play well if he has to hunt for what he wants and when he finds it half is missing. His things need organizing just as efficiently as a kitchen or a real laboratory.

Toy cupboards hide a mess from your visitors, but they also hide his possessions from the child and encourage you to let a mess build up. Many parents grumble that their children have hundreds of toys that they never play with. Usually it is because the toys are incomplete, broken or simply forgotten. Try to arrange to have toy shelves in his main play-space and take pride in their organization. Big toys stand at the bottom so that he can get them without breaking his toes; other toys can stand direct on the shelves where they will look very attractive; vital collections of small objects – cars, stones, counters – can be kept sorted into cardboard boxes, plastic ice cream cartons or plant trays. If you stick one of each item on the outside of the box, the toddler will be able to see for himself what lives where.

The child's toys stay interesting to him for longer if he cannot see all of them all the time. He will feel that he has more variety if some of his things are kept in the particular places where they are used. A special drawer in the kitchen for his "cooking" things will keep him from turning yours out. A basket of bath-toys could live by the bath, while outdoor toys could have their own place on the balcony or in the shed. Especially nice books, difficult puzzles and records will probably be better appreciated if they are kept in the living room, to be used when he has an adult's attention, while things he likes to use in bed can live in his room. The toddler is only just old enough to have his own new ideas about what to do with playthings or how to combine them to make them more interesting. An "odds and ends" box in which you squirrel away packaging materials, scraps of cloth, ribbon and string, cardboard tubes, plastic jars etc., will ensure that you can produce a new cereal-packet garage for cars that have become boring or a new costume for a doll who has lost her novelty-value.

Joining in with
your child's play

Your toddler wants to be near you as he plays and often he will welcome your help and participation in what he does, but he does not need or want to be told what to do. His play is exploration, discovery and experiment. If you insist on showing him what particular toys are "for", demonstrating the "right" way to do things and telling him the answers to questions he has barely formulated, you will spoil the whole process. The art of joining in a toddler's play is to let him be play-leader.

Provided your dignity will alow you to take this subordinate role you can enrich his play enormously:

Give physical help. He is very small and physically incompetent. Often he has a plan in his mind but is frustrated by his physical inability to carry it out. Lend him your coordinated muscles, your height and your weight, but make sure that you stop when his immediate problem is solved. He wanted you to carry the watering can to the sandpit, but did he ask you to wet the sand?

Offer partnership. Some games require a partner – and you are elected. He cannot play "chase" if nobody will run (slowly) after him. He cannot practise rolling and receiving a ball if nobody else will play.

Try, sometimes, to offer unlimited time for these games. Many toddlers have to nag ceaselessly in order to get a grudging game from an adult. Then they spend most of the ten minutes allotted to them waiting for the dread words "that's enough". You cannot play with him all day but try sometimes to seem willing, or even eager, to play, and to let him have the luxury of going on until *he* is ready to stop. He learns by continuous repetition. If ball-rolling is on today's play-work agenda, he may need to roll a ball for half an hour at a time.

Offer casual demonstrations and suggestions. He can use any number of these provided they are not made bossily or at tactless moments. If he is playing with ping-pong balls and you happen to have the cardboard tube from a toilet roll to hand, pick up a ball and show him the interesting thing that happens if you roll it through the tube. He can take up the suggestion or not, just as he pleases.

If he is playing with some paper, show him what happens if you scribble on it with a chalk. He may or may not want to have a try himself. But don't bustle up with the ping-pong ball or the chalks when he is busily engaged with his bricks. If you do, you are rudely implying that what he is doing has no importance. You are interrupting him.

Help the toddler to concentrate. He will find it difficult to concentrate for more than a few minutes at a time on anything that he finds at all difficult – especially if it means sitting still. That means that he will not be able to get very much satisfaction out of his most advanced new activities like doing puzzles or fitting toys. If you will sit with him, talk, support and encourage him, he will be able to go on for longer, perhaps for long enough to get the tremendous satisfaction of completing his self-imposed task.

Help your child to manage with other children. He is not ready to play with other toddlers but he will get great pleasure (and many new ideas) out of playing alongside them. Be prepared to conduct the party for them both. They are not old enough to be left to "fight their own battles" or to "play fair", "take turns" or "be nice to visitors". They need protecting from each other so that neither has to watch a "friend" destroy a mysterious arrangement of counters or break down a careful sand castle. Give them similar materials and let each do what he wishes, guarded from interference. Both will play, pausing now and then to watch the other; enjoying each other's presence and making the interesting discovery that there are other children in the world who do the same kinds of things but do them just a bit differently. . . .

Older children can be wonderful company for a toddler but playing at the younger level comes very hard on the older ones. They have their own play, different from, although just as important as, the toddler's. An eight year old may let the toddler "catch" her three times in a game of tag but the fourth time her natural desire to win will overcome her. The game will end in tears. Older children should not be expected to entertain toddlers except for short periods as a spontaneous gesture of affection.

Where circumstances demand that a mixed age group play together, you can help them to find a game which has a natural role for the toddler. He can play at his level, the older children can play at theirs, and everyone will be satisfied. On the beach, wave-jumping suits everyone from the ripple-splashing baby to the breaker-jumper. At home, any variety of "mothers and fathers" or "hospitals" gives the toddler a natural position as baby or patient.

Playing alongside another child is the first step towards making friends. But each child will need his or her own materials and you must be ready to act as peace-keeper.

Learning language

Toddlers cannot really join the human race until they can understand and use language. Until that time they are part of a baby-race, needing to be "talked to" with special gestures, little words, lots of physical contact. And until that time their needs and wants have to be guessed at too. He is whining. What does he want? Is he tired? Hungry? Bored?

Once a child can really understand and use speech, you can discuss things with him or her. Things that are there to be seen like that naughty dog stealing the chicken off the table; things that are not there but will be, like Jane who will soon be home from school; things that will never be "there" in the sense of being visible, like thunder or electricity or joy.

Understanding language

Language is for communication; for people to talk with each other. It is not just one person saying words. A few separate words on their own are not even very useful, as you will know if you have ever faced a foreign country armed with a phrasebook. The book will tell you how to say "where is a hotel?" but it cannot tell you how to understand the answer.

Understanding language is far more important to your toddler than actually speaking it. Once he really understands, he will communicate with you. If you try to teach him to imitate word-sounds before he understands their meaning, you are treating him like a parrot, not a person.

Helping your child to understand language

As we have seen, a baby has an inbuilt interest in human voices with a natural tendency to listen and to concentrate when someone is talking. You can build on this as you did earlier.

Talk as much and as often as you can directly to the child. Look at him while you talk. Let him see your face and your gestures.

Let the toddler see what you mean, by matching what you do to what you say. "Off with your shirt" you say, taking it off over his head; "Now your shoes" – removing them.

Let the toddler see what you feel by matching what you say with your facial expressions. This is no age for teasing. If you give him a big hug while saying "Who's mummy's great horrible grubby monster then?" you will confuse him. Your face is saying "Who's mummy's gorgeous boy?"

Help your child to realize that all talk is communication. If you chat away to yourself without waiting for a response or looking as if you want one; or if you don't bother to answer when he or another member of the family speaks to you, he is bound to feel that words are just meaningless sounds.

Don't have talk as background noise. If you like to have the radio on all day, try to keep it to music unless you are actually listening. If you are listening, let him see that you are receiving meaningful communication from the voice he cannot see.

Act as your toddler's interpreter. You will find it much easier to understand his language than strangers do and he will find it much easier to understand you and other members of the family than to understand strangers.

Help the child to understand your overall communication; it does not matter whether he understands your exact words or not. If you do some cooking, lay the table, take off your apron and then hold out your hand to him saying "It's lunch time now", he will understand that his lunch is ready and will come to his high chair. He probably would not have understood the words "lunch time now" if he had not had all those other cues to go with them. He will learn the meanings of the words themselves through understanding them, again and again, in helpful contexts.

Using words   As we have seen (see p. 264) babies' first words are almost always labels; they are names for people, animals or other things that are important to them. Once babies have attached name labels to a person or an animal or two they are likely to add a label for a favourite food. It will not be a word like "supper", produced out of hunger. Hunger will lead to whining, not talk. It will be a name for some treat food or for something giving special emotional pleasure. "Bopple" and "Biccit" are very usual ones.

Toddlers' attention often turns next to their own clothes. Shoes are a firm favourite for early naming. They have novelty value because the first pair has only just been introduced and they stay in sight much more than do sweaters or pants!

Many children do not get further than this before the middle of their second year. New words come very slowly at first, being added, perhaps, at a rate of only one or two each month. But the child is storing up understanding of language and eventually, often at around twenty months, will burst out with a positive spate of new words. It is not unusual for a child who says only ten words at eighteen months to be using two hundred by the second birthday.

The new spate of words will almost all be centred on the child himself. He is most interested in the things which are part of, or concern him, and these are the things he chooses to talk about. He will learn the names for parts of his own body. He will find his hairbrush and name it, avoid his face flannel while naming it and escape from his cot, by name. When he begins to extend his words to things that belong outside his own home they will still be things that are important to *him*. He may learn to name the birds he enjoys feeding with crumbs but he will not bother to speak of the school that is important to his sister!

Although these single words are all simple name-labels for familiar objects that the child can see, he uses them in an increasingly varied way as he readies himself for the next stage of speech. You can help him along by paying attention not only to the word he says but to the way he says it. He may label the family pet "dog" and you acknowledge that he is indeed a dog. But next time he uses the word he puts a question mark after it. "Dog?" he says, watching him trot across the garden. Answer

Outdoors brings freedom to her play . . .

. . . freedom from restrictions about making a mess

. . . freedom to create miniature worlds of her own.

. . . freedom to play alongside others, and make a noise,
– and maybe find it's tuneful . . .

the question mark: tell him where the dog is going. He may even make moral judgments with his single words. Watching the dog scratching in your flower bed he may say "Dog!" in tones of deep disapproval. Make it clear that you have understood him by agreeing that the dog is doing wrong.

Using more than one word at a time

Once he has acquired a good collection of single words and has learned to use them with varying intonations and meanings, your toddler will move on to the two-word stage without any prompting. But do not expect his first phrases to be grammatically correct. He adds a second word in order to communicate a fuller or more exact meaning, not in order to speak more "properly". He will not go from "ball" to *the* ball because "the" adds nothing to what he wants to say about the ball. Instead he will say "John ball" or "more ball". Don't try to correct him. If you do, you will limit his pleasure in communicating with you. Try to make him feel that each new effort he makes in this difficult business of talking is worthwhile. When he says "ball" he may mean one of a number of things, but when he says "John ball" it is much easier to guess that he means "Is this John's ball?" or perhaps "Will John play ball?"

Two-word phrases make it much easier to understand the toddler's thought processes. You will be able to see, for example, that he is beginning to be able to think about things which are not actually visible (see p. 342). If he wanders around the room saying "Ted?", "Ted?" you may guess that he is thinking about his teddy bear, but once he wanders around saying "Where Ted?" you will know that he is searching for it. You will be able to hear his early concepts forming too (see p. 341). If he has been at the stage where all animals were called "Pussy" and he now meets an Alsatian dog and says, in tones of doubtful amazement, "*BIG* pussy?" you will know that while he still does not have a separate word for dogs or for animals-that-are-not-cats, he does have a clear concept of cats themselves and is quite aware that this large dog does not fit into it!

Sentences and grammar

Once he has begun to make two-word phrases your toddler will soon add another word or two and make sentences. But he will not do this by copying the things he hears you say. His sentences will follow strictly communicative and *logical* rules of grammar which will usually be quite different from the "correct" grammar of whatever language you happen to speak.

Don't try to correct your child's grammar. He will not alter what he says to suit your instructions, but your disapproval will put him off. He needs to feel that any message he communicates is welcomed for itself, so just listen to him instead.

Listen to the order of the child's words. He rarely gets this wrong. If he wants to tell his sister she is naughty he will say "naughty Jane". But if he wants to tell you that his sister is naughty, he will say "Jane naughty". If he wants to tell you that he has seen a bus he will say "see bus", but if he wants you to come quickly to the window and see the bus for yourself, he will say "bus, see".

Listen to the way your child makes past tenses. Most English verbs are made into the past tense by adding a "d" sound. The toddler extends the rule and says "he goed" and "I comed".

Sometimes for good measure he adds the "d" sound to a verb that is already in the past tense so that he says "I wented" or "she beened".

Listen to the way plurals are made. Most English words are made plural by adding an "s" or a "z" sound. The toddler extends this logically to all words and says "sheeps", "mans" and "mouses".

Listen to your toddler using phrases as if they were all one word. Phrases which the toddler has understood for many months often seem like single words to him. When he comes to use them with another word, he cannot separate the first two to get the grammar right. He has heard "pick up", "put on" and "give me" over and over again. Now he says "pick up it", "put on them" and "give me it".

Learning to get grammar right

A toddler's early sentences are his very own original telegraphese, developed out of his desire to communicate interesting and exciting things rather than imitated from teaching adults. Convincing evidence of this came from a small boy who was taken to see a football match. Thrilled by the scene he said "See lots mans!" It was the first time he had ever said anything of that kind and he could not possibly have copied the sentence from adult speech. An adult would have communicated the same message with the sentence: "See what a lot of men". If you compare the sounds of the two sentences you will find that they have almost nothing in common. The little boy had thought up his sentence all for himself.

Your child will speak his language and he will listen to you speaking yours. Your quick and understanding response to the things he says will keep him interested in communicating with you, while your correct speech keeps a model in front of him to which he will gradually adapt his own. When he rushes into the kitchen saying "Baba cry, quick!" you know that he means his baby sister is crying and you should go to her at once. You show that you understand his language but you answer in your own: "Is Jane crying? I'd better come and see what's the matter."

If you insist on correcting your toddler's telegraphese and making him say things "properly", you will bore him and hold up his language development. He is not interested in saying that same thing more correctly; he wants to say something new. Let him speak in his own way and don't pretend that you do not understand him when you do.

If you reply to your toddler only in his own "baby talk", you will also hold up his language development because you will not be providing him with new things to say. So along with letting him speak his way, make sure that you speak your way, too. Let him ask you for a "biccit" if that is his word for it; let him tell you that he has "eated it". But you offer him a "biscuit" and ask him whether he has "eaten it" yet. As long as you both understand each other and as long as you both say plenty to each other, all will be well.

In the toddler years . . .

She looks to you to interpret talk, just as she looks to you to interpret the world.

the language of strangers is always hard to understand.

Only when you have translated for her can she respond for herself. In this way she will learn in time to meet the outside world without your mediation . . .

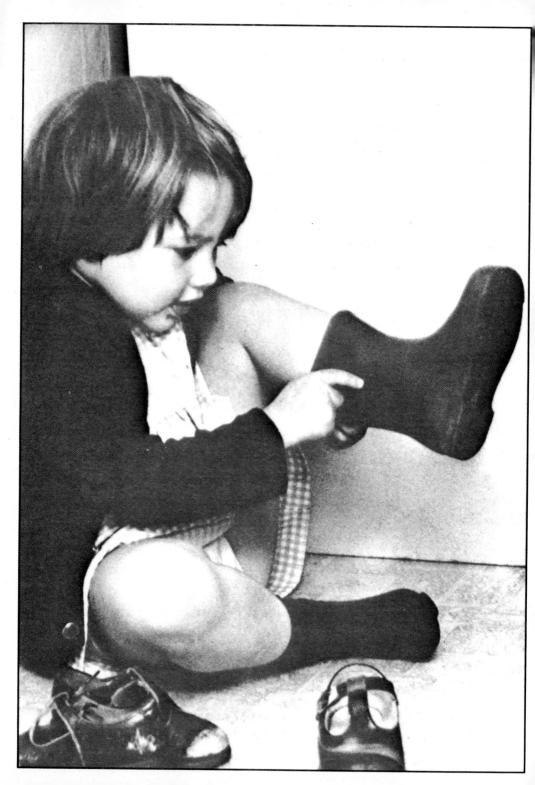

CHAPTER SIX

THE PRE-SCHOOL CHILD

From two and a half to five

A pre-school child does not emerge from your toddler on a given date or birthday. He becomes a child when he ceases to be a wayward, confusing, unpredictable and often bolshy person-in-the-making, and becomes a comparatively cooperative, eager-and-easy-to-please real human being – at least 60 per cent of the time.

Children change and grow up gradually. They do not transform themselves overnight, turning from caterpillars to butterflies under our eyes, but this particular change from toddler to pre-school child, whether it takes place at $2\frac{1}{2}$ or 4, does have a sudden and magical quality about it. The pre-school child has, in some almost mystical way, "got there". He has made it safely through infancy and toddlerhood into the beginning of real childhood. The changes that take place within him between, say, $2\frac{1}{2}$ and $3\frac{1}{2}$, are not actually as great as the changes of the second year, but they seem tremendous because he is suddenly so much easier to live with and to love.

A lot of the magic lies in his language. Grown-up people do very little and say a great deal. We use words instead of actions, telling off ourselves and others with conscience-searching and with scolding rather than with hair-tearing and blows. We tell our troubles rather than howl. We make lists rather than get ten items one at a time. Everything we feel and do is mediated through words. Toddlers say very little and do a great deal. They express themselves in action and demand action from us. With a toddler you cannot explain, you have to show. You cannot send, you have to take. You cannot control with words, you have to use your body.

Although pre-school children are still very physical in their reactions to their feelings and to the world, still readily capable of tears and tantrums, they have learned enough language and enough of the thinking that goes with it to be able to join us in using words as well.

At last you can talk to your child, have what you say listened to, understood and accepted, get reasonable answers back. The great block in communication between you has finally come down, and this, more than anything else, makes the child seem like a "real person".

Compared with the toddler, your pre-school child has built up a lot of experience and a lot of accomplishment. He can wash his face (if you tell him); put on his boots (if you leave them right way round); get his own drinks (if he can reach the tap) and climb in and out of chairs, cars and trouble. As his abilities increase, your routine work diminishes. As he feels more able to manage his world and himself in it, so you can devote increasing time and energy to the exciting business of introducing him to a wider world and its ideas.

As he uses the kaleidoscopic pieces of what he has learned, shaking them together in his mind to form and re-form different patterns of thought, he begins to remember from day to day. He applies what he learned yesterday to what he does today and he looks forward to tomorrow. Because he can look forward he can wait a bit, too. The offer of a game when you have finished what you are doing no longer drives him into a frenzy because he wants to play *now*. He can enjoy simple choices, asking himself what he enjoyed last time, wondering what he feels like now. He can begin to understand (though not to keep) promises; to recognize (though not reliably to tell) the truth, and to acknowledge (though not always to respect) the rights of other people.

He can begin to acknowledge your rights because his feelings of individuality have extended from himself to you. He not only sees himself as a separate person from you, he also sees you as a separate person in yourself. You are no longer simply an appendage or slave whose desire to do other things than look after him is at best incomprehensible, at worst bitterly hurtful. He may not understand *why* you should want to talk to adult friends, but he sees that you do; sees that your wish is similar to his own desire to play with his friends; sees the reasonableness of your case. So this is the age of bargaining, of practical and emotional trade. "If I do this, will you do that?" appeals directly to his finely-balanced sense of justice and makes it easy to find ways around almost every potential clash.

Seeing you as a real whole person gives his love for you a new quality and one which brings it much closer to adult ideas about love. He becomes capable of genuinely unselfish sympathy and concern; capable of offering something because he thinks you might want it rather than because he feels like giving it. If he should see you crying, he will not simply be frightened and angry at the feelings your tears call up in *him*, he will be sorry for you because of the feelings the tears suggest you are experiencing. He would like to help you; like to have some part in making you feel better. If he comes and hugs you, it will not be an attempt to reclaim your attention from

*She is able now to recognize how you feel
– and she can offer you sympathy too . . .*

whatever is bothering you back to himself, but an attempt to soothe you with his own attention. He gives as well as takes.

As he watches you and the other adults who are close to him or who catch his imagination, the pre-school child strives to understand their roles and their behaviour towards each other. This is the age of identification. Your child will "be" all kinds of people from his own baby sister to the elevator man, but above all he will try to "be" you. However hard you try to keep activities and play bi-sexual, the child may insist, during this period, in adopting the most sexist aspects of family life, seeming always to be involved in domestic play when he is "Mummy" or with mechanical matters when he is "Daddy". The accuracy of his observations may be uncomfortable. As he looks at you, you will sometimes see his father's, supposedly private, coaxing expression on his face. As he cares for his doll-family you will hear your own turns of phrase and the expressions you are least proud to have recognized as yours!

It is through identification with adults in general and with you, his special people, in particular, that the pre-school child takes in and makes part of himself the instruction and demands which have previously come from you, outside him. Now he begins to scold himself (and anyone else below him in status) for carelessness you had not even noticed. He warns himself against actions you had not known he was contemplating and he tries to run everything just the way he thinks you want it. Because he is very young and inexperienced, he will sometimes go too far so that he sounds bossy and smug. Sometimes you will find yourself positively looking forward to his more babyish and less virtuous moods, or even being tempted to squash him when he asks yet again: "That's right isn't it, Daddy?" or "I'm good aren't I?"

But this new behaviour, even if it is sometimes irritating, is a triumph for his development and a golden star for the relationship between you. It means that he at last consciously wants your approval, wants you to be pleased with him and is actually prepared to put some effort into seeing that you are. You know that your toddler *needed* love and approval but he often seemed not to care whether he got it or not and never seemed to know how to earn it. Your pre-school child is positively asking you to tell him what does and does not earn approval, so he is ready to learn any social refinement of being human which you will teach him. Since that was what you were aiming at all along, his obvious desire to please should make it easy to be patient and gentle with him. He knows now that he wants your love and he has learned how to ask for it. Give it to him in full measure.

Feeding and growing

The pre-school period sees a further slowing in growth rate. Your child will probably gain around 5lbs (2.3kg) and $3\frac{1}{2}$ inches (8.9cm) in the third year, dropping to $4\frac{1}{2}$lbs (2kg) and $2\frac{1}{2}$ inches (6.4cm) during the fifth. Don't worry if the gradual change from being a stocky, curvy two year old to a slimmer, straighter five year old makes the child look comparatively thin for a while. The toddler plumpness will eventually be replaced by muscle but this takes time. In the meanwhile legs and arms may look positively fragile.

Weighing and measuring

There is no point in frequent weight and height checks now. But twice yearly weighing and measuring is sensible. If both rise together (see chart p. 508), you will know that growth is proceeding normally. If weight rises much faster than height, you will know that the child is getting fatter. If the height does not rise perceptibly during six months, you should measure your child again three months later. If there is still no increase, take chart and child to the doctor. A very few children do lack a particular hormone which is vital for growth. It can be given to them at a "growth clinic" and will re-start normal growth, but it may not be able to make up for the height the child has already failed to gain. So get advice before much growing time has been lost.

How to measure. Measuring a child's height accurately is difficult. Don't try to use a tape measure directly. Instead, stand the child up against a wall or door, heels flat on the floor and touching the wall, head straight so that he or she is looking directly in front. Now put something flat and rigid (such as a book) on the top of the head so that it flattens any sticking-up hair. Make a mark on the wall, and then use a tape to measure from the floor to your mark. If you always use the same wall or door for measuring your children, you can name and date your marks so that over the years you accumulate a permanent record of who measured what at which age.

Lithe and leggy, the pre-school child's proportions are quite different from the dumpy toddler or large-headed baby...

Food and eating

Pre-school children who have not got food and eating mixed up in their minds with love and discipline (see p. 286) are often real trencher-people. They use up an enormous amount of energy in their daily lives and they eat to match it. Provided there is enough food available, a child like this will certainly take in enough calories. Hunger will see to that. If the offered food is adequate in proteins, vitamins and minerals, the child will also select a diet that is well-balanced for his or her needs. As we have seen, refusal of particular, valuable foods like meat, eggs or green vegetables will not matter provided that the child can get their value from other sources such as cheese and fruit. As a useful "rule-of-thumb", a child who is eating as much as he or she wants of an ordinary family diet and is having a pint of milk and a correct dose of multivitamins every day will be getting everything needed.

So you need not push particular foods, but neither need you hold back. There is no food which is ordinarily served to your family which your child should not have. If he or she likes curry and you like serving it, let the child have it too. A few foods may still disagree with him or her, but unless your doctor confirms an allergy to one of them (see Enc/Allergies) you need not worry unduly even about these. The child will not "eat himself sick" either. A child who always eats enthusiastically will stop where greed ends and gluttony begins.

Helping your child to eat sociably

Your child is enthusiastic about food because you have not spoiled the natural relationship between feeling hungry and enjoying food. He or she is ready, now, to start to fit in with the social aspects of mealtimes. But go easy. If you suddenly change your attitudes, insisting on a vast improvement in table manners overnight, you could still spoil eating for the child and make problems for yourself.

Teach table manners by example rather than by exhortation. On the whole he will come to behave as the rest of the family does, so if you are suddenly irritated by his eating with his fingers and leaning his elbows on the table, make sure he is not watching the rest of you doing the same thing!

Promote the child to eating arrangements like your own. He will imitate adults more readily if he sits on an ordinary chair (or a small but extra-tall version specially made for young children) rather than in a high chair, and if he has a place setting like everybody else. He cannot learn to take care of china and glass and to manage a fork, spoon and eventually a table-knife if he is only given plastic.

Help your child to acquire a sense of occasion. Few families can have every meal together, elegantly served at a perfectly set table. Life is not long enough. But if every meal is a kitchen-scramble, with mashed potatoes dolloped from saucepan to plate and people coming and going at different times, your pre-school child will get no chance to see how people behave on more formal occasions. He is bound to "let you down" when you most want him to behave nicely. In a busy household it may be a good idea to make one weekend meal deliberately more formal. The child could be involved in making the table look pretty – perhaps picking flowers for the middle or folding paper napkins – and he could change into clean, tidy clothes for the meal. If the grown ups have a drink beforehand, a special drink for him adds to the fun. During the meal food is served on dishes and everyone, including the child, helps themselves and each other. It is obviously an occasion for something specially nice to eat and for at least some conversation which will particularly interest him.

In this kind of atmosphere the child will not feel nagged at if you show him a more conventional way to manage a fork or get peas to his mouth. He will feel much more adventurous if you are letting him in on the grown up world. It is realistic too. Why shouldn't he eat potato chips with his fingers when he is having supper alone in front of the television and there is nobody there to see? What matters is that he should be able to behave inoffensively at table when the occasion demands it.

Help the child to acquire new tastes. If your pre-school child knows, from bitter experience, that he will be made to eat anything that is put on his plate, he will probably refuse even to try new foods, in case he does not like them. He will feel much more adventurous if you allow him to taste before the meal or to have a tiny bit of the new food on a teaspoon and decide whether he wants to be served with it or not.

Get the child used to foods which will make life easier for you. A child who is generally enthusiastic about food will accept new foods if you start off by introducing them as part of ordinary family meals. Accustom him to whatever will be available on camping trips, picnics or in restaurants. Above all, try to get him used to eating cheese. Bread or biscuits with cheese and an apple is a perfectly balanced meal which takes 30 seconds to prepare and another 30 seconds to clear up. It is easily portable and available in any roadside pull-in in any western country. If he will happily eat that combination you need never interrupt a day's activities in order to think of something for his meal.

There is more to meal-times than just food now. You can help her to see them as social occasions by letting her join in their preparation . . .

"Faddy" eaters

Real eating problems now are almost certainly a hangover from the toddler period and need handling similarly (see p. 287). But a lot of pre-school children get labelled "faddy" or "difficult eaters" when they are only trying to exercise the same rights to personal taste and appetite which adults take for granted. In our well-fed society most of us would rather stay hungry than eat what we dislike. Yet because we are adult we seldom face the choice. We buy and/or prepare what we do like. Only very young children are faced with food prepared by someone else and are then expected to "eat what is put in front of them".

So allow for the child's dawning tastes in food. Where those tastes are similar to yours they will be accepted without question; it is when a child's tastes differ from everyone else's that he or she tends to be called "faddy". If no member of the family eats bacon fat, the child's rasher will be trimmed without question; but if other people eat the whole rasher, the child may well be labelled "fussy" when he or she leaves the fat.

While every family will work out its own attitudes to individual food tastes, there is a reasonable middle-road which will go a long way to avoiding mealtime trouble for all concerned:

From the child's point of view	From your point of view
It is unreasonable to serve a meal or dish you know the child dislikes and then be irritated when she leaves it. Make sure you serve something she normally eats, even if it means substituting an egg or some cheese for the family main dish.	*It is not reasonable to pander to momentary whims. The child must make her meal out of whichever items she normally eats that are available today. If the menu is liver and bacon which she normally enjoys, she does not have the right to demand egg and bacon instead. If she does not want liver today she must make do with the bacon.*
Remember that you will never help her to like a particular food by forcing her to eat it. Many adults still cannot face foods which were forced on them because of war-time or other restrictions.	*It is not reasonable to allow the child all of the best part of a family dish. If she only wants the crisp brown top of her helping, fine. Don't give her any underneath. But don't feel that you have to give her the crisp brown top of everyone else's helping too.*
It is unreasonable to insist that the child eat all the food on her plate if you put it there. Let her say how much she wants or help herself. She may then come back for more.	*It is not reasonable to let the child spoil food. If there are iced cakes and she does not want any cake but only icing, she has the right to the icing off one cake – she has simply eaten what she wanted of it – but this does not give her the right to nibble the icing off a plateful.*
It is unreasonable to insist that the child eat at all if she says she is not hungry. She may be sickening for something or having an unhungry day. She has the right not to eat, just as you have.	

Eating between meals

Most pre-school children genuinely need to eat more often than the adults in the family. If you are using up that much energy, it is a long time from breakfast to lunch and from lunch to supper.

Children who are hungry at other times need food-fuel. A formal mid-morning and mid-afternoon snack will almost certainly be routine, but problems arise because hunger gets confused with greed. Usually it is our fault. The child says he is hungry and we give him a chocolate biscuit. Next time, he does not say he is hungry, he says he wants a chocolate biscuit. Is he hungry or is he greedy?

The easiest way to keep out of this kind of dilemma, once your child is old enough to understand, is to have certain foods which the whole family knows to be available at any time they want them. There might, for example, be a biscuit tin which is kept filled with plain biscuits, and a fruit bowl with apples and bananas. Equally there might always be bread and butter for the asking or a piece of cheese or a handful of raisins. Different families with different tastes and budgets will find their own basics, but for all families the point is the same. These are "I'm hungry" foods. Anyone who cannot wait for the next meal can have some.

If you do follow this idea, other foods which the child asks for between meals can be seen as being asked for from greed rather than hunger and you can decide for yourself whether you feel indulgent or not. If you have just baked a batch of buns and the smell is driving the child mad with greed, you may decide to give him one at its warm best or to make him wait until teatime. Either way you are not depriving him of food when he is hungry.

Sweets If you have managed the kind of approach to sweets which was outlined in the previous section (see p. 290), they will probably never be a major issue in your household. But sometimes, as children get older, spend more time with other children and are able to compare what they get with what others get, sweet-trouble does begin. If you have to formulate a sweet "policy", remember that it is usually the parents who try for the strongest and most righteous line who have the most trouble. Strict rationing, for example, tends to focus attention on what is *not* allowed. Those who can stay coolest about the matter suffer least.

The policy which most often seems helpful is the simple one of never keeping sweets in the house. If you have not got any sweets you can say so, calmly and honestly, when the child asks. Willingly buying the child a small packet of the least damaging type of sweets (see p. 291) at some regular times (such as on the way home from shopping) also gets you out of a lot of difficulties. The child knows there will be some sweets then, so your refusal to buy any right now will probably be accepted quite calmly. You can also make sweets seem nice-but-ordinary by occasionally using them as part of meals – serving chocolate with pudding or using jelly beans to decorate a cake. When your child does have some sweets, you can reduce the damage they do both by banning the most damaging types (such as toffees and lollipops) and by encouraging him to finish what he wants of them all in one go just as he would finish with a slice of cake.

Your whole attitude to especially-nice-things-to-eat will have an effect on the ease or difficulty with which you handle the sweet problem. If you want him to regard sweets as just one more nice thing in a life full of nice things, some of which are foods, encourage him, sometimes, to buy himself a different kind of food-treat. The actual shopping is half the point. Many small children only get the chance to shop for themselves from the sweet shop, but being allowed to choose and buy a beautiful red apple from the greengrocer or a shiny brown bun from the baker can be just as much fun.

Fat pre-school children

The natural growth pattern tends to slim children down now, so obesity becomes less usual and fat children all the more conspicuous. Really fat children are often made a butt by others, so try to produce a slimmer contour before it is time for your child to start infant school.

The aim of slimming fat children should be to slow their weight gain down so that as they grow upwards, less and less of them bulges out. Over the next eighteen months or so your child will get about 5 inches (13cm) taller. If you can hold the weight gain over that period down to only 2–3 pounds (0.9–1.4kg), you will end up with a much thinner-looking child.

It may be a good idea to start your "slimming campaign" by taking your child to the doctor. Take the growth chart with you so that he can see whether the obesity is new or part of a long-term pattern, and so that he can help you to work out by how much the weight gain is outstripping the gains in height.

Slimming

The principal ways in which you can help a pre-school child slim down are similar to those suggested for toddlers (see p. 293). But the child's greater age makes some differences:

Fat consumption has probably gone up because the child now shares family meals which may mean more fried foods and more bread and toast. Remember that almost all foods you normally fry in butter or oil can be dry-fried with no extra fat at all if you use a non-stick pan. Frying by this method is better for everybody. Remember, too, that many foods which your child likes crisp can be made that way by being dry-baked in an oven. Crisp bacon cooked by this method actually *loses* most of its fat.

Not everything that is spread on bread need be fatty and fattening. The child is old enough now to experiment with spreads that need no extra butter at all such as peanut butter or cream cheese.

Although the child may drink less milk than before, he or she may be drinking a great many fizzy drinks. Serve plain water at meals. If fizz is the point of treat drinks, mix squash with plain soda water. Ice cubes often make simple drinks seem fun.

Obviously you will try not to let a child who is already fat eat a great many sweets and fattening snack foods which are extra to meals. But cutting down on these sweet and enjoyable foods takes tact if the child is not to be made miserable. A very useful trick is to buy, make or serve miniatures. Ten tiny sweets seem more to a child than three big ones. Three finger biscuits seem plenty yet will not contain the calories of one full-sized one. You can even make home-made cakes in paper sweet cases. . . .

By the time fat children are three or four years old, they may have fallen into a vicious circle over exercise. They do not run about much and this is partly because they are fat, but they are fat partly because they do not run about much. Where a *toddler* will normally be very active provided he or she is allowed physical freedom, a *pre-school child* may have grown out of running for its own sake. Your child needs people to run with, after and away from. When he or she must play alone, encourage kicking a ball, rolling a hoop or skipping rope. Even indoors the child can dance to music, set records for hopping on one leg, and learn to turn somersaults.

Sleeping

Problems over going to bed are almost universal among toddlers, but pre-school children tend to divide neatly into those who make no fuss about it at all and those who make a very great deal. If your child is in the first group, you are lucky. Go on doing whatever it is that you have been doing up to now and hope that it lasts! If your child is in the trouble-group, it may help if you take an honest look at the whole business of bedtime.

A lot of children spend a great deal more time in bed than they spend asleep. They are put to bed because their parents want peace in the evening. If you can admit that it is you who wants the child in bed rather than the child who needs to be there, you will see that it is worth it to you to make bed, and going there, as pleasant as possible for the child.

Making bedtime pleasant

Pre-school children are rapidly developing a sense of ownership and the beginnings of feelings of privacy. They really need a place they can call their own. Whether you decide to do up a room specially or merely to spend a weekend reorganizing to make a sleeping corner, consult with the child about the grand new arrangements, and make it clear to the rest of the family that this place now belongs to him or her. Older brothers and sisters should not be allowed to barge in without permission and it should be left to the child to show it to any visitors.

Remember that the child will spend at least half the time in this special place. It should therefore be kept just as bright and clean and pretty as the more public parts of the house. However much children like their rooms they will not, at this age, keep them tidy themselves. If you do not do so, the room will soon become so littered that it is totally unappealing.

The child's bed should be the centrepiece. This is probably the sensible moment to promote him or her from a cot to a "big bed". Don't use bunk beds unless child-space is really tight. One or other child will always feel that the other one has the best layer and it is difficult to feel private when two of you sleep on top of one another. Another disadvantage is that nursing a child in a top bunk is impossible so every time your child is ill he or she will have to be moved. Two separate beds are infinitely better, even if they make the room crowded. Don't buy a "junior" bed. Your child will grow out of it long before its useful life is over. Buy a full-sized single bed and if the absence of the accustomed cot sides worries him or her, use a removable safety rail for a while.

Make the bed itself as attractive as you can. Don't decide that it is not worth buying pretty bedding and smart pyjamas while the child still wets the bed: the pretty ones wash just as well as shabby old ones. If you are buying new bedding, take a serious look at Continental quilts. They suit a small child's instinct to snuggle, and they make bed making easy too. Make the bed properly whenever the child gets up, whether it is in the morning or after a nap. A child will not want to return to a muddle of bedding any more than you would.

A careful arrangement of possessions around the bed will complete a sort of "mini-home" to which – you hope – your child will look forward to returning each night and in which he or she will be happy to spend time awake each morning. Tastes vary, but these are some of the things which make their sleeping quarters attractive to many children:

A light, safely screwed to the wall and within the child's reach. It can have a 15 watt bulb for leaving on all night or a dimmer switch he can work for himself.

Pictures on the wall or on a pinboard, and mobiles over the bed and hung in the airflow from the window.

A bedside table or shelf stocked with his own books. Picture books meant for pre-school children are fine; strip-cartoon annuals meant for older children are also excellent because a non-reader can follow the picture-stories.

Special bed-toys which usually fall into two groups: soft toys for friendship and comfort, and puzzles and fitting toys which he may attend to better in bed than he does during the day.

A musical box or a cheap radio. The source of friendly noise will probably be switched on the moment the child is left for the night and the moment he wakes in the morning.

A means of communicating with you. This may just mean an open door or it may, in a large house, mean a baby alarm or intercom.

Using this special place

The point of all this trouble is to make your child a place which feels pleasant for relaxing, playing and going to sleep. You will ruin it all if you *ever* use it as any kind of punishment. Don't send your child to the bedroom or to bed because of naughtiness. Don't even suggest such a thing indirectly by saying "you must be overtired or you wouldn't be so silly. I think you'd better have an early night...."

Try instead to make nice things happen in his room. If a letter or postcard should come for him, put it on his bed for him to find. If you have bought him a new sweater, spread it there ready for him to try on. Keep magazine pictures for him to put on his wall or draw him a message sometimes and put it there for him to see at bedtime. If he asks to play with something of yours which he is not normally allowed – like your costume jewellery or a pack of cards – tell him he can borrow them to play with in bed.

If you are going to put all this thought into making bed a nice place to be, you obviously want to make the business of getting there enjoyable too. Make sure that the child has plenty of notice when bedtime is coming up. As with younger children (see p. 295) a definite evening routine usually works best, but, whatever your family pattern, don't expect the child to break off in the middle of a game or television programme and come instantly to bed.

Tell or read a bedtime story with the child actually in his bed. If you tell or read it downstairs, the story is just one more nice thing which has to be left at bedtime. Read upstairs it is something nice to look forward to in bed.

When you leave the child in bed give (and keep) a definite promise of your return. You might say something like "I'm going down to have my supper now. I'll pop up and see if you're asleep when I've finished." The child knows that if he does not go quickly to sleep you will be back before long. As a result he is likely to be fast asleep before the allotted time is over.

Once the child is in bed, getting out again should be banned or, better still, never considered. But if you want him to take it for granted that once he is in bed he stays there, you will have to be prepared to wait on him a bit. If you expect him to get out of bed to fetch his own drink of water you cannot be surprised if he also gets out to tell you something interesting. He must know that if he wants something and calls, one of you will always come. At around three and four, urination may cause difficulty. The child may worry in case he wets himself or he may use needing to go to the lavatory as an excuse for getting up. A pot beside the bed with permission to call for company if he needs to use it together with a plastic sheet on the bed and a relaxed attitude to "accidents" will usually avert problems.

Sleeping problems

However attractive you can make going to bed, there are some night-time problems which are very common during this age period. You will all be exceptionally fortunate if your child never experiences any of them.

Nasty thoughts These are a kind of half-asleep nightmare which many children experience when they are drowsing off. The child himself will not be sure whether he was awake or asleep. After quite a long period of silence from his room (so that you probably thought he was fast asleep) the child either starts to cry or calls you and says that he cannot go to sleep.

It sometimes helps to ask the child what is bothering him. He may be able to tell you what monster is besetting him and make himself feel better by talking about it. But your reassurances need to be very simple and definite. If the trouble is "nasty men getting in . . ." remind him that nobody who does not belong in his family could possibly get in; the doors are locked and need a key to open them, the windows are too high even for a ladder to reach them. . . .

Preventing "nasty thoughts" Unlike nightmares (see p. 378), nasty thoughts often arise directly out of stories the child has heard, or seen on television. It is as if his mind replays the story to him and then, as his controls relax towards sleep, his powerful imagination takes over and embroiders it. Censoring his viewing and his bedtime stories, so that he goes to bed with his head full of pleasant everyday matters rather than mysteries and miseries, may help.

Overheard snippets of real life can cause "nasty thoughts" too. A half-understood telephone conversation about Aunt May's operation; a half-heard quarrel between you two or the sound of his mother in tears can all impinge on the child so that as sleep approaches he is flooded with anxiety. Once again it may help to talk and explain but it will not help to lie. If he did overhear a quarrel or tears, it is much better to admit it and tell him a suitable version of what it was about. He will accept that quarrels and upsets need not be frightening and do not mean that you don't love each other any more, if you remind him that he too sometimes has quarrels with his friends, or his brothers and sisters, and that grown ups, too, can cry.

Nightmares Nightmares definitely take place during sleep and you will seldom be able to relate them directly to real happenings or stories. They are a sign of anxiety but a normal one. Every child has things he is anxious about (see p. 391) and from time to time his fears will surface in this way. They often come in phases so that the child has a nightmare almost every night for weeks on end and then has none at all for months.

The only vital point in handling nightmares is to get to the child *quickly* when he cries out. The sound, sight or touch of you will reassure him immediately. But if he has the chance to scream himself fully awake, the sound of his own frightened crying in the night-quiet will frighten him all the more and the fact that he is alone will add a new dimension of terror. You, or someone he knows and trusts, must be there if he surfaces. If you cannot easily hear him when you are downstairs, use a baby alarm. If you go out leaving him with a baby-sitter, make sure you choose someone he knows and someone you can trust to go to him at the least sound of fear.

Night terrors Night terrors are much rarer than nightmares. Most children never have them. Very few have them more than once in a while.

Your first warning of a night terror is the same as of a nightmare – frightened crying or screaming. But when you reach the child you find him neither asleep nor awake, but in a strange state which is rather like the delirium which can accompany a high fever.

Typically, the child is sitting up, eyes open, "looking" at some non-existent "thing" in the corner of the room. He seems not only afraid, but terrified. If there is anger mixed in with the fear it will be real, hating anger. If there is grief, it will be desolation.

Although he looks awake, the child is not really conscious and he is difficult to "bring to himself". Instead of being instantly comforted by your arrival he will either ignore your attempts at comfort or actually involve you in his terrified fantasy. He may make you into one of the enemy with horrified screams of "go 'way, go 'way", or make you into a companion victim, crying "look, oh look. . . ." Sometimes he will actually scream piteously for you: "Mummy, Mummy, I want my Mummy" even as you hug and pat him and try to make him conscious of your presence.

Handling a night terror Such extreme fear is infectious and there is something eerie, too, about a child who seems wide awake but is not in touch with reality. You will probably feel a prickle of unease up your spine and have to fight a tendency to gaze with the child into the corner he has peopled with horrors.

Put all the lights on. This will steady your nerves and may alter the room enough to begin to dispel whatever images the child is seeing. Even if the light has no effect on him now, it will reassure him if he comes to full wakefulness before the incident is over.

Don't argue with the child. He is not awake so he is not open to reasonable statements about monsters being made-up or there being no huge wolves in the room. Just burble soothingly along "it's all right darling" lines. If he is conscious of your voice at all, it will only be the tone he hears.

Don't take any notice if the child says hurtful things. He is not conscious, so he is not responsible for anything he says. If he shouts about hating and killing you, ignore it. He doesn't mean *you*, he means whatever you stand for in his night terror.

Don't do anything in particular to awaken a child who stays in bed. The terror will probably recede, letting him drift straight back into normal sleep without ever knowing what has happened. You will probably need a cup of coffee but he will be quite unharmed.

If he gets physically involved in the terror so that he gets out of bed, runs away or begins to throw himself about or knock things over, see whether he will let you pick him up without increased panic. If he will, carry and rock him so that he wakes to warmth and comfort rather than to the shock of pain when he runs into a doorpost. If he fights you, don't capture him by force, but follow him, putting on lights as you go, and pick him up as soon as he will permit it. If all else fails, a warm wet washcloth wiped over his face will probably wake him by its cooling evaporation.

If you do have to wake the child from a night terror, especially if he has ended up in a different room, he will probably be very surprised. Don't let relief at having him "normal" again make you at all dramatic. Just tell him he had a bad dream and ask if he would like a drink or to go to the lavatory. He may now be so wide awake that you have to put him to bed all over again as if it were the beginning of his night. If he remembers his strange awakening next day, dismiss it matter-of-factly: "You had a nasty dream...."

Nobody knows exactly why some children have night terrors and others do not, or even exactly where a nightmare ends and a night terror begins. Children who do have them seem to be most susceptible when a high fever is already making them a bit "wandery"; when they are given a sedative medicine for any reason, or when they have had a severe physical and emotional shock such as being involved in a car smash. Night terrors need to be handled by parents or at least by calm and experienced adults. Don't leave your child with a teenage baby-sitter if previous experience and present circumstances give you any reason to suppose that he might have one tonight.

Sleep talking A great many children mutter in their sleep. Some speak clearly enough for you to hear words. The child may even laugh, or talk in a tone of voice that suggests teasing. It all sounds a bit eerie, but it does not matter unless the child is obviously having a nightmare or starting a night terror.

Night-talking children who are calm don't need waking and they don't need listening to either. It is better not to tell them funny stories next day of the peculiar things they said, as most children find the idea of talking when they were not conscious rather scary. A talking child may wake a brother or sister who shares the room. A very young one may be frightened. If so, you may have to find other sleeping arrangements because once children start to talk in their sleep, they usually go on doing it from time to time right through childhood.

Waking in the night for no obvious reason

Occasionally a child will wake, after several hours of sleep, for no reason that either you or he can see. He has not dreamed – as far as he knows – he is not afraid and does not need anything. He is simply wide awake and so amazed at finding himself the only conscious being in a silent house that he has to call you to make sure that the world has not emptied around him.

A reassuring visit and permission to look at a book until he is sleepy again will be all he needs, but if it happens often you may be able to explain to him that most people like to stay asleep all night and that it is a pity to wake them unless he really needs something. His room can be arranged like the early waker's room (see below) and he can be encouraged to look after himself.

But he may not be able to bear the solitude. He may have to see that there are other people left in his world. If so, being put to sleep with a brother or sister (even a tiny baby one) may work wonders. He is asked not to wake the brother or sister so he stays very quiet, but he can see his or her sleeping, breathing form and he knows he is not alone.

If you have no brother or sister available, there are other forms of "company" that may work. I have known various families successfully use each of the following:

A bowl of goldfish; a hibernating tortoise; a "noddy clock" with a friendly face that moves with each tick; a special lampshade (designed for a low wattage nightlight) with stars or pictures which flick on and off, and a photograph of the whole family.

If all this fails and the wakeful child simply has to announce that he is conscious, you may not have to get out of bed if his room is nearby and doors are open. Just calling to him may be enough.

Early waking

If your child is fond of his special place and his bed with all its things around it, early waking need not be a problem now. He cannot stay asleep just to please you – so it is no good being irritated with him for waking up – but he can play quietly without disturbing you. Soon after his third birthday he will probably be able to understand that he must not wake you, except for a special reason, until he hears your alarm clock or the radio or hears you moving about.

Of course he may wake you by mistake because you hear him talking to brothers or sisters, dolls or teddy bears. That is different. He cannot be expected to stay totally silent. You will just have to put your heads under the pillows and revel in your last half hour. If he insists on calling for you, it may be because he wakes wet, urgently needing the lavatory, hungry or thirsty.

If he calls because he is wet, it is not fair either to ignore or to scold him. It is a good sign that he is aware of being wet (see p. 383), and once he begins to move around in play he will get very cold in wet pyjamas and sheets. You will have to go to him but you need not go through the palaver of changing his bed until later. Hand him dry pyjamas to struggle into while you put an old drawsheet or towel over the wet patch on the sheets.

If hunger and/or thirst is the problem, try leaving a drink in his old "teacher-beaker" and a couple of rusks or biscuits by his bed. Helping himself to this morning mini-picnic is good entertainment as well as meeting the need.

Toilet training and after

Many children will be completely reliable about using the lavatory or a pot, both for urinating and for bowel movements, before they reach their third birthdays. Then you can help them to *generalize* their accomplishment so that they can manage the whole business of excretion under almost any circumstances.

Getting used to lavatories

Your child may have been using the lavatory for months, but many children infinitely prefer their pots and manage the early stages of training better if they are allowed to use them exclusively. Now it is time your child got used to lavatories so that he or she will be able to manage anywhere, without you having to carry a pot with you.

The first step in the switch-over is to give that familiar pot a new home right next to the lavatory so that the child gets used to going in there just as you do. When the child is calm about this change in routine, buy a child-size lavatory seat that clips over the big one and find a box or stool that is the right height for climbing on and off the lavatory alone and for planting the feet on while sitting there. Encourage your child to use this new set-up, but don't actually remove the pot until it is voluntarily abandoned.

Once he or she is happy to use the lavatory at home, you can cultivate interest in lavatories all over the place. Show the lavatories at friends' houses; take the child to the "Ladies" in shops or at the swimming pool. He or she should even make the acquaintance of less elegant toilet facilities in public places. It is most distressing for a child who would not dream of wetting to be faced with a dirty, smelly lavatory on a train or in a wayside garage. Eventually the lavatories at school may even upset him unless he has met the lack of privacy and hygiene before.

Most three and four year olds will prefer a parent to go with them to a strange lavatory, especially one in a public place. No one will object to a very little boy accompanying his mother to the "Ladies" but fathers and little girls are in a more difficult situation as rows of strange men using urinals can be a bit put-off and off-putting. Most of Europe already has Unisex public facilities. Let us hope it spreads.

Managing out of doors

However reliable the child is, his or her waiting time will still not be very long. Every child needs to learn how to urinate outdoors if family picnics or long drives are not to be ruined for everybody.

Boys don't usually find this difficult. They can copy Daddy and urinate against a tree or even beside the car in a layby if necessary. Girls are at an unfair disadvantage. One who went on a picnic with a boy cousin expressed it neatly: "Why won't Mummy get *me* one of those useful things to take on picnics?"

Very small girls may find it easier if they are "held out" with a parent supporting them in a squatting position. Four and five year olds may prefer to remove their pants altogether as they find it difficult to hold pulled-down pants out of the way. All ages will be thoroughly put off if they find themselves amid nettles!

Urinating positions Most little boys urinate sitting down during the toddler years but begin to copy fathers, older brothers and friends during these pre-school years. It is a good idea to help him achieve this position before he starts at a pre-school group. If you point out that urinating standing up means that he need not take down his pants, the ease and speed will probably appeal to him. Do keep him in elastic waisted trousers or shorts until peer-group fashion makes him yearn for zip flies. Elastic is both easier and safer for him (see Enc/Penis). Once he stands to urinate, start teaching him to lift the lavatory seat beforehand. Make sure the surrounding floor is easy to clean; his aim will often be inaccurate.

If a little girl sees a boy standing to urinate, she will probably try too. When that experiment proves messy and frustrating she may urinate sitting backwards astride the lavatory. Don't fuss. She will soon realize that her body works best if she sits normally. Accepting this is part of accepting that she is female and that female bodies are not the same as male ones.

The child's bowel rhythm Remember that many children do not need to move their bowels every day but will do so quite naturally every two or three days. Equally naturally some will regularly go twice or three times a day. The child's pattern is individual and, ideally, it is none of your business.

If the child seems to like to go after breakfast, this makes good physiological sense, as eating after the long fast of the night often sets up a reflex need to move the bowels. Later on it may make social sense, too. Many children do not like using school lavatories so are better off if they open their bowels at home. But if this is not your child's natural pattern, do not try to impose it. Children should go when they feel the need, just as they urinate when they need to.

Managing alone At home, the child will feel more secure and independent when he or she can manage completely alone in the lavatory. Most will still prefer a parent to wipe their bottoms after a bowel movement, but they should gradually learn to manage even this alone so that they are not caught out later on, at school.

Little girls must be taught to wipe from the front backwards, never the other way around. Wiping forwards brings traces of the faeces into contact with the vaginal area and the urethra and can lead to urinary infections.

Problems with staying dry Children vary widely in the age at which they can manage to stay dry all day. If your child still shows no signs of being "trained", he may simply be a late developer in this respect. Look back to the toddler section (see p. 307) and see whether he is following the ordinary *sequence* for learning control, even if he is doing so later, or more slowly, than most. If he is, you have nothing at all to worry about. All children, except the severely mentally or physically handicapped, learn to stay dry in the end. So will yours. If despair makes you doubt this, ask yourself whether you have ever seen a child start big school in nappies. . . .

There is some evidence that being late in acquiring bladder control runs in families. If you can check up on your own achievements, by asking your respective mothers to search their memories, the answers may comfort you. There is also evidence that boys tend to be later than girls in perfecting control – so if your worry is partly due to comparing a girl who was dry early with this sopping wet boy, stop. They are not comparable.

If your child constantly dribbles urine so that he is always damp rather than occasionally soaking, it is just possible that there is a physical reason why he is not yet "trained". His sphincter should function in such a way that it is either firmly closed or entirely open. If it is permanently in-between, he cannot learn to control it. Brief your doctor privately so that the child need not suffer the embarrassment of listening to you describe his damp pants, and then take the child to see him.

If the child seems totally oblivious to pots, lavatories or indeed to urine, make sure that he or she does in fact understand what you want:

Take the child out of nappies altogether in the daytime. Those accustomed wads of padding may be concealing the whole business from his or her attention.

Make it clear that you want the child to use the pot or lavatory. You may have been so anxious to avoid toilet training pressure that you have quite neglected to convey this message!

Make sure that the child sees family and friends using the lavatory. You do not want to rub his or her nose in the fact that everybody else stays dry, but imitation can be a great help.

Otherwise there is nothing you can do to hurry the process. Relax and help your child as if he were a two year old (see p. 308).

"Accidents" Many three and four year olds have frequent accidents. Even five and six year olds have enough to make a supply of spare pants standard equipment in infant schools.

Once a child is basically "trained", wet pants are much more embarrassing for him or her than they are for you. They are uncomfortable too. So be sorry for the child.

Some children, especially boys, have a small bladder capacity. They need to urinate very frequently until their bladders mature both in their capacity and in their ability to concentrate the urine. Some authorities believe that you can speed up this development by getting the child to tell you every time he needs to urinate and then to wait a few more minutes by the clock. Although this seems to work for some children it inevitably focuses a great deal of attention and anxiety on what should be an entirely natural and matter-of-fact part of life. It is probably better to let his bladder mature in its own time.

Like most adults, children urinate most frequently when they are nervous or excited so don't be surprised if your child chooses all the worst times for accidents, such as birthday parties or trips to the dentist. Many also ignore signals from their bladders if they are deeply involved in play. A tactful reminder may save a flood.

Very occasionally a child under emotional stress will hold urine for so long that the bladder becomes overfull and he or she is unable to empty it. This occasionally happens, for example, if an unready child is left with strangers and is determined not to use the lavatory without mother. The answer is water. The sound of a fast-running tap may release the flow. If it does not, put the child into a warm bath. It is easy to urinate there.

Urinating at night

Many children need nappies at night well past their third birthdays. If your child still urinates every couple of hours during the day and always wakes with a wet nappy in the morning, you can be quite sure he is not ready to stay dry. After all, the urination that takes place while he is asleep is not within his control. You cannot *teach* him either to hold all the urine until morning or to wake up to the signals from his full bladder. Only greater maturity will enable him to do either or both. Wet beds seem more of a "problem" than wet nappies, so don't hurry.

Timing the giving up of night nappies

Wait until he sometimes wakes up dry after a whole night's sleep, sometimes goes for three or four hours without urinating in the daytime, and occasionally wakes in the early morning because he needs to urinate. Even when you see some or all of these signs of growing up, don't insist on leaving nappies off if he prefers to wear them. If you make him anxious about night-time urination, you will make wet beds and eventual problems more likely.

When you and he together do decide to abandon nappies, do encase the mattress in a proper plastic protective cover. Small plastic sheets get horribly wrinkled and uncomfortable and they usually manage not to cover part of the flood area. Show the child the covered mattress and explain that because it is there it does not matter at all if he should wet in his sleep.

If you have just bought new pyjamas and/or bedding, casually emphasize their washability, and *don't* describe them as making a "lovely bed for a grown up, dry boy". If he gets the idea that wetting his bed will spoil these nice new things, he will be anxious before the event and heartbroken after it.

Helping your child to stay dry

Distinguish between trying to keep the child's *bed* dry and helping him to keep *himself* dry. "Lifting" a child to urinate late at night and early in the morning may help avoid wet sheets, but it does nothing for the child's control. If he wakes when you lift him, he will be aware that you, not he, are responsible for his night-time urination. If he does not wake, but urinates, almost asleep, while you hold him out, you are actually encouraging the very thing you are trying to avoid: peeing in his sleep. It is probably best to avoid lifting, at least until a five or six year old becomes worried about wet beds and asks for your help. At that point you can agree, but make sure you wake the child enough to register full bladder signals for himself.

Never restrict evening drinks. A child who goes to sleep thinking thirstily of water is far more likely to wet the bed.

If a child wakes because he needs to pee, this is an excellent sign that control is coming. Make sure he has a pot in his room and enough light in the room to keep the bogeys that live under the bed in their places. He may need company, though. Getting out of bed alone frightens many small children. If he is not allowed to call, he may not get out until too late. He is bound to have some wet and some dry beds. Don't comment on either.

Congratulation for dry beds and silence on wet ones is almost as bad as scolding him for wetting. If you tell him he is "good" when he is dry, he himself will feel that he is "naughty" – or at least "not good" – when he is wet. You can avoid praise and blame altogether by explaining honestly that people's bladders grow up along with the rest of them and that eventually his will be grown up enough to hold all the urine all night.

Coping with wet beds

Night-time accidents are usual until around five and common until around seven – especially in boys. Don't be in a hurry to decide that your child has a problem.

If you find that you worry about wet beds when your child is four or five, you have to decide whether you can afford to keep calm and keep the child calm, while he or she matures, or whether you ought to seek help from your doctor or clinic.

If the child is wet because of a continuous dribble of urine, there might be a physical problem. A medical check would be worthwhile. If, as well as being wet, there seems to be a lot of bottom scratching at night, the child might have picked up pinworms (see Enc/Worms). These are common in small children and have nothing to do with dirty living conditions, but they do cause a lot of itching. Coming half awake to scratch sometimes makes bedwetting more likely. Your doctor can prescribe a medicine for the whole family which will rid the household of the infestation.

Sometimes children will themselves become worried about bedwetting – usually following tactless comments by overnight guests or hostesses. They may find it difficult to accept your assurances about soon growing out of it, and put more faith in the identical message given with more authority by a doctor. If you brief your doctor privately, explaining that it is your child who is concerned, not you, he can concentrate on reassurance, and the promise of further help being available if it is needed later (see Enc/Bedwetting).

If bedwetting suddenly starts again when your child has been dry for months, it may be a reaction to stress in daily life. A new baby in the family may give the child an unconscious wish to be a baby again even though his or her conscious wish is to be grown up enough to stay dry. A separation from you, a stay in hospital, the loss of a beloved grandparent or any other major unheaval can shake a child's confidence and make him or her temporarily less able to cope. If there is any obvious stress, you may be able to relieve it by talking about it and babying the child a little. If you can see that the child is tense and anxious but you cannot quite see the cause, your doctor may be able to help you work out what the trouble is.

Soiling

Since bowel control usually comes more easily, quickly and finally than bladder control (see p. 306) bowel accidents are rare after the end of the toddler period. A sudden attack of diarrhoea can catch a child out; curiosity can lead to an episode of smearing, but a preference for passing movements in pants or on the floor in a child who has been using a pot or the lavatory can be a sign of disturbance. Soiling is deeply upsetting to most parents and most children. If it happens in your family seek help early (see Enc p. 490).

Everyday care

During the pre-school years children will and should become increasingly aware of their own individuality: it shows clearly in their sense of physical dignity. They resent their bodies being treated like objects belonging to you or like poodles to be brushed and be-ribboned.

Of course you still have overall responsibility for your child's general cleanliness, health and well-being. But the more you can help him or her to manage the details of daily routines alone, the less you will offend that sense of autonomy. Practically this will be good for both of you. Every task the child performs is one less for you. Every piece of self-care is preparation for school when you will not be there to do it. And habits set up now may last a lifetime.

Don't expect fast learning; the chores are boring and repetitive. But there will be gradual progress. Children who will wash their faces, with a parent standing over them, at three, will wash, if they are told to, at four, and may go and wash just because they are dirty by the time they are five. . . .

Making things easy at home

If your child is to try to do things independently, you need to make it physically possible. In a dark house most children will refuse to run their own errands; lit corridors make it possible. If a child is to cope in the lavatory the door handle must be in reach and the lock manageable or out of reach. Walk around considering your child's size and safety. Is the water hot enough to scald? Are the drawers too heavy to open? Can the child reach that toothbrush without touching razors or pills, reach a cup without breaking your best glasses? Children cannot do the impossible and will not do anything that is accompanied by frantic exhortations to "be careful" so arranging their independence is up to you. If there are no coat hooks they can reach, how can they hang their coats up?

Giving choices

Making decisions is part of growing up. Your child must learn to think, rather than simply doing (or not doing!) what you say, But in these early days you cannot leave choices entirely to the child, because he or she will often make decisions that are bad for health (like "deciding" only to clean teeth weekly) or intolerable to you (like "deciding" to play in the mud in "best clothes").

The trick is to organize life so that your child has complete freedom of decision between a carefully limited set of choices. He or she can clean teeth now or after a story; go to the lavatory now or later; wear any of the clothes you have left in the cupboard or choose between the two dishes you are offering for supper.

Making clothes easy to manage

Your child is developing a taste in clothes and he or she will loathe garments which are heavy or "smothery". Stretchy materials will still be most comfortable while adding extra light layers will avoid the heavy sweaters most children hate. Avoid heavy overcoats in favour of quilted anoraks which allow freedom of movement and freedom to get dirty. Buy in the colour the child prefers and always with comfort and independence in mind.

Go for buttons or toggles the child can manage alone rather than slot-in zips which are difficult. Until he or she pleads for zip flies, try for elastic waisted trousers, shorts and skirts. Keep tiresome extras like gloves and hats to a minimum and sew on essentials so they do not get lost. Buy slip-on or buckle shoes so that the child need neither face those knotted laces nor continually come to you for help.

Coping with the boring chores

Most pre-school children still hate having their hair washed or even thoroughly combed through, while fingernail and toenail cutting is boring and teeth are often brushed in a hurry. A weekly "spring cleaning", undertaken on a regular, agreed evening, chosen *not* to clash with a favourite TV programme, and conducted with pleasant ceremony, is often the easiest way for both of you. Set aside plenty of time; rushing will make the child bolshy. You must have time to let him or her try everything and the child must feel that there is lots of relaxed attention in return for cooperation.

Nailcare: At this stage children cannot cut their own nails; but you can give them some control over the process. Let your child use an emery board to smooth one hand while you cut the other. Toenails should be cut straight across, not in a curve. The child can clean them with an orange stick.

Teeth: To finish off, make a game of "how well have you cleaned your teeth this week?" Your child will enjoy using a disclosing agent which stains areas of remaining plaque bright pink. Getting that pink off is a real challenge and when it is done you will know that the teeth really are clean, for now.

Hairwashing: Hair has got to be washed but if washing it causes problems let the child decide the

easiest way. He or she may choose any of the tricks suggested for toddlers (see p. 313) but just being allowed to choose is what matters. Offering a choice of shampoos or the use of your personal comb may help too. At the foamy stage, let the child do the rubbing, design soap "hairstyles" and have a mirror to look in. Teach him or her to check adequate rinsing by "squeaking" hair between the fingers. A cream rinse afterwards will help with tangles, but if knots are a problem a short style might be better both for the hair and your tempers.

Clean all over and taught some useful things, let the spring cleaning end in little luxuries: a sprinkle of your talc; clean pyjamas; a story while the hair dries . . . not spoiling but a way of ensuring cooperation next week!

Teething

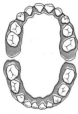

At around $2\frac{1}{2}$ years old your child will have a complete set of first (milk) teeth consisting of ten teeth in each jaw: two molars (double teeth) on each side, one canine (eye tooth) each side and four incisors across the front.

The second molars, the double teeth right at the back, are the last to be cut. Like the first molars cut at around a year (see p. 316) they can make a child's jaw ache while they are coming through.

Preventing cavities

The completion of the set of teeth makes tooth cleaning even more important than before. Each tooth now has another one butting up to it and food debris can easily become trapped in between. A small toothbrush, used with an up and down motion, will clear it. Even better is a battery-operated toothbrush which makes tooth cleaning more enjoyable and does a more thorough job. Make sure the back teeth are cleaned as well as the front ones! Make sure that his teeth are thoroughly cleaned after his last food in the evening so that he does not spend all night with food debris between his teeth. Make cleaning them after breakfast a regular habit too, and then try to see that he has a drink of water, which will at least rinse his mouth, after meals. Remember that sweet foods which stay in his mouth for a long time are the worst for his teeth, so try to keep sticky sweets like toffee and long-lasting ones like lollipops away from him and, when he does have sweets, encourage him to eat what he wants and get the whole thing over rather than nibbling over a long period.

Fluoride can do a great deal to strengthen the enamel of your child's teeth and help it to resist the acid which causes decay. Unless you live in an area whose water supply is high in fluoride, he should have a correct dose by mouth every day. Once he has his full set of first teeth your dentist may also suggest treating them with "topical fluoride" which can be applied in various ways. Don't rely only on a "fluoride toothpaste" to provide for your child's needs. While the fluoride in these products may be marginally better than nothing, it is by no means enough.

Going to the dentist

Having made a familiarization visit to the dentist during his second year (see p. 317) your child should start regular check-ups at least every six months by the time he is two and a half.

First teeth are vitally important. The second set do not even start to come through until he is around six, so these first ones have to last for years. Furthermore they keep the proper spaces open for the later teeth, and help his jaws to grow to their intended shape. So don't take a happy-go-lucky approach to early dentistry. Above all, don't wait to make an appointment until the child has toothache. Pain means that you have missed the stage where only superficial enamel was affected and a repair would have been easy and painless. The pulp is damaged and the cavity is much larger than it need have been. Try to find a dentist who enjoys working with very young children. Some find them time-wasting and tiresome but others pride themselves on this skill. If your pre-school child can build an interested and interesting relationship with his dentist before he first requires treatment, he is far more likely to accept later fillings trustingly.

First fillings   However much your child likes his dentist he is not going to enjoy his first filling. Don't make a drama out of it but don't pretend that it is nothing either. A superficial cavity in the enamel probably will not hurt even when it is drilled, but a cavity as deep as the pulp may. Even if there is no pain, the noise and vibration of the drill are hard for a child to bear, especially if it is a top tooth which is affected.

Explain what the drill is for and, with your dentist's cooperation, show the child his cavity in the mirror. It feels huge while it is being drilled; seeing how tiny it really is can be comforting.

Help him to feel that he has some control over the situation by arranging with the dentist to stop drilling at once if the child signals (perhaps by raising his hand) that he needs a rest. This is really important. If he feels helpless and tortured he may panic, now, or the next time he sits in that chair.

With tactful handling most pre-school children will tolerate any dental treatment that is needed, but a few will find it impossible to cooperate. Discuss any problems privately with the dentist. He cannot work on your child by force so the two of you have to decide whether to leave the cavity for a few months, hoping that the child's nerve will improve, or whether the treatment is urgent and should therefore be carried out with the help of a mild sedative or even a very light general anaesthetic. If an anaesthetic is to be used, make sure that a qualified anaesthetist will administer it. If your dentist insists on giving it himself, find another dentist.

Accidents and   Teeth are not rooted directly into the child's jawbone but into a
teeth   strong pad of highly elastic tissue which acts as a shock absorber. It takes quite a hard bang to knock a tooth out.

Occasionally a direct blow will drive a milk tooth back into the gum from which it emerged. You will probably be able to see or feel its top, just as you could when he was first cutting it. In most cases the tooth will emerge again of its own accord. If the nerve has been damaged, the tooth may "die" and this will mean that it turns a dull yellowish colour. Show it to your dentist, but don't be too worried about it. Even a "dead" tooth can usually safely be left to do its job until the second teeth begin to come through.

A tooth which gets broken or chipped is more serious. The sharp edge may cut the child's tongue as he eats or even cut through his lip next time he falls. Take him to the dentist. He will file the sharp edge down or he may decide to "cap" it.

If a tooth is knocked out, or if it is left still attached but out of place, take child and tooth and go straight to your dentist or to the nearest dental hospital. Baby teeth can sometimes be put back into position, so that they re-attach themselves, if you get dental help quickly enough. If the tooth cannot be replaced, your dentist must decide whether to leave your child with a gap until his second teeth arrive to fill it, or whether to make a single false tooth for him.

Crying and comforting

Becoming a pre-school child implies that some of the acute emotional stresses which are typical of toddlers have been left behind. But the child has not changed his personality. If he was tense before, he will still be tense. If he was bolshy before, he will not have become entirely sweet and biddable. But whatever he is like, his ability to cope with the stresses of everyday life and with the feelings they call up in him will have improved.

You will probably see the improvement most clearly in his reactions to separation from you. A few months ago he was bedevilled by separation anxiety. Now, although his passionate dependence on you is as strong as ever, he is able to hold himself calm through minor separations.

Words help him to cope. When you leave the room saying "I'm just going down to the clothes line" he can understand you and see the clothes line and you going to it in his mind.

The beginnings of a sense of time help too. If you say you will be home by lunch time, he cannot count the hours that must pass but he knows that they will.

Experience of other adults makes the world seem more secure. He has discovered by now that there are other nice people in the world. A grandmother can mend a hurt knee, a babysitter can bring a drink of water, and an older child can hold hands on the way to the swings.

His own growing competence is reassuring too. He knows that he can manage a good many things for himself. He is no longer dependent on you for anything he might need at any moment of the day. He is beginning to value playmates of his own age and when he plays with them he accepts that you are only a background figure.

But perhaps it is time and experience which give him most help in coping. He has lived as your child for long enough now to begin to trust you. Over and over again you have left him (for a minute, an hour or a day); over and over again you have come safely back to him. As long as he feels absolute security in your dependable presence and affection, he can afford to take some of his concentrated attention off you and focus it instead on the outside world.

If you can make your child feel that it is safe to venture a little away from you now, to make tiny flights out from under your protection, you will be laying the best possible foundations for the time when he has to venture out into school. But take care. His ability to cope without you is only in the bud and it is rooted in security. If you make him feel that you expect more independence than he can comfortably manage, or if something happens in his life to make him feel less secure, the coping will shrivel and he will revert to anxious clinging. As usual you have to strike a sensitive balance. You have to allow him all the independence he wants without forcing too much on him, and foresee the things which are likely to worry him without being so over-protective that you deprive him of the opportunity to try to manage them.

Typical fears and worries

Although every individual child has special fears and worries of his or her own, there are some anxieties which are very general among children of both sexes at this particular age and stage.

Worry about disasters

The child is riding on a crest of imagination in everything he does. This makes him liable to all kinds of "supposing..." fears. Where a toddler does not worry about getting lost until he sees a likelihood of being so, the pre-school child looks at his small self in the big park and wonders *what it would be like* to be lost. In the same way he may worry about all kinds of improbable possibilities like the house catching fire, both his parents dying or the dog going berserk.

Worry about injury

Awareness of self, as a whole separate person inside a body which belongs to him or her, tends to make the child temporarily very anxious about getting hurt. Sex comes into this exaggerated fear of even minor injury. The child is aware now of which sex he or she belongs to. A little boy usually feels that his penis is both a precious and a vulnerable part of him; despite explanations, he finds it hard to believe that girls are meant to be without these organs, so the removal of his own seems to him to be a real possibility. A little girl is usually also puzzled by her own lack of a penis; despite explanations she may believe that her body has already been damaged by having its penis removed. So for both sexes, injury seems to start up terrible images of being broken, damaged for ever or having lost a part of their precious selves.

The focus of terror is often blood. Pre-school children get through more boxes of sticking plaster than any other age-group because they cannot get on with their lives until that dreaded blood is safely hidden. But pain is a focus too. A routine injection, which would have evoked nothing but a brief cry a year ago, may be dreaded, hated and remembered with horror. It may take all your tactful skill to get a splinter out of that finger.

Worry about breakages

This fear of injury to themselves spreads, in many children, to a shivery horror of injury to anything else. Your child may be disproportionately upset if he breaks anything. If he comes across a headless doll, he may react as you would react to a dead rat. A few children cannot even enjoy jigsaw puzzles because they so dislike the incomplete and "broken" pictures.

Worry about adult words

Although the child's language helps him to tell of his fears, his understanding of language also causes some. He overhears fragments of adult conversation and understands the words without their context and without allowing for the dramatizations and shorthand which adults allow themselves when they are gossiping. If he hears you reply to a conventional "How are you?" with "Not long for this world I'm afraid...", he may not take it as the wry joke which you intended. He may panic. The same applies to half-heard and partially understood fragments of radio or television programmes. Pathetic child-victims of war or famine confirm his anxious feelings that the world is a dangerous place.

Stories of the monster-horror type may be too much for him too. He has only the vaguest grasp of the difference between fantasy and reality. Green-eyed monsters are as menacing to him as robbers or terrorists. You may need to censor his viewing and his stories and be alert to the possibility of his overhearing conversation which was not meant for him. A casual explanation given at the time can de-fuse an anxiety-bomb.

Dealing with your child's fears

You can help him best by letting him lead the way towards independence whenever you can. You can help him too by keeping a firm and even control over him and his life, making it clear that you do not expect him to take the responsibility for his own safety; that is still your job. If he asks permission to do something – such as go to the playground alone with a friend – and you can see that he is not happy about it, say "no" quite firmly. He will be enormously relieved to find that you don't feel he *ought* to be ready for the new experience.

When he is afraid, give him reassurance in full measure. Do not ever tease him or let anyone else mock his fears. If you do, he may learn to hide them, or to mask them under a layer of cockiness, but they will still bother him inside.

Your pre-school child's fearfulness will cure itself when he has had enough experience of being able to cope with whatever happens to him. Gradually he will discover that grazed skin always heals, that falling off a tricycle does not break him into pieces, that mother never loses him, forgets him or goes off without telling him, that baddies do not break into the house at night and that he stays quite safe and in control of whatever is asked of him. But the less he is frightened in the meanwhile, the faster he will reach that happy state of confidence in himself.

Common stressful experiences

Pre-school education

With your child's third birthday in sight, you have to decide whether or not to send him to a pre-school group. Nobody can tell you categorically that such a group will or will not be good for your child. Experts argue about their value. The fact that they argue makes it clear that there is no general answer! Happy experience in a good group probably is valuable: perhaps even better than staying at home full-time in an "average" family. Unhappy group experience is not good but, if your circumstances are especially difficult, you may have to help your child weather it. Only you can judge. If freedom from part of his daily care is a prime consideration, a group which he will *tolerate* may be acceptable to you. If positively valuable experience for him is your aim, then only a group which gives him *more than home* will do.

If you decide not to use a pre-school group or if you cannot find one, don't feel that you are necessarily depriving him of anything vital. A good group gives him playmates, new helpful adults, a wide range of interesting occupations and the valuable experiences of getting on with a group and of managing without you. You can give him all these things from home if you are prepared to put some time and effort into doing so. If you decide that you do want your child to have pre-school group experience, for his own sake, the first step is to decide whether or not he is ready. Most groups accept children from the age of three but many children who start then become bored with the group's small world before it is time for "big school". So if you are not sure that he is ready for the inevitable stresses of starting group life, delay.

Judging your child's readiness for pre-school

One of the most important signs of readiness is your child's willingness to be away from you and/or from his home for short periods. If he still clearly prefers to spend every waking moment within your sight, managing without you will be a tremendous effort for him.

Being willing to be away from you will probably mean that he is able to talk easily with other familiar adults, no longer needing you as constant interpreter (see p. 363). A child who has reached this point will obviously find it easier to make friends with a teacher than a child who is still desperately shy.

Interest in other children whom he sees playing in the park or playground is also a sign of readiness for group life. Even if he has not yet had much opportunity to join in their play, his interest means that he is ready to try out relationships with people his own age rather than devoting his whole attention to adults.

Apart from these psychological points, you also need to consider more practical aspects of his readiness. He needs to be more or less clean and dry, for example. Although a few puddles will be calmly accepted in any good pre-school group, the child will feel uncomfortable if he cannot use the pots or lavatories provided just as the other children do.

Deciding what type of group

Playgroups or community groups try to provide enriching experience for children and their parents. They will expect co-operation and may insist on participation from you. They will have no sympathy with attempts to use them as a baby-sitting service. On the other hand they will involve themselves sympathetically in your child's social and emotional development and in any family problems which may affect him.

Nursery schools or kindergartens tend to see themselves as more directly "educational" and therefore as doing something, with and for your child, which is separate from the job you do with him at home. They will probably expect less from you but they will also give less. They may be more interested in his intellectual development and behaviour than in his feelings.

Day nurseries or centres exist to provide all-day care for children who cannot get it at home, either because both parents are working or because only one is available. They tend, therefore, to see themselves as fulfilling your role for you rather than providing something extra for your or the child's benefit. Children who are in a group all day need a lot of physical care. The staff may not be able to give as much time and thought as the other types of group to their charges' play or learning. Although the staff will do their best to make the group a happy one, your child's happiness may not be of as much concern to them as his physical well-being. It will be assumed that he is there because he has got to be there rather than because you expect him to derive positive enjoyment or benefit from membership.

From these notes comparing the main characteristics of these types of group, you may get some idea of the kind which will suit you. But do remember that any group depends on the staff. You can only select the right one for your child by going to see it.

Playgroup/neighbourhood group	Nursery school/kindergarten	Day nursery/day centre
Run by and for the local community. Trained person in charge assisted by rota of mother-volunteers.	*May be owned and run for profit by private individual, or run by Education Authority in conjunction with a school. Professional staff.*	*May be run by private individuals, groups or local authorities. These exist more for the benefit of parents than of children. Their principal role is looking after the child, often all day, while both parents work. Professional staff.*
Inexpensive, non profit-making; charges often adjusted to parents' income.	*Private ones are often very expensive.*	*Expense varies; local authorities adjust fees to income.*
Usually a waiting list. Priority often given to children in difficult circumstances, via local Health/community worker.	*Some have waiting lists. Priority usually only given to brothers and sisters.*	*Almost all have waiting lists. In Britain priority goes to children with mothers in essential services (teaching, nursing etc.) and those who must work (single-parent families etc.).*
Hours usually short: as little as 2 hours twice a week to as much as 3 hours each weekday.	*Hours vary widely but sessions are always daily. Some offer midday lunch and a full "school day" at four years.*	*Most offer a full day designed to cover the whole period from mother leaving for work in the morning to her return at night. Children can attend shorter hours if preferred.*
Emphasis on parent participation and on child's full development, rather than on "teaching". Lots of individual attention; help with mixing with other children etc.	*Generally rather more emphasis on actual teaching, with number work etc. More emphasis on child learning to conform to group rules etc.*	*Emphasis has to be on caretaking rather than on the child's development or her education.*
May be open all year or school terms only.	*School terms only.*	*All year.*

Assessing a group Make an appointment to visit the group, without your child but during its open hours. Meet the person in charge, by all means, but if the group is split into various sub-groups or "classes" make sure you also meet the person who will be directly responsible for talking to, comforting and disciplining your child. Do you like her? Does she seem really to like small children, speaking sympathetically of them and not being too ready to joke with you at their expense or to dismiss them as "all the same at that age"?

Ask to be allowed to watch the group in action. Do the children seem happy and busy? Do they talk freely to each other, to themselves and to the adults? Does there seem to be some choice of activities so that a child who does not want to join in a song can play, rather than sit in a corner as if in disgrace? Is there adequate tactful supervision during "free play", or are these periods a chaos of fights, tumbles and tears?

Consider the accommodation. A dreary building is not a sensible reason to turn down a group that is otherwise good: it is people who make or mar a pre-school group, not buildings. But if you have any choice, you will obviously prefer a group whose facilities offer things which you feel your child particularly needs. Outdoor play-space may not matter to a child with a garden at home but it can be a big plus to a child from a high-rise apartment. A large multi-group school might overawe a shy child but be an advantage to a confident one who needs a wide range of children to make friends with and the possibility of "promotion" with age.

Getting ready to start pre-school Rising threes cannot usually be directly prepared for this big new experience. It is totally new so there is nothing similar in their previous lives with which you can compare it in talk or with which the child can compare it in his mind. Unless he is unusually advanced in both speaking and understanding you may even put him off the whole idea if you make too much of it. Take him to visit the group; make sure he registers "his" teacher or helper by some permanent (you hope) feature, like her long dark hair, and then be content with occasional references to the group: "Look at that rocking horse. It's just like the one they have at playgroup. . . ."

But if his first days are going to go smoothly, you may need to think ahead about how *you* are going to manage:

If you are pregnant, arrange for him to start well before the birth, or resign yourself to keeping him at home until several months after it. If you launch him into group life just when the new baby comes into his life, he is bound to feel banished and rejected. If you try and lauch him immediately afterwards, you will not have the time or energy to support him properly through his first weeks. If you confide your pregnancy to the group leader, she may even agree to take your child before his third birthday so that he can be well-settled before the baby arrives.

Get the taking and fetching organized. If the group is only a short walk away, you may be able to manage alone, but if it is far, the double journey at 9.30 and again at midday will drive you mad. If you do it by car, there will be days when it is being serviced. . . . You need a rota, a friend who will share, or at least somebody who will take and fetch for you in emergencies. Making this kind of arrangement may be an excellent excuse to strike up acquaintance with other parents whose children are starting at the group. They will all benefit by getting to know each other on their home ground.

Think carefully about how you will use your new free time. Unless the two of you can stand in for each other or you have tame relations near by, a demanding part-time job is risky. The child will be exposed to a barrage of germs. He will probably have more colds, sore throats and middle ear infections during his first couple of terms in the group than at any other time in his childhood. Since you cannot send him when he is unwell you will need a great many days off. Work which you can bring home if necessary, a study course which you can catch up on at night when you must, or a part-time job which you can persuade a forward-looking employer to let you share with another similarly placed mother, will probably be safer.

First days at a pre-school group

Most three year olds reckon to be able to cope with almost anything as long as Mum is there, so if your child is starting in a group that encourages you to stay with him until he is ready to be left, you should not have much difficulty.

Mention casually, about a week ahead, that his first day is coming up. Remind him the day before, and answer any questions. Make it clear that you will be with him. If, for example, he asks what the other children will be like, you can say something like "I'm sure they will be very nice, but anyway we shall see tomorrow shan't we?"

Be honest with the child about your movements. If you mean to stay all morning, every morning, until he is happy to be left, tell him so and mean it. Don't suddenly decide to slip away after all in the middle of the session because he seems so happy. Later on, if you mean to stay for half an hour, tell him that too and say "goodbye" when you are leaving. He cannot concentrate on group activities if he is continually looking over his shoulder to see if you have vanished.

Try, over the first few sessions, to become more and more invisible. If you play with the child, get things out for him and take him to the lavatory, you make yourself into a barrier between him and the other adults as well as between him and the other children. He may need you to stand between him and them on the very first day, but after that you have to help him behave as if you were not there, ready for the day when you will not be. If he keeps coming to you to show you things, try saying "It's lovely, why don't you show it to Miss Jones?" If he tells you he needs to go to the lavatory, say "I'm sure Miss Jones will take you, just as she does the others". Above all, don't interfere between your child and the others. The teachers will protect him if he needs protecting, or control him if they think he is being too rough.

When you and the teacher decide that the time has come for you to leave him for the first time, do tell him. Remind him, by name, of all the people he knows there now and of all the things he likes doing. Point out that only new children have their mothers with them and that he is not new any more.

Give him something from home to take with him. If the group prefers children not to bring toys from home in case they get lost or appropriated, he can have the handkerchief out of your handbag, to keep in his pocket, or even just an apple out of the home fruit bowl to eat at snack time.

Take the child to the group yourself, leave him with his teacher and say that you will be there, on that same spot, to take him back again at going home time. The idea is to make him feel quite sure that there will be no gap at all between his being in your care and in the teacher's.

Go back early on the first two or three days. He does not, of course, know the actual time, but you should aim to arrive there before the last activity of the session ends and therefore before he even has time to start looking for you.

Do not be late in collecting him, at least during his first few weeks. Children left waiting with a teacher after every other child has gone feel abandoned. The teacher's justified irritation (which the child will sense, however kindly she conceals it) will not help. Your child may then decide that it is not safe to let you leave in the first place.

Don't tell him about interesting things that happened while he was away. If you tell him about beloved visitors who came and have now left or fascinating dramas involving plumbers or stray dogs, you will make him feel that he is missing too much by going to his group. Make your routine sound as ordinary as possible. You can even be clever and mention casually that you have finished up all your most boring jobs so that you now have time to bake a cake or play a game.

Once he is settled, don't take parting tears too seriously. Many children who are genuinely enjoying and benefiting from group life find the parting moment hard. A good teacher will tell you honestly whether your child cheers up and joins in as soon as you have left. If you are not sure you believe her, arrange a bit of spying over the garden wall or through the door crack. If he is drearily watching the door and sucking his thumb, spy again next day in case you picked a bad moment. If it is the same sad sight, talk to the teacher again, making it clear that you do not want the child to come to group unless he enjoys it. If the worst comes to the worst, you may have to take him away and see whether, after a few weeks, having discovered that home is still just the same, he asks to go back.

But probably, if you spy, you will see your child happily doing whatever the others are doing. If it is only "goodbye" which is causing trouble, don't let the child think you take his tears too seriously or he may deduce that letting you go really is dangerous. Instead, try to find another mother and child to travel with so that the two children can rush in together. If that is impossible, experiment to see whether he finds it easier to part from his father, having left you where (in his view!) you belong: at home. Either way, confide in the teacher. She may find a regular job – like paint-mixing – for your child to do the moment he arrives. His busy importance will probably solve the whole problem.

A new baby Parents who love their first child and look forward to the second often find the idea of the older child being resentful and jealous almost unbearable. They are pleased; they want their child to be pleased too. Natural though this is, pretending to yourselves that your present child looks forward to and will love the coming one will not make him or her more likely to do so. Things will go more smoothly if you can honestly accept the fact that you are asking your child to put up with being supplanted and that, however you dress the facts up, he or she is going to mind. Just for fun, imagine your husband coming home to tell you that he was proposing to take on a second wife as well as you and imagine him using the various phrases that are frequently used to break the news of a coming baby to a child:

Parent to child	Husband to wife
"We're going to have a new baby, darling, because we thought it would be so nice for you to have a little brother or sister to play with."	*"I'm going to take a second wife, darling, because I thought it would be so nice for you to have some company and help with the work."*
"We like you so much we just can't wait to have another gorgeous boy or girl."	*"I like you so much I just can't wait to have another gorgeous wife."*
"It'll be our baby; it'll belong to all three of us and we'll all look after it together."	*"It'll be our wife. It'll belong to both of us and we'll both look after her together."*
"I shall really need my big boy/girl now, to help me look after the tiny new baby."	*"I shall really need my reliable old wife now to help me look after this young new one."*
"Of course I shan't love you any less, we'll all love each other."	*"Of course I shan't love you any less, we'll all love each other."*

You wouldn't feel exactly mollified, would you? When we love people we want to be enough for them. The fact that they want another person makes us feel jealous and pushed out. So assume that your child is going to feel jealous and don't try to induce pleasurable anticipation of an event which he or she can barely understand and would not look forward to anyway. Concentrate instead on increasing the child's ability to cope with the stress of the new baby. That means getting the relationship between all of you as secure and happy as possible; getting the child's own life running as smoothly and independently as possible and doing what you can to induce a general interest in babies.

Don't tell the child about the coming baby at once. Use the early months of pregnancy for talking generally to him about families; point out his friends' brothers and sisters and find a very young one to talk about. The idea is to get your child to accept that most families do have more than one child in them, so that when his does too he feels that it is normal, rather than a particular punishment for which he has been singled out.

Tell the child yourself before someone else lets it out. Wait until around six months if you can, but tell him sooner if you cannot trust friends not to drop hints or comment on your shape in front of him. He himself will notice nothing until you are too huge to play crawling games on the floor any more.

Do everything you can to get the child's independent life going well. If you plan pre-school for him and he will be three by the time the baby arrives, consider starting him now. If he is not going to pre-school or is too young to start yet, work at establishing a network of friends he likes to play with and other houses he likes to go to. He is going to need things to think about other than you and that baby; places to escape to and ways of showing himself how different he is from the baby.

Foresee the weeks around the birth. You must get him used, now, to whatever new arrangements he will have to put up with then, under stress. If he is to spend a few days with Granny, arrange a couple of one night visits in advance and let them be treats. If his father is going to look after him, let him practise getting the bacon just the way the child likes it. Tiny details of routine will matter a great deal to him when he is upset.

If you have always taken the major share of his day-to-day care, try to integrate his father more and more. When there are two children, two parents become life-saving, but nothing is more hurtful than a pre-school child who says "but I want *Mummy*" when his father offers to do something for him.

Tell the child where the baby is and let him feel her move. Once he has accepted the fact that there is going to be a new baby, physical evidence of her existence will help him to face the reality and to get interested in the whole affair.

Try to make the baby real for him by discussing names and speculating about sex, but don't describe it as "a brother or sister for you to play with". It will not be that for months. Instead, talk ruefully about how helpless it will be and how it will cry and wet its nappies. Tell him that he was just the same when he was tiny; show him some photographs of himself as a baby and think up some funny stories about his infant misdeeds like the time he peed on Granny's dress, sicked up in the bus or bit the doctor. Aim to inculcate an attitude of tolerant and amused superiority in the child.

About a fortnight before the expected date, tell the child your arrangements. Don't make any promises you may not be able to keep. If, for example, you tell him that you will only be away for three days and it turns out to be a week, it will be a disaster for him. So play safe. At two and a half he will not be able to understand the time scale anyway so keep it to "I shall be in the hospital and Daddy/Granny will look after you until I come home again". At three and a half you can talk about it in terms of "less than half of a week".

When labour starts, say "goodbye" even if you have to wake the child up to do so. Let him face what he has to face rather than waking up one morning and discovering that you have gone.

Let the child visit if the hospital will allow it. Seeing you will help him if you have to be away for more than 24–48 hours. But think carefully if you have a drip set up or a lot of stitches so that you cannot move without wanting to screech. Your child wants to see his familiar you. If you cannot yet be that familiar person it will be better to wait until you can.

The early jealous days

When you come home, remember that it is you the child wants, not the baby. He is going to have to accept that baby's presence and the care you give her, but there is no need to rub his nose in it. Come into the house without the baby and concentrate on him, leaving the new person to somebody else for a bit. During the first few days there are a few practical things you can do to ease him into the situation:

Try not to breast-feed in front of the child for the first couple of days until he is used to having you safely home again. Whoever is helping you can be briefed to lure him away to some fascinating entertainment at feeding times. After a day or two, or when he refuses the lure, show him how a new baby feeds, reminding him that he fed like that too when he was tiny. He may ask to try some breast milk. You do not have to let him if you hate the idea, but try not to look shocked. You can always give him a taste on your finger so that he can see he is not missing nectar.

Do with the child as many as possible of the things you did before. When you cannot, do not make the baby the reason too often. When the baby clearly is the reason, come right out into the open and say what you know the child is feeling: "I'm sorry but I've got to feed the baby first, I know that it must seem unfair, but little babies can't wait for their food as older people can, so I must do it now. She will go to sleep after her feed and then you and I will be able to play together."

Accept any offers of help from the older child, but don't make too much of the "you're my big boy" line. He may not be feeling at all big. Indeed he is probably feeling that his bigness is his whole trouble; if he were tiny he would be getting all the attention like that beastly baby. To have to help in order to get your approval may be the last straw.

Offer the child chances to behave in a babyish way for a bit, and make it clear that far from having to be "grown up" to keep your approval, you love him devotedly even if he decides to be more babyish than the newcomer. You could offer him a turn in the baby bath and a sprinkle of the baby powder. You can cuddle him, pat his back and sing to him. It may sound absurd but from the child's point of view it is not. You want him to feel that while the baby gets a lot of things he does not normally get, she is not getting anything he *cannot* have, but only things which he has *grown out of*. You want him to think "I can have a bottle too if I like, but I'm old enough to have orange juice in a glass and it tastes much nicer than that baby milk".

Make sure that there are some practical advantages to suddenly being "the oldest" to balance the inevitable disadvantages. This may be the moment for a few new privileges. Pocket money, perhaps, or a later bedtime or a regular Saturday expedition with Dad and without the baby.

Their father can make all the difference to the elder child's reactions to the new baby if he is prepared to take a full part in the care and companioning of both of them. There are two children and two parents. He can make the pull between their differing needs much less obvious and painful by being prepared to cope with the baby while you do something with the older child and to do exciting things with the older one while you are busy with the baby. Some fathers find that they cement their whole relationship with the first child during this period; he is under stress, needs father and turns to him because at this moment he feels let down by his mother's involvement with the newcomer.

Don't make the older child feel guilty about jealous feelings. Don't ask him to love the baby. He cannot. If you ask him to, he will feel guilty and think that you would hate him if you knew what he really felt. Accept, even suggest, that the baby is a considerable nuisance to him while assuring him that one day the two of them will be friends and companions.

Don't let the child hurt the baby. He will feel guilty however nice you are to him about it or however much you pretend to think it was an accident. So don't let it happen. Watch very carefully when he makes approaches to the baby and use a cat net, which he will think is against cats, to prevent those by-accident-on-purpose occasions when a ball gets thrown into the pram. Never leave the older child to "take care of the baby" outside a shop. It is not fair to put him in a position of responsibility.

Work to make the child feel that the baby likes him. We all find it easier to like people who seem to like us; your child will find it much more possible to love his new sister if the affectionate advances seem to come from her. Fortunately this is easy parent-upmanship. The baby will smile at the child if he puts his face close to hers and makes noises. Once she smiles you can play it up a little. "Mark is the one she *really* likes" you can say to admiring visitors. If the child says "I'll keep her quiet for you, Mummy, she'll stop crying for *me*", you will know you are over the worst.

With any luck, two or three months of tactful handling and lots of affectionate attention from you both will carry the child through to a point where he can be amusedly patronising about the baby. Try very hard to get him to this stage well before the baby gets mobile. While she lies in a cot she is only a nuisance to him in the emotional sense of taking up your time and attention, but once she can crawl into games and snatch toys she will be a practical nuisance too. If your child can say "Oh isn't she silly!" or "She's trying to copy me!", their relationship will survive. If he simply dislikes her, you will be in for a difficult couple of years.

Balancing both their needs
Even when first jealousy has blown itself out and your older child has forgotten what life was like when he was the only one, balancing their needs goes on needing thought. If one starts school while the other starts playgroup, both will need all your emotional support and you will have to share it out or overdraw on your resources. There will be problems in suiting treats, expeditions and holidays to their differing age/stages; problems in nursing one without neglecting the other, and problems in coping fairly with one who gets her own way by charm while the other fails to get it by bullying. Do remember that as long as they both depend on you emotionally there will be jealousy *on both sides.* The younger one's jealousy can be just as painful so don't overdo it in guarding the older child from the green-eyed monster.

Try not to assume, even as they grow older, that they love each other. Parents often take this love so much for granted that they insist that the children are "very close really" even when constant quarrelling and bitter complaints suggest otherwise. Both children have to tolerate each other and behave decently, but they do not have to love each other and, given the inevitable jealousies, they may not. Don't force them into each other's company. If you let them work it out, they may eventually surprise you with their mutual affection and loyalty.

Respect both children's dignity. If you can make it clear that you love them both as individuals and will never make them feel or look small to each other or to outsiders, you will not go far wrong. Do not compare them. There is no more point than there would be in comparing oranges and apples. They are simply nice-but-different. Never hold one up as an example to the other. The charming manners or neat habits that come easily to one may be almost impossibly difficult for the other to learn.

Getting on with other children

Although a two year old is usually interested in watching, and then in playing alongside, other children (see p. 354), he or she will not be ready for the beginnings of cooperative play until well into the third year. If he has always played where there are other children, he may slip into an active participation without you even noticing, but if he is not used to others there may be problems. He has to learn the vital lessons of taking turns, of sharing, of giving way. He has to discover that it is all worthwhile; that many games are more fun with a group and two can often succeed where one fails.

Gentle, cooperative, social behaviour is a tremendous effort for most small children and those who are making the effort successfully tend to be hard on a child who cannot yet manage. If a group has just discovered how to make a sand village without trampling each other's contributions, it will be quick to turn on the big-footed newcomer who does not know the rules. So don't expect other small children to "be nice" to yours. If there is trouble, don't waste energy on being hurt and angry with them for "picking on him". Look at his behaviour; see what it is that he does or does not do which makes him unacceptable to the group, and teach him how to manage better. He can learn acceptable group behaviour just as easily as he can learn table manners or new words.

Behaviours that make for trouble

Some pre-school children take out on other children all the stresses they are feeling at home.

If your three or four year old bites, hits, kicks, attacks younger children, pockets other people's toys and generally makes it impossible for anyone to like him for a playmate, look to his life at home. Is he hitting strangers because he longs to hit the new baby and dare not? Does he steal their toys because he feels he has unfairly few of his own or because he feels that their toys mean they are loved, while he is not sure that he is? Does he disrupt their games because he wants to get back at you for being too bossy over him?

Some children have been over-carefully handled at home so that they find the rough-and-tumble of group life amazing. If you have always arranged for your three year old to win at "Snap",

It takes time to learn
that someone else's feelings . . .

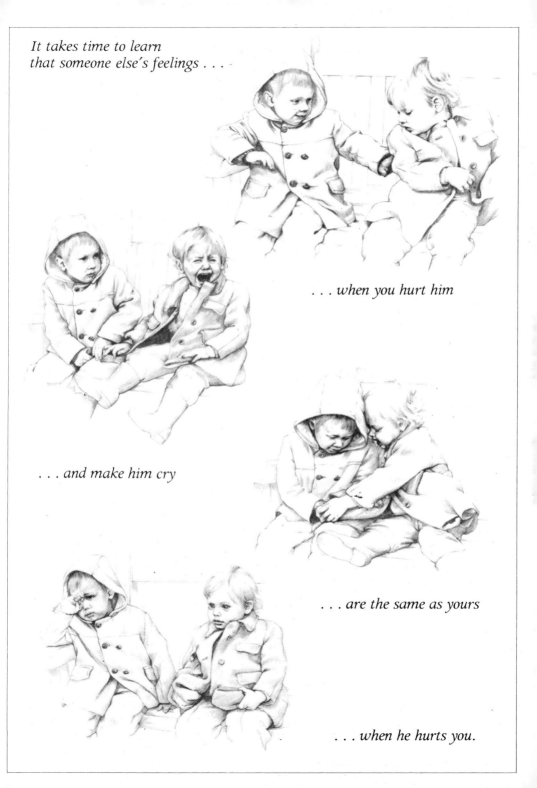

. . . when you hurt him

. . . and make him cry

. . . are the same as yours

. . . when he hurts you.

have the biggest strawberries and think himself stronger than you, he is not going to take kindly to playing with other children who expect justice and reality. "But I *want* to go first" he will say, amazed that anyone else should claim the privilege. "Fall *down*" he will command, pushing at a stalwart opponent.

Helping your child to learn to get on with others

As he comes out of toddlerhood, it is important to teach the child the basic principles of "do as you would be done by". If you can help him to understand that every child wants to win and only one can; that each would like to lead and only one can; that all would like the biggest cake and only one can have it; he will at least see *how* to play nicely, even if he cannot manage to play that way all the time. Help him to see that there is a real point to good social behaviour. It may seem obvious to you that it is wrong to kick other people. It is not obvious to your child at this age.

He will learn it best if you take every opportunity to show him that other people's feelings are generally the same as his. For example, if he complains that a particular little boy is a sissy and a tell-tale, always running to Mummy, suggest that the child may be a bit shy and not very used to other children yet. Remind him of a time when he felt a bit like that. If he pops someone's balloon and gets clobbered for it, kiss the bump but then point out that everyone likes to keep or pop their own balloons.

Don't expect pre-school children to play in company without supervision. Their social controls are not strong enough. Tempers are still precarious and new forethought can be lost in the heat of the moment. If one child lays another's head open with a tennis racket, both will suffer. It is your absolute duty to keep everyone reasonably safe from their own and other children's aggression.

But supervision needs to be subtle. Do not sit and watch them like a policeman watching a demonstration. Find something to do within their vicinity; busy yourself but be prepared to step in before things get out of hand. If everyone is armed with a plastic sword and the battle is hotting up, it is no use exhorting them to "be careful". Take the swords away and suggest something else.

If a group is playing on something – such as a climbing frame – which could be dangerous, you cannot rely on their good sense to take turns and not push. Go and **supervise** directly, saying "you can only use this if you do it properly; it's one at a time up the ladder, and one at a time down the slide, now, who's first?"

When things go wrong, concentrate on getting them going right again, rather than on finding out the rights and wrongs of the situation. It does not matter who began the fight. It matters only that the fight has spoiled play for everyone, so it must stop.

"One at a time" is a valuable lesson in taking turns as well as a safety precaution when groups are using large equipment.

An easy relationship with the children who live nearby is beginning to be important to your child now and will be increasingly important all through childhood. So think carefully before deciding that the local children are not suitable friends. If you really cannot accept your local community on your child's behalf, you may have to move house rather than commit him or her to a lonely and isolated childhood.

But the children you see around and with whom your three year old tries to play may be too old for him. He cannot mix well with a group of schoolchildren, for example. They may tolerate him from time to time as slave labour – fielder of the ball but never bowler – but they will hurtfully reject him most of the time. He needs younger friends. There may be other pre-school children living close by whom he does not know because they seldom appear without an adult escort. If so, a well-timed birthday party or a few invitations to coffee issued to child *and* mother when you meet at the shop or chat over the back fence, may help him.

If there really are no young children available, you may have to make the effort to take him where there are some. Your local town hall will know of any nearby clubs or playgrounds for the under-fives. Failing any facilities of that kind, absence of playmates is a good reason for considering some form of playgroup for him.

Once he is old enough to spend much of his time playing with other children, make it clear to him that he is welcome to bring them in. If he seems to prefer visiting their houses to using his own with them, ask yourself why. He may feel that you do not really like having lots of children in and out, that you resent the noise or the muddle. He may be afraid that you will embarrass him in front of them or that the discipline he is accustomed to will seem severe to them.

If he is to have a comfortable, secure feeling about his own community and his own street, all the way through his childhood, it is important to get these things right, now, while he is feeling his way into the outside world. Pride in you both and in his own home is going to be important to him. You do not have to be grand; it does not have to be luxurious. But he does have to feel that it is truly friendly and welcoming.

You cannot make friends for her but you can help her to make her own. . . .

Using his or her body

Pre-school children have won the battle to get onto their feet and to get their bodies under reasonable control. Now they are ready to use those bodies. They are their bodies; that arm does not only belong to the child, it is the child.

Because pre-school children feel at one with their bodies they do not separate physical activities, thinking activities and feeling activities as adults tend to do. Doing helps them think; thinking makes them do. Doing helps them to understand what they feel and to stand the strength of their feelings; so feeling also makes them do.

They are always on the go. But as they rush around they are learning. Physical activities are just as important to a child's development and intelligence as other kinds of play (see p. 422).

Testing self-limits
Since children feel that their bodies are "themselves", bodily strength and efficiency is very important to both sexes. A child whose body fails at a task feels that he or she personally has failed.

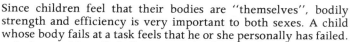

So he sets himself challenges, testing his own limits. He knows he can walk, but needs to see how far; he knows he can run, but needs to find out whether he can run faster than his friends. He knows he can climb, but he has to find out whether that particular tree will defeat him. While he measures himself against these continual challenges, he learns vital lessons about managing his physical self. He learns where the main strength of his body lies. He finds, for example, that a bed which he cannot move when he pushes from the wrist, shifts a little when he pushes from the shoulder. If he lies on the floor and pushes with his feet, his straight legs, powered by his hips, can move it freely.

He learns how to nurse his body along so as to get the most out of it. If he carries something heavy in one hand, the muscles tire; when he changes hands, the fresh muscles work better. When he changes back again, the first set of muscles are rested and ready for more. He discovers his most vulnerable spots too. He learns to guard his head with his arms when he falls and to let his knees take the brunt of life rather than falling flat on his belly. Painfully he discovers that his private parts need respectful clearance when he climbs over sharp chair arms or climbing frame bars!

Gradually he discovers more about what he can and cannot do with this body. It is solid enough to stop a rolling ball if his feet are together but if they are apart it will roll through. His hands can make a cup efficient enough to carry wet sand but inefficient when the sand is dry and hopeless for water. Gravity affects his body: he can run downhill and jump down steps but he learns that he cannot get far upwards. He experiments continually with balance or, as he probably sees it, "how not to fall down"! He can walk along a bench with both arms outstretched but if one hand comes inwards to put a lollipop in his mouth he will wobble. He can lean just so far over a fence to reach something but when he leans farther he is off-balance and cannot get back. By the time he is three he can stand on one foot but only while he concentrates; doing anything else at the same time is impossible.

The child's body and feelings

Pre-school children have to involve their bodies as well as their minds in order to understand the world and its experiences. Watching television, the four year old shoots the baddies, cheers the hero and gallops round the room with the horses. He neither can nor should sit quietly. If he may not engage his body as well as his mind, he will switch off.

His own emotions affect him in the same way. He must vent his anger in shouts and stamps, howl out his misery as he throws himself dramatically on the floor, or hop and squeak to let out just enough joy to stop himself exploding.

Unfortunately for small children, this kind of emotional display shocks and embarrasses many adults. We tend to take pride in controlling ourselves, in using words instead of actions and in concealing our feelings from others. So many parents try to impose a separation between body and feeling on children who are at the stage where the two are totally intermixed. Imposing physical restraint of this kind can totally spoil things for him. If he may not roar with laughter and drum his heels when the clown enters the circus ring, he will stop finding him funny. It can make feelings harder to bear, too. If a sudden disappointment leaves him crying bitterly and you say "Oh don't cry, lovey", you make him feel that it is his actual tears that distress you rather than his disappointed feelings.

If, instead of trying to squash his physical displays of feeling, you can accept and even encourage them, you will help him to recognize what it is that he feels and to learn to cope with it. Instead of telling that disappointed child not to cry, you could say, "It has made you sad, hasn't it? Come and sit with me for a bit until you don't feel cryey any more. Then when you feel better we'll do something else. . . ." You show the child that you accept his disappointed feelings; that tears are a perfectly acceptable response to them; that you will support him through the feelings/tears; and that when the tears end, the feelings will have become manageable. On happier occasions you can even play pretend-feelings with him. He is a natural actor and will throw himself eagerly into a game of "Be a very tired old woman; be a very angry man; be a child who's lost his puppy. . . ." He will deliberately tense and distort his face and body, striving for the feeling-image your words have conjured up. As he does so he is learning to understand the feelings through his body; making them familiar; making them safe.

Your body and your feelings

Pre-school children are so tuned in to bodies and to physical behaviours that they read the "body language" of adults with uncanny skill. Where a toddler needs to see your face to know whether you are happy or sad, a pre-school child will often read your headache in your drooping back.

He will hardly ever be wrong about *what* you are feeling but he will often be wrong about what you *want him to know* you are feeling. If you are trying to conceal a serious quarrel, a death or work problem from him, he will know that you are miserable. Your bright, forced smile will not fool him but it will confuse him. He knows you are sad, yet you pretend to be happy. You make him doubt the evidence of his own senses. He will be better reassured by a simplified version of the truth than by attempts at total concealment of it. "Mummy is sad because her Daddy is ill" is a far less worrying thought for a small child than: "There's something odd about Mummy and I don't understand her today. . . ."

The child who detects sadness in your body will use his own to try and comfort you. The best comfort he knows is the comfort he himself wants when he is miserable: a big hug. Tied up in your own problems you may feel quite unable to use a hug just now. If you reject his efforts too often, he may stop trying. Try and accept what he offers with a good grace. Giving your stubbed toe over to be "kissed better" is part of parenthood!

Safety Physical adventures mean a chance of physical accidents, but while it is your job to keep your child safe, it is also your job to keep your caretaking to a minimum. If you continually fuss at the child to "get down from there" or "hold my hand or you'll fall", you get between him and his body. You prevent him from finding out what he can and cannot do: by preventing him from learning, you may even cause the very kind of accident you are working so hard to avoid.

It is often helpful to remember that you could only certainly prevent all possibility of accidents by literally imprisoning your child – following him around and holding on to him all day. So try to accept the fact that a few bumps and grazes are all in the day's work for a pre-school child. Concern yourself with preventing *serious probabilities* but don't drive yourself mad thinking about the thousand and one *trivial possibilities*.

Trust a child who is playing alone. He will almost certainly stay within his own limits. He will not climb four rungs of the climbing frame until he can manage three. Let him set his own pace. Remember that muscles improve with use; balance improves with practice; and nerves steady with experience of success.

Watch out when other children tease. The taunt of "baby" will drive the most sensible child to heights of idiotic daring. He needs you to remind him of the line between bravery and folly.

Be careful of leaving your child in the charge of older children. He will long to emulate their exploits and they will find it easier to take him with them to the lake than to find him a safe occupation nearer home and keep coming back for him.

Be wary of machines. At a stage when he is discovering the workings of his own body you cannot expect him to have much idea of the workings of machines. They have quite different properties. Pedal cars will amaze him by being more difficult to stop from high than from low speed. He will not remember to keep his fingers out of tricycle spokes or his toes away from wheelbarrow wheels. Objects like lawnmowers and hedge clippers will be highly dangerous because he will not easily understand the relationship between switching a switch and distant blades whirling round.

Above all, watch out for traffic. However sensible he seems about "road drill" (see Enc/Safety), he is totally incapable of assessing the speed or intentions of a moving vehicle. However obedient he seems to your instructions to stay on the pavement, he will forget when anything distracts him.

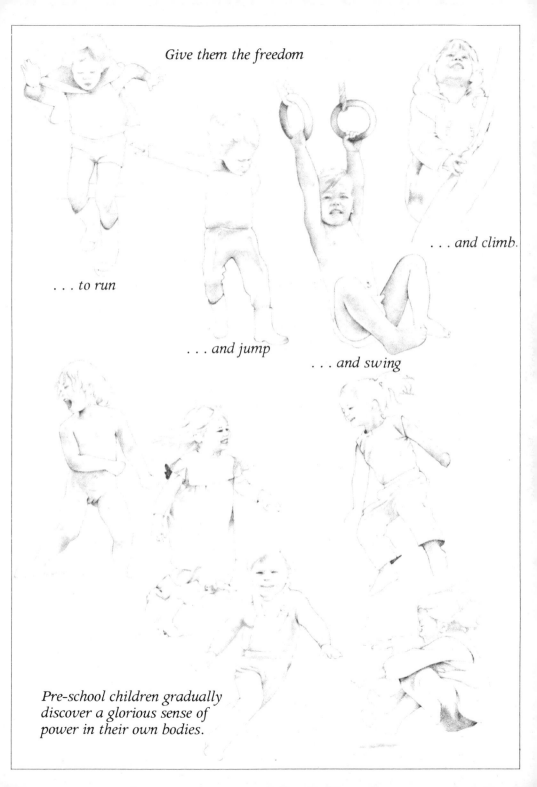

Give them the freedom

. . . and climb.

. . . to run

. . . and jump

. . . and swing

Pre-school children gradually discover a glorious sense of power in their own bodies.

Holidays and trips away from home

A lot of small children who can keep themselves reasonably safe at home come to grief when they are away. A new environment offers new hazards. The child has never met them before and therefore can neither anticipate nor even recognize them. You have to do both for him. At the seaside, for example, local children will have learned about tides and collapsing sand tunnels. Your child has not learned. He will see no significance in a dwindling beach, the increasing pull of a current around his legs or the tell-tale trickles of sand from a tunnel that is about to cave in.

When you take your child on holiday you will probably long to let him run free, but if his freedom is to be unsupervised you need to choose your place very carefully indeed. Even that innocent country cottage may have a bull in the next field, deadly nightshade in the hedge, a well in the garden or a delightful haystack with a pitchfork for him to jump on.

Put yourself in your child's shoes. Think of this new environment and all the things in it he has never met before. Try to foresee how they will strike him.

Make a tour of inspection when you arrive. Visualize your child running around and try to spot the traps lying in wait for him.

Be an undemanding but willing escort, ready to go with him over the rocks or down to the pool, into the ocean or over to the farm. With you as his watchdog he can have freedom.

Fatigue and illness

Your pre-school child, whose whole life involves maximum effort, is more liable to accidents when he or she is physically below par.

The more tired or unwell he becomes, the more liable he is to frustration. If he has been trying to ride a two-wheeler all afternoon and his performance gets worse as suppertime approaches, he will be furious. "I can, I can do it" he roars, setting off yet again. Left to try and fail and try again, he will get rasher as he gets crosser. If you mind him coming to grief, you have to find a tactful way to make him stop until he is rested again.

"Accident prone" children

Some children seem unusually accident prone all the time. The local casualty department may even come to know them by name, so often do they appear for a couple of stitches, a plaster cast or a night's observation.

A few of these children may be being distracted by worries or anxieties or made careless of their own safety and bad at managing their bodies by long-term unhappiness. If you suspect that your child's liability to accidents is due to unhappiness and tension, you may need to offer extra protection while you try to discover and sort out the trouble.

Some children are just less well-coordinated than many others, so that they come to grief during ordinary play. You can offer practical help. Show him safe ways to climb a ladder; teach him to wait until he has got his balance before trying to walk along a wall and to sit down when he feels himself wobbling; set him little obstacle courses on his bike to improve his steering.

If he seems really clumsy, he may benefit from actual lessons in bodily control. You may be able to enrol him in "music and movement", dancing, gymnastic or even judo classes.

A few children seem neither unhappy nor clumsy but unreasonably fearless. Nothing frightens them. They do not only climb too high into trees, they also jump out again and break their legs. Speed does not frighten them so they win all the bike races at the expense of bits of skin.

A child like this will learn his own lesson in time, but you want him to do it as cheaply as possible. Never congratulate him on his outrageous performances even when relief that he has come through safely makes you want to cheer. Instead of clapping his Tarzan leap, point out that his success was pure luck and that trying was stupid. If you can make him feel that his rashness is babyish and silly, he may take some notice.

Physical anger and aggression

Even the most tolerant parents rightly draw the line at being hit or kicked because the child is angry. He has the right to use his body to act out his feelings, but he does not have the right to use it to hurt anyone.

A lot of parents believe that a child who deliberately hurts should be hurt back. The idea is that if he is shown what a good smack feels like he will not do it any more. If he does still do it then he deserves painful punishment.

This is a completely illogical argument from the child's point of view. If he smacks you and you smack him back, he sees that you have done exactly the same thing as him. He cannot possibly take you seriously when you punctuate your slaps with "I will *not* have you *hitting* people!"

The force of your argument is much stronger if nobody in your house ever hits anyone. When he hits you, you take his hands and say "No, I know you're angry but we don't hit people. Hitting hurts and that's horrid. . . ."

You are bigger and stronger than the child. You don't have to hurt him to stop him attacking you. If you also suggest some other way that he can vent his pent-up fury, he will stop. Some families have a special pillow or cushion for angry pummelling. Some actually encourage other, harmless, signs of anger, saying "go on, shout, see how loud you can shout. . . ." The vital thing is to make it clear to the aggressive child that it is not the *anger* you disapprove of but only his particularly painful way of showing it.

Aggression against other children

The child who is accustomed to using physical violence to get his own way, or to having it used against him when other people want their way, is the one who is most likely to hurt other children on purpose. He may accompany cries of "that's mine" with a good wallop to reinforce the point, or he may gratuitously attack smaller children just because he feels angry inside. Although problems of this kind can arise however carefully you teach your child non-violence, they are much less likely if you teach him that there are no circumstances under which it is right to hurt anyone deliberately, and that accidents which hurt merit apologies all around. It goes without saying that this philosophy will only be effective if he sees it continually applied by and to all members of his family.

Once he starts at playgroup or mixes freely with other children you will meet the "hitting back" dilemma. Morally, it is obviously less reprehensible to hit *back* than to hit *first*. But even hitting back is not useful. A hits B so B hits A. Inevitably A will hit B again and the fight could go on forever because neither child can bear to accept the last blow and retire. I actually overheard one panting four year old plead "Oh do just let me hit you one more time so that I can stop..."!

Perhaps you can bring morals and practical considerations closest together if you suggest that while straight revenge is not a good reason for violence, hitting a bully in order to escape, or pushing a child so as to get out of his clutches is acceptable.

Physical punishments and caresses

Your child's body is his or her own. Nobody has the right to hurt it, hold it prisoner or force it in any way except fleetingly to prevent it damaging itself or somebody else. Being physically hurt or forced cuts at the centre of a child's new sense of self. Because this phase of development is so very physical he or she cannot say (as some prisoners of conscience have said), "Do what you like with my body, you cannot touch my mind." Whatever you do to your child's body, you are doing it to your child's mind too.

Of course even the most non-violent parent can get caught out by his or her temper and deliver a slap. While it will not do any good, it need not do any permanent harm either. The important thing is to make it clear to the child that you lost your temper and did something that you disapprove of. "I'm sorry, I lost my temper. I should not have hit you...."

From the child's point of view, being forced to make gestures of physical affection is almost as bad as receiving physical punishment. The child who is forced to kiss Aunt Mary, whom he dislikes, is being asked to betray himself through his body; to use it to express an emotion he does not truly feel.

Sometimes even parents, whom the child does love, demand too many kisses and hugs. The little boy who loves to sit on Mummy's knee wants to (and should) do it when his feelings tell him to. If she grabs him and snatches kisses as he passes on other business, he feels that she is using his body for her own pleasure rather than accepting love when it is offered to her. Don't demand physical affection or force it on your child. If you truly yearn for a cuddle, you can always ask for one to be freely given.

Physical sex differences

An only child takes the shape of his or her own body for granted. He or she tends to assume that all other children are made in the same way. Mummy and Daddy are usually also taken for granted; they are just themselves and the child sees no similarity between their big hairy bodies and his or her own smooth little one.

First questions usually come up when the child notices a child of the opposite sex naked. "What's that?" All he wants is its name – vagina – and perhaps the matching name for what he has instead – penis.

There is no reason why the subject should get loaded with embarrassment if you take it calmly and concentrate on giving accurate information that exactly answers the specific question you have been asked. You do not have to "get the whole business over" by telling all. It is much better to let the child realize which parts he does not understand and ask, in his own time, for the missing links. He may be six or seven before he asks that crunch question: "How does the Daddy put the seed in the Mummy's va-what do you call it?" After years of brief specific answers you will find it perfectly easy to reply "By putting his penis into it."

If you do let a deadly serious "special" atmosphere build up every time your child asks a question that touches on sex, you may land yourself with pure farce. One child rushed into the kitchen saying "Quick, Mummy, tell me where I came from. Sarah's waiting to know." Taking a deep breath, her mother launched into her long-prepared lecture, watched with amazement by her daughter who at last interrupted: "Mummy, I only said where did I come from? Was it Colchester like Sarah?"

Some families make a point of letting their young children see them naked so that they get the chance to see the difference between the sexes when they are adult. Other families make an equal point of not displaying themselves. Where sex and young children are concerned it is probably best not to make a point of anything. It does not matter whether or not your child sees you naked as long as the atmosphere is relaxed and casual. An exaggerated modesty that leads you to scream and clutch for a towel if he comes into the bathroom is liable to make him wonder why you are so embarrassed. Equally, a carefully staged nude parade will probably embarrass *him* because he will not know how you want him to react. So behave as you always have behaved and don't be deliberately "old-fashioned" or self-consciously modern.

Deliberate displays which are intended to show children that they are made just like their parents of the same sex can misfire badly. To a child's eye there is no similarity between a small, smooth hairless girl and a fully developed woman nor between a little boy with a tiny penis and almost invisible scrotum and a fully mature man. Looking at a same-sex parent, the child may actually worry about his or her own inadequacy. Looking at an opposite-sex parent, he or she may actually worry at the thought of making a baby with someone like that. If your child says anything which suggests that he or she is bothered in this way, it is comforting to say that all the parts of people's bodies grow at just the right rate to keep up with the rest. The child is just the right size and shape now and will be just the right size and shape when he or she is grown up.

But at this stage it is better if children are not especially encouraged to think about *themselves* and the sex act. Intercourse is just one more peculiar thing people get up to when they are adult. That is why sexy teasing and jokes about "boy friends" and "girl friends" are much better avoided.

Language

Most parents are as thrilled with their children's first words as with their first steps. But just as it is wrong to assume that a newly walking child will now use walking just as adults do, so it is wrong to assume that once the first words come, the rest of language will follow automatically.

Using language becomes more, rather than less, difficult once children have passed the toddler stage. They learned their early words as labels for, and comments on, interesting things that they could actually see. But now they begin to use language for its uniquely human purpose: for talking about things that are not in the room but in their heads, and for expressing ideas that are theirs alone.

Pre-school children are tremendously busy finding out how things work, finding out what they themselves can do, and putting themselves, imaginatively, into other people's places. The more language they have, the faster thinking will progress. But the more thinking they are doing, the more language they will use. So language and thought, even language and "intelligence", are intimately entangled. A very bright child will be, or at least will become, advanced in talking: he will need language for his thoughts. A child who is helped to use language well will use all the brightness he has to good effect. His talking feeds his intelligence.

How you can help The more conversation you have with the child the better. But to be really useful, it must be genuine, two-way conversation, not just talk. If you just let him burble at you while you keep the flow going with "uh-huh" and "really?", the talk is not true communication. He will realize that you are not really listening to him. Monologues from you are not very useful either. If you do not leave pauses for his contributions, and listen and react to them, your talk is no more than pleasant background noise like a radio left on when nobody is listening. He will soon realize that you do not care whether he listens or understands you or not; he will stop bothering.

Provided you are having attentive two-way talk, you can help your child enormously by providing him with labels for things or ideas at the moments when he needs them. Whether he already has a large vocabulary or still uses only a few words, he needs more and more.

Suppose that he is struggling to move a fresh bag of sand towards his sandpit. He obviously needs physical help, but you can give him language-learning help at the same time by labelling his problem for him. If you just say "Let me help you", he learns nothing new. If you say "Let me help you to carry that bag of sand, it is too heavy for you", he is offered several new language ideas. It may not previously have occurred to him that sand in a bag is called a "bag of sand". Above all, he will probably not have realized that he was unable to move it himself because it was "too heavy". You have just taught him the label for an idea (weight) which he could sense but could not express.

You can do the same with all kinds of other ideas. You reach something for him because you are "taller"; you take some ketchup off his plate because he has taken "too much"; you dropped a dish because it was "very hot" and you rejected one of his sweaters because it had got "too small".

You can help him with words about colour, shape and number in the same way. If you offer him a bag of sweets and he selects a pink one, you *could* say "You're going to have that one are you?" – friendly chat, but not actually helpful. If instead you say "You're going to have the pink one are you?" you supply him with the word for a colour he obviously likes the look of but probably did not know was called "pink". Two sweets give you the chance to elaborate with "Two sweets! One sweet for this hand and one sweet for that hand. Two sweets for two hands. . . ." If both are pink but one is oblong and the other round, you can add that into your comments too.

His imaginary games give you scope for providing words, too. Equipped with a tiny pair of gloves and a huge umbrella, he announces "I'm Daddy". He knows that his father often goes out and he is obviously playing a Daddy-going-out-game in his head. "Is Daddy going to the office or is he going for a walk?" you ask. You have supplied him with name-labels for two of the places Daddy might go; you have helped him to elaborate his thinking within his own game.

You can carry on with this kind of elaboration almost whenever your child speaks to you. There is nothing difficult or phoney about it. Indeed if you are *really* listening to what the child is saying, what he is trying to communicate, you may find yourself doing it automatically. It is the opposite of the "uh-huh" approach to children's talk. He says "Look! Big dog!" It is clearly an exclamation; he has obviously seen something notable about the dog. You try to see what it is and to offer him an elaboration both of the thoughts and of the words that will express them: "Yes, it is a big dog isn't it? And just look how fast he is running. . . ."

He runs to you, showing his grazed knee, crying "Bad bang, bad bang". Embroidery and comfort can go together with "Poor love, you have banged your knee haven't you? But it isn't really very bad; it's only a bit bad. See, there isn't any blood, just a bump. . . ."

Although your child probably does not need you now as constant interpreter when he speaks to other people (see p. 356), you can still help him to get the most out of conversation with them. If his father comes home and asks "What have you been doing today?", he probably means the question to be rhetorical. Without your help the child will not answer because the question was incomprehensibly general. But you can help him. "Are you going to tell Daddy about the squirrel we saw in the park?" Launched into telling, the child's account will be jerky and incomplete, but you can smooth it out and keep it unrolling for him with the same elaborating technique:

"Squirrel comed . . . frightened . . . I say 'OOOH'. . . ."

"Yes, you did say 'Ooh' didn't you? And then what happened? The squirrel ran back into the . . . ?"

"TREE!" supplies the child delightedly.

Learning to use pronouns

With this kind of conversation going on, the child adds the nouns which label things, the adjectives which describe those things and the verbs which tell what they do, at a rapid rate. But he finds words like "me", "you", and "him" extremely confusing because their meaning depends on who is talking and your ordinary elaborations therefore get in a mess. *I* am writing this book for *you* to read. But if you tell someone else about it, you will say "I am reading this book that she wrote". I am still me and you are still you. But I have become "she" and you have become "I"!

Because this is so confusing, children usually go on using proper names (their own and other things), thus avoiding pronouns altogether: "Johnny will get Teddy" rather than "I will get him". Trying to correct this will get you both into a monstrous mess. You say: "Say, 'I'll get Teddy', darling". The child will look at you in amazement and reiterate his first statement: "Johnny will get Teddy". What he means is that it isn't *you* who will get him, but he. Yet you said "I". Oh dear.

Don't try to make him use pronouns but take trouble, now, to use them correctly yourself, saying "Shall I help?" rather than "Shall Mummy help?". He will gradually sort it out for himself.

Asking questions

By the time he is three the child knows that he needs more words and he asks you for them by continually demanding "What's that?". He is asking you to tell him or remind him of the *name*, so don't confuse the issue by launching into elaborate answers to a different question, "What's that for?". If it is the washing machine he is pointing to, say "That's the washing machine". Don't embark on "That's my special machine for washing clothes. . . ."

Soon you will be into "why?".

Several hundred "why?" questions per day of the "why can't I?", "why is it hot?", "why has Daddy gone out?" type can be very wearing. But remember that the child is asking because he *needs to know*. He is adding to his store of knowledge and understanding and he is doing it in the most efficient possible way – by using words. "Why's" are a clear sign of growing up. As a toddler he would either have tried to find out by doing or he would not have thought of the question in the first place.

Some "why's" are unanswerable either because the child, without realizing it of course, is tapping the edges of human knowledge, or because he is tapping the edges of yours!

"Why does it thunder/rain/blow?"
"Why is Daddy a man/big/brown?"
"Why is that lady on my TV?"
"Why do lights switch on?"
"Why won't the sun switch on?"

Try not to fall back on "because that's the way it is". If the question is answerable, answer it briefly. But don't muster everything you know about the workings of television and launch into a lecture. His question is casual; the phenomenon of the TV showing that particular picture has just caught his attention. "Because she is the lady this programme is about" is probably all he needs. If the question is answerable, but not by you, don't be afraid to say so. There is nothing but good in telling the child: "That's an interesting question but I don't know myself; let's ask Daddy/ let's look in a book...."

Some "why's" land you in a sort of "Alice in Wonderland" world.

"Why am I John?"
"Because when you were a new baby
we decided we liked that name,
so that's what we called you."
"Why?"
"Because it seemed like a nice name for a super boy."
"Why?"

The "why's" may simply be a device to keep your attention, keep the conversation going, or the child may have long ago stopped meaning literally "why?" and be meaning "tell me more". You can break it up by saying "Shall I tell you more about when you were a new baby?"

Often, he asks "why?" but is unanswerable because "why?" is not the right question. He is using the word wrongly so it is meaningless: "Why are bulls?". Try not to say "I don't know what you mean". Try instead to think what he is likely to mean. Is it *what* are bulls? What are bulls for? Are bulls dangerous? Are you frightened of bulls and should I be?...A general "I'm not quite certain what you want to know, but let's talk about bulls and see. Do you know what a bull is? It's a man cow..." will start him off on the conversation he is really seeking.

Using words to control his or her own behaviour

After years of having their behaviour controlled and managed by you, pre-school children begin to take over for themselves (see p. 434). You will probably notice this new self-discipline first in what he says to himself as he plays. He uses the same kinds of controlling phrase he hears from you to his toys or imaginary companions: "Careful now!", "Up you come", "Don't touch...." He is a hard taskmaster. You will overhear much fiercer tones than you are conscious of using.

Later on he begins to talk to himself in the same way, but his warnings come after the event. He kicks his ball into the flower bed and scolds himself: "Not in the *flowers*, John". A little while later he warns himself in advance. Poised to kick that ball, he says "No John, not in the flowers" and just as if someone else had spoken, he turns and kicks it the other way.

This is an excellent sign that he really is taking your instructions and rules into himself and applying them alone. But if you often hear him fiercely instructing himself but *disobeying his own instructions*, saying "Mustn't hurt the dog, John" as he yanks its tail, try to listen to yourself for a few days. You may be issuing streams of nagging instructions without making the reasons clear or making sure one is obeyed before the next is given.

Using words to control the behaviour of others

Being on the receiving end of controlling talk, the child is bound to try out this use of language for himself. Four year olds, in particular, tend to sound very bossy. "Stop it at once", he yells at the surprised baby; "Come here immejitly" he commands the unheeding dog. He is trying to find someone below him in the status hierarchy so that he can be boss as well as being bossed. He is also trying to see whether his words have as much power over other people's behaviour as yours have over him. So be tolerant of this tiresome phase. He does not mean to be unpleasant. If his bossiness really upsets you, teach him to soften his commands and exhortations with "please" and "thank you" and look to the way you both speak to him....

Using words to boost his or her self-esteem
Boasting is another typical four year old trait and not to be taken too seriously. Two children together will often have a boasting session that is almost a verbal tennis match – and recognized by both to be a game:

"My house is bigger than yours."
"My house is bigger."
"My house is as big as a palace."
"My house is as big as a park."
"My house is as big as, as, as *everything*!"

Although listening adults often sadly recognize that one or the other child does, in reality, have a smaller house, father or income than the other, you need not worry about hurt feelings. This kind of thing is recognized by both children as verbal play.

If your child boasts continually, you may wonder whether he needs to make himself sound very grand and big and rich because he really feels rather humble and small and poor. Lots of love and more congratulation and praise than criticism and reproof may be the right prescription.

Using words to ask for approval
Four year olds often sound goody-goody as well as bossy. "John's a *good* boy" he says, smugly. Try not to be sharp with him for being so. It is a good sign for his future behaviour that he wants you to think him "good". And it is also a good sign of language development that he wants to use words to talk about the idea. Don't sit on him, saying "Well, I don't know about that...." You will hurt his feelings and confuse him.

Sometimes this talk means that the child wants assurance that you love *him* even when you do not love *what he does*. He is still very literal about language, so these distinctions are important to him. If he and his sister have been racketing around until you feel that the noise will drive you crazy, try to avoid saying "Do go out into the garden you two, you're driving me round the bend." Separate *them* (whom you love) from their noise (which you do not) and say "Do go out into the garden you two if you are going on with that game. The noise is driving me round the bend...."

Problems–large and small

As we saw in an earlier chapter (see p. 356), there is an enormous variation in the age at which individual children learn each stage of speech. One child may stay wordless until he is two and a half and then produce three-word sentences; another will have several words at ten months and add very few more during his second year. Yet another will start talking at around a year and progress fairly steadily.

If your child is not talking *at all* by the time he is two and a half, take him to your doctor or clinic and ask for a developmental check-up. You may be sent to a special speech clinic. If there is any serious reason for the child being slow to speak (such as deafness or mental retardation), they will tell you. If they find nothing amiss (and they probably will not), they may ask you to bring him back in six months time.

Slower than average speech development

If your child has a few words, you almost certainly have nothing to worry about. Take him or her for a check-up by all means if it will prevent you from worrying, but the child is probably acquiring speech more slowly than average for one of the following reasons:

He is giving his concentration and energy to acquiring some other skill.	*He cannot do everything at once. He may talk more when walking is perfected.*
He is a twin or has a brother or sister very close to him in age.	*The problem is not "private language" but too little individual attention from adults.*
Because he is a boy and not a girl.	*Boys' developmental programming is slightly different, so don't compare across the sexes.*
He has several older brothers and sisters.	*Older children may interpret too skilfully, so that he has little need or time to speak for himself. Their talk may be so continuous that he has little chance for face-to-face talk with you.*
He is in group care with too low a ratio of adults to children.	*He may lack face-to-face talk with a familiar caretaker and/or be unhappy.*
He may be cared for by a foreign helper or "au pair".	*Both may find gestures easier than words. He needs a fluent adult model.*
His family may be bi-lingual.	*Learning two languages at once will take him longer than learning one.*

Stuttering

The pre-school child's ideas are bigger than his vocabulary. He finds it difficult to express his thoughts smoothly, especially when having to search for the right word holds up the flow of what he wants to say. When he is excited or upset, he wants to pour something out but the words keep hiccuping.

Jerky uneven speech happens to almost every pre-school child sometimes but only rarely does it turn into a real stutter which lasts. The important thing is to stay calm yourselves (even if one of you stuttered as a child so that you are sensitized to the possibility) and remain completely accepting of the way the child talks. If you can avoid making him nervous or self-conscious about speaking, he will almost certainly talk his way out of this phase (see Enc/Stammering).

The chatterbox

Most three and four year olds talk all the time. With perhaps 500 words in his vocabulary, the child may utter 20,000 words in a single day. That is an awful lot of repetitions. Some parents get extremely bored with it.

But he *must* talk, because he has to practise *making* the actual sounds. He has to try out different inflections for his words and he has to try them in different combinations.

The child will practise using every word he can think of that will go with one particular one. He may say "Daddy gone" as father leaves for work. Then, he starts casting around the room for other words he can use with "gone": "Breakfast gone", "water gone", "dog gone". When he has run out of things he can see that have gone he produces more "gone" things out of his mind: "tree gone, Jack gone, bed gone, house gone, me gone. . . ." It is nonsense, of course, in that what he says is not *true*, but it is sense all the same because he is making sense of the use of the word.

Join in and make a game of it. He does not *really* think the tree has gone; after all, he is looking at it while he says it. He is playing with words, so you play with them too. Look straight at him and say "trousers gone?" or put yourself half behind the curtain and say "Mummy gone?". He will probably roar with laughter and embroider the game even further.

Baby talk   Some children do go on with baby talk for a very long time. It is as if they refuse to accept adults' words and expressions in certain areas and insist on going on using the "words" they started out with a year or more ago. "Biccit-a-baby" demands the four year old who is perfectly capable of saying "I want a biscuit".

Usually such a child has discovered that grown ups think his baby talk is "sweet". Maybe when he uses it, your face softens. Perhaps you use it back to him. Perhaps he has overheard conversations in which you have proudly maintained to uncomprehending visitors that you "understand every word he says".

Suddenly you realize that most people *cannot* understand him and that that will make trouble when he goes to pre-school or to big school. Or you look at him one day in his new jeans and his Snoopy sweat-shirt and realize (rather late) that his talk is not appropriate to his age.

Obviously it is very hurtful to the child if you suddenly take against talk which up to then you have seemed to encourage. So don't do anything sudden. Vow never to imitate or melt to baby talk any more, and translate everything he says in it into proper English, so that you put his version alongside yours. Over a few months he will drop it.

Some other kinds of baby talk are positively useful though. When the child does not know the word for something he wants to mention, he will often coin a highly descriptive word. That cereal which is advertised as going "Snap, crackle, pop" was christened "snapples" by my own children long before the advertisers had the same idea. A small girl who was anxiously excited by the sound of an ambulance asked if it was the "bellvan". Words of this kind show that the child is actually *thinking* about words and making them *work for him*. They often get adopted into family speech, and why not? They make a bridge between the child's language and the language of adults, and their use by other people shows him that he can produce good, meaningful words of his own. It is easy to tell him the "proper" name for it while letting everyone have some pleasure out of his.

Nonsense and naughty-nonsense

Words are powerful things. Being able to use them makes the pre-school child feel much more able to control the world.

If he can find some words which have a particularly powerful effect on other people, he is liable to use them over and over again. "Pee-pee" he shouts. If he gets a nice strong reaction, he will add in "Wee-wee" and "Piss, piss, piss" for good measure.

If you ignore him, it will probably not get out of hand. If you scold, you will get into very deep water. What are you scolding for? A word? *Can* a word be naughty? No, obviously not. If you start trying to explain that this particular word is naughty except when used in its "proper" context, you will really confuse him.

If this kind of thing bothers you, the best way to cope is to substitute your own equally absurd but less "naughty" nonsense for the child's. "Squashed tomatoes to you" is the kind of response that never fails!

All pre-school children love nonsense rhymes and nonsense words. "Niddle, naddle, noddle nee" they chant, enjoying the rhythm and the sounds and practising both difficult consonants and new emphases. If this chant drives you crazy, suggest a new one: "double, double, toil and trouble," for example.

A child who enjoys nonsense rhymes is ready to be introduced to the sounds and rhythms of poetry too, even if he cannot understand all the words. You could read him some of "Hiawatha" with its regular beat and lovely sounds. It will all help him to listen and think and enjoy words. He will be off to a flying start when he meets "creative writing" at school.

Insults and angry talk

We try to teach pre-school children to use words instead of blows. The trouble is that having taught these lessons parents often don't much like the angry *words* either. The child gets into trouble for going for you as if he would like to kill you, but he also gets into trouble for standing stock still shouting "I'll kill you...".

A child who says this kind of thing is usually frightened. His own powerful fury frightens him and he is still very unsure just how great his power is. He does not know that it would be virtually impossible for him really to damage you. He longs for you to prevent him, to keep control of him while he is out of control of himself. If you let yourself get angry because of his words and shout back at him, you add to his alarm. You have no real reason for anger. He is using great self control in using words instead of physical attack. Try calmly to assure him that he will not kill you, could not kill you, but that you realize he feels very angry just at the moment and you are sorry for him.

Lesser insults can usually be turned into a joke if you can remember that it is a little *child* who is calling you a "silly old cow". You really don't need to react as you would if an adult insulted you! "If I'm a silly old cow, you're a cross little calf" will often bring the whole episode to a giggly close.

It is important to avoid giving the child the idea that words are ever bad in themselves. You want him to use words, to like words, to enjoy his own and other people's words. So try to apply – and even teach – that old adage "sticks and stones may break your bones but words will never hurt you". It is not entirely true, of course, but it is useful with this age-group.

Playing and thinking

The stages through which your child's playing and thinking will pass during the pre-school years are neither so clear-cut nor so easy to see as those that passed during the toddler period. As an explorer discovering his small world and then as a scientist experimenting with its properties and behaviour (see p. 335), he learned an enormous number of separate facts and facets. At the same time he began to develop the ability to think about the things he was finding out. Now, in the pre-school years, it is this ability to think, to imagine, to create and to "play in his head" which dominates his play-learning. It is rather as if his toddler years had been spent gathering together the separate tiny pieces which go into a kaleidoscope, and his pre-school years see him able, at last, to put all the pieces into his kaleidoscopic mind and shake them around to form new and different patterns at will.

It is not only his ability to think which is maturing. His body, and especially his manual dexterity, is growing up too. Increasingly he will be able to do the things he can now think of. He can think about how something works and make it work; he can think about colour and apply it to paper; he can imagine himself as Mummy or the milkman, the midwife or Mr. Jones, and manage the "props" which help the game along.

Expanding your child's world

The play-conditions which were outlined for your toddler in the previous chapter will still be entirely appropriate for him. He still needs that suitable play-space, the undemanding company, willing partnership and varied equipment which he needed then. But it will not be enough for him. His immediate world has become familiar, he needs more scope. With home and all its familiar things as a solid background, he needs new experiences, new people, new objects, to feed that imagination.

Organizing an expanded world

Your family circumstances will dictate how much you need deliberately do to broaden his daily life. If you live in the country, with adult activities like farming or market gardening going on around him and the seasons bringing their own change and drama to life, he will promote himself at his own pace. He will move gradually from the shelter of the house towards the barns and fields, joining in with adult activities, making relationships with whoever is around working the land. You do not have to plan special trips for a child who has haymaking or root clamping, sheep shearing or the apple crop coming up.

If you live in a close community with many other children around, the same sort of automatic expansion of his life may take place. He will join the other children more and more, gradually being included in their group movement from house to house, garden to garden. Sometimes you will find yourself laying on an impromptu tea party for seven; at other times you will have no child at all because he will be "camping" in the Jones' garden or setting up a wild flower stall or made-up fairground with the Robinson children....

Sadly, most children live in cities, and few of them experience a close community. You are likely to have to choose between expanding your child's life through some form of pre-school group or working at it yourself. What is needed from home if home is the whole world will be totally different from what is needed from home if it is the backcloth to new group experience.

What your child needs from home when home is all of every day	What your child needs from home when a group is added to it
The whole of her enjoyment, occupation and learning is in your hands. She will experience nothing new unless you arrange it; she will go almost nowhere unless you take her; she will have no fresh play materials unless you provide them nor friends of her own age unless you find them for her. Each day you have to ask yourself what new material for thought and action you have fed her.	Much of his interest and his energy is being mopped up at the group. His teachers present him with new experiences, take him on expeditions, provide fresh play materials and help him to work with a group of children his own age. He is probably stretched to his limits. Your job is to keep home and its familiar objects and people just as they were before.
Her day is no longer broken up by naps so it needs breaking up and structuring by complete changes of activity and place. Solitary play indoors while you are busy in the morning needs a recognizable end with a morning snack and then something different — a walk or active play in the garden. She needs a routine that is both predictable and varied.	His day is totally broken up by group attendance. Time before group in the morning is just waiting time. After group, at lunch time, he may need an actual nap or at least a rest. For the remainder of the day he needs time just to be himself; to contemplate, to mess around.
Although you are the most important people in her life you are not enough. She needs to meet every sort and kind of person. She needs individual adults to make friends with; she needs individual children to be a pair with; she needs groups of children to see what group life is like and how it works.	He did not have you at group. He will need a chunk of your time and attention now. He may have had enough of all other people and need peace and solitude rather than tea parties.
Without your direct and concentrated help she probably will not muster the effort and persistence needed to conquer tasks she finds really difficult or frustrating. She needs time with you to master that puzzle, cut out a crown neat enough to satisfy her or to finish her clay model with paint.	Group activities will usually include all the concentrated careful work of which he is capable. Spurred on by the other children and by skilled teachers he will be stretching himself on "educational" play. Home play will need to be easy, as well as fun.
Without ideas and information from you whole worlds of play-learning will stay closed to her. She cannot conjure the idea of a book, a record or a radio programme out of her head. She needs you to introduce her.	Different groups will emphasize different types of activity. He will need from you what the group does not provide. He may have had enough of stories and music and may need garden-romps instead or he may have climbed and swung and pedalled all morning and need stories from you.
Every human being needs high-spots and holidays in life. Break up her week, her winter and her year as well as her days. Saturdays or Sabbaths may be special; people's birthdays are important. Even the official first day of Spring can make a marker.	Group life may be full of special days; there may be Mother's day celebrations, little concerts, end of term shows, exhibitions of children's work . . . let the home-weeks roll calmly on.

When it is all up to you

Gradually broadening your child's horizons without much help from outside demands a new level of communication between you. By listening to him and thinking about his questions (see p. 416), you can keep abreast of his thought processes. By talking to him you can both feed in information and ideas and you can involve him directly in the things you do and see together. If you can stay alert to the way he is likely to be thinking, and awake to his comments, you can make even the most casual encounters fascinating. An ambulance, for example, is likely to cause comment. "Why" he asks you "does it make that noise?" You can use his question to bring alive the whole drama of hurrying sick people to hospital. You could talk to him about the fact that ambulances take priority over other traffic. If he goes on asking questions you could take him, then or another day, to see your nearest hospital with its uniformed nurses.

You can involve him in routine things too. The supermarket has long been a favourite place but now he can look for specific items for you, fetch things which are within reach, push the trolley instead of riding in it, and even choose which particular kind of biscuits you should buy.

With words you can help him to think about people. The milkman, to a toddler, is a man with an interesting van, a cap and a lot of milk bottles. To your pre-school child he can also be somebody who has to get up very early in the morning, carry heavy crates, read people's scribbled notes and cope with their barking dogs. You, too, can become "real" to him. Let him think about you as a person. Which of the things that he sees you doing every day do you actually enjoy? What are you looking forward to?

With his interest and his imagination well fed by new things to see and feel and understand, you will notice his play change. If you watch and listen, unobtrusively, you will be able to find areas in which he is ready to use help and ideas from you.

Dramatic play

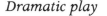

The pre-school child is usually being somebody else. He tries out every activity he notices among adults, not simply copying what they do (as a toddler might) but trying to put himself into their place and be them. When he is a builder, it is not just sand and bricks he is thinking about but sweat and language too.

Although he may love dressing up, he does not need elaborate costumes. He changes character in his head. More useful than clothes are "props". A detective needs a magnifying glass, a mother a house, and a knight a sword.

Sometimes he will use dramatic play to re-live incidents which were emotionally important to him. With practice you can see these coming. A night in the hospital, for example, is bound to mean a spate of hospital games, and merits a doctor set or nurse's outfit. You will hear him assuring his Teddy that "this is only my listening thing; keep still, it won't hurt – much".

Don't insist on listening to, much less taking part in, dramatic play. There is only room for one author and that is the child. If he plays hospitals, he does not want you to be nurse while he plays patient. This is his script and he is the doctor. His patient will be a junior and shadowy figure, a doll or soft toy or even an imaginary someone from out of his head. If you have a role at all,

Play belongs to the child.
It is not for us to know who
he is being when he dresses up . . .

. . . whether she sees "a picture"
in her mind's eye or simply
enjoys the process
when she is painting

. . . who inhabits this, her own small
world, as she plays "house"

. . . how she feels as she hands on to others the care she herself receives

*. . . what they see in their imaginations
as they build higher than themselves.*

it is entirely subordinate. You may be required as dresser, or as provider of "pink medicine". Otherwise keep discreetly away. This is his private world which he is making for himself out of the raw material of the real world you show him.

Arts and crafts

Making and creating things with his hands is vitally important to the pre-school child. As a toddler he wanted to discover how things like scissors and felt-tipped pens worked. Now he gradually discovers how to make them work for him. The child deliberately snips a piece of paper. Don't ask him what he has made. The obvious answer is a piece of paper with snips in it. But by asking for an identification you suggest to him that it "ought" to be something else. After some practice, he may look at his most recent piece of snipped paper and decide that it is "lace". He will have reached yet a further stage in creation when he decides *in advance* that he is going to snip the paper into lace. The same applies to drawing and painting. He begins by exploring the materials. He wants to paint in order to make a painting, not in order to make a painting of a house. For a long time the medium is the message.

Colours are important. As he learns their names and relationships, finding that pink is somehow linked with red, he will explore them deliberately. He may paint 57 rainbows in a week. Give him the materials and stand back. If he asks for comments, stick to what you can see on the paper: "I like those colours" is safe appreciation. "Is that Daddy?" is a question which will either make him think you ineffably stupid (since representational painting has not entered his mind) or make him feel inadequate: "Ought it to be Daddy?"

His drawing goes through definite learning stages without anyone teaching him. At three, he finds vertical lines and circles much easier than horizontal lines. His drawings are therefore either up and down scribble or round and round scribble.

Soon the day comes when he sees something in the scribble that reminds him of a person. If he has made a circular drawing, he will add some lines for limbs and perhaps some dots for eyes. Then he will announce his first representational drawing: "A man".

By the time he is four, he will actually set out to draw a person, rather than scribbling first and labelling afterwards. His man will have a big roundish head, with eyes and perhaps a nose and mouth too. Straight out of the head will poke legs. The man has no separate body yet and probably no arms either. During his fifth year, his man gets more and more lifelike. By the time he is five it may have a separate head and body; legs with feet, arms with hands, and even some clothes indicated by buttons or a waistband.

"Messy" play

Play with water, clay, mud, dough or sand often spans dramatic and creative play. It can be either one or both together. To some extent your child can expand these activities for himself using only his own imagination. He may spend all afternoon in the sandpit but now he is not just experimenting with the sand, he is mixing "cement" and using it to fill every crack in the paving stones.

But he needs help in expanding and applying the lessons he has learned about natural materials. His knowledge of volume is

*Whatever the mess, it is time for him
to put his play-skills—like pouring—
to real use . . .*

growing, but he need not think about it much when he is pouring water as part of water play: an overflow is just part of the game. He needs to discover that his mug will overflow in just the same way if he does not stop pouring milk in time.

He needs to use all these skills in ways which are obviously useful as well as "just" fun. He has messed around with dough. Now it is time for real scraps of pastry. He has mixed sand and water, now it can be cupcakes and endless questions about why they "blow up" in the oven.

Building, fitting and counting play

This is the most obviously "educational" play and, perhaps as a result, it is the kind for which most toys are bought. But it is also a kind of play which many pre-school children find pointless. Where there is a cupboard full of barely-used toys most of them will certainly be construction sets, jigsaw puzzles and fitting toys.

Your child need not use "educational" toys to educate himself. He will carry out all the intellectual activities which these toys are supposed to encourage if he is given materials which lend themselves also to more imaginative and multiple uses. He probably already owns a good many of them, such as bricks.

Expanding this kind of play means helping him to use his knowledge and skills in contexts where he can see that they are useful. Counting on an abacus is a game. But counting out spoons for supper or tins of cat food at the supermarket has obvious point.

He need not use a construction set to construct. He can build with his bricks; make your clean sheets into a neat stack in the linen cupboard or put together a castle out of cardboard boxes.

Careful, exact fitting is part of managing life. If he can fit the cutlery into its compartmented drawer and learn how to open the front door with your key, he may scorn a "mere toy".

Gradually he can be helped to use an increasing number of adult tools. Your sharing will give him pleasure; the lessons will teach him manual dexterity, and learning how to use these things will mean fewer careless accidents later on. He can use a whisk to beat eggs for his omelette; learn to handle a small knife and make a start with lightweight gardening and carpentry tools.

Physical play

As we have seen, the child continually tries out his physical limits as well as having to involve his body in all his activities. But even here you can help him to expand his play so that some of it overlaps the real and serious adult world. If he can climb a ladder, he can go up the step-ladder to fetch what you need from that high shelf. If he can run fast, he can be the one to get to the telephone before it stops ringing. If he can jump, he can ford the stream by those stepping stones and he can add his small proud strength to yours in mastery of that shopping bag.

Physical skills acquired in the pre-school years are seldom completely lost. Look ahead: think what he will need to be able to do later, that you could teach him now. He can certainly learn to swim – the earlier the better. He can master a two-wheeler with patient help. He can enjoy the basic playground games like hopscotch or skipping which will make him feel at home when he goes to "big school", and if offered the opportunity he can learn to ski, ride a pony or skate.

Music Every human being has a sense of rhythm; all life, after all, is based on it, from the seasons to our heartbeats. But while every child with normal hearing can also perceive the different sounds that make up music, it has only recently been discovered that teaching can help him learn to interpret them; to hear them as music and reproduce them as such with his voice. The music of completely foreign cultures tends not to sing to us because we have not learned to hear it.

The older child who cannot carry a tune or sing on key is not a child with an inbuilt defect, but a child who was not taught. You can teach your child to be musical even though you cannot teach him that still-mysterious thing called "musical talent". Listening with you and singing simple melodies is part of it. But your child needs more structured teaching too. A tuneful xylophone, bought from a music shop rather than from a toy shop, is probably his best tool. With and without your help, he will make and listen to pure sounds which get higher and lower, louder and softer, are the same as or different from each other. He will discover for himself that two notes an octave apart are the same-only-different, while two notes seven tones apart are simply different. Two and three year olds learn to play violins in Japan; British infant schools teach the recorder as a matter of course. If your three or four year old gets as interested in those sounds as in colours or somersaults he could learn to play the piano. . . .

Books Where books are concerned the child really does need your direct help. He does not know what books there are nor what they say. He cannot imagine what pleasure they can give him. He cannot "invent" them out of his own head.

Almost every toddler enjoys looking at picture books as well as hearing stories read aloud. But the pre-school years are the ideal time to expand your child's acquaintance with and affection for books and all that they contain. They are going to be vital to his later education.

He needs three kinds of book. Picture books are important. By "reading" pictures he prepares himself for reading words later on. Both are symbols after all, the words are just a further abstraction from the pictures. Look at them with him. Help him to milk each illustration of its last detail. How many birds are in that tree? What is the little boy in the background doing? Try to find him books with big, colourful, detailed illustrations rather than the sterile conventional A is for Antelope type.

Highly illustrated story books are important too. If you choose good ones, he will be able to follow the story you are reading him on the picture pages, or at least stop you in mid-sentence to study the highlights of the plot. You have read about the children getting ready for the party. Now on this page he can study the party itself, discover what the children wore and had for tea. . . .

Your books are important too. He needs to get the idea that books are important to you – to the adult world – as well as to children. If you read for pleasure anyway, this will happen automatically. If not, try sometimes to look up the answer to one of his questions in a book, or to find him a picture of something that interests him. Help him to see them as useful as well as fun.

Problems with play

A child's play-world is his or her very own. Ideally what your child does within it should be nobody else's business provided the child does not hurt anybody or anything. But there are some troublesome issues which do arise.

Guns, war and violence

Pretend-war and blood-curdling deeds are part of the universal currency of play for both sexes in all cultures. If you do not buy your child guns, swords and shields, he or she will make do with sticks and your bread board. If you try to forbid war games, you will find yourself confused as to where to draw lines. "Soldiers" is obviously a war game, but so, in a sense is "tag", not to mention "cowboys and Indians". Our history, and therefore our culture, with all its fairy tales and folk heroes, is full of blood and battle. Even if you kept your child's acquaintance with literature to the Bible only, he or she would find plenty of war-stories to play out.

Try to accept the games as games. The child has not and could not have any idea what it would *really* be like to shoot somebody. Your child has no concept of killing. "Bang-bang you're dead" means no more and no less than "You're It".

Sex differences

Children are human beings who happen to be either male or female. They should clearly have the opportunity of exploring all aspects of human behaviour as children. Make no difference between "boys' toys" and "girls' toys" or the games that are associated with them. If your son wants to dress up as a queen, why shouldn't he? You would probably be happy to let your daughter dress up as a cowboy. As to dolls, why be shocked at a little boy's tenderness? When he is grown up you will admire him for his actively involved fatherhood.

Your child's eventual sexual predilections will not be changed by swapping roles in childhood. He or she is going to act out every possible role. If you try to make the child stick to the "right" sex, you deprive him or her of half the world.

Television

In our anxiety lest children lose playing or reading time for television, we tend to lose sight of its benefits. Selective viewing can increase your child's knowledge of the world and available fuel for thought enormously. How else can he visualize a lighthouse or a wild elephant?

Until your child can read the programme guides for himself, television should cause no problems. You tell him what is on; when it is over you turn the set off. Unless yours is a family where it is kept on as a background to life, or unless older children view hour after hour, he will neither know nor care what he is missing.

You can encourage now a selective and critical attitude to viewing which should stand you in good stead later. Don't ever yield to the temptation of using a soap opera as a babysitter and don't turn the set on casually "just to see what's on". You want him to feel that watching television is a positive activity rather than something to do when there is nothing to do. You can make it even clearer that it is an activity with a purpose if you watch with him as often as you can and talk with him about what he has seen.

Learning how to behave

As children move out of toddlerhood and into childhood, they have to begin to learn behaviour which will enable them to be accepted by a wider world than the family. Society has countless expectations for peoples' behaviour and while nobody will expect a three year old to meet all of these all the time, the pre-school years are the ideal period for coming to terms with them.

Small children will learn almost anything adults try to teach. They like to learn because they want to know and they particularly want to know how to behave because they very much want to please you. But a process which ought to be agreeable and interesting both for you and the child is often bedevilled by the heavy word "discipline" with all its related spectres such as "disobedience" and "dishonesty".

If you like your child, if you are proud of him and pleased with yourselves for having done a good job as parents so far, you may be able to get right through his childhood without ever thinking about "discipline", as a topic, at all. The child has moods and so do you. He makes mistakes just as you do and he sometimes does what he wants instead of what he ought, just as everybody does. If you are just moving along happily together treating each other as human beings, that may be all there is to it. If so, do not bother with this chapter. It is meant for the millions of parents who do not feel able to take this casual approach because they feel that they have problems with discipline.

What is discipline?
Dictionaries define the word as "teaching rules and forms of behaviour by continual repetition and drill. . . ." A disciplined person is defined as "one whose obedience is unquestioning. . . ." The word itself, with all those grim, punitive connotations, has bedevilled our attempts to show children how to behave. You can make sure that your child obeys you, tells you the truth, behaves as you say and fears your displeasure. But none of that will help to keep him safe, honest and good when you are not there to tell him what to do. And you are not going to be with him forever.

True discipline is aimed at building up within the child what we call a conscience. This is the *self-discipline* which will one day keep him doing what he should and behaving as he ought, even when there is nobody to tell him what to do or to notice if he does wrong. Telling a child what he must and must not do is only a means to that end. The things that you teach him are only of value once he takes them inside himself and makes your instructions his own instructions to himself.

Learning self-discipline takes time. When he was a baby you had to *be* him. You acted for him in all the ways he could not act for himself and thought for him when he could not think for himself. When he became a toddler you had to combine letting him begin to be himself with keeping a total control over his safety, his security and his social acceptability. Now that he is a pre-school child he is ready to begin to learn how to keep *himself* safe, secure and socially acceptable. You will show him how to behave in countless different situations and circumstances. You will teach him that all those different items of behaviour add up to a few basic and vitally important principles. Then, bit by bit, you will withdraw your control, leaving him to apply the principles for himself because he has taken them in and made them his own.

Showing your child how to behave

The very first rule for trouble-free and effective discipline is "do as you would be done by". The child will not give you more politeness, consideration and cooperation than you give him. There can be few double standards here. If he asks for help with his puzzle and is told you are too busy; trips over your feet and gets screamed at, he will not readily help you to lay the supper table nor quickly forgive you when the comb pulls his hair.

Make sure that good behaviour gets rewarded and that bad behaviour does not. It sounds obvious, but it is not. If you take your child shopping and he whines for sweets, you may well buy him some for the sake of peace. If you take him shopping and he does *not* whine for sweets, does he get any?

Be positive: "do" works better than "don't". Small children like action and hate inactivity. They respond much better to being told something positive that they should do than to being told *not* to do things. "You can't leave your tricycle there" is a challenge. It makes him think "I can, too. Just watch me." But "Put your tricycle over by the wall so that nobody trips over it" tells the child something positive that he ought to do.

Be clear. Even positive instructions don't work very well if they are vague. "Behave yourself" sounds like a positive instruction, but it is meaningless to a child of this age. What you really mean is "don't do anything I don't like" which is an impossible command because he does not know what you don't like!

Always tell your child why. Apart from emergencies, when reasons must wait until later, it is an insult to the child's intelligence to tell him to do something without telling him why. "Because I say so" is the kind of answer that makes sure that the child will not learn anything useful from what you say. Without a reason, he cannot fit this particular instruction into the general pattern of "how to behave" that he is building up in his mind.

"Put that shovel back" you say crossly.

Why? Because it is dangerous? Dirty? Breakable? Because you want to be sure of being able to find it next time? If you tell him that it belongs to the builders who have a right to find it where they left it, he can apply that thought to other occasions. But if you just say "Because I say so", you teach him nothing.

Keep "don't" for actual rules. Telling the child not to do things really only works when you want to forbid a specific action once and for all. If you only want to forbid a piece of behaviour now, under these particular circumstances, you will do better to turn it around and phrase it positively. For example: "Don't interrupt while I'm talking" is useless. There are lots of times when you actually want him to interrupt – to tell you the potatoes are boiling over, his sister is crying or that he needs to go to the lavatory. Better to say "Wait a minute until we have finishing talking".

Specific "don'ts" become rules. As long as you keep them to a minimum the child will probably accept them easily, especially if you explain your reasons.

"Don't ever climb in that tree, it's not safe." If you stick to it and don't let him risk it "just for once", that particular tree will be recognized as forbidden.

"You mustn't cross any roads without a grown up." Once again this is an acceptable rule just as long as you don't send him to the corner shop for a newspaper because the road concerned is only a small one and anyway you want the paper!

Rules are very useful in keeping a small child safe. But they don't really play much part in teaching him how to behave. They are too rigid and inflexible to be very useful in ordinary life. So try to keep rules to small, definite issues and try not to make them about the big things that really matter.

Trust your child to mean well. If your child feels that you are always standing over him, ready to correct or instruct him, he probably will not bother to think very much about what he ought or ought not to do. So within the limits of his age and stage try to pass as much responsibility for his own behaviour as you can over to him, and make him feel that you know you can trust him to handle it.

If he is to go to a friend's house, for example, don't smother him with anxious instructions such as "remember to say thank you for having me" and "don't forget to wipe your feet". If you are willing to let him go at all, you must be willing to let him take charge of himself. Your exhortations will not help him to behave nicely, they will merely make him feel uneasy about going.

Be consistent in your principles. You obviously cannot show your child how to behave if you are not yourselves sure how people *should* behave. But this is the only kind of consistency that really matters. Your child is not a circus animal, being taught always to respond to a specific signal with a particular trick. He is a human being, taught to respond as best he can to a vast range of signals. He will accept that circumstances alter cases. Sweets ad lib at Christmas will not make him expect them when the holiday is over, nor will permission to jump on Granny's bed make him demand to jump on your forbidden one. Even disagreement between you two need not matter if it is honestly discussed in his presence so that he cannot play you off against each other.

When you are wrong, admit it. Since small children are watching how you behave, and modelling themselves, to some extent on you, it is important to be willing to admit and apologize if you make a mistake.

A useful family phrase, used in excuse, apology or forgiveness, is "everybody's silly sometimes". If your child is brought up to accept the truth of this statement, he will not set unreasonably high standards for you, for himself or for his friends, and he will not be shocked and disillusioned the first time he catches you in a real mistake, an injustice or a "white" lie.

Suppose you accuse him of breaking a glass and refuse to believe his denial. You later discover that you were wrong. By all the standards you are trying to teach your child, you owe him a sincere apology. There is no escaping it. No way to save your face. You were wrong; you were unfair and you refused to believe him when he was speaking the truth. If you ask him to forgive you, he will respect you more, not less.

Problems of behaviour

If you are truly thinking about "discipline" as a matter of showing your child how to behave, you will find that most of the problem issues of discipline cease to look like problems at all. Disobedience becomes an irrelevance, because you will not be issuing unexplained orders nor will you resent questions of the "why should I?" kind.

Disobedience Instant and unquestioning obedience probably kept life peaceful for Victorian parents, but it cannot produce children who think for themselves and can therefore be trusted to look after themselves from an early age. The difference was sharply illustrated when three small girls were abducted in a car from outside their infant school. A fourth child ran home, and raised the alarm. They were home again four hours later and one distraught father asked:

"Darling, why did you go with the man in the car? We've *always* told you not to go with strangers...."

"But the man said 'Your father says you're to come with me at once. He sent me to fetch you'. So I did. You always say 'you must do what I tell you'. You always say it."

The child who raised the alarm was questioned by police:

"What made you run home instead of going too?"

"I don't know, but Daddy and Mummy are always saying 'think!' They say 'You've got a mind of your own, use it'. So I thought. I thinked that if Daddy really wanted us he'd have come and I thinked that the man only said one Daddy and we've got three Daddies, all of us have I mean. So I ran."

Getting rid of "obedience" and "disobedience" and thinking instead of the child cooperating, defuses the whole issue.

Sometimes he will not do what you want because he wants to do something different. He will not go to bed because he wants to finish his game. It is not his disobedience that is causing trouble, it is a simple conflict of interests. Instead of yelling "Do as I say this moment", find a compromise like "five more minutes".

Sometimes he will not do what you want because he has not understood what you do want. Told to stay at the table until lunch is finished he may get down when his plate is empty. He did not realize you meant that he was to stay put until everyone had finished. He has not failed to obey, he has failed to understand.

Occasionally he will not do what you want because he is out to annoy you. He feels like showing his independence. He feels bolshy. You tell him not to touch your new book and he goes straight to it. This, and out of all these examples *only* this, is true disobedience. It is a deliberate attempt to provoke and best defused by refusing to rise to the bait. "Fancy you being so silly as to go straight off and do the one thing I asked you not to. You must be in a silly mood" will take the wind right out of his sails. Where is the argument he was looking forward to?

Lying   Denying wrongdoing is the kind of lie that usually gets children into trouble. Your child breaks his sister's doll by mistake. Faced with it he denies the whole incident. You are probably angrier with him for the lie than you are about the breakage.

But what matters is that he should recognize the mistake he has made. Confessing is not nearly as important.

If you do feel strongly that your child should confess when he or she has done something wrong, do make it easy. "This doll is broken, I wonder what happened?" is much more likely to enable him to say "I broke it, I'm sorry" than "You've broken this doll, haven't you, you naughty, careless boy."

If your child does admit to something, either because you force it out of him or of his own accord, do make sure that you don't overwhelm him with anger and punishments. You cannot have it both ways. If you want him to tell you when he has done something "wrong", you cannot also be furious with him. If you are furious, he would be a fool to tell you next time, wouldn't he?

Tall stories get some children into trouble too. Pre-school children are not often very good at telling reality from fantasy or what they wish had happened from what really did. They can happily accept stories about the Easter Bunny while keeping a quite unmagic rabbit of their own; they see no conflict between the two.

If you are going to read your child fairy stories and help him to enjoy Santa Claus, it is unreasonable to jump on him for lying when he comes in from a walk with an elaborate story of his own about meeting a lion and taking a thorn out of its paw. Enjoy the story. Such fantasies are not *lies* in the moral sense.

Parents sometimes complain that their children simply seem to have no regard for the truth at all. They may overhear them casually mentioning Mummy's new dress when she hasn't got one, or announcing that they were sick last night when they weren't, or just telling a friend that they are going out for the day when they aren't.

There are lots of reasons for this kind of casual inaccurate talk. But an important one is that the child hears his parents doing it. Adults lie out of tact, kindness, a desire to avoid hurting other people's feelings. The child hears them. He hears you agreeing with old Mrs. Smith that the weather is much too hot when you have just told the child how much you like the heat. Unless the reasons for these being "white" lies are explained to him, he cannot be expected to see why he must never exaggerate or falsify when you can.

If your child tells so many stories and adds so much embroidery to his accounts of daily life that you really cannot be sure what is true and what is not, then it is time to make it clear to him *why truth matters*. Don't fall back on it being "naughty" to tell lies. Instead try him with the story of "The boy who cried wolf". It is a good story. He will enjoy it. Having told it you can discuss it with him. Point out that if you cannot distinguish between what is true and what is untrue, you might not know when something really important had happened to him or when he was really feeling ill. Phrase the whole conversation so that he feels you only care about him telling the truth because you care about *him* and want to be sure that you look after him properly.

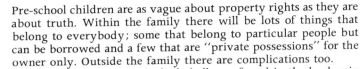

Stealing

Pre-school children are as vague about property rights as they are about truth. Within the family there will be lots of things that belong to everybody; some that belong to particular people but can be borrowed and a few that are "private possessions" for the owner only. Outside the family there are complications too.

It is all right to keep the little ball you found in the bushes in the park but it is not all right to keep money. It is all right to bring your painting home from nursery school but not a piece of plasticine. One can take leaflets from shops but not packets of soup.

Obviously you want to be careful that your child does not appear to steal, because other people are liable to make such a song and dance about it. But don't make it a moral issue at this age. Probably it is a good case for rules:

Don't bring anything away from somebody else's house without asking. Always ask a grown up if it is all right to keep anything you find.

Try not to be especially moralistic about *money*. If he takes some from your handbag, stop and ask yourself what you would have said if it had been a lipstick that he took and then say the same about the money. To him it is the same. It is treasure. He knows money is precious because he hears you talking about it and sees you exchange it for nice things. But to him it is like one of those tokens you put in slot machines. He has no concept of *real* money.

The child who is forever pinching things, behaving like a magpie, collecting other people's possessions in a bottom drawer, may be in emotional trouble. In a symbolic way he may be trying to *take* something that he does not feel he is being *given* – it is probably love or approval that he feels short of. Instead of being furious and upset and making him feel disgraced, could you try to *offer* what he needs? If you cannot and if his stealing goes on, you would probably be sensible to ask for help from your local Child Guidance Clinic. They will help you to see the problem calmly and to put it right.

Arguing and bargaining

Some children, especially rather intelligent ones, catch on to the idea that if you want them to do something they don't want to do, they have bargaining power. Rather than go silently upstairs to change into a clean shirt, your son may say "If I get clean cos you want me to will you get out my paints cos I want you to?" Unfortunately, parents often feel that this is in some way "cheeky". They have the right to tell him what to do and they don't want to concede him the right to do the same. "Do as your mother tells you and don't argue!" roars father. We are really back with instant obedience.

Bargaining can be a very useful form of human exchange – as every adult society throughout history has discovered. But you will obviously get bored with it if the child tries to exact a return for every single thing you remind him to do. Keep bargains for *exceptional* requests or ones that are unusually tiresome for the child, and then use them yourself, sometimes, rather than always waiting for him to propose them. "I know you're comfy in those jeans but they're dirtier than I can stand. Will you go and put on some clean ones if I get your bike out for you to save time?"

Problems of handling

Punishment The idea of "punishment" belongs with "discipline" rather than with "learning how to behave". A punishment may show your child what you will not put up with today but it says nothing about the behaviour you want, today and always.

There is nothing good to be said of physical punishments. For a start they can be dangerous. That "light" smack can catch the child off balance and knock him down or land on his spine rather than his bottom. A boxed ear can mean a burst eardrum, while a shaking can lead to whiplash injury to his back or even to concussion as his brain is jarred inside his skull. Even if the first round of punishments do your child no harm, they will do no good. Because they are ineffective, they will probably escalate. Most of his wrongdoing is due to impulse and forgetfulness. You smack him for trampling the flowers after six warnings but tomorrow he does it again. Logically you will have to smack again – harder. But if you carry on like that, today's careful slap can easily become next year's real spanking. . . . Research has shown that smacked children can never remember what they were smacked *for*. Pain and indignity make them so angry that they go away seething with anger rather than full of repentance. You cannot get his cooperation through blows.

Confining a child to his room is a silly punishment too. If it upsets him, it may put him off that "special place" for a long time. If it does not upset him, it is not a punishment. In that case you may be tempted to try a different kind of confinement next time; your punishments will escalate in the same way as smacking.

Punishments designed to make the child feel silly or undignified are just as dangerous emotionally. If you take away his shoes because he ran away from home, or make him wear a baby's bib because he spilled down his clothes, you assert your own power and his powerlessness in the crudest possible way. You make him feel helpless and worthless; incapable of being "good".

If you genuinely are trying to show him how to behave, you will not need to hurt or shame him. Behaviour which is truly anti-social carries its own uncomfortable results. Exposing him to them, after careful warnings, is the only sensible kind of "punishment".

If he will insist on throwing his toys around in a rage, one of them will eventually get broken. He will be sad and you can be just as sympathetic and quick with the glue as you would have been if you had broken the toy yourself. He has learned the lesson; discovered how *not* to behave if he wants his toys to stay intact. His "punishment" is the result of his own action; it is nothing to do with your power.

A gradual and gentle exposing of the child to the results of his own ill-advised actions is the only ultimate sanction you need. Any other kind of punishment is revenge and power-mongering. It will make him less inclined to listen to what you say and to do what you want. You are trying to teach him to control *himself* and take responsibility for his own behaviour. Later on, when he faces problems without you, there will be nobody there to jog his memory with a sharp slap, so manage without it now, and keep him on your side, learning willingly how to behave.

Spoiling Everybody knows that spoiled children are a misery to themselves and to everyone else, and most people assume that they reflect badly on their parents good sense. But few people stop to consider what it is that makes them consider a child "spoiled" or what it is that the parents have done to him or her. As a result, "spoiled" is a sort of spectre haunting parents who live in dread of hearing the word used either of their child or of their child-handling. Some even deliberately withhold treats and presents from their children because "we don't want him getting spoiled. . . ."

This is sad because true spoiling is nothing to do with what a child owns or with the amount of attention he gets. He can have the major part of your income, living space and attention and not be spoiled, or he can have very little and be spoiled. It is not what he gets that is at issue. It is how and why he gets it. Spoiling is to do with the family balance of power.

The pre-school child sees himself as an individual among other individuals and he is deeply concerned about the extent to which he can manage them as well as himself. So this is the age when power-games begin. He tests the limits of his influence just as he tests the limits of his muscles.

It is right that he should discover that he has some influence over people; he cannot grow up if you keep him totally subservient. But it is not right that he should discover that he can override your power by bullying. There is a balance to strike.

The secret lies in deciding what *you* consider it reasonable or sensible for him to have or do, and then in being honest. If he manages genuinely to change your mind by reasoned argument or charming persuasion, that is fine. He is using real influence to good effect. But if, despite tears and tantrums, he does not alter your real opinion, don't give in. Think of yourself as a judge. You are always prepared to listen patiently to your child-witness, but you insist, as a judge does, on reasonable behaviour in court, and your final verdict depends only on the evidence. Has he convinced you that he needs another ice-lolly because he is so hot and thirsty, or do you secretly still believe that he is just being greedy? Another ice-lolly will not spoil him, but winning things he wants against your better judgment may.

React more favourably to reason and charm than to tears and tantrums. Although self-control is still very difficult for him, you want the child to realize that while you are never prepared to be frightened into saying "yes" to a request, you are often prepared to be charmed into it. "Getting round people" is a very valuable skill to teach him. Encouraging him to use reason is important, too. If he can think and say why he so badly wants something, he not only gives you a chance to weigh his wanting against your policy, he also makes it possible for you to soften an eventual "no" by thinking of some other way of meeting his clearly expressed need. If he simply whines "play with me" over and over again, he is likely to get anger as well as no game. If he says "I'm bored of being by myself, will you play with me?", you can say "I can't come and play just now because I'm doing the ironing, but if it's company you want why not bring your teddy over here and iron his clothes too?"

Let your child join in decision-making processes. As he gets older there will be an increasing number of policy-decisions to make. He will discover what is permitted to other children of his age, hear about television programmes he has never seen and generally seek new privileges. Because these are new issues you will not have ready-made answers. Don't pretend that you have by giving quick answers off the top of your head. Discuss them with your partner *and* your child. Whether the matter goes for or against him, he will know that the two of you are agreed and he has had his chance to speak too. He will not feel that a spontaneous "no" can probably be altered by an equally spontaneous yell!

Balance the child's rights against yours just as you balance the rights of one child against the rights of another. If you want to spend the afternoon gardening while he wants to go for a walk, there is a problem. Discuss with him the genuine conflict of interests. If you cannot stand the idea of a walk, say so clearly. If you waver and hover, he is bound to feel that just a little more pressure might swing you his way. If you feel that his request is reasonable, work out a compromise between his wishes and your own. You might suggest a half-hour walk for him and then gardening for you. But if you make a plan of this kind, do carry out your side of what amounts to a bargain, willingly. If you make it clear that every step you take on that walk is under protest, you will ruin the whole idea. You will spoil his pleasure in the walk so that you will not truly have played your part in the compromise. And you will make him feel that he forced you into coming. And that is the one thing that you want him to believe is impossible.

Help your child to understand other people's feelings. The more interested you can make him in how other people feel and in how similar their feelings are to his own, the more sensitive to them he will be able to be. Understanding the feelings of others is the root of unselfishness and therefore the opposite of being spoiled. When an opportunity comes up, grab it. Talk to him about what the little girl next door felt when the big ones stole her bike. If he says, calmly, that she can buy another, point out that parents often want to buy things for their children but cannot always afford to. When you are making family plans, let him in on the difficulties of arranging treats and holidays so that all the different people involved get what they enjoy. You can even help him see that while it would be unfair to *him* if you served the cabbage he hates every night of the week, it is equally unfair to his *father* if you never serve what happens to be his favourite vegetable....

Your pre-school child longs for conversation with adults and information of all kinds. As long as you don't do this kind of teaching as a set of lectures, each cued off by some misdemeanour of his own, he will enjoy it enormously. You are doing him the honour of discussing feelings with him as well as things. You are helping him in the age-appropriate task of putting himself into other people's shoes. And you are calling his attention to a whole area of experience he might not have noticed for himself. The more you can do this, the sooner and the more clearly will he come to understand that he is one very important and much-loved person in a world of equally important other people.

Your child is not spoiled if . . .

Whatever you may overhear people saying when your child throws a tantrum in the supermarket; however guilty you may feel about that pile of birthday presents, your child is not spoiled if you enjoy him or her and he or she enjoys life.

If you enjoy spending time with him, arranging treats and buying him things he wants, he must be a nice person. If he were spoiled, you might still do these things, but they would be duties and trouble averters, not pleasures.

If he enjoys everything extra-nice, nice and just ordinary that you offer, he cannot be spoiled. If he were, his mind would be on how to get the next thing rather than on enjoying this one.

If he accepts a "no" with reasonable grace – usually – he cannot be spoiled. However many things he asks you for, he clearly understands that you have the right of decision.

If you have your mind changed – however frequently – by reasonable argument but never by obnoxious scenes, you are not spoiling him. If you are not sure where to draw that line between "reasonable" and "obnoxious", ask yourself whether once your mind is changed to his advantage, you are willing or reluctant to act on what the child wants. If you feel willing, all is well.

If you can face a scene when you must, you are not spoiling him. Giving way, with a bad grace, rather than living through a semi-deliberate tantrum, is something every parent does sometimes but no parent should do too often. You do not want the child to learn that *that* is the way to behave. . . . !

Bribes and prizes

People who are shocked at the idea of bargaining with a small child will probably find the idea of bribing one even more horrifying. After all, a child *ought* to do anything you say without question. . . .

But bribery or, if you think it sounds less immoral, prizes, can be very useful. Small children have a clear sense of justice and are clear-sighted about other people's goodwill. If you have to make the child do something he very much dislikes, offering a prize will both make it seem worth his while to cooperate and make him realize that you are trying to soften the blow.

Suppose, for example, that it is a hot afternoon and he is enjoying himself in his paddling pool. You have run out of potatoes and must go to the shops. You cannot leave him behind because there is nobody in the house. What is wrong with a simple bribe honestly proposed? "I know you'd rather we stayed at home but we can't because I've got to get some potatoes so we'll have to go to the shops. What about coming home by the baker's and choosing a bun for tea? Would that help?" It is a bribe but it is also a perfectly reasonable bargain provided he wants a bun.

An actual prize sometimes makes all the difference to a child who has to put up with something genuinely unpleasant. A child who has to face an anaesthetic or stitches in his head may be carried through the experience by thoughts of the prize to come. It is not the *object* that matters, it is having something nice dangling just the other side of the nasty few minutes. Don't make this kind of prize conditional on good behaviour though. If you offer a prize "if you don't make any fuss", you put him under terrible strain. He may *need* to make a fuss. And he certainly needs to feel that you will support him however he behaves.

Launching into life

Your child's world with you, with his family, his home and his immediate community, is now secure. His foundations are laid in his relationship with you and all that you have taught him. They are steady, solid, confident. Ready to bear the weight and balance of whatever superstructure of life and personality is to be built upon them.

The wider world is waiting for him, waiting to add its part to what you have already made. With it wait some of the greatest pleasures you will ever know. The pleasure of watching him become a child among children; leader, follower, one of the gang. The pleasure of watching him try out on teachers and other adult friends the techniques he has perfected on you; the charm, the wheedlings, the arguments and explanations. The pleasure of watching that lithe, coordinated body that you have cherished and nourished, cleaned and patched, arcing through the air in its first dive; gliding, giggling across the tarmac on its first roller skates or parading proudly in its first real play. The pleasure of watching him through the eyes of other people; seeing him regarded as "my friend"; as "always sensible"; as "such a sweet child" or, quite simply, as "the nice-looking one over there". The pleasure, above all, of his pleasures; so intimately entangled with your own that you no longer know whether you enjoyed that circus, because he enjoyed it with a joy that was more than enough for you all.

His sadnesses will be yours too and there will be some. But even here there is gladness. Because he has you; because you care and he knows that you care, his sadnesses need never be solitary; his despair need never be desolation. Whatever the world must do to him, he has a safe haven in you.

You have made the most important thing there is: a new person. New though he still is, he is ready to start being a person among other people just so long as you are always there for him to come back to. When he was a crawler he left your feet to journey to the sofa and bring you a ball. When he was a toddler he left your side to journey across the grass and bring you a leaf. When he was a pre-school child he left your garden to journey next door and bring you back his neighbour's doll. Now he will journey into school and bring you back pieces of his new world.

He will bring you his teachers, holding them up to you for comment with cries of "my teacher says. . . ."

He will bring you his friends and his enemies, recounting their games, boasts and exploits, waiting for you to help him fit them into the jigsaw puzzle of people.

He will bring you proud and disunited facts to be admired and put into context. Above all, he will bring you himself, to prepare for his next launching.

His journeys are all outwards now, into that waiting world. But he feels the invisible and infinitely elastic threads that still guide him back to you. He returns to the base that is you, seeking rest and re-charging for each new leap into life.

With you they have built security.
Now they will go out into a wider world . . .

. . . and from that world they will bring you
their bangs and bumps and scratches

. . . their triumphs and their new-found strengths

*. . . returning to recharge
the bond for each
new leap into life.*

Encyclopedia/Index

A

**'ACCIDENT-PRONE'
CHILDREN** 410-411
**ACCIDENTS, EMERGENCIES
AND FIRST AID** *see* BITES;
BLEEDING; BLISTERS; BRUISES; BURNS
AND SCALDS; CHOKING; CONCUSSION;
CUTS AND GRAZES; DISLOCATIONS;
DROWNING; ELECTRIC SHOCK;
EYES/Injuries; FINGER AND TOE
INJURIES; FIRST AID SUPPLIES;
FRACTURES; HEAD INJURIES;
MOUTH-TO-MOUTH RESUSCITATION;
MULTIPLE MINOR INJURIES;
NOSEBLEEDS; PENIS/Caught in zip
fastener; POISONING; SHOCK;
SPLINTERS; SPRAINS AND STRAINS;
STINGS; SWALLOWED OBJECTS;
UNCONSCIOUSNESS; EMERGENCIES
pp.510-512

Your general approach to accidents is important. The minor bumps and grazes are an everyday part of your exploring child's learning-by-experience. If you try too hard to protect him from them you will make him less able to avoid them for himself. If you offer too much sympathy too soon you will make him feel that getting even slightly hurt is a serious matter and/or a way of getting attention. More serious accidents obviously have to be treated on their merits but even here your attitudes are almost as important as your actions.

Minor accidents
☐ Don't overdo hygiene. If you clean, use only water; antiseptics are unnecessary and can be damaging.
☐ Don't overdo dressings. If you do dress a wound, use plain adhesive dressings and don't make them airtight.
Serious accidents
☐ Try to appear calm: pain and fear form a vicious circle, each increasing the other.
☐ Keep first aid to a minimum. Your job is to get medical attention for him quickly and to make sure that matters do not get worse in the interim. Leave elaborate bandaging, splinting etc. to the experts.
☐ Watch the child; the effects of shock can have serious consequences.
☐ Stay with him while he is treated. Only your presence will assure him that you approve of his treatment.

ADENOIDS

These are bodies of 'lymphoid tissue' to either side of the base of the child's nose. Like the tonsils, they guard against infection.

Enlarged adenoids can make a child breathe through his mouth or have a perpetually 'stuffy' nose. More importantly, they can contribute to repeated ear troubles. They are so placed that they can partially block the eustachian tubes which run from the back of the throat to the middle ear, and block the free passage of matter down the nose. The result can be infection of the middle ear called 'otitis media'. Otitis media can damage hearing by causing repeated scarring of the inside of the ear. So if enlarged adenoids are contributing to the attacks, their removal may be recommended.

Adenoidectomy Removal of the adenoids will be carried out without the tonsils being touched if the child is under four. If he is older than this then both his adenoids and his tonsils will be removed at the same operation. Equally, an older child who is having his tonsils removed will probably have his adenoids taken out at the same time.

If a child under, say, seven faces removal of tonsils and adenoids, it is a good thing if you can go into hospital with him and share in his care until he is recovered. *See* FEAR

ALLERGIC RHINITIS

The child is allergic to something he breathes. The mucous membranes in the nose swell and discharge clear fluid. The eyes may also be red and watery. He may sneeze.

Hay fever This is the most common type, the allergen being one of the many pollens released during spring and early summer.

Seasonal allergic rhinitis This occurs in the autumn. The allergen is one of the moulds which form on plants as they die down and on root crops brought in for winter storage.

Perennial allergic rhinitis This can be due to many allergens. The house mite is especially suspect if the condition worsens in winter.

Distinguishing allergic rhinitis from a head cold depends on noting the nasal discharge. In a cold the nose is obstructed by a thick discharge. In rhinitis it is obstructed by internal swelling, while the discharge is watery.

Although seldom more than tiresome in itself allergic rhinitis can presage asthma in a child generally prone to allergy. So consult your doctor during his first attack.

Avoidance of the allergen if it is known is the best 'treatment', otherwise medically supervised use of nasal decongestants and/or antihistamine medicines may give some relief.

ALLERGIES food 139, 141, 210, 370 *see* ALLERGIC RHINITIS; ASTHMA; ECZEMA; URTICARIA

The world and everything in it teems with micro-organisms. Most are harmless and cause no reaction in the body. Potentially harmful ones induce our bodies to manufacture antibodies against them.

An allergic individual's body fails to differentiate between harmless and harmful substances. An allergic child may manufacture antibodies against house dust or pollen as well as against illness-inducing bacteria and viruses.

Allergen This is the term used to describe any substance causing an allergic reaction. Most allergens are proteins, ranging from familiar food proteins such as egg white to unexpected or invisible ones like fleas or fungus spores.

When allergen meets antibody Local reaction causes small blood vessels to dilate and leak fluid into surrounding tissue, which swells. Excess mucus is produced. There may be muscle spasm.

Allergic symptoms The local reaction is always the same but the symptoms to which it gives rise depend where in the body the 'fight' is located. If allergen meets antibody in the nose, the child will have allergic rhinitis; if in the bronchi he will have asthma; if on the skin he may have urticaria or eczema. Although allergic disorders seem very different from each other they are all due to the same syndrome of over-reactivity.

Inheritance A tendency to allergic reactions runs in families although the form taken may differ; a father with hay fever due to pollens may have a child with frequent urticaria due to foodstuffs.

Factors affecting allergic illness The particular disorder to which an allergic child is liable varies with outside circumstances.

☐ Age is important. Untreated, he will probably have infantile eczema as a baby, asthma as a child and hay fever as an adult. Both the allergens which trigger his allergic responses, and the parts of his body which react, change with age.

☐ The degree of exposure to allergens is important. Intolerance of cow's milk protein can make a baby newly weaned from breast to bottle violently ill. Substitution of soya bean milk not only improves his symptoms but may make him able to tolerate a little cow's milk in his other foods.

☐ Infections play an important though ill-understood part. The child may be allergic to the actual agents of infection, made more susceptible to infection by his allergy or have his sensitivity to other allergens increased by the presence of infection. Whatever the causal connection, a cold is likely to precipitate asthma or a vaccination a major exacerbation of eczema in susceptible children.

☐ Stress and high emotion exacerbate allergic symptoms too. But this is a difficult area because over-protection can lead to invalidism and further stress while the attacks themselves (especially in frightening disorders like asthma) *cause* stress. Unless symptoms are so severe that they must be avoided at any cost, it is usually best to play down this aspect, treating allergic reactions to stress much as you would treat another child's stress reactions in the form of tantrums or comfort habits.

Diagnosis and treatment There is no treatment for the allergic tendency. We cannot force the child's body to confine its manufacture of antibodies to harmful substances. The aim must be symptom-control.

☐ Mild disorders may diagnose themselves (like the hay fever that occurs when, and only when, the pollen count is high) and vanish without treatment like transient urticaria.

☐ Some serious allergies (especially to foods and to drugs like penicillin) can only effectively be dealt with by avoidance. If some unidentified item of diet is upsetting a child, the doctor may ask you to record the relationship between meals and symptoms and then to exclude suspect foods one at a time, until the allergen becomes clear. If the food to be avoided is a socially difficult one, like cow's milk or chocolate, he will work with you to reintroduce minute quantities, slowly, hoping to persuade the child's body to tolerate enough for him to have a normal diet.

☐ You cannot always avoid stings etc. so life-threatening allergic reactions like anaphylactic shock will mean de-sensitization after the first emergency. The doctor will test the child with a series of much diluted poisons until he finds the one that causes a red weal to rise on the site of his test-scratch. Then a series of injections of diluted allergen will be given, increasing in strength but staying within his body's rising tolerance. The aim is to persuade him to produce special extra antibodies which will bind to the injected allergen thus preventing a reaction between his sensitizing antibodies and any new dose.

☐ Symptomatic treatment without diagnosis is the best that can be offered if the child is sensitive to many common substances. Attempts to identify, avoid and/or de-sensitize him against numerous dusts etc. would cause more distress than do the symptoms. The doctor will rely on medicines (such as antihistamines) to reduce the reaction during attacks of hay fever or urticaria, and on various ointments to relieve the itching of skin reactions such as infantile eczema.

Overall management Many allergic children have at least one stage in their lives when no single approach is adequate. The doctor will use some avoidance, some de-sensitization and some medication in order to keep allergic attacks as few and as mild as possible. If he is to do the best possible job, he needs to know the child and all his circumstances well; if you have an allergic child, you need a doctor whom you like and trust with the family skeletons as well as the family 'flu'.

ANGER AND FRUSTRATION
156, 158, 194, 233-235, 266, 407, 411; in achieving independence 288, 311, 314, 323, 411, 421; with objects 177, 323-324, 423; with own body and size 241, 243, 324, 327, 410; at physical punishment 440; with playmates 402-404, 408, 411-412; releasing in physical play 348; in tantrums 291, 318-319, 324-327, 441, 442-443 *see* CRYING AND COMFORTING

ANIMALS *see* PETS

ANTIBODIES in breast milk 49, 50 *see also* ALLERGIES; IMMUNIZATION; RHESUS DISEASE

ANXIETY and
accident-proneness 410; in baby whose needs are not met 194, 199, 200, 218; at night 221, 302, 377-379; in pre-school period 390-392; about sex 413; about talking 420; in toddlers 318-322, 327, 330; about wetting himself 383-385 *see* ATTACHMENT TO YOU; CRYING AND COMFORTING; FEAR; SOOTHING

APPENDICITIS *see* APPENDIX; STOMACH-ACHE

APPENDIX
The appendix is a small blind tube leading off the lower part of the intestine. It seems to serve no purpose and, being a 'dead end' with no through drainage, is liable to infection. Infection leads to inflammation, with pain, often vomiting, sometimes fever. The child has appendicitis.

Appendectomy If a child really has got appendicitis it is essential to remove the appendix before it becomes so inflamed and infected that it bursts, spreading infection through the abdomen.

Diagnosing appendicitis is difficult but because it can be so serious if neglected, doctors will 'play safe' and therefore sometimes find themselves removing a normal appendix.

Provided the appendix has not burst, the operation is simple and the child recovers quickly. Although he will have considerable pain for two or three days after surgery, it is important that he should breathe deeply and cough freely to prevent pneumonia. Constipation can be a problem, too, as the child is terrified to strain. If you are rooming-in at the hospital or at least spending all day with him, you can help with these vital matters under direction from the nurses. They know what should be done, but you know the child.

APPETITE *see* FEEDING

ARTIFICIAL RESPIRATION *see* MOUTH-TO-MOUTH RESUSCITATION

ASTHMA
Asthma is an allergic condition. The allergen is in the air the child breathes and the reaction with his antibodies takes place in the bronchi (breathing tubes), leading to an outpouring of mucus, which gives his breathing the characteristic 'wheeze', and to muscle spasm, which makes the process of breathing (especially breathing out) difficult. A severely asthmatic child may always be wheezy and breathless on exertion, but an asthma attack is a different and dramatic event.

Attacks These usually take place at night. The child wakes, unable to release his breath in order to take in the next. Panic tenses muscles and tears take breath he cannot spare.

What to do
☐ On the first occasion summon the doctor urgently. There are other causes for frightening breathlessness. He must make sure it is asthma, if so, he can cut the attack short.
☐ While you wait, sit the child up and calm him as much as you can. If he is old enough to understand, assure him that whatever it feels like enough air *will* get through. Explain that the more he can relax the easier it will be. Reading aloud may help.

After the first attack With your doctor's help, identify at least the principal allergens so as to avoid heavy concentrations. Feathers, down, animal hair and natural wool are all common ones, but most common of all is the 'house mite', a microscopic creature which lives off shed dead scales of human skin in house dust.

You cannot clear any house of mites but you can reduce the population especially in the child's bedroom. Plastic foam mattresses and upholstery, hard floors with washable rugs laundered weekly, unlined cotton curtains and synthetic continental quilts instead of conventional bedding will all prove inhospitable to the mites. Damp dusting will prevent their precipitation into the air, while frequent washing of clothing etc. will prevent a build-up. In a serious case the child may have to keep toys, books etc. elsewhere so that he does not spend all night breathing their inevitable dust.

Work is being carried out on de-sensitizing children to the house mite but the procedure has not so far proved satisfactory.

Treatment of subsequent attacks It may not be necessary to call the doctor for each attack once the diagnosis is established. He will instruct you on the administration of drugs to relax the muscle spasms, liquefy the mucus and/or relieve his anxiety. They can be administered by mouth or by inhalation if he cannot swallow. During a severe attack administration by the doctor via injection or suppository works faster.

Overall treatment of the child Repeated severe attacks of asthma can eventually damage a child's lungs and produce a 'pigeon chest'. Physiotherapy to clear mucus from the bronchi and to teach the child correct breathing techniques is vital.

If the asthma is often precipitated by infections your doctor may ask to be called at each sign of illness so that he can give antibiotics early if they are appropriate. Long-term antibiotic treatment may be given to protect the child during winter.

The doctor will also want to discuss emotional and environmental precipitating factors. Don't be offended when the consultation turns to your discipline and your dust. *See* ALLERGIES

ATHLETE'S FOOT *see* RINGWORM
ATTACHMENT TO YOU
119-124, 197-200; clinginess 197-200, 275, 318, 319, 332, 333, 390, 393, 396-397, 441; distinguishing you from others 32, 120, 197-200, 232-233, 275, 424, 441; through listening to voices 32, 51, 114-115, 120, 180, 181, 182, 260-261; through looking at faces 32, 51, 114-115, 119-120, 155, 180; making you special 34, 36, 120, 122, 155, 195, 197-198, 215-216, 267, 273, 390; shyness 200, 319, 393; smiling 116, 120, 180, 182, 198, 200; *see* FEAR

B

BABY ALARM 93, 304, 378
BABY BATTERING
Every parent shares the feelings of acute irritation, frustration and stress which lie behind the actions of the few who are violently cruel to their children.

Battering of babies is usually the result of continual crying. Battering of older children usually starts as 'discipline'. Both form a vicious circle. The baby cries and will not stop; losing control, the parent shakes him so he cries more and is shaken harder. . . . The child soils his pants and is walloped. Shaken and furious, he wets himself. His apparent defiance earns him worse 'punishment'. . . . Recognize the edges of the circle and you can still escape; let yourself be drawn in and you are trapped in a whirlpool.

Many parents do recognize the edges. Women leave the house at 2 am not from negligence but from fear of throwing their crying child from the window. Doors are locked not to keep children in but to keep parents, who have used the last of their self-control to turn that key—out.

If you feel the edges of that whirlpool ask for help *now*. Your feelings are nothing to be ashamed of and you have not taken shameful action yet.

If you know someone trapped in it, ask for help for him or her. Just dismissing the battering parent as a monster helps nobody—least of all the child. No parent chooses to be cruel. *See* USEFUL ADDRESSES
BABY BOUNCER 158, 349 *see*
PLAYTHINGS
BABYFOODS *see* FOODS
BABYMILKS *see* MILK/Formula
BABY-SITTING 122, 295, 378, 379, 393-394, 419
BABY TALK 183, 265-266, 362, 420-421 *see* TALKING
BABYWALKER 330, 349 *see*
PLAYTHINGS
BACTERIA *see* HYGIENE;
GASTRO-ENTERITIS
BATHING first days 84, 96, 105; first six months 152-153; six months to one year 226-227; one year to two and a half 312
BEDROOM child's own 216, 268, 375-376; heating 81, 221; moving baby from your room 93, 94; night lighting 92, 223, 301, 376; sharing 223, 375, 379, 380
BEDS AND COTS drop-side cots 93, 302-304; making baby's 93; double bed as play-place 190, 349; promoting to big bed 304, 375; types 93 *see* PRAMS

First beds A cradle or Moses basket is the conventional first bed but is not a necessity. You will probably find a carry cot is more convenient. If you use a carry cot on a stand, check that the stand itself cannot tip and that it has rails at all four sides, into which the cot drops, so that it cannot be tipped off.

A carry cot is not well insulated and not all have a hood. The baby cannot sleep outside in it unless the weather is superb. Used with a 'transporter' the baby may have a very rough ride because in the less expensive models the wheeled base is not sprung. All in all a carry cot and transporter do not add up to a pram. They are ideal for indoor use and for car travel.

A detachable pram top with a folding chassis can be used both as carry cot and pram. Remember, though, that the top may be too heavy for you to carry by yourself. You may need a carry cot as well.

Cots The baby needs a drop-sided cot by the time he is beginning even to try to sit up—usually at 4-5 months. He could sleep in one from birth, but it is difficult to make him cosy in such a large draughty space, and a bed you cannot move from room to room will exclude him from family life.

451

Most babies get very attached to their cots, so don't hurry to transfer him to a big bed. He could stay in his cot until he is three. If another baby is coming along, buy or borrow a second cot; otherwise promote him well before the birth so that the toddler does not feel that the new baby has got 'his' cot. Best of all put it right away for a few months and then repaint it so that the toddler never takes in the fact that it used to be his.

Beds His first real bed should be a full-sized one. Junior beds only last for about 5 or 6 years and are not really worth the money. Detachable safety rails (which fasten under the mattress and run about one third of the way along the bed) will both make the child feel safer since he is used to being 'railed in' and will discourage climbing or falling out.

It is vital that a child should have his own bed to sleep in. If a space-problem is otherwise insuperable, a double bunk set may solve it, although sleeping on top of each other will reduce each child's feeling of privacy. Put your oldest child in the top bunk and make sure that the safety rail is adequate. If it is not you can add a rail made of 1½ in. × 1½ in. (3.8 cm × 3.8 cm) timber, yourself. Bed-making will be much easier with fitted bottom sheets and continental quilts (duvets).

Folding guest beds or divan sets where one bed fits under the other during the day save space but deprive the child of his own constantly available safe place of retreat. *See* SAFETY

BEDWETTING 375, 377, 380, 384-385
This is usual until three years, common until five and by no means rare until seven, especially in boys. The wetting is involuntary so no system of punishment/reward is effective; it may make matters worse by increasing the child's tension. The matter is best ignored unless the child himself asks for help. If he does, 'lifting' him last thing at night may help. If he is really concerned, a doctor can recommend a 'bell and pad' system. When the pad beneath him is moistened with urine the bell rings and awakens him. Over weeks/months he learns to wake to the sensations alone without help from the alarm bell. It does not work for all children; it is dependent on the child's willing cooperation and should be reserved for over-sevens.

BIBS *see* FEEDING EQUIPMENT
BICYCLES AND TRICYCLES
349, 408, 410, 431; *see* PLAYTHINGS; SAFETY
BIRTH 26-29

BIRTH/Formalities after
The Medical Officer of Health must be notified of every birth within 36 hours. If the baby is born in hospital this is done by the staff. If he is born at home, the doctor or midwife who delivers him will do it. Should you deliver a baby without medical help, you must notify the Medical Officer yourself.

Registration Every baby also has to be registered, so that he can have a formal birth certificate. Most hospitals arrange regular visits from the local registrar so that the child can be registered before he is taken home. A baby born at home must be registered at your local town hall within six weeks of the birth.

Other documents Along with the birth certificate you are given a medical card so that the baby can be added to a National Health Service list, as well as a card for the Department of Health and Social Security, which allows babyfoods and vitamins to be bought at child health clinics.

BIRTHMARKS 42
BIRTHWEIGHT 37-41, 78; average 37; heavy 38; light 38; *see* GROWTH; 506-508

BITES
Families travelling abroad should always get information in advance about the hazards such as snake bites etc. of the specific area to which they are going.

Many children find minor bites and stings more frightening than a more serious injury from another cause because they feel 'attacked'. Reassurance is vital.

Cats and dogs A bite or scratch which has only just broken the skin can be treated at home.
□ Wash the wound under cold running water, dry it and cover with a dry adhesive dressing.
□ Inspect it next day to make sure there is no redness around it which might suggest infection.
□ A deep bite, a single tooth puncture whose bottom you cannot see, or a severe scratch should be treated as above, but also shown immediately to a doctor or hospital casualty department. Treatment may be needed to prevent infection and the child may have to have an anti-tetanus booster injection, especially if the injury was caused by a dog.

Guinea pigs, hamsters These small pets often bite but very seldom do more than make a tiny graze in the skin or a pin prick puncture.
□ Wash the wound under cold running water. Dry and cover with an adhesive dressing.

Horses Many ponies and horses 'nip'. Such a bite may bruise but seldom breaks the skin.

Snakes Very small children are usually the worst affected by snake bites. If you are in an area infested with venomous snakes, take local advice on recognition and action. If a child is bitten he should be treated as follows:
□ Reassure and comfort the child. Fear may induce SHOCK even if there is little poison in the system. The bite will hurt.
□ Lie him down. If he keeps still the spread of poison will be delayed.
□ Wash the wound to get rid of any venom which may still be on the skin around the puncture. If you have no water gently wipe it, using your own saliva.
□ Get the child to hospital keeping the bitten limb as still as possible. An injection of anti-venin or anti-tetanus may be given and a small child may be kept in hospital overnight.
NB Avoid heroic measures like cutting open the wound. You are more liable to do harm than good.

BLACK EYE *see* EYES/Injuries
BLADDER CONTROL *see* BEDWETTING; TOILET TRAINING

BLEEDING
Although your child may hate the sight of it, blood which oozes is never dangerous and is usually valuable in carrying dirt etc. out of the wound.

Heavy bleeding Blood dripping from a cut or running down an injured limb will take a very long time to reach critical levels. You can easily stop it with pressure which will seal the cut edges of the blood vessels while the escaped blood clots to form a self-seal.

What to do
□ Press gently on the wound with the inner side of a clean ironed handkerchief or with a piece of gauze dressing. Two minutes pressure should stop it.
□ Remove pressure gently and dress the wound with an adhesive dressing.
□ If bleeding has not stopped but is still oozing, dress it all the same and wait to see whether blood comes through the dressing. It probably will not.

□ If blood is still dripping steadily after pressure, try for two more minutes. If it still drips after that, take the child to your local casualty department. The bleeding itself is still not dangerous, but the wound may be deep enough to require stitching to help it heal.

Dangerous bleeding If blood spurts from a wound, it suggests a cut artery. Each heart beat is sending blood through the cut as it pushes it around the body. Because of the blood pressure, such bleeding cannot clot to seal the wound.

What to do This is an emergency; a time to forget hygiene and even to ignore the child's pain.

□ Press directly on the spurting wound—hard. Use a handkerchief if you have one, your fingers if not. Raise the injured part above heart level to reduce the flow of blood.

□ If blood spurts around your pressure, you must find an underlying bone to compress the cut vessel against. Try just above the wound. If the spurting slows, you have found the right 'pressure point'. Don't move your fingers or relax the pressure.

□ If the wound is in a place you cannot span with pressing fingers, such as the groin or armpit, lie the child down and use your closed fist or a balled handkerchief to press the wound up against the bone.

□ If you can carry the child without releasing your pressure, take him to the telephone or to a place from which you can shout for help.

□ If you must leave him to get help, replace your pressure with pressure from something hard. Outside you may be able to reach a smooth stone. Press that on the wound and bandage on tightly with your scarf or any garment you can get off. Indoors, the bowl of a spoon bandaged on with a tea towel will do. Check that your 'pressure bandage' has stopped the spurting as your hand did, then go for help—fast.

NB Don't drive the child to hospital yourself if there is any other hope of help. If the pressure should fail and spurting start again, you would have to stop.

Don't try to use a tourniquet to control arterial bleeding. It is far more difficult than old-fashioned first aid manuals imply and it is also very dangerous as a successful tourniquet cuts off blood from all the vessels to the damaged area, not just from the cut one.

See 510-512; CUTS AND GRAZES; NOSEBLEEDS; SHOCK; STITCHES

BLISTERS sucking 44
Apart from burns, friction is the most usual cause of blistering. The outer layer of the skin separates from the inner layer. Fluid from the inner layer seeps out. Eventually the fluid inside the blister is reabsorbed, and the dead outer skin peels away, leaving a new layer of healed skin underneath.

What to do
□ Don't remove or prick the blister. The skin underneath it will be raw and extremely sore.

□ Protect it from further friction by covering it with a 'ring doughnut' shape of dry lint with an adhesive dressing over it, or with a ring-shaped corn plaster.

□ Check the shoes that caused the blistering. If the fit is wrong, discard them. If the child simply wore them without socks, try them, with socks, when the foot is completely healed.

BLOOD TESTS *see* INJECTIONS AND BLOOD TESTS

BOILS AND PIMPLES
Every hair grows from its root to the surface of the skin along a channel called a 'hair follicle'.

Pimples If an infection starts where the hair emerges from the skin a white pimple forms containing a tiny amount of pus which will discharge itself in a day or so. Let it alone.

Boils Infection occurs lower down near the root of the hair. The boil starts as a hard red tender lump which gets bigger and more painful until it makes a 'head' and the pus escapes. This usually takes two or three days. Since infection spreads very easily from one hair follicle to another, boils often appear in crops. They are especially likely if a child has been ill or is below par for some reason when his resistance will be lowered.

What to do Take the child to the doctor if:
□ A boil does not come to a head within five days.

□ It is in an awkward place such as the ear, the armpit or on the bottom of a child in nappies.

□ You can see red streaks under the skin running from it.

□ The child has swollen tender glands in the area.

For home treatment:
□ Clean the skin around the boil with surgical spirit; this may help to prevent one boil turning into a crop of boils.

□ Dress the boil by stretching an adhesive dressing across it; this will lessen the pain by preventing too much movement and pulling by the surrounding skin.

N.B. Don't squeeze a boil. You may force the pus downwards. Don't use hot fomentations. They hurt a great deal and may also spread the infection. Don't use antiseptic or ointments unless prescribed by a doctor. They do no good, and they too may spread the infection.

BREASTS abscesses in 53; baby's 44; breast pump 41; care of in breast-feeding 62; engorged 52-53, 63; hard, sore lumps in 53; leaking milk 54, 62, 63, 127; nipples: cracked 53, 54, dry and flaky 62, hardened 62, soggy 62, sore 53, 61, 62; overfull of milk 54, 63, 127, 202; size and shape 51, 52, 61; *see* BREAST-FEEDING; MILK

BREATH HOLDING 325
Occasionally a child who is having a tantrum or screaming with pain holds his breath for so long that he turns from scarlet to greyish blue. He may even go into a convulsion. Breath holding looks alarming but is not dangerous. It is quite impossible for anyone to hold their breath long enough to harm themselves. If he holds it for so long that he becomes unconscious, reflex breathing will instantly take over. Don't make dramatic attempts to force the child to draw breath. The more attention he gets this time, the more likely he is to do it next time. Breath holding can become a habit, indulged in whenever he is in a rage.

BRIBES AND PRIZES 443
BRONCHITIS *see* COLDS
BROTHERS AND SISTERS *see* GETTING ON WITH OTHER CHILDREN
BRUISES
A bruise appears when blood vessels under the skin are crushed or broken and blood escapes into the tissue. The area looks red at first then bluish/black. As the escaped blood is broken down and reabsorbed the area looks greenish-yellow. It may take as much as two weeks for all signs of a bruise to disappear.
Trivial bruises These are a normal part of childhood needing no treatment. A very cold swab of cotton wool or gauze held over the place for half an hour may make the bruising less dramatic, but few children would think the effort of keeping still worthwhile.
Extensive bruising If a child has a fall so bad that he bruises himself over a large area, you will probably have to treat him for minor shock, and have him checked by a doctor.
  Remember that the bruising does mean that the child is bleeding even though he is doing it inside so that you cannot actually see the blood.
Excessive bruising Parents sometimes worry because their child seems to bruise very easily—out of proportion to the knocks and bumps he takes. Small children's skin is soft compared with older people's. Very fair children's skin

shows marks which would not be visible on a darker child. If you are really concerned about this, by all means take the child to your doctor and let him decide whether there is any problem, but unless he also bleeds excessively, or for a long time, from minor cuts etc., there almost certainly is not.

BURNS AND SCALDS
These do not only affect the skin you can see. Heat penetrates to blood vessels below the skin, dilates them and lets the colourless part of the blood (the plasma) escape. In a minor burn this escaped plasma becomes trapped in a blister. In a burn that removes the skin altogether plasma weeps from the raw area. Although only the clear part of the blood is lost, its loss reduces the total volume of fluid available to the circulation. This is why large burns and scalds so often lead to shock and why fluid-replacement by transfusion is such a vital part of hospital treatment. Judge the seriousness of a burn or scald by its area, not its depth.

☐ If a burn covers more than half a square inch of skin, show it to a doctor.

☐ If a burn covers an area more than the size of your hand, it is potentially serious. Rush the child to hospital.

First aid
☐ Stop heat from burned skin penetrating deeper tissues by instantly cooling the whole area. Put a finger under the cold tap or a seriously burned child into a cold bath. Continue cooling for ten minutes. This will help blood vessels which have been damaged already to close up again and prevent further loss of plasma. Cooling will also stop the pain—temporarily.

☐ If clothes are soaked in boiling water, oil, acids or alkalis, the heat or chemicals will be trapped by them. Tear the clothes off as you run the cold tap.

☐ If the burned or scalded area merits medical treatment, wrap the cooled child in a freshly laundered sheet to keep air-borne bacteria from his raw skin. Get him to hospital immediately.
  For burns small enough to treat at home: Don't interfere with a blister. It protects raw skin from infection and prevents further plasma-leakage. Don't use any ointment or grease. Apply nothing but a sterile adhesive dressing to protect it from rubbing.

Scalds can mislead you If a large area of skin is reddened but no blisters form, you may be tempted to assume no damage has been done. Don't. Fluid leakage is taking place slowly under the skin. Cool the skin and rush him to hospital. Scalds in the mouth are best cooled by sucking ice. If none is available, get the child to sip icy cold water through a straw (so it emerges near the burned area) or from a bottle.
Electrical burns look trivial You can usually only see a blackened pinpoint because the electrical contact has closed up the skin's blood vessels so there can be no superficial blister. But underneath the current will have fanned out. There may be a big wedge of burned tissue under that normal-looking skin. All electrical burns should be seen by a doctor at once.
Pain may surprise you Burns and scalds hurt more than any other kind of wound. Even tiny ones upset children badly. Muster all the calm comfort you have. *See* SAFETY; SHOCK; 510-512

BURPING *see* FEEDING

C

CAR JOURNEYS *see* PLAYTHINGS; TRAVEL SICKNESS; SAFETY
CARRY COTS *see* BEDS AND COTS
CAT-NET 93, 401
CHAIRS for car *see* SAFETY; high chair 144, 192, 239; infant seat 144, 163, 239; starting to use ordinary chairs 144, 370
CHEWING importance of learning 154-155, 211; pureed foods 141; suitable foods for 145, 154-155, 214, 231
CHICKENPOX
Incubation period 17–21 days
First signs
☐ Possibly slightly off colour for 1–2 days, but often no warning at all.
Definite signs
☐ Small dark red pimples appear and within hours turn into blisters that look like drops of water on the skin. The fragile blisters rub off, leaving raw places which then scab. While the first batch are changing, a new batch of pimples is appearing. This goes on over 3–4 days so that the child has spots in every stage of development and healing.
Degree of illness
☐ Usually very minor; child may not feel ill at all. Older children can be extremely ill with high fever.
Possible complications
☐ A really copious rash may cover the child including scalp, inside the mouth, ears, vagina and anus.

The tremendous itching/scratching can mean very disturbed nights and infected blisters which will leave scars.

What the doctor may do
□ Prescribe an ointment to help prevent infection of scratched spots in nappy area.
□ Possibly consider a sedative for extreme itching at night.

What you can do
□ Help the itching by giving frequent lukewarm baths with a cupful of bicarbonate of soda dissolved in each. In between dab spots with calamine lotion—a pre-school child may like to have his own lotion and cotton wool; being allowed to do it himself may prevent him scratching.
□ Leave a baby without nappies as much as possible.
□ Keep the fingernails short and as clean as you possibly can. *See* NURSING

CHILD ABUSE *see* BABY BATTERING

CHILLING 80-81; disturbing baby's sleep 90, 93, 97, 148, 220-221

CHOKING 61, 74, 93, 140, 145, 155, 158, 203
Choking occurs when food, drink or a foreign body goes into the passage to the lungs instead of the passage to the stomach. Coughing and spluttering is the body's very efficient method of getting it back up into the throat.

What to do
□ As long as the child keeps coughing and is not turning blue or grey in the face, there is nothing to worry about. He is getting plenty of air past the obstruction and he will 'cough it up' for himself. A series of sharp pats on his back, between his shoulder blades, may speed things up. Coughed back food or drink may be expelled so violently that it actually goes up into his nose. It is painful (especially if the substance is acidic) but not dangerous.
Choking on objects can be much more serious as something round, such as a button or marble, can become wedged at the back of the throat blocking the air passage.
□ If the child is coughing, don't worry too much; he must be getting some air past it or he could not cough. Put him across your forearm or knee so that his head and chest are lower than his legs and hips, and pat him smartly between the shoulder blades until the object is coughed out.
□ If the child is not coughing but is gasping, turning scarlet and then

greyish, with an expression of panic, act fast. Open his mouth and put your finger boldly in to the back of his throat in case you can hook out the object. If you make him retch so much the better; this may dislodge it.
□ If you cannot hook it out immediately, call an ambulance, telling the despatcher that your child cannot breathe, or drive him to hospital yourself.
N.B. Carry him in the head down position all the time and keep banging his back.

CIRCUMCISION 47
A minor operation removing the foreskin from a boy's penis. Very seldom advisable in babies on medical grounds, it may be required for religious or social reasons. If a baby is not circumcised, his foreskin should be left strictly alone. Attempts to retract it for washing can cause tiny splits whose healing leaves scar tissue which may eventually fix the foreskin to the penis and make natural retraction impossible later. This is the most usual reason for circumcision becoming necessary in an older boy.
If your child must be circumcised after infancy, it may be better to leave the operation until school-age. It will very seldom be a medically urgent matter and the psychological upset to a toddler or pre-school child can be very great. *See* HOSPITAL

CLEANLINESS *see* EVERYDAY CARE; HYGIENE

CLIMBING out of bed 302-304; as physical play 348, 351, 406, 408, 411 *see* PLAYING AND LEARNING; PLAYTHINGS

CLINGINESS *see* ATTACHMENT TO YOU

CLOTHING 78, 80, 83, 226, 242, 314-315, 382, 387; dressing and undressing 83, 311 *see* NAPPIES; SHOES AND SOCKS

COLDS
These are caused by virus infection. Sitting in a draught, having wet feet, or going out without a coat cannot *cause* a cold, although severe chilling might possibly lower a child's resistance to an infection that his body was already fighting. Babies may be upset by even mild colds: they find the mouth-breathing necessitated by a blocked nose difficult, and need to breathe through their noses in order to suck. A doctor may recommend nose drops to clear the baby's nose so that he can at least feed comfortably.
Children often run a fever, or even vomit, at the beginning of a

cold. But once it is established they are seldom ill—only uncomfortable. It helps if the child is shown how to blow his nose effectively, by closing one nostril with a finger while he blows down the other. If he relies on sucking a dummy or his fingers or thumb for getting to sleep, there may be a case for using nose drops at bedtime for him too. But don't use them more often than your doctor recommends.

Complications Colds often get worse before they get better, because once the viruses have a foothold, they lower the child's resistance and can therefore multiply. Complications occasionally set in if, because of this lowered resistance, harmful bacteria enter, leading to 'secondary infections', like bronchitis, pneumonia or a middle ear infection. Suspect secondary infection if the child runs a fever after the first day, has a thick greenish-yellow nasal discharge; a thick or wheezy cough, sore throat, earache or deafness, or seems ill, lethargic, lacking in appetite.
While a doctor cannot prescribe medicines which are specifically against *viruses* he can prescribe antibiotics against *bacteria*. Call him as soon as a common cold begins to look unusual.

COLD SORES (HERPES SIMPLEX)
Some people, children and adults, are carriers of a virus called herpes simplex. Most of the time the virus remains dormant, although the child can pass it on and nothing can be done to stop this.
When he is run down, usually when he has a cold (which is where this infection gets its popular, but inaccurate, name) the virus attacks. The first attack usually takes the form of a crop of extremely painful ulcers in the mouth (*see* Mouth ulcers). Later attacks take the form of unpleasant sores round the mouth or nostrils, starting as red patches, becoming open and weepy and then forming crusty scabs which tend to crack.

What to do Cold sores are very liable to become infected. Your doctor may prescribe an antibiotic ointment with a greasy base which will protect against infection and cracking. The cold sore will vanish in about a week.

COLIC 101-102, 148
COLOSTRUM *see* MILK/Breast

COLOUR BLINDNESS
This affects about eight in 100 boys and one in 200 girls. The usual confusion is between red and green but others are possible.

Diagnosing it early is difficult as the child confuses the names given to colours and may seem colour-blind when he is not. The problem should be obvious by the time he is four years old.

Warn all teachers. Colour coding is extensively used in teaching—especially maths. Help will be needed. Remember that traffic lights are red/green and that 'red for danger' is a common signal on machinery etc. Protect him.

COMFORT HABITS 216-218; cuddlies and soft toys 190, 217, 218, 220, 301, 318, 319, 347, 376; dummies 100, 157, 167, 203, 217, 301, 317; ear-twisting 218; finger and thumbsucking 50, 100, 157, 203, 204, 217, 306; head banging 218; hair-twiddling 218; manipulating parts of own body 218; nightlights 92, 216, 301, 319, 380, 384; rituals 218, 220, 295, 300, 319, 347, 376; rocking 99-100, 217, 218; sweets 291, 373; *see* HEAD BANGING; MASTURBATION; NAIL-BITING; SUCKING

It is good for a baby or small child to be able to give himself comfort. It means that he can be a little more self-reliant; not quite so dependent on the adult world with all its whims. Nearly all babies use sucking or cuddlies for this sort of comforting. A great many adopt rhythmical habits, such as rocking, pulling their hair, twisting their ears, or grinding their jaws. But needing to comfort himself a great deal, especially in the daytime when there are potentially comforting adults around, means that something is not quite right for the child: either things are making him frequently miserable or the adult world is not offering him enough of the kind of comfort he needs so he is being forced to invent his own. See whether offering lots of extra company, cuddling and play reduces his use of comfort habits to sleep times and occasional day-time use only. If he appears to *prefer* his own solitary rocking to your affectionate attention, seek advice from your clinic or doctor.

CONCEPTS AND ABSTRACT IDEAS formation of, in toddler 278, 336, 341-342, 344-347, 353; development of, in pre-school child 366, 399; and language 341-342, 361, 414-417, 422, 424, 429-431

CONCUSSION
The skull protects the brain. A bang on the head or a tremendous shaking can cause the brain to bang itself against the skull. The result is concussion.

A concussed child will lose consciousness for anything from a second to many days. Even momentary loss of consciousness should be taken seriously. Lie the child down. Treat him for shock.

Occasionally what seems to you and the doctor to be a very mild concussion, requiring only a few hours rest, may turn out to be more serious. Some of the blood vessels inside the brain may have been damaged. They may bleed, slowly. The blood is trapped inside the skull so that as it clots it presses into the brain's surface. This possibility means that you should keep a careful eye on a child who has been concussed, over the subsequent 24 hours. If he develops severe headache, dizziness, impaired vision or odd-looking eyes, difficulties with balance or speech, vomiting, exceptional drowsiness or confused or irrational behaviour, send for an ambulance.

If a blood clot (sub-dural haematoma) is diagnosed, it may have to be removed surgically to relieve the pressure on the brain. *See* HEAD INJURIES; UNCONSCIOUSNESS

CONJUNCTIVITIS ('PINK EYE') *see* EYES/Infections

CONSTIPATION 88, 149, 224 *see* LAXATIVES
Left to themselves, the bowels empty by reflex as soon as the rectum is full. Each individual has his own pattern. It may be perfectly normal for a child only to pass a stool every three or four days, so constipation cannot correctly be diagnosed by the infrequency of stools, but only by their consistency. A dry, hard stool that is difficult and/or painful to pass is a constipated one.

CONTACT COMFORT need for in newborn 36, 82-83, 97-100, 101, 104, 105, 113, 120, 151, 156 *see* COMFORT HABITS

CONVULSIONS
Convulsions or 'fits' in young children are usually caused by a sudden rise in body temperature at the beginning of an illness. The sudden fever irritates the brain, which is less stable in young children than in older people. The irritated brain gives abnormal 'messages' to the nerves which, in their turn, 'instruct' the muscles to clench and contract.

The tendency to feverish convulsions usually runs in families. The first episode generally occurs between the ages of 2 and 3, and once the child has had one, he may

be liable to have another any time he runs a high temperature. He will outgrow the tendency by the time he reaches school age.

While one convulsion does the child no harm, a big one every couple of months is not good for him. The doctor may advise you to try to keep the child's temperature down whenever he is unwell and to give him a prescribed sedative medicine at the first signs of illness. During a period when he is completely well he may suggest that he should be tested to make quite sure that the convulsions *are* only fever convulsions, with no epileptic illness behind them.

Recognizing a convulsion The child may suddenly 'have a fit' while playing. He will become rigid, and then the muscles of his arms, legs and body will relax and clench again so he jerks and twitches. His entire body may be involved or only his limbs, his face may grimace and his teeth clench.

More often the child will have been asleep or dozing, perhaps twitching a little and seeming restless. In this case picking the child up or waking him will probably start the convulsion.

What to do The child will not die of the convulsion. It looks much worse than it really is. But it could be dangerous to leave him while you telephone or run for help.

□ Stay with him in case he vomits and inhales the vomit or injures himself by banging his head or by falling into the fire.

□ Put him on the floor if he is not already in bed on his side or on his front with his head turned.

□ Don't try to control his thrashing limbs; you may wrench a muscle or even cause a fracture.

□ Don't try to force open his mouth in case he bites his tongue; you are much more likely to damage his jaw than he is to damage the tongue.

The convulsion will only last a few seconds, or a minute or two at most. As soon as it ends, the child will either wake up and then drop straight into sleep, or he will pass straight from the unconsciousness of the convulsion into sleep. As soon as he is peaceful phone the doctor. While you wait for him, start cooling the child. Don't bother to take his temperature as the convulsion itself will have put it up. Just assume that it was too high. Take off all clothes except a bare minimum for comfort; cover him only with a sheet; sponge his face, arms and neck with warm water and let it dry. *See* FEVER

COT DEATHS

This term is used when a baby is put to bed in good health and then found dead. After the first week of life, cot deaths kill more babies than do illnesses and accidents put together. Causes are still not known; they are the subject of much research. But a cot death cannot be foreseen by anyone, not even by a doctor. Some victims have been pronounced healthy only hours before the tragedy. A cot death cannot be confused with death by violence or neglect. It is not the result of suffocation or careless babycare. There is no way such a baby could have been secretly damaged by his parents. A cot death must, by law, be subject to police enquiries and an inquest. This is because, by definition, the death is unexpected and unexplained. It is not because the parents are suspect.

Preventing cot deaths This will be impossible until the causes are unravelled, but there is some evidence that breast-fed babies are at lesser risk than bottle-fed ones, even if breast-feeding is brief. Pillows were used in a high proportion of cases; they did not smother the babies but may possibly have made breathing more difficult once it began to fail. More deaths take place in winter than summer. There is no evidence to suggest that cold is, or is not, a factor, but it is possible that temperatures perfectly adequate for a baby under normal circumstances make it more difficult for him to combat whatever condition it is that leads to his sudden death.

COTS *see* BEDS AND COTS

COUGHS

A child coughs because there is extra mucus somewhere in his upper respiratory system. The cough reflex is designed to rid his body of the mucus and is therefore valuable in itself.

The most usual reason for coughing is a simple cold. Mucus which does not appear as nasal discharge trickles down his throat, tickles and makes him cough. But the mucus may not be in his nose. It could be anywhere from deep in his lungs upwards. And it may not be caused by a cold. It could be caused by asthma, croup, bronchitis, whooping cough, pneumonia . . . so don't try to diagnose a cough yourself. Let the doctor do it.

Coughs with vomiting Usually mean only that the child has swallowed enough coughed-up mucus to

make him sick. As he vomits, his stomach muscles will press on his lungs and air passages, pressing out more of the mucus that is bothering him. So although unpleasant, the vomiting is not a bad thing.

Coughs with difficult breathing If the coughing child's breathing is noisy, difficult or painful, sucks in his lower ribs and/or distends his nostrils, he may have serious respiratory trouble. Ring the doctor immediately. *See* WHOOPING COUGH

CRADLECAP 42

CRADLES *see* BEDS AND COTS

CRAWLING across the floor
240-241; alternatives to 240-241; beginnings of 161, 164; and independence 233-234; and other 'milestones' 160,197, 240, 243; reflex in newborn baby 108; safe freedom to practise 197, 242, 267-268; toys for 241

CRIBS *see* BEDS AND COTS

CROUP

A form of laryngitis which has dramatic effects in babies or small children simply because their breathing tubes are so small. Infection from a virus cold moves downwards to the voice box (larynx) and the windpipe (trachea). In an older person this would lead to hoarseness, a tickly throat and a cough. In babies and small children the inflammation of the larynx can cause enough swelling to obstruct the passage of air through it. Instead of ordinary laryngitis the child has croup which is an emergency.

Symptoms The child wakes in the night with a hard, painful hacking cough, usually followed by crying. As he draws in his breath to cry he makes the extraordinary barking noise which is diagnostic of croup. In severe croup the child's breathing will be extremely laboured and his lower chest will suck in with every breath. He will be able to speak only in a hoarse whisper, if at all.

What to do You need a doctor urgently, but if you follow the emergency steps below you can relieve the child's breathing while you wait.

☐ Try to calm the child. He is short of oxygen and the feeling makes him panic, but the more he struggles and cries the more oxygen he will need. If you can get him to keep still and quiet (and even better to relax), he will discover that the reduced amount of oxygen he is getting is enough.

☐ Take him to a window and let him take six breaths of night air.

Cold or moist air will reduce the swelling of the larynx enough to let a little more air past.

☐ Then carry him to the bathroom, close the window, and turn on every hot tap so that the room fills with steam. Stay in the steam filled room for ten minutes. If you have no hot water supply an electric kettle will steam up a small room quickly.

The cold air and the wet air will usually relieve the child's breathing within ten minutes, so that you can ring the doctor if he is not already on his way. Stay in the steam filled room till he arrives, even if the child seems better. If you cannot get hold of a doctor quickly, ring for an ambulance or take the child by car to your nearest casualty department.

When the emergency is over Your doctor may want you to keep the child in a steamy atmosphere for several hours as dry air can start the trouble all over again. You can improvise a steam tent by draping a bed sheet around his cot or bed and boiling an electric kettle or pan of water on a camping stove just inside it. But this is not ideal. The steam is hot. The child must be guarded every minute and the heat will tend to drive his fever higher.

If steam is needed for more than a few hours, ask your doctor if he can arrange the loan or hire of a 'cold steam vaporiser' which blows a stream of *cold* wet air.

If two attacks convince you that your child has a tendency to croup it would be worth buying a vaporiser. You can safely leave it on beside the child all night. Used routinely whenever he has a feverish cold, it will usually abort attacks.

CRUISING *see* WALKING

CRYING AND COMFORTING
birth 29; early days 95-102; first six months 156-159; six months to one year 232-235; one year to two and a half 318-327; two and a half to five 390-405; from anger *see* ANGER AND FRUSTRATION; anxiety about separation from you 193-194, 216, 218, 220, 233, 273, 299-300, 333, 375, 390, 392, 393, 395, 396, 397, 399; boredom 158-159, 194; causes and cures, first six months 32, 36, 95, 102, 157, 158; and cold and warmth 81, 95, 97, 100, 148, 159, 221, 301, 329; colic 101, 148; as communication 95, 115, 156, 193-194, 232, 233, 261; and contact comfort 48, 97-100, 151; from year 82, 96, 103, 105, 113,

115, 232-233, 273, 321-323; of strangers 233; from helplessness 233-234; and hunger 50, 51, 72, 75, 92, 94, 95, 96, 115, 127, 132, 134, 136, 140, 156, 194-195, 301; nasty thoughts 377; newborn patterns of sleeping, feeding and 73, 106-107; nightmares 221, 301-302, 320, 378; night terrors 378-379; and nightwandering 302-304; and pain 95-96, 115, 151, 154, 156, 221, 291, 315, 316, 388-389, 391, 407; and playing with other children 354; and rhythmical comfort 99-100; sucking *see* SUCKING; and temperament 104, 156, 184-189, 235; and teething 152, 231, 316; and waking: early in the morning 148, 223, 304; from naps 193, 296; in the night 220-231, 300-301

CUDDLIES AND SOFT TOYS *see* COMFORT HABITS

CUPS *see* FEEDING EQUIPMENT

CUTS AND GRAZES

What to do Minor cuts need little treatment. Bleeding will carry germs out of the wound and seal it as it clots.

☐ If you want to do something, put it under a gently running cold tap. Don't use antiseptic. If it is strong enough to kill germs it will damage cut tissue too. Don't use ointment. It will delay formation of a protective scab.

☐ If an adhesive dressing is needed to conceal the wound from the child, remove it as soon as he will let you, so that the wound can harden in the air.

Cuts on the face These should be seen by a doctor if they penetrate more than the top layer of skin. Even if the wound is trivial, stitches may be advisable to minimize scarring.

Gaping or jagged cuts elsewhere While serious ones should be seen by a doctor, even trivial ones will leave scars unless stitched. With these you can balance beauty against the trauma of stitching. A scarred knee may not matter. You can help such a cut to heal neatly by cleaning it under running water, laying a layer of gauze over it and then using strips of adhesive plaster to hold its edges together.

Puncture cuts Those wounds made when a child steps on a nail are very liable to infection because they are deep for their size. Any germs have been carried well into the tissue; there is little bleeding to carry them out again and you cannot reach the bottom of the 'hole' with running water. A deep wound, especially if it was made by

something dirty, should be seen by a doctor. He may give the child an anti-tetanus booster injection.

☐ A smaller, cleaner wound, made perhaps by a glass splinter, should be considered carefully. If it is deep, play safe. Take him to the doctor. Thorn or needle punctures do not need medical aid.

Grazes While trivial these are usually painful because a large area of raw tissue is exposed to the air. If the child does not show you a graze at once leave it alone. Bleeding and oozing will have carried out most of the dirt. Any that remains will be incorporated and lost in the scab which will already be forming.

Grazes with embedded grit These usually come from falls on gravel, some of which penetrates deeper than the superficial skin. If the surface is open and the grit visible, remove what you can with moistened cotton wool under a running tap. It will be painful. An older child may prefer to do it himself.

It will need protecting from friction by clothes etc., but the more air it gets the faster it will heal. Cover it with gauze taped to the child's skin.

The scab will probably be yellowish, showing some local infection and remaining dirt, but this will clear by itself.

If the surface has pockets of skin with grit beneath them, cleaning and dressing is a professional job as the pockets must not be allowed to heal with dirt trapped inside. Take the child to your doctor or casualty department.

Any graze on the face which has visible dirt or grit in it should be professionally cleaned. Dirt can stain the tissues leaving an unsightly scar.

D

DAY NURSERIES 392-397
DEAFNESS 182, 260-261 *see* EARS/Hearing problems
DECISIONS AND CHOICES learning to make 278, 366, 386, 387, 412, 442
DEHYDRATION *see* DIARRHOEA; FLUIDS; VOMITING
DENTIST 231, 291, 317, 388, 389; *see* TEETH; TEETHING

DEPRESSION AFTER BIRTH
31, 39, 41, 119
However thrilled with your new baby you may be, you will probably experience a degree of 'let down' when the drama of birth is over. A sudden bout of weepiness round about day three or four is the most

common. Feelings of exhaustion and being unable to cope when the time comes for leaving hospital and/or taking full charge of the baby are common too.

There are physical causes such as the hormonal upheaval which takes place as your body returns to a non-pregnant state and either establishes lactation or adapts to its artifical suppression. Your body will not have settled down until at least six weeks after the birth.

Practical causes are numerous too. Among these are having to put up with post-birth discomforts such as stitches, and the necessity of caring for the new baby at night, when rest is so badly needed.

Emotions also run riot. A new baby is a total and long-lasting responsibility; it means rethinking your own image, it means a change in your relationship with your partner. It also means offering constant care to a baby who cannot yet reward you with signs of recognition and affection.

Practical assistance and emotional support together with acceptance of your own feelings as both 'normal' and transient are vital. Above all, don't let guilt creep up on you. If you cannot love the baby yet, offer him adequate care and don't worry. Love will come. If you cannot feel sexual desire yet, ask for the support you need instead and don't worry. Lust will return. If you cannot cope with everyday life *and* the baby yet, get what help you can, let what does not really matter go, and don't worry. In a few days or weeks you will have settled into the new pattern of your life and everything will seem quite ordinary again.

If you are still beset by tears and fears by the time your post-natal check-up is due, confide in your doctor. He can help you.

DIARRHOEA 89, 149, 224, 385
see GASTRO-ENTERITIS; SOILING
In diarrhoea the contents of the intestine are hurried through, so less water is absorbed through the intestinal walls. The reason for this can be illness; food poisoning or even an emotional upset. If the child seems perfectly well and has a normal appetite, disregard the diarrhoea. You need only consider it as a symptom:

☐ If he seems ill.
☐ If he has griping pains.
☐ If he has no appetite.
☐ If he is also vomiting.

Diarrhoea and vomiting combined lead to rapid loss of fluid and require urgent medical help.

DIET/What nutrients your child needs

	For babies of 14 lb (6.4 kg) i.e. large baby at 3 months; average at 4½ months; small at 6 months.	For babies of 19 lbs (8.6 kg) i.e. large baby at 6 months; average at 9 months; small at 12 months.	For toddlers weighing about 25-30 lbs (11.4 kg) i.e. aged about 1-3 years	For pre-school children weighing around 35 lbs (15.9 kg) i.e. aged about 3-5 years.
Energy	760 kcal	950 kcal	1,200 kcal	1,600 kcal
Protein	20 g	20 g	30 g	40 g
Minerals				
Calcium	600 mg	600 mg	500 mg	500 mg
Iron	6 mg	6 mg	7 mg	8 mg
Vitamins				
A (Retinol)	450 μg	450 μg	300 μg	300 μg
D	10 μg	10 μg	10 μg	10 μg
Thiamine (B1)	0.3 mg	0.3 mg	0.5 mg	0.6 mg
Riboflavine (B2)	0.4 mg	0.4 mg	0.6 mg	0.8 mg
Niacin (Nicotinic acid)	5 mg	5 mg	7 mg	9 mg
C (Ascorbic acid)	15 mg	15 mg	20 mg	20 mg

Notes
□ Infants require approximately 1.5 g of protein and 52 kcal per day for every 1 lb of their weight.
□ Minimum protein levels, i.e. those below which there is a possibility of protein deficiency, are approximately two thirds of the above figures.
□ **kcal** = kilocalorie (often incorrectly abbreviated to 'calorie' in nutrition). This is the amount of energy required to heat 1 litre of water 1°C (1 pint of water 3°F)
g = gram = 1/28 oz
mg = milligram = 1/1000 g
μg. = microgram = 1/1000 mg
□ **Vitamin A** in a diet consists roughly of 2/3 retinol and 1/3 carotene, a related chemical. The measure is therefore in 'retinol equivalents'.

Need	Source	Examples
CALORIES (energy) Calories are a measure of the amount of energy our bodies take in. We need energy to keep our bodies ticking over and warm, to keep our hearts, lungs and digestions working. We need more when we are awake and moving around. We need most when we do heavy physical work. Children need more calories than adults, weight for weight, both because they use a lot of physical energy and because they need a surplus for growing. If your child gains no weight for three months, or actually loses weight, you should check with your doctor or local clinic.	*All* foods contain calories. Whatever your child eats will provide him with calories. His appetite will accurately control his intake, so if he eats as much as he is hungry for he will be taking enough, while if he eats from greed not hunger he will get fat. Some foods contain more *concentrated* calories than others. Fats are the most concentrated, then sugar, and other carbohydrates like flour and cereals; least concentrated are leafy vegetables.	1oz **butter** = 211 calories; 1oz **sugar** = 112; 1oz **beef** = 89; 1oz **bread** =72; 1oz **boiled potatoes** = 23; 1oz **boiled cabbage** = 2. But looking at calories per ounce of food is not very useful, because you would probably not eat a whole ounce of butter or sugar at once, whereas you would eat much more than an ounce of potato or beef. So the calorie content of a meal made from the above might be: 3ozs **beef** = 270 calories; 6ozs **potatoes** = 138; 4ozs **cabbage** =8; 1oz **bread (1 slice)** =72; ¼oz **butter spread on bread** = 53; **2 teaspoons sugar in tea** =50.
CARBOHYDRATES Carbohydrates provide energy for maintaining body functions and for powering activity. If not enough carbohydrates are eaten, the body will burn proteins instead. In a growing child especially, this can mean that protein needed for body growth is used for energy. Carbohydrate foods also provide the bulk of our diet, and this bulk is important in proper digestion/excretion. Sugar is, of course, pure carbohydrate and offers the body nothing except calories. But most carbohydrate foods contain other nutrients as well. Although the nutrient concentrations may be low, large quantities are consumed, so they are useful sources.	Apart from sugar and products sweetened with it, potatoes, other root vegetables, bread, all flour and flour products, all cereals and cereal products are high in carbohydrates. There are lower proportions of carbohydrate in milk and in other vegetables and fruits.	½oz **blackcurrant concentrate** = 8g; 10ozs **milk** = 14g; 1oz **bread** = 15.5g; 2ozs **boiled potato** = 11.2g; 3ozs **chipped potatoes** = 31.8g; ½oz **spaghetti** = 11.9g; ½oz **flour** = 11.4g; ½oz **rice** = 12.3g; 1oz **cereal** = 24.9g; 1oz bar of **chocolate** = 15.5g; ½oz **sugar** = 14.9g. The "protein sparing" function of carbohydrates will best be fulfilled when he eats traditional combinations of foods, such as a hamburger in a bun, a hot dog in a roll, fish and chips, or milk and biscuits.

Need	Source	Examples

PROTEINS

Our tissue and muscle are made of protein. We therefore need it so that our bodies can heal and repair themselves. Children especially need protein because they are making new tissue. Proteins are made up of various combinations of chemical substances called 'amino acids'. There are 9 particular amino acids which a child must eat complete, and all at the same time, because his body cannot construct these out of others. We call certain high-protein foods "first-class" because they contain these essential substances in the correct balance. Proteins in other foods are called "second-class", because, while the amino acids they contain are just as useful in themselves, the balance between them is not exactly right or else one or more of the vital 9 are missing.

"First class" protein is animal protein. Most concentrated in meat, fish, eggs, milk, cheese and other dairy produce, it is available also in any food manufactured from animal foods, such as fish fingers, sausages, or luncheon meats. Many foods which are not commonly thought of as high in protein contain egg, milk etc. with the other ingredients. "Second class" protein is from vegetable sources. Both the concentration and the balance of the various amino acids vary so that, for example, soya bean protein is an almost-perfect substitute for animal protein; nuts are excellent sources and the amino acid balance of both potatoes and wheat (from which pasta as well as bread is made) has been shown to sustain growth well over long periods.
Vegetables such as beans and peas contain high concentrations of some amino acids, although some of the vital ones are lacking. Combinations of vegetables eaten together can give the child protein which is just as good for his growth as the protein in animal foods. This is the basis of a good vegetarian diet.
Since many sources of vegetable protein only just fall short of the body's requirements, a very small quantity of animal protein can balance the mixture. The addition of milk to potato, for example, produces an amino acid combination which is just as good for the child as butcher's meat.

A toddler is adequately served by 25 grams of protein (first class or completed second class) each day. Ordinary cow's **milk** yields almost 1 gram per fluid ounce so if he takes 1 pint of milk (in drinks and/or cooking) he will get 20 grams of protein. At this level he could not go short of protein whatever else he did or did not eat.
If he hates milk and takes none at all, each of the following food portions will give him one third of his day's requirement:-
1 tablespoon **minced beef**; 1 tablespoon **minced liver**; 1 tablespoon **white fish**; 1 standard 2oz **egg**; 1 tablespoon **grated cheese**/1 slice from vacuum pack; 1½ large **sausages**/3 chippolata; 2½ slices **luncheon meat**; 2-3 rashers back **bacon**; 2 slices **ham** from vacuum pack; 8ozs (2 pots) natural **yoghurt**; 7ozs (3 small brickettes) **ice cream**; 3ozs **milk chocolate** (medium bar).
The following food portions will each yield one third of his day's requirements, either in the form of a mixture amounting to first class protein, or by containing vegetable proteins known to be adequate in the presence of minute quantities of animal foods.
3 slices from cut **white or brown bread**; 4 medium size **potatoes**; 6 level tablespoons **baked beans**; 1 heaped tablespoon **roast peanuts**; 8 average sweet or **chocolate biscuits**; 4 small slices **madeira cake**; 5 individual (1oz) bag **potato crisps**.

FATS

The only *need* human beings have for fats is for tiny traces of three 'fatty acids', which occur in all animal or vegetable fats and oils. It would be impossible to go short of these as long as you were eating anything at all. There is therefore no need for table fats and frying oils. Because they have so many calories concentrated in them, fats can be useful in feeding a child who cannot eat much bulk. They also contain the "fat soluble" vitamins A and D.

Most of our fat intake comes from butter and margarine, cooking fats and oils, lard, dripping and meat fat. There is also a considerable amount of fat in cream, milk and egg yolk. Vegetable sources include most nuts and seeds.

Fats are the most concentrated of all sources of calories.
1 slice of **bread** = 72 calories, but, with ¼oz of **butter** added to it, it equals 125.
A serving of two **boiled potatoes** = 80 calories, but with ½oz butter added this becomes 185, while turning the same potatoes into **chips** makes them yield 240 calories.
An 8oz glass of **milk** = 144 calories. A 2oz serving of **double cream** = 256 calories.

Need	Source	Examples
VITAMINS **B Group** The process by which our bodies get a smooth and continuous supply of energy from our carbohydrates is controlled by these vitamins. We need a daily intake as the body cannot store them.	These vitamins are distributed in such a wide variety of foods that a shortage would be most unlikely in anyone except an adult on a violent slimming diet. Most of our intake comes from milk and milk products, flour and flour products, other cereals and cereal products.	Almost everything he eats will contribute to his daily intake of these vitamins.
Vitamin A Vitamin A is important to the processes of vision and in the protection of mucous membranes. Children need it especially as it also contributes to the processes of growth. It is stored in the liver. If your child drinks milk, likes butter, margarine or cheese, eats fortified baby cereal or liver occasionally, he will not go short. If he rejects all these things *and* dislikes carrots, he could go short. That is why vitamin A is included with the recommended multivitamin supplement.	Liver and fish liver oils are a rich source of this vitamin. Milk and milk products are a good source too. Carrots contain a substance called 'carotene' which can be converted by the body to vitamin A.	A pre-school child needs about 450 micrograms daily. 1 pint of **milk** = $220\mu g$ 2ozs **butter** = $564\mu g$ 1 **egg** = $170\mu g$ 1oz **cheddar** = $119\mu g$ 1 small **carrot** = $500\mu g$
Vitamin C This vitamin is important in maintaining the structure of the body's connective tissue; it aids wound healing and possibly helps in developing resistance to infection. The body cannot store vitamin C so daily supplies are important.	This vitamin is present in most fresh fruits and vegetables, but unfortunately it is soluble in water, destroyed by heat and destroyed by sunlight. This means that cooked vegetables and fruits are not a reliable source because they lose much of their vitamin C in the cooking water and have much of what is left destroyed by heat. Salads displayed outside the greengrocer may have lost most of their vitamin C through being exposed to sunlight. Citrus fruits are probably the best source: their skins protect them from sunlight and they are eaten raw.	Your child needs about 20mg per day. The juice of one orange (2ozs of orange juice) will meet this need. If fruit juices or fortified fruit syrups do not agree with your child, you will have to rely on vitamin drops or tablets.
Vitamin D This vitamin enables the child's body to absorb and use the calcium and phosphorus it needs (see below) to build bones and teeth. The body can store this vitamin.	The body can manufacture vitamin D for itself through the action of sunlight on bare skin, so a deficiency is unlikely in a white child who spends a good deal of time outdoors during the summer months; the pigmentation which protects a dark child from sunburn also prevents efficient manufacture of this vitamin, so even in summer such a child risks deficiency. In winter, from diet alone, this is the most difficult vitamin to provide in adequate quantities. It is present mostly in fatty fish— like herrings and sardines—and in eggs, but unless a child is very fond of these you will have to rely on supplementation.	Fortified baby cereals and fortified margarines may provide sufficient, but many children go short as soon as they stop drinking a fortified milk formula. He needs about 10 micrograms each day. 1 **egg** = $1\mu g$ 1oz **herring** = $6\mu g$ 1oz **sardines** = $2\mu g$ 1oz fortified **margarine** = $2.5\mu g$ These quantities make clear that a vitamin D supplement is necessary for him, especially in winter.

Need	Source	Examples
MINERALS **Calcium** Calcium is vital to the proper clotting of blood and to muscle function. Children need it especially as it plays a vital part in laying down healthy bones and teeth. A baby's need for calcium starts in the womb, so it is important that pregnant women eat a diet containing adequate amounts.	Milk is by far the most useful and adequate source. There are useful amounts in bread, flour and other cereals too, but not enough taken on their own. If he rejects milk other milk products such as yoghurt are good too, but cheese is the best and most concentrated.	He needs about 500mg per day 1 pint of **milk** = 680mg (more than the requirement) 1oz **cheese** = 230mg 1oz **white bread** = 28mg 1oz **white flour** = 41mg
Phosphorus Phosphorus is also important to growing bones and teeth.	This is found in the same foods as calcium.	A child who is getting enough calcium will be getting enough phosphorus too.
Iron Unlike most essential nutrients, iron intake is not a daily concern, because it is stored in the liver and can be used and re-used. Babies accumulate stores in their livers while they are still in the womb, enough to last for three or four months, which is lucky, as milk contains almost none. So you will only need to concern yourself with providing an 'iron rich' diet during the early months of weaning. Iron is a vital part of the haemoglobin, the constituent of red blood cells which carries oxygen round the body. People who are anaemic as a result of iron deficiency feel exhausted and weak because their muscles are not receiving enough oxygen.	Fortified cereals and flours, eggs, meat, some fruits and vegetables, all contain small quantities of iron. Chocolate and cocoa powder are rich sources, and drinking water contains variable amounts.	The average recommended daily intake is about 8mg, but this is only approximate, as various types of dietary iron are variously absorbed. 1 portion of fortified **cereal** = 3mg 1 small slice of **liver** = 6mg 1 tablespoon of **minced beef** = 1mg 1 **egg yolk** = 2 mg 1 small bar of **chocolate** = 1mg 1 slice of **white bread** = 0.5mg 1 slice of **wholemeal bread** = 1mg

DIET/Problems of weaning and switching to milkman's milk

Don't be in too much of a hurry to wean your baby from sucking breast or bottle. Weaning usually means a drop in the baby's milk intake and hence his nutrient intake. Switching from breast/formula milk to cow's milk will add to this problem, since ordinary (cow's) milk is less nutritious than either breast or formula milk. If you look at the table below you will see that even if your baby drinks 32 ozs (910 ml) of cow's milk (his maximum capacity) he will be short of calories, iron and vitamins A, C and D. If his milk intake goes down to 1 pint (20 ozs-570 ml) he will not be getting enough protein or thiamine either. If his milk intake goes down to ½ pint (10 ozs-285 ml), he lacks some of every single vital nutrient except riboflavine. He will need a complete solid diet.

	Energy (kcal)	Protein (g)	Calcium (mg)	Iron (mg)	Vitamin A (µg)	Vitamin D (µg)	Thiamine (mg)	Riboflavine (mg)	Niacin (mg)	Vitamin C (mg)
What the 6 month baby needs	800	20	600	6	450	10	0.3	0.4	5	15
What the baby gets: From 32ozs (910ml) of a full-cream formula milk	556	28	1,000	4	900	10	0.3	1.2	9.6	32
From 32ozs (910ml) of cow's milk	576	29	1,100	0	350	trace	0.3	1.2	9.6	0
From 20ozs (570ml) of cow's milk	360	18	680	0	220	trace	0.2	0.8	6	0
From 10ozs (285ml) of cow's milk	180	9	340	0	110	trace	0.1	0.4	3	0

DISLOCATIONS

In theory any movable skeletal joint can become dislocated. The hip joint, for example, is formed with a 'ball' at the top of the thigh bone which fits into and rotates within a 'socket' of bone at the base of the pelvis. If the 'ball' becomes wrenched out from its socket, the joint is dislocated.

In practice dislocations are rare without fractures because the muscles and ligaments which hold them together are stronger and more resilient than the bones themselves. There are two exceptions to this. Firstly, the shoulder joint is extremely mobile. The 'ball' at the top of the upper arm bone can be twisted out of its socket in the shoulder, especially if the arm receives a sudden jolt when fully stretched above the head. A child who falls from a height and, on landing, instinctively throws up his arms to protect his head may dislocate his shoulder. Secondly, the lower jaw can sometimes be dislocated by an extremely deep yawn although an injury to the jaw seldom has this effect and is more likely to fracture the bone.

Recognizing a dislocation There is little point in trying to work out whether your child has dislocated a joint or fractured a bone. Only a skilled doctor and an X-ray can differentiate one from the other or see whether the child has suffered both together. Re-aligning the joint is a comparatively simple job provided it is done *within two or three hours of the injury*. If more time passes, the surrounding tissues tend to swell.

What to do
☐ The child needs comfort and urgent medical attention because he will be in great pain. The displaced parts of the joint press on nerves and over-stretch ligaments and muscles at the slightest movement. The pain of a 'simple' dislocation may in fact be greater than the pain of a simple fracture of one of the long bones. If his jaw is dislocated it is just possible that it will click back into place of its own accord as he cries. If so, and if the child can then open and close his mouth freely without any pain, assume that all is well.

☐ If his shoulder is dislocated, the child will probably be holding the arm across his chest. Secure it there with a sling made out of a big scarf folded into a triangle and tied round the child's neck. Take him to the nearest hospital casualty department as soon as possible.
☐ Don't give the child anything to eat or drink—he will almost certainly need an anaesthetic. Don't let him use the dislocated part; any attempt at movement may lead to further damage to the tissues around the joint.

Although fractures are commonly considered more serious than dislocations, the opposite is often true. Even after a joint has been slipped back into its proper position there will be torn ligaments and bruised tissues to heal. The joint may have to be immobilized for several weeks, and it may be more painful during this healing period than a fracture.

Occasionally a bad dislocation leaves a joint weakened and more liable to further dislocations, because the holding ligaments and muscles fail to heal to quite their original strength and elasticity. In such cases, the child may need further treatment to strengthen it.

DISOBEDIENCE 437 *see* "DISCIPLINE"

DOCTOR

Choosing Like anyone else, a doctor likes some parts of his work better than other parts. You need one who enjoys pediatrics and tolerates anxious parents. A doctor who runs his own child health clinic and undertakes ante-natal care will be one of these. You can also get useful recommendations from health visitors, your local clinic and from other parents.

Using Try and get to know your doctor. If you can ask him what he feels about making home-visits, giving advice by telephone or being called in the night, you can also tell him what you feel about these things and then reach agreement. A doctor who makes you feel a nuisance or who does not trouble to explain things properly is not the right one for you. But just as he has an absolute duty to explain in a way you can understand, so you have a duty both to listen to what he says and to tell him if you have not understood. A meek 'yes Doctor, I see . . .' when you don't see will lead to muddles that are both your faults. Ask and go on asking until you are sure. If you are afraid of looking silly you need a different doctor.

When to call
For brand-new babies who have not yet settled down, call whenever you find yourself worried. Your doctor must act as your teacher; if your worry was unnecessary this time you will learn something for next time. If you need support, he may ask the health visitor to see you regularly until you feel more confident. He is not fobbing you off; just sharing the load.
For any age baby Pay attention to your feelings about him. If he does not 'seem right' to you, he may not *be* right even if you cannot put your finger on the exact symptom. On the other hand a baby who looks and feels to you just as he always does, and seems cheerful and as active as usual is unlikely to be very ill.

Get your doctor's advice if:
☐ He will not feed or suck water and/or he has vomiting and/or diarrhoea. Refusing or losing fluid will quickly dehydrate him.
☐ Breathing is noisy. His air passages are tiny so even a little mucus rattles, but a doctor should check that it is not in his chest.
☐ Breathing sucks in his lower ribs; this does suggest respiratory trouble. Bare his chest and watch for a full minute. If the sucking-in goes on for that long, get immediate help.
☐ He has high fever; a new fever of 101° or more is reason for calling that same day. An established fever that has gone 2° higher than the doctor knows or has overtopped 103.5° is reason to contact him immediately.
For babies and young children The following are all good reasons for calling the doctor whatever the time of day or night. He can, of course, be ill without having any of these, and he can have these without being really ill. But they are signs which need checking for safety.
☐ Vomiting and/or diarrhoea which goes on and on so that the child is clearly losing more fluid than he is taking in.
☐ Breathing which is painful, noisy, sucks his ribs in, does not seem to get him enough air.
☐ High fever, especially if he also seems trembly and/or 'wandery' (delirious).
☐ Headache *with* any stiffness of the neck, eyes that look odd or different from each other, or violent dislike of light.
☐ Stomach-ache violent enough to make him scream *or* continuous over 8 hours *or* intermittent over a whole day.

☐ Earache severe enough to wake him up and/or to make him cry.

☐ Blood in spit or phlegm (unless the child has just had a nose-bleed), vomit, stool or urine.

☐ Inability to use any part of his body, even when you have distracted his attention or offered a lure.

☐ Convulsions or 'fits'.

☐ Unconsciousness, however brief.

Night calls It is in the small hours that decisions about calling the doctor are most difficult. If your child has none of the listed symptoms but you are still worried, your call is legitimate if:

☐ You feel you would have to take the child to the nearest casualty department if you could not reach your doctor.

☐ You would accept his advice if he came and recommended hospital admission for the child.

☐ You would willingly dress and go out in search of medicines if he came and prescribed them.

If you do not feel that your child is as ill as that, your call can probably wait until morning.

Telephone advice Once you and your doctor know and trust each other, time may be saved by telephone contact, especially in continuing illnesses where it is a question of 'is he progressing as well as can be expected?' Ask your doctor what he feels about being consulted by phone and ask what time of day he prefers. Do remember that if you report *new* illness by telephone, you put him under heavy pressure to see the child even if you do not ask him to. If he does not, and the child later turns out to be seriously ill, he will feel very responsible. If you are concerned enough to want to speak to him it is better to take the child to see him.

DRAUGHT REFLEX 54, 63, 128
DRAWING AND PAINTING 259, 350, 429 *see* PLAYING AND LEARNING: PLAYTHINGS
DRINKS *see* FLUIDS

DROWNING
If your child falls into deep water Shout for help and don't be discreet or a heroine. Don't jump into the water yourself until you are sure it will not drown both of you and/or that there is no alternative such as a nearby lifebelt, rope or boat. If you do jump in, work out which way the current and/or tide is taking the child and jump ahead so that he is swept to you. Keep shouting for help.

If he falls out of a boat Don't leave it without a rope/lifebelt. When manoeuvring to retrieve him, switch off engine when you get close. Hold out an oar/rope to hold him until you can lift him over the stern—don't lift him over the side, you may capsize.

If a boat capsizes Stay with it. Fasten the child to you with belt/tie and lie across the hull. The boat will support you and rescuers from the air will see it.

If an airbed or inflatable toy boat drifts Don't go after it if retrieval means swimming; it will be too fast for you. Shout to the child to stay on it; he is safer and more visible there than in the water. Shout, send or run for help.

First aid If he is coughing, choking or vomiting he is breathing. If someone else will go to call an ambulance, put him in the 'recovery position', cover him with any clothing you have and wait for its arrival. If alone, carry him, with his head lower than his chest to help water drain out, and make for the nearest helper/telephone.

If he is not breathing Start the 'kiss of life' if you are competent. Otherwise put him head down over your shoulder and make for help. *See* MOUTH-TO-MOUTH RESUSCITATION; SAFETY; 510–512

DUMMIES *see* COMFORT HABITS

E

EARACHE 316 *see* EARS/Infections
EARS in newborn 44, 84

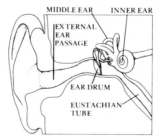

MIDDLE EAR   INNER EAR
EXTERNAL EAR PASSAGE
EAR DRUM
EUSTACHIAN TUBE

The opening of each ear leads, by a short passage, to the ear drum. On the other side of this membrane is a small 'compartment' known as the middle ear. It is connected by a long passage, the eustachian tube, to the back of the throat. Beyond the middle ear lies the inner ear containing structures concerned with both hearing and balance.

EARS/Drops
The part of the ear which is most subject to infection (the middle ear) cannot be reached from outside as it is protected by the ear drum. Medicines intended for the middle ear must therefore be given nasally. (*See* NOSE DROPS)

Ear drops may be prescribed for an infection of the outer ear. If wax is impacted in the canal, a doctor may instil drops to soften it prior to washing the wax out.

To give ear drops
☐ Lie the child across your lap with his head turned to one side. Put the correct number of drops into his ear.

☐ Keep him still for two minutes before repeating for the other ear. The medicine instilled will drain out if the child starts moving around as the ear canal is a dead end.

N.B. Never put *anything* into your child's ears without direct orders from your doctor. 'Home remedies' for earache such as warmed olive oil are as dangerous as they are useless.

EARS/Hearing disorders
Deafness New babies can be born completely deaf or with any degree of 'hearing loss'. Deafness is surprisingly difficult to detect because until at least six months a baby will make a normal number and range of sounds himself even though he is not hearing them. It is only later that a deaf baby's sound making will begin to seem different from others of the same age. This unfortunately is after the optimum time for noticing that a baby is deaf. The earlier you can detect hearing problems the more the baby can be helped, so it is worth making a definite effort to be sure that he can hear normally from the earliest weeks.

At around five to six weeks a baby should react to a sound by turning his eyes or even his head towards it. Try speaking to the baby or shaking a rattle when he is unaware that you are beside him. Don't use very loud and sudden sounds; not only will the baby be startled but he may be able to hear loud noises while still being deaf to normal speech tones. If there is any doubt of the results of these 'tests' mention them to a doctor.

Older children can become temporarily partly deaf after a middle ear infection or even after a heavy cold which blocks the eustachian tubes. If the child seems deaf after, say, a week, take him to a doctor.

Repeated middle ear infections can cause permanent damage to the hearing. This is why any acute pain in the ears should always be reported immediately to a doctor. Permanent deafness or severe impairment of the hearing is a handicap but it is one which hearing aids and therapy can do a great deal to ameliorate. *See* COLDS; MUMPS; USEFUL ADDRESSES

EARS/Infections
In a small child the eustachian tubes are relatively wide. Since a baby spends much of his time lying down, it is easy for germs, or even part of a vomited milk feed, to find their way from the throat up the eustachian tube into the middle ear. This often leads to middle ear infection.

Inflammation of the middle ear (otitis media) This can make a baby or child extremely ill very quickly, with high fever and great pain. A doctor should be called immediately if an ear infection is suspected. Treatment, usually with antibiotics, will prevent a burst ear drum and possible damage to hearing. The child may be ill without making it obvious that his ear is the cause: this is why a doctor will always examine an ill child's ears even if they do not appear to hurt.

Inflammation of the outer ear (otitis externa) This can be due to infection, perhaps after swimming or because the child has poked something into the ear, or even scratched the ear passage with a dirty fingernail. It is extremely painful; moving the ear or even lying on it will hurt; you may also be able to see inflammation or discharge. The child should see a doctor immediately.

Discharge from ears A neglected middle ear infection may lead to a build up of pus which eventually bursts through the ear drum and produces a visible discharge. This is an emergency. The child must have urgent treatment or the perforated ear drum may damage hearing on that side.

Earache Although unimportant causes, such as water in the ears after swimming, can cause temporary pain in the ear, most earache is due to infection either of the outer or the middle ear. If infection is present, treatment is urgent.

While waiting to consult your doctor, do nothing.

Don't give pain-relievers; they may confuse the diagnosis.

Don't put anything in the ear. Home remedies such as warm oil are useless and can be dangerous.

Don't apply external heat. A hot water bottle to lay his head against may feel comforting but if there should be a boil or abcess in the ear the heat can speed it towards bursting point.

Babies can have severe ear infections without being able to localize the pain to the ear. To complicate matters further, a baby who happens to be teething may be thought to put his hand to his face because of teething discomfort when in fact the trouble is in his ear.

If he keeps pawing at his face, grizzles and seems off-colour, take him to the doctor.

If he also has fever and/or loss of appetite, contact him urgently.

EARS/Problems
Wax in ears Sometimes it is difficult to distinguish between wax and pus. Wax coming from the ear is perfectly normal—the body's way of clearing dust from the passage—but if you are uncertain whether it is wax, take the child to a doctor.

Objects pushed into ears If a child pushes a bead or other round object firmly into his ear, don't try to remove it: you may push it further in and damage the ear drum. Take the child straight to a doctor or to the nearest casualty department. If the object is irregularly shaped or soft, it may be removed with tweezers. But one gentle try is enough: if this fails leave it to a doctor.

Water in ears This may feel uncomfortable or even make a child temporarily deaf, but it will do no harm unless he already has an infection of the outer ear. If it worries the child encourage him to lie with the affected ear downwards, so water can drain.

'Blocked' ears Changes in air pressure which occur for example when travelling in an aeroplane or when driving in high mountains, can make the ears feel blocked and deaf. Swallowing will equalise the pressure and cure the problem. A sweet to suck will force a child to keep swallowing. A baby can most easily be kept comfortable under these circumstances by being given the breast or a bottle to suck.

EAR-TWISTING *see* COMFORT HABITS

ECZEMA
Infantile eczema is an allergic complaint and tends to run in families. There will probably be a close relation susceptible either to eczema or to some other allergic complaint such as hay fever or asthma. Like all allergic conditions it will be made temporarily worse by anything which upsets the child: a separation from home, for example. The vast majority of children outgrow the eczema (although not necessarily the tendency to allergic complaints) by the time they are three years old.

The disorder usually begins with bright red, scaly and wildly itching patches on the cheeks. There may well be scurf on the scalp and this may lead to bad patches of itchy rash behind the ears. Occasionally the rash spreads to cover large areas of the body, but it is usually concentrated in the moist creases of the body; in the groin, behind the knees etc. When the eczema is very active, acute inflammation makes the scaly red patches moist. Eczema itches continually and scratching will make the patches sore and may infect them. The baby is likely to be desperately miserable.

What to do There is no cure, but you can do a great deal to keep infantile eczema manageable.

☐ With your doctor's help, look for a cause. Extensive testing for allergens is not helpful, but occasionally the child is allergic to cow's milk protein. Suspect this particularly if the eczema began when he was weaned from breast milk. Your doctor may recommend you to try feeding him on soya bean milk instead of cow's milk.

☐ Soap and water often make the skin worse. Use mineral oil or baby lotion on cotton wool instead.

☐ Avoid rough or scratchy clothes; several layers of thin silky materials will be better than a big woolly sweater.

☐ Keep fingernails very short and very clean, so that his scratching rubs the skin rather than cutting it.

N.B. Don't put him into mittens or splints however bad his skin becomes. It will be torture for him if he cannot even rub the place.

☐ Provide masses of entertainment and occupation to distract him from the itching. He must have special attention for the moment, so try to give it to him yourselves or find someone else who will. If you don't expect him to play peacefully by himself or to drop calmly off to sleep every night you will not be quite so maddened by his continual frenzies of itching-scratching-crying.

☐ Stay in touch with your doctor. If you get desperate or the eczema suddenly gets very bad, there are extreme measures he can take to help you all over the bad patch. He may, for example, prescribe a cortisone preparation for the skin or give the child a sedative for a few days to help the itching and get him (and you) some rest. For an older child he may be able to arrange a priority place in a playgroup if you and he both feel this would help. Severe infantile eczema can be an overwhelming burden for all of you, so don't suffer alone and in silence.

ELECTRIC SHOCKS
When you plug an appliance into a wall socket, you complete a circuit between the 'live' and 'neutral' wires, allowing the current to follow its natural path back to the source, but tapping it, to make your fire or your light or your washing machine work.

Electric shocks or burns occur:

☐ If the child sticks his finger or a piece of wire or any other reasonably good conductor of electricity into the 'live' hole of a socket.

☐ If the child sticks one end of a piece of wire into the 'live' hole of a socket and the other into the 'neutral' hole. The shock will not go through his body but because he is holding that wire he will feel the current as a shock in his fingertips and the wire may get so hot that his fingers are burnt.

☐ If instead of the circuit remaining complete, the wires inside the appliance touch its casing and the child touches that.
NB If the appliance has an 'earth' wire (and all appliances should have these) any current running into the casing would at once take the line of least resistance down the earth wire. Instead of being 'live' the appliance would fuse.

☐ If the child touches an appliance or wall socket with wet hands and water gets behind the plug and into the live socket.

☐ If faulty or broken wires of a live appliance, such as an electric water heater, accidentally touch a good conductor of electric current, such as a cold water pipe and the child touches the pipe.

What to do The severity of an electric shock depends on how much resistance the child offers to the current passing through him. It will be worst if he touchs the electric switch with damp hands, as water is an excellent conductor of electricity.

Minor shocks A minor electric shock will have upset the child and left him shaky. He will probably cry. Treat him for minor shock.

Major shocks As an electric shock passes through the body, it causes muscles (which are 'electrically' controlled anyway) to contract. Usually the contracting muscles either merely twitch or throw the child away from the electric source. But occasionally, especially if his hand was already curled around the 'live' object, the contracting muscles clench round it, so that the current is holding him as part of the electrical circuit.

Electric current that goes on passing through the body is a life-threatening emergency. He cannot 'let go' until it is turned off or he is bodily forced from it.

☐ If the child is touching an appliance which is plugged into a wall socket, immediately switch off the socket or pull out the plug.

☐ If the child is touching a live wire, wall switch or something where you cannot cut off the electric current, pull him away. He himself will be 'live'. So do not touch him with your bare hands — you cannot help him once you too are being shocked. Use something which will not conduct the electricity through you. Try rubber gloves, a rubber doormat, your rubber soled shoes or rubberized mackintosh or a pair of wellington boots held like pincers.

☐ If there is nothing like this to hand, try to push him free using something that will not conduct electricity. Try a wooden chair, a broom handle or a big cushion.

☐ If the child has stopped breathing, give him mouth-to-mouth resuscitation or get him to someone who can do this.

☐ If the child is unconscious but breathing, lie him face down with one arm forward and one leg drawn up and turn his head well towards that side.

☐ Summon medical help.
See SAFETY

EMERGENCIES 510-512

ENEMAS
Liquids injected into the rectum. The best-known enemas are used to wash out the lower bowel, but the same technique is sometimes used to give an anaesthetic to a baby or small child or to give other drugs to a child who is vomiting. The medicine is absorbed into the body through the mucous membrane of the lower bowel instead of being absorbed from the stomach or being put straight into the bloodstream by an injection. No enema should ever be given except on instructions from a doctor.

These may be prescribed for minor eye irritations or infections. If giving eye drops, do not expect much cooperation from the child because however much he means to keep still and hold the eye open, reflex action will make him blink and turn his head when he sees the dropper coming. The doctor may prescribe an ointment instead. Applying ointment will be easier and more pleasant for the child.

To give eye drops
☐ Lie the child across your lap, or, if he is old enough to be cooperative, lie him on a bed instead.
☐ Draw up the right amount of the solution into the dropper.
☐ Put your left arm around the back of the child's head so that your hand reaches round his face.
☐ Gently use finger and thumb to hold the eyelids apart.
☐ Poise the dropper about two inches above the eye, and then wait until he blinks. As he does so, drop the solution into the inner corner of his eye.
☐ Keep him lying still for a few seconds to allow the solution to spread over the whole eyeball. Repeat for the other eye.

To give eye ointment Eye ointments are usually sold in tiny tubes with a very fine nozzle on the end.
☐ Lie the child down, bring the nozzle to the inner corner of his eye, and squeeze out the correct amount. Don't worry about the child blinking; the ointment can even be applied when his eye is closed.
☐ Keep the child still for a few minutes: the feeling of the ointment in his eye will be uncomfortable; if you let him free he will probably wipe it away. As he blinks you should see a fine film of the dissolving ointment spreading round the inside of the lids and filming over the eyeball.
☐ If the ointment does not go inside the corner of his eye, but simply stays on the outside, repeat the application. Treat the other eye in the same manner.

Eye drops and ointments have a fairly short shelf life: they should never be kept and used again. Furthermore eye infections are highly contagious. Never use the same dropper or ointment tube for anyone else.

EYES focusing 44, 116, 119, 168, 177; in newborn 43-44; *see* LOOKING; SEEING HAND-EYE COORDINATION;

EYES/Infections

Conjunctivitis ('Pink eye') The conjunctiva which lines the outside of the eyeball and inside of the eye lids is inflamed. The eye may be weepy and reddened. After sleep, the discharge forms dry yellowish crusts in the eyelashes. There may be pain and/or gritty discomfort.

Irritation from dust etc. can cause conjunctivitis, but so can a variety of infections including the 'pink eye' which rages through schools. Take your child to the doctor; drops or ointment will quickly clear up the infection. Make sure the infected child uses only his own face-flannel and towel—the infectious varieties can easily spread.

Stye A stye is a tiny boil developing from infection at the base of an eyelash. The infection often passes from one lash or eye to another, producing a succession of styes. Your doctor can prescribe an ointment to prevent this.

What to do You can relieve the pain of a single stye if the child is old enough to cooperate and keep still.
□ Look at the stye carefully in a good light until you see which specific eyelash is growing through it.
□ Remove the lash with tweezers—it will come out easily as the root is infected; a tiny drop of pus and complete relief of pain follow.
□ Bathe away the pus with cotton wool, avoiding the other eye.
□ Sterilize the tweezers before using for anything else. Any child with a stye must keep to his own washing flannel and face-towel to avoid infecting anyone else.

EYES/Injuries

Any injury to the eyeball itself should be seen at once by your doctor or local casualty department. A tiny scratch on the white of the eye may not be serious but will need treatment to prevent infection. Even the tiniest scratch on the pupil is very serious indeed; treatment is urgent.

Cover the affected eye if that makes the child more comfortable. Do nothing else. Don't even bathe it; hurt eyes are for experts.

Black eye A blow around the eyebrow, nose or cheekbone may lead to rapid swelling and a fearsome-looking black eye. The eye itself is seldom damaged: eyes are set in bony sockets to prevent just this. But if eye-damage seems a possibility, take the child to a doctor or casualty department quickly. The swelling may more or less close the eyelids and make examination impossible.

EYES/Problems

Foreign bodies in eye If dust, sand or an insect gets into the child's eye it will water. If the child cries this will help the flushing action and the matter will probably right itself.

If it does not, try licking. Hold the child's head between your hands, your two thumbs gently holding the lids apart. Sweep your tongue right over the eyeball. Your wet slippery tongue cannot damage the eye as the corner of your handkerchief might.

If you still cannot see the foreign body, gently turn down the lower lid to see if it is trapped there, then lift the upper lid a little to help anything there to float down.

If there is still discomfort and no sign of the object, cover the affected eye with a pad and try to distract the child. If the child is still uncomfortable after half an hour, take him to a doctor or local casualty department.

Stinging substances in the eye Soap, shampoo etc., will not damage eyes although it will hurt and may leave the eye looking red and sore. Licking is the quickest way to get such substances out.

Any other stinging substance is dangerous or should be treated as such just in case (e.g., household cleaners, deodorants, insecticides). The eye must be washed out with plain water, over and over again, until no trace of the stinging, possibly damaging, substance remains. Ignore protests and the mess. If he has a strong acid or alkali in his eye his sight is at stake.

□ Rush him to the nearest tap. Turn it on about half strength. Put him under the stream with the affected eye underneath so that nothing runs from it into the other eye. Hold him there with one hand, holding his lids apart with the other. Shift the position of his head from time to time so that you swill every part of the eye from every angle. Go on for at least ten minutes.

□ If anyone else is in the house, get him to phone your doctor or local

hospital while this is going on. He should read the doctor the label of the container. If he is told it is harmless, you can stop the water-treatment. If not, you may be advised to take the child to hospital after ten minutes irrigation. If you are alone, irrigate for ten minutes and then telephone yourself.

EYES/Vision disorders; squinting 43-44; 'wandering eye' 44
Most vision problems are due to faults or peculiarities in the shape of some or all of the working parts of the eye, rather than to disease.

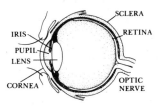

The eyeball is covered with a thin, transparent membrane called the 'conjunctiva' which extends to form the inner lining of the eyelids. Beneath this is the opaque white of the eye known as the 'sclera'. Its centre is transparent and forms the disc-shaped 'cornea'. The cornea helps to bend rays of light as they enter the eye and also serves to protect the parts of the eye which lie directly beneath it. It is highly sensitive, its reactions ensuring that any foreign bodies are removed before they can do damage.

Beneath the cornea lies the circular coloured portion of the eye—the 'iris'. (At birth the iris is usually bluey-grey. Permanent eye colour is not established until about six months of age.) The iris contains many tiny muscles which control the opening and closing of the 'pupil', the little dark hole in the centre of the iris. It is through this opening that light rays enter the eye. If light is bright the pupil closes up; if dim it opens fully.

Directly behind the pupil lies the 'lens' whose muscles adjust shape so as to focus light rays from objects at varying distances on to the light-sensitive 'retina'. Layers of sensory nerve cells within the retina respond to impinging light rays by building up images of the thing being looked at. These are transmitted along the optic nerve from the back of the eye to the brain. Here they are interpreted and converted into a 'picture'.

Astigmatism A child may be born with a cornea which does not refract (bend) light rays uniformly as they pass through to the pupil and lens. If the cornea is not perfectly curved, for example, light rays will not reach the retina in a point, as they should. The shapes of objects may be distorted so that round objects look oval.

Focusing problems Occasionally the lens of the eye does not become adequately adjusted to focus on objects, whatever their distance from the eye. If the lens allows an image to fall in front of the retina, the child will only clearly see objects which are close at hand. He will be 'short-sighted' or 'myopic'. If an image falls behind the retina the child will only see clearly objects which are at some distance from him. He will be 'long-sighted'.

Treatment Problems of this kind can all be corrected with opthalmic glasses. Small children adapt surprisingly well to wearing glasses, but many will also accept contact lenses, whose design is being rapidly improved. If you prefer the idea of these lenses for your child, ask your opthalmologist to consider their suitability.

Squinting Although a baby should focus briefly on objects brought within eight inches of his eyes, from birth, one eye may 'wander' from the focus of the other. The muscles are not yet strong enough to hold them in alignment. By three months the eyes should be permanently aligned. A 'fixed' squint or an eye that still 'wanders' should be reported to the doctor.

Fixed squints need urgent treatment. The retinas of normal eyes receive images from slightly different angles. The two fuse to give the brain a single composite picture to interpret. If the eyes squint, these images cannot fuse. The baby's brain receives two images but because it cannot interpret both at once it rejects one, interpreting, for example, only the 'messages' from the left optic nerve. Over time the right eye will go blind from lack of use. Don't let the phrase 'lazy eye' make you feel it is not serious. It is. The baby may have to wear a pad over the good eye to force his brain to accept images from the other. When old enough he will be given exercises to strengthen the eye muscles. Later he may need surgery to adjust the lengths of the eye muscles so that they move properly together. See SEEING.

468

F

FALLS 82, 162, 238-239, 245, 247, 267, 296, 329, 408-411
FAT BABIES AND CHILDREN 49, 66, 78, 130, 133, 137, 203, 209, 211, 287, 292, 293-294, 374
FEAR of anger 115, 261, 273, 280, 318-319, 324-325, 326, 327, 421; of the bath 84, 227-228, 312; of blood 391; of the dentist 389; of falls 82, 189, 239, 245, 247, 329; and general anxiety 275, 302, 318-323, 327, 377, 392; lack of in accident-prone children 410-411; of lavatories 309, 381; in the night 221, 301-302, 377-379, 386; and phobias 321-322; of separation from you 158-159, 194, 198-200, 215, 216, 220, 221, 223, 299-300, 318-319, 330, 332-333, 390, 396, 397, 398; of specific objects 189, 232, 298, 313, 320-321; and startling in the newborn 83, 96, 97, 103, 105-106; moro response 109, 113, 114, 180, 232; of strangers 200, 232-233, 263, 319; of the unexpected 232-233, 335; and worries in pre-school children 391-392, 407-408, 421
FEARLESSNESS see BRAVERY AND FEARLESSNESS
FEEDING first days 48-79; first six months 126-145; six months to one year 201-214; one year to two and a half 281-295; two and a half to five 369-374; appetite 32, 76, 132, 136, 209, 284, 370; and attachment to mother 48, 125, 203; avoiding discipline in 286-287, 290, 370; beginning 50, 51; bringing up milk 75; burping or bringing up wind 74-75; changing from baby milk to ordinary milk 201-202; choosing to bottle or breast-feed 48-49; convenient timing without scheduling 135, 142; and crying and sleeping patterns 72, 73, 296, 301; and eating between meals 292-293, 372-373; and eating with fingers 143, 145, 212, 214, 288, 370-371; and growing see GROWTH; helping her to eat sociably 370-371; in illness see NURSING; and mealtime behaviour 286-287, 370-371; mixed 137-145, 209-214; 'good mixed diet' 282-286; night 49, 134-136, 195; premature babies 38, 41, 126; self 212-213; sleepy babies 51; spoonfeeding 137, 140-141, 145; and starting family meals 282, 370, 371; and sucking, importance of 32, 50, 51, 90, 125, 140, 202, 203, 209
FEEDING EQUIPMENT bibs 144, 145, 214; bottles and bottle equipment 66, 69-71; chairs and tables 145; cups 143, 144, 204, 209, 214; dishes 144, 145; high

chairs 144, 192, 239; spoons 140, 144, 145, 212, 288; teacher-beakers 144, 145, 209, 304
FEET athlete's foot *see* RINGWORM; flat 281; in newborn 42, 81; care of 315, 387

FEVER
Most children can have a high temperature without seeming especially odd or ill, but have a sort of 'critical level' above which the fever seems to overwhelm them, affecting their level of consciousness and their nervous systems. For many children past babyhood the level seems to be somewhere around 103°F (40°C).
Complications
□ Once your child's fever has gone too high for *him* he may, if he is inclined that way and the rise has been sudden, have a febrile convulsion.
□ Even if he is not liable to convulsions he may be trembly; his limbs may judder; he may over-react to everything you do, jumping when you touch him, crying as if in pain when you sponge his mouth.
□ Without becoming completely unconscious, he may 'wander' so that in the middle of an apparently normal conversation he says something quite irrational.
□ He may talk in his sleep and then, when you try gently to waken him, be completely delirious.
□ He may vomit back any pills, medicine or even drinks which you try to give him.
□ He may vomit anyway, sometimes quite suddenly without apparent nausea.
□ Unless his control has been established for a long time, he may wet himself.
What to do
□ If your child suddenly shoots a high temperature you cannot foresee it. But once you know he is ill you have to try to keep the fever down below his critical level. Keep his room fairly cool—67°F (19°C) is enough for a very feverish child. Dress and cover him lightly. Sponge him from time to time.
□ Try to stay calm because if he is very jumpy obvious anxiety from you will make him much worse. Nursing a delirious child is alarming, but fever alone is not dangerous; it will drop eventually and he will then either suddenly wake and seem normal again or go off into natural sleep.
□ If he has ever had a convulsion you will naturally be terrified that it is going to happen again. It is only likely to do so at the very beginning of the fever. However,

once your child has had a febrile convulsion you have every right to ring your doctor any time he has a high fever. Even if he does not think it necessary to come he will stay in touch with you and tell you where he can be reached.

□ Stay with him in case he gets up and wanders about in a delirious state or is sick, but let him sleep or doze as much as he can. You will get more rest at night if you either sleep in his room or bring him into yours, so that you are right there if he needs you. If you are alone in the house with him and really worried, a friend or relative who can share the watches of the night with you can make all the difference. Choose his least feverish moments to give him the water he must have and any medicine prescribed, as well as aspirin to reduce the fever.

Reducing fever
□ Make sure that the room is cool. Open all windows etc.
□ Take all coverings off the child's bed or 'nest' and replace them just with a sheet.
□ Take off the child's clothes, down to the minimum in which he feels comfortable. In hospital he might be stripped naked, but most children find this very distressing because they feel so exposed. A nappy and vest, or short sleeved tee shirt and underpants will do.
□ Get a bowl of warm water and a face-cloth; sponge the child's face, neck, the inside of his arms and legs (where you can see the blood vessels close to the surface of the skin). Leave the skin wet. This is much more effective and less unpleasant for the child than sponging with cold water and then drying him. The water feels pleasant instead of freezing, and cools the child by evaporation.

If the sponging makes him cry, shiver and generally seem very distressed (which it may do as the skin can be hyper-sensitive to touch in high fever), try using a fan to cool him instead. Most hot air blower heaters have a cold setting and this is very satisfactory; alternatively a small electric fan can be used or even hand fanning in an emergency. Aspirin will help to reduce fever but don't give it without orders from your doctor; within 4 hours of a previous dose; if he is a baby and in pain; if he is vomiting or if he has any stomach symptoms. Any fever over 102°F (38.5°C) should drop a little with these measures. Take his temperature again half an hour after you have finished ministering to him.

If it has risen further, ring your doctor. If it has stayed the same, do everything all over again except the aspirin.
□ If this second bout of nursing still does not reduce the fever, ring your doctor and report. *See* CONVULSIONS; DOCTOR; TEMPERATURE.

FINGER AND TOE INJURIES
If a child catches his finger in a door, shout to him to keep still. Any attempt to pull the finger out will increase the damage.
□ Open the door and release the finger. If the skin is unbroken and the finger appears normal, put it at once under a cold water tap and keep it there for at least two minutes. Cooling will cut down the amount of bleeding under the nail and so reduce the intense pain.
□ If the skin is broken, the nail dislodged or the finger misshapen, take the child to the nearest casualty department. Don't give him anything to eat or drink—he may need an anaesthetic.
□ If a child drops a heavy object on his toes and there is bleeding under the nail, take him immediately to the nearest casualty department. The doctor will probably try to release the trapped blood by making a tiny hole in the toenail; this will alleviate the pain.
□ If the nail appears unaffected but the toe itself took the blow, wait and see whether the pain lessens over half an hour or so. If it does not, take the child to the hospital. He may have fractured a bone.

Fingers and toes have a liberal nerve supply. Injuries will be very painful for the child.

FINGER-FOODS *see* FOODS
FINGERNAILS AND
TOENAILS biting *see* NAIL-BITING; cutting 151, 313, 387
FINGERS eating with 143, 145, 212, 214, 288, 371; opposing fingers and thumb 257, 258; sucking *see* COMFORT HABITS; trapped *see* FINGER AND TOE INJURIES
FIRE *see* BURNS AND SCALDS; SAFETY 510-512
FIRST AID *see* ACCIDENTS, EMERGENCIES AND FIRST AID

FIRST AID SUPPLIES
Medical supplies should all be kept together in one place so that you (or anyone else who may be left in charge) know exactly where to find them in any kind of emergency. A medicine cabinet is the obvious choice. Buy the kind that has two or three sections, at least one of which locks. Use the locked section for medicines.

Keep first aid equipment simple. There is no point in storing a whole range of bandages, slings etc. An injury that requires an elaborate dressing will need medical attention anyway. Include:
□ A large box of assorted sizes of adhesive dressing—the kind that has each one sealed into a sterile packet is best. These should be used for covering small wounds while scabs form and for concealing blood from a scared child until he has forgotten his fright.
□ A packet of sterile gauze—useful for cleansing dirty grazes; for helping grit out of eyes and for dressing wounds (especially grazes) that are too large to be adequately covered by the lint patches on ready-prepared adhesive dressings.
□ A roll of adhesive strapping—use in strips to hold gauze dressings in place, or to make a neat finish for a bandage. N.B. Never put strapping all the way round an arm, leg or finger. It could hinder the circulation.
□ Two 1 in. (2.5 cm) bandages; two 2 in. (5 cm) bandages—these may be useful to provide temporary protection, over plenty of gauze, for wounds or minor injuries (such as finger and toe injuries) which are going to be shown to a doctor but must be protected meanwhile, and again over plenty of gauze, for dealing with a knee or elbow so badly grazed and bruised that any form of adhesive dressing would be extremely painful to remove.
□ A large, freshly laundered, ironed (and therefore sterile), handkerchief, in a sealed plastic bag—this is for emergency use to cover a serious wound, such as a burn or a compound fracture, during transport to hospital.
□ A bottle of plaster remover—a kindly way to remove adhesive dressings especially from hairy areas and more convenient, sometimes, than soaking the dressing off in the bath.

In the locked section you need:
□ A pair of scissors—for cutting gauze, adhesive strapping etc.
□ An insect sting reliever spray.
□ A soothing cream for nettlestings etc.
□ An anti sunburn cream or oil.
□ A soothing lotion for sunburn.
□ A clinical thermometer.
□ A pair of square-ended tweezers and a packet of needles (and the matches for sterilizing them)—for getting thorns and splinters out.

The medicine section should be kept simple too. The more patent medicines you keep in the house the more chance there is of something poisonous being left around where a child might take it. The more unfinished prescribed medicines you hoard the more temptation there is to use them for another member of the family instead of giving the doctor a chance to prescribe (or not prescribe) especially for him or her.

If you are tempted to keep medicines 'just in case they are useful another time' remember that many drugs have a short shelf-life, so that bottle you unearth from the back of your packed cupboard may be quite useless. You may want to include:

☐ A pain-reliever such as soluble aspirin or paracetamol. The kind that has each tablet separately wrapped in foil is safest. You will need both adult and children's (junior) strengths.

☐ A travel-sickness remedy if this is one of your child's problems. Ask your doctor's advice; buy the type he prescribes or advises and use strictly according to instructions.

☐ An antiseptic liquid—for your own hands.

☐ A bottle-sterilant—for thermometers etc.

☐ A nappy rash cream.

☐ Multivitamins—liquid or tablets according to your child's age and the advice given.

N.B. Don't stock laxatives unless you yourself are hooked on them. Your child should never need them.

Don't keep things like eye ointment or nose drops in stock. Buy and use them when and if they are needed, but throw away whatever is left.

Don't bother with cough medicines. Cough syrups are ineffective (although soothing): expectorant or codeine containing cough medicines should only be given on your doctor's advice.

Don't keep antibiotic medicines prescribed for the child; they lose their efficacy with storage. Furthermore they are only effective if the whole amount prescribed is given.

If you have room in this locked section, it is a good idea to keep here all the dangerous 'toiletries' you both need in the bathroom: deodorants, shaving tackle; contraceptive pills or jellies; depilatory sprays or creams.

FITS see CONVULSIONS

FLAT FEET see FEET; SHOES AND SOCKS

FLEAS see ALLERGIES; PETS

FLUIDS importance of 43, 50, 64, 66, 76, 89, 133, 134, 149, 224, 231, 282, 294, 316, 374; sugar water 89, 93, 94, 95, 114, 136, 149; vitamin C enriched syrups 76, 133, 134, 149, 282, 286, 294, see MILK; THIRST; see DIARRHOEA; VOMITING

FLUORIDE 231, 316, 388 see TEETH;

FONTANELLES 18, 43

FOOD POISONING see GASTRO-ENTERITIS

FOODS allergies to 141, 212 see ALLERGIES; finger-foods 143, 145, 214; first solid 139-143; fluids, importance of 50, 69, 76, 133, 134, 136, 137, 301, 384; in 'good mixed diet' 282-286; milk see MILK/Breast; MILK/Cows; MILK/Formula; preferences 114, 139, 201, 209, 210, 211, 282-283, 370-372; salt/seasoning, avoiding in baby foods 66, 141, 210, 224, 282; snacks 143, 292-293, 372-373, 374; sugar, avoiding excess in 89, 139, 141, 224, 294, 317; sweets 290-291, 294, 373, 374, 388; for weaning 209-212

FOOTWEAR see SHOES AND SOCKS

FRACTURES

Greenstick fracture A greenstick fracture is not usually as serious as a fracture in an older person. Because the affected bone only bends and cracks like a green twig rather than snapping like a dry one, there are no sharp ends of bone inside the limb to damage blood vessels and muscles. The bone cannot get out of alignment so it does not need complicated 'setting'. Nor will movement make it much worse.

Symptoms Your child will complain of pain in the limb and probably refuse to use it. The limb may look swollen or bruised. But many of these signs may be present in a severe sprain too. For confirmation of a fracture an X-ray is usually needed.

What to do If you want to avoid taking the child to hospital unless it is absolutely necessary, you can afford to wait for half an hour or so to see whether he starts to use the injured limb.

☐ Comfort the child and lie him down if he seems at all shocked.

☐ Put the affected limb in whatever position seems most comfortable. Don't encourage him to use it, but don't stop him either.

N.B. Don't give him anything to eat or drink because if it is fractured he may need an anaesthetic.

☐ If after half an hour he can use the limb and does not complain any longer of acute pain it is safe to assume that all is well.

☐ If he cannot use it, or if it hurts

very much when he tries to do so, take him to a hospital casualty department. Even if it is only a sprain it is obviously bad enough to merit medical attention.

Serious fractures The fracture will be more serious if the break is complete. There may be a real risk of damage to the blood vessels, muscles etc., as the broken ends of bone move around, and/or the fracture is 'compound' and there is a wound exposing the broken bone to the outside world so that there is a risk of infection.

Symptoms The child will clearly be badly hurt, shocked and unable to use the affected part: you will need to get him to hospital straight away.

What to do

☐ Don't move him unless he himself gets up and you are therefore quite sure he has not damaged his spine or his pelvis or a bone in his thigh. Make him as comfortable as you can where he is until an ambulance arrives.

☐ If the child can walk, but has obviously damaged an arm, collar bone or ribs, get him as comfortable as his injuries allow and then keep him still. The more he moves, the more those ends of broken bone are going to damage him, and the more difficult the fracture is going to be to set.

☐ If you have to move him yourself to hospital (perhaps because the accident happened miles from anywhere) try and keep the injured part from moving by fastening it to the child himself. If he has broken his collar bone he will instinctively hold the arm bent at the elbow across his chest. Tie it in that position. An injured leg can be tied to the sound leg in several places well away from the apparent break, so that the sound leg splints the broken one.

☐ If he must be carried, carry him flat as if he were on a proper stretcher. If there is no convenient hurdle or removable car seat to use as a stretcher, an adult's coat will do provided you and your helper keep it stretched tight so that the child is lying flat.

A bone which has broken through the skin, or a wound which goes right through to the broken bone does carry a very real risk of the bone itself getting infected.

☐ If you are at home, cover the whole area with a big sterile dressing. Don't attempt to wash or interfere with such a wound, that is a hospital job.

☐ If you are out, try and think of

470

something which is likely to be sterile or at least clean. The inner folds of a newly laundered handkerchief will do fine.

Your child will almost certainly be shocked. Keep him calm, quiet, lying down and covered up until help arrives. (see Shock).

N.B. Don't give him anything at all to eat or drink, he will need an anaesthetic.

Plaster casts A limb in plaster can make a child believe that the limb has actually been removed or at least that it will be permanently stiff and heavy. Try to prepare for this common emergency by talk and play at home in advance. If it happens, warn the child, before he has the anaesthetic for setting the limb, that it will be in plaster when he wakes up. Point out, when he comes round, that his thigh is still visible one end and his toes the other; the rest of his leg is still there. It is just safely covered up to keep it still while it heals.

Traction Sometimes, after a bad fracture, your child's arm or leg has to be stretched for a while so that the bones are held end-to-end, rather than overlapping, while they re-fuse.

Lying on his back with his leg raised on a pulley and weights suspended from it, the child is trapped. He cannot sit up, turn over or do anything for himself. He may have pain in the limb during the first days, and muscle discomfort later. He needs constant reassurance that his leg is still whole under the cast and that when he next sees it, it will be perfectly normal. He also needs careful explanations as to what is happening and why and continual company and entertainment. Do room-in with him if you possibly can even though traction usually means a long stay. *See* HOSPITAL

FRUSTRATION *see* ANGER AND FRUSTRATION

G

GASTRO-ENTERITIS 49, 65, 88, 150, 224
GENITALS in newborn 47; care of 84, 151; *see* MASTURBATION; PENIS; UNDESCENDED TESTICLES; VAGINA

GERMAN MEASLES (RUBELLA)
Incubation period 14–21 days
First sign Usually none.
Definite signs
☐ Flat pink spots start behind the ears and spread to the forehead and then over the body, merging, often in a few hours, so that the skin merely looks flushed. The whole rash may pass so rapidly that you never notice it and/or have no time to show it to a doctor.
☐ Swollen glands high up on the back of the neck, just below the skull, may be sore to touch. They often stay swollen for weeks.
Degree of illness
☐ Usually nil. This 'illness' often passes unnoticed.
Possible complications
☐ None for the patient, but infection of a mother in the early weeks of pregnancy can be disastrous to her baby. This is why this mildest of all infectious diseases is the subject of a campaign for the immunization of all girls before or at puberty.
What the doctor may do
☐ Nothing for the child but he may try to diagnose the illness so that you can warn any possibly pregnant women who have had contact with him.
What you can do
☐ Nothing for the patient. Keep him away from places where young women congregate; warn anyone you know to be in early pregnancy or who later tells you that she is pregnant, having had contact with your child. The worst foetal effects happen if infection takes place during the first weeks when the mother may not even have had the pregnancy confirmed. If told later, she can be tested for immunity. *See* NURSING

GETTING ON WITH OTHER CHILDREN 352, 354, 396, 399, 402-405, 408, 411-412,422-423; brothers and sisters 223, 228, 265, 288, 296, 299, 304, 306, 329, 351, 375, 377, 379, 380; *see* PRE-SCHOOL GROUPS; JEALOUSY OF NEW BABY

GRASPING AND LETTING GO development of 167-179, 248-259, 335 *see* NEWBORN REFLEX BEHAVIOUR

GRAZES *see* CUTS AND GRAZES

GROWTH first days 76-79; first six months 126; six months to one year 201; one year to two and a half 281; two and a half to five 369; birthweight as starting point for 37-39, 41, 76-77; birthweight, loss and regain through 50, 79; birthweight, significance of average 78; chart for your child's 506-508; expected height/weight-basic concept of 76-78, finding 79; hormone 369; measuring 77-78, 79, 201, 281, 369; normal patterns of 79, 126, 201, 281; changes and exceptions 78; obesity 49, 78, 133, 209, 292, 296, 374; rate of 76, 79, 126, 138, 201, 214, 281, 369; weighing 77, 79, 138, 201, 281, 369; test weighing 59, 129
GROWTH CHART FOR YOUR BABY 506-508

GUM BOILS
These are hard, painful red swellings at the margin of the gum, where a tooth sticks up. They are not really boils at all, but abscesses which have formed under the actual tooth and are trying to make a 'head' through the gum.

Make an emergency appointment with the dentist that same day. If you delay, your child may lose the affected tooth as well as having an extremely painful night.

H

HABITS *see* COMFORT HABITS
HAIR-TWIDDLING *see* COMFORT HABITS
HAIRWASHING 151, 228, 313, 387

HANDEDNESS
All babies start out using either hand with equal facility. Until he is around two, a child will go through phases of doing particular things with one or other hand. His handedness will not be decided until well into toddlerhood.

Left-handedness About one boy in ten and rather fewer girls are finally left-handed. They are a minority in a right-handed world with everything from doorknobs to tools wrongly placed or designed for them. Learning to write will be especially difficult; writing from left to right, the left-hander's work is covered (and smudged) by his hand.

What you can do While your toddler behaves ambidextrously, conduct life right-handedly, hoping that he will settle down to it. But if, in his third year, he consistently swaps everything you offer to his right hand into his left, accept that he is left-handed. A left-handed child should never be pressured to change. His handedness is controlled by the part of the brain that controls language, spoken, written or read. If you interfere he could develop speech difficulties as well as trouble later with reading and writing.

Help him instead. Lay his place setting the right way round for him. Get him 'left-handed' scissors. Make sure nursery school teachers know that he is left-handed and show him, from the beginning, the easiest ways to hold pencils and manage paper.

HAND-EYE COORDINATION
development of 165-179, 248-259
see HANDS

HANDICAPPED CHILDREN
Mental and physical handicaps In babies and very young children the distinction is not very useful, because the development of intelligence and physical abilities go together. A mentally retarded child may be slow to learn to walk so that he appears physically handicapped. On the other hand a child with a specific physical defect may be equally slow to get moving and because he cannot explore as normally crawling babies do, his mental development is slowed up and he may appear mentally retarded when the real cause of his trouble is only in his lack of control of his limbs.

A vital aim of treatment—the experts' and yours—is to minimize these spin-off effects, compensating for the child's handicap so that all his faculties which can develop normally do so. A child with cerebral palsy, for example, need not be mentally subnormal unless his physical disability and strange appearance are allowed to cut him off from opportunities to learn and develop intellectually.

Slow development Even if development is slower than normal, it still takes place, so do not give up. A seven year old with the vocabulary of a two year old may never speak normally, but with enough help he could speak like a seven year old by the time he is adolescent. Some speech is better than none.

Getting help early If you are uneasy about any aspect of your child's development, tell your doctor or clinic and don't accept reassurance unless it convinces you. Ask for a full assessment by a pediatrician. Early help makes all the difference. Once a diagnosis is made, do go on asking questions until you fully understand it. Ask your own doctor to be interpreter if you cannot get clear information from the hospital.

Once you understand your child's problem and the proposed treatment, you can do a great deal to help him. With the therapist's guidance, you can carry into everyday life the 'treatment' she is giving twice-weekly.

Seek out both state aid to which you may be entitled, and parent-support groups. You have a demanding job ahead and you have a right to and a need for all the help you can find. *See* USEFUL ADDRESSES

HANDS coordinating with eyes 165-179; coordinating with speech 181; finding 100, 165-166, 248; importance of leaving free 99; reflex grip 113; using 248-259, 335-342, 429-431; washing 230, 313, 387; see FEEDING; PLAYING AND LEARNING; PLAYTHINGS; SUCKING

HAY FEVER *see* ALLERGIC RHINITIS

HEADACHES
A baby or toddler whose head appears to hurt him may have a headache but equally he may have earache, toothache or swollen sore neck glands. Neither you nor he will be able to tell so you need a doctor.

An older child may tell you that his 'hair hurts', or he may now copy your term.

Headaches can mean nothing or almost anything. If the child seems well in every other way and the pain is transient, you need offer nothing but sympathy. If the pain persists, keep an eye on him: the headache may herald a fever. Don't give him pain-relievers at this stage; they may mask symptoms of illness. If the headache is so bad that you cannot bear to withhold relief, call the doctor.

If he does become ill and headache remains a tiresome symptom, a pain-reliever such as soluble aspirin or paracetamol will relieve it.

Headache severe enough to make the child want to lie still, especially if it is associated with high fever, unusual sleepiness, dislike of light or a stiff neck should always be reported to your doctor. The whole group of symptoms is often associated with nothing worse than measles or tonsillitis, but he should see the child now, rather than tomorrow morning, as his symptoms could be due to one of the illnesses which affect the central nervous system and require immediate treatment.

Headaches are never due to 'eye-strain'. A child who frequently announces that his head aches, especially in association with going to school, is more likely to be in need of help in coping without you than of spectacles. Have his eyes tested if it will relieve you, but look for the solution to the headaches in some aspect of his life which is causing tension.

HEAD BANGING 218
In head banging the baby rhythmically knocks his head against something hard—usually the cot bars. Often he keeps up the rhythm by rocking on hands and knees. He bangs hard enough to hurt himself but he does not cry—only the marks tell you there must have been pain.

This kind of head banging is not normal because 'enjoying' pain is an abnormal reaction. It suggests that the child has a lot of anger, aggression or hurt inside him which he is trying to express by turning it on himself. In practical terms, of course, you can pad the end of his cot. But more important is to try and discover why he needs to do it.

Sometimes, if you pay him a lot of extra loving attention, encourage him to express all his feelings in play, and make sure that you never leave him alone in his cot until he is absolutely ready for sleep, you will find that the habit ceases almost overnight. Eventually he may express a lot of aggression towards you instead of against himself. But sometimes nothing you can do seems to stop the habit and you may find that he starts to bang his head against walls or furniture during the day, too, and refuses to be distracted. If this is the case, go to your child health clinic for help and don't be put off by being told that 'lots of children do it'. Only a few do and they are not happy or secure.

HEAD CONTROL 82, 108, 160

HEAD INJURIES
Babies and small children have heads that are heavy in proportion to their bodies so when they fall, heads often suffer. Most bumps and bangs are nothing to worry about. They look worse than they are because the scalp is richly supplied with blood vessels and tightly stretched. Even a graze bleeds copiously while a tiny cut gapes and bleeds freely.

If the child seems normal in every way except for furious crying, he is not badly hurt. Comfort him and let him get on with life. Cotton wool wrung out in cold water may help reduce the swelling of a bump.

If the child seems dazed and shaken, put him to lie down, cover him with a light blanket and watch him while you read a story or otherwise entertain. He will probably go to sleep. That is fine provided his colour and breathing remain normal. If he remains or becomes very pale or his breathing seems unusually harsh, rapid or sounds like snoring, wake him up. If he is easy to rouse, don't worry. If it is difficult or impossible to rouse him, phone for medical advice.

During the hour or so after the bump, watch for any of the following signs:

☐ Vomiting (if he is lying down, make sure he does not inhale the vomit).

☐ Eye peculiarities such as difference in pupil size or failure of both to move together.

☐ Clumsiness or inability to use a limb.

☐ Blurred or irrational speech or strange sounds from a pre-verbal child.

☐ Failure to recognize you or to react normally to his surroundings.

☐ Complaints of continuing headache, separate from the obvious soreness of the bump itself.

☐ Bleeding from ears, nose or mouth (except from a bitten tongue or lip).

If any of these occur, phone your doctor. If you cannot reach him, play safe and take him to the nearest casualty department. You can use your own car if you have someone else to hold him. If not, phone for an ambulance.

Skull Fracture An X-ray may show a hairline crack in your child's skull. Such a fracture will heal spontaneously. Its presence does not mean that the head injury is worse than you had realized. A fracture of the skull is no more serious in itself than a fracture of any other bone. What matters is the damage, if any, that has been done to the brain beneath.

Very occasionally the skull is fractured in such a way that part is forced inwards putting pressure on the brain. Called a 'depressed' skull fracture, this is a serious matter. The depressed portion of bone will probably have to be lifted back into line surgically. Provided its pressure has not done serious injury to the brain it will then heal normally. *See* CONCUSSION; SHOCK; UNCONSCIOUSNESS

HEALTH VISITORS 405

These are fully qualified nurses with special training in most aspects of baby and child care; many are also qualified to help handicapped people. They are based on a community health centre, child health clinic or the practice of a local group of doctors. A health visitor will visit you within ten days of your baby's birth. She will be notified of the birth by the hospital or attending midwife and come of her own accord. How often she comes after that first visit is up to you.

A health visitor's principal role is in preserving health. If your baby is sick she will help you to get him to a doctor or to hospital. If he is well but some aspect of his care or behaviour is bothering you she will listen to you, advise you and help you. She is the person who has time for those questions that seem too silly or trivial to bother a doctor with. She is the person who can act as a bridge for you between home and hospital if things go wrong. She is also the person who can tell you about local facilities; put you in touch with pre-school groups or child-minders or help you to get financial help if your child needs special care.

HEARING adult conversations 377, 391; and copying 264; and making sounds in newborn 114; and reacting to loud sounds in newborn 105, 232; recognizing deficiency in 181, 260; and talking in settled baby 180-183; *see* EARS; LISTENING; TALKING

HEATING *see* WARMTH

HEIGHT GAIN first days 78, 79; first six months 78, 79, 126; six months to one year 201; one year to two and a half 281, 293; two and a half to five 369, 374; *see* GROWTH; WEIGHT GAIN; 506-508

HEPATITIS *see* JAUNDICE

HERNIA IN NEWBORN 47

HERPES SIMPLEX *see* COLD SORES

HICCUPS

Spasmodic involuntary contractions of the diaphragm which draw air through the larynx into the lungs. With each contraction the glottis—the opening at the top of the larynx—suddenly closes, making the characteristic 'hic' sound. Young babies get hiccups frequently. They will neither bother nor harm the baby. No action is necessary. Older children can be irritated by a long-lasting attack.

Most remedies for hiccups depend on forcing the lungs to work harder for a time by holding the breath or by giving the child a fright (which makes him gasp). The most effective remedy requires a paper (not plastic) bag; get the child to breathe into and out of it for about half a minute. Gradually the amount of oxygen in the bagged air will decrease. This makes the child's lungs work harder to get more.

HIGH CHAIRS *see* FEEDING EQUIPMENT

HIVES *see* URTICARIA

HOME HELPS

Most local authorities have arrangements with Home helps who lend a hand with housework, shopping, washing etc., in a household that really needs them. Home helps are scarce. Elderly and handicapped people usually have priority, so having a baby may not qualify you for this service, but it is worth enquiring at your ante-natal clinic. The arrangements are usually fairly informal. Some Home helps will take over and cope with anything that needs doing so that you can rest and devote yourself to the baby. Others may only do basic house-cleaning. As you will be expected to pay for the Home help on a scale adjusted to your income, it may not be any cheaper than finding a 'daily'.

HORMONES mother's causing newborn problems 44, 47; growth 369; milk-producing 52-53, 54; and depression after birth 31, 39

HOSPITAL emotional after-effects 215, 217, 302, 385, 424

Preparing for child's admission If your child faces a planned stay in hospital, perhaps for tonsillectomy, you can do a great deal to prepare him for the experience.

Find out from the specialist whose hospital your child will enter: whether you can room-in with your child; whether you can visit him at any time of day or night and stay as long as you like; whether you will be allowed to stay with him while he is prepared for the operation and to be there waiting for him when he first comes round from the anaesthetic; and whether you will be allowed to stay with him during medical procedures such as injections, dressings etc.

If it seems that the hospital only wants you to hand over your child and then keep out of the way except for a formal visit each afternoon, consider asking your doctor to refer you to another hospital. You can find out which hospital in your area has the best facilities for young children by writing to the National Society for the Welfare of Children in Hospital. *See* USEFUL ADDRESSES

Try to visit the ward to which your child will be admitted, meet the ward Sister, and find out about:

☐ Play facilities: will your child be expected to stay in bed, or are children allowed to play around the ward or to use a special playroom? Are there good play facilities, equipment and toys?

□ Clothes: will your child be allowed to wear his own pyjamas or must he wear hospital ones? If he must wear hospital clothes may he at least keep his home clothes in his locker as a link with home?

□ Food: if your child is particular about what he eats, try to find out whether any choice is offered, and, above all, whether, if he will not eat what is offered, the staff are likely to put pressure on him.

□ Company: find out how big a ward he will be in and the age range which it takes.

□ Lavatory and washing arrangements: will he have to use a bedpan or do the staff allow all children to be taken to the lavatories unless they are really too ill to move? Will he have to have a bath immediately he arrives? What are the baths and lavatories like?

□ His bed: will he be in a cot, a bed with sides or an ordinary bed?

If the answers to these questions are not what you would have chosen, there is obviously nothing you can do to change them. But at least if you know what is in store for the child you can do something to prepare him.

On your last visit to the specialist before the child is admitted, find out everything you can about what will be done to your child. Things that adults accept as simple routine are new and frightening to children:

□ Will he have a routine blood test or X-ray?

□ How will his 'pre-med' (the medicine given just before the operation to make him relaxed and sleepy) be given? By injection, by enema or by mouth?

□ What time of day will the operation take place and therefore over what period of *waking time* will the child not be allowed food or drink?

□ What procedures will he face after the operation? Will there be dressings/gargles/ physiotherapy/ medicines by mouth or by injection etc?

□ What will the child notice about himself when he wakes up? Will he be in pain? In plaster? Will he have visible stitches etc?

Preparing the child Do everything you can to prepare your child for the experience with honest information tailored to be as unalarming as possible.

If he is to have his tonsils out he must know that when he wakes up he will probably bleed a little from his mouth and that his throat will

feel very sore. Stress that the bleeding is just like the bleeding he sees when he cuts himself and that the soreness will not last long and will be helped by medicine and by nice things like ice to suck and ice cream to eat.

Try, in play, to prepare him for hospital life. If he will wear hospital clothes, play at it in a game of dressing up. If he must use a bedpan, play at that too: a boy could even try peeing in a bottle in his own bed. Play 'doctors and nurses' and be the doctor yourself, listen to his chest and pretend to give him an injection.

If he is old enough, get from the library one of the many books about children in hospital designed to familiarize new patients in advance.

When the admission is imminent, do everything you can to make it clear to the child that he will be coming home again shortly. Taking his coat to the cleaners 'so that it will be all nice for you when you come home', or putting a nearly flowering plant by his bed 'so that it will be flowering when you come home', or arranging a tea party 'for a treat when you come home' will all make the child feel that going to hospital is only a break in his safe, ordinary life.

Don't make any promises you may not be able to keep. Equally important, keep any promises you have made, at almost any cost. For example 'it won't hurt a bit' is a silly promise: it may. But 'you will feel better again very soon and if it hurts, the nurses will give you something to make it feel better' is just as reassuring as well as more accurate; it may be up to you to see that they do.

Decide whether you are going to stay with the child or not. If you are not going to 'room-in' decide how much time you are going to spend with him. Make sure he knows, and stick to it.

Rooming-in If he is under seven (or even more important, if he is under four) do room-in if you possibly can. If you do then all the detailed points about daily life on the ward lose their strangeness for him. What is more you will be there to explain all the things that happen to him when they happen. And when he is miserable he will not have to add his desperate missing of you to his other miseries. The payoff for you will be that you will not have to face the behaviour disturbances which are so likely if you 'abandon' him.

Visiting Do spend as much time as you possibly can with him every day however upset he gets when you leave. A child who sits silently without his parents is not 'settled', he is grieving. Left to grieve he becomes convinced that he has been abandoned forever. When his parents finally do appear he is furiously angry at them for betraying him. If you spend a large part of each day with him you can avoid all that. Of course he cries when you leave. But it is right and normal that he should feel that way, and as long as you always reappear when you said you would, he will survive.

Sudden admission to hospital If your child has to go into hospital as an emergency, you obviously have no time for long and careful preparation. Because the child is acutely ill, he is in no state to take in elaborate explanations or to tolerate stress. It is essential that you go with him and that you stay. No hospital has the right to stop you going into the ward with him nor to prevent you from sitting by his cot or bed—all night if necessary. Say that you want to stay by him until you can talk to the doctor about what treatment is planned for your child or at least until your child is awake enough, or calm enough or better enough to understand what is happening and why.

Asking questions Just as you have the right to be with your child when he is ill in hospital, so you have the right to know what is the matter with him and what treatment is proposed. But finding out can be tricky, especially as you must be cooperative and calm so as not to give the staff the feeling that your child is being unnecessarily fussed or other children upset by you.

There are two useful approaches to getting information. The first is to start by asking to speak to the top of the hierarchy. Ask the doctor you see around the ward doing routine tests etc., whether you may see the consultant. He will at least arrange for you to see the person one step down the ladder—the registrar. The other approach is to start from the bottom; make friends with that junior doctor. He is not in charge of your child in the sense of controlling his treatment, but he has access to his 'notes' and is free to question his superiors. You can use the same techniques on the nursing staff who control daily life on the ward. Ask for the sister, or befriend the student nurse.

Emotional after-effects Your child's reaction to having been in hospital will depend on his age, what was done to him and, perhaps above all, whether or not you left him (in his terms 'deserted') or whether you stayed. Expect at least some upset. He may be more clingy than usual; he may be inclined to nightmares or in need of constant bottles. He may revert to being generally more babyish for a while.

If you did have to leave him, expect some anger at you, too. It is a good thing if he can express it, so if he is of talking age do encourage him to talk about what he felt each time you went away.

HUNGER *see* FEEDING

HYGIENE 36, 63, 65, 66, 69, 70, 71, 84, 85, 87, 88, 140, 144-145, 151, 157, 167, 201, 203, 204, 211, 212, 217, 224, 225, 229, 230, 242, 311, 313, 382, 386

I

IMAGINATION being other people 342, 347, 368, 404, 424, 433, 442; in pre-school child 377-378, 391-392, 407-408, 414, 415, 422, 424, 433, 438; in toddler 334-335, 342, 346, 347

IMITATION copying your activities 258-259, 270, 334, 381, 382-383, 411, 435, 438; demonstrations for child 259, 353, 370-371; identification in pre-school child 347, 368, 370-371, 417, 434; imitative stage 264, 342, 354; *not* learning words by 182, 260, 264, 361-362

IMMUNIZATION (VACCINATION)
When a child 'catches' an infectious disease his body fights the invading 'germs' by producing antibodies. When a child is immunized, he is given the 'germs' in a very much weakened (or a killed) form. His body produces antibodies just as it would do if he had been infected with fully active 'germs', but because they were so weakened, he is not ill. If he later comes into contact with the infection he will have the weapons to fight it already formed and will either not get the disease or will get it in a very much reduced form.

If whole populations of children are immunized, the infection becomes rare but the 'germs' still exist. If parents decide not to bother with immunization because a particular disease has become so rare, they risk being partly responsible for starting it up again.

If you are taking your child abroad, tell your doctor. He may alter the immunization programme to make sure that your child has the necessary protection. Keep a record of the dates of your child's injections.

Triple vaccine (DPT) This is a combined vaccine against diphtheria, pertussis (whooping cough) and tetanus, given in three doses as an injection in the arm. The intervals between doses are critical so that if your baby is very late in having his second or third shot he may have to start all over again. If the baby is ill when the shot is due the doctor may defer it. On the other hand if the baby keeps getting bad colds etc., he may decide that the child is particularly in need of protection.
The usual recommended schedule is:
☐ First injection at six months; second injection at eight months and third injection at twelve months.
☐ Booster: at around five years when the child is about to start school, but this booster will not include immunization against whooping cough since by five years a dangerous attack of this disease is unlikely and there is a risk of unpleasant reactions to the vaccine by this age.
Reactions The baby may have a small sore lump at the injection site and be slightly grizzly. If he is feverish or seems ill ring your doctor. The baby may be reacting badly to the pertussis (whooping cough) part of the triple vaccine in which case your doctor should know so that he can decide whether to leave it out of the child's next shot.
Poliomyelitis (infantile paralysis)
☐ The vaccine is given as a syrup to babies and on a lump of sugar to older children, at the same time as the triple vaccination.
☐ Booster: this is given when the child is around five years.
Reactions None.
Measles This is a serious and extremely unpleasant disease. What is more, since most small children *are* immunized, the child who is not may fail to catch it when he is very young (because there are few children to catch it from) but may catch it when he is older and is then likely to be affected even more seriously.
☐ A single injection given during the second year when the immunity received from the mother has waned will protect the child for life. Do not decide to miss it out.

Reactions A slight fever and a mild rash are common about one week after the injection but the child will not be infectious.

A very few children suffer convulsions after the injection. If this should happen to your child remind yourself that such reactions are much more common during a full scale attack of real measles. Because of this very small risk, a child who has had feverish convulsions will not be given the injection. Be sure to discuss any such episodes with the doctor who is to immunize the child.

German measles The illness is so mild that there is no need to immunize small children against it, but this immunization should be offered routinely to all girls before puberty, through their schools, so that there is no chance of them catching German measles during the early months of a pregnancy, when the virus can have devastating effects on the growing foetus. Do not refuse it even if you think your child has already had German measles. You may be wrong as this illness is difficult to diagnose.

Smallpox Routine vaccination is no longer recommended since the disease has been almost eradicated. The slight risk of complications from the vaccination are thought to outweigh the risk of a child catching the disease.

Some countries still demand that everyone entering should have a certificate of up-to-date vaccination, so if you mean to travel with your child he may have to be vaccinated. Certain groups of children, such as those who have had eczema should not be vaccinated. Your doctor will help you weigh the risks. Sometimes a medical certificate of exemption will be accepted instead of a certificate of vaccination.

If your child should come into contact with smallpox your doctor will decide whether he should be vaccinated or not.

Tropical diseases Your travel agent will tell you the legal immunization requirements against such diseases as typhoid, paratyphoid, cholera and yellow fever for any particular country, but only your doctor can help you decide what should be done for your particular child. If your work takes you to such a country then the reactions which can follow full immunization are probably worthwhile. But for the sake of a brief holiday it may not be advisable. *See* INJECTIONS AND BLOOD TESTS

IMPETIGO

The first signs of this disorder are little red spots usually on exposed parts of the skin such as the hands, legs or face. They quickly develop little watery heads and then change into large brownish crusts.

Impetigo can be cleared up by antibiotics (ointment, medicine or both) so take your child to the doctor the moment you suspect it. Left untreated it will spread rapidly. It is also extremely contagious, so other children in the family are likely to get it if you don't act promptly. Keep the infected child's face-cloth, towel etc., separate from everyone else's.

INCUBATION PERIOD see
INFECTIOUS DISEASES
INCUBATOR 38, 39-41

INFECTION IN WOUNDS

You cannot keep wounds bacteria-free (sterile) because there are bacteria everywhere including on the broken skin and on whatever injured it. Washing and covering with a sterile dressing will prevent more bacteria getting in, but minor infection in small wounds and grazes is common. The wound may look wet and weepy. The scab that forms may be yellowish. But the body's defences are coping. Only the superficial skin layers are affected and when the scab falls off healing will be complete.

Warnings If the body is not coping well, the wound will become more painful and the edges will be red and inflamed. There may be some oozing of yellow or white pus. If the wound is small, keep a check on it. If it is large or does not start to heal cleanly in a further 24 hours, show it to your doctor.

Danger signs Occasionally, instead of infected material being carried up out of a wound to harden into a scab, it is carried into the bloodstream and can be extremely serious. Take the child immediately to the doctor if:
☐ Reddish streaks run away under the skin from the edges of the wound.
☐ The skin around it is tight, hot and shiny.
☐ There is continuous, throbbing pain.
☐ There is swelling around the wound.
☐ Pus is oozing from beneath a hardened scab.

INFECTIOUS DISEASES

The common childhood diseases are measles, mumps, whooping cough, scarlet fever, chickenpox, German measles. They are thought of as 'childish complaints' because they are extremely infectious and the immunity your child got from you wears off during his first year so that he will probably catch each disease the first time he comes into contact with it. He is less likely to catch them when he is older because most of the children he mixes with will already have had them—or been immunized.

The incubation period This is the interval between the time when the child 'catches' the illness—takes the 'germs' into his body—and the time when symptoms appear.

Measles	8–14 days
Mumps	14–27 days
Whooping cough	8–14 days
Scarlet fever	1–5 days
Chickenpox	17–21 days
German measles	14–21 days

Quarantine Schools, nurseries etc., used to insist on strict quarantine for children who had been in contact with one of the infectious diseases and might be incubating it. It has been found that quarantine has little effect on the spread of infection, so it is now normally only enforced in the case of 'notifiable infections' such as smallpox. Local Health authorities, nurseries and schools vary in their regulations, so check with them or with your doctor.

Preventing the spread of infection A child with one of these diseases is most infectious at the end of the incubation period and at the beginning of the illness. Unfortunately, incubation periods are so variable that you cannot isolate him 'in case'. But you can warn visitors of the chance that he is infectious—and above all keep him away from pregnant women while he may be brewing German measles. Not every woman is immunized. Within the family it is almost impossible and probably not worth even trying to keep other children from catching what one child has. What is more it is probably just as well for the other children to get the disease over while they are young, and easier to nurse a series of cases all at once.

If you particularly want to protect another child (because she is very young/convalescent/facing a vital exam etc.) it may be worth a try. You could send an older child to stay with a relative or friend, for example. *See* CHICKENPOX; GERMAN MEASLES; IMMUNIZATION; MEASLES; MUMPS; ROSEOLA INFANTUM; SCARLET FEVER; WHOOPING COUGH

INJECTIONS AND BLOOD TESTS

Most injections are quick so if you warn the child that there will be a prick, it will be over before he has time to be very frightened. Try not to let him see the hypodermic. It looks worse than it feels.

Local anaesthetic injections are an unfortunate exception. A rather large volume of fluid has to be injected slowly and directly into the nerve-tract. The needle may have to go between knuckles to numb a finger or between jawbones to numb a tooth. The child will have to be firmly held. A baby or toddler is best supported through it with simple reiterated 'nearly over'—type soothing. An older child may feel better about it if he has something to do. Try getting him to say 'Ouch' as the needle goes in and then to count, loudly, until it is taken out again.

Blood for testing If only a little is needed it may be taken by pricking the child's finger and then squeezing out a drop. The prick only hurts for a second. Warn him, but don't let him see it coming; the fear is worse than the pain.

If more blood is needed it will be taken from a vein—usually one of the veins in the crook of his elbow. Putting the needle into the vein hurts but withdrawing the blood does not. If the doctor gets the needle in first try it will not be too bad, but several tries build up both pain and fear. Check with the doctor that it is essential. Blood tests are occasionally taken as 'routine' on hospital admission. If it is a matter of routine, you can refuse. If it is necessary, hold the child really firmly to give that first try every chance. But if the doctor finds it difficult to get the needle into his tiny vein, don't allow him to go on and on trying until the whole thing becomes a hysterical struggle. It could give the child a terror of hypodermics that lasts for years. When he has had all you think he can take, stop it. Ask for someone more practised.

J K

JAUNDICE

One of the many functions of the liver is to deal with red blood cells when their normal lifespan of about three months is over. The haemoglobin in these 'finished' cells is converted by the liver into bile which is then passed into the intestine and excreted.

If the liver is working inefficiently, bile is not made and got rid of quickly enough. Yellow colouring matter from the breakdown of those finished red blood cells accumulates and can be seen as a yellow tinge to the skin and eyes.

Newborn 'normal' (physiological) jaundice Many newborn babies, especially premature ones, have some jaundice in the first few days of life while the liver builds up to its full working capacity.

Often no treatment is needed although the baby may be a little sleepy and slow to feed and the hospital staff will test his blood from time to time to make sure that the jaundice is getting better, not worse. If the jaundice is severe or slow to clear up, the baby may be treated with ultra-violet light ('phototherapy'). His eyes will be bandaged to protect them and he may only be allowed out of his cot in the nursery for feeds. He may need extra water in addition to whatever he takes from the breast.

Infectious hepatitis is Infection of the liver (hepatitis) is a rare cause of jaundice in small babies. If the mother has this infection there is little purpose in taking the baby away because the incubation period for the various viruses responsible is so long that the baby will probably have caught it, if he is going to, before the illness in the mother is even recognized.

Infectious hepatitis in an older baby or child can be mild or very serious. The yellow jaundice will not develop until the child has been obviously ill for some time.

Other infections causing jaundice In a young baby infection of any organ of the body can eventually cause jaundice because the infection prevents the liver from doing its work efficiently. In such cases yellow jaundice will not be the first sign of ill health. The baby will have gone off his feeds and will probably be already seriously ill.

Antibiotics have done a great deal to reduce this kind of jaundice: infections can now be dealt with at an early stage, long before there is any effect on the liver.

Congenital defects causing jaundice In very rare cases malformation of the liver or bile duct may cause jaundice. It will usually appear when the baby is about ten days old.

If it is only the channel (bile duct) outside the liver which is missing or deformed, surgery may put matters right. If the trouble is within the liver itself there may be nothing that can be done.

JEALOUSY OF NEW BABY 302, 312, 318, 395, 398-402; coping with first days 400-401; inevitability of 395, 398, 401, 402; preparation for 398-399; regression in 400
'JUMPY' BABIES 103, 105-106
KINDERGARTEN see
PRE-SCHOOL GROUPS
'KISS OF LIFE' see
MOUTH-TO-MOUTH RESUSCITATION

L

LANGUAGE see TALKING
LAXATIVES 224, 307 see
CONSTIPATION; EXCRETING
No child should ever be given a laxative without specific instructions from the doctor. His intestine will empty itself when it needs to do so. That may be twice every day or once every four days. There is no relationship between daily bowel movements and good health.

Trying to force a daily pattern with laxatives may upset the whole system, and laxatives tend to be habit forming too. You dose your child on Tuesday because he has not passed a motion since Sunday. He will pass a large motion on Wednesday and his bowels will then be abnormally empty. It may be Saturday before it is ready to empty again, but you have dosed him again on Friday.

If the child is genuinely constipated, so that his motions are not only infrequent but also hard and painful to pass, then the doctor may prescribe a laxative to make things more comfortable for him.
'LAZY EYE' see EYES/Vision disorders
LEFT-HANDEDNESS see
HANDEDNESS
LENGTH see HEIGHT GAIN
'LET DOWN' REFLEX see
DRAUGHT REFLEX
LIBRARIES
Books Almost every public library now has a children's section and most have a Children's Librarian, skilled in finding the right book for the right child. Your child should be an acceptable member from babyhood.
Records Usually lent from the same library as books. Many children's libraries have children's records.
Toys The Toy Libraries Association is starting more and more schemes for lending toys to children who particularly need them. Child-minders may be able to get a selection; parents of retarded or in any way handicapped children may be eligible too.

LICE see NITS
LISTENING and learning to recognize familiar sounds 182, 304, 321, 335; and talking in older baby 260-266; helping him to listen and talk 264; importance of, in learning to talk 260, 355; in newborn 32, 99, 107, 115; to music 350, 432; to rhythmical sounds 99, 115; to voices with pleasure 115, 180, 220, 221, 260, 380 see EARS; HEARING
LONG-SIGHT see EYES/Vision disorders
LOOKING at books 183, 350, 423, 432; at television, 377, 407, 433; and learning by imitation 259; toys for 107, 158, 161
LYING 278, 366, 436-437, 438

M

MASTURBATION
Babies have to find out about their own bodies just as they have to find out about everything else. Their genitals tend to come as a pleasant surprise to them because they are usually covered with nappies—so nakedness can mean an instant exploring hand. Later on the child discovers that touching and rubbing his or her genitals feels nice.

Masturbation will not harm the child in any way, nor does an early interest in it suggest that the child is particularly 'highly-sexed'. If he or she sometimes occupies those boring times awake in bed by masturbating, that is a private and personal matter. If you walk in and find the child red faced and panting you will probably be shocked, but that is because adults prefer to believe that small children have no sexual feelings, not because they either do or do not or should not have any!

Masturbation in public is embarrassing. You can usually divert a very small child before he or she gets started. An older child can be told, quite simply, that it is not something to do in front of other people. It may help if you use the term 'private parts'. But keep the whole matter on a par with picking his nose; a question of acceptable behaviour not moral outrage. Very occasionally a young child, usually a boy, becomes a compulsive masturbator and uses this as a comfort habit, masturbating frequently. He is turned in on himself and the pleasure he can give himself, rather than being open to the world and the pleasure other people can give him. Ask for help from your doctor or clinic.

MEALS see FEEDING; FOODS

MEASLES

Incubation period 8–14 days

First signs

□ A 'bad cold' with runny nose, reddened, watery eyes and a cough.

□ Fever which gradually rises rather than dropping as you would expect in a genuine cold.

□ Child complains of feeling ill.

Definite signs

□ 'Koplik's spots', which look like grains of salt, appear on the inside of the cheeks about day 3 or 4.

□ Rash proper appears on day 4 or 5, as small dark red spots starting behind the ears and spreading and becoming blotchy over the face and body.

Degree of illness

□ He may be exceedingly ill from about day 3 until day 5 or 6 when the rash is fully out.

□ Very high fever with delirium is quite usual.

□ Dry irritating cough disturbs him.

□ Sore eyes are distressing.

Possible complications

□ Acute conjunctivitis with intolerance of light. (Light will not damage his eyes but may make them feel worse.)

□ Sore throat spreading to middle ear.

□ Secondary infection leading to bronchitis or pneumonia.

□ Inflammation of the brain, leading to encephalitis.

What the doctor may do

□ Confirm the diagnosis.

□ Prescribe lotion for eyes.

□ Prescribe antibiotics to protect against/treat secondary infections.

What you can do

□ Free yourself from housework etc. for intensive and continuous nursing for at least a week; much longer if there are complications.

□ Bathe eyes often using lotion or boiled water on cotton wool.

□ Keep fever to reasonable level.

□ Keep fluid intake up with frequent small drinks.

□ Report immediately to the doctor if: he has earache; breathing becomes laboured; cough becomes thick, with sputum; fever rises sharply once it has begun to drop; he seems suddenly iller after seeming a little better; he becomes semi-conscious or difficult to rouse. *See* NURSING

MEASURING YOUR CHILD 369

MECONIUM *see* STOOLS

MEDICINE/Giving dosage by weight 78; *see* DOCTOR; ENEMAS; FIRST AID SUPPLIES; LAXATIVES; PAIN RELIEVERS

Your doctor prescribes medicine because your child needs it. If he needs it at all he needs every dose. Don't stop giving it because he seems better or because he dislikes it. If you really cannot get it down him or he vomits it, tell the doctor immediately. Most medicines (such as antibiotics) are supposed to be given at regular intervals so that the level of the drug in the child's bloodstream stays constant. Ask the doctor whether the child must be woken at night to take medicine, or whether the stated number of doses can be fitted in while he is awake. Write down the times you give it. It is easy to forget a dose or to get muddled especially if you are giving two drugs on different dose schedules.

Liquid medicines These are usually prescribed for small children in preference to pills but often taste nasty with synthetic fruit 'concealing' a bitter drug. Sit him up on a chair or on your lap (never give medicine with the child lying down; he might choke) and put a glass of his favourite drink beside him ready to wash the taste away. Measure the proper dose into a big spoon (it will spill from a small one), get the child to open his mouth and just pour it in well back.

If he simply hates it, try concealing the taste by mixing the proper dose into a spoonful of something soft but strong tasting like apple sauce or chocolate mousse. Tell him it is medicine but that it does not taste nasty this way and then proceed on the assumption that he will take it. Don't pretend it is just apple sauce or the funny taste may put the child off apple sauce as well as medicine. Don't try to hide the medicine in a drink. It will only sink to the bottom and stick to the sides. Even if he empties the glass he will not have had it all. If he still will not take it you can try:

□ *Force* Wrap the child in a blanket so that he cannot bat the spoon out of your hand and then calmly wait him out. Pop it in the minute he opens his mouth either to cooperate or protest.

□ *Bribery* With an older child you can often strike a bribe/bargain, perhaps a sweet immediately afterwards, a comic he badly wants or the promise of a game.

Changing the medicine Your doctor may sound a bit scornful if you admit that you cannot get the medicine down the child. But it can be extremely difficult: maybe

he has not had to try recently. He can certainly prescribe the same drug in a different form.

Pills and capsules If the child wants to cooperate, but simply loathes the taste of the liquid, try capsules or pills (sugar-coated if possible). Some children manage to swallow these at a surprisingly early age. Wetting the capsules to make the gelatine coating slippery makes them easier to swallow. Explain that the bit of his tongue which tastes things is at the front and that if the pill or capsule goes at the back of his tongue he will not taste it. Give him a drink to hold, get him to open wide, pop it right back on his tongue and encourage him to empty that glass.

If he cannot or will not cooperate, capsules are useless as they must never be opened or crushed. Tablets can be crushed to a really fine powder. Put a layer of anything slippery and strong tasting that your child really likes—jam, honey, chocolate spread—in a small spoon. Dump the powder on top, all in one place, and cover it with another delicious layer. The spoonful should simply slide down the child's throat and he will never taste the powder at all. If you cannot think of anything the child will want to eat a whole spoonful of, try *mixing* the powder with a very small amount of yeast extract or something with an equally strong or salty cover-up taste to make a sort of pellet no bigger than a salt spoon. If you are still stuck, there is one more trick to try with a whole pill. Push it into the tiniest piece of banana which will hold it. Pop it in and encourage him to swallow this 'banana pill' straight down. Don't use this technique with a grape or cherry. It could lead to choking.

MEMORY AND

FORETHOUGHT development of 235, 259, 269, 272, 273; in toddler 276, 335, 342; in pre-school child 366, 390, 392, 417; in toilet training 305-308

MILK/Breast banks for 41; colostrum 49, 50, 52, 64; changing to cow's milk from 201; compared to cow's and formula 49, 64, 134, 137, 202; expressing of 41, 53, 54, 59, 61, 63, 128; production of 52, 54, 63; storage of 63; *see* DIET

MILK/Cow's changing to from breast or formula 201, 209; compared to breast and formula 49, 64, 134, 137, 202; cooking with 139, 145, 210, 285; nutrients in 209, 214, 282, 285, 286, 294; *see* ALLERGIES; DIET

MILK/Emergency feed for baby
If you should be caught out without a supply of your baby's usual formula or without breast milk for a breast-fed baby, you can put together an emergency feed.

Evaporated milk Any brand of unsweetened evaporated milk will do. Do not use sweetened condensed milk.
☐ Boil water.
☐ Mix with milk in proportion of one ounce (28 ml) of milk to two ounces (57 ml) of water.
☐ Add a flat teaspoon (5 ml size) of sugar to every 4 ozs (115 ml) of this made-up mixture.

Fresh milk
☐ Pour off any visible cream.
☐ Boil water.
☐ Boil milk.
☐ Mix together in equal quantities.
☐ Add one flat teaspoon (5 ml size) of sugar to every five ounces (140 ml) of this made-up mixture. If you have no bottle, feed, slowly in an upright position, by spoon.
N.B. Neither of these emergency formulae will be adequate and digestible for a baby over a long period. Get formula or medical advice as soon as possible.

MILK/Formula choosing a 49, 64-65, 89; compared to breast and cow's 49, 64, 134, 137, 202; making up accurately, importance of 64, 66, 70, 77, 78, 88, 89, 133; storing 65, 70; transporting 71 *see* DIET
'MISERABLE' BABIES 104-105
MITES *see* SCABIES
MIXED FEEDING *see* FEEDING
MOBILES 107, 161, 168, 178-179, 190, 376 *see* PLAYTHINGS
MORO RESPONSE *see* NEWBORN REFLEX BEHAVIOUR
MOTIONS *see* EXCRETING; STOOLS; TOILET TRAINING
MOUTH exploring with 155, 166-167, 177, 179, 192, 230, 248, 258, 336; *see* BURNS AND SCALDS; COLD SORES; GUM BOILS; MEASLES; MOUTH ULCERS; PLAYTHINGS; SUCKING; SUCKING BLISTERS; THRUSH; TONGUE-TIE

MOUTH-TO-MOUTH RESUSCITATION ('KISS OF LIFE')
When a child stops breathing the blood which his heart is pumping around his body stops having its oxygen renewed. His brain will be damaged within about 3-4 minutes. He will be finally dead soon after.
Older methods of artificial respiration tried to force the victim's own lungs to take in air. Mouth-to-mouth puts air into his lungs from your own. Your 'used' breath still contains enough

oxygen to keep him going until natural breathing starts again or help arrives. Started quickly and kept up until a doctor says it is unnecessary, the kiss of life can be the one thing that will save your child. BUT THE KISS OF LIFE NEEDS SKILL. If you ever need it, there will be no time to read instructions or fumble preparations. Get yourself taught the technique at an approved 'life-saving' course.

MOUTH ULCERS
Single mouth ulcers may appear as a sore red a*ea with a yellowish-white centre on the inside of the child's cheek, on the gum or beneath the tongue. They are very painful indeed. They take about 10 days to clear up. The most useful treatment is usually a cortisone ointment which your doctor may prescribe.
Several shallow white ulcers appearing together on the roof of the child's mouth, inside the cheeks, or on the gums, may be a first attack of the herpes simplex virus; later attacks will take the form of cold sores. This first attack is extremely painful. The child will probably refuse all solid food; he may even find it difficult to drink. A straw will help. Vaseline applied gently to each ulcer may help a little by protecting them from rubbing against the teeth.

MULTIPLE MINOR INJURIES
Bumps and bangs, cuts and grazes are part of a child's everyday life when they occur singly. But the kind of tumble that leaves a child with a bumped head, a cut elbow, a wrenched shoulder and a skinned hand and knee is a slightly different matter. Each of the injuries is trivial in itself, but taken together they add up to a nasty shock and to a very uncomfortable day or two. If the child seems upset and miserable, treat him for shock and when he feels better after an hour or so, encourage him to pass the rest of the day quietly, perhaps rather as you would encourage him to rest if he were convalescent.

MUMPS
Incubation period 14–28 days
First signs
☐ May seem generally off colour for 1-2 days.

Definite signs
☐ Swollen, painful gland running from behind the ear to beneath the jaw bone.
☐ Dry mouth (the affected glands normally make the saliva and now do not).
☐ Acute stinging pain on swallowing anything acid.

☐ Increasing swelling, changing the whole shape of his face.
Degree of illness
☐ Minor, unless there are complications, but pain on swallowing will be troublesome and he may be self-conscious.
Possible complications
☐ The illness may affect each side of his face in turn so that the other side swells just as you thought he was recovering.
☐ Deafness; often overlooked, so check.
☐ Very rarely inflammation of the spinal cord 'mumps meningitis' starting about 10 days afterwards with high fever, delirium and stiff neck.
What the doctor may do
☐ Diagnose; check hearing.
What you can do
☐ Be tactful; don't let other children laugh unless he himself thinks his face looks funny.
☐ Remember that opening his mouth/swallowing are really painful. Give bland nourishing drinks (ice cream milkshakes, drinking chocolate etc.) through a straw. Help him rinse out his dry mouth.
☐ Give pain relievers if pain keeps him awake.
☐ Keep an eye on him during the week after recovery so that you recognize meningitis quickly. *See* NURSING

MUSIC 99, 115, 189, 263, 269, 350, 423, 432; *see* PLAYTHINGS

N

NAIL-BITING
A great many pre-school and older children bite their nails at least sometimes. Some combine nail-biting with bedwetting, frequent nightmares and other signs of stress or insecurity.
If your child is one of these it may be as well to think through his daily life and the happenings of recent weeks and see whether you can identify any reasons for his feeling anxious just now. But many children who bite their nails show no other signs of insecurity. They simply find it an enjoyable occupation when they are bored or fed up, and irresistible if they happen to have a sharp or chipped nail. You will not stop the habit by nagging but you may be able to lessen it by making sure that the child's fingernails are kept comfortably smooth (teach him to use an emery board for himself) and by offering a girl colourless nail varnish which she may want to

keep unchipped. Don't put the child to bed in mittens or paint nasty-tasting medicine on his fingers. You may turn a casual and unimportant habit into a real issue between you.

NAPPIES changing 86, 229, 311-312; giving up nappies by day 309; giving up night-time nappies 384; types 85, 229; washing and sterilizing 85, 87

NAPPY RASH 84, 87, 151, 221, 229 *see* RASHES

NAPS *see* SLEEPING

NEIGHBOURHOOD GROUPS
Bringing up a child can be an exciting job but it can be a lonely one too. A neighbourhood group can help you to meet up with other local people in the same situation. Self-help community groups are starting up in many areas. You may find one that suits you through your Health Visitor, on your Newsagent's or Clinic noticeboard or at an actual community centre nearby. If not, try some of the organizations listed under SOME USEFUL ADDRESSES. *See* PRE-SCHOOL GROUPS

'NEO-NATAL COLD SYNDROME' 81 *see* CHILLING

'NEO-NATAL URTICARIA' 42 *see also* URTICARIA

NETTLE RASH *see* URTICARIA

NEW BABY preparing child for 398-402; as cause of stress in child 302, 322, 330, 347, 385, 395

NEWBORN CHARACTERISTICS 42-47; and appropriate handling 103-104, 126, 189; jumpiness 105-106, 157; miserableness 104-105, 156, 157, 158, 194, 235; sleepiness 106; suckiness 50, 100, 157; wakefulness 106-107, 158-159, 223 *see* CRYING AND COMFORTING

NEWBORN POSTURES 108-113, 160-161

NEWBORN REFLEX BEHAVIOUR 32, 50-51, 55-58, 61, 71, 108-113

NIGHT FEEDS *see* FEEDING

NIGHTLIGHTS *see* SLEEPING

NIGHTMARES *see* FEAR; SLEEPING

NIGHT TERRORS *see* FEAR; SLEEPING

NIGHT WAKING *see* FEAR; SLEEPING

NIGHT WANDERING *see* SLEEPING

NIPPLES *see* BREASTS

NITS
The tiny sticky white eggs of a louse which can infest a child's hair. A child is more likely to acquire lice from an infested friend if his hair is dirty and greasy. Make sure it is regularly shampooed.

What to do Special shampoos kill the lice and prevent hatching of the nits which can be combed out with a very fine metal comb. Consult chemist, doctor or school for the right shampoo for any given outbreak as lice-sensitivities are changing rapidly.

NOISE *see* SOUNDS

NOSEBLEEDS
Nosebleeds caused by a blow on the head or nose should be seen by a doctor. Minor nosebleeds can be caused by the child picking his nose, or by the spontaneous rupture of a tiny blood vessel inside it.
What to do
☐ Reassure the child. Most hate the sight of their own blood so sit him up leaning forward over a washbasin with the tap running fast so that it is continually washed away. Don't let him swallow the blood: it will make him feel sick.
☐ If bleeding is heavy or goes on for more than two minutes, pinch the nostrils firmly together for two minutes during which time the blood should clot.

☐ Don't let the child blow or fiddle with his nose for at least an hour even though the clotted blood will feel uncomfortable.
☐ If the child has repeated nosebleeds for no apparent reason he may have a fragile blood vessel in his nose. It may eventually have to be cauterized. *See also* HEAD INJURIES

NOSE BLOWING
This technique is hard for a small child to learn. You are doing well if he can manage it efficiently and discreetly by the time he goes to school. Teach him always to block one nostril with his finger and then to blow down the other. Blowing down both nostrils at once may force mucus into the eustachian tubes and lead to middle ear infections.
Remember that disposable paper handkerchiefs are more hygienic than washable ones. *See* EARS

NOSE DROPS
A small baby who has a heavy cold may get frantic because he cannot breathe through his nose and therefore cannot suck properly.

Your doctor may prescribe drops which will temporarily reduce the stuffiness in his nose and let him suck more comfortably. Don't use them unless they have been prescribed. Don't use more often than the doctor advises or for more than two days without checking with him. Sometimes these drops have a rebound effect; they dry up the nasal secretions so efficiently that the body makes extra mucus to make up and the nose becomes even more stuffy than before.
Giving drops
☐ If the dropper in the bottle is glass or rigid plastic, buy a separate soft rubber dropper, which will not damage the baby's nose should he move his head suddenly.
☐ Use the bottle's own dropper to draw up the right number of drops and drop them into a clean spoon, then suck them into the soft dropper.
☐ Lie the baby across your lap with his head hanging down a little over your thigh. Hold his head still with one hand, turning it a little to one side.
☐ Use the other hand to drop the right number of drops into the upper nostril. Hold him still for a minute or two and then turn his head a little the other way and put the drops into the other nostril.

NOSE PICKING
All children pick their noses from time to time and eat the product. The most you may be able to do is to teach him not to do it in public.
Children who frequently pick their noses as a nervous habit can make real scabs and sores inside the nostrils which make picking even more irresistible. Keeping the fingernails short is the best solution—but let him assume that you are cutting them because they need cutting, not as a punishment.

NURSERY SCHOOLS *see* PRE-SCHOOL GROUPS

NURSING
Going to hospital is always upsetting for babies and small children. The more confident you can become, as a nurse, the more likely it is that the doctor will let you keep him at home. If you are panic-stricken by an attack of croup or a raging fever, he will have the child admitted for your sake. If you can cope, the majority of illnesses can be managed with the help of visits from him and/or a nurse who will perform any necessary technical procedures.
Caring for an ill child is like caring for a well one only more so. He needs proper food, warmth,

company, but he needs them adapted to his physical condition and brought into line with the doctor's orders.

Food Unless the doctor orders otherwise, he can have anything he wants to eat and need have nothing he does not want. But liquids are vital, especially if the illness involves vomiting and/or diarrhoea. If you are worried because he drinks little or vomits what he drinks, ask your doctor for a target quantity for each day. Give it to him in tiny glassfuls, varying the liquid from plain iced water through fruit juices to plain and flavoured milk. An almost weaned baby will probably drink more if allowed to use his bottle. A child may enjoy a straw to drink through.

Warmth An ill child needs all his energy for getting better. Your aim is to keep him at a temperature which prevents him needing to use any for keeping warm or cool. This means a *steady* temperature.

☐ If he goes from an overheated living room to an icy bathroom, his body must work hard to adapt.

☐ If he is in bed, the pyjamas that keep him comfortable every night will be right now, too. If he is up, ordinary indoor clothes are fine. If he is neither one nor the other, he needs a compromise such as pyjamas with a light jersey and slipper socks.

☐ Keep rooms warm but airy. Open windows will keep fresh air circulating.

☐ Don't snuggle a feverish child up. His body can cope with the excess heat much better if he is very lightly dressed under very few covers. If you are actually working to reduce a fever, you want free air circulation all round his skin. Leaving him naked with only a sheet to lend an illusion of safe comfort is ideal but if he feels too exposed, find him a thin porous tee shirt and pants to wear.

Bed or not? Only in very rare cases will your doctor order bed-rest. If he does not, leave it to the child.

Babies will want snuggling They will want lots of cuddling and holding. When they cannot have that, they need a soft nest somewhere near you. Don't put a baby who is ill away in his cot. Put him in his pram nearby.

Children need nests A child who feels very unwell, has a headache etc., may want to lie down. But unlike an adult he will want company, not privacy.

☐ Make him a nest of pillows on the sofa or, ideally, use a folding guest bed which can be easily erected anywhere in the house or garden and is just the right height for him to get in and out of as he pleases.

☐ If he is ill enough to spend a lot of time in it, you can move bed and child from time to time to give him a change of scene, such as access to the television. If you have no such bed, a thick eiderdown or air bed on the floor will do as well.

☐ Having him with you will save you endless trips up and downstairs. It will also keep his real bed as the place he goes at night, just as usual. If he has not spent all day in it he will not be sick of the sight of it and you will more easily be able to keep to normal bedtime routines.

Passing the time Both being ill and nursing soon become boring. If the illness is very brief—a bad cold, for example—you can probably keep him happy and stay sane yourself if you just drop everything while you read to him, watch television with him and play games. But if the illness is something longer-term like a bad attack of measles, it will be easier for you both if you get organized.

☐ Cancel any engagements that you are doubtful you can make.

☐ Arrange for someone to get in food for easy meals.

☐ Try and find some things you can do which will amuse you, while keeping you available to the nested child. A bout of cooking for the freezer, jam-making, dress-making or even cupboard turning-out can give you a sense of accomplishment and amuse him.

Handling the child Feeling unwell will make him irritable and easily frustrated. While you do not want him to feel that persuading you that he is ill means total licence and your undivided attention, it is no good expecting his most reasonable and grown up behaviour. A happy medium means treating him as if he were one stage younger than his actual age, dropping the top demands of the moment. Treat a crawler like a baby, a toddler like a crawler, a pre-school child like a toddler. . . . But within those concessions, ask for, or rather behave as if you take for granted, ordinarily civil behaviour.

Routines The child will feel more ordinary and behave more normally if you keep some pattern to his day. Don't let the hours drift past unmarked.

☐ Get him up in the morning even if it is only into clean pyjamas and his nest instead of bed.

☐ Make small ceremonies of meals even if he is only having a drink.

☐ Put him to bed for his usual naps and keep bedtime just as usual even if you know that you will be up and down to him all night.

Play While your company and attention will be what he really craves, the following ideas may help to relieve his boredom and give you at least a little time to get on with other things:

☐ A 'being ill box' is a good idea especially during the pre-school years when many children seem to get one cold or throat infection after another. Assemble all the surplus things your child is given, like his second painting book or those felt-tip pens; odds and ends that he has had and lost interest in, like trinkets won at a fair; things you might have put in the 'odds and ends box' but did not because they were too good — like pretty boxes or tinsel ribbon from Christmas — plus a few small items you buy from time to time, like a new drawing block, some plasticine, coloured sticky labels and transfers.

☐ If you want to be more elaborate than this, order a parcel of tiny toys from a wholesaler; they are mostly junk, but just right for novelty for a bored, miserable child. Add one or two toys that your child is not usually allowed to have. They might be things that you find too expensive to keep replacing, like a battery-operated torch, or something too noisy, like a mouth organ. Alternatively present him with a 'comforting person' which is any soft toy that you have prevented from becoming part of your child's regular 'family' but which appears each time he is ill, and with anything entrancing of your own that the child would not normally be allowed to play with like costume jewellery or discarded make-up.

Put the whole lot into a box and hide it. The whole point is lost if the child knows what is in it. Dip in, or let the child dip in, either at regular intervals through the day, or just whenever you think he really needs a new distraction.

☐ A small child needs interesting things to look at and to fiddle with. Try a mobile; the family goldfish bowl to keep him company, and something 'fiddly' like a small abacus, a string of beads or a squeaky toy.

☐ When you cannot be with him he may enjoy the radio, preferably tuned to something like a 'talk-in' rather than just music which will soon become a background blur. If he is in the same room with the television, this is the one time when casual watching might be allowed.

□ When he is a bit better but does not want to be up he must have a proper play surface. A large tray on his knee will do but a swing-across bed-table is better because he does not have to keep still.

□ If you put a large plastic tablecloth right over the bed, he can do almost anything in bed that he likes doing out. Try a bowl of sugar for 'sand play', a mixing bowl and marbles to whizz round and round it, pastry to make into 'men', your old make-up and a mirror to watch his own transformation in, and a propped up tray to whizz his cars down.

□ When you cannot play with him, try starting him off on activities and then setting him tasks to complete while you are busy. Show him old photo albums and ask him to find all the pictures of himself; make a string of paper dolls and then ask him to colour them; set all his toy animals out and then ask him to put them in their proper families; help him find some pictures of cars in a magazine and then ask him to find as many more as he can; start a bead necklace and leave him to finish it or bring him the shells you collected on holiday and ask him to sort them out.

□ Being confined and inactive is often a time when the child learns a lot because he does not get distracted by his desire to rush off and be physically active. Read to him; show him how to cut out neatly or to colour accurately; talk to him and use books to look things up in; introduce him to a new puzzle or bring out a construction set that he has never taken much interest in and see if now is the time for him to find he can do it.

□ Choose some playthings that do not slide about and get lost in the bedclothes all the time. He may enjoy those cut-out shapes that miraculously stick, all by themselves, on to sheets of special felt. He may enjoy a magnet and things to 'catch' with it.

□ Glove puppets are excellent company in bed. You may find that the child will use a glove puppet to tell you what he is feeling: some children find it much easier to express misery, headache, dread of medicines etc., through 'someone' else. You can make glove puppets very simply or, if bought puppets are too expensive, you can gradually accumulate a collection of 'finger

puppets' which most small children find easier to use. See FEVER

NUTRIENTS *see* DIET
NUTRITION *see* DIET; FEEDING; FOODS

O P Q

OBESITY *see* FAT BABIES AND CHILDREN
OPERATIONS *see* ADENOIDS; APPENDIX; CIRCUMCISION; HOSPITAL; TONSILS
PAIN *see* CRYING AND COMFORTING
PAIN RELIEVERS
Babies should not be given any pain relievers without a doctor's instructions. If your baby is in pain, call the doctor. Pain relievers may 'cover up' something that needs treatment, such as earache. They may even make him worse: aspirin for a stomach-ache, for example, can be really dangerous as the drug has an irritating effect on the stomach-lining which may already be inflamed.

For an older child, the correct dosage of aspirin or paracetamol can relieve the pain of toothache, headache, sunburn, sprains and strains, a newly set fracture etc. Use a liquid or soluble product meant for children; in the exact dose suggested for his weight and at no more than the intervals recommended. Give with plenty of fluid. Avoid giving it on an empty stomach. Do not continue regular doses for more than 24 hours without consulting a doctor. See MEDICINE/Giving

PAINTING *see* DRAWING AND PAINTING
PARALLEL PLAY *see* GETTING ON WITH OTHER CHILDREN; PLAYING AND LEARNING
PENIS 47, 84, 391, 413; *see* CIRCUMCISION

PENIS/Caught in zip fastener
What to do
□ Don't try to unzip. Take the weight of the trousers in one hand and, with the other, lie the child down so there is no added pull on his trapped skin.
□ If the end of the penis of a circumcised child is caught, keep him absolutely still while you call an ambulance, or carry him carefully to the car if you have someone who can drive you to hospital.
□ If only the foreskin or superficial skin of the shaft is caught, cut the trousers from the waistband downwards, on each side of the zipper. Once you can see the piece of metal pinching his skin, you should be able to lift it free. If one try doesn't do it, make for hospital.

The child will need plenty of reassurance that no permanent damage has been done.

PETS 93, 230, 336, 356-357 *see* BITES; PLAYTHINGS; RINGWORM; SAFETY
PHENYLKETONURIA (PKU)
This is a biochemical disorder affecting only about 1 in 10,000 babies. Although it is so rare, the results of untreated PKU are disastrous, including extreme mental retardation as well as various physical difficulties. Provided it is recognized very early on, a special (and difficult) diet can prevent these effects altogether, so in the UK every baby has a blood test for it on the sixth day of life.

PHOBIAS *see* FEAR
PHYSICAL ACTIVITY first days 108-113; first six months 160-179; six months to one year 236-247; one year to two and a half 328-333, 348-349; two and a half to five 406-413; emotional importance of 311, 348, 386-387, 407-408, 444; importance of outdoors 190, 268, 270, 351-352, 422-423; kicking for fun 146, 158, 161, 189, 226-227; pleasures of naked play 152, 190, 229, 308; romping 184, 268, 348-349; setting himself challenges 296, 298, 406, 431; suggestions for indoors *see* PLAYTHINGS; PLAYING AND LEARNING
PICTURES 116, 218, 298, 341-342, 350, 352, 376, 429
'PINK EYE' *see* EYES/Infections
PLASTIC dangers of 93, 144; pants 81, 85, 151, 229, 308; surfaces 99, 377, 384; *see* SAFETY; SMOTHERING
PLAYGROUNDS 296, 298, 319, 351, 405 *see* USEFUL ADDRESSES
PLAYGROUPS *see* PRE-SCHOOL GROUPS; USEFUL ADDRESSES
PLAYING AND LEARNING first six months 184-192; six months to one year 267-271; one year to two and a half 334-354; two and a half to five 422-433; adjusting play to early temperament 103-107, 158-159, 184, 189; coping with emotions through 347, 406-408, 411-412; effect of physical abilities on 161-163, 267-270, 272-273, 296, 298, 335-336, 408-409, 431; hands as playthings 99, 165-167, 181; hand-eye coordination and play-learning 168-177; imagination in 342, 347, 368, 422, 424; importance of 184, 267-268, 334-341, 422-424; interaction between language and 181, 335, 341-342, 414; mental concepts formed through 334-336, 341-342; other children and 351, 354, 393, 396, 399, 400, 402-403,

404-405, 412, 423, 433; providing partnership for 183, 184-185, 189, 190, 223, 257, 259, 268, 270, 298, 347, 350, 353-354, 410, 429; providing play-space 158, 238-239, 242, 259, 267-268, 272, 351-352; providing playthings for 165-166, 178-179, 190, 192, 222-223, 227, 258, 259, 268, 304, 324, 330, 334, 350, 376

PLAYMATES *see* GETTING ON WITH OTHER CHILDREN; PLAYING AND LEARNING; PRE-SCHOOL GROUPS

PLAYROOMS 267-268, 351

PLAYTHINGS *see* 498-505

POISONING

If a child eats or drinks something poisonous he must be treated quickly. The longer the poison stays in his stomach, the more of it will be absorbed into his bloodstream and the more seriously ill he will be.

But the treatment is extremely frightening and unpleasant for the child. It will involve making him violently sick and/or passing a tube into his stomach and siphoning out the contents. He will probably be kept in hospital overnight to be watched for effects of poison already absorbed. So while you must play safe, do be sure that he really has eaten or drunk something dangerous before you rush him to hospital. It would be tragic to put him through all that, if the pills you thought he had eaten were on the floor all the time.

Pills and medicines Assume that anything your child takes from the medicine cupboard may poison him: e.g. very few sleeping pills/ tranquillizers/anti-depressants are needed to kill a child. Painkillers, such as aspirin, kill many children every year. Anti-histamines and travel sickness tablets contain powerful and dangerous drugs. Even medicines (like vitamins or iron tablets) which may be good for a child in controlled doses can kill him if he takes much more.

Household cleaning products Assume that all are potentially dangerous. They may be alkalis such as bleach, ammonia or caustic soda, acids such as carbolic soap, or disinfectants and petroleum products such as dry cleaning fluid or liquid polish. The first two groups burn the throat and stomach. The third group releases poisonous gas which can be fatal.

Garden products Any insecticide, weedkiller or fungicide is dangerous. Some can be fatal if even a tiny quantity is tasted.

Garage and workshop Oil-based paints, paint removers such as turpentine, car polishes, metal polishes, petrol and paraffin are only a few of the serious poisons he might find and take.

Garden Yew berries, laburnum seeds, deadly nightshade (and the more common woody nightshade and enchanter's nightshade) are all extremely poisonous. Privet and laurel berries are less dangerous but still a serious matter.

Adult pleasures Tobacco is a lethal poison if swallowed. A single cigarette could kill a one year old. Alcohol is also surprisingly poisonous. A good swig of neat spirits can kill a toddler.

What to do

If your child has swallowed any pills, medicine, tobacco, alcohol or berries:

☐ Clear his mouth of any bits he has not yet swallowed. Put him face down across your knee with his head lower than his hips, and put two fingers right to the back of his throat and wiggle them until he vomits. If he retches but nothing comes up, make him drink a big glass of water or milk and then try again. Be bold.

☐ Whether you have managed to make him sick or not, give up your first aid after three minutes and get him to hospital. Take the poison with you.

N.B. Don't give him an emetic like salt or mustard and water. They take too long to prepare; too long to force down the child; often don't work and are dangerous anyway. Don't make him sick lying down on his back, or if he seems drowsy. He might breathe his vomit and choke.

If the poison is any form of household cleaner, garden spray, paint solvent, petrol or paraffin, vomiting it up will burn his throat more and he might breathe it in, so don't make him sick.

☐ Try to dilute the poison so that it does not damage his stomach so badly. Give him as big a drink of milk as you can persuade him to sip quickly. Don't force him or he may vomit.

☐ Swill his mouth out and sponge his face to get rid of any chemicals that are still damaging his skin. Rush him to hospital. Take the poison with you. *See also* SAFETY

POLIOMYELITIS *see* IMMUNIZATION

POSSETTING

This term is often used to describe a young baby's tendency to 'bring back' a little milk during or immediately after feeds. *See* VOMITING

POST-NATAL DEPRESSION *see* DEPRESSION AFTER BIRTH

POTS *see* TOILET TRAINING

PRAMS cat-net 93, 401; choosing 238-239 *see* BEDS AND COTS; leaving outside 80, 93, 97, 100; playthings for 178-179; pushchairs 239, 243, 333; *see* SAFETY

PREMATURE BABIES 38, 41, 43, 78, 80

PRE-SCHOOL GROUPS 392-397, 411-412, 423; assessing 395, 419; first days at 396-397; informal neighbourhood 352; preparation for 395-396; readiness for 393, 399, 405, 420; types of 393-394 *see* GETTING ON WITH OTHER CHILDREN

PUNCTURE WOUNDS *see* CUTS AND GRAZES

PUNISHMENT 273, 278, 290, 291, 293, 326, 376, 411-412, 438, 440

PUSHCHAIRS *see* PRAMS

PYLORIC STENOSIS *see* VOMITING

QUARANTINE PERIOD *see* INFECTIOUS DISEASES

R

RASHES

Children quite frequently produce dramatic skin rashes, with no other symptoms. They go away as suddenly as they came. Some of these are probably allergic reactions; some may be caused by viruses. Your doctor may not be able to diagnose such a rash but once he has assured you that it is nothing serious, it really does not matter what it is. *See* CHICKENPOX; ECZEMA; GERMAN MEASLES; IMPETIGO; MEASLES; RINGWORM; ROSEOLA INFANTUM; SCARLET FEVER; URTICARIA.

REACHING OUT *see* HAND/EYE COORDINATION

READING ALOUD 183, 298, 350, 376, 423, 432

REINS 331

RHESUS DISEASE

About 15% of women have blood which is Rhesus negative. If such a woman has a baby by a man who is Rhesus positive her baby's blood group may not match her own. While the placenta is under pressure during labour some of the baby's red blood cells can be squeezed through into the mother's circulation. If this happens and if the baby's red cells are Rhesus positive, the mother's blood will form antibodies to deal with these 'invading' cells.

Although this does no harm to the mother or to that first baby, a second or later child who is Rhesus positive may not be so lucky. As the mother's blood crosses the placenta to nourish the new foetus, these antibodies will attack the new baby's red cells. The dead red cells have to be processed into bile by his liver. If the liver cannot cope with the overload, the bile will not be excreted and he will get jaundiced. Having his red cells killed will also make him anaemic. In the past Rhesus disease killed many babies in the womb and caused death or brain damage in most of those born alive, but it can now largely be prevented and most babies born with it have an excellent chance of survival.

Preventing Rhesus disease Any Rhesus negative woman whose first baby is Rhesus positive should be tested immediately after the delivery to see whether any of the baby's red blood cells have entered her circulation. If so, she should be given an injection of Rhesus positive antibodies prepared from the blood of another person. These will neutralize the 'foreign' blood cells from her baby and thus prevent her from making any antibodies of her own. If this was done routinely for all Rhesus negative women having Rhesus positive babies the problem would be wiped out.

Coping with Rhesus disease A Rhesus negative woman will be carefully watched during pregnancy and her blood tested to see if she has any Rhesus positive antibodies. Her baby must be delivered in hospital. A baby born with Rhesus disease may receive an 'exchange transfusion': his own blood being gradually taken out while fresh Rhesus negative blood is put in. The transfusion washes out most of the antibodies that have reached him in the womb, while giving him Rhesus negative blood ensures that if any antibodies are left they will not attack the new red blood cells which will also deal with his anaemia. This will be repeated until the level of jaundice drops.

RHYMES 350, 421

RINGWORM
This is a fungus infection which has many forms affecting different parts of the body. Some types can be caught from animals, so if you have a case in the family get your vet to check any pets. Usually it is passed on from another child.

Tinea capitis (ringworm of the scalp) The child has one or more small bald areas usually round or oval in shape. They are covered with dry greyish scales and you can see the stumps of broken off hair among the scales. The doctor will

confirm the diagnosis by shining a special light on the scalp and/or looking at a scraping of the scales under a microscope.

Treatment with a recently developed antibiotic prevents further growth of the infecting fungus. The hair will recover completely in about three weeks. During this time the child will have to be kept away from nursery, playgroup or school. Other children in the family are likely to catch it, but the risk can be minimized by strictly separating his hairbrushes, towels etc. If the bald patches embarrass the child a boy can wear a baseball cap or a girl a bandeau.

Ringworm of the body This produces circular or oval areas with tiny bumps round the edges. Your doctor will probably prescribe a special ointment or paint. Treatment is easier and quicker than for the scalp, but you must check for hidden sites of the infection such as between the toes.

Athlete's foot This is by far the commonest form of ringworm. It can occasionally be the cause of ringworm of the body. Athlete's foot makes the skin between the toes look white and sodden. It itches desperately and scratching removes the sodden skin revealing raw sore areas underneath. It is extremely contagious and spreads rapidly through schools.

To treat athlete's foot, a special cream, available from your chemist, should be applied all over the affected area three times daily. The child should not go barefoot in the house until it has completely cleared up. On the other hand socks and shoes make the feet sweaty and give the fungus a good environment for growth, so encourage him to wear open sandals without socks.

RITUALS *see* COMFORT HABITS; SLEEPING

ROAD SAFETY *see* SAFETY

ROCKING *see* COMFORT HABITS; CRYING AND COMFORTING

ROLLING enjoying physical movement of 189, 190, 236; from back to side 162; from side to back 162; and other milestones 160; over and over 240, 349

ROSEOLA INFANTUM
Incubation period 7–14 days
First signs
☐ Inexplicable high fever for about 3 days.
Definite signs
☐ Small, separate pink spots appear all over the body but vanish so quickly that they may be missed altogether.

Degree of illness
☐ Depends on the height of the fever and his reactions to it. In a susceptible child, it may cause febrile convulsions Once the rash appears there is no further illness.
Possible complications None.
What the doctor may do. Nothing, unless you need his help early on because of convulsions.
What you can do Nothing is needed except nursing of the fever stage.
See NURSING; FEVER

ROUNDWORMS *see* WORMS
RUBELLA *see* GERMAN MEASLES
RUNNING 331, 348, 352, 353, 374, 406, 410, 431; *see* WALKING

S

SAFETY-HARNESS 144, 163, 238, 239, 303-304

SAFETY/In the home 93, 192, 197, 239, 242, 245, 246, 267, 268, 272, 276, 331, 348, 349, 351, 386, 408-411
Some of the worst accidents to babies and young children take place in their own homes. The setting that is safe and comfortable for an experienced adult can be a death trap to a child. You have to think ahead: to stay one jump ahead of your child's abilities; to see 'interesting' things before he sets out to explore them; to notice him watching you and realize that he may imitate you, and to bear in mind all the time that a child's safety is not his own business: it is yours. The best tip for accident prevention is always to take the child around with you rather than leave him alone in a room. Tuck him under your arm or plonk him on your hip if you have to answer the phone or the door bell. Some other traps for the unwary are:
☐ Furniture which is not solid or steady enough for a newly standing child to pull himself up on— that spindly coffee table will spell disaster.
☐ Things that pinch fingers: deck chairs, ironing boards, clothes horses etc., can all blacken nails or break fingers if the child tries to set them up or play with them.
☐ Door hinges pinch worse than the closing side and it is much easier to miss the fact that the child's hand is at risk.
☐ Swinging doors or those with automatic closures will always bang or squash a toddler: he cannot time his exit with its swing.
☐ Plate glass windows and French doors can lead to horrible injuries if they are kept so clean that the

child does not notice the glass and tries to walk through it. Let it get covered with finger marks or stick transfers or paper strips on the glass to show it is solid. Glass doors with panes are far safer: safety glass is a good precaution.

☐ Falls from windows still happen. If you don't want bars, fit 'acorn fasteners' which allow the window to be opened only a few inches.

☐ Watch out for anything which dangles within the toddler's reach or which he can pull down on himself—an iron for example. Watch out too for what will happen if he goes for the bottom of a pile of things. The chairs you stacked up while you washed the floor might knock him out.

☐ Be careful of anything he can get into but not out of. Chest freezers make a deadly hiding place. You will not even hear him call because of the insulation. Keep them locked. Be sure that if he can get into cupboards he can get out again. Bathrooms and lavatories should have their locks too high for him to reach or have the sort of lock that can be opened from the outside with a coin.

☐ Make sure your garden is safe too, with no access to the road, ready for the day when he learns to open the front door.

☐ Some things are safe when whole, but dangerous if broken: a favourite mug can turn into a deadly weapon if banged too much.

Animals

☐ A few dogs (usually long-established pets) are bitterly jealous of a baby, occasionally even to the point of attacking it. Watch out for warning signs like the dog always wanting attention when you are holding the baby etc.

☐ Dogs vary in how much mauling they will take from a small child. Some will put up with anything; others treat the crawling child like a puppy (and that means a few reproving nips), a few get cross and snap. To play safe, don't leave dog and child alone together.

☐ Various skin and parasitic complaints can be caught from dogs. Keep yours in tip-top health; clean, regularly 'wormed' and free from fleas. Mention his existence to your doctor if your child gets any puzzling illness.

☐ Cats are not usually emotionally concerned about a baby, but use a cat-net over the pram to make sure the cat cannot curl up on top of him, and watch out for scratches if an older child captures the cat and mauls it.

☐ Small mammals like hamsters and guinea pigs should not be given to a tiny child to hold—for both their sakes. Let the child watch them, and stroke them while someone else does the holding.

☐ Fish tanks are unhygienic; fish are liable to all kinds of fungus diseases. A child should not be allowed to dabble in the water.

Burns and scalds

☐ All fires must have fixed 'safety approved' guards. Don't use portable bar electric fires unless you put them into a guarded corner.

☐ Even guarded fires need caution. Don't put anything on or above the mantlepiece that might make the child want to climb up there. Don't let the child see you poke things into a fire, use a spill of paper to get a light for your cigarette from it, use a newspaper to make it draw or do anything to the fire that he might imitate. Gas fires should be self igniting in case the child turns on the gas tap.

☐ Paraffin heaters have been responsible for more serious burns, often fatalities, than any other single factor in the home. They are almost impossible to make entirely safe; even the best of them can be tipped over. The paraffin itself is both a fire hazard and a poison. Bottled gas is far safer.

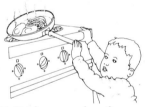

☐ Watch your cooker: there are 'pan guards' on the market which are safety rings that drop over the burners, and then hold saucepans safely so they cannot be tipped over. Failing that, always turn the handles of pans inward, and use the back burners if possible. Remember that some ovens are so badly insulated that a child can burn himself just by leaning on the door. Never leave anything frying on the stove in the same room as the child without you: hot fat can spit; hot oil can catch fire and an oil burn is even worse than a boiling water scald.

☐ Remember that things like irons and fires hold their heat for some time after you have turned them off. They are not safe until they have cooled.

☐ Never fill a hot-water bottle with water hot enough to scald the child if it should leak or burst. Better still, only use it to warm the bed—take it out when the child gets in.

☐ Check your hot water temperature. If your domestic hot water or central heating runs at too high a setting, radiators and hot taps can lead to burns and scalds.

☐ Discipline yourself if you are a smoker. A lit cigarette can inflict a painful (if minor) burn; your lighter or your matches must not be left lying around. A lighter on a thong round your neck is safest if you have no pockets.

☐ Tea or coffee can scald a child even if not actually boiling. Teapots and coffee pots should never be put on low tables where a child could reach or knock them, nor on a high table with a cloth. Pulling off the cloth and the pot has scarred many a little chest and tummy for life.

☐ Remember that oven-to-table dishes stay hot for a long time, hot enough to cause damage. Keep high chairs well back from the family table; don't use tablecloths that could be pulled off. Serving from a side table may be safer.

Choosing baby equipment Baby equipment can cause accidents through bad design. The exact angle of road on which a pram brake will hold; the exact balance that will allow a carry cot to be safely carried by its handles are highly technical matters. But the results of someone getting it wrong matter to you. Whenever you buy a piece of equipment check that it is "safety approved". If in doubt, consult your local Consumer council. Then play safe. If a piece of equipment says it is safe up to 24 lbs, stop using it when the baby weighs 20 lbs. If the pram brake is supposed to be safe on steep hills, wedge something under the wheel all the same.

Electricity A shock from the mains can kill a small child.

☐ Make not touching plugs or switching on appliances one of your few definite rules.

☐ Don't buy toys that are powered from the mains even via a transformer, at least until he is old enough to appreciate how the power source works. Transformers can go wrong.

☐ Don't let a child use an electric blanket—a wet bed or a spilt drink can make it dangerous.

☐ Have all appliances earthed: this means 3-core cable and 3-pin plugs.

□ Keep switched sockets in the 'off' position — then even if the child turns the mixer on, it will not mangle his fingers.

□ Use shuttered square pin 13 amp plugs or buy dummy plugs and keep one in every unused socket so the child cannot poke things into the holes.

□ Use correct ampage fuses as indicated on appliances.

□ Have the flexes of appliances repaired if they are fraying.

□ Use 'flex holders' to keep trailing wires out of the way of tripping feet or clutching hands.

Medicines Children between about one and five years old will eat any pills that they "discover", however difficult they are about taking medicines that have actually been prescribed for them.

□ Buy a medicine cabinet with a safety lock made to 'safety approved' standards. Nowhere else is really safe. A high cupboard can be a challenge to a climber, an ordinary lock and key can be an entrancing game to a fiddler, while a hiding place will be discovered in the end by your favourite explorer. Keep all medicines, even 'harmless' ones like the children's own vitamins in the cabinet, and put them back immediately after use.

□ Don't keep medicines (even oral contraceptives) in the room just to remind you of a regular dosage; write yourself a message instead.

□ Don't carry medicines in your handbag unless you have a chronic condition for which they are essential. If so ask your chemist for a child proof container.

□ Don't let the child play with empty medicine containers. It only increases the chances of a mistake.

□ Don't get caught out in other people's houses. Grandparents' houses can be especially dangerous: all too often there are sleeping pills by the bed, 'heart pills' in the pocket and laxatives beside the washbasin.

□ Be extra careful when travelling. A vanity case or briefcase which locks is probably safest.

□ Guard against your own mistakes as well as the child's: don't give medicine in the dark: check the label. Don't give medicines from one illness or one child to the next. Don't rely on breaking adult tablets to arrive at a child's dose. Rewrite any label which gets smudged so that you know, for sure, what is in the bottle.

Poisons Cleaning, gardening and beauty products are so many and various that you cannot hope to know exactly what is in everything. Play safe. Assume that all these things can harm a child.

□ Keep all cleaning materials in a cupboard too high for the child even to climb up to. Remember that even if he did not actually drink the bleach or the oven cleaner, he could spray it in his eyes and blind himself.

□ Garden sheds, garages or workshops must be kept locked. Even so the really dangerous things like insect and weedkillers, paint-strippers and cleaners, paraffin etc., should be kept in locked cupboards in case you leave the door open 'just for a minute'.

□ Keep potentially dangerous beauty products in the medicine cabinet. A good go at your surplus hair remover will do the child no good at all.

Steps and stairs

□ Beware of rugs on polished floors, especially near stairs.

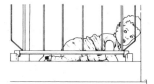

□ Until your child can go safely up and down stairs, you need safety gates at the top *and* bottom. If you only gate the top he may climb all the way up from the bottom and tumble all the way down again.

□ Steps in gardens etc. are a particular hazard for a child on a tricycle or other ride-on toy. You may need a safety fence across the top until he learns to use his brakes and can *always* judge a halt.

□ Ban socks without shoes; they make an ordinary plastic floor into a skating rink.

□ Watch out for banisters: older children will slide down them if they are slideable. If there is a real drop you need a safety net or uprights at frequent intervals ruining the run.

Suffocation Even a new baby will turn his head if he cannot breathe, but this will not remove all obstructions. Avoid plastic—especially the thin filmy kind that clings. Take it off cot mattresses etc. before you ever use them. Tear up and throw away plastic bags—or if you want to re-use them, lock them away like poisons. Use stiff plastic bibs and take them off as soon as a meal is over. Keep plastic pants well out of his way.

□ Don't give him a pillow when he is sleeping. If you want to prop him when he is awake use a pillow under the mattress.

□ Don't leave him alone with food or with a bottle. He may choke. Put him to sleep on his tummy so that if he sicks up some milk it will run harmlessly out of his mouth and not be inhaled.

□ Don't let a baby or small child play with anything small enough to be swallowed, especially if it is round and smooth. A half swallowed marble could wedge across his throat, cutting off all air and being too smooth for you to get out. A little soldier will hurt if it gets half swallowed and stuck, but at least it will not block the air off completely.

Tools and kitchenware When your child is very small, everything sharp enough to do damage, especially if he puts it into his mouth and falls down, has to be kept completely out of reach. But the sooner he learns to use all these properly and safely the sooner you will be able to stop locking them away. Properly taught, a four year old can be safe with real (but small size) carpentry tools; it is the child who has never had the chance to learn who is a menace to himself and everyone else with his first saw.

□ Knives, scissors, screwdrivers etc. are best kept along a magnetic rack which can be screwed to the wall out of the child's reach.

□ Cutlery, especially forks, need to be kept safe too. If he plays in the kitchen, keep them in the dining room—or vice versa.

□ Sewing materials, especially needles, should be kept in a high or locked drawer or cupboard. A Victorian writing box makes an excellent workbox and has a lock.

□ Keep pencils and fountain pens locked away, and let him have free access to non toxic, washable felt-tip pens and/or chubby crayons which are quite safe.

□ Be especially wary of electrically powered appliances such as grass cutters, hedge trimmers, or saws that could cause serious injury if a child suddenly ran into them.

Water Children can, and do, drown in a couple of inches of water. Unlike older people, a toddler who finds his face submerged takes a breath to yell . . . only he does not get air.

The sooner you teach your baby to swim the sooner he will learn to hold his breath instead of breathing water—and the safer he will be in all kinds of water. Many public swimming pools have 'mother and baby' sessions. Some even heat the water a welcome extra few degrees.

If you have ornamental garden pools or water butts while your children are tiny, they should be carefully guarded. A water butt can have a heavy wooden cover, with a hole only just big enough for the downpipe. A pool will probably need a fence.

☐ Paddling pools should be taken down or emptied at the end of every supervised play session; otherwise invest in one of the large 'splasher pools' which have sides too high for a small child to climb without help.

☐ If you take a toddler to a public paddling pool you must be prepared to paddle too.

☐ Never leave a baby or small child alone in the bath. Babies need holding until they can sit steadily: hovering over right through the just-standing and toddling phase, and keeping in sight until they are around 3½.

☐ Gravel pits, sewage beds, farm slurries or even road works can become rain-filled and dangerous. Rivers, canals, lakes and reservoirs are all irresistible play-places. Don't let him go near any of these without an *adult*. Older children may not allow for his incompetence.

☐ At the sea or lakeside try to bathe near lifeguard stations. Don't do more than paddle if 'caution flags' are flying. Don't even paddle if red danger flags are flying. Always take local advice about tides, shelving beaches etc. before bathing off a deserted beach.

☐ Always keep inflatable water toys on a line. Wind or tide may carry them away from shore.

☐ Always make children wear life-jackets when boating on anything deeper than a junior boating lake.

☐ If you spend a lot of time on or near water see that your child studies for his 'Personal Survival Badges.' Your local authority swimming pool will give you details of classes. By the time he has taken his bronze medal he will be competent to look after himself under normal circumstances in water—but he may be nine or ten years old before he takes that medal.

SAFETY/On the road

Nearly a quarter of the 55,000 children under 15 involved in road accidents in Britain each year are under five. A quarter of them are hurt while out *walking*.

A toddler can begin to learn that the kerb is a safety line between him and traffic. But don't trust him any more than you would trust him on the edge of a deep lake. Hold on to his hand or reins, he can dart out in a second.

Until you can absolutely trust your child to stay on the pavement, don't let him out alone at all. Children under 5 should never be allowed to cross any road alone. They are unpredictable, easily distracted or attracted and forgetful. Even when concentrating they cannot usually distinguish right from left, judge how far away approaching traffic is, how fast it is moving or whether it is parked. They cannot anticipate unexpected driving manoeuvres such as U-turns or right-turns across the traffic.

Older children who are ready for school still only learn these things gradually, and through example and experience. They may be fully able to learn and apply the Green Cross Code yet still be caught out by unexpected traffic lights failure or non-appearance of a crossing patrol. They are subject to moods and distractions, and very liable to fatigue, especially if the school day has gone wrong. Give them experience with you but don't regard them as road-proof until you have months of evidence.

The Green Cross Code If you live in a quiet area, you may be able to teach your child to use the Code as a set of absolute rules. If so you must obey them too—always. In a city it may be difficult for the child ever to follow it simply because there may be no safe places to cross and the road may never be clear. You will have to fill in the gaps.

Code

☐ First find a safe place to cross such as a pedestrian crossing; patrolled crossing, subway or controlled lights. (There may be none).

☐ Stand on the pavement near the kerb. Look all round for traffic and listen. (There may be traffic everywhere).

☐ If traffic is coming, let it pass. Look all round again.

☐ When there is no traffic near, cross. (There may always be traffic in daytime).

☐ Keep looking and listening for traffic while you cross.

Adapting the code for your child Decide what regular journeys you want the child to make alone on foot and work out yourself:

☐ Where he should cross.

☐ When he should cross: find markers that the child can use as his signal that approaching traffic is too close, like 'don't cross if there is anything closer than the red brick house' or 'don't cross if there is anything your side of the bridge'.

☐ How he should cross: if there are likely to be parked cars, you may have to teach him to stand between them holding the outside edge of one bumper while he peers both ways.

☐ What he is to do if he cannot cross because of road works etc: is he to walk on to an alternative crossing place or wait until an adult comes and then ask for help?

Walk each route several times with the child. Make a game out of testing him—when he thinks he knows one you could make him take you. Then you could let him go alone within sight and calling distance of you. Then you could let him do the easiest half of the walk and meet you half-way. Carry on until you are sure he is no more likely to get run over than you are yourself.

Gradually, generalize this very special teaching which has kept him safe on particular roads, to other roads. Don't worry if it is two years from the time he first goes to school alone before you let him go wherever he pleases on the roads.

Tricycles Tricycles and other self-propelled vehicles are toys. They are not meant for riding on roads, even quiet ones. A child on a trike is too low down for even the most careful driver to see him in time.

☐ On the pavement, watch out. He is bad at steering, bad at using brakes (even if he has them) and slow to spot or react to emergencies. He may go off the kerb.

☐ In the park, watch out for hills. Putting his feet down to stop can pitch him over the handlebars on to his head.

☐ In the garden, guard steps if you have them. Neither riding down nor pitching down will do him any good. A temporary safety fence or set of boards 4 in. (10 cm) high and set at least 2 ft. (60 cm) back from the top step may be needed.

Bicycles for fun Your child will probably manage to balance a two-wheeler by the time he is five: it may be a status-symbol and heart's desire.

If there is safe fun-riding space

in parks etc. teach him to push the bike along the pavement to it. Make it clear that if he rides it on the road it will be confiscated.

Bicycles for use Big cities are just not safe for cycling any more except where special 'Cycle lanes' have been made. Whatever your child's road sense on foot, he will be in danger on a bike with traffic. It is easier to teach a young child safe use of public transport for necessary journeys to school etc.

If you live in the country and he really needs a bike:

□ Buy one that fits him, not one he will 'grow into' unless it is the kind that can be made larger.

□ Have it safety-checked even if it is new; many come from factories with faulty brakes etc.

□ Have him properly taught to ride it; most schools have schemes.

□ Take or have him taken on several trial rides before you let him go alone.

□ Don't allow him to ride after dusk. Teach him to telephone if something keeps him late at school in winter.

□ In case of unforeseen circumstances keep his lights in top condition (don't make him buy batteries out of pocket money) and sew reflective strips on his clothing. The police will tell you where to get these locally.

In the car Children may not legally sit on an adult's lap on the front passenger seat even if that adult is wearing a seat belt. This position is the most dangerous in the whole car. In a crash, his body will protect yours...

In the back, babies who cannot sit alone should travel lying in carry-cot or pram-top fastened to the seat with proper safety straps. Children who sit but weigh less than 40 lbs (18 kg) need a special approved car safety seat. These have the tremendous advantage that they are raised off the ordinary seat so that the child can see out. Between 40 lbs and 80 lbs (18–36 kg) the child needs one of the approved 'trainer harnesses' properly bolted to the car by a garage. Over 80 lbs (36 kg) the child can wear an adult-type safety belt, but try to keep him in the back of the car all the same. Belt or no belt it is safer.

□ Hook over the seat 'car chairs' for babies and toddlers are not strong enough to hold the child in a car smash.

□ Remember that friends may not

have safety harnesses: it is worth checking on this before you let your child ride in their cars.

□ Don't carry more children than your car has harnesses.

□ Have safety locks fitted in the back of your car.

□ Remember it can be dangerous to let a child lean out of the window, or put out an arm.

SALT 66, 141, 210, 224, 282

SCABIES

The itch mite 'sarcoptes scabie' lays its eggs under its victim's skin, leaving secretions which cause small, intensely irritating pimples, normally in warm areas such as the groin or between the fingers.

As the mites hatch, they are easily passed to other people, while scratching often leads to secondary infection in the skin.

Consult your doctor about any persistent itching. If scabies is the cause, disinfestation is easily carried out with a special cream or lotion. Treatment of the entire family together with sterilization of bedding etc. may be necessary.

SCALDS *see* BURNS AND SCALDS

SCARLET FEVER
Incubation period 1–5 days
First signs
□ Scarlet fever is a bacterial (streptococcal) throat infection which happens to produce a rash. First signs are similar to an attack of tonsillitis. There may be fever, loss of appetite and vomiting.

□ Complaints of stomach-ache may be due to swollen glands in the abdomen.

Definite signs
□ On day 2 or 3, tiny red dots appear on skin which has an overall red flush. The rash starts on the chest and neck, then spreads to the whole body. There are no spots or flushing around the mouth so, in contrast with the rest of the face, this area always looks strikingly pale. When the rash fades after about one week, the skin flakes.

Degree of illness
□ He will be about as ill as with a bout of tonsillitis.

Possible complications
□ Middle ear infection.

□ Without treatment, there is a chance of the bacteria spreading to infect the kidneys or cause rheumatic fever.

What the doctor may do
□ Give antibiotics or sulphonamides to control the bacteria and prevent complications. Although the illness itself is not severe the complications can be.

SHOCK
Shock can range in severity from the slight and short-lived pallor and shakiness of a child who has had a nasty fright to the progressive failure of circulation, and eventually breathing, of a child who has been severely injured. You need to know how to cope with the first. You need to know what you can do to prevent the second.

Minor shock In minor shock the child's brain is temporarily starved of blood as in a faint. Because it cannot function efficiently he is shaky and feels 'odd'. The blood vessels to the skin close up to preserve blood for the vital organs inside the body. This causes the pallor or cold clamminess of the skin. It can result from purely emotional causes such as hearing bad news or seeing a bloody accident to mixed emotional/physical ones such as getting slightly hurt in frightening circumstances.

This kind of shock is much increased by fear and by pain. A comparatively minor burn may cause more shock reaction than a bad cut simply because it hurts more and goes on hurting. The child cries and goes very pale, cold and shivery. There may be beads of sweat on his face, and he may feel faint, giddy or sick, and vomit.

What to do
□ Lie the child down with his head

lower than his feet to help adequate blood return to the brain.
□ Keep his head turned to one side so that if he should vomit he will not choke.
□ Loosen any tight clothing so that his breathing is not restricted.
□ Cover with a blanket or coat to preserve his body warmth.
□ Comfort and make much of him so that he stops being frightened.

N.B. Do not give hot, sweet drinks or indeed anything to drink at all until he is completely back to normal. He cannot digest anything while his body is fighting shock. Do not warm with hot-water bottles etc. Artificial warming will force the blood vessels in the skin to re-open. His colour will improve, but at the expense of his vital organs which, for the moment, need extra blood.

Even five minutes lying quietly should reverse this minor kind of shock. The child's colour will improve and his tension relax. He will either drop off to sleep (in which case all you have to do is watch that he does not vomit, and make sure that he does not choke) or sit up and get on with life.

If he does not seem normal within half an hour, call your doctor. It is just possible that the incident which led to the shock was more serious than you had thought.

Medical shock following serious accident or acute illness The child's brain is being starved of blood as in minor shock, but simply lying down cannot give it adequate help because some physical cause such as very heavy bleeding (external or internal), extreme dehydration, a severe scald or burn, uncontrollable sickness or diarrhoea, has reduced the amount of blood or body fluid in the circulation. Damage to the brain or nervous system may also disrupt the brain's control of the heart and circulation, producing a state of medical shock.

Because the circulation is short of blood, the heart automatically pumps harder but because it has less than the optimum amount to pump, it gets less efficient so that decreasing amounts of blood reach the brain wtose control circuits therefore get even more inefficient. Without treatment, acute medical shock leads eventually to failure of the circulation and of breathing.

The signs of serious medical shock are similar to those of minor shock but more pronounced. The child looks and acts 'collapsed'.

Dizziness and faintness may be so pronounced that the child is barely conscious. He may behave as if delirious; rambling and not recognizing you. He may be extremely restless and anxious, behaving like a child with a night terror.

N.B. Lying down does not produce immediate improvement: the child is obviously getting worse.

What to do
□ Recognize the likelihood of shock developing;
□ Send urgently for medical help;
□ Treat the cause if this is obvious (by stopping heavy bleeding for example) and minimize the effects while waiting for help by treating the child as for minor shock.

SHOES AND SOCKS 247, 264, 315, 329, 356, 387
In cultures where people go barefoot there are few deformed feet and no corns and bunions. Let your child go barefoot as much as you possibly can. Babies don't need anything on their feet until they are walking outside and need shoes for protection. If you think your baby's feet will get cold, use a sleeping bag or put him in a sleeping suit with big roomy feet. Feet that are cool to the touch don't matter; if your baby's bare stomach and thighs feel warm then he is warm enough. If floors are too cold for your newly standing baby, use slipper-socks.

Shoes These must be properly fitted for length and width by a trained fitter in a reputable shoe shop. Your child's feet must be remeasured and the fit of his shoes checked at least every three months. Never keep a pair that is small for 'special occasions'.

At first shoes will feel strange, heavy and slippery to your child and they will prevent his 'feeling' the ground with his toes, so buy the lightest and most flexible ones you can find and watch out for tumbles until he is used to them. Never let him wear socks without shoes — they are slippery — or shoes without socks — they may rub.

The fit of your child's socks is just as important. Throw away any that are too small so you will not put them on one morning when you are in a hurry. Check cotton socks after the first washing to make sure that they have not shrunk. Socks or shoes that cramp your child's feet will not cause him any pain; the bones are still so flexible that they will squash up quite comfortably causing damage without the child complaining.

Don't pass shoes down between children. Even if the sizing of a secondhand shoe is right, the fit will have moulded to the first wearer's feet.

Special shoe problems A generation ago many children were prescribed shoes to stop them 'toeing in' or to correct 'flat feet'. Now most authorities believe that time and growth will correct problems of this kind. Flat feet and curious walking are normal for young toddlers anyway. If you are really concerned about some such peculiarity, consult your doctor. He may recommend that your child runs barefoot as much as possible so that his foot muscles strengthen.

Sloppy shoes Healthy feet don't need shoes which 'support' them. Any shoe which protects them, without putting damaging pressure on them, will do. But be careful, especially with older children, about shoes which are so loose and 'comfortable' that the child actually screws his toes up or shuffles to keep them on. A well-fitting pair of plimsolls or open sandals is fine. But these cheap summery shoes are usually only made in whole sizes and one width. If your child needs a half size or an extra wide or narrow shoe, they cannot be right for him.

SHORT-SIGHT focusing range of newborn 116, 168 *see* EYES/Vision disorders

SHYNESS *see* ATTACHMENT TO YOU

SITTING beginnings of independent 162-163, 236-239; down from standing 243; helping him practise 162, 179, 236-239, 267-268; independent 238; in a chair up to meals 144, 214, 286, 288, 370-371; and other 'milestones' 160, 197, 240; in a chair up to play 177, 179, 189, 192, 259; propped up 158, 163, 238; still for rest without sleep 243, 298, 350; suitable chairs *see* CHAIRS

SKIN *see* ALLERGIES; NAPPY RASH; RASHES; SUNBURN

SKULL FRACTURES *see* HEAD INJURIES

SLEEPING AND WAKING first days 90-94; first six months 146-148; six months to one year 215-223; one year to two and a half 295-304; two and a half to five 375-380; bags 148, 221, 246, 301, 303, 304; and cold and warmth 80-81, 92, 98, 148, 158, 220-221; and colic 148; difficulty in settling for 203-204, 215-220, 298, 299-300, 317, 319, 375; disturbances to 82-83, 92, 97, 98, 105, 220-222, 300-304; and

489

feeding 51, 73, 94, 125, 133, 140, 142, 146, 148, 194-195, 204, 215; early separation from wakefulness 90, 92, 146, 148; hours 82, 94, 106, 134, 146, 158, 193, 215, 295; keeping himself from 215, 298; and naps 107, 146, 148, 193, 215, 223, 295-296, 423; waking from 296; 'nasty thoughts' 377; and night-lights 92, 216, 301, 319, 321, 380, 384; and nightmares 301-302, 319, 378; and night terrors 378-379; and night wandering 302-304, 377; and overtiredness 99, 104, 215, 296, 298, 301; patterns of 32, 72, 73, 134-135, 142, 146, 148, 214, 221, 223, 295-296; places to sleep 90, 92, 93, 94, 148, 216, 303-304, 375-377; sharing 223, 375, 380; positions for 74, 93, 158; resting without 243, 298; 'sleepy' babies 51, 106, 133; soothing and 98-100, 157, 216-218, 319; talking during 379; wakeful babies 106-107, 147, 148, 158, 223; waking early in the morning 148, 223, 261, 304, 380; waking in the night 220-221, 300-301 *see* COMFORT HABITS; CRYING AND COMFORTING

SLEEP TALKING *see* SLEEPING

'SLEEPY' BABIES 51, 106, 133

SMACKING 273, 278, 299, 347, 411, 412, 440

SMALL-FOR-DATES BABIES 39, 41, 78

SMALLPOX *see* IMMUNIZATION

SMELLING not sharing adults' opinions 307; sense of smell in newborn 114; sense well-developed by toddler stage 335, 373

SMILING 116, 120, 180, 182, 198, 200, 401

SMOTHERING 93, 108, 144, 239, 410 *see* MOUTH-TO-MOUTH RESUSCITATION; SAFETY
It is impossible for a baby to smother himself just by lying face down in a bed that has no pillow or by going under the bedclothes. He will turn his head clear when he needs air, and sufficient air will come through blankets and sheets even should he get tangled up.
Plastic Plastic may cause smothering because it is both air tight and clingy. If a child puts a plastic bag or thin plastic sheeting over his face, the first breath he takes in causes the plastic to cling and mould itself closely over his mouth and nose so that he cannot rip it off.
What to do
☐ Speed is what matters. Rip off the material. He may take a great gasping breath and all will be well.
☐ If he does not breathe, don't waste a second. If you know how to

do mouth-to-mouth resuscitation, start instantly, and give him six full breaths. Phone for an ambulance, dialling between breaths.
Continue until help arrives. If you don't know how to give mouth-to-mouth resuscitation don't waste time trying. Rush him to hospital or phone for an ambulance, whichever will be quicker.
Earth, sand or cement Fine grainy material can collapse on the child, covering his chest and head and filling his mouth and nostrils. Efforts to breathe only pull the material into his air passages.
Never let him tunnel in sand or piles of earth. Don't even encourage games of burying each other in sand at the seaside. Sand dunes make heavenly playgrounds but sand falls are always possible; he should be watched every moment.
What to do
☐ Speed is essential. Dig him out, clearing his complete chest as well as his face. He cannot breathe with weight on his rib cage.
☐ Rapidly clear all the sand you can out of his mouth, throat and nose. He may start to choke and splutter in which case all will probably be well, though he should be rushed to hospital as he may have sand in his lungs.
☐ If he shows no sign of breathing but is still a normal colour, rush him to hospital.
☐ If he shows no sign of breathing and is already greyish blue, start mouth-to-mouth resuscitation if you know how to do it. You risk blowing more sand into his lungs, but that risk is worth taking if his colour tells you that immediate oxygen is the only chance. If you don't know how to do it, don't waste time. Rush for hospital.

SNACKS *see* FOODS

SOCKS *see* SHOES AND SOCKS

SOFT TOYS *see* COMFORT HABITS

SOILING 385 *see* EXCRETING; TOILET TRAINING
Bowel training is normally complete by three years. Once complete, 'accidents' (except in sudden diarrhoea) are rare, although slightly soiled pants may result from inefficient wiping.
Once he is able to pass his motions in a pot or lavatory, a child who insists on passing them elsewhere (in pants, on the floor etc.) is usually making an unconscious protest either against your pressure on him to become clean or against your general power over him. He shows you that however much you may control the rest of him you cannot control his bowels.

A child who refuses to pass his motions at all may appear to have diarrhoea rather than constipation. He withholds his faeces for so long that they become dry, hard and impossible to pass. What you see on his pants is leakage of liquid faeces from around what has become a blockage. He too is protesting but more passively. He does not put his motions where he pleases, he simply refuses to give them up, to you.
Soiling is a problem which is usually deeply entrenched in the relationship between you and the child. Don't wait for him to grow out of it. His self-disgust and the disgust of other people, children and adults, will become more extreme and damaging as he gets older. Sorting it out before he starts pre-school or real school is vital. Brief your doctor privately in advance to give him every chance to handle the matter tactfully. Tell the child that the doctor knows and understands his problem and that you are all going to work together to find ways of coping with it. Then take him to see him.

SOOTHING 51, 72, 80, 95-100, 104, 105, 115, 134, 157, 180, 184, 194, 203, 216-218, 221, 378

SOUNDS attracting baby 168, 180; disturbing baby 51, 96, 180, 189, 220; getting used to 232; hearing and making 114-115, 181-182, 260-263 *see* TALKING

SORE THROAT *see* COLDS; COUGHS; TONSILS

SPEECH *see* TALKING

SPLINTERS
What to do
☐ If the end of a splinter or thorn stands proud of your child's skin it can be removed using tweezers.
☐ If there is no end to get hold of, but the splinter is clearly visible lying under the skin, look carefully to see the direction in which it entered. Squeezing gently from the other end may persuade it to come back through its own hole. If not, you may be able to tease it out, using a fine needle, sterilized in a match flame.
☐ If the splinter has penetrated below the skin into the tissues, or if it has entered directly downwards so that only the pin-point head is visible, the needle-technique will hurt. Unless the splinter is painful it may be best left alone. It will work its own way out in time.
Splinters of glass or metal should always be removed by a doctor. All sides will be sharp. Attempts to remove it may therefore cause additional damage.

'SPOILING' loving and 193, 195, 221, 441-443; mistaken ideas of 193, 387, 441; recognizing 443

SPOONFEEDING see FEEDING

SPOTS see BOILS AND PIMPLES; INFECTIOUS DISEASES; 'NEO-NATAL URTICARIA'; RASHES; URTICARIA

SPRAINS AND STRAINS

These are rare in small children. A sudden fall may cause severe wrenching of a joint such that supporting ligaments become torn. This is a sprain. The ankle, knee, wrist and shoulder joints are all susceptible to this type of injury.

A strain is the over-stretching or tearing of muscle fibres (as opposed to ligaments), and occasionally results from the sudden, vigorous movement of a limb.

What to do

☐ Treat either a sprain or a strain as for greenstick fractures. Don't bother with cold compresses or with bandaging the affected part. If the limb is fractured you will do more harm than good. If it is not, the hospital will certainly undo your careful work to inspect the limb, probably X-ray and certainly re-bandage it.

A sprain is a more serious injury than a strain. The swelling and pain will be more intense and the child will probably be unable to use the affected limb. However, a strain may take longer to heal.

SQUINTING 43, 44 see EYES/Vision disorders

STAMMERING

A tendency to speech hesitations, repeated syllables and pauses while he searches for a new word, is almost universal among children in the pre-school period. The development from this of a confirmed and disabling stammer is almost invariably due to parental anxiety. Stammering tends to run in families, not because of a genetic tendency to speech difficulties, but because parents with painful experience of them tend to be over-conscious of their children's speech. Stammering is often created by attempts to prevent it.

☐ Listen to what your child is saying, not to how he is saying it. Don't ever hurry him; don't finish sentences for him; don't tell him to speak more clearly or slowly. While speech is a conscious thing, the processes that produce speech sounds are unconscious. If you make him think about *how* he produces a word you will cause stumbling, just as your breathing becomes erratic if you think about how your chest goes in and out.

☐ Make it clear that you enjoy him talking. If he feels it is 'not good enough' for you he will become self-conscious.

☐ Make communication easy for him. If he always has to say everything six times or shout down his sister to make you listen, repetition and a word jam become more likely.

If a stammer is turning from a normal stage in speech development into the beginnings of a problem, you will probably see him making conscious efforts to control the muscles of his face, lips and tongue, so that he grimaces whenever his words stumble.

☐ Listen to him talking to himself when he is alone. If he is fluent without an audience then it is your pressure which is making trouble.

☐ Take all the pressure off him. Consider other areas of stress as well as speech. He may be feeling generally disapproved of; this will show in his increasing stammer.

☐ Unless this policy rapidly improves his speech flow so that you notice some difference within 6 weeks, and so that talking to you becomes an easy and automatic thing again, ask your doctor to refer you to a speech therapist. Your child must have help quickly. Lack of confidence in his ability to communicate will rapidly sap his confidence in all other areas too.

STANDING alone 245, 328; in a baby bouncer 158; beginnings of 164; on one leg 332; and other 'milestones' 160, 243; to pee 382; position for everyday care 311; pulling himself up to 243, 245, 330; safe freedom to practise 245-247, 267; and sitting down from 243; see WALKING

STEALING 439

STERILIZING dummies 157; bottle-feeding equipment 65, 69, 201, 224; nappies 87; teacher-beakers 145

STERILIZING/Nursing equipment etc.

In most home nursing and first aid cleanliness is important, but sterilizing is not. There is no point in killing every bacterium on the scissors you use to cut adhesive dressings. Clean dry metal is not a breeding ground for bacteria, and the ordinary ones, that are on the scissors, are on the knee too . . .

Thermometers A clean dry thermometer will not nourish germs, but it is idiotic to put the same instrument straight from one child's mouth into another's. They may be harbouring the same germs or they may not. Have two

thermometers. Sterilize them by standing, mercury downwards, in bottle-sterilant.

Tweezers, needles etc. These should be sterile before being used to cope with thorns and splinters or you may introduce germs into the puncture. Hold in a match flame for 30 seconds.

Handkerchiefs For children's use, ban washable ones if you can in favour of hygienic paper. Otherwise sterilize in nappy-sterilant.

Dressings Ordinary adhesive dressings are sterile until they are opened. In an emergency you may want to cover a large wound which is very liable to infection in order to keep the air (with its bacteria) off it until you get medical help. You can buy sealed packets of sterile dressings for this purpose—don't open them until you need one. Alternatively you can sterilize an ordinary handkerchief by soaking it in nappy solution. Wrap in plastic film and keep it in the medicine cupboard.

In an emergency if you have nothing prepared, unfold a clean ironed handkerchief and use the inside surface. Ironing will have sterilized the material and the inside surface will not have been in contact with the air.

Personal towels Keeping special towels, face-cloths, brushes etc. for a child who may have some highly infectious skin trouble is easier said than done in many households. You can lessen the risk by allotting him two of everything, and sterilizing one set while he uses the other.

'STICKY EYE' 43

STINGS

Fear and panic are usually the worst aspect of insect stings.

What to do

☐ Calm the child. Tell him that the pain he feels now, this minute, is the worst he is going to feel.

☐ Remove the sting if you can see it.

☐ Spray the area with one of the special products available, if you can reach it quickly. Otherwise cool the area as best you can.

A little swelling is to be expected, but if there is a great deal take the child to the doctor.

Stings in the mouth These may lead to swelling which can obstruct the child's breathing. Give him a piece of ice to suck and take him straight to the doctor or hospital.

Very occasionally a child reacts to a sting with general collapse, becoming pale, sweaty and faint. This is called 'anaphylactic shock' and is a full-scale emergency requiring a rush to hospital. A child who reacts in this way once may need further treatment, once the emergency is over, to 'desensitize' him so that later stings do not have the same effect. *See* ALLERGIES

Multiple stings These may lead to so much poison being injected into the child that his body cannot cope. He will be in severe pain. Remove clothes from the affected area and wrap in a cold wet sheet to relieve the pain. Rush him to hospital.

STITCHES (Sutures) 410, 443; *see* BLEEDING; CUTS AND GRAZES
The edges of wounds are held together with stitches either to control bleeding so that clotting/healing can take place or to ensure a neat rather than a wide, jagged scar.

Where cosmetic considerations predominate, you have some choice. A scar on a boy's knee may not matter as much as the stitches; his face is a different matter. Increasingly, hospitals use 'skin closures' — highly adhesive strips — instead of stitches. They are painless. Having stitches hurts. Don't pretend it is not going to or your child will feel betrayed when it does. Don't pander to yourself by staying outside, either. He needs your support; and he needs to know you approve of what is being done to him.

The doctor may use a spray anaesthetic to deaden the skin; the spray will not hurt but the stitches still will—a little. If he uses an injected local anaesthetic, the injection will hurt — often quite a lot as it must reach the right nerves which in a hand, for example, means putting the needle in between the knuckles. But the stitches really will not then hurt.

STOMACH-ACHE 95-96, 101
Stomach-ache is a difficult symptom to cope with because it can herald an acute abdominal emergency (such as appendicitis); an illness in some quite different part of the body (such as tonsillitis) or nothing at all. Don't try home-diagnosis. Decide whether or not to call the doctor on the basis of:
How severe the pain is.
How long it lasts.
How ill the child seems.
Any other symptoms.

Babies Stomach-ache makes a baby scream and draw his legs and thighs up to his tummy. But so does anger. If cuddling comforts him and he seems otherwise well,

you can afford to wait for other symptoms.

If cuddling does not comfort him although he seems otherwise well, he may have colic. Talk to your doctor but not as an emergency.

If he has fever, diarrhoea, vomiting and/or seems ill, call the doctor.

Young children They often cannot locate pain accurately or differentiate pain from nausea. If the child seems very ill, has other symptoms as well or has such severe pain that he cries, lies curled up and walks bent double, call the doctor at once.

If the pain is milder and/or there are no other symptoms, you can afford to wait and see. Ring for advice if it is still bothering him after two or three hours.

Acute intussusception This is a very rare but acute abdominal emergency in babies between three months and two years. A small portion of the intestine telescopes into the portion in front causing total blockage. When natural intestinal movements press on the blockage the pain is so intense that the baby goes grey/white and seems beside himself. It goes off after two or three minutes, but happens again about 20 minutes later. He may vomit between attacks. Don't wait for a third attack. Rush him to hospital.

Emotional causes Some children get periodic bouts of stomach-ache and/or vomiting as a reaction to stress. Have him checked by the doctor the first time, to make sure there really is no physical cause. Then treat him with sympathy (the pain hurts just as much as if it was caused by a germ) and try to relieve the stress-cause. If the idea of a party gives him stomach-ache he probably should not go.

Although you need not bother your doctor for every one of your child's periodic stomach-aches, be careful. Proneness to stress pains does not protect him from all other possible causes. You will have to consider each one on its merits or you may miss the one that *is* appendicitis.

STOOLS 47, 88-89, 149, 224 *see* CONSTIPATION; DIARRHOEA; EXCRETING; SOILING; TOILET TRAINING

STORIES *see* BOOKS; PLAYING AND LEARNING; READING ALOUD

STRAINS *see* SPRAINS AND STRAINS

STRANGER ANXIETY *see* FEAR

STRANGERS *see* FEAR; TALKING TO STRANGERS

STUTTERING 419; *see* STAMMERING

STYES *see* EYES/Infections

SUCKING 44, 50-51, 55-58, 61, 71, 74, 100, 125, 140, 143, 144, 157, 202-204, 217, 316-317, 330

SUCKING REFLEX 50-51, 55-58, 61, 71

'SUCKY' BABIES 50, 157

'SUDDEN DEATH IN INFANCY SYNDROME' *see* COT DEATHS

SUGAR 139, 141, 224, 282, 284, 291, 294, 374; in bottle-feeds 64, 66, 88, 89; water *see* FLUIDS; and tooth decay 290, 317 *see* DIET; FAT BABIES AND CHILDREN; FOODS

SUNBURN 93, 229
Sunburn needs to be taken just as seriously as other burns. It does not show or hurt until after the damage has been done, so don't rely for prevention either on looking at your child's skin or on what he says.

Prevention

☐ A fair skinned child will burn more easily than a darker child and his skin will take longer to build up a protective tan. You may have to guard against sunburn right through the summer.

☐ Sun is reflected off water as well as beating down on to it, so take particular care when you are beside the sea, or out in a boat. Veiled sun can burn. Wind can keep you cool when the sun is bright, and the drying effect of wind on skin is making sunburn more likely.

☐ Skin which is least often exposed to the air and the sun is most liable to burn. Watch out especially for your toddler's bottom. If you strip him off on the beach, he will spend a good deal of time with his bottom in the air as he digs and examines shells. That scarlet bottom may ruin the rest of your holiday.

☐ If your child is used to running naked in the garden, his skin will probably take the sun fairly easily. Otherwise, half an hour a day in the full sun is all he should have for the first two or three days, or until you can see him going brown. Let him wear a light cotton shirt or tee shirt in the water over his swimsuit. If there is no shade on the beach, hire or even buy a beach umbrella so that he is in the shade when he wants to sit still. A wide brimmed hat will shade the back of his neck and shoulders. If you cannot persuade him to stay covered up enough, cut down your time on the beach, especially in the middle of the day.

☐ Protective creams, lotions or oils will help, but unless you use a cream which cuts out almost all the ultra-violet rays and therefore prevents tanning as well as burning, you cannot rely on them completely. A preparation which cuts out most of the shorter ultra-violet rays (which burn) allowing the longer ones (which tan) to get through is probably the best. To be really effective these need to be reapplied every time he goes into the water.

What to do

☐ In a mild case, the child's skin will be red and hot to the touch. Apply calamine lotion liberally, and cover him with something really soft—such as his softest tee shirt or a gauze nappy.

N.B. Keep the burned area out of the sun. The merest touch of the sun's heat will be painful.

☐ In a more serious case blisters may form. The child will be in real pain. He will need a doctor's attention unless the area is small and he seems perfectly well. Get a doctor at once if he is feverish and/or seems ill. An appropriate dose of junior aspirin will help the pain. At night stretch his under-sheet very tightly to help prevent friction, and use a silky covering if you can, rather than ordinary bedclothes.

SUPPOSITORIES 224

These are little bullet-shaped tablets containing drugs. They are inserted into the child's rectum where they melt. Suppositories should not be given to a child without specific instructions from a doctor. This includes the 'soap sticks' so beloved of nannies long ago, who used them to make babies have bowel movements.

SWADDLING *see* WRAPPING NEWBORN BABY

SWALLOWED OBJECTS

Provided the object your child has swallowed is neither poisonous nor sharp, the chances are that it will pass through him without doing him any harm. If it was small enough for him to swallow it will be small enough for him to pass with his bowel movement. Your doctor may suggest that you watch out for its reappearance and tell him if it has not arrived within 24 hours.

Sharp objects It is difficult for a child to swallow a really sharp object like an open safety pin, without it sticking in his throat and causing a great deal of pain. It is worth making sure that it is not still in his mouth or hand or on the floor before you rush him to hospital.

The hospital staff will probably X-ray the child to try and see where the object is. They may decide that they can safely let it pass through him, or they may decide that they must operate to remove it before it can damage the lining of his stomach or intestines.

Poisonous objects Sometimes a child swallows something like an ink cartridge from a pen that is not actually a medicine or a poison but which might be extremely bad for him all the same. If you are not sure whether it is poisonous or not, don't take chances, but go to your nearest outpatient department. *See* POISONING

SWEETS *see* FOODS

SWIMMING 313, 323, 410, 431 *see* SAFETY

SWINGING 233, 349 *see* PLAYTHINGS

T

TABLE MANNERS *see* FEEDING

TALKING first days 114, first six months 180-183, six months to one year 260-266, one year to two and a half 355-356, 361-362, two and a half to five 414-421; asking for approval 418; babbling 181-182, 261; 'baby talk' 183, 265, 266, 310, 362, 420; boasting 418; chatterbox 419-420; crying as communication 95, 114, 156, 233; first non-cry sounds 180; first words 263-264; from babble to jargon 261-263; helping him to be talkative 182-183, 260-266, 355-356, 414-415; insults and anger 421; jargoning 263, 335; nonsense and naughty nonsense 421; questions 416; in sentences 361-362; in single words 356; in sleep 379; slow development of 418-419; stuttering 419; and thinking 327, 335, 341, 390, 414, 424; in two-word phrases 361; *see* LISTENING

TALKING TO STRANGERS

Children under five will not be safe from traffic and other hazards if they are allowed to leave the house and garden alone, so protection from the possibility of assault by mentally disturbed adults only *begins* now. But it is a good idea to lay the groundwork:

'Never talk to strangers' is not the most useful approach. No child will come to harm through *talking* and a child forbidden to speak will not be able to ask the way or reply politely when asked the time. Instead, teach him that he must 'never go anywhere with a stranger'. Couple this with teaching him to report back to you

before going *anywhere*. If you can get these ideas into his head, the man who beckons over the fence and tells him to come outside and see his puppy will not stand a chance. If he is a total stranger, he will know he must not go. If he recognizes him as someone who always smiles at him in the street, he will still know he must pop in to the house and tell you before going with him.

As he comes near school age, reinforce both rules. Explain that while most people are nice and like children, some are not and don't. Stress that nice people know that children are not supposed to go anywhere without telling an adult, so anyone who tries to persuade him to do so cannot be nice.

As he begins to go to friends' houses nearby or to the corner-shop alone, absolutely insist that he always tell you where he is going and that having done so, he go straight there and only there. Diversions and delays are forbidden unless he reports back to you first. Make sure he applies this rule to going with, or into the houses of, friends as well as strangers. Although a 'stranger' is the obvious hazard, most assaults are in fact carried out by acquaintances, neighbours or relations.

TANTRUMS 291, 318-319, 324-327, 365, 441, 442-443

TAPEWORMS *see* WORMS

TASTING commercially-prepared foods and home-prepared foods 211; early preferences 139; first solids 138; poisonous substances 230; presenting new tastes 371; developing personal tastes 214, 284-285, 288, 291, 372; sense of taste in newborn 95, 114, 291; sense well-developed by toddler stage 335, 336

TEACHER-BEAKERS *see* FEEDING EQUIPMENT

TEATS *see* BOTTLE-FEEDING

TEETH avoiding decay 158, 203, 231, 290-291, 316-317, 388; and chewing 154-155; cleaning 231, 291, 316-317, 386, 387, 388, 389; first fillings 389; milk and permanent 388; order of eruption 154, 155, 231, 316, 388; toothache 316, 388; toothbrush 316-317, 386-388 *see* DENTIST

TEETHING first six months 154-155; six months to one year 231; one year to two and a half 316-317; two and a half to five 388-389; and illness 154, 316; ring 69, 154

TELEVISION 263, 350, 376, 377, 387, 392, 407, 433, 447

TEMPERAMENT 32, 103-107, 119, 156, 189, 235, 320-321, 326, 390, 401, 402, 410-412

TEMPERATURE/Taking *see* CONVULSIONS; FEVER

How to read thermometer
☐ Hold mercury end between left forefinger and thumb; glass end between your right. Rotate it until the numbers and marks are on your side. Now rotate a little more and you will see a thick column of mercury appear under the numbers. The point where that column ends is the temperature.

How to take temperature
☐ Holding thermometer by glass end, flick your wrist sharply to shake mercury down well below the "normal" (98.6°F) mark. The mercury can only run *up*, not down, so if you start with last months 102°F you will not discover that his temperature is normal today.
☐ Put the mercury end into the child's armpit, fold the arm across his chest to seal it in, hold him still for three minutes then read off.
N.B. Mercury is poisonous; broken glass is dangerous. Don't take his temperature by mouth or rectum nor leave him with a thermometer in reach.

TESTICLES of newborn 47 *see* UNDESCENDED TESTICLES

TEST WEIGHING 59, 129

TETANUS *see* BITES; CUTS AND GRAZES; IMMUNIZATION

THIRST 50, 66, 133, 134, 136, 301, 384

THREADWORMS *see* WORMS

THRUSH
The fungus candida albicans is a normal inhabitant of the mouth, intestines and vagina. It is usually harmless but occasionally it sets up the infection known as thrush.

If you have a candida infection of the vagina, the fungus can reach your baby's mouth during birth or later on via ill-washed hands or inadequately sterilized bottles and teats. It produces white patches on the inside of a baby's cheeks and sometimes on his tongue and the roof of his mouth. The patches look like milk but if you try to wipe them off they either stick or come away leaving raw patches underneath. The mouth is usually extremely sore so that the baby cannot suck comfortably.

Treatment for thrush consists of either painting the patches with gentian violet or dropping an antibiotic solution on to them. A baby with thrush should have his nappies changed very frequently, as his stools will contain the fungus, and if they are left in contact with his warm wet bottom for long he may develop thrush around the anus. Treatment is again by painting with gentian violet.

THUMB-SUCKING *see* COMFORT HABITS

TOE INJURIES *see* FINGER AND TOE INJURIES

TOENAILS *see* FINGERNAILS AND TOENAILS

TOILET TRAINING 305-310, 381-387; avoiding early 'potting' 225; bladder control by day 307-310, 382, 383; bowel control 306-307, 385; choosing lavatory terminology 310; coping out of doors 381; from pot to lavatory 381, 393; staying dry at night 384-385 *see* BEDWETTING; EXCRETING; SOILING

TONGUE-TIE 44 *see* THRUSH

TONSILS
The tonsils are bodies of 'lymphoid tissue' on either side of the top of a child's throat which act as a filter and trap for harmful organisms. Tonsils are always small in the first year and enlarge after that. Large tonsils are not harmful, indeed their large size may suggest that they are actively doing their job of protecting the child against infections.

Tonsillitis When the tonsils 'trap' harmful bacteria or viruses which, had they got past the throat, might have affected the child's breathing passages or lungs, the 'battle' between tonsils and 'germs' gives rise to tonsillitis.

The tonsils swell and the throat looks red. Young children seldom complain of pain in the throat but older children may be tormented by the discomfort. In an extreme case, small yellow-white spots may be seen on the outside surfaces of the enlarged tonsils. The child will be feverish and obviously unwell. His breath may smell unpleasant. He may vomit as the fever rises. He may complain of stomach pain due, it is thought, to glands in other parts of the lymphoid system becoming swollen.

What to do Call the doctor. Infection can easily spread from the tonsils to the middle ear; the doctor must check that there is no ear inflammation; if there is, it must be treated early.

The doctor may, or may not, prescribe antibiotics for straightforward tonsillitis. It is a gamble because if the infecting organisms are bacteria, antibiotics are highly effective, but if they are viruses, the child is being dosed to no purpose.

He can discover what type of 'germ' is responsible by taking a 'throat swab' from the tonsil surface. But laboratory analysis of such swabs usually takes longer than spontaneous recovery so this is seldom done in a simple case.

Nurse the child as for any other feverish illness.

He will not be infectious in the sense of passing on his inflammation of the tonsils, but he can, of course, pass on whatever 'germs' have caused it.

Chronic infection in the tonsils, or repeated severe attacks of tonsillitis may eventually leave the tonsils scarred and useless. But their removal is never recommended nowadays before the child is four years old as they will still be performing at least part of their function. Most surgeons will defer operating as long as possible. Many children who have been very prone to tonsillitis in the early school period get fewer and fewer attacks as they reach the age of 7 or 8. Even if they still need the operation by this age they will be better able to cope.

Tonsillectomy Removal of the tonsils is not pleasant for the child. He will have an extremely sore throat and feel ill and miserable for a couple of days. Inevitably there is some bleeding from the site of the tonsils; usually there is some vomiting from the anaesthetic. The combination can be very frightening for him.

Because the main risk from tonsillectomy is of heavy bleeding during this recovery period, some hospitals insist that the child be kept as quiet as possible while he comes round. You may even be asked not to visit until the day after the operation. But this is bad advice. Your child is much more likely to sleep the anaesthetic off quietly, and to stay calm if he vomits, if you are with him. Crying for you is the most likely cause of bleeding.

If hospital policy is to keep parents out and you want to be with your child when he wakes up, ask your doctor to refer you elsewhere. See HOSPITAL

TOOTHACHE see TEETH

TOPPING AND TAILING see BATHING

TOUCHING AND TEXTURE coordinating touching with looking 167-177; exploring textures 270, 335-336, 344-346, 351; finding his hands 100, 104, 165; importance of contact comfort to newborn 97-99; importance of novelty in playthings 190; over-stimulation of newborn 96; sense of touch in newborn 114; sense well-developed by toddler stage 335; touching as refinement of grabbing 248, 258; toys for touching 178-179, 190, 192, 268; see CONTACT COMFORT

TOY LIBRARIES see LIBRARIES; USEFUL ADDRESSES

TOYS see PLAYING AND LEARNING; PLAYTHINGS

TRAINER PANTS 308 see TOILET TRAINING

TRANSITIONAL COMFORT OBJECTS see COMFORT HABITS

TRAVEL SICKNESS
This is thought to be caused by motion upsetting the delicate balance mechanism of the inner ear. Rough motion (such as that on a boat in choppy seas) makes most people sick. But many children feel, or are, sick with the much gentler motion of a car, bus or aeroplane. Travel sickness can begin as young as six months. It tends to peak in middle childhood and to get much less or to vanish in adolescence.

Prevention Your mode of travel is important. Few children feel sick in trains; almost all the sickness-prone ones hate coaches, while hard-sprung cars are usually better than soft-sprung ones.

☐ Sitting in the front of the car helps most children but has to be balanced against safety. If your child is badly affected it may be worth fitting a safety-harness in front for him. Otherwise lying down may help, so try making him a 'nest' on the back seat.

☐ Early morning is usually the worst time to travel; afternoon or evening the best.

☐ Give the child a light meal well before you start your journey and allow snacks such as dry biscuits, salty crisps, barley sugar etc., while travelling. Fizzy drinks are best avoided. Ice cold water from a thermos flask is the best drink.

Symptoms Silence in the midst of chattering or singing, pallor and sleepiness are early signs in most children. Tears, visible sweat and heavy watering of the mouth mean that vomiting is imminent.

Cure Only time will provide the permanent cure, but your doctor can prescribe a drug to prevent sickness on individual journeys. Follow the dosage carefully as there can be uncomfortable side-effects. An alternative is to travel at night and to ask your doctor whether he will prescribe an antihistamine drug. These both lessen nausea and induce sleep.

TRICYCLES see BICYCLES AND TRICYCLES

TROPICAL DISEASES see IMMUNIZATION

TWINS
There are two kinds of twin. Fraternal twins are formed from two separate eggs fertilized by two sperms, both at the same time. They may be of the same or of opposite sexes. They are no more alike, from the genetic point of view, than any other pair of brothers and sisters. Identical twins are formed when a single already-fertilized egg splits into two identical parts and develops into two babies. They will always be of the same sex and are identical from the genetic point of view.

Incidence of twins
☐ Identical twins are conceived by about 3 or 4 mothers out of every 1,000 who get pregnant. This number is very little affected by any outside factors such as the mother's race, age or number of previous pregnancies.
☐ Fraternal twins are conceived by white American and European mothers at a rate of about 1 in every 100 pregnancies. Unlike identical twins fraternal twins really do 'run in families'. A mother who has one pair is five times more likely to 'twin' again. If she, or a close female relation, is a twin, her chances of 'twinning' are about twice the average.

☐ The incidence of fraternal twins increases with the mother's age and with her number of previous pregnancies. There is also a racial variation. Negroes have the highest twinning rate, with African negro women producing about 1 pair of twins in every 40 pregnancies in some tribes. Caucasians come next, while people of Mongolian origin (Japanese, Chinese, American Indians) produce only about 1 twin pair in every 160 pregnancies.
☐ Drugs administered to induce ovulation in women who have previously been unable to conceive a child, because no eggs were released for fertilization, have led to many multiple births.

Preparing for twins As soon as you know that twins are on the way, do start preparing for the fascinating but infinitely exhausting task ahead of you. Bringing up twins is not just twice the work of bringing up one baby. It is a quite different task which will use all your intelligence and ingenuity as well as your patience and stamina. You might start by getting hold of a copy of 'Twins and Supertwins' by Amram Scheinfeld which is published as a paperback by Penguin books. You might also make contact with your health visitor and ask her to introduce you to any mothers of twins whom she knows: watching how they manage will give you plenty of ideas. A few areas even have 'Twin clubs' whose members not only offer each other mutual support but the loan of all those expensive items of vital equipment like twin prams and pushchairs.

U

UNCONSCIOUSNESS
What to do
☐ A child who is unconscious for any reason, even for a second, needs medical attention urgently. Send for your doctor or an ambulance, whichever will be quicker.
☐ Until he is conscious, guard against choking and assist circulation by putting the child in the recovery position—on his tummy with his head turned to one side and the leg on that side drawn well up, with the arm bent at the elbow so that the hand lies opposite the face. In this position his tongue cannot fall back in his mouth and obstruct his breathing and any bleeding or vomit will drain out of his mouth.
N.B. Do not try to give anything to drink, you may choke him.

☐ When he 'comes to', let him move into a more comfortable position if he wishes, but keep him lying down until a doctor has seen him. *See also* 510-512

UNDESCENDED TESTICLES
The testes of a male foetus develop in his abdomen and migrate, late in the pregnancy, through a passage in the abdominal muscles into the scrotal sac.

In some baby boys, the testes have descended normally but their passageway into the abdomen has remained open. One or both testes will retract back inside when the scrotum is touched, especially if the touch is cold. A retractable testis will almost invariably fix itself in the scrotum, its passageway closing behind it, during the early years.

Occasionally one or both testes fail to descend before birth. Usually the descent will take place spontaneously, but it is important to check as a testis which remains in the abdomen cannot develop its sexual function.

If the testes are descended and fixed, you will be able to feel them as separate walnut-shaped objects inside the loose scrotal skin. If they are descended but retractable on touch, you will be able to see their shape clearly when the baby lies on his back with his legs in the air.

The presence of both testes will be checked by the doctor on routine medical examinations. If one or both have failed to descend or become fixed by the time he is eight, surgery, which is simple although it can be psychologically upsetting, will be advised.

URINARY INFECTIONS 89, 382
URINATING *see* EXCRETING; NAPPY RASH; TOILET TRAINING
URINE newborn baby's 47, 89 *see* EXCRETING; NAPPY RASH; TOILET TRAINING

URTICARIA (HIVES; NETTLE RASH)
A general term for an allergic skin reaction. White weals surrounded by reddened areas appear. The skin itches furiously. If the reaction is intense, the weals may become large swollen white patches which make the child's face or body look misshapen.

The weals and the itching usually vanish within a few hours but new ones can appear as the old ones wane so that the child has urticaria for days at a time.

Many children have a single attack of urticaria and nobody ever knows the cause. If it recurs frequently, however, the misery of the itching and the damage done

to the skin by scratching may make it necessary to search for the allergen. This is frequently a food (such as shellfish or strawberries), a drug (such as aspirin or penicillin) or an insect bite. In a few allergic children emotional tension clearly predisposes the skin to react in this way.

Relieve the itching with calamine lotion or a bath containing two tablespoons of sodium bicarbonate. If the urticaria goes on for several days your doctor might prescribe antihistamine medicines. These directly help a few sufferers and their sedative side-effects can help others to sleep through the irritation.

Angio-neurotic oedema An uncommon but dramatic form of urticaria. A single large area of skin, commonly around the eye, lip or penis, suddenly puffs up into a large white weal. The swelling usually goes down in a few hours and the allergen is seldom discovered.

Occasionally angio-neurotic oedema affects the soft tissues of the throat and causes difficulty in breathing. Any sign of obstructed breathing should, of course, lead you to take the child straight to the nearest source of emergency help.

Papular urticaria An allergic reaction of the child's skin to the protein in animal fleas. The white weals on reddened skin look a little like normal urticaria except that each weal is topped by a round spot with a little blister of clear fluid on it. The weals will disappear in a few hours, but the spots may stay longer and since they itch, the child may scratch the blisters off and infect them.

Calamine lotion will help the itching, but the trouble will recur if the child has any contact at all with animal fleas. Touch is enough; he need not be bitten.

☐ Dust all pets against fleas.
☐ Keep the child out of places like hay barns which are likely to have a flea population.

If you have real trouble with this minor but tiresome complaint take your child to the doctor. He may think antihistamine drugs worth a trial. *See* ALLERGIES

V

VACCINATION *see* IMMUNIZATION
VAGINA 47, 89, 382

VAGINA/Foreign Bodies in
A child exploring her body may poke something into her vagina.

Beads and small objects The first you will know of this will probably be a whitish, possibly nasty-smelling, discharge which will mean that some infection has been set up. It is seldom a serious matter, but take her to the doctor who will check for the object and prescribe treatment.

Larger objects Poking her fingers or other objects into her vagina is harmless (unless infection starts) but very occasionally the child may partially split the hymen, causing a small amount of bleeding. In a child who still wears nappies, check with your doctor as the minute tear will easily become infected by contact with faeces. In an older child you can safely ignore the whole matter. A little silicone barrier cream over the whole area will protect against stinging caused when she pees.

VERRUCAS AND WARTS
These are harmless small growths on the skin caused by a virus and often come in crops. The kind which appear on the feet are called verrucas. They are contagious, so the infected child should not go to public swimming baths or walk around barefoot until they have been treated. Verrucas can be painful because the growth presses into the foot during walking.

Your doctor may suggest cutting or scraping out the wart, but this is unnecessarily painful for a small child; verrucas can be dealt with more gently and gradually by repeated applications of a special ointment.

VISION *see* EYES; LOOKING; SEEING

VOMITING 47, 75, 89, 149, 224
The forcible expulsion of the contents of the stomach; it is usually preceded by feeling sick (nausea) and accompanied by retching. Some children vomit easily; at the beginning of almost any illness; from excitement or nervous tension; in moving vehicles; or for no apparent reason. Vomiting seldom means anything very important. Take it seriously:
☐ If it happens more than twice in one day.
☐ If your child feels ill and nauseated even after vomiting.
☐ If it is accompanied by diarrhoea.
☐ If it follows head injury.
☐ If your child has stomach pain (which can be difficult to detect as very young children cannot tell stomach-ache from nausea).
Otherwise just keep a casual eye on him. You will soon see whether he is ill or not.

W X

'WAKEFUL' BABIES 106-107, 147-148, 158, 223

WAKING see SLEEPING AND WAKING

WALKING first days 113; first six months 164; six months to one year 243; one year to two and a half 328-333; two and a half to five 406; alone 328-332; beginnings of 164, 242; 'cruising' round supports 245, 247, 328; getting overtired while learning 296-297; and other 'milestones' 160, 243; playthings for 324, 330, 348, 349; reflex in newborn baby 113; safe freedom to practise 329-331; stages of learning 328-329; toddlers' peculiar use of 332-333

WARMTH 32, 36, 38, 39, 80-81, 92, 93, 97, 98, 100, 104, 148, 151, 153, 158, 221, 316 see CHILLING

WARTS see VERRUCAS AND WARTS

WATER see FLUIDS

WEANING balancing quantities of milk and solids 138, 209, 294; bottle-fed babies 203-204, 221, 231; breast-fed babies 202-203, 221, 231; older baby from bottle 203, 317

WEIGHT GAIN first days 50, 64, 76-79; first six months 126; six months to one year 201; one year to two and a half 281, 293; two and a half to five 369, 374 see FAT BABIES AND CHILDREN; GROWTH; HEIGHT GAIN

WETTING see BEDWETTING; EXCRETING; TOILET TRAINING

WHINING 275, 291, 296, 332, 355, 435, 441

WHOOPING COUGH

Incubation period 8–14 days

First signs

☐ An ordinary-sounding cough which may, or may not, be accompanied by a runny nose. The child may seem slightly off colour and the whole phase may drag on for several days.

Definite signs (In an *immunized* child diagnosis may be very difficult as the typical features are lacking).

☐ The cough worsens and becomes paroxysmal so that the child coughs several times on a single breath.

☐ Typically, the cough takes him unawares, with no time to breathe in before coughing out. As a result he becomes distressed for air. The diagnostic 'whoop' is a trick he learns to cope with this situation. He forces air in while the larynx is still in spasm. Because the larynx is partly closed the inrushing breath makes the whooping sound.

☐ Very young babies may never learn to whoop. As a result they do become very short of oxygen with each coughing fit. They may turn bluey-grey in the face during the attack and vomit after it.

Degree of illness

☐ Very ill indeed and for a long time, especially if he is under one year old and/or is not immunized.

Possible complications

☐ The frequency of coughing bouts and the vomiting after them may make it extremely difficult to get and keep enough liquid and food down the child. Exhaustion, dehydration and prostration are real risks.

☐ Middle ear infections and broncho-pneumonia are common.

What the doctor may do

☐ Confirm the diagnosis with throat swab and/or blood test, especially in a child who has been immunized or is too young to whoop.

☐ Give antibiotics which are effective in modifying the disease if they are given *early*.

☐ Show you how to tap the child's chest while he lies head down, so as to move the phlegm to a position from which he can more easily cough it up.

☐ Recommend hospital admission if the child (especially a baby) is getting dehydrated or exhausted, or if you have nobody with whom to share continuous, demanding nursing.

What you can do

☐ Nurse him continuously, making sure he is never left alone even at night. Panic makes breathlessness worse so your reassurance during coughing fits is vital. Inhaled vomit is dangerous so you must be there to hold his head.

☐ Keep him quiet, especially during the acute phase. Active play will make him cough.

☐ Give tiny drinks and things to eat immediately *after* a coughing/vomiting fit. This gives the best chance of at least some of it being absorbed before the next attack brings it up again. Keep accurate notes of the quantities of liquid the child has had. Even though you do not know how much he has vomited, these will help your doctor decide if he is getting something near enough.

☐ Be prepared for a long bout of intensive care and even after that, for what may be weeks of convalescence.

☐ Protect unimmunized or very young babies from contact with the patient. See NURSING

WORDS see TALKING

WORMS 385

Any child or adult can get worms. They do not indicate dirty habits, and treatment is quick and final.

Threadworms These are the most common type and look like little white threads. You can sometimes see them in the motion or around the anus because the females come out to lay their eggs. Threadworms can cause irritation around the anus, or around the vagina of little girls, who may transfer a few by scratching. Occasionally bedwetting is caused by the irritation which half wakes the child and makes him scratch. The infection is passed on, because the child scratches himself and gets eggs on his fingers. He may then either reinfect himself by putting his fingers in his mouth or pass them on to a new host.

What to do Your doctor will prescribe a drug specifically for threadworms which should be taken simultaneously by the whole household. One dose usually kills all the worms and eggs, but everyone must take a second dose two weeks later.

Help the child who has worms not to scratch around his anus. Close-fitting pants or a pair of stretch swimming trunks to wear for a few nights may prevent him scratching in his sleep. Keep his nails really short, and take trouble about handwashing, especially after using the lavatory.

Roundworms These are rare except in tropical countries. They look like whitish earthworms and are often up to six inches (15.2 cm) long. They are usually passed in the stool, but occasionally if a child has a heavy infestation he will vomit one.

Tapeworms These are rare, and appear as flat white moving segments in the stool. The source is usually undercooked pork.

WOUNDS see BLEEDING; CUTS AND GRAZES

WRAPPING NEWBORN BABY 92, 93, 97, 98-99, 100, 101, 105, 148, 151, 158, see CONTACT COMFORT; CRYING AND COMFORTING

X-RAYS

Having an X-ray can be frightening for a child. Do explain that all that machinery is only a kind of camera and that when he puts his head between the plates, he is not going to be hurt.

It is a good idea to get him used to the idea of X-rays before he ever needs one. Find an X-ray picture to show him if you can.

Playthings The following pages will help you to provide the playthings that will keep your child interested, happy and learning fast at each stage of his development.

	What he needs	Why he needs it	Suitable 'toys'
First weeks	He needs as much contact with people as possible. Objects mean nothing to him at this stage. Physical and visual contact are what matter.	His survival depends on human care. He is programmed to attend to people's voices and faces.	He does not need objects. His "entertainment", apart from sucking etc., is in listening to your voice and in studying your face. His best focusing distance is only 8-10 in. (20-25 cm) from the bridge of his nose.
From about five weeks . . .	Contact with you and the chance to study faces are still his prime needs. Hold him close, put his pram or chair near you so he can watch your activities.	He has seen nothing, so variety and change are what matter. He will practise focusing his eyes on things at different distances, and begin to learn the appearances of things.	Mobiles, washing, or moving leaves, seen from his pram; things strung across his cot. His own hands, left free to suck when he can "find" them.
From about three months . . .	He needs things to hold as well as to look at, and things which sound as he waves them about. Go for variety of shape and colour.	When his random waving makes a rattle sound, the sound makes him look and see the clever thing he is making happen. He is learning to find his hands by touch and by eye; they are his best toy, don't conceal them in mittens or wrappings.	Small plastic or metal pots filled with dried peas, sugar or paper clips all sound different and give variety. Make sure the lids are securely on. Fill a transparent plastic bottle with coloured water and detergent. It looks pretty and makes an interesting swooshy sound as well.
	He needs things to reach out for and things to swipe. His best reaching out will take place when he is supported sitting on your lap or in his chair.	Batting at hanging objects gives him practice in getting his hand to something he can see and the lovely power of making it move.	Woolly balls, partially blown-up balloons; a shiny plastic ball, tiny soft animal toys, paper streamers, a chiming ball.
	He needs things to get hold of. They will go into his mouth, so watch out for toxic paints etc. as well as for sharp edges.	Once he can get hold of things, mouth and handle them, he can explore his world, object by object.	Seal a single marble in a plastic bottle (such as a washed out detergent bottle). It thuds and alters its balance as the marble moves inside. Make your own bean bags with crunchy cornflake or dried pea filling. Make chewable books by putting magazine pictures into clear plastic wallets. Provide some big objects to get hold of; soft toys or even cushions or loaves of bread.
	He needs physical play–give him games like 'this little piggy' counting his toes, or 'this is the way the farmer rides,' bouncing his whole body.	He is learning about his whole body, where it ends and the "outside me" world begins, how it feels, what he can make it do.	Your lap is his best gymnasium, his own body the perfect floor toy, with rolling over to practise. Bounce or roll him on your bed: it is as exciting as a trampoline. Buy or borrow a baby bouncer, it will stay in use right through toddlerhood.

498

	What he needs	**Why he needs it**	**Suitable 'toys'**
From about six months . . . Many of the playthings he already has will still be popular, but he will increasingly *use*, as well as merely examine, them. So provide at least some toys with which he can actually do something and from which he can learn something specific.	*Everyday household objects especially those used in his care.* 	*He is deeply attached to you and will soon be highly imitative. If he is encouraged, through play, to take part in his own care he will feel less overwhelmed and bullied later.*	*Bath equipment: washcloth, toothbrush. Feeding equipment: own spoon, beaker etc. 'Helping Mum': dusters, brushes etc. Clothes: a try at getting his own socks on etc.*
	Toys with a definite cause and effect.	*He needs to feel that he has power to affect his world. He needs to feel 'because I do this, that happens. I do it; I make it happen.'*	*Toys that squeak when squeezed, pots and pans or drums and tambourines to bang. Miniature cars to pull, paper to tear.*
	Objects that behave in different ways when they are treated in the same way.	*Once he has grasped his own power to make things happen he can learn a lot about his world by discovering that objects have basic characteristics which differentiate them from each other whatever he does.*	*Things that roll when they are pushed and things that don't: a ball and a brick. Things that crumble when banged and things that don't: a biscuit and a piece of bread.*
	Toys which are fun at the baby level of looking, sucking, banging, but have built-in potential for more advanced play.	*He will often acquire new skills by first making something happen by accident and then, because it was fun, teaching himself to do it again on purpose.*	*A pull-string musical box, nesting toys, containers and things to put in and out of them. Boxes, jars and bottles with lids to remove; 'pop-up' toys.*
	Games you can play with him.	*He learns by watching and by imitating what you do. The ability to watch and copy will be important to all his later education. You can foster it now.*	*Build brick towers for him to knock down; soon he will build too. Post ping-pong balls down a cardboard tube. Eventually he will learn to angle the tube so they roll in particular directions. Roll a ball for him to retrieve; soon he will roll it back to you. Play the piano and let him bang the keys, and make loud or soft, high or low discords.*
	Once the baby can crawl, much of his play will be crawling for its own sake, but some kinds of playthings are ideal at this stage. He needs toys big enough to see across the room and crawl to, and toys he can have fun with when he reaches them.	*Being a crawler can be frustrating. He needs to work off on suitable objects the inevitable frustrations of having unsuitable ones removed from his explorations.*	*Big wheeled toys, wooden lorries etc. Really big soft toys and cushions that will stay still while he pummels them. Beach balls or balloons which may escape when he pushes them. Quoits or rings which he will eventually learn to pick up and throw.*
	He needs his own special possessions, like, but distinct from, everyone else's.	*As he nears his first birthday he begins to feel himself to be a separate and unique individual. Possessions can help to encourage this vital sense of self.*	*A safety mirror set in a moulded frame with finger holes. He can see something he is realizing is 'me'. Eventually he will make faces at himself. Photographs of himself with and without you. His own special plate, mug, books, pictures, etc.*

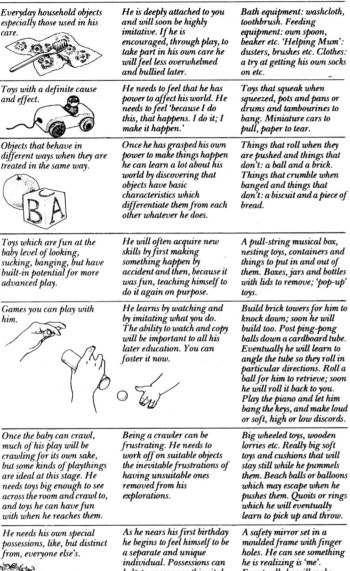

**Playthings from about
one year . . .**
Your child is ready for more
elaborate toys, but safety is a very
real factor, for he is pulling himself to standing and about to
become a biped. Almost every
child will enjoy the following types
of toy; they are safe and he will use
them long enough to make the
investment worthwhile.
Babywalker This small push-cart is
designed so that it neither tips
when the child pulls himself up by
the handle nor runs away when he
toddles with it. It gives him mobility indoors and out during the
cruising stage and has years of life
ahead as first doll's pram or
wheel-barrow. The design is crucial—don't try to make your own.

Pull-toys Once he walks steadily he
can pull a wheeled toy along at the
same time. Would-be pet owners
will enjoy a realistic dog with
wagging tail and wobbling tongue.
Ride-on toys Any toy for him to sit
on, and push himself along by his
feet, should have castors, which
will safely take pressure in any
direction, not wheels, which will
tip when he pushes randomly.

Push-toys These are unsafe until he
can get to his feet without using
anything to pull up by, and understands that when riding, he must
push straight with his feet. Then a
wheeled animal with a handle will
be very popular.
Romping toys Soft toys nearly as big
as himself are fun to romp with and
a safety valve for feelings too, as
they get punched and strangled.
Save money by using a ready-to-
sew 'novelty cushion kit'. There are
huge snakes, teddy bears and even
a snail big enough to ride on.

Fitting toys Although he is concentrating largely on getting mobile,
hand control is developing too. He
needs a few toys which hold his
attention while he sits still for a
change. Follow the rule: the smaller the hands the bigger the pieces
should be. Of the many available
the following best combine fun
and lasting play value.
□ Rods-on-a-stand, with big coloured balls that slide on to them.
The rods take different numbers
of coloured balls—a first counting
and colour learning toy.

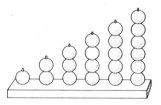

□ Very simple nesting toys, such as
a set of graduated beakers.
□ A version of the traditional
hammer peg toy—wooden frame
with holes through which pegs are
banged with a mallet. Then the
frame is turned over and they are
banged back again.

□ Simple take-apart toys, such as
wooden vehicles with interchangeable top parts which can be
lifted off a hole and peg attachment, or with interchangeable peg
'men' fitting into holes in the body.
Moulded plastic 'people' sold with
a variety of vehicles and equipment, into which they slot, are
even more versatile, and the 'people' can populate later games.

**Playthings suitable for
toddlers and pre-school
children . . .**
The bewildering variety of toys on
the market together with claims to
special educational advantages
makes choosing good toys hard.
  The more a toy is played with
the better its value. As a fun-guide,

you can work out play value, by
dividing purchase price by
minutes of play. You may find that
expensive equipment such as a
climbing frame, that is played with
over years, and small cheap toys,
that are played with intensively
over the first days of their novelty,
both work out better than the
medium priced toys—such as construction sets. One such "educational" set only received 2 hours
play in total over a year. Those two
hours cost over £2 per hour . . . .
Choosing toys While every child
should sometimes have a particular toy just because it fulfils a
heart's desire, many such yearn-
ings will be inspired by misleading
advertising. Always have the package opened before you buy. Does
the toy work? Does it do what the
child expects? Will he be able to
use it or does it need more space
than you have available, more help
from you than you are prepared to
give, or weather you cannot expect
at this season? Consider whether
the toys will stand up to your
particular child's play-of-the-
moment. A plastic plane used as a
missile can turn into a lethal
weapon when it breaks. A "talking" doll will not "talk" for long if
all dolls in your house have frequent baths!
  Don't refuse to buy "more of the
same". If a girl likes dolls her idea
of enough will not be the same as
yours.
  If you want to buy something he
has never had before, choose
something that particularly suits a
time in his daily life when he is
often bored, such as a sitting-down
toy for the early morning if he is
bored in his cot.
  Try not to buy toys that are too
delicate/expensive/noisy for him to
use as he pleases. If you are going
to say 'ssh' or 'careful' every time
he uses that drum or doll's house,
don't buy them. If you buy a toy
with many pieces which are easily
mislaid, check the availability of
spares and if possible buy some
extras; a marble run that will only
take its own marbles can be useless
in a week if they all get lost.
  Provided they look nice, children don't care if toys are second-
hand or home-made. Buying from
jumble sales or ads in your local
paper may mean you can afford
more and better toys for him.
Many toys are ludicrously over-
priced. Lift ideas ruthlessly from
toyshops and catalogues and provide the same play value for much
less money by cobbling things
together yourself (see Presents).

Playthings to save
up for, or make

These comparatively large and expensive items are not, of course, *necessary* to your child. But each will give him hours of fun over many years. In terms of value for money they will be worth every penny. . . .

A paddling pool Buy the biggest you can afford. The inflatable type is safest as there are no sharp sides to fall against.

SAFETY NOTE—stay close by. Empty between sessions.

Splasher pool You might save money in the end by buying a 'splasher pool' (10 ft/3 m in diameter, 2 ft 6 in./76 cm deep) instead of a paddling pool. It will last for years, your children can learn to swim in it and because it is above ground you can safely leave it full all summer without fear of them falling in.

SAFETY NOTE Go in with toddlers, provide water wings for older non-swimmers and stay close.

A home-made 'wallow' Take the biggest plastic sheet you have got, spread it on the lawn and roll the edges up round garden canes, lilos or whatever you have. Fill from the hose and you have a large expanse of water only about 1 inch deep (2.5 cm). It will leak away but not before the child has had a lot of fun. Provide ping-pong balls and paper boats to float on it.

SAFETY NOTE It will be slippery, so make sure there is nothing he can bang his head on when he falls.

Climbing frame A climbing frame will cost a lot of money but will repay it over and over again. Don't try to make one yourself unless you are an experienced carpenter. The child's safety for years to come depends on its stability. A freelance carpenter might make you one to fit your particular garden (perhaps even incorporating a well placed tree) for less than a shop will charge you. Choose between tubular metal and wood. Metal lasts longer but is cold, slippery when wet, and does not easily allow

you to make your own accessories. Wood will outlast your family if you periodically check that all joints are still tight and perhaps add a coat of wood-preservative every couple of years. Buy the biggest frame you can get. Choose a position that gets all the sun there is and is in full view of the house: you may want to keep an eye on it.

SAFETY NOTE Put your frame on grass if you can. Falls are rare, but more likely to be serious on concrete or paving.

Extras Your small child will be safer just climbing at first. Later you can buy a slide to fit.

Platforms You can make your own: measure across one of the bays of the frame; buy a rectangle of timber one inch bigger than the space. Sandpaper and paint it with wood-preservative. Mark on its underside exactly where it crosses the bars, and screw on stout clips that will fit the bars tightly. It can now be clipped securely in place, and is easily removed when the frame is wanted for climbing.

Swing A rope about 1½ inches (3.8 cm) in diameter can be tied to the top of the frame for climbing. A big knot at the bottom makes a simple swing. Turn it into a monkey swing by cutting, or getting cut, a circle of timber about 1 inch (2.5 cm) thick and 15 inches (38 cm) across. Drill a hole in the centre, thread the rope through and knot the end. You can suspend a small car tyre for standing or swinging on, but if you leave it out it will fill with water which is surprisingly difficult to get out.

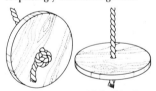

Cover A cover (an old double sheet will do) right over the frame makes a fantastic house or tent.

Gym set A rope ladder, trapeze bar and swinging rings can be bought as a set, complete with ropes fitted with clips at either end, so they are interchangeable and easy to hang, indoors or out.

Balancing planks Make these exciting extensions to the frame. Buy 8 in. x 1 in. (20 cm x 2.5 cm) planks 6 to 8 ft (2 to 2.5 m) long. Sandpaper them and paint with wood-preservative, and screw a pair of clips to the underside of one end so it can clip safely to the climbing frame bars.

On a low bar a small child can balance up the gentle slopes. On a higher bar you can make an exciting angle for older children.

Playhouses

A proper 'Wendy House' made of wood and designed to live permanently in the garden will cost as much as a garden shed. A plastic or cotton 'playhouse' cover that slips over a collapsible metal frame is a better and cheaper buy, but check that the material is fire resistant.

A small tent makes a good house out of doors. A wigwam is more adaptable, since it is self-supporting and can be put up anywhere, including the living room! If space and money are no problem, wooden fold-away houses designed to serve as houses, shops and puppet theatres, suit a wide age range. A competent handy-person could copy one of these designs easily. The structure is no more than a series of hardboard panels hinged together, with refinements like doors, windows and counters added. You could make a simpler version by cutting windows etc. in an old-fashioned screen. Even easier is a 'clothes horse' house, made from the kind of clothes horse that opens into three wings. Cover each wing by stapling material around the top and bottom bars, and across the top if wanted.

If you buy a new cooker, fridge or freezer, make a house from the box it comes in. It will not last forever but will give enormous pleasure until it collapses. If you like handiwork you could transform one of these boxes into something a bit more permanent. Seal the whole thing with size and then with paint, and strengthen all edges and folds with insulating tape. Use simulated brick wallpaper, stick-on flowers etc. to decorate it. Treated like this your house should stand up to months of use.

Making bricks

Bricks are irreplaceable. He must have them, and he must have plenty. Choose a big plain set sold by a good toy suppliers in their own kit bag rather than a cheap small coloured set. Try to buy enough all at once. If you add more later their measurements may have been changed so the child cannot learn, for example, that one big one takes up the same space as two medium or four small.

To make your own: Decide on your basic 'module.' A 2 inch (5 cm) cube is about right. Buy 2 in. x 2 in. (5 cm x 5 cm) timber—each brick will need only one saw cut. Cut a few 'doubles' of 4 in. x 2 in. x 2 in. (10 cm x 5 cm x 5 cm) and a few 'halves' of 1 in. x 2 in. x 2 in. (2.5 cm x 5 cm x 5 cm). You may like to add some flat pieces too, cut from ½ in. (1.3 cm) thick wood and measuring 4 in. x 2 in. (10 cm x 5 cm) or 2 in. x 2 in. (5 cm x 5 cm). Sandpaper each block so that it is safe for sucking, and paint or varnish (with non-toxic material) so they can be washed. It is easiest to spread them all on newspaper and spray the lot with aerosol varnish. Don't do the underside until the tops are dry. Provide a container which comfortably holds the whole lot—a drawstring bag or a plastic laundry basket will do.

Making a sandpit

If you have a garden, a sandpit is a worthwhile investment. It should be at least 4 ft x 4 ft (1.2 m x 1.2 m) with seats in the corners. It can be wood or moulded plastic.

You can save money by making a wooden one. Buy four lengths of timber each measuring 4 ft x 9 in. x 1 in. (1.2 m x 23 cm x 2.5 cm). Screw them together at each corner. Screw a further piece of timber across the two front corners to give added rigidity and make 'seats.'

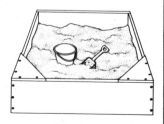

Use washed or silver sand, not ordinary builder's sand which stains everything orange. Provide a cover to keep out animals, leaves and so on. A sheet of hardboard will do, or a sheet of heavy plastic folded over the corners of the sandpit as if wrapping a parcel, and stapled so that it can be slipped on and off. Use something (perhaps a bucket) in the centre to act as a 'pie funnel' so that water runs off the cover.

If you install your sandpit on concrete or paving it will drain adequately. On earth, you will need to put a plastic sheet down first, studded with little drainage holes. Choose a sunny place close to your own garden activities.

Provide buckets and spades, a rake, a sieve, a big plastic spoon or flour shovel, and a variety of plastic containers. Provide somewhere to store the toys so the child can get a clear start at the sand.

SAFETY NOTE: Teach the child never to throw sand and don't let two or more toddlers play in the sandpit on their own. Sand in the eyes can be dangerously scratchy.

Playing and long distance travel

Every form of transport has its problems with young children, but cars are the worst as well as the most usual. Adapt these ideas if you are going by train or plane.

Safety comes first Babies should have their own car-safety seats, older children 'trainer' seat belts in the back.

Comfort is vital Define shares of the back seat with rolled blankets or pillows between children; these double as head rests for sleeping and prevent physical fights, if not quarrels. Keep clothes comfortable. Tee shirts and stretch trousers are better than fiddly belts and tight jerseys. Give each child a large plant tray as a play-table and don't forget his 'cuddly'.

A surprise bag Although it may seem extravagant, a 'surprise bag' full of small cheap treasures collected over previous weeks makes all the difference. The collection can be used in various ways to suit different ages. You might collect:
☐ A balloon to blow up and let down with a squeal.
☐ A tiny notebook and crayon.
☐ A small car, doll or animal.
☐ Plasticine or playdoh.
☐ A bubble blowing kit—bubbles stream beautifully from a partly opened car window.
☐ A new book or comic.
☐ A puzzle or drawing book.
☐ A kaleidoscope to hold to the window or a telescope for looking out of it.
☐ Carefully chosen snacks—not chocolate!

Using the bag Give a very small child a parcel whenever his boredom drives you to screaming point. Build older children's parcels into a game to last the whole journey. Tell him he can have one at each of the following place names, write out the names for him and make him compare the letters on town signs and say when a parcel is due. Or set a number of miles apart for each parcel and make him consult the milometer or milestones. Say he can have a parcel each time he sees a school bus full of boys or a car with an H registration or six horses in a field. . . .

More toys specially for cars The back windows are an excellent surface for drawing on with felt-tip pens. A new set and a damp sponge will pass minutes. Stick-on peel-off plastic shapes sold to make 'scenes' on a background will stick on the window too. Pocket puzzles of the kind that let the child compete against his own record are a good idea: 'pin ball' lets you set challenges like 'try and score 500 with three balls.' Many children (of both sexes) travel happily if allowed to 'shoot' passing motorists out of the window. Perhaps this sure-fire game shocks you, but if not, include a toy gun in the surprise bag.

Games Car games depend on family tradition and your patience. Try the 'silence' game. Hand a watch with a second-hand to an older child, a kitchen timer to a younger one. Challenge him to keep silent for a whole minute. He enjoys watching time pass, you get at least 20 seconds peace and it sometimes ends in sleep. Elaborations include timing breath holding or nursery rhyme-chanting.

Using a tape recorder If you have a portable cassette recorder or car tape-deck, record a tape specially for the child in advance. You could include stories read by each or both of you, favourite songs off a record, idiotic jokes and riddles. . . . You may find that a tape like this stays in demand long after the journey is over.

Even if you have no garden, you can teach your child about the living world, by bringing outdoors indoors . . .

Plants You can buy many kinds of children's 'propagator', ready supplied with suitable seeds.
Mustard and cress will grow on any piece of absorbent paper or material, if it is kept damp. The child could sow someone's name for a birthday. Or eat his own harvest.

Mung beans are quick and easy to grow. After the first two days the child can see daily progress, and eat the shoots a week later . . .
A bean or pea, put between the sides of a jam jar and a lining of damp blotting paper, grows fast too. No crop, but fun to watch the roots going down, the shoots up.

Creatures Leaving 'real pets' aside, the child can get a lot of interest without giving you much work through:
A snailery Collect snails off the plant they are eating and make a note of it; they may eat nothing else around. Keep in a shallow plastic tray with food-leaves, stones, other greenery.

A wormery You can buy these, but a small aquarium or large pyrex dish filled with earth will do. Use fine wire mesh for a lid. If the worms stay invisible water the soil lightly and they will surface.

Ant farm It is best to buy special containers (from school equipment suppliers or pet shops) as it is difficult to make an ant-proof one yourself. If you manage to get a colony established it is fascinating to watch and the child will enjoy feeding them.
Tadpoles Collect frog spawn and water. Put into a large container and add rocks, gravel and pond weeds. Top up with pond water if possible, rain water if not.

Tap water will kill the developing tadpoles. Once they are swimming free feed them tiny quantities of fish food meant for baby fish. Raw meat leads to stinking water and dead tadpoles.

Whether you have a garden or not, your child will benefit from having somewhere to climb and swing indoors . . .

Climbing set Failing a climbing frame you can make your own climbing set. You need at least two (more if you have space) sturdy wooden boxes big enough for the child to get right inside. Tea chests are the easiest to find. Be careful to remove all nails, and to flatten down any sharp pieces of metal binding before using.

Now buy a board, about 6 ft (2 m) long by 8 inches (20 cm) wide and at least 1 inch (25 cm) thick. Sandpaper it carefully, and paint it and your boxes with long-lasting, non-toxic paint in a bright colour.

The child will use this collection separately and together, for years. The boxes will be hidden in, climbed on, jumped off, put together for a train and on top of each other for a ship's bridge. The board will be walked along on the floor, put across the boxes for a bridge, jumped off and balanced along. With one end on a box it is a slide; with the middle over a box it is a see-saw.

If you cannot store such a set, it is still worth making just the board. A pile of magazines each end makes it a bridge and balancing bar, one end propped on a chair makes a slide. When the child is not using it himself he will run cars down it or sit dolls on it.

Hooks in the ceiling You may already have one of these from his baby bouncer. If so, add another about 15 inches (38 cm) away and you have tremendous potential for years to come. A gymnastic set consisting of rope ladder, trapeze bar and swinging rings is the best bet to use with them. The quick-change clip-ropes make the various items quick and easy to hang. An ordinary rope about 1½ inches (3.8 cm) in diameter can have a permanent loop made to slip over the hook at the top, and a big knot for sitting on at the bottom. It can even have a monkey-swing seat (see p 501) for a change. Elastic cord left over from his baby bouncer or bought (for luggage racks) from a car-accessory shop will give him quite a new experience. Holding on to this he can jump, and seem to defy gravity.

If the floor beneath your hooks is stone or quarry tiles, you may be happier if you provide the child with a soft landing. A sheet of 1 inch (2.5 cm) thick foam rubber will do a great deal to protect him and can be neatly rolled away in an elastic band for storage. Such a gym mat will also encourage lots of physical adventures on its own, like learning to turn head over heels and to stand on his head.

Pre-school Presents

Collections of things can make presents which are cheap, original, geared to your child's particular tastes and infinitely more fun than most "bought" toys. Even if your child already owns some of the separate items, he will enjoy the collection. Make them as elaborate or as simple as you please.

Play cooking

A sophisticated version of mud pies helps the child to find out what happens when he mixes this and that, and is good practice in measuring and using utensils.

Collect many small plastic containers—and lids. Scrub off labels (scouring pads remove print from the plastic.)

Fill pots with flour, sugar, cereal, chocolate vermicelli, with as much variety of texture and colour as you can manage.

Collect small plastic spoons, measuring scoops, miniatures of salt, jam and so on.

Provide a plastic mixing bowl. Add extras like patty tins, a toy food mixer, or egg whisk.

Buy a plastic tray about 18 in. x 12 in. x 3 in. (45 cm x 30 cm x 75 cm). Assemble and present everything in it. Washing up is part of the game!

Shops

The stock for a shop will delight any child of this age. It can be simple, or as ingenious as you like.

Refill the jars of a toy 'sweet shop' with real sweets, such as chocolate drops or jelly tots.

To make a general store fill containers as for play cooking. Stick-on labels make it seem more real.

Dolls' house cakes make a baker's shop. Or bake tiny loaves from flour and water dough.

Make fruits for a greengrocer's department with marzipan and food colouring.

For a grander present, buy scales, a till and play money. A box covered with sticky-backed plastic holds everything and becomes the counter when emptied and turned upside down.

Post office

Your own set, using real stationery, can be cheaper as well as better than a ready-made one.

Collect trading stamps, play money, paper clips, sticky labels. Use bank slips for official looking forms.

A date stamp, or inkpad and stamp set add a final touch of grandeur.

Play dough

Make dough from equal parts plain flour and salt, enough water for pastry.

Colour, using food colouring in the water or powder paint with the flour. Pack in matching lidded pots—½ pint (285 ml) ice cream pots are perfect. Stick on coloured labels to match the contents.

Add pastry-making 'extras'. Pack in box, with a plastic tablecloth. Keep in the refrigerator.

Montage

Give a special collection for cutting, sticking and making pictures and patterns. The basics: different coloured sugar paper, a glue pen, round-ended real scissors. The extras: coloured tissue and foils, lacy doilies, stiff card, sticky papers, shiny and matt. The trimmings: pipe cleaners, sticky stars or labels, paper streamers, small balls of wool, scrap-book pictures.

Finger paints

Mix small quantities of non-toxic wallpaper paste, made up to cheese-sauce consistency, with dry powder paint.

Choose bright and subtle shades, black and white too. Put in plastic jars with close-fitting lids or in screw-top jars covered with sticky-backed plastic (so the glass will not splinter free if it breaks).

Leave a strip clear to see the colour. Keep in the refrigerator. Add a square of white formica covered board, plastic mirror or glossy lino to paint on, a comb, plastic fork or biscuit cutters to vary the patterns he makes.

Painting sets can give your child new ideas. Even if used to ordinary poster paints and brushes, he will enjoy some of these.

Folded paintings
Buy big sheets of drawing paper. Crease each one down the middle.

Provide an eye dropper, plastic spoon, drinking straw. Help him to drop paint on one half,

then fold for a mirror-image 'print'.

Drippy paintings
With same tools as for folded paintings, the child drops paint on thin card and tips it to make patterns.

Air paintings
The child drops paint on shiny card and disperses it by blowing through a wide plastic tube

or uses a 'squeezy bottle' to apply it. Or (more exciting) he can apply thin paint from a garden sprayer.

Print painting
Letter printing sets are too fiddly at this age. Buy ink pad sets with animal stamps, or make your own set. Saw ½ in. (1.3 cm) softwood cubes. Chip away all of the surface except the shape to be printed, which stands proud of surface.

Or glue shapes to the block: curtain rings, matchsticks, string squiggles or balsa wood chips. For the pads, line pots or tins (such as adhesive dressing tins) with ¼ in. (0.6 cm) sorbo rubber. Soak each in a different brilliant colour of washable ink. These pads can also be used with potato cuts.
Other prints can be taken from any textured object:
☐ A sponge, dipped in paint and pressed on the paper.

☐ A paint roller, tied to make stripes or with chunks cut out to make a line with holes in it.

Negative paintings
The child puts an interesting shape on his paper, paints over paper and shape and then removes shape which appears as white amid the colour.

Lacy doilies, paper dolls or leaves (stuck with a dab of glue to remain steady for painting) all make lovely patterns.

Making things
Pre-school children long to make things, but are not ready for most commercial 'kits.' You can prepare one to fit his interest and abilities along the lines of the ideas given here.

Woodwork

If you cut out the basic shapes of boats, doll's house furniture etc. from softwood (balsa is easiest) and present them with dowelling strips, sandpaper, glue, scraps of material for cushions etc. the child can finish and decorate them himself.

Dressing up
Cut masks, crowns etc. out of stiff cardboard.

Make holes for eyes and give with paint or sticky paper, and elastic for the child to complete. He can even adapt the shapes with scissors.

Sewing doll's clothes
Make basic dresses with elasticated necks so that they fit a wide variety of dolls.

Present with a collection of pretty buttons, fringing, lace, ribbons. The child can then make them as elaborate as he likes with little sewing.

Soft toys
The boring part for the child is making the basic shape. Sew this for him and give with a bag of foam crumbs for stuffing, buttons for eyes, bits of fur fabric etc. for him to finish.

Felt needs no hemming and can be glued. You can even cut felt shapes ready to stick on.

Polystyrene
Buy polystyrene balls and blocks and present them with orange sticks, dowelling, glue, paint, wool and material scraps.

He can assemble "people" by pushing the sticks into the poly-styrene, and then give them hair and clothes. The balls can also be painted gold or silver for Christmas decorations.

Box modelling
For extra glamorous junk modelling, collect stout, pretty boxes (chocolate and shoe boxes are best), match-boxes, cardboard tubes.

Add a good paper glue, felt-tip pens, paints, treasury tags and stamp hinges, paper fasteners and ring reinforcements. Coloured string, sticky tape and a small stapler are useful too. Give him a good start by presenting a model with the kit.

Use it yourself growth chart
Birth to one year

Fill these charts in regularly for a permanent record of your baby's growth and an instant comparison between his actual weight and length gains and those expected of a baby of his birthweight and length.

Recording weight Find your baby's weight up the scale on the left of the chart and his age along the bottom. Make a dot where the weight and age lines cross. You can join successive dots to make a weight curve.

Recording length Tape measures drop down the chart at "0 weeks" (birth) and then at three-monthly intervals. Rule his birthlength off on the first one and then record his

new length on each successive tape.

Comparing your baby with the charted ones The expected weight for boys (heavy lines) and girls (light lines) are charted in three groups: "heavy babies" (solid lines) are heavier than 90% of all babies. "Average babies" (dashed lines) are heavier than 50% while "light babies" (dotted lines) are heavier than 10%.

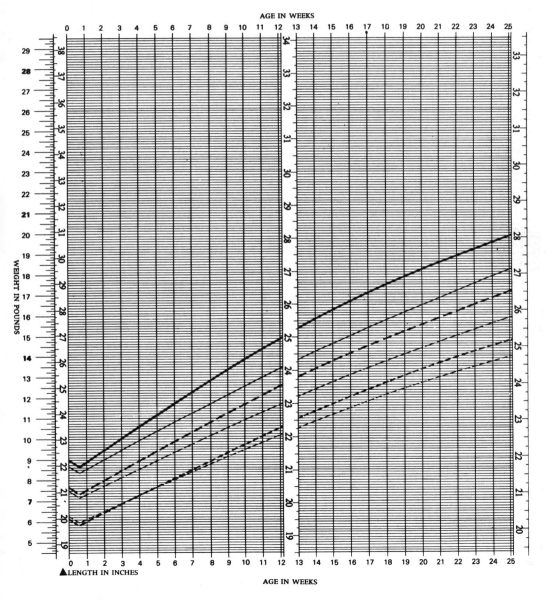

AGE IN WEEKS

WEIGHT IN POUNDS

LENGTH IN INCHES

AGE IN WEEKS

When you mark in your baby's birthweight you can see where it puts him in relation to these. The expected weight lines cross the tape measures at approximately the expected lengths, so you can see whether your baby is the expected length for his birthweight and age, too.

You can spot obesity coming – by noticing if his weight curve is rising faster than expected while his length gains stay at the expected points. You can also spot underfeeding, by noticing if his length gains are as fast, or faster, than expected while his weight gain is slow.

But don't expect any individual baby **exactly** to follow these curves and points. Small "wiggles" in your curve or differences in your length points are bound to occur. If your baby's overall pattern is like these in shape and stays roughly in the same place relative to them, he is doing fine.

AGE IN WEEKS

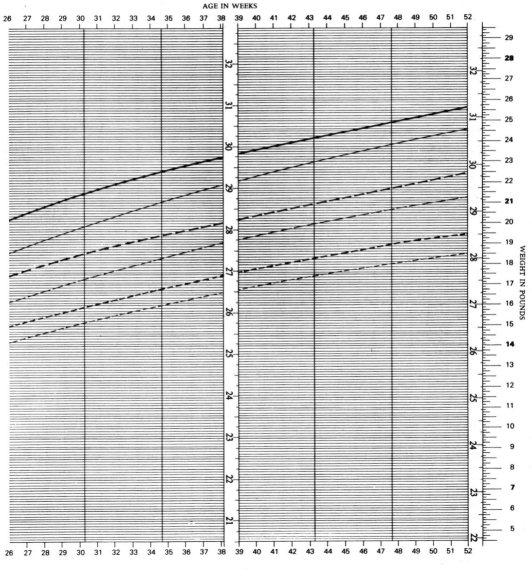

AGE IN WEEKS

Use it yourself growth chart
One to five years

This chart can be used in the same way as the previous one to record your child's growth from 1-5. The scale has changed to accommodate the less frequent measurings recommended for these age periods.

(The figures on this chart and on the chart on pp.506-507 are adapted from Tanner, J.M., Whitehouse, R.H. and Takaishi, H.: "Standards from Birth to Maturity for Height, Weight, Height Velocity and Weight Velocity: British Children", *Archives of Diseases in Childhood*, 41, 613, 1966.)

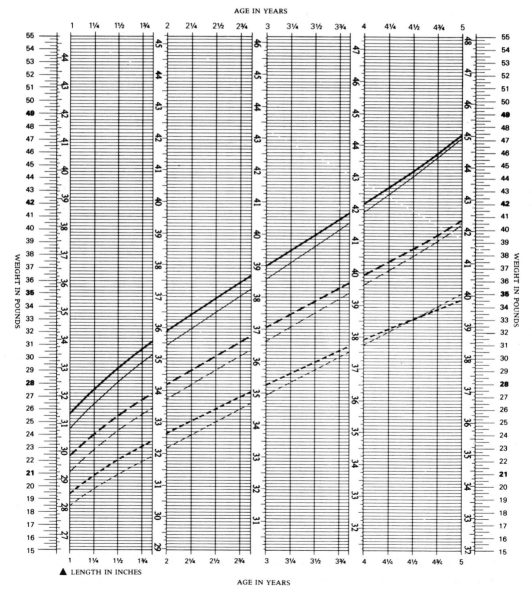

AGE IN YEARS

WEIGHT IN POUNDS

▲ LENGTH IN INCHES

AGE IN YEARS

SOME USEFUL ADDRESSES

Britain has many services for young children and their parents, but not all are available everywhere and it can be difficult to know where to start looking for them. These are Headquarters addresses and telephone numbers. If you contact them, you will be told what is available to you locally, and how to find it.

The Advisory Centre for Education, 18 Victoria Park Square, London E2. 01-980 4596
Information/advice on all stages and aspects of education plus parents magazine WHERE

British Red Cross Society, 9 Grosvenor Crescent, London SW1. 01-235 5454
Local branches provide a wide range of facilities including equipment loans, hospital/home visiting, recreational clubs and help with transport.

Child Poverty Action Group, 1 Macklin Street, London WC2. 01-242 9149
Campaigns for better welfare state benefits and will help you sort out which you are entitled to and help you get them.

Family Planning Association, Margaret Pyke House, 27-35 Mortimer Street, London W1. 01-636 7866
Local branches provide advice and practical assistance not only on contraception but also on a wide range of sexual problems.

Gingerbread, 9 Poland Street, London W1. 01-734 9014
A self-help association for one-parent families of both sexes. It is equally concerned with morale and with practical issues such as housing and baby-minding. If you have no nearby branch, headquarters will help you start one.

Good Samaritans, St. Stephen's Church, Walbrook, London EC4. 01-626 9000
This is the number to ring if you are in despair. It is manned 24 hours per day and even if you are miles away the voice that answers will know of somebody close by who can help now.

Independent Adoption Society, 160 Peckham Rye, London SE22. 01-693 9611
With no religious affiliations or geographical limitations, it concentrates on finding adoptive parents for older children or those with handicaps. Works closely with natural parents and provides permanent follow-up service for those who adopt.

La Leche League, PO Box B.M. 3424, London WC1.
Publishes information about breast-feeding and arranges practical help/ support for women planning, or experiencing difficulty with, breast-feeding.

MIND, The National Association for Mental Health, 22 Harley Street, London W1. 01-637 0741
Contact this organisation if your child is disturbed or mentally or physically handicapped. It offers a wide range of personal advice and guidance services. It also acts as a clearing-house for the many organisations which exist to help parents of children with specific disorders. If its staff cannot help you themselves, they will certainly be able to tell you exactly who can.

National Association for Gifted Children, 27 John Adam Street, London WC2. 01-839 1861
Recognises that children of exceptionally high intelligence and/or special talent may experience and present both social and educational problems. Provides counselling for parents and special activities for children.

National Association for the Welfare of Children in Hospital, 7 Exton Street, London SE1. 01-261 1738
Provides a national information service through publications and a local counselling and help service through its many branches and groups. If your chid must go into hospital they will give up-to-date information on visiting/rooming-in facilities locally; help you prepare the child for admission and, if necessary, help you with transport, baby-minding or other practical problems.

National Childbirth Trust, 9 Queensborough Terrace, London W2. 01-229 9319
Provides a nation-wide advisory service with many publications, together with locally organised ante-natal classes preparing parents for childbirth. Through local branches, many services such as help with breast-feeding, mothers support-groups and parents clubs are available. If there is nothing in your area, Headquarters will help you to get something started.

National Citizens' Advice Bureaux Council, 26 Bedford Square, London WC1. 01-636 4066
Local Bureaux staff will advise and assist you not only with legal and financial problems but also with personal and family ones.

National Council of Voluntary Child-care Organisations, 85 Highbury Park, London N5. 01-226 6592
Voluntary organisations offer a wide range of services which are often unfamiliar to those who could use them. This organisation will guide you through the maze to what is available in your area.

National Society for Mentally Handicapped Children, Pembridge Hall, 17 Pembridge Square, London W2. 01-229 8941
Provides playgroups, holiday homes and other services for mentally retarded or otherwise mentally handicapped children and support and counselling for their parents. Many new schemes are getting under way so contact headquarters even if you know of nothing in your locality.

National Society for the Prevention of Cruelty to Children, 1 Riding House Street, London W1. 01-580 8812
Give warning of danger to a child: your message will be kept anonymous and nobody will blame you if it is a false alarm. But Local Inspectors are concerned to prevent cruelty rather than punish it. Sympathetic advice and help is available to any parent whose practical or emotional difficulties are making life with a child difficult.

Pre-School Playgroups Association, Alford House, Aveline Street, London SE11. 01-582 8871
This organisation has done more than any other to provide local community facilities for parents and children under five. Publishes pamphlets and magazines CONTACT and UNDER FIVE; organises courses for play-leaders and interested parents all over the country and, of course, gets playgroups going. Headquarters will put you in touch with your local branch, tell you where your nearest playgroup is or how to go about planning to start your own.

Society of Compassionate Friends, 50 Wood Way, Watford, Herts. 92-242-97
Puts parents who have suffered the death of a baby or child in touch with others who know what it is like. Whether your tragedy is a stillbirth, a sudden death in infancy, a fatal accident or illness or a condition you know is hopeless, contact this organisation if you would like help and support yourself or if you feel that you could help somebody else who lives near you.

Note
Every Local Authority has a Social Services Department whose Social Workers are there to advise and help you. Contact it through your Town Hall. In an emergency, outside office hours, ask for the "Duty Social Worker".

Health Visitors from your Local Child Health Clinic will put you in touch with the service you need if your problem is outside their scope.

General Practitioners work in close cooperation with Health and Welfare services. They, too, can tell you where to go for help.

Probation Officers are trained to help the public in every kind of social difficulty. You can see the Duty Probation Officer, without an appointment, at any time in office hours. If your problem requires help from another social agency, he or she will make any necessary appointments for you and see that you get the assistance you need.

Although elaborate first aid is best left to the experts, there are a few circumstances in which if you know what to do and can bring yourself to do it – fast – you could save your own or another child's life.

If a child's clothes should catch fire

Remember that heat and flame rise. If the bottom of a skirt catches fire and the child is standing up, the flames will soon rise to engulf the rest and reach her face and hair. If she runs around in panic she will fan the fire. If you throw her down on the burning part of her dress, trying to smother the fire, flames will lick upwards round her body.

Put the child on the floor with the flames uppermost

Unless you have water to hand and can dowse the fire you must smother it:

Smother the flames with the nearest rug, coat or towel

If there is nothing else within reach you can smother the fire with your own body but if you are going to be as brave as this you must find the courage to lie absolutely flat upon her so that your body presses down on all of the fire. If you half-kneel so that there are air pockets between her body and yours, flames will funnel up and burn you both.

If there's nothing else, smother the fire with your own body

If a child is receiving a continuous electric shock

Something has prevented him from being thrown clear of, or jumping away from, the power source. His finger may be trapped in the socket down which he poked a hair-pin; he may be entangled in a "live" wire or the muscular contractions which go with electric shock may have clenched his hand around a faulty appliance. Remember that as long as he is receiving the electric charge he is part of the circuit.

Don't touch him with bare hands or you will receive the shock, too

If you can find your mains switch quickly, or see that the source of the shock is a switched plug:

Switch off the power

If you cannot switch off, you will have to push the child clear, avoiding anything metallic which might conduct current.

Push the child clear using a broom, cushion, wooden chair...